IRELAND
AND THE
EUROPEAN UNION:
CONSTITUTIONAL
AND
STATUTORY TEXTS
AND
COMMENTARY

AUSTRALIA

The Law Book Company
Brisbane * Sydney * Melbourne * Perth

CANADA

Carswell
Ottawa * Toronto * Calgary * Montreal
Vancouver

AGENTS

Steimatsky's Agency Ltd, Tel Aviv
N.M. Tripathi (Private) Ltd, Bombay
Eastern Law House (Private) Ltd, Calcutta
M.P.P. House, Bangalore
Universal Book Traders, Delhi
MacMillan Shuppan KK, Tokyo
Pakistan Law House, Karachi, Lahore

Ireland
and the
European Union:
Constitutional
and
Statutory Texts
and
Commentary

by

GERARD HOGAN
B.C.L., LL.M.(NUI); LL.M.(Penn.); M.A., Barrister
Fellow, Trinity College, Dublin

and

ANTHONY WHELAN
LL.B. (Dub.), LL.M. (Cantab.), Barrister

LONDON
SWEET & MAXWELL
1995

Published in 1995 by
Sweet & Maxwell Limited of
South Quay Plaza, 183 Marsh Wall
London E14 9FT

Typeset by
MFK Information Services Ltd, Hitchin, Herts.
Printed and bound in Great Britain by
Butler and Tanner Ltd, Frome and London

No natural forests were destroyed to make this product;
only farmed timber was used and replanted

A CIP catalogue record for this book is available from the British Library

ISBN 0 421 52940 7

PREFACE

This book aims to provide a comprehensive guide to the provisions of Article 29.4.3–6 of the Constitution of Ireland, the European Communities Acts, 1972–1995 and to the amendments made to the Treaty of Rome by the Maastricht Treaty of European Union. A number of theoretical issues arising from the inter-action of Irish constitutional law and Community law are also discussed in detail. As will be seen from the Introduction, the book is composed of three elements—the Irish constitutional commentary (chiefly by Anthony Whelan), the statute annotations (chiefly by Gerard Hogan) and the annotation of the Treaties. We are especially indebted to Paul Beaumont and Gordon Moir who permitted us to use their Treaty annotation from a similar book on the reception of European Community law in the United Kingdom: *European Communities (Amendment) Act 1993 with the Treaty of Rome (as amended): Text and Commentary* as the substantial basis of a slightly updated and hibernicised version in this work.

We must also thank Professor Kevin Boyle of the University of Essex who, in his capacity as editor of the *Irish Current Law Statutes Annotated*, first suggested that we produce a book of this kind. We are especially grateful to Anthony Collins (Court of Justice) and Eoin O'Dell (Law School, Trinity College, Dublin) who read through the Irish constitutional chapters in their entirety and offered myriad helpful comments. Alex Schuster (Law School, Trinity College, Dublin) also read and commented on many of these chapters at varying stages of preparation. Numerous conversations with Dr Diarmuid Rossa Phelan (Law School, Trinity College, Dublin) helped to identify a number of vital issues and problems and Diarmuid McGuinness, Barrister, made a number of helpful suggestions. Advocate General Nial Fennelly, Kieran St. Clair Bradley and Nicolas Lockhart (all at the Court of Justice) each commented on a number of chapters. Dr John Temple Lang of the European Commission was extremely helpful with Chapter 6. Philip McDonagh of the Department of Foreign Affairs, Anthony Coughlan, Professor Patrick Keatinge and Dr Ben Tonra (all at Trinity College, Dublin) were helpful with earlier versions of Chapter 7 and Dr Clive Symmons (Law School, Trinity College, Dublin) advised on a large number of delicate points. James Kingston kindly allowed the adaptation of a previous collaboration with Anthony Whelan in Chapter 9. Niamh Hyland (Court of Justice) and Claire Loftus (Chief State Solicitor's Office) collaborated with Anthony Whelan in the study of citizenship. James Bergeron (Law Faculty, University College, Dublin) and Leo Flynn (King's College, London) were sources of interesting ideas. Our respective colleagues in the Law School, Trinity College, Dublin and the *Cabinet* Fennelly in Luxembourg, the libraries of Trinity College, Dublin, the Court of Justice, the Institute of Advanced Legal Studies in London, the University of Cambridge and at the Centre Méditerranéen d'Études Françaises at Cap d'Ail have all been helpful and tolerant. Anthony Whelan would like to thank Philip Allott at Trinity College, Cambridge, who inspired interest in this field five years ago.

Parts of the constitutional section are adapted from earlier work. Chapters 6 and 7 draw on earlier *Irish Current Law Statutes Annotated* annotations. Chapter 3 is an expansion of Gerard Hogan's article "The Supreme Court and the Single European Act" (1987) 22 *Irish Jurist* 55; Chapter 4 updates Anthony Whelan's note on *Meagher v. Minister for Agriculture & Food* (1993) 15 *Dublin University Law Journal* 152; Chapter 5 develops the same author's "Article 29.4.3 and the meaning of 'necessity' " (1992) 2 *Irish Students Law Review* 60. Chapter 9 uses some elements of James Kingston and

Anthony Whelan, "The Protection of the Unborn in Three Legal Orders—Part IV" (1992) 10 *Irish Law Times*.

Since the book was first written, the authors have had occasion to reflect on the legal significance of Article F(2) of the Maastricht Treaty (which commits the Union to respecting fundamental rights as protected by the European Convention of Human Rights). As the authors' note in the main text indicates, this provision is excluded from the jurisdiction of the Court of Justice by Article L. However, the suggestion has been made that even though the Court of Justice is denied jurisdiction in respect of this provision, that a national court might be called upon to give effect to it as part of its general duty to enforce Community and/or Union law. But it must be noted that Article F (in common with the other provisions of Title 1 of the Maastricht Treaty) has never been given force of law in this State: see section 1(p) of the European Communities Act, 1972 (as inserted by section 1(1) of the European Communities (Amendment) Act, 1992). Therefore, by virtue of Article 29.6 of the Constitution, Article F(2) would seem to have the same status as any other international agreement to which the State is a party but which has not been made part of the domestic law of the State, even if all due allowances are made for the exceptional character of the Treaty in question. This would not, of course, prevent the courts giving this provision a form of indirect legal effect: see Kelly, *The Irish Constitution* (1994) at 298–9. Of course, it might be argued that Article 29.4.4 itself suffices to give the Maastricht Treaty the complete force of law in this State, but this argument fails to have regard to the fact that this constitutional provision simply enables (and does not coerce) the State to ratify the Treaty.

Although Anthony Whelan is now a *référendaire* at the Court of Justice, the views expressed by him are purely personal.

We have sought to state the law as of February 1, 1995 for the Treaty annotations and September 1, 1995 for the constitutional sections.

Gerard Hogan
Anthony Whelan

September 21, 1995

TABLE OF CONTENTS

Preface	v
Table of Irish Cases	xi
Table of European Cases	xiii
Table of References to the Constitution of Ireland	xvii
Table of Statutes	xix
Table of Statutory Instruments	xxi
Table of European Treaties	xxiii
Table of European Legislation	xxxiii

Introduction	1

Part 1: Irish Constitutional Material

Article 29.4.3–6, Constitution of Ireland	5

Chapter One
INTRODUCTION: THE RECEPTION OF EUROPEAN COMMUNITY LAW IN IRISH LAW	7

Chapter Two
ARTICLE 177 E.C. AND THE INTEGRITY OF COMMUNITY LAW IN IRELAND	17
Campus Oil Ltd. v. Minister for Industry and Energy	17
Article 26 of the Constitution and the *Renvoi Préjudiciel*	21

Chapter Three
CROTTY V. AN TAOISEACH: THE TESTS OF ESSENTIAL OBJECTIVES AND OF LEGAL OBLIGATION	25
Crotty v. An Taoiseach: "necessitated" measures	30
Does every amendment of the Community and Union Treaties require a separate constitutional amendment?	39
Crotty v. An Taoiseach: freedom to conduct foreign policy	42

Chapter Four
MEAGHER V. MINISTER FOR AGRICULTURE AND THE IMPLEMENTATION OF COMMUNITY LAW	51
Meagher v. Minister for Agriculture: The High Court	58
Meagher v. Minister for Agriculture: The Supreme Court	60

Chapter Five
REVIEW OF THE CONTENT OF IMPLEMENTING MEASURES	69

Chapter Six
COMMUNITY COMPETENCE AND MEMBER STATE OBLIGATION: MIXED AGREEMENTS	79
(i) Mixed agreements and Community Law	80
(ii) Mixed agreements and Community Responsibility	84

Chapter Seven
THE ELEVENTH AMENDMENT AND THE EUROPEAN UNION   89
   (i) Union Acts and Obligations
       Article 29.4.5 of the Constitution and the European
          Union: Preliminary Issues   90
        (a) Secondary obligations under the Treaty on
           European Union
           Co-operation in the fields of judicial and home
              affairs   91
           Common Foreign and Security Policy   93
           The Common and Final Provisions   95
        (b) Acts of the Union or of the Member States in
           Common?   98
        (c) Direct applicability and the force of the law in
           the State   106
   (ii) The Union and Fundamental Rights   109
        (a) "Prior restraint" of the Government   110
        (b) Supervision by the European Court of Human
           Rights   113
   (iii) The Exclusion of the European Court of Justice   116
       Conclusion   119

Chapter Eight
"THE MIRROR CRACK'D FROM SIDE TO SIDE": NORMATIVE
   CONFLICT AND CONSTITUTIONAL INTERPRETATION   121
The Principles of Constitutional Interpretation   121
   (i) The Literal Approach   122
   (ii) The Teleological Approach   123
   (iii) The Harmonious Approach   123
   (iv) The Historical Approach   124
   (v) The Natural Law Approach   126
Normative Conflict and the Interpretive Role of the Irish
   Courts: Article 29.4.5 *Redux*   128

Chapter Nine
RENVOI IN REVERSE? PROTOCOL NO. 17 TO THE MAASTRICHT
   TREATY   143
Protocol No. 17 and Community Law   144
Protocol No. 17 and the Treaty on European Union   151

Third Amendment of the Constitution Act, 1972   155
Tenth Amendment of the Constitution Act, 1987   159
Eleventh Amendment of the Constitution Act, 1992   160

Part 2:   Irish Statutory Material and the Treaty on European Union

INTRODUCTION   165
European Communities Acts, 1972–1995   165
   European Communities Act, 1972   166

Contents

European Communities (Confirmation of Regulations)
Act, 1973   181
European Communities Act, 1973   182
European Communities (Amendment) Act, 1977   183
European Communities (Amendment) Act, 1979   184
European Communities (Amendment) Act, 1985   185
European Communities (Amendment) (No. 2) Act,
1985   186
European Communities (Amendment) Act, 1986   187
European Communities (Amendment) Act, 1992   189
European Communities (Amendment) Act, 1993   190
European Communities (Amendment) Act, 1994   195
European Communities (Amendment) Act, 1995   196

The Treaty on European Union   198
The Treaty on European Union (TEU)   199
Background   199
Structure of the New Union   201
The Pillars of a common foreign and security policy
and co-operation in the fields of justice and home
affairs   202
The Scheme of the Treaty on European Union   206
Amendments to the Treaty of Rome establishing the
European Economic Community   206
Institutional Reform   211
The European Parliament (Arts. 137–143 E.C.)   211
The Commission (Arts. 156–163 E.C.)   212
The European Court of Justice (Arts. 165–184 E.C.)   213
The Committee of the Regions (Art. 198a–198c E.C.)   213
The Council of Ministers (Arts. 145–154 E.C.)   213
Legislative Procedures   213
Economic and monetary union (Arts. 102a–109m E.C.)   215
1996 and enlargement   218

The Treaty on European Union   220

Part 3:   The E.C. Treaty   245
Index   479

ix

TABLE OF IRISH CASES

Agra Meat Packers Ltd v. Minister for Agriculture and Food (High Court, December
    14, 1994) 61, 176
Att.-Gen. v. Hamilton (No. 1) [1993] 2 I.R. 250 125
—— v. —— (No. 2) [1993] I.L.R.M. 821 .... 66, 125
—— v. Mc Bride [1928] I.R. 451 .... 193, 194
—— *ex rel.* S.P.U.C. (Ireland) Ltd v. Open Door Counselling Ltd [1988] I.R. 593 ... 124, 129
—— v. Paperlink Ltd [1984] I.L.R.M. 348 123
—— v. X [1992] 1 I.R. 1 .... 23, 124, 130, 133, 143, 147, 148, 150

Boland v. An Taoiseach [1971] I.R. 371 110
Brennan v. Attorney-General [1984] I.L.R.M. 355 76
Browne v. Bórd Pleanála [1989] I.L.R.M. 865 54

Cahalane v. Murphy [1994] 2 I.R. 262; [1994] 2 I.L.R.M. 383 194
Cahill v. Sutton [1980] I.R. 269 30
Campus Oil Ltd v. Minister for Industry and Energy [1983] I.R. 82 ...... 7, 17, 18, 19, 20, 21, 58,
    121, 129, 131, 138, 140, 142
City View Press Ltd v. AnC.O. [1980] I.R. 381 .... 51, 64
Condon v. Minister for Agriculture, High Court, October 12, 1990; [1993] I.J.E.L. 151   72, 75
Cox v. Ireland [1992] 2 I.R. 503 194
Crotty v. An Taoiseach [1987] I.R. 713 .... 13, 25, 28, 30, 31, 32, 33, 34, 35, 36, 37, 38, 39, 42,
    43, 44, 45, 46, 47, 48, 49, 51, 52, 66, 69, 71, 72, 74, 89, 92, 93,
    97, 110, 111, 112, 121, 122, 123, 126, 133, 142, 156, 159,
    160, 161, 187, 202

Desmond v. Glackin [1993] 3 I.R. 1 .... 108, 140
Doyle v. An Taoiseach [1986] I.L.R.M. 793 .... 22, 142
D.P.P. v. Byrne [1994] 2 I.R. 236; [1994] 2 I.L.R.M. 91 194
—— v. Logan [1994] 3 I.R. 254; [1994] 2 I.L.R.M. 229 194

E. v. E. [1982] I.L.R.M. 497 32
E. v. F and Ireland [1994] I.L.R.M. 401 .... 15, 141
East Donegal Cooperative Livestock Marts Ltd v. Attorney-General [1970] I.R. 317   61, 181

Fakih v. Minister for Justice [1993] 2 I.R. 406 .... 32, 92, 108
Finn v. Attorney-General [1983] I.R. 154 140
Finucane v. McMahon [1990] 1 I.R. 156 124

G. v. An Bórd Uchtála [1980] I.R. 32 140
G. v. Director of Public Prosecutions [1994] 1 I.R. 374 194
Greene v. Minister for Agriculture [1990] I.L.R.M. 364; [1990] 2 I.R. 17 .... 56, 71, 72, 73, 74,
    75, 142
Gutrani v. Minister for Justice [1993] 2 I.R. 427 108

Hibernia Meats Ltd v. Minister for Agriculture (High Court, July 29, 1983) 22
Hutchinson v. Minister of Justice [1993] I.L.R.M. 602 105
Hyland v. Minister for Social Welfare [1989] I.R. 624 .... 75, 76

Kajli v. Minister for Justice, High Court, August 21, 1992 108
Kerry Co-operative Creameries Ltd v. An Bord Bainne Co-operative Ltd [1991]
    I.L.R.M. 851 22

Lawlor v. Minister for Agriculture [1990] 1 I.R. 1; [1990] 1 I.R. 356; [1988] I.L.R.M.
    400 .... 56, 71, 74, 142

Mallon v. Minister for Agriculture, *The Irish Times*, July 28; July 29, 1994 .... 74, 177
McDaid v. Sheehy [1991] 1 I.R. 1; [1989] I.L.R.M. 342 .... 52, 59, 180
McDonald v. Bord na gCon [1965] I.R. 217 70
McGee v. Attorney-General [1974] I.R. 284 .... 125, 127, 140

McGimpsey v. Ireland H.Ct. [1988] I.R. 567; S.Ct. [1990] 1 I.R. 110 .... 32, 46, 47, 48, 80, 93,
110, 135
McKenna v. An Taoiseach (High Court, June 8, 1992) 134
Meagher v. Minister for Agriculture [1994] 1 I.R. 329; [1994] 1 I.L.R.M. 1 .... 13, 20, 33, 51,
56, 58, 59, 60, 62, 63, 65, 66, 67, 69, 71, 74, 78,
121, 123, 129, 131, 142, 165, 172, 175, 176, 178,
179, 180, 181, 193, 194
Murphy v. Attorney-General [1982] I.R. 241 .... 35, 58
Murphy v. P.M.P.A. Insurance Co. [1978] I.R.L.M. 725 141
Murray v. Ireland [1985] I.R. 532 127

Norris v. Attorney-General [1984] I.R. 436 .... 32, 126, 140

O'B. v. S. [1984] I.R. 316 32
O Domhnaill v. Merrick [1985] I.L.R.M. 40 108
O Laighléis, Re [1960] I.R. 93 32
Open Door Counselling Ltd v. Ireland (Series A, No. 246; (1993) 15 E.H.R.R. 244)   130

People (Director of Public Prosecutions) v. O'Shea [1982] I.R. 384 .... 122, 123, 126, 135
People v. Shaw [1982] I.R.1 124
Pigs and Bacon Commission v. McCarron, High Court, June 30, 1978; (1978)
J.I.S.E.L. 77 .... 7, 12, 142

Quinn v. Wren [1985] I.R. 322 124

Re Article 26 and the Emergency Powers Bill 1976 [1977] I.R. 159 52
Re Article 26 and the Regulation of Information (Services outside the State for Ter-
mination of Pregnancies) Bill, 1995 [1995] 2 I.L.R.M. 81 .... 15, 21, 126, 141, 144
Re Electoral (Amendment) Bill, 1983 [1984] I.R. 268 272
Russell v. Fanning [1988] I.R. 505 .... 124, 135
Ryan v. Attorney-General [1965] I.R. 294 70
—— v. Ireland [1989] I.R. 177 13

Society for the Protection of Unborn Children (Ireland) Ltd v. Grogan [1989] I.R.
753 .... 17, 20, 33, 112, 113, 128, 129, 130, 133, 134, 136, 142, 148
State (Director of Public Prosecutions) v. Walsh [1981] I.R. 412 108
State (Gilliland) v. Governor of Mountjoy Prison [1987] I.R. 201 .... 32, 62, 80, 154
State (Woods) v. Attorney-General [1969] I.R. 385 70
Sullivan v. Robinson [1954] I.R. 151 123

Tate v. Minister for Social Welfare [1995] 1 I.R.L.M. 507, 521 .... 11, 14

TABLE OF EUROPEAN CASES

France (*Conseil constitutionel*)
Ratification of the Treaty on European Union, *Re* [1993] 3 C.M.L.R. 345 ....   28, 40

Germany (*Bundesverfassungsgericht*)
Brunner, *Re* [1994] 1 C.M.L.R. 57 .... 44, 66, 95, **104**, 107, **109**, 111, 117, 118, 126,
                                                             136, **137**, 146, 198
Freistaat Bayern v. Bundesregierung [1990] 1 C.M.L.R. 649 ....   111, 113
Internationale Handelsgesellschaft mbH v. Einfuhr- und Vorratsstelle für Getreide
    und Futtermittel [1974] 2 C.M.L.R. 540   138
M. GmbH v. Bundesregierung (BVerfG, May 12, 1989) [1990] 1 C.M.L.R. 570 ....   77, 111,
                                                                       112, 115
Wünsche Handelsgesellschaft "Solange II" [1987] 3 C.M.L.R. 225 ....   110, 112, 113, 115, 138

Italy (*Corte Constituzionale*)
Frontini v. Ministero delle Finanze [1973] Giur. Cost. 2041   138
Spa. Granital v. Amministrazione Finanziaria [1984] Giur. Cost. 1098   138

United Kingdom
Hastings and Folkestone Glassworks Ltd v. Kalson [1949] 1 K.B. 214, 2 All E.R. 1013   176
Maclaine Watson & Co Ltd v. Department of Trade and Industry and the Inter-
    national Tin Council [1989] 3 All E.R. 523 ....   118, 149
R. v. H.M. Treasury, *ex p*. Smedley [1985] Q.B. 657; [1985] 2 W.L.R. 576; 129 S.J. 48,
    [1985] 1 All E.R. 589; [1985] 1 C.M.L.R. 665   111
R. v. Secretary of State for Foreign and Commonwealth Affairs, *ex p*. Rees Mogg
    [1994] 1 All E.R. 457; [1993] 3 C.M.L.R. 101 ....   43, 44, 151, 152, 190, 199

European Court of Human Rights
C.F.D.T. v. E.C., E.C. States collectively and E.C. States individually [1979] 2
    C.M.L.R. 299   114
Dufay v. E.C., E.C. States collectively and E.C. States individually (Application No.
    13539/88, January 19, 1989)   114
European School in Brussels: D. v. Belgium and the E.C., *Re* (11055/84), [1987] 2
    C.M.L.R. 57   114
M. v. Germany (Application No. 13258/87) Decision of February, 1990 ....   114, 115, 116

European Court of Justice
Acciairie San Michele Sp.A. v. High Authority (9/65 and 58/65), [1967] E.C.R. 1 .....   26, 33, 34
Amministrazione delle Finanze dello Stato v. San Giorgio (199/82), [1983] E.C.R.
    3595; [1985] 2 C.M. L.R. 658   24
Amministrazione delle Finanze v. Simmenthal (106/77), [1978] E.C.R. 629; [1978] 3
    C.M.L.R. 263 ....   8, 22, 23, 24, 146
Antonissen (C–292/89)   149

BASF A.G. v. Commission (T–79/89)   398
Bachmann v. Belgium (C–204 & 300/90 2), [1992] I.E.C.R. 379   362
Bellamy (T–179)   34
Blaizot v. University of Liège (24/86), [1988] E.C.R. 379; [1989] 1 C.M.L.R. 57   362
Bresciani v. Amministrazione Italiana delle Finanze, (87/75), [1976] E.C.R. 129   81

Criminal Proceedings Against Casati (203/80) [1981] E.C.R. 2 595; 1 C.M.L.R. 365 .   293, 297
CILFIT Srl v. Ministry of Health (C–283/81) [1982] E.C.R. 3415; [1983] 1 C.M.L.R.
    472 ....   21, 131
Commission v. Belgium (102/79), [1980] E.C.R. 1473; [1981] 1 C.M.L.R. 164   54
Commission v. Belgium (300/90), [1990] I E.C.R. 249   300
Commission v. Council (ERASMUS) (242/87); [1989] E.C.R. 1425; [1991] 1
    C.M.L.R. 478   362
Commission v. Council (E.R.T.A.) (22/70), [1971] E.C.R. 263; [1971] C.M.L.R. 335   80, 81,
                                                                          84, 99, 435

Table of European Cases

Commission v. Council (Generalised Tariff Preferences) (C–45/86), [1987] E.C.R. 1493; [1988] 2 C.M.L.R. 131 258
Commission v. Council (Titanium Dioxide) (C–300/89), [1991] I E.C.R. 2867 215
Commission v. Denmark (C–302/86) [1988] E.C.R. 4607 379
Commission v. France (42/82). [1983] E.C.R. 1013 300
Commission v. Italy (39/72), [1973] E.C.R. 101; [1973] C.M.L.R. 439 .... 10, 11
Commission v. Italy (145/82), [1983] E.C.R. 711 54
Commission v. Italy (22/87) [1989] E.C.R. 143 404
Commission v. Netherlands (236, 85), [1987] E.C.R. 3989 54
Commission v. United Kingdom (32/79), [1980] E.C.R. 2403 .... 37, 258
Commission v. United Kingdom (Fishery Conservation Measures (No.2) (804/79) [1981] E.C.R. 1045 .... 84, 257, 258
Costa v. Ente Natzionale per l'Energia Elettrica (ENEL) 6/64 [1964] E.C.R. 585; [1964] C.M.L.R. 425 .... 8, 11, 23, 403

Defrenne v. SABENA (43/75), [1976] E.C.R. 455; [1976] 2 C.M.L.R. 98 .... 58, 255
Demirel v. Stadt Schwäbisch Gmünd (12/86), [1987] E.C.R. 3719) 82, 83, 86, 174, 257
Denkavit v. Minister für Ernährung Landwirtschaft and Forster (251/78) [1979] E.C.R. 3327; [1980] 3 C.M.L.R. 513 300
Deutsche Milchkontor GmbH v. Germany (Joined Cases 205–215/82) [1983] E.C.R. 2633 .... 53, 56, 57
Duff v. Minister for Agriculture (C–63/93) [1993] 2 C.M.L.R. 969; [1994] I.J.E.L. 247 .... 74, 78, 134

Elliniki Radiophonio Tileorassi, (C–260/89), [1991] E.C.R. I, 2925 69
Emmott (C–208/90), [1991] I E.C.R. 4269; [1991] 3 C.M.L.R. 894 24
Eridania v. Minister of Agriculture and Forestry (230/78), [1979] E.C.R. 2749 51
European Economic Area (No. 1) (Opinion 1/91) [1991] E.C.R. I, 6079 .... 8, 153, 172, 255

Foto-Frost v. Hauptzollamt Lübeck-Ost (314/85), [1987] E.C.R. 4199; [1988] 3 C.M.L.R. 57 .... 34, 73, 118
France v. United Kingdom (C–141/78), [1979] E.C.R. 2923; [1980] 1 C.M.L.R. 6 37
Francovich and Boniface v. Italy (C–6, C–9/90), [1991] E.C.R. 5359; [1992] I.R.L.R. 84 .... 15, 24, 57, 64, 197, 213, 257, 376, 404

GATT (Opinion 1/94, [1994] I.E.C.R. 1 .... 37, 80, 81, 82, 151, 257, 262
Gravier v. City of Liege (293/83), [1985] E.C.R. 593; [1985] 3 C.M.L.R. 1 362
Groupment des Industries Sidérurgiques Luxembourgeoises v. High Authority (C.7 & 9/54), [1956] E.C.R. 175 151
Gutmann v. Commission (C–18, 35/65), [1966] E.C.R. 103 261

Haegemann v. Belgium (C–181/73) [1974], E.C.R. 449; [1975] 1 C.M.L.R. 515 79
Hauptzollamt Mainz v. Kupferberg [1982] (104/81), E.C.R. 3641; [1983] 1 C.M.L.R. 1 ..... 79, 81, 86, 153

I.L.O. Convention No. 170 (Opinion 2/91), [1993] 3 C.M.L.R. 800 .... 81, 261
Ideal Standard (C–9/93), [1994] I E.C.R. 2789 37
Internationale Handelsgesellschaft GmbH v. Einfuhr- und Vorratsstelle für Getreide und Futtermittel (C–11/70) [1970] II E.C.R. 1125; [1972] C.M.L.R. 255 .... 34, 76, 138

Jongeneel Kaas v. The State (Netherlands) and Stichting Centraal Orgaan Zuivel-controle (C–237/82), [1984] E.C.R. 4893 74

Les Verts-Parti Ecologiste v. European Parliament (294/83), [1986] E.C.R. 1339; [1987] 2 C.M.L.R. 343 .... 8, 405
Luisi and Carbone v. Ministero del Tesoro (286/82, 26/83), [1984] E.C.R. 377 297

M. GmbH. v. Bundesregierung (BVerfG, May 12, 1989) [1990] 1 C.M.L.R. 570 .... 77, 111, 112, 115

Marleasing SA v. La Commercial Internacional de Alimentation SA (C–106/89),
  [1990] E.C.R. I 4135.. 15, 64, 108, 403
Marthe Klensch and Others v. Secrétaire d'État à l'Agriculture et à la Viticulture
  (C–202/85) [1986] E.C.R. 3477; [1988] 1 C.M.L.R. 151..................................... 69
Micheletti v. Delegación del Gobierno en Cantabria (C–369/90), [1992] I E.C.R. 4239   268
Ministère Public v. Lambert (C–203/80, 286/82, 26/83), [1988] E.C.R. 4369.............. 297

Natural Rubber Agreement (Opinion 1/78) [1978] E.C.R. 2871................................ 80, 81
Netherlands v. Commission (C–28/66), [1968] E.C.R. 1, 12–13.............................. 255
Nold K.G. v. Commission (C–4/73), [1974] E.C.R. 491; [1974] 2 C.M.L.R. 338.......... 138

Parliament v. Commission (C–445/93).. 149
Parliament v. Council [1985] (13/83), E.C.R. 1513; [1986] 1 C.M.L.R. 138................. 406
Parliament v. Council (Comitology) (302/87), [1988] E.C.R. 5615 405
Parliament v. Council (Chernobyl) (C–70/88), [1990] E.C.R. I–2041 405
Parliament v. Council (C–295/90), [1992] I E.C.R. 4193................................... 58, 265, 270
Physical Protection of Nuclear Materials (Ruling 1/78) [1978] E.C.R. 2151............... 81, 85, 87
Pogglien (C–297/92).. 149
Polydor and R.S.O. Records Inc v. Harlequin Record Shops and Simons Records
  (C–270/80) [1982] E.C.R. 329; [1982] 1 C.M.L.R. 677..................................... 153
Procureur du Roi v. Royer (C–48/75), [1976] E.C.R. 497; [1976] 2 C.M.L.R. 619   76
Pubblico Ministero v. Ratti (C–148/78), [1979] E.C.R. 1629; [1980] 1 C.M.L.R. 96....   403

R. v. Secretary of State of Health (C–11/92), [1993] O.J. C174/1 364
R. v. Secretary of State for Transport, ex p. Factortame Ltd (C–213/89), [1990] I
  E.C.R. 2433; [1990] 3 C.M.L.R. 1.. 24
Razanatsimba (C–65/77), [1977] E.C.R. 2229; [1978] 1 C.M.L.R. 246   83
Rewe v. Landwirtschaftskammer Saarland (33/76), [1976] E.C.R. 1989; [1977] 1
  C.M.L.R. 533.. 24
Reyners v. Belgium (2/74), [1974] E.C.R. 631; [1974] 2 C.M.L.R. 105 300
Rheinmühlen-Düsseldorf v. Einfuhr und-Vorratsstelle Getreide (146, 166/73) [1974]
  E.C.R., 139; [1974] 1 C.M.L.R. 523.. 18
Rhine Laying-up Fund (Opinion 1/76) [1977] E.C.R. 741................................... 81
Roquette Fréres S.A. v. Council (C–139/79), [1980] E.C.R. 3393 .... 204, 422
Rouja v. Council (T–584/93), [1994] II E.C.R. 587.. 34

S.C.S. Peterbroeck v. Belgium (C–272/93) 23, 24
S.P.U.C. (Ireland) Ltd v. Grogan 159/90 [1991] E.C.R. I 4685.............................. 22, 130, 143
Spain v. Council (C–350/92) 37

Tedeschi (Carlo) Denkavit Commerciale SRL (5/77), [1977] E.C.R. 1556; [1978] 1
  C.M.L.R. 1.. 360
Thieffry v. Conseil de l'Ordre des Advocats (C–71/76), [1977] E.C.R. 765; [1977] 2
  C.M.L.R. 373.. 37

United Kingdom v. Council (68/86), [1988] E.C.R. 855; [1988] 2 C.M.L.R. 543.......... 82, 151
United Kingdom v. Council (84/94) 76

Van Duyn v. Home Office (C–41/74) [1974] E.C.R. 1337; [1975] 1 C.M.L.R. 1 .... 64, 403
Van Gend en Loos v. Nederlandse Belastingadministratie (C–26/62), [1963] E.C.R. 1;
  [1963] C.M.L.R. 105.. 8, 403
Van Schijndel v. Stichting Pensioen fonds voor Fysiotherapeuten (C–430, 431/93)...   23, 24
Von Colsen and Kamann v. Land Nordrhein-westfalen: C–14/83. [1984] E.C.R. 1891;
  [1986] 2 C.M.L.R. 430 .... 108, 403

Zuckerfabrik Franken GmbH v. Federal Republic of Germany (C–77/81), [1982]
  E.C.R. 681.. 69
Zwartveld (C–2/88), [1990] I E.C.R. 3365; [1998] 3 C.M.L.R. 457 257

TABLE OF REFERENCES TO THE CONSTITUTION OF IRELAND

Irish Constitution——
  Preamble 138
  Art. 1 138
     2 135
     3 135
     5 .... 127, 138, 156
     6 .... 52, 138
     10 156
     12 138
     12.2.2 42
     15 .... 13, 59, 138, 156, 193
     15.2 .... 51, 53, 56, 61, 64, 193
     15.2.1 .... 64, 106, 107, 178
     16 138
     16.2 272
     16.2.ii 41
     26 .... 17, 21, 22, 23
     26.2.1 21
     27 155
     28 .... 138, 156
     28.3.1 41
     28.3.3 .... 13, 52, 53
     29 134
     29.1 47
     29.4 161
     29.4.1–2 35
     29.4.1 25
     29.4.2 .... 29, 47
     29.4.3–4 .... 37, 38
     29.4.3–5 .... 11, 14, 19, 20, 23,
                     128, 137
     29.4.3–6 .... 7, 16, 121, 122, 125,
               126, 155, 161, 165
     29.4.3 .... 16, 18, 19, 20, 26, 27,
             29, 30, 31, 36, 38, 52,
             71, 89, 117, 119, 123,
             129, 135, 136, 156,
             159, 160, 161, 166,
                        193
     29.4.4 .... 38, 39, 40, 41, 42, 89,
                     93, 161
     29.4.5 .... 13, 14, 15, 16, 19, 20,
             21, 28, 30, 33, 34, 35,
             36, 37, 38, 42, 44, 51,

Irish Constitution—*cont.*
  Art. 29.4.5—*cont.*
              52, 53, 56, 59, 60, 61,
              63, 64, 65, 66, 69, 70,
              72, 73, 78, 79, 80, 83,
              84, 87, 89, 90, 91, 97,
              98, 103, 104, 105,
              106, 108, 109, 110,
              112, 116, 117, 118,
              119, 120, 121, 123,
              124, 125, 127, 128,
              130, 131, 132, 133,
              134, 135, 138, 139,
              140, 142, 143, 144,
                145, 153, 154,
              161, 170, 178, 264
     29.4.6 .... 37, 89, 161
     29.5–6 .... 35, 42, 105
     29.5 47
     29.5.1 105
     29.5.2 .... 25, 32, 93, 105,
                     112, 171
     29.5.4 104
     29.6 .... 32, 105, 106, 156,
                     165, 166
     34 .... 17, 18, 19, 156
     34.1 .... 27, 36
     34.3.2 22
     34.3.2 128
     34.3.3 22
     34.4.3 .... 17, 19, 126
     34.4.5 .... 60, 62
     38.2 177
     38.5 74
     40.3 .... 71, 126, 127, 135
     40.3.3 .... 20, 129, 130, 133,
              135, 140, 143, 144,
              145, 146, 147, 152,
                  153, 154
     41 .... 71, 75, 126, 127
     41.1.1 127
     42 .... 126, 127
     43 .... 71, 72, 126, 127
     46 .... 135, 141, 156

TABLE OF STATUTES

1851 Petty Sessions (Ireland) Act.   62
      s.10(4) (14 & 15 Vict., c. 93) 59, 194
1927 Public Safety Act (No. 31)—
      s.3.   193
1951 Criminal Justice Act (No. 2)—
      s.2.   194
1957 Statute of Limitations (No. 6)   108
1965 Extradition Act (No. 17)—
      Part II. 32, 154
      s.11   108
      s.50   124
1972 European Communities Act
      (No. 27). 32, 52, 53, 56, 57,
                        60, 61, 106, 156, 165,
                        166, 169, 171, 174,
                        176, 178, 180, 181,
                        183, 184, 185, 193,
                                          195
      s.1. . . . . .   121, 156, 165, 166, **167**,
                                     170, 171
      (2).   177
      s.2. . . . . 13, 14, 15, 19, 51, 55, 59,
                    60, 62, 64, 79, 121, 166, **171**,
                                     172, 174
      (1). 7, 11, 19, 35, 80, 87,
                                     106, 174
      (2). 87, 106, 172, 174, 175
      s.3. . 51, 60, 64, 165, 166, 172, 174,
                175, 176, 178, 193, 194
      (1). 51, 59, 179
      (2). . . 51, 52, 56, 58, 59, 61, 67,
                    131, 142, 176, 194
      (3). 62, 176, 195
      s.4. . 55, 57, 59, 165, 166, 172, **177**,
                178, 179, 180, 182, 193, 196
      s.5. . . . . 166, **181**
      s.6. . . . .   **181**
      Third Amendment of the Con-
        stitution Act. . . 13, 31, 155, 161
      Preamble **155**
      s.1. . . . .   **155**
      Local   Elections   Act
        (No. 12)—
      s.1.   271
1973 European   Communities
      (Amendment)   Act
      (No. 20)   179,
                                    182, 196
      s.1. . . . .   177, **183**
      (2).   177
      s.2. . . . .   **183**
      European Communities (Con-
        firmation of Regulations)
        (No. 5) Act 55, **181**
      ss.1–2   182
1977–1993 European   Parliament
        Election Acts   272
1977 European Assembly Elections
        Act (No. 30)   188

1977 European   Communities
      (Amendment)   Act
      (No. 5). 39, 165, **183**
      s.1. . . . . 167, **184**
      s.2. . . . .   **184**
      s.3.   271
      s.7.   271
      Protection of Young Persons
        (Employment)   Act
        (No. 9)   65
1979 European   Communities
      (Amendment)   Act
      (No. 32). 165, 169,
                                          184
      s.1. . . . . 167, **185**
      s.2. . . . .   **185**
1984 Ninth Amendment of the Con-
        stitution Act 41, 272
      European Assembly Elections
        Act (No. 6)   188
1985 Electoral (Amendment) Act
        (No. 1)   41
      European   Communities
      (Amendment)   Act
      (No. 1).   165,
                                     169, **185**
      s.1. . . . .   **186**
      s.2. . . . .   **186**
1985 European   Communities
      (Amendment) (No. 2)
      Act (No. 19). 169, **186**
      s.1. . . . . 168, **187**
      s.2. . . . .   **187**
1986 European   Communities
      (Amendment)   Act
      (No. 37). 26, 27, 29, 30, 39,
                        48, 49, 126, 160, 161,
                        165, 169, 170, 187
      s.1. . . . .   **188**
      (1).   168
      s.2. . . . .   **188**
      s.3. . . . .   **188**
1987 Tenth Amendment of the
        Constitution Act. . .   13, 25, 30,
                                     159, 161
      s.1. . . . .   **159**
1991 Contractual   Obligations
      (Applicable Law) Act
      (No. 8)   36
1992 Electoral Act.   175
      s.8(2)(a).   272
      (3).   272
      s.9.   271
      s.10.   271
      Eleventh Amendment of the
        Constitution Act. . .   13, 37, 39,
                                     135, **160**
      s.1. . . . .   **161**
      s.2. . . . .   **162**

1992 European Communities
(Amendment) Act
(No. 23). 106, 165, 170,
172, **189**
s.1. . . . . 170, **189**
(1). 168
s.2. . . . . **189**
s.3. . . . . **190**
1993 Animal Remedies Act
(No. 23). 66, 176, 178
s.9. 58
ss.20–22. 62
s.22(2). 194
s.23(1)(b). 177
European Communities
(Amendment) Act
(No. 25). 165, 170, 175,
190, 193
s.1. . . . . **191**
s.2. . . . . 175, **191**
(1)(b) 168
s.3. . . . . 171, 174, **192**
s.4. . . . . 175, **192**
(1). 174
(2). 174
s.5(1)–5(3) 193
s.5. . . . . **192**, 193
(1). 193, 194
(2). 193, 194
(3). 193, 194

1993 European Communities
(Amendment) Act—*cont.*
s.6. . . . . 178, **196**
(1). 177, 197
(2). 178
s.7. . . . . **195**
European Parliament Elec-
tions Act (No. 30) 188
1994 Criminal Justice (Public
Order) Act (No. 2). . . . 178
European Communities
(Amendment) Act
(No. 30). 165, 170, 171,
195, 196
s.1. . . . . **196**
(1). 168
s.2. . . . . **196**
Local Government Act
(No. 8)—
s.23. 271
Road Traffic Act (No. 7)—
s.48. 194
1995 European Communities
(Amendment) Act
(No. 6). 165, **196**
s.1. . . . . 55, 177, **196**
s.2. . . . . **197**
(1). 197
(2). 197

TABLE OF STATUTORY INSTRUMENTS

1975 Food Standards (Certain Sugars) (E.C.) Regulations (S.I. 1975 No. 188)—
    reg. 5. 180
1976 European Communities (Statistical Surveys) Regulations (S.I. 1976 No. 223) 181
1977 European Communities (Road Traffic) (Compulsory Insurance) Regulations (S.I. 1975 No. 178) 181
1980 European Communities (Safeguarding of Employees Rights on Transfer of Ownership) Regulations (S.I. 1980 No. 306) 65
1982 Fuels (Control of Supplies) Order. 17
1985 European Communities (Milk Levy) Regulations—
    Art. 40(3). 71
    (5). 71
1986 European Communities (Amendment) Act, 1986 (Commencement) Order, 1987 (S.I. No. 170). . . 160, 188
    European Communities (Life Assurance Accounts, Statements and Valuations) Regulations (S.I. 1986 No. 437)—
    reg. 4. 181

1988 European Communities (Material and Articles in contact with Foodstuffs) Regulations (S.I. 1988 No. 60)—
    reg. 4. 181
    European Communities (Control of Oestrogenic, Andogenic, Gestagenic and Thyrosatic Substances) Regulations (S.I. 1988 No. 218) 58, 59
    Art. 16. 58
    32(8). 58
1990 European Communities (Control of Veterinary Medicinal Products and their Residues) Regulations (S.I. 1990 No. 171) 58, 59
    Art. 11(4). 58
1993 European Communities (Amendment) Act, 1992 (Commencement) Order (S.I. 1993 No. 304) 190
1994 European Parliament Elections (Voting and Candidature) Regulations 1994 (S.I. No. 14) 272

TABLE OF EUROPEAN TREATIES

1951	European Coal and Steel Community Treaty....	166
	Art. 41..............	34
	Art. 84..............	151
1957	Convention on Institutions Common to the Communities..........	166
	Euratom Treaty.........	166
	Art. 102.............	80
	Art. 141.............	35
	Art. 142.............	35
	Art. 150.............	34
	Art. 207.............	151
	European Community Treaty (Treaty of Rome)....	166
	Preamble............	254
	Art. 1............	100, **254**
	Arts. 2–3...........	332
	Art. 2.... 153, **255**, 257, 320, 330, 360, 376, 389, 391	
	(1)............	356
	(2)............	207
	(6)............	211
	Art. 3.... 208, 254, 255, **256**, 258, 259, 294, 391	
	(*a*)............	257
	(*b*)............	257
	(*c*)............	257
	(*d*)............	258
	(*e*)............	257
	(*f*)............	257
	(*g*)............	257, 258
	(*h*)............	257
	(*i*)............	258
	(*j*)............	258, 264
	(*k*)............	258
	(*l*)............	259
	(*m*)............	258
	(*n*)............	258
	(*o*)............	258
	(*p*)............	258
	(*q*)............	258
	(*r*)............	258, 259
	(*t*)............	259
	Art. 3a.... 215, 256, **259**, 320, 330	
	(1)............	259
	(2)............	259
	(3)............	215
	Art. 3b.. 59, 76, 80, 137, 208, 256, **260**, 261, 331, 377	
	Art. 4. 96, **263**, 264, 330, 332, 392, 409, 410	
	Art. 5. 9, 13, 15, 16, 20, 30, 37, 38, 42, 53, 58, 64, 66, 74, 86, 87, 93, 113, 154, 174, 256, **265**, 275, 389, 404	

1957	European Community Treaty (Treaty of Rome)—*cont.*	
	Art. 6...... 211, **265**, 362, 393	
	(1)............	294
	(2)............	301
	Arts. 7–16...........	332
	Art. 7a–c............	267
	Art. 7........... **265**, 347, 362	
	Art. 7a... 198, 205, 216, 257, 262, 269, 294, 311, 312, 315, 366	
	Art. 7b.............	**267**
	Art. 7c.............	**267**
	Arts. 8a–c...........	267
	Arts. 8a–d...........	267
	Arts. 8–8e......... 41, 100, 209	
	Art. 8...... 266, 267, **268**, 269	
	Art. 8a... 198, 216, 257, 262, 268, **269**, 270, 294, 311, 312, 315	
	8a(1).............	269
	(2)............	14
	Art. 8b.... 42, 175, 268, **270**, 271	
	(1)............ 42, 271	
	Art. 8c....... 268, **272**, 273	
	Art. 8d............ **273**, 387	
	Art. 8e.. 41, 42, 269, 270, **274**, 275	
	Arts. 9–37...........	209
	Arts. 9–130y........	275
	Art. 9............. **275**, 343	
	Art. 10............ **275**, 394	
	(2)............	397
	Art. 11.............	**276**
	(1)............	351
	Art. 12............. **276**, 397	
	Art. 13............. **276**, 397	
	Art. 14............. **276**, 398	
	Art. 15.............	**277**
	(1)............	343
	(4)............	343
	Art. 16.............	**277**
	Art. 17............. **277**, 332	
	(1)............	392
	(2)............	392
	Art. 18......... **278**, 332, 394	
	Art. 19.............	**278**
	(1)............ 332, 334	
	(2)............	332
	Art. 20............. **278**, 332	
	Art. 21.............	**279**
	Art. 22............. **279**, 332, 334	
	Art. 23............. **279**, 332	
	Art. 24............. **280**, 332	
	Art. 25.............	**280**
	Art. 26............. **280**, 332	
	Art. 27.............	**280**
	Art. 28.............	**280**
	(1)............	332
	Art. 29.............	**281**

1957 European Community Treaty
       (Treaty of Rome)—*cont.*
       Art. 29(2).   332
       Art. 30. . . . . . .   17, 268, **281**, 365
          (1).   330
          (4).   332
       Art. 31. . . . .   17, **281**
       Art. 32. . . . .   **281**
          (2).   332
          (4).   332
          (6).   332
       Art. 33. . . . .   **281**
       Art. 34. . . . .   **282**, 332
          (3).   332
       Art. 35. . . . .   **282**
       Art. 36. . . . . . .   17, **283**, 300, 332
       Art. 37. . . . .   **283**
       Arts. 38–46.   257
       Arts. 38–47.   209
       Art. 38. . . . .   **283**
       Art. 39. . . . .   262, **284**
       Art. 40. . . . .   **284**
       Art. 41. . . . .   **285**
       Art. 42. . . . .   **285**
       Art. 43. . . . .   **285**
       Art. 44. . . . .   **286**
       Art. 45. . . . .   **287**
       Art. 46. . . . .   **287**
       Art. 47. . . . .   **288**
       Arts. 48–52.   269
       Art. 48. . . . .   **288**, 289
       Art. 49. . . . .   **288**, 415, 421
          (2).   414
       Art. 50. . . . .   **289**
       Art. 51. . . . .   **289**
       Arts. 52–66.   300
       Art. 52. . . . .   **289**, 290, 300
       Art. 53. . . . .   **289**
       Art. 54. . . . .   **289**, 290, 421
          (2).   415
       Art. 55. . . . .   **290**, 300
       Art. 56. . . . .   130, 145, **291**
          (2).   415
       Art. 57. . . . .   **291**
          (1).   415
          (2). 291, 415
       Art. 58. . . . .   **291**
       Art. 59. . . . .   **292**
       Art. 60. . . . .   130, 136, **292**
       Art. 61. . . . .   **292**
       Art. 62. . . . .   **292**
       Art. 63. . . . .   **292**, 421
       Art. 64. . . . .   **293**
       Art. 65. . . . .   **293**
       Art. 66. . . . .   **293**
       Arts. 67–73.   293
       Art. 67. . . . .   216, 293, **294**
          (1).   297
          (2).   297
       Art. 68. . . . .   **294**
       Art. 69. . . . .   294, **295**, 301
       Art. 70. . . . .   **295**, 298
       Art. 71. . . . .   **295**, 296
       Art. 72. . . . .   **295**, 296

1957 European Community Treaty
       (Treaty of Rome)—*cont.*
       Arts. 73a–h. 209, 296
       Arts. 73b–g. 293, 297, 302
       Art. 73. . . . .   **295**, 296
          (1).   296
          (c).   304
          (2). 296, 298
       Art. 73a. 293, 297
       Art. 73b 217, 293, 296, **297**, 299, 300
       Art. 73c. **298**
          (1). 296, 297
          (2).   297
       Art. 73d. 296, **298**, 299
          (1).   296
          (2).   296
          (3).   296
       Art. 73e. 217, 294, **300**
       Art. 73f. 296, 297, 301
       Art. 73g. 296, 297, **301**
          (1). 296, 302
          (2). 296, 302
       Art. 73h. 297, **302**, 303
       Art. 74. . . . .   **303**
       Art. 75. . . . .   262, **303**, 421
          (1).   304
          (3).   304
       Art. 76. . . . .   **304**
       Art. 77. . . . .   **304**
       Art. 78. . . . .   **304**
       Art. 79. . . . .   **304**, 421
       Art. 80. . . . .   **305**
       Art. 81. . . . .   **305**
       Art. 82. . . . .   **305**
       Art. 83. . . . .   **305**
       Art. 84. . . . .   **306**, 421
       Arts. 85–94.   209
       Art. 85. . . . .   173, **306**
          (1).   114
       Art. 86. . . . .   173, **307**
       Art. 87. . . . .   **307**
       Art. 88. . . . .   **307**, 403
       Art. 89. . . . .   **307**
       Art. 90. . . . .   **308**
       Art. 91. . . . .   **308**
       Art. 92. . . . .   **308**
          (3).   209
       Art. 93. . . . .   **309**
       Art. 94. . . . .   209, **310**
       Art. 95. . . . .   268, **310**
          (2).   399
       Art. 96. . . . .   **310**
       Art. 97. . . . .   **310**
       Art. 98. . . . .   **310**
       Art. 99. . . . . . .   207, 214, **311**, 421
       Art. 100. . . . . .   207, **311**, 365, 421
       Art. 100a . .   54, 210, 257, **311**, 363,
                              364, 365, 372, 412, 421
          (3).   365
       Art. 100b. **312**
       Art. 100c 27, 92, 203, 204, 258, **312**,
                              313, 316
          (1). 258, 313, 314
          (2). 206, 258

1957 European Community Treaty
       (Treaty of Rome)—*cont.*
       Art. 100c(3) 313, 314
           (6)   313
           (7) 313, 314, 315
       Art. 100d **315**, 316
       Art. 101 . . . . **316**
       Arts. 102a–104c 215, 317
       Arts. 102a–109   209
       Arts. 102a–109m 215, 259
       Art. 102 . . . . 262, **316**
       Art. 102a 39, 255, 318, **319**,
                                 320, 321
       Art. 102c   321
       Art. 102d   321
       Art. 103 . . 215, 318, **320**, 321, 322,
                          325, 326, 336
           (2) 95, 318, 320, **322**
           (4) 216, 327, 340
       Art. 103a   207
       Art. 104–104b   318
       Art. 104c(3)–(14)   318
       Art. 104 . . . 217, 318, **323**, 324, 341
       Art. 104a 217, **323**, 341
           (2)   324
       Art. 104b **323**
           (2)   323
       Art. 104c 318, **324**, 326, 328,
                             329, 341, 370
           (1) . . . 216, 325, 326, 328
           (2) 318, 325, 327, 328, 347
           (5)   327
           (9) 326, 328, 349
           (11) . . 216, 318, 326, 349
           (13) 327, 328
           (14) 326, 329
       Arts. 105–109   215
       Arts. 105–109m   318
       Art. 105 . . . . 318, **329**, 336
           (1) 330, 349
           (2) 330, 349
           (3) 330, 349
           (4)   330
           (5) 331, 349
           (6) 214, 330, 334
       Art. 105a **331**, 349, 352
       Art. 105a(2)   331
       Art. 106 . . . . 318, **331**, 338
           (1)   332
           (2)   337
           (3)   332
           (5) 214, 332
           (6) 330, 334
       Arts. 107–109   318
       Art. 107 . . . . . 318, **332**, 337, 347
       Art. 108 . . . 294, **333**, 346, 347, 349
       Art. 108a **333**
       Arts. 109a–b   318
       Arts. 109a–d 264, 318
       Arts. 109e–m   319
       Art. 109 . . . 330, **335**, 340, 346, 349
       Art. 109a **337**
           (2)(b)   349
       Art. 109b(3)   322
       Art. 109c 318, 327, **338**

1957 European Community Treaty
       (Treaty of Rome)—*cont.*
       Art. 109c(1) 327, 337
           (2)   327
           (3)   326
           (4)   340
       Art. 109d 318, **340**
       Art. 109e **340**
           (1) 217, 319
           (3) . . . 217, 319, 322, 323,
                          326, 329
           (4) 217, 326
           (5)   217
       Art. 109f 319, **341**
           (2)   319
           (3)   319
       Art. 109g **344**
       Art. 109h . . 301, 340, **345**, 346, 350
           (3)   336
           (5)   336
       Art. 109i 301, **346**, 350
       Art. 109j 217, 218, 321, 327,
                           340, **346**, 352
           (1) 319, 349
           (2) 319, 349
           (3) . . . 218, 319, 349, 351
           (4) 217, 319, 349
       Art. 109k **348**, 351
           (2)   218
           (4)   335
           (6)   346
       Art. 109(1)   336
       Art. 109l **350**
           (4)   345
           (5) 340, 351
       Art. 109m **352**
       Arts. 110–116   352
       Arts. 110–130y   209
       Art. 110 . . . .   **352**
       Art. 111 . . . . 352, **353**
       Art. 112 . . . .   **353**
       Art. 113 . . . . 258, 262, **353**, 354,
                              410, 435
           (3)   353
           (4)   435
       Art. 114 . . . .   **354**
       Art. 115   354
       Art. 116 . . . .   **355**
       Arts. 117–122 . . . . 201, 210, 355
       Art. 117 . . . . 210, 355, **356**
       Art. 118 . . . . 210, **356**
       Art. 118a 210, 211, 355, 356,
                              357, 421
       Art. 118b **357**
       Art. 119 . . . . 210, 211, **357**
       Art. 120 . . . .   **358**
       Art. 121 . . . .   **358**, 421
       Art. 122 . . . .   **358**
       Arts. 123–125 . . . . 362, 368
       Art. 123 . . . .   **358**, 359
       Art. 124 . . . .   **359**
       Art. 125 . . . .   **359**
       Art. 126 . . . . 208, 359, **360**, 361,
                              371, 421
           (4) 206, 208, 361, 415

1957   European Community Treaty
       (Treaty of Rome)—*cont.*
       Art. 127 . .   208, 355, 359, 360, **361**,
                        362, 363, 371, 421
             (1).   361
             (2).   362
             (4).   206
       Art. 128. .   208, 359, 361, **362**, 363,
                        372, 421
             (2).   363
             (5). 208, 415
       Art. 129 206, 264, 265, **363**, 421, 422
             (1).   364
             (4). 208, 364
       Art. 129a. 259, **364**, 365, 421
             (2). 206, 415
       Art. 129b **366**
       Art. 129c **366**
             (1). 259, 366
             (3)   366
       Art. 129d. .   206, 208, 366, **367**, 421
             (1).   415
       Art. 130. . .   259, 264, **367**, 421, 422
       Art. 130a–e   258
       Art. 130a. 366, **368**, 422
       Art. 130b. **369**, 421, 422
       Art. 130c **369**
       Art. 130d. 258, 359, 366, **369**,
                        370, 421
             (1).   214
       Art. 130e. **370**, 421
       Arts. 130f–q   371
       Art. 130f. 371, **372**
             (1)   372
       Art. 130g. 371, **372**
             (5)   370
       Art. 130h **373**
       Art. 130i. 371, **373**, 415, 421
             (1). 374, 415
             (3). 371, 374
             (4). 371, 374
       Art. 130j–l   206
       Art. 130j **374**
       Art. 130k **374**
       Art. 130l **374**
       Art. 130m **375**
       Art. 130n **375**
       Art. 130o. 371, **375**
       Art. 130p. 374, **375**
       Art. 130q. 371, 374, **375**
       Art. 130r–t   375
       Art. 130r. **376**, 378
             (2). 258, 375, 377
             (4)   377
             (5)   377
       Art. 130s. 206, **377**, 378, 421
             (5)   376
       Art. 130t. 375, 376, **379**
       Art. 130u–y   379
             (1). 379, 381
       Art. 130v. 379, **380**
       Art. 130w. 206, **380**
       Art. 130x **381**
       Art. 130y   380

1957   European Community Treaty
       (Treaty of Rome)—*cont.*
       Art. 130(3). 259, 368, 415
       Arts. 131–136a   258
       Art. 131 . . . .   **381**
       Art. 132 . . . .   **382**
       Art. 133 . . . .   **382**
       Art. 134 . . . .   **383**
       Art. 135 . . . .   **383**
       Art. 136 . . . .   **383**
       Art. 136a **383**
       Arts. 137–143   211
       Arts. 137–198e   209
       Art. 137. . . . .   211, **383**
       Art. 138. . . . .   275, **384**
             (3). 272, 385
       Arts. 138a–e   385
             (2). 214, 384
             (3).   207
       Art. 138a **385**
       Art. 138b. 212, **385**
       Art. 138c. 211, **386**
       Art. 138d. 273, **387**
       Art. 138e. 207, **387**
             (4)   385
       Art. 139 . . . .   **389**
       Art. 140 . . . .   **389**
       Art. 141 . . . .   **389**
       Art. 142 . . . .   **389**
       Art. 143 . . . .   **389**
       Art. 144. . . . .   212, **389**, 398
       Arts. 145–154   213
       Art. 145 . . . .   **390**
       Art. 145, indent 3   436
       Art. 146. . . . . .   96, 99, 113, **391**
       Art. 147 . . . .   **391**
       Art. 148 . . . .   **391**
             (1).   435
             (2). . . .   328, 336, 350, **392**
             (3).   350
       Art. 149 . . . .   **392**
             (1).   411
             (2)   208, 214, 289, 290, 291,
                        411, 413, 417
       Art. 150 . . . .   **392**
       Art. 151. . . . .   316, 327, **392**
       Art. 152. . . . .   340, 386, **392**
       Art. 153 . . . .   **393**
       Art. 154 . . . .   **393**
       Art. 155 . . . .   **393**
       Arts. 156–163. . . . .   212, 393
       Art. 156. . . . .   **393**, 394
       Art. 157. . . . .   212, **394**
             (1).   395
             (2).   95, 333, 395, 397, 419
       Art. 158. . . . .   212, 390, 393, **395**
             (1).   397
             (2). 390, 396
             (3). 395, 396
       Art. 159 . . . .   **397**
       Art. 160   395
       Art. 161 . . . .   **398**
       Art. 162 . . . .   **398**
       Art. 163 . . . .   **398**

1957 European Community Treaty
(Treaty of Rome)—*cont.*
Art. 164. . . . . 146, 149, 228, 263,
273, **399**
Arts. 165–184 213
Art. 165. . . . . 207, **399**
Art. 166. . . . . 207, **400**
Art. 167. . . . . 95, **400**
Art. 168. . . . . **400**
Art. 168a. 213, 399, **400**, 401
Arts. 169–171 213
Art. 169. . . . 35, 58, 274, 298, 314,
328, 344, 387, **402**,
403, 407, 408
Art. 170. 35
Art. 170. . . . . . 35, 58, 314, 328,
402, 403
Art. 171. . . . . 212, 213, 257, 334,
402, 403, 404
(2). 399
Art. 172. . . . . 334, **405**
Art. 173 . . . 58, 210, 261, 263, 264,
334, 344, 357, 401,
405, 406, 408, 422
Art. 174. . . . . 58, **405**
Art. 175. . . . . 76, 344, 406
Art. 176. . . . . 344, **406**
Art. 177. . . . 17, 18, 19, 20, 21, 22,
30, 34, 38, 73, 78, 117, 129,
131, 142, 154, 314,
344, 401, **406**, 407
Art. 178. . . . . 344, **407**, 431
Art. 179. . . . . 401, **407**
Art. 180. . . . . . 265, 344, **407**, 408
Art. 181 . . . . **408**
Art. 182 . . . . **408**
Art. 183 . . . . **408**
Art. 184 . . . . **408**
Art. 185 . . . . **408**
Art. 186 . . . . **408**
Art. 187 . . . . **408**
Art. 188 . . . . **408**
Art. 188a–c. 168, 263, 409
Art. 188a. **409**, 428
Art. 188b **409**
Art. 188c **410**
Art. 189. . . 53, 55, 64, 66, 72, 274,
321, 334, **411**
Art. 189a. 322, **411**, 413
(1). . . 327, 336, 414, 415
(2). 336, 415
Art. 189b . . 52, 207, 208, 211, 214,
274, 289, 290, 291, 312,
361, 363, 371, 383, 405,
408, 411, **412**, 413, 414,
415, 417, 418, 436
(2) 414
(a) 414
(b) 414
(c) 414
(d) 414
(3). 412, 414
(4). 412, 414, 415

1957 European Community Treaty
(Treaty of Rome)—*cont.*
Art. 189b(5) 412
(6) 415
(7). 414, 415
(8). 219, 415, 439
Art. 189c. 208, 214, 265, 289,
290, 291, 304, 322,
357, 362, 414, **416**,
436
(3) 51
Arts. 190–192 334
Art. 190. . . . . 334, **417**
Art. 191. . . . . 415, **417**
(1) 417
(2) 417
Art. 192. . . . . 115, **418**
Arts. 193–198 213
Art. 193 . . . . **418**
Art. 194 . . . . **418**, 419, 421
Art. 195 . . . . **419**
Art. 196 . . . . **419**, 420, 421
Art. 197 . . . . **419**
Art. 198 . . . . **420**, 421
Art. 198a–c 213
Art. 198a. 419, **420**
Art. 198b. **419**, 421
Art. 198c. 420, **421**
Art. 198d. 264, **422**
Art. 198e. 264, **422**
Art. 199 . . . . **423**
Art. 200 . . . . **423**, 429
Art. 201 . . . . 207, **423**, 424
Art. 201a **424**
Art. 202 . . . . **424**
Art. 203 . . . . **425**
Art. 204 . . . . **427**
Art. 205 . . . . **427**
Art. 205a **427**
Art. 206. . . . . . 168, 263, 409, **428**
(2)–(10) 410
Art. 206a. 409, 411, 428
Art. 206b 428
Art. 207 . . . . **428**
Art. 208 . . . . **429**
Art. 209 . . . . **429**
Art. 209a. 264, 411, **429**
Art. 210. . . . . 90, 100, **430**
Art. 211. . . . . 90, 103, **430**
Art. 212 . . . . **430**
Art. 213 . . . . **430**
Art. 214 . . . . **430**
Art. 215. . . . . 149, **431**, 344
(2) 431
Art. 216 . . . . **431**
Art. 217 . . . . **431**
Art. 218 . . . . **431**
Art. 219 . . . . **431**
Art. 220. . . 36, 37, 38, 93, 275, **431**
Art. 221 . . . . **431**
Art. 222 . . . . **431**
Art. 223 . . . . **431**
Art. 224. . . . . 302, **431**
Art. 225 . . . . **431**
Art. 226 . . . . **431**
Art. 227 . . . . **431**

1957 European Community Treaty
(Treaty of Rome)—*cont.*
Art. 227(5)............ 434
Art. 228..... 79, 80, 86, 174, 204,
208, 228, 335, 353,
380, 381, **434**, 435,
436
(1)........... 435
(3)...... 214, 353, 439
(5)........... 439
(7)...... 79, 82, 83, 84
Art. 228a..... 99, 107, 149, 301,
302, 380, **437**
Art. 229............. **437**
Art. 230............ 229, **437**
Art. 231............. **437**
Art. 232............. **438**
Art. 233............. **438**
Art. 234......... 113, 114, **438**
Art. 235...... 9, 28, 37, 40, 134,
137, 207, 214, 255,
256, 361, 363, 364,
365, 372, 275, **438**
Art. 236 . 28, 30, 97, 173, 199, 237,
275, 436, 438
Art. 237. 28, 97, 207, 237, 438, 439
Art. 238....... 86, 257, 435, **439**
(3)........... 436
Art. 239..... 143, 151, 211, **439**
Art. 240............. **439**
Art. 241............. **439**
Art. 242............. **439**
Art. 243............. **440**
Art. 244............. **440**
Art. 245........... . **440**
Art. 246............ . **440**
Art. 247............. **440**
Art. 248............. **441**
Protocols 1–16....... 442 *et seq.*
Protocol on the Statute of the
European System of Cen-
tral Banks and of the
European Central Bank... 264
Art. 1 .... **442**
Art. 2 .... **442**
Art. 3 .... **442**
Art. 4 .... **443**
Arts. 5(1)–(3)......... 332
Art. 5 .... **443**
(4) 332
Art. 6 .... **443**
Art. 7 .... **443**
Art. 8 .... **444**
Art. 9............. 264, **444**
Art. 10............ 338, **444**
Art. 11............ 338, **444**
Art. 12............ 338, **445**
Art. 13............. **446**
Art. 14............. **446**
Art. 15............. **446**
Art. 16............ 331, **446**
Art. 17............. **447**
Art. 18............. **447**
Art. 19............. **447**
Art. 20............. **447**

1957 European Community Treaty
(Treaty of Rome)—*cont.*
Art. 21............. **447**
Art. 22............. **448**
Art. 23............. **448**
Art. 24............. **448**
Art. 25............. **448**
Art. 26............. **448**
Art. 27............. **449**
Art. 28............. **449**
Art. 29............. **449**
Art. 30............. **450**
Art. 31............. **450**
(2)............. 330
Art. 32............. **450**
Art. 33............. **451**
Art. 34............. **451**
Art. 35............. **452**
Art. 36............. **452**
Art. 37............. **452**
Art. 38............. **452**
Art. 39............. **452**
Art. 40............. **453**
Art. 41............. **453**
Art. 42............. 332, **453**
Art. 43............. **453**
Art. 44............. **453**
Art. 45............. 351, **454**
Art. 46............. **454**
Art. 47............. 351, **454**
(3)............. 351
Art. 48............. **454**
Art. 49............. **454**
Art. 50............. 351, **455**
Art. 51............. **455**
Art. 52............. **455**
Art. 53............. **455**
Protocol on the Statute of the
European Monetary
Institute
Art. 1 .... **456**
Art. 2 .... **456**
Art. 3 .... **456**
Art. 4 .... **456**
Art. 5 .... **457**
Art. 6 .... **457**
Art. 7 .... **458**
Art. 8 .... **458**
Art. 9 .... **458**
Art. 10............. **459**
Art. 11............. **459**
Art. 12............. **460**
Art. 13............. **460**
Art. 14............. **460**
Art. 15............. **460**
Art. 16............. **460**
Art. 17............. **461**
Art. 18............. **461**
Art. 19............. **461**
Art. 20............. **462**
Art. 21............. **462**
Art. 22............. **462**
Art. 23............. **462**

1957 Protocol on the Excessive
  Deficit Procedure
  Art. 1 . . . . 317, 328, **462**
  Art. 2 . . . . 328, **463**
  Art. 3 . . . . 329, **463**
  Art. 4 . . . . 329, **463**
Protocol on the Convergence
  Criteria Referred to in
  Article 109J of the EC
  Treaty
  Art. 1 . . . . **463**
  Art. 2 . . . . 327, **463**
  Art. 3 . . . . 348, **463**
  Art. 4 . . . . **464**
  Art. 5 . . . . **464**
  Art. 6 . . . . **464**
Protocol Amending the Proto-
  col on the Privileges and
  Immunities of the Euro-
  pean Communities
Sole Article **464**
  Art. 23 . . . . **464**
Protocol on Denmark **465**
Protocol on Portugal **465**
Protocol on the Transition to
  the Third Stage of Econ-
  omic and Monetary
  Union **465**
Protocol on Certain Provisions
  Relating to the United
  Kingdom of Great Britain
  and Northern Ireland . . **465**
Protocol on Certain Provisions
  relating to Denmark . . . **467**
Protocol on France **467**
Protocol on Social Policy . . . **468**
Agreement on Social Policy . **468**
  Art. 1 . . . . **468**
  Art. 2 . . . . **469**
  Art. 3 . . . . **469**
  Art. 4 . . . . **470**
  Art. 5 . . . . **470**
  Art. 6 . . . . **470**
  Art. 7 . . . . **470**
  Declaration 1 . . . . **471**
  Declaration 2 . . . . **471**
Protocol on Economic and
  Social Cohesion **471**
Protocol No. 16 264
Protocol on the Statute of the
  European Investment
  Bank 170
  Declarations **473**
Declaration on Civil Protec-
  tion, Energy and Tourism **473**
Declaration on Nationality of
  a Member State **473**
Declaration on Part Three, Ti-
  tles III and VI, of the
  Treaty Establishing the
  European Community . **473**
Declaration on Part Three, Ti-
  tle VI, of the Treaty,
  Establishing the Euro-
  pean Community **473**

1957 Declaration on Monetary Co-
  operation with Non-com-
  munity Countries **473**
Declaration on Monetary
  Relations with the
  Republic of San Marino,
  the Vatican City and the
  Principality of Monaco . **474**
Declaration on Article 73D of
  the Treaty Establishing
  the European Com-
  munity **474**
Declaration on Article 109 of
  the Treaty Establishing
  the European Com-
  munity **474**
Declaration on Part Three, Ti-
  tle XVI, of the Treaty
  Establishing the Euro-
  pean Community **474**
Declaration on Articles 109,
  130R and 130Y of the
  Treaty Establishing the
  European Community . **474**
Declaration on the Directive
  of 24 November 1988
  (Emissions) **474**
Declaration on the European
  Development Fund . . . **474**
Declaration on the Role of
  National Parliaments in
  the European Union . . **474**
Declaration on the Confer-
  ence of the Parliaments . **475**
Declarations on the Number
  of Members of the Com-
  mission and of the Euro-
  pean Parliament **475**
Declaration on the Hierarchy
  of Community Acts . . . **475**
Declaration on the Right of
  Access to Information . **475**
Declaration on Estimated
  Costs Under Commission
  Proposals **475**
Declaration on the Implemen-
  tation of Community Law
  . . . . **475**
Declaration on Assessment of
  the Environmental
  Impact of Community
  Measures **476**
Declaration on the Court of
  Auditors **476**
Declaration on the Economic
  and Social Committee . . **476**
Declaration on Co-operation
  with Charitable Associ-
  ations **476**
Declaration on the Protection
  of Animals **476**

1957	Declaration on the Representation of the Interests of the Overseas Countries and Territories Referred to in Article 227(3) and (5)(A) and (B) of the Treaty Establishing the European Community	**476**
	Declaration on the Outermost Regions of the Community	**477**
1965	Merger Treaty	
	Art. 1.	101, 166
1968	Brussels Convention on Jurisdiction and the Enforcement of Judgments in Civil and Commercial Matters	161
1970	First Budgetary Treaty	166
1972	Treaty of Accession of Ireland to the EEC and Euratom	166
1974	Second Budgetary Treatment	165, 168, 183
1984	Brussels Treaty.	169, 185
1985	Treaty of Accession	
	Art. 2	169
1986	Single European Act.	25, 26, 30, 93, 159, 160, 161, 165, 169, 171
	Preamble	39
	Titles I–IV	25
	Title I.	25, 169
	Title II.	25, 27, 48, 49, 149, 169, 170
	Title III.	25, 26, 28, 29, 30, 43, 45, 46, 47, 48, 49, 100, 102, 161, 165, 169, 170, 187, 200, 202
	Title IV	25
	Art. 1.	28, 48, 49
	Art. 3(1).	25, 188
	Art. 20.	39
	Art. 30(1).	28
	(2)(a).	28
	(b)	28
	(c).	28
	(3)(a).	98
	(5).	437
	Art. 31.	25, 149
	Art. 32.	25, 149
	Art. 33.	26
	(2).	187
	Single European Act Declarations Annexed to Final Act	148
1989	Community Patents Convention	161
1992	European Economic Area Agreement	172
	Pt. II	173
	Pt. III	173
	Pt. IV	173
	Pt. V	173

1992	European Economic Area Agreement—*cont.*	
	Pt. VI	173
	Pt. VII.	172
	Art. 2(c).	83, 174, 175
	Art. 4	175
	Arts. 102–104	192
1993	Protocol Amending the European Economic Area Agreement	172
1993	Act Amending the Protocol on the Statute of the European Investment Bank	170
1994	Corfu Treaty.	165, 170
	Title I	171
	Art. 2	171
1995	Treaty on European Union	**220**
	Title I.	116, 206
	Title II.	152, 206
	Title III.	152, 199, 206
	Title IV.	152, 199, 206
	Title V.	41, 43, 89, 91, 92, 93, 96, 98, 99, 102, 103, 105, 106, 108, 109, 112, 116, 119, 149, 152, 153, 170, 203, 302
	Title VI.	89, 91, 92, 96, 98, 99, 102, 103, 105, 106, 108, 109, 110, 112, 116, 119, 152, 153, 170, 203, 206
	Title VII.	151, 206
	Arts. A–F.	116, 198
	Art. A.	89, 92, 100, 110, 120, 170, 199, 206, **226**, 260
	Art. B.	40, 153, 211, **226**
	Art. C.	100, 101, 102, 109, 202, 211, **226**
	Art. D.	95, 96, 202, **227**
	Art. E.	99, 101, 102, **227**
	Art. F.	**227**, 267
	(2).	109, 116, 138, 205, 228
	(3).	95, 96, 137
	Art. G.	206, **229**
	Art. H.	**229**
	Art. I.	**229**
	Arts. J–S	198
	Art. J.	40, 41, 43, **230**
	Arts. J(1)–(11)	206
	Art. J(1)	94
	(1)	93
	(2).	93, 109, 116
	(3)	94
	(4).	97, 98
	(2).	93, 94
	(1)	98
	(2).	94, 98, 104
	(3)	94
	(3).	41, 94, 95, 104, 153
	(1).	94, 98
	(2)	103
	(3)	94

1995 Treaty on European Union—
        cont.
     Art. J(3)(4). 92, 94
             (5)   94
             (6)   94
          (4)   439
             (1). 40, 41
             (2). 40, 41
             (3). 41, 153
             (6)   40
          (5)(2)   99
             (4)   94
          (6). 94, 100, 272
          (8)   95
             (1)–(2).   93
             (2). 104, 423
             (5)   204
          (11).   94
             (2). . . . 94, 98, 102, 153,
                           204, 423
     Art. K **233**
          (1). 203, 313
          (1)–(6). 204, 314
          (1)–(9)   89
          (1)(7)–(9)   204
          (1). 91, 109
             (2)   107
             (7)   314
             (8)   314
             (9)   314
          (2)(1). 109, 110, 116
          (3)   205
             (1). 91, 98
             (2)   92
             (*a*)–(*b*). 98, 104
             (*b*)–(*c*)   104
             (*b*).   103
             (*c*). . . . 42, 93, 94, 98,
                  103, 107, 110, 112,
                           116, 274
          (4). 204, 316
             (3)   423
          (5)   336
          (8)(2). . . . 94, 98, 102, 107,
                           204, 423
          (9). . . . 42, 92, 94, 203, 204,
                           313, 314

1995 Treaty on European Union—
        cont.
     Art. L. 34, 90, 97, 106, 107,
                  108, 109, 116, 149,
                  152, 205, **236**
          (*c*).   33
     Art. M. . . . 95, 106, 133, 152, **236**
     Art. N. 28, 30, 33, 34, 35, 36,
                  40, 42, 97, 98, 146,
                  150, 173, 202, **236**,
                  237, 275, 314, 436,
                           438, 439
     Art. N(2). 40, 218
     Art. O. 28, 97, 98, 108, 207,
                           214, 439
     Art. P. 106, **237**
     Art. Q **237**
     Art. R. 151, **237**
          (1)   198
          (2). 190, 198
     Art. S **237**
     Protocol Annexed to the
        Treaty   on   European
        Union and to the Treaties
        Establishing the Euro-
        pean Communities. . . .   **238**
     Asylum. **241**
     Disputes Between the ECB
        and the EMI and Their
        Servants **242**
     Police Co-operation **241**
     Practical Arrangements in the
        Field of the Common For-
        eign and Security Policy   **238**
     Use of Languages in the Field
        of the Common Foreign
        and Security Policy. . . .   **239**
     Voting in the Field of the Com-
        mon Foreign and Security
        Policy. **238**
     Western European Union . .   **239**
     Protocol 11. . . . . 52, 209
     Protocol 12. . . . . 52, 209
     Protocol 17. .   13, 130, 133, 135, 139,
                           143–154
     Declaration of 1 May 1992. . . .   144,
                           149, 150
     Declaration No. 31   313

TABLE OF EUROPEAN LEGISLATION

Regulations

Regulation 1969/88, [1988] O.J. L178/1—

Art. 11 345

Regulation 2052/88 [1988] O.J. L185/9................................. 358, 359, 370

Art. 1 359

Regulation 4253/88 [1988] O.J. L375/55—

Art. 14(2) 359

Regulation 4254/88 [1988] O.J. L374/15................................. 359

Regulation 4255/88 [1988] 359

Arts. 1–9.. 359

Regulation 4256/88 [1988] O.J. L374/25.. 359

Regulation 792/93, [1993] O.J. L79/74.. 370

Regulation 2081/93 [1993] O.J. L193/5–47..................................... 358, 359, 370

Regulation 2083/93 [1993] O.J. L193/34..................................... 359, 370

Regulation 2084/93 [1993] O.J. L193/39..................................... 359, 370

Arts. 1–9.. 359

Art. 1 360

Art. 5 359

Regulation 2085/93 [1993] O.J. L193/44..................................... 359, 370

Regulation 32741/93 437

Regulation 3275/93 437

Regulation 3604/93 [1993] O.J. L332/1.. 323, 329

Regulation 3605/93 [1993] O.J. L332 329

Regulation 40/94 [1994] O.J. L11/10 37

Regulation 566/94 [1994] O.J. L72/1 370

Regulation 1164/94 [1994] O.J. L130/1.. 370

Directives

Directive 64/22 [1963–64] O.J. 117 ... 270

Directive 68/369 [1968] O.J. 520 270

Directives—*cont.*

Directive 75/34 [1975] O.J. L14/10.... 270

Directive 75/35 [1975] O.J. L14/14.... 270

Directive 75/129 [1975] O.J. L48/29.. 65

Directive 75/268 [1975] O.J. L128/1.. 71, 75

Art. 6 .... 71, 72

Directive 77/187 [1977] O.J. L61/26.. 65

Directive 79/893 181

Directive 80/987 404

Directive 81/602 58

Directive 81/851 [1981] O.J. L317/1.. 58

Directive 85/358 .... 58, 62

Arts. 1, 3, 6.................................... 62

Directive 86/469 [1986]..................... 58

Directive 88/146 58

Directive 88/299 [1988] O.J. L128/36 58

Directive 88/361 [1988] O.J. L178/5.. 216, 293, 294, 296, 297, 301

Art. 1 296

Art. 3 296

Art. 4 299

Directive 88/378 [1988] O.J. L187/1.. 365

Directive 89/391 [1989] O.J. L183/1.. 356

Directive 90/364, [1990] O.J. L180/26 270

Directive 90/365, [1990] O.J. L180/28 270

Directive 90/366 [1990] O.J. L180/30 270

Directive 92/59, [1992] O.J. L228/24. 365

Directive 92/85 [1992] O.J. L348....... 210, 357

Directive 92/122 [1992] O.J. L409/33 294, 301

Directive 93196 [1993] O.J. L317/59. 270

Directive 93/109 [1993] O.J. L329/39 271, 272

Decisions

Decision 93/591 [1993] O.J. L281/18. 101

Decision 93/728/C.F.S.P. 153

Decision [1994] O.J. L327................. 107

Decision 94/366/C.F.S.P. [1994] O.J. L165.. 107

This book is divided into three parts, which are designed to give an account of the principal constitutional texts which govern Ireland's membership of the European Union and of the Communities comprised therein. In each part, the relevant constitutional text is accompanied by a commentary of varying extent. The term "constitutional" is used advisedly in this context, and in the title of the book, and is intended to apply to all of the materials published in the book. The reference in the title to "constitutional *and treaty* texts" is a response to the risk that the subject-matter of the book would otherwise be too narrowly construed by those who first encounter it. It is the constitutional character, in different senses, of the texts published in this book which unites them.

It is natural that the material in Part 1 of the book should be termed constitutional. Part 1 concerns Articles 29.4.3-6 of the Constitution of Ireland (introduced and altered by the Third, Tenth and Eleventh Amendments), which set out the conditions for the reception of European Community law, and of European Union obligations, in the Irish legal order established under the Constitution. A detailed account is attempted of those conditions, which are for most purposes very accommodating, but which nonetheless pose problems in certain exceptional cases which can only be resolved by the Irish courts or ultimately by the People. Protocol No. 17 to the Maastricht Treaty on European Union is also discussed in this part, as its operation is expressly made dependent on the application of Article 40.3.3 of the Constitution of Ireland.

Part 2 begins with material which a British reader would certainly have no difficulty in recognising as constitutional in character, the European Communities Acts, 1972–95. While these Acts (the texts of which appear in full) govern a miscellany of matters related to Ireland's membership of the Communities, their chief purpose is to create the institutional or constitutional framework for the application of Community law in Ireland, *viz.* the incorporation of the Treaties and of the present and future acts of the institutions into Irish law on the conditions required thereby, and the facilitation of the implementation of Community law by the appropriate Irish authorities, consistently with the conditions set out in the Constitution itself.

The latter half of Part 2, and Part 3, comprise the annotated texts of the two most significant Treaties on European integration: the Maastricht Treaty on European Union of 1992, which established the European Union; and the European Community Treaty (the Treaty of Rome) of 1957, as amended most notably by the Single European Act and by the Maastricht Treaty. The European Court of Justice has described the European Economic Community Treaty (as it was before Maastricht) as "a constitutional charter". It is evident, even had such terms not been employed by the Court, that in the areas governed by the Treaty, the relationship of the Member States with the Communities, and with each other, has been transformed since the 1950s from the plane of the international relations of sovereign States to that of the constitutional relations of the elements in a polity which has many federal characteristics. Not all observers are happy with this outcome, or with the manner in which it was reached, but its occurrence can scarcely be doubted. The term "constitutional" is applied less confidently to the Treaty on European Union, which appears to have been designed to placate the fears of Member States that the sensitive areas of foreign and security policy, and judicial and home affairs co-operation, would also be removed from their sovereign control by the operation of the Community legislative method and the constitutionalising influence of the Court. Nonetheless, it is argued in the text that even the Union Treaty cannot be seen simply as another international agreement; as will be seen, this point is reinforced by the terms of the

1

Eleventh Amendment of the Constitution in 1992. This is hopefully sufficient to justify the use of the term "constitutional" in this instance as well.

Part 3 is based on the commentary published by Paul Beaumont and Gordon Moir in 1994 in a similar book on the British European Communities (Amendment) Act 1993. Some substantive changes have been made, and the opportunity was taken to up-date the text to take account of the coming into force of the Maastricht Treaty, but these parts remain the product for the most part of their labours. The Treaty on European Union and the European Community Treaty are set out in the same manner as in the European Community's unannotated text, *Selected Instruments from the Treaties*, Volume 1, Book 1.

The commentary on the Treaty on European Union is the least extensive in the book, because of the overlap with the discussion in other parts. The non-Community provisions of the Union Treaty are comprehensively analysed in Chapter 7 of Part 1, on the Eleventh Amendment of the Constitution of Ireland. The provisions amending the Treaty of Rome are in turn discussed in Part 3. For reasons of space, and of their marginal relevance to Ireland, the Treaties establishing the European Coal and Steel Community, and the European Atomic Energy Community, are not published, nor are they or the amendments thereto under the Maastricht Treaty discussed.

Part 3 gives a commentary only on those provisions of the Treaty of Rome which were amended by the Treaty on European Union. Immense works have been devoted to the analysis of the European Community Treaty over the years, and the authors did not feel qualified, or able in a book with so wide a remit, to attempt to discuss the constitutional development of the Community since 1957. The predominantly institutional focus of the Maastricht amendments also indicated that such time and space as was available, in the preparation of a book with a constitutional theme, should be devoted to these most recent developments.

PART 1: IRISH CONSTITUTIONAL MATERIAL

CONSTITUTIONAL PROVISION FOR MEMBERSHIP OF THE EUROPEAN COMMUNITIES AND THE EUROPEAN UNION

ARTICLE 29.4.3-6

THE EUROPEAN COMMUNITIES AND EUROPEAN UNION

3° The State may become a member of the European Coal and Steel Community (established by Treaty signed at Paris on the 18th day of April, 1951), the European Economic Community (established by Treaty signed at Rome on the 25th day of March, 1957) and the European Atomic Energy Community (established by Treaty signed at Rome on the 25th day of March, 1957). The State may ratify the Single European Act (signed on behalf of the Member States of the Communities at Luxembourg on the 17th day of February, 1986, and at The Hague on the 28th day of February, 1986).

4° The State may ratify the Treaty on European Union signed at Maastricht on the 7th day of February, 1992, and may become a member of that Union.

5° No provision of this Constitution invalidates laws enacted, acts done or measures adopted by the State which are necessitated by the obligations of membership of the European Union or of the Communities, or prevents laws enacted, acts done or measures adopted by the European Union or by the Communities or by institutions thereof, or by bodies competent under the Treaties establishing the Communities, from having the force of law in the State.

6° The State may ratify the Agreement relating to Community Patents drawn up between the Member States of the Communities and done at Luxembourg on the 15th day of December, 1989.

3° Tig leis an Stát a bheith ina chomhalta den Chomhphobal Eorpach do Ghual agus Cruach (a bunaíodh le Conradh a síníodh i bPáras an 18ú lá d'Aibreán, 1951), de Chomhphobal Eacnamaíochta na hEorpa (a bunaíodh le Conradh a síníodh sa Róimh an 25ú lá de Mhárta 1957) agus den Chomhphobal Eorpach do Fhuinneamh Adamhach (a bunaíodh le Conradh a síníodh sa Róimh an 25ú lá de Mhárta, 1957). Tig leis an Stát an Ionstraim Eorpach Aonair (do síníodh thar ceann Bhallstáit na gComhphobal i Lucsamburg an 17ú lá d'Fheabhra, 1986, agus insan Háig an 28ú lá d'Fheabhra, 1986) do dhaingniú.

4° Tig leis an Stát an Conradh ar an Aontas Eorpach a sínigheadh i Maastricht ar an 7ú lá d'Fheabhra, 1992, do dhaingniú agus tig leis do bheith ina chomhalta den Aontas san.

5° Ní dhéanann aon fhoráileamh atá insan Bhunreacht seo aon dlíghthe d'achtuigh, gníomhartha do rinne nó bearta le n-ar ghlac an Stát, de bhíthin riachtanais ná n-oibleagaidí mar chomhalta den Aontas Eorpach nó de na Comhphobail do chur ó bháil dlíghidh ná cosc do chur le dlíghthe d'achtuigh, gníomhartha do rinne nó bearta le n-ar ghlac an tAontas Eorpach nó na Comhphobail nó institiúidl díobh, nó comhluchtaí atá inneamhail fá na Connarthaí ag bunú na gComhphobal, ó fheidhm dlíghidh do beith aca sa Stát.

6° Tig leis an Stát an Comhaontú maidir le Paitínní Comhphobail a tarrainguigheadh suas idir Ballstáit na gComhphobal agus a rinneadh i Lucsamburg ar an 15adh lá de Nollaig, 1989, do dhaingniú.

5

CHAPTER ONE

INTRODUCTION: THE RECEPTION OF EUROPEAN COMMUNITY LAW IN IRISH LAW

This commentary on the terms of Articles 29.4.3-6 of the Constitution of Ireland is concerned with the reception in Irish law of European Community law (and of the "law" of the European Union). The Third Amendment to the Constitution (later supplemented by the Tenth and Eleventh Amendments to give the present text) was designed to ensure that this reception would be as smooth as possible, and that any State measures necessitated by Community membership, and any legislative or administrative acts of the Community institutions, would be free from constitutional scrutiny. The result was an astonishingly wide immunity clause accompanying the formal authorisation of Community membership: wide in terms both of the class of measures to which it applied, and of the breadth of immediate or potential application of such measures. This was accompanied by the European Communities Act, 1972, section 2(1) of which provides that the "constitutional" Treaties of the Communities and the existing and future acts of the Community institutions are to be part of the law of the State under the conditions laid down in those Treaties (see the annotation below of the Act for a list of the Treaties). This innovation was "sweeping" in effect, and took the "form of [a] *carte blanche* the implications of which cannot be measured in advance .... It is as if the people of Ireland had adopted Community law as a second but transcendent Constitution, with the difference that Community law is not to be found in any single document—it is a living growing organism and the right to interpret it and give it conclusive judicial interpretation is reserved to the institutions of the Community and to its Court" (Henchy J., "The Irish Constitution and the E.E.C." (1977) D.U.L.J. 20, at 21, 23).

Why was this done? It was done because Community law requires that it "takes effect in the Irish legal system in the manner in which it itself provides"—which Costello J. stated was the effect of the constitutional innovations just described, in *Pigs and Bacon Commission v. McCarron* (High Court, June 30, 1978; (1978) J.I.S.E.L. 77). His remarks would seem to indicate that Community law has been effectively received on its own very demanding terms in Irish law. It would however be foolhardy to accept such a conclusion without further inquiry, for at least two reasons. First, one must always be mindful of the possibility of contrary judicial interpretations of the Irish law. As the relevant constitutional and legislative provisions derive their authority from the Constitution of Ireland, it is the courts established under that Constitution which must interpret them. Chapter 8 below details some of the possible problems that could be presented by a less *communautaire* judicial attitude than is currently displayed by the Irish courts. The discussion of *Campus Oil Ltd v. Minister for Industry and Energy* [1983] I.R. 82 in Chapter 2 is also of relevance to this question.

Secondly, the vehicles for the reception of Community law—the Irish constitutional and legislative provisions—may be very accommodating, and nonetheless seem to belie by their very existence the constitutional claims of Community law. The European Court of Justice has long indicated that the Treaties are not to be treated simply as international agreements instituting a very advanced form of co-operation between sovereign States. The Treaties are the constitutional charter of a new legal order, characterised by the supremacy and direct applicability in the law of the Member States of many of the provisions of the Community Treaties and of derived Community legislation. The Member States have irrevocably transferred a number of sovereign powers to the Communities. As with any constitution, the Treaties are both a necessary and a sufficient basis for the obligations of Community law to be effective throughout the territory governed by its legal order, and require no further national act after that of ratification of the Treaties for them to have this constitutional effect (See Case 26/62, *van Gend en Loos v. Nederlandse Belastingadministratie* [1963] E.C.R. 1; Case 6/64, *Costa v. ENEL* [1964] E.C.R. 585; Case 106/77, *Amministraziane delle Finanze dello Stato v. Simmenthal Sp.A.* [1978] E.C.R. 629; Case 294/83, *Les Verts v. Parliament* [1986] E.C.R. 1339; Opinion 1/91, *European Economic Area (No. 1)*: [1991] E.C.R. 6079; see among the vast literature Stein, "Lawyers, Judges, and the Making of a Transnational Constitution" (1981) 75 A.J.I.L. 1; Weiler, "The Community System: The Dual Character of Supranationalism" (1981) 1 Y.E.L. 267, and "The Transformation of Europe" (1991) 100 Yale L.J. 2403; Mancini, "The Making of a Constitution for Europe" (1989) 26 C.M.L.Rev. 595; Lenaerts, "Constitutionalism and the Many Faces of Federalism" (1990) 38 A.J.C.L. 205; Temple Lang, "The Development of European Community Constitutional Law" (1991) 13 D.U.L.J. 36; Everling, "Reflections on the Structure of the European Union" (1992) 29 C.M.L.Rev. 1053; Jacobs, "Is the Court of Justice of the European Communities a Constitutional Court?" in Curtin & O'Keeffe eds., *Constitutional Adjudication in European Community and National Law* (1992) 25; *cf.* Wyatt, "New Legal Order or Old?" (1982) 7 E.L.R. 147; Handoll, "The Protection of National Interests in the European Union" (1994) 3 I.J.E.L. 221; Phelan, *Revolts or Revolution: the Constitutional Boundaries of the European Community*. Ph.D. Thesis, E.U.I., Florence (1995) (hereinafter, Phelan, *Revolution*)). The words of the Court of Justice in *Costa v. ENEL* give the rudiments of its position (Case 6/64, [1964] E.C.R. 585, at 593; authors' italics):

> "By contrast with ordinary international treaties, the EEC Treaty has created *its own legal system* which, *on the entry into force of the Treaty*, became *an integral part* of the legal systems of the Member States and which their courts are bound to apply."

If the Treaties are the *grundnorm* or ultimate source of authority of Community constitutional law, that law does not in its own terms require an act of reception. The Community legal system is often likened to that of a federation. One rarely if ever finds in the constitutions of the component states of federal states a provision for the reception and supremacy and direct applicability of federal law. This arises automatically from the federal constitution itself, which is a single *grundnorm* for the legal order of a federal State polity. (The term *grundnorm* is employed rather loosely, as the Treaties acknowledge, as do most constitutions, an amending process which in the Community case is probably original rather than derived. Most of the Member States contend that the amending process under the Treaties leaves them with ultimate sovereign power over the development of the Communities: hence their claim to be *Herren der Verträge*, or "Masters of the Treaties"; *cf.* Opinion 1/91 *European Economic Area (No. 1)* [1991] E.C.R. I-6079, and Curtin, "The Constitutional Structure of the Union: A Europe of Bits and Pieces" (1993) 30 C.M.L.Rev. 17, discussed in Chapter 9 below.) Yet all of the Member States (with the possible exceptions of Belgium and Luxembourg) receive Community law, including the Treaties, in their national laws only by virtue of national acts of reception. This may arise from a general constitutional reference to international organisations or international law (*e.g.* in the Netherlands, and originally in France), or from a specific accommodation of the Community legal order (*e.g.* in Ireland, Germany, France and, in a special sense, the United Kingdom). There are at least two reasons for this. First, it was not envisaged at the point of establishment of the Communities that they would develop into a *sui generis* federal polity. Later adherents such as Ireland (and Member States which have made later constitutional amendments, such as Germany and France) acknowledge expressly or by implication (*e.g.* in the use in Article 88 of the French Constitution of the term of art *transferts de compétences*) many of the incidents of the constitutional claims of the Communities as expressed by the European Court of Justice (see generally Hartley, *Foundations of European Community Law* (3rd ed., 1994) pp. 238–65 (hereinafter Hartley, *Foundations*)). They do not really accept the basis of these claims, however, in so far as these constitutional provisions and other acts of reception are still considered, as a matter of national law, to be necessary for Community constitutional law to have force in the national legal order and legal "space". This is largely attributable to a second, more fundamental reason than the original expectations of the High Contracting Parties to the Treaties, which will now be discussed.

The European Communities are generally considered to have limited competence, or *compétence d'attribution*. They can only act with the powers and in the fields entrusted to them by the Treaties, which though "ever-widening" are also perceived to be limited (see *e.g.* Article 36 E.C.). The Communities are not generally considered to have *compétence de la compétence*, or *Kompetenz Kompetenz*, that is, the power to decide on their own powers. While this point may be obscured by Article 235 E.C. (and increasingly by Article 5 E.C. as well; see Temple Lang, "Community Constitutional Law: Article 5 EEC Treaty" (1990) 27 C.M.L.Rev. 645), the terms of Article 235 do seem to disclose some limits (the necessity and appropriateness of measures adopted thereunder to attain one of the objectives of the Community and the Treaty) on its use (see also on this point Phelan, *Revolution*, at 162). This must mean that there are matters of exclusive Member State competence, however difficult to identify, which are unaffected by Community law (although *cf.* Chapter 6 below).

The constitutions of federal states often make provision for exclusive competences of the component states, so this is not determinative. What is more important is the source of such competences. This emerges from the following analysis by Handoll ("The Protection of National Interests in the European Union" (1994) 3 I.J.E.L. 221, at 222–3):

> "It is true that elements of the Community 'constitution' elaborated by the Court of Justice have a 'federal' flavour. The Court is, however, bound to recognise that the Community has an existence and powers limited by the Treaty and that the Member State retains its independence in crucial State-defining fields. However, the idea of federalism as providing a framework for solving conflicts between Community and national legal orders does not work unless it can be seen as an idea embracing the totality of the central and national orders. This can only be so where the original actors—the Member States—agree that an over-arching federation exists (or should exist). They have not done so."

Member State exclusive competences must continue to derive from the national constitutional order. This has resulted in multiple sources of sovereign authority, as Temple Lang has observed ("The Development of European Community Constitutional Law" (1991) 13 D.U.L.J. 36, at 47; there were then 12 Member States):

> "States' powers are not derived from the Community constitution: the Treaty is the basis of the Community's constitutional law, but not that of the States' constitutions. There are 13 *grundnorms* in the Community. But in so far as Community rules now form part of the States' constitutional laws, the States can alter them only by amending the Treaty."

The development of the doctrine of divisible sovereignty has been one of the contributions of the Communities to modern political and legal thought (see Louis, *The Community Legal Order* (2nd ed., 1990) pp. 11–16). However, it poses problems for legal systems long accustomed to locating sovereign authority solely within their own constitutions. From the national constitutional perspective, Community law can be superior, directly applicable, and so on, only if the national constitution permits this in some *nationally effective* fashion. In the Constitutional orders of certain Member States, Community law is not as a matter of principle conceded to be superior to constitutional law, but Community law is in fact given the precedence it claims by the practice of adopting specific constitutional amendments to pre-empt conflict between the two legal orders (this is particularly true of France and Spain—see the contribution of the European Parliament Legal Service to a Symposium of the European Parliament Legal Affairs Committee, *Les relations entre le droit international public; le droit communautaire et le droit constitutionnel des Etats Membres* (1995; PE 213.411) p. 9).

There may be no nationally effective way of receiving certain Community obligations. For example, transfers of sovereignty which undermine the federal and democratic nature of the German State and its protection of human dignity, or the republican nature of the French State, or which are perceived to entail the irrevocable limitation of the powers of the United Kingdom Parliament, would all be nationally ineffective without some doctrinal shift in the political and constitutional doctrine of those States—what Ackerman calls a "constitutional moment" (in *We, the People* (1993)). As will be seen immediately below and in Chapter 8, similar arguments can be made for the ineffectiveness of any purported transfer of power to override the principles of individual rights and the common good, or of natural law recognised in the Constitution of Ireland. Phelan has argued in *Revolution* that there would be a constitutional revolution in Ireland if the primacy of Community law were to be accepted by the Irish courts in a situation of profound normative conflict with such fundamental features of the Irish constitutional order—features which he sees as so fundamental as to be unamendable within the paradigm of the existing Constitution. However, as is pointed out in Chapter 8 below, it can as easily be contended that Ireland's constitutional "moment", or "revolution", took place in 1972 when the Third Amendment was adopted by the People. In either case, however, the revolution is (or would be) incomplete, because the final machinery of reception is (or would remain) intact.

The Community legal order, operating in the legal "space" of the territory of the Member States, is simultaneously both federal and not federal. From the Community perspective, the Community legal order has its own authority and is supreme and (where necessary) directly applicable by virtue of that fact. National competences are residual and are not opposable to the application in its field of action of Community law. The field of action of Community law is determined by the Treaties as interpreted by the Court of Justice. *Within its field of action*, the Community legal order is a federal legal order, *i.e.* within that field it corresponds to Handoll's requirements of federalism. From the national perspective, Community powers, however extensive, are exceptional. The obligations of membership of the Communities (including the "constitutional" requirements of supremacy, direct applicability, etc.) are accommodated by special concessions within the national constitutional order. The national constitutional order remains the over-arching source of authority of both national competence and, *within its territory*, of Community competence, however deferential it may be *de facto* to Community law.

Phelan has suggested that this paradoxical situation, in which the same legal rules can have differing ultimate sources of legitimacy in the different legal orders (national and Community) in which they take (simultaneously) effect, is contrary to Community law (*Revolution*, at 461; see also at 364–367).

> "The present situation is one of permanent disobedience to European Community law because national courts do not accept the doctrine of direct effect [in this context, that Community law takes effect *ex proprio vogore*]. Their reliance on national provisions is not only contrary to European Community constitutional law in the abstract, it is contrary to the principle enunciated in Case 39/72 *Commission v. Italy* [1973]

E.C.R. 101 because the legal nature of the [Community law] right is brought into doubt."

In case 39/72 *Commission v. Italy*, the Court of Justice found that the transportation of Community regulations into Italian law by parliamentary enactments enactments was contrary to E.C. law because it disguised the nature and origin of Community law rights [1973] E.C.R. 101, at paras. 17–18. However, one can take issue with both the particular analogy and the general point posed by Phelan. As regards the former, there is a difference between dressing up directly applicable Community law measures as national law, without attribution of source (thus disguising not only the nature of the rights but also quite possibly, the avenues available for their enforcement in the event of denial), and giving full effect to Community law, acknowledge as such, in a national legal order by virtue of a national provision authorising such effect. It is nowhere indicated that Community law is thereby a species of national law rather than an autonomous legal order, although its force in the national legal order may be (from the national point of view) dependent on national law.

Nor is it evident that the dependence of Community law (as a matter of natural law) on national acts of reception is contrary to Community law in the abstract, precisely because it is only in the national legal order that this dependence is manifest. It is inherent in an order approach to law—the principle that differing legal orders can make differently legitimated claims to regulate the same subject matter, each justified in its own terms—that legal orders may accommodate (or conflict) each other on different bases, each consistent with its own paradigm. The Court of Justice has never claimed that the Community legal order has entirely subsumed the national legal orders, and replaced their legitimating principles with its own. As the paradigmatic quotation above from *Costa v. E.N.E.L.* illustrates, it views Community law as a system, or order, at once distinct from the national legal orders and an integral part of them. Community law claims that integral position as of right, pursuant to the ratification of the Treaties and the accompanying transfer of State sovereignty. It does not follow that it requires a different legal order, which cannot be expected to operate on the same fundamental organising principles, to accept it on its own terms, so long as it is accorded *in fact* the position and priority it claims in national law. Although the concrete claims of Community law are more extensive than those of public international law, both in range and volume and in manner of compliance required (see *e.g.* Phelan, *Revolution*, Chapter 3), there is nothing to support that, as in the case of public international law, Community law cannot be fully accommodated on terms different from but not in practical terms inconsistent with its own by national constitutional legal orders. (Phelan's rejection of this possibility is consistent with another position he implicitly takes, which the authors also find unconvincing, that the Community legal order must evolve into a federal state with a single source of legitimacy, or relapse into public international law; see *e.g. Revolution*, at 19, 26, 107, 172.) It must therefore be unnecessary as well as foolhardy for Community law to require the suppression of national acts of reception which are the means by which its claims are given effect in the national legal orders—acts which, in the words of Carroll J. In the High Court in *Tate v. Minister for Social Welfare* [1995] 1 I.R.L.M. 507, 521 are "the conduit pipe through which Community law became part of domestic law" [as a matter of domestic law].

The fundamental difference in perspective between Community law and national law is obscured in a number of Member States, including Ireland, by what Rawlings has called, in the United Kingdom context, "the principle of the mirror image" ("Legal Politics: The United Kingdom and Ratification of the Treaty on European Union" [1994] P.L. 254, at 258). While Community law is operative in the United Kingdom legal order, as in that of Ireland, only

by virtue of the relevant incorporating provisions of the European Communities Acts (section 2(1) in the Irish case, as supplemented by the terms of
Article 29.4.3-5 of the Constitution), it is sought by that act of incorporation
to grant to Community law the effect in the national legal order which it itself
requires. Thus, the daily interaction of national and Community law, operating on fundamentally different premises, should be conflict-free. While
Costello J.'s remarks in *Pigs and Bacon Commission v. McCurran and
McCurran* on the receipt of Community law in Irish law on its own terms are
therefore inaccurate (see Phelan, *Revolution*, at 364) a possible pretence is
made of doing so consistently with the Irish constitutional paradigm.

The problem with this attempted solution is that the mirror may be flawed.
This is most likely to arise in the Irish case, despite the terms of the relevant
national constitutional and legislative provisions, in a case of deep normative
conflict between the still unharmonized legitimising theories of Community
law and national law. This can best be illustrated by an extensive quotation
from Phelan's discussion of the problem ("Two Hats, One Wig, No Halo" in
Treacy & Whyte eds., *Religion, Morality and Public Policy* (1995) 130, at
130–1):

> "Judges have a European Community law duty to apply E.C. law. This
> duty is direct and does not depend on provisions of national law.
> According to E.C. law, a judge in a Member State who is required to
> apply E.C. law in a case is exercising an E.C. law function pursuant to an
> E.C. law duty.... E.C. law requires that [E.C.] rights take precedence
> over any conflicting right, principle, doctrine or custom of Irish law and
> that they be effectively enforced by the judge.
> Judges have an Irish law duty to apply Irish law. In particular, they have
> a constitutional duty to uphold the Constitution. A judge applying con-
> stitutional law is exercising a constitutional function pursuant to a con-
> stitutional duty.... Constitutional law requires that [constitutional]
> rights take precedence over any conflicting right. However, consti-
> tutional law also provides that no constitutional provisions prevent E.C.
> law having the force of law.
> Some written rights and some unenumerated rights are stated or recog-
> nised by judges to be natural rights, antecedent and superior to positive
> law.... As a matter of Irish law, then, natural rights may prevent an E.C.
> law having the force of law in the State. The judge in such a situation
> faces a conflict of duties [which] is more than a problem resolvable
> within the single legal order of the Constitution....
> What is a judge, experiencing a conflict between the duties imposed by
> two legal orders, to do in order to decide which right to uphold? The two
> legal orders make the same form of command—uphold the right based
> on their respective legal orders—but the result is conflict."

It is beyond the scope of this work to inquire into the philosophical resolution of such normative conflict, but it is essential that the possible legal
effects of such conflict be recognised. They are inherent in the manner in
which Community law is received in Ireland, even if it should never transpire
in practice.

This work has the more limited object of analysing the relationship of
Community law and national law "within the single legal order of the Constitution", but by reference to the "constitutional" requirements of Community
law. (Chapter 9 on the "Irish" Protocol to the Maastricht Treaty on European Union is an exception, but for reasons that are outlined therein.) It will
examine how the constitutional and legislative acts of reception are interpreted in the light of the obligations of Community law, and how they might
be interpreted in future cases (including cases of fundamental conflict). In
effect, it is sought to assess how well the principle of the mirror image has
worked in Ireland. The experience of other national jurisdictions is drawn

upon (especially that of Germany), but *caveats* must be attached to any comparative conclusions due to differing constitutional contexts, and possibly different normative stances in respect of the national acceptance of Community obligations in cases of fundamental conflict.

Much of this commentary (and especially Chapters 4 and 5) proceeds on the basis of a normative presumption (at least outside cases of fundamental conflict) that constitutional protection and constitutional judicial review in Ireland should be limited to the degree, *but only to the degree*, that is required by Community law. The decision of the Supreme Court in *Ryan v. Ireland* [1989] I.R. 177 suggests that immunity clauses (in that case Article 28.3.3 of the Constitution) should be read parsimoniously. Thus, the authors broadly favour the test of "legal obligation" which is derived in chapter 3 from the Supreme Court decision in *Crotty v. An Taoiseach* [1987] I.R. 713), and which is asserted in Chapter 4 to have been misapplied in *Meagher v. Minister for Agriculture* [1994] 1 I.R. 329. However, the jurisprudence on Article 5 E.C. indicates that a test of legal obligation need not be narrowly legalist in effect. For example, Chapter 6 deals with a special case, where the legal obligations of the State under Community law can possibly be extended to fields outwith the limited competence of the Communities by the operation of Article 5 E.C. and the public international law doctrine of State responsibility. Chapter 7 addresses the grievous problems presented by the reception in Irish law of obligations arising from membership of the European Union on the same terms as Community law.

Chapter 8 examines how the principle of the mirror image may break down in cases of profound normative conflict between the national and Community legal orders, and how the acts of reception (in particular Article 29.4.5 of the Constitution) could be interpreted by a judge committed to a normative position inconsistent with the unfailing supremacy of Community law. Chapter 9 analyses a special case, in which a looming normative conflict was sought to be resolved by securing changes in the "constitution" of the Communities, via Protocol No. 17 to the Maastricht Treaty on European Union. This "reception" of Irish constitutional law in Community law encounters problems similar to those which affect the reception of Community law in national law. The substantive commentary is followed by brief annotations of the individual Acts which resulted in the present text: the Third Amendment of the Constitution Act, 1972; the Tenth Amendment of the Constitution Act, 1987; and the Eleventh Amendment of the Constitution Act, 1992.

A few further introductory remarks are necessary on two topics. One is the relationship of the first and second clauses of Article 29.4.5 of the Constitution with each other and with section 2 of the European Communities Act, 1972; the other concerns terminology in the discussion that follows. Phelan has made a number of points in relation to the constitutional and statutory machinery of reception of Community law in Ireland, some of which it is sought to address here (without prejudice to Chapter 8, where many of his ideas on the interpretation of the first clause of Article 29.4.5 of the Constitution are discussed). Phelan makes three remarks (in *Revolution* at 367–370) about section 2 of the European Communities Act, 1972, which states the Community Treaties and the existing and future acts of the Community institutions to be part of the domestic law of the State under the conditions laid down in those Treaties. First, the Act cannot prevent its later repeal by another Act of the Oireachtas; this, of course, is true (save in the extreme case that the legislative power of the Oireachtas under Article 15 of the Constitution is seen as being among the provisions of the Constitution disabled from preventing Community law having the force of law in the State), but it is not in practical terms very important. It is implicit in the continued autonomous subsistence of a legal order which accommodates itself to the

13

existence and claims of another (rather than accepting those claims in their own terms) that the *possibility* persists of abandoning that accommodation; until that occurs, however, the accommodation, if well-conceived in the terms of the accommodating legal order, should proceed smoothly.

Secondly, Phelan suggests that section 2 leaves "the conditions laid down in those [Community] Treaties" open to interpretation by the Irish courts, who might interpret them differently to the Court of Justice. This analysis is stated to be reinforced by the fact that section 2 itself is not required by the Treaties, as interpreted by the Court of Justice, which as a matter of Community law take effect upon ratification and are not dependent on an act of reception. This, however, fails to appreciate the operation of the principle of the mirror image in a situation, admittedly paradoxical but not intolerably so, where the national legislator wishes to accept Community law and all its incidents (including those of primacy and direct effect) within the context of the national legal order. A bridging provision is required, or, as Carroll J. put it, a conduit pipe. Before Community law is received into national law, by an act of incorporation supported by a constitutional amendment designed to save it from unconstitutionality, it has no foothold in that system; its claims (immediately binding upon ratification as a matter of Community law) cannot be heard, especially where the national legal system is dualist and so does not even grant them domestic status as a species of public international law. After reception (if it proceeds on the mirror image principle, as the Irish measures clearly do), Community law should operate as if its claims had in fact been accepted after all. The purpose of the act of reception is to ensure that this pretence can be maintained. Thus, it would be contrary to the object of section 2 of the 1972 Act (which should be read as part of a project or reception of which Article 29.4.3-5 is the other element) to read it as permitting national interpretations of the Community Treaties other than those adopted by the Court of Justice, even though the section itself is otiose from the point of view of Community law. The section can be said to be self-abnegating, in that its chief purpose is to engender a state of affairs in national law which permits the national judge to act in compliance with the requirements of the Community legal order, and thereby to act, as a matter of Community law, as if the section did not exist. This appears to be consistent with the analysis of Carroll J. in *Tate v. Minister for Social Welfare* [1995] 1 I.L.R.M. 507, at 521. After the above-quoted remark, she continued:

> "The Constitution was amended to enable accession to the Community, the European Communities Act, 1972 was passed and the Treaty of Accession was agreed, and thereby the whole body of Community law, past, present and future was incorporated into domestic law. But Community law did not thereby become constitutional law or statute law. It is still Community law governed by Community law but with domestic effect. And it is in that form that it is part of domestic law."

Furthermore, this view enables one to argue that the Act is necessitated by the obligations of membership of the Communities, the test of constitutional immunity in the first clause of Article 29.4.5 of the Constitution, even while maintaining that that test is in all other respects a test of the obligations of Community membership as determined by Community law and thus by the Court of Justice (see Chapters 3 and 8 below in particular). The test of necessity is an Irish constitutional test, which operating within the context of Irish law requires the incorporation of Community law before its obligations can be activated: therefore, the continued validity of the act of incorporation is necessary, on the analysis above, to enable the Irish courts to enforce Community law after incorporation apparently on its own terms, and to protect State acts necessitated by Community law, as a matter of Community law, from invalidation.

Thirdly, Phelan states that section 2 of the 1972 Act cannot give to

Community law a status higher than its own, *i.e.* the status of statute law. However, even presuming this to be the case, its foreseeable practical effects are limited because higher law, *i.e.* constitutional law, will, on a straightforward reading of Article 29.4.5 of the Constitution, be barred from obstructing the operation of the section. (As is pointed out in Chapter 8 below, any effect of natural law independent of the provisions of the Constitution has been discountenanced in *E. v. F and Ireland* [1994] I.L.R.M. 401 and in *Re Article 26 and the Regulation of Information (Services outside the State for Termination of Pregnancies) Bill, 1995,* [1995] 2 I.L.R.M. 81; the effect of the preamble—which is not a constitutional provision as such—is unknown.) Phelan returns to this point when discussing the second clause of Article 29.4.5 of the Constitution (*Revolution*, at 389–391). He states that this bar to constitutional impediments to granting the force of law to Community measures does not mean that the 1972 Act can confer on Community law a status superior to a subsequent statute. This returns us to the first point above, which is relevant only in the event of action on the part of the national legislator to abandon adherence to Community law. (One assumes here, as has been done in the United Kingdom, that the Community law requirement of primacy—which is introduced into Irish law by section 2 of the 1972 Act— will be found, in domestic terms, to exclude *implicit* amendment by an inconsistent later statute of the 1972 Act or of Community law introduced into domestic law by its terms.) One might add, in any event, that the second clause of Article 29.4.5 may indeed, on another construction give constitutional force to Community law, once incorporated; this task of incorporation being left to ordinary legislation because of the frequency with which it must occur, very often for relatively unremarkable amendments (see the annotation below of the various European Community (Amendment) Acts).

The meaning of the phrase "the force of law in the State" in the second clause of Article 29.4.5 must also be discussed more generally. The use of the phrase in the Community context must relate it primarily to the direct applicability in the domestic legal order of certain secondary legislative instruments, *e.g.* E.C. regulations, and some Community agreements with third countries. On the other hand, the first clause appears to relate to the transposition by the national authorities of certain Community measures, such as E.C. directives, into the domestic legal order. A possible supplementary reading of the second clause (of "the force of law in the State"), also in the Community context, is that certain laws, acts or measures of the Communities that are not ordinarily directly applicable, such as E.C. directives, can have legal force in the State in that the courts must take certain steps to ensure their effectiveness in the absence of proper implementation in the State (see the principle of direct effect of directives, and the decisions in Case C-106/89, *Marleasing S.A. v. La Commercial Internacional de Alimentacion S.A.* [1990] E.C.R. I-4135 and Cases C-6, C-9/90 *Francovich & Bonifaci v. Italy* [1991] E.C.R. I-5357). Such innovations in the domestic legal order could, however, be justified quite as easily by their description as obligations of membership of the Communities which necessitate certain action by the courts as judicial organs of the State. One might also speculate about whether the second clause of Article 29.4.5 ensures that Community acts which are executive rather than legislative in character are seen as *lawful* in the State, the provisions of the Constitution notwithstanding. However, the first clause of Article 29.4.5 could in any event protect the administrative measures of the Communities from judicial review in accordance with domestic constitutional principles: such administrative measures are lawful as a matter of Community law provided they are within the competences set out in the Community Treaties and any relevant secondary legislation, and are not in breach of the general principles of Community law. It is then an obligation of membership of the Communities (*e.g.* under Article 5 E.C.) for the courts to reject any domestic challenge, in order not to jeopardize the attainment of the objectives of the Treaties. Even the direct applicability in national courts of E.C. regulations and of provisions of the Treaties could be protected by the first clause on this basis.

An extended interpretation of the first clause of Article 29.4.5 could rob the second clause of virtually any utility. It is not impossible, of course, that the first and second clauses of Article 29.4.5 should overlap in their fields of application. Nonetheless, for ease of exposition in the analyses that follow, the direct applicability of Community law will be treated as being secured in the first instance by the second clause of Article 29.4.5, and the term "the force of law in the State" will be used in its primary meaning of direct applicability. This matter will be further discussed in Chapter 7 in the context of laws, acts and measures of the Union.

The consistent use of terminology is made difficult by changes in both Irish and Community law over the years. The content of the original Third Amendment, Article 29.4.3 of the Constitution, has been expanded, and now spreads over Article 29.4.3-6. This commentary will deal with the present text of the Constitution concerning membership of the European Communities and the European Union and certain ancillary matters. Wherever possible, constitutional provisions are referred to under their present numbering. It has occasionally been necessary, when quoting from judgments or other commentators, or because the context requires it, to refer to relevant provisions by earlier numberings; on such occasions, it has been sought to make this clear.

As regards Community law, it has been sought to follow a consistent practice (from which readers will no doubt notice many unconscious departures). The three Communities are referred to as "the Communities"; the abbreviation "E.C." which formerly could be used for this purpose is now used to refer to the European Community (formerly the European Economic Community). Similarly, Treaty provisions are identified by an abbreviated suffix: Article 5 E.C. identifies that Article of the European Community Treaty (post-Maastricht), and Article 5 EEC its predecessor. "The Community" also indicates the European [Economic] Community, unless the context indicates otherwise. The use of the term "Community" to describe other things, *e.g.* Community law or Community agreements, relates to all three Communities, unless it is indicated otherwise. The term "Union" causes special problems. It is sometimes used to embrace the Communities as well as the other two pillars (common foreign and security policy, and co-operation in the fields of judicial and home affairs), but this should be made clear in the text. It will nearly always be used to indicate matters governed by the Treaty on European Union other than Community matters. It has again been sought to make this clear, by referring to "the non-Community pillars of the Union", but considerations of style have precluded use of this unwieldy formula in all cases. The abbreviated suffix "E.U." identifies provisions of the Treaty on European Union, *e.g.* Article A, E.U. The term "Union law", in so far as it is appropriate at all, is used to describe the legal obligations arising under or pursuant to the operation of the Treaty on European Union other than those arising from Community law. It is not a synonym for Community law, but the opposite, as the two are treated as being mutually exclusive.

CHAPTER TWO

ARTICLE 177 E.C. AND THE INTEGRITY OF COMMUNITY LAW IN IRELAND

The *renvoi préjudiciel* or preliminary reference procedure under Article 177 E.C. is one of the central elements of the protection and projection of the primacy and uniformity of Community law by the European Court of Justice. Its use has not occasioned great difficulty in Ireland, but was the occasion for the first case in which the relationship of Irish and Community law was considered in any detail: *Campus Oil Ltd v. Minister for Industry and Energy* [1983] I.R. 82. One must also address the question of how the procedure is accommodated in Irish judicial proceedings which were developed before accession to the Communities. Special questions are raised by the procedure under Article 26 of the Constitution, whereby the President can refer Bills to the Supreme Court before signature for a decision as to whether they are repugnant to the Constitution.

Campus Oil Ltd v. Minister for Industry and Energy

The decision of the Supreme Court in *Campus Oil Ltd v. Minister for Industry and Energy* [1983] I.R. 82 arose from an appeal from the High Court against a decision by Murphy J. to make a reference to the European Court of Justice under Article 177 EEC. Article 34.4.3 of the Constitution states that "[t]he Supreme Court shall, with such exceptions and subject to such regulations as may be prescribed by law, have appellate jurisdiction from all decisions of the High Court". Murphy J. had sought a preliminary ruling from the Court of Justice on the application of Articles 30, 31 and 36 EEC to the Irish regulatory requirement (under the Fuels (Control of Supplies) Order, 1982) that importers of oil products into the State purchase from a State-owned refinery up to 35 per cent of their requirements of petroleum oil. The Supreme Court decided that there could be no appeal against a decision by the High Court to make a reference.

Walsh J. (O'Higgins C.J. and Hederman J. concurring) stated that a request for a reference was in no way an appeal to a higher court, but a non-contentious request for an interpretation of the Treaty for the benefit of the national judge. He remarked in passing that in Irish law, no appeal lies against the decision of any judge to state a consultative case, and concluded that "in my view the reference made by Mr. Justice Murphy in this case is not a decision within the meaning of Article 34. He made no order having any legal effect upon the parties to the litigation" [1983] I.R. 82, at 86-7. Thus, the Supreme Court's decision was based primarily on a question of Irish constitutional law, that is, whether the innovation of the preliminary reference to the Court of Justice could be deemed to be a decision of the High Court for the purposes of Article 34.4.3. The analogy with the case stated procedure was probably apposite. One can of course criticise the decision on practical grounds, for example, because of the effect on the parties of an unnecessary reference, disposal of which takes, on average, eighteen months. However, the decision to refer and the question of domestic interlocutory remedies are distinct issues, as was made clear in *S.P.U.C. (Ireland) Ltd v. Grogan* [1989] I.R. 753 (discussed in Chapter 8 below). In that case, the Supreme Court granted an interlocutory injunction restraining the defendants from supplying information constituting assistance in obtaining abortions outside the State, on appeal from the High Court where Carroll J. had made an Article 177 EEC reference to the Court of Justice without making such an order. The Supreme Court did not consider her decision to make the reference, although some judges were critical of it.

It is certain *obiter* remarks of Walsh J. in *Campus Oil* that have won most attention. He continued, "even if the reference of questions to the Court of Justice were a decision within the meaning of Article 34 of the Constitution, I would hold that by virtue of the provisions of Article 29.4.3 of the Constitution, the right of appeal to this court from such a decision must yield to the primacy of Article 177 of the Treaty. That Article, as a part of Irish law, qualifies Article 34 of the Constitution in the matter in question" ([1983] I.R. 82, at 87). This statement would probably be an unexceptionable statement of the primacy of Community law, mediated into the Irish constitutional order by Article 29.4.3 of the Constitution (as it then was) if the Treaty required that there be no appeal against Article 177 references.

Walsh J. stated that "[t]he very purpose of... Article 177 of the Treaty is to enable the national judge to have direct and unimpeded access to the only court which has jurisdiction to furnish him with such interpretation. To fetter that right, by making it subject to review on appeal, would be contrary to both the spirit and the letter of Article 177 of the Treaty" ([1983] I.R. 82, at 87). However, the Court of Justice has expressly stated that the order for reference remains "subject to the remedies normally available under national law", over the recommendation to the contrary by Advocate General Warner, who felt that the existence of a right of appeal constituted an improper fetter on the power of the national court to make a reference (Cases 146, 166/73, *Rheinmühlen-Düsseldorf v. Einfuhr-und-Vorratsstelle Getreide* [1974] E.C.R. 33, 139, at 147). One could argue that the Supreme Court in *Campus Oil* did make the reference procedure subject to the remedies normally available, having approximated it to the consultative case stated. (Jacobs and Durand have contended that the *special* provision for appeals against an order for reference in the United Kingdom, in R.S C. Ord. 114, r. 6, is contrary to Community law, in *References to the European Court* (1975) p. 171; *cf.* Collins, *European Community Law in the United Kingdom* (4th ed., 1990) p. 152; Collins & O'Reilly, "The Application of Community Law in Ireland 1973-1989)" (1990) 27 C.M.L. Rev. 315, at 329.) However, the statements of Walsh J. now under consideration were in the alternative to that position, and expressly disdained the applicability to the Irish case of the earlier decisions of the Court of Justice ([1983] I.R. 82, at 87, authors' italics):

> "It is as a matter of Irish law that Article 177 of the Treaty confers upon an Irish national judge an unfettered discretion to make a preliminary reference to the Court of Justice. [He then gave the interpretation of Article 177 quoted above, reviewed the contrary decisions of the Court of Justice on the point, and continued.] These cases are of interest as showing the views that were expressed by the Court of Justice in examining the question *as a question of Community law*. I do not seek to rely upon any of the statements in those cases because, for the reason I have already given, this matter must be decided *as a question of Irish law*."

This aspect of the decision has been widely criticised. O'Keeffe described it as being *"plus royaliste que le roi"* ("Appeals against an Order to Refer under Article 177 of the EEC Treaty" (1984) 9 E.L. Rev. 87, at 97). Hogan and Whyte have denounced the decision at length (Hogan & Whyte eds., Kelly, *The Irish Constitution* (3rd ed., 1994), pp. 284–5):

> "This case seems to be a questionable example of harmonious interpretation of the Constitution. First, this interpretation of Article 177 of the Treaty of Rome has never been laid down by the European Court of Justice, which does not consider an appeal against a decision to refer to be 'contrary to the spirit and letter of Article 177'. Secondly, and more fundamentally, the decision proceeds on the premise that the Treaty of Rome has been incorporated by reference into the constitutional order,

18

and that the Treaty of Rome may be invoked to qualify the language of the Constitution itself. This is a questionable premise given that Article 29.4.5 does no more than (i) allow the State to become a member of the European Community and (ii) provide a shield against constitutional attack for Community and domestic legislation and executive acts necessitated by obligations of Community membership. The *Campus Oil* case goes much further than this, and would appear to approach the radical proposition that Article 29.4.3-5 has the effect of scheduling every Article of the Treaty of Rome to the text of the Constitution."

Reid added (although approvingly) that "in the Supreme Court's view, the Amendment rather than scheduling the Treaties to the Constitution, has the effect (within the areas of competence of the Communities) of scheduling the Constitution to the Treaties" (*The Impact of Community Law on the Irish Constitution* (1990) p. 16 (hereinafter Reid, *Constitution*)).

A different construction of the views of Walsh J. is possible: one which, far from being more *communautaire* than the Community, is subversive of the Community legal order; but is also fraught with contradictions. The Supreme Court opined that Article 177 EEC operated as part of Irish law: "The national judge, by virtue of this power conferred upon him by the Treaty, exercises a function under Irish law in making such a request". This of course is true, as Community law has to be applied where relevant in national courts, and is part of the domestic legal systems of the Member States; and this in turn is recognised by section 2(1) of the European Communities Act, 1972. Yet Walsh J. appears to have drawn from this the conclusion that Treaty provisions have a dual existence, as part of Community law and as part of national law, and that they are capable of different interpretations within the two legal orders. In so far as the then Article 29.4.3 of the Constitution might permit Article 177 EEC to qualify Article 34 of the Constitution, it is a question of Irish law contingent on the interpretation of Article 177 by the Irish courts, which are free to differ from the European Court of Justice. Once the Irish court decides that it is an obligation of membership of the Communities that there be no appeal against Article 177 references by national judges, Article 29.4.3 permits that "obligation" to override the normal requirements of Article 34.4.3 of the Constitution.

If that was the position of the Supreme Court, it sits uncomfortably with the earlier statement in Walsh J.'s judgment that the Court of Justice is the only court having jurisdiction to give binding interpretations of the Treaty. (This self-contradiction has also been remarked upon by Phelan, *Revolution*, p. 392, n. 241.) That statement may of course have related to the exclusive interpretative authority of the Court of Justice *as a matter of Community law*. That is an issue which the Supreme Court appears to have deemed to be separate from the interpretation of the Treaty for the purpose of Irish constitutional adjudication.

If this is a correct construction of Walsh J.'s judgment, its ultra-*communautaire* result in the instant case may be accidental, and incidental to its real significance. It would mean that the determination of the obligations of Community membership, in so far as they require to be given effect in Irish law through the medium of section 2 of the European Communities Act, 1972 and to be protected from constitutional invalidation by Article 29.4.3 (now 29.4.5) of the Constitution, would be a matter for the Irish courts. The Irish courts could, from case to case, interpret the provisions of Community law more narrowly rather than more broadly than the Court of Justice, leading to a diminution of the primacy of Community law. The Community Treaties would indeed have been scheduled to the text of the Constitution, but would thereby have become subject to the exclusive jurisdiction of the Irish courts to interpret the terms of the Constitution.

It may have been purely fortuitous that a direct conflict with Community law did not occur in *Campus Oil* because the Supreme Court viewed Article 177 E.E.C. as being more intrusive on the autonomy of national judicial systems than did the Court of Justice itself. The possibility of a narrower approach being taken by the Irish courts was disclosed by Walsh J. in *S.P.U.C. (Ireland) Ltd. v. Grogan* [1989] I.R. 753, when he argued that the interaction of the Third Amendment (Article 29.4.3) and the Eighth Amendment (Article 40.3.3, on the right to life of the unborn) was a matter for the Irish courts, and that "it cannot be one of the objectives of the European Communities that a Member State should be obliged to permit activities which are clearly designed to set at nought the constitutional guarantees for the protection within the State of a fundamental human right" ([1989] I.R. 753, at 769; see further Chapter 8 below).

It is ironic, of course, that a conclusion about the relationship of Irish and Community law which was arguably subversive of the uniformity and primacy of Community law should be reached in a case the immediate effect of which was to remove obstacles to references by Irish courts to the Court of Justice. This fact alone must cause one to question whether the alternative analysis offered of the *Campus Oil* decision truly reflects the thinking of the Court, despite the reasoning given. It has been argued (by Phelan, "Necessitated by the Obligations of Membership? Article 29.4.5 of the Constitution" (1993) 11 I.L.T. 272, at 273) that the decision of the Supreme Court in *Meagher v. Minister for Agriculture* [1994] 1 I.R. 329 betrays a similarly national conception of the obligations of Community membership, but it is contended below that that case in fact prioritises the primacy of Community law, a principle long cultivated by the European Court of Justice, and is ultimately to be faulted chiefly for its misconstruction of Community law and for its flawed appreciation of the Irish factual situation. Whatever may have been intended in *Campus Oil*, any suggestion arising therefrom that Article 29.4.5 of the Constitution gives the Irish courts the right to interpret the Treaties, and to determine the obligations arising therefrom, in a manner which conflicts with the interpretation of the Court of Justice, has been undermined by later jurisprudence. As will be seen, it will always be possible as a matter of Irish law, by virtue of the contingency of the primacy of Community law in Ireland on the act of reception (Article 29.4.3-5 of the Constitution), for Irish courts to adopt a restrictive or conditional view of the applicability of Community law in cases of conflict with other provisions of the Constitution which is inconsistent with their role as Community courts. However, the jurisprudence to date shows little sign of the Irish courts taking such a stance.

Walsh J.'s later remarks in *Grogan* notwithstanding, it may be that the *Campus Oil* principle (of domestic interpretation of Community obligations as a matter of Irish law) operates in one direction only, *i.e.* only from the threshold of the obligations of Community membership as construed by the Court of Justice. Thus, Irish courts could deem certain laws or acts to be required even when the Court of Justice had indicated that they were not, if it were thought that they were necessary in the Irish context to comply with the spirit and objectives of the Treaties; but would not question any finding by the Court of Justice that certain measures *were* required. Such an approach by the Irish courts could be said to be in keeping with the spirit of Article 5 E.C., and with a broad teleological approach to Community membership. However, in the absence of an objective requirement as a matter of Community law, it would diverge from the apparently more limited purpose of Article 29.4.5, as described above by Hogan and Whyte, and as emerges from the Dáil debates on the Third Amendment (see below), of securing constitutional immunity only for laws, acts or measures legally required of the State as a matter of Community law.

Article 26 of the Constitution and the Renvoi Préjudiciel

One does not need to adopt the expansive approach of the Supreme Court in *Campus Oil* to the interpretation of Article 177 E.C. to see that it, and other provisions of the Treaty, can have unforeseen effects on the Irish legal system. This was one of the reasons for the adoption of a general immunity clause rather than a line-by-line amendment of the Constitution in 1972 (see the annotation of the Third Amendment below). For example, Robinson has remarked that the time constraints in Article 26 of the Constitution would prevent the making of a reference by the Supreme Court to the Court of Justice under Article 177 after a Bill was referred to it by the President for a decision as to whether it is repugnant to the Constitution ("The Constitutional Problem in Ratifying the Community Patent Convention", in Robinson ed. *Intellectual Property* (1989) p. 69, at 74). The Supreme Court has only 60 days in which to reach a decision (Article 26.2.1).

However, the constitutionality of a Bill, otherwise unconstitutional, may turn on whether it is necessitated by the obligations of membership of the Communities. In that case, and if the case does not fall within the *acte clair* doctrine (see Case 283/81, *CILFIT Srl v. Ministry of Health* [1982] E.C.R. 3415), the Supreme Court may be under a duty to make a reference to the Court of Justice. This duty could arise as a matter of Community law and independently (or interdependently), as a matter of Irish Constitutional law. Despite the manner in which the Bill reaches the Supreme Court for consideration of its validity, and the lack of parties properly so called, the Court can probably be said to be engaged in the judicial resolution of the question before it. It exercises ultimate as well as original jurisdiction on the question. A straightforward reading of Article 29.4.5 of the constitution indicates that the validity of the Bill will turn, in the circumstances described, on the interpretation of the Treaty or on the validity or interpretation of the acts of the institutions of the Community which are claimed to necessitate the enactment of the Bill in question. The question of what State laws, acts or measures are necessitated by the obligations of membership of the Communities is a question in Irish constitutional law, the answer to which is provided by Community law. (A variety of other possible readings of Article 29.4.5 is considered in Chapter 8, but that just described is contended to be that obtaining at the moment.) Even if the Supreme Court is only concerned with whether the Bill under consideration is the means of implementation of the relevant Community obligation most consistent with the Constitution (a question discussed further in Chapter 5), it may need to know if alternative means of implementation are adequate to fulfil that Community obligation. Thus the resolution of a question in Irish Constitutional law entails a question of Community law, which entails in turn, in a court of ultimate jurisdiction, an Article 177 Reference to the European Court of Justice. In that case, the 60 day limit would presumably have to give way to the requirement of the Treaty and of Article 29.4.5 of the Constitution. (This is also suggested in Hogan & Whyte eds., Kelly, *The Irish Constitution* (3rd ed., 1994), p. 218, n. 27).

If it were alleged, on the other hand, that the Bill, even if constitutional, was contrary to Community law, the situation would be more difficult. No constitutional court in any of the Member States has ever referred such a question to the Court of Justice.

Such a question could have been raised in *Re Article 26 and the Regulation of Information (Services outside the State for Termination of Pregnancies) Bill*, 1995, [1995] 2 I.L.R.M. 81. Sections 6 and 7 of the Act make it unlawful for a person, otherwise authorised, to provide abortion information if such a person provides what are termed pregnancy termination services or has an interest in a body providing such services; and make it unlawful for such a person to obtain directly or indirectly any financial or other benefit or advantage from any person who provides pregnancy termination services outside the State or who has an interest in a body providing such services. In Case 159/90 *S.P.U.C. (Ireland) Ltd v. Grogan* [1991] I E.C.R. 4685, the European Court of Justice indicated that the provision of information about what it deemed to be abortion services would fall within the field of application of Community law in precisely the sort of circumstances prohibited by sections 6 and 7 of the 1995 Act. A right to provide abortion information in such circumstances can be claimed as a matter of Community law. It may in turn be subject to a derogation in pursuance of the State's public policy, but permissibility and extent of such a derogation is also a matter of Community law. One can therefore devise arguments that sections 6 and 7 of the 1995 Act are contrary to Community law, in whole or in part. No such arguments were entertained by the Supreme Court, in the event, nor does it appear that any were presented.

The Supreme Court is not given jurisdiction under Article 26 to entertain any wider question than that of repugnancy to the Constitution. It does not apply the Bill under review to litigation *inter partes*. The question of disapplication of the subsequent Act for breach of Community law (see Case 106/77, *Amministrazione delle Finanze v. Simmenthal* [1978] E.C.R. 629) is not prejudiced by a finding of constitutionality, and by the normal prohibition on questioning the validity of laws after a decision in their favour under Article 26 (see Article 34.3.3 of the Constitution): the distinct nature of constitutional judicial review and of disapplication of conflicting national law is made evident by the competence (and duty) of the District and Circuit Courts in respect of the latter, although they are expressly precluded from the former jurisdiction (Article 34.3.2 of the Constitution; see further Casey, *Constitutional Law in Ireland* (2nd ed., 1992) p. 166).

Perhaps the strongest argument against disapplication of a Bill in Article 26 proceedings (and any related Article 177 reference) is that such proceedings take place *in abstracto*. In general, in deciding litigation *inter partes*, the Irish courts avoid issues of Community law where possible. Henchy J. stated in *Doyle v. An Taoiseach* [1986] I.L.R.M. 793, at 714 (Finlay C.J., Walsh, Griffin and Gannon JJ. concurring):

> "Just as it is generally undesirable to decide a case by bringing provisions of the Constitution into play for the purpose of invalidating an impugned law when the case may be decided without thus invoking constitutional provisions, so also, in my opinion, should Community law, which also has the paramount force and effect of constitutional provisions, not be applied save where necessary for the decision in the case."

Similar sentiments motivated the decision of Barron J. not to make a reference to the Court of Justice in *Hibernia Meats Ltd v. Minister for Agriculture* (High Court, July 29, 1983), and have been repeated by Finlay C.J. in *Kerry Co-operative Creameries Ltd v. An Bord Bainne Co-operative Ltd.* [1991] I.L.R.M. 851, at 854, speaking for the Supreme Court on the approach of the court to the making of references:

> "It is for this court to reach a decision as to whether the resolution of any question concerning
> (a) the interpretation of the Treaty, and/or
> (b) the validity and interpretation of acts of the institutions of the Community, and/or
> (c) the interpretation of statutes of bodies established by an act of the Council where those statutes so provide,
>
> is necessary to enable this court to give judgment. That decision is of course a matter of national law necessarily governed by a consideration of the principles applicable in that law to the issues which must be deter-

mined in order for this court to give judgment on the issues between the parties."

This *dictum* was followed subsequently in *Att.-Gen. v. X* [1992] 1 I.R. 1. It also appears to be in conformity with the views of the Court of Justice on when courts against whose decisions there is no judicial remedy under national law should make a reference (see Case 6/64, *Costa v. E.N.E.L.* [1964] E.C.R. 585), although Hogan and Whyte have suggested that Irish courts are overly reluctant to make references (Kelly, *The Irish Constitution* (3rd ed., 1994) p. 293). As there is no issue between parties in an Article 26 reference to the Supreme Court other than that (between the Attorney-General and counsel assigned by the Court) of the constitutionality of the Bill in question, such cases should not, it seems, give rise to any need for a further reference to the Court of Justice other than to resolve a point under Article 29.4.3-5 of the Constitution, as discussed above.

However, the effect of the competing imperatives of *Simmenthal* and of the protection of the integrity of the Community legal order, is difficult to assess. National courts are at all times under a duty to disapply national laws which conflict with Community law, which duty could extend to the Article 26 proceedings. While this is not within the normal scope of the Article 26 jurisdiction, the obligation is one which affects all courts irrespective of limits on their powers under national law – hence the role, just mentioned, of the District and Circuit Courts. The fact that a Bill is not yet law should not affect the matter. This gives the Supreme Court an even better opportunity to ensure from the outset that the integrity of the Community legal order and of the entitlements of individuals thereunder is not disturbed. Indeed, the judgment of the European Court of Justice in *Simmenthal* seems almost directly in point (although it concerned a national law which had passed through the national legislative process in full), when it states that Community law "preclude[s] the valid adoption of new national legislative measures to the extent to which they would be incompatible with Community provisions", and continues ([1978] E.C.R. 629, at paras. 17 and 18; authors' italics):

> "*Any* recognition that national legislative measures which encroach upon the field within which the Community exercises its legislative power or which are otherwise incompatible with the provisions of Community law had any legal effect would amount to a corresponding denial of the effectiveness of obligations undertaken unconditionally and irrevocably by the Member States and would thus imperil the very foundations of the Community."

This would suggest that in this case also, the Supreme Court should where necessary make a reference to the Court of Justice from Article 26 proceedings, irrespective of the normal time limits.

On the other hand, the recent Opinions of Advocate General Jacobs in Case C-372/93 *S.C.S. Peterbroeck v. Belgium* and in Joined Cases C-430-431/93 *Van Schijndel v. Stichting Pensioenfonds voor Fysiotherapeuten* (both on June 15, 1995) adopt a less radical approach to *Simmenthal*. *Peterbroeck* concerned the question whether a national court must set aside a national procedural rule preventing it from considering a point of Community law raised by one of the parties after the relevant deadline. *Van Schijndel* gave rise to the question whether a national court should apply provisions of Community law of its own motion where the party to the proceedings which has an interest in the application of those provisions has not relied upon them, where by doing so the national court would go beyond the passive role assigned to it by national procedural rules in considering grounds in excess of the parties' claims and calling for further factual evidence in support of those grounds. In an earlier Opinion in *Peterbroeck* (of May 4, 1994, after which the oral procedure was reopened in the case), Advocate General Jacobs remarked that it has "long been established by this Court's case-law [citing, *e.g.* Case 33/76 *Rewe v. Landwirtschaftskammer Saarland* [1976] E.C.R. 1989; Case 199/82 *Amministrazione delle Finanze dello Stato v. San Giorgio* [1983] E.C.R. 3595; Case C-208/90 *Emmott* [1991] I E.C.R 4269; Joined Cases C-6 & 9/90 *Francovich* [1991] I E.C.R. 5357] that, in the absence of Community rules, it is for the domestic legal system of each Member State to determine the courts having jurisdiction and the procedural conditions governing actions intended to ensure the protection of directly effective Community rights, provided that those conditions fulfil two requirements: they are not less favourable than the conditions relating to similar actions of a domestic nature; and they do not render virtually impossible or excessively difficult, the exercise of rights conferred by Community law" (at para. 17). "Those requirements are intended to establish a balance between the need to respect the procedural autonomy of the legal systems of the Member States and the need to ensure the effective protection of Community rights in the national courts (Opinion of June 15, 1995 in *van Schijndel*, at para. 18).

Advocate General Jacobs distinguished the facts in *Simmenthal* and in Case 213/89 *R. v. Secretary of State for Transport, ex p. Factortame Ltd* [1990] I E.C.R. 2433 from those in the instant cases. In the former, "the Court [of Justice]'s intervention was necessary in order to enable national courts, *before which claims based on Community law had been properly brought*, to perform effectively the task conferred upon them under the system established by the Treaty" (*van Schijndel*, at para. 22; authors' italics): in *Simmenthal*, because "[i]f the Constitutional Court alone had jurisdiction to set aside national law conflicting with Community law, [involving long complex and expensive proceedings,] that would undoubtedly have constituted a major impediment to the application of Community law ... by the Italian courts, [and] would have deterred individuals from seeking enforcement of their rights under Community law" (at para. 19); in *Factortame*, because of the "compelling need for the Court [of Justice] to remedy the inadequacy of the judicial protection of Community Rights afforded by national law", *viz.* the non-availability of interim relief in the form of suspension of the application of provisions of a United Kingdom Act of Parliament contended to be incompatible with Community law while a ruling was being sought from the Court of Justice (at para. 20). Advocate General Jacobs continued that "as regards procedural rules, the primacy of Community law does not require that they should be overridden in all circumstances so as to allow Community law to enter the arena at any stage in the proceedings ... [I]t is sufficient that individuals are given, by the national procedural rules, an effective opportunity of enforcing their rights" (at para. 25). An effective opportunity, one can take it, need not mean every conceivable opportunity, if this would involve changing the nature of the proceedings in question in order to enable a Community law point to be raised. The contrary view "could be regarded as infringing the principle of proportionality and, in a broad sense, the principle of subsidiarity, which reflects precisely the balance which the Court has sought to attain in this area for many years" (at para. 27). There was therefore no need, as a matter of Community law, to abandon or alter the national procedural rules at issue in *van Schijndel* or, by extension of reasoning, in *Peterbroeck*. Similarly, the exclusion in the specialised context of an Article 26 reference of points of Community law which may require the disapplication (*in abstracto*) of the Bill in question can probably be tolerated so long as the Irish courts at all levels remain willing to consider the compatibility of the national legislation with Community law even after a positive ruling on the constitutional validity of the Bill by the Supreme Court.

CROTTY V. AN TAOISEACH: THE TESTS OF ESSENTIAL OBJECTIVES AND OF LEGAL OBLIGATION

The decision of the Supreme Court in *Crotty v. An Taoiseach* [1987] I.R. 713 has been described as one of the most extraordinary ever delivered by that Court, and as a remarkable display of judicial activism (Hogan, "The Supreme Court and the Single European Act" (1987) 22 Ir. Jur. 55, at 55 (hereinafter Hogan, S.E.A.)). A majority of the Court (Walsh, Henchy and Hederman JJ.; Finlay C.J. and Griffin J. dissenting) held that it would be unconstitutional for Ireland to ratify the Single European Act (S.E.A.) on the ground that to do so would fetter the freedom of the Government to conduct foreign policy in the manner provided for in Article 29.4.1 of the Constitution. Although this decision was reversed in part by the passage of the Tenth Amendment of the Constitution Act, 1987 (which simply allows the State to ratify the Single European Act; see further the annotation of the Act below), the judgments in *Crotty* remain of vital importance for the light they cast on the relationship of Irish constitutional law, Community law and international law. In particular, the decision indicates that amendments to the constitutional Treaties of the Communities are constitutionally acceptable without a referendum if within the essential scope and objectives of the original Treaties; and that observance of Treaty amendments is necessitated by the obligations of membership of the Communities only after their ratification and entry into force.

The Single European Act consisted of a Preamble, four Titles and a Final Act consisting of 20 Declarations adopted either by the Intergovernmental Conference, the Commission or individual Member States. Title I concerned the formal recognition of European Political Cooperation (E.P.C.), the European Council and institutional changes, such as changing the title of the "Assembly" to the "European Parliament". Title II amended the Treaties establishing the European Communities. It provided, *inter alia*, for the creation of a Court of First Instance; greater powers for the European Parliament, *viz.* the operation of the co-operation procedure in certain circumstances; new provisions on the environment; and internal market provisions with altered voting rules designed to achieve an integrated market by 1992. Title III concerned the codification of the existing foreign policy co-operation of E.P.C., outside the framework of the Communities (see further below), and Title IV contained general and final provisions. (For further analysis, see Murphy, "The Single European Act" (1985) 20 Ir. Jur. 17, 239 (hereinafter Murphy, S.E.A.).)

Although Ireland had made a (political) commitment to ratify the Single Act by January 1, 1987, together with the other Member States of the Communities, the European Communities (Amendment) Bill, 1986 was only published on September 23, 1986. The Bill sought to give effect in domestic law to Title II of the S.E.A., as well as to those parts of the other Titles which affected E.C. law and institutions, *viz.* Article 3(1), Title I (changing the name of the Assembly to "the European Parliament") and Articles 31 and 32, Title IV (delimiting the jurisdiction of the European Court of Justice and the effect of the S.E.A. on the E.C. Treaties). The Bill was passed by both Houses of the Oireachtas and was signed into law by the President on December 23, 1986. The Dáil had earlier passed a separate motion approving the terms of the entire Single European Act, to comply with the terms of Article 29.5.2 of the Constitution. (See further the annotation of the Act below.)

On December 24, 1986, Barrington J. granted an injunction in the High Court to the plaintiff Mr Raymond Crotty, a private citizen, who had sought an order restraining the Government from depositing the instrument of ratification with the Italian Republic in accordance with Article 33 of the Single Act. Mr Crotty alleged that if ratified the S.E.A. could not be challenged because it would benefit from the protection of the Third Amendment of the Constitution, whereas the substantive amendments to the E.C. Treaties involved further diminution of the legislative, judicial and executive powers of the State. The order sought was granted by Barrington J. with some hesitation, as the effect of the injunction was to preclude the State from complying with the January 1 deadline. However, the plaintiff had made out a strong arguable case, and the decision of the European Court of Justice in Cases 9/65 and 58/65, *Acciairie San Michele Sp.A. v. High Authority* [1967] E.C.R. 1 suggested that the courts could not subsequently look behind an instrument of ratification, so that the action could probably not be pursued at a later stage; thus, the balance of convenience lay in the plaintiff's favour.

The matter then came on for hearing before a Divisional High Court, but on this occasion the plaintiff was to fail. Barrington J. (with whom Hamilton P. and Carroll J. concurred) based his reasoning on the language of Article 29.4.3 (as it then was). Barrington J. described the first sentence of Article 29.4.3 as granting the State "a licence to join a living dynamic Community". The immunity referred to in the second sentence referred only to "legislative and administrative measures taken in the day-to-day running of the Community". If the plaintiff had established that the European Communities (Amendment) Act, 1986 had gone beyond the licence granted by the first sentence,

> "[i]t [would be] open to challenge, in an appropriate case, as being invalid having regard to the provisions of the Constitution. Should such challenge be successful, such Acts of the institutions of the Community as depend on it for their status in domestic law would lose that status and would be of no effect in domestic law. Such a result might be embarrassing for the Government, and might involve the State being in breach of its international obligations, but such considerations should not prevent this Court from fulfilling its constitutional duty should the matter be made out in a case properly before it."

As the mere deposit of the instrument of ratification did not prevent a future challenge to the validity of the 1986 Act or "of such provisions of the Single European Act as depend on it for their status", Barrington J. concluded that it would be premature to grant the injunctive relief sought by the plaintiff. Having failed on this point, he had no standing to attack the constitutionality of the 1986 Act as he was not "immediately affected or threatened by any of the other matters which he seeks to raise". Although the court did not want to prejudge the outome of any such future challenge, Barrington J. was nonetheless

> "unconvinced that there is anything in the Single European Act which is outside the terms of the licence granted by the Third Amendment [or which] extends the scope of the objectives of the European Communities, poses any new threat to any rights guaranteed by our Constitution or represents anything other than an evolution of the Community within the terms of its original objectives."

The plaintiff, however, appealed successfully to the Supreme Court. The judgment of the Supreme Court was in two parts. Finlay C.J. delivered the judgment of the Court upholding the constitutionality of the European Communities (Amendment) Act, 1986. Separate judgments were given in relation to the proposed ratification of the Single European Act, addressing those parts of the S.E.A. not covered by the 1986 Act. A majority of the Court (Walsh, Henchy and Hederman JJ.) held that it would be unconstitutional for the State to ratify Title III without submitting the issue to a referendum; Finlay C.J. and Griffin J. dissented.

The reasoning of the Court in upholding the validity of the 1986 Act differed markedly from that of Barrington J. Neither the Single Act nor the 1986 Act enjoyed at that juncture any immunity from constitutional challenge as it was conceded that neither measure was "necessitated" by the obligations of Community membership. The question, therefore, was whether any of the amendments effected by the Single Act went beyond the "essential scope or objectives" of the Communities. This can be described as a purposive or teleological interpretation of the licence to join the Communities (see further the discussion of the principles of constitutional interpretation in Chapter 8 below). As such, it is probably an appropriate mode of construction of a constitutional provision authorising ratification of Treaties to the interpretation of which the same interpretative theory is applied. Finlay C.J. observed in the judgment of the Court:

> "To hold that the first sentence of Article 29.4.3 does not authorise any form of amendment to the treaties after 1973 without a further amendment of the Constitution would be too narrow a construction; to construe it as an open-ended authority to agree, without further amendment of the Constitution, to any amendment of the treaties would be too broad."

The Court then proceeded to consider *seriatim* the various grounds of invalidity alleged by the plaintiff in relation to Title II. The creation of a Court of First Instance attached to the European Court of Justice was not an infringement of the judicial power contained in Article 34.1 of the Constitution as it did not affect "in any material way the extent to which the judicial power has already been ceded to the European Court". The court also rejected arguments that other changes proposed in Title II such as qualified majority voting to allow for the approximation of laws concerning the provision of services, the working environment, health and safety of workers, or co-operation on economic and monetary policy, went beyond the terms of Article 29.4.3; and it also considered that the new powers given to the Community to deal with the environment did not go beyond the original objectives of the Communities:

> "In many instances the Treaty of Rome provided a requirement that a decision on a particular topic should be unanimous, but would after the expiry of a particular stage or the transitional stage require only a qualified majority. The Community was thus a developing organism with diverse and changing methods for making decisions and an inbuilt and clearly expressed objective of expansion and progress, both in terms of the number of Member States and in terms of the mechanics to be used in the achievement of its agreed objectives. Having regard to these considerations, it is the opinion of the Court that neither the proposed changes from unanimity to qualified majority, nor the identification of topics which, while now separately stated, are within the original aims and objectives of the European Community, bring these amendments outside the scope of authorisation contained in Article 29.4.3."

Finlay C.J. added however that it did not follow that "all other decisions of the Council which now require unanimity could, without a further amendment of the Constitution, be changed to decisions requiring less than unanimity". In much the same vein, the French *Conseil Constitutionnel* took the view that the provision made in Article 100c E.C. for qualified majority voting after January 1, 1996 in respect of visa requirements for entry into the Union from third countries would affect the exercise by the State of powers which form part of the essential conditions of its sovereignty, and would thus be unconstitutional unless the French Constitution were appropriately amended (*Re Ratification of the Treaty on European Union*, (1993) 3 C.M.L.Rev. 345; see further Boyron, "The *Conseil Constitutionnel* and the European Union" [1993] P.L. 30).

This *dictum* of the Supreme Court might mean, for example, that a constitutional amendment would be required if Article O, E.U. (formerly Article 237 EEC) were changed to provide for majority voting (as opposed to the present unanimity requirement) in relation to the admission of new Member States to the Union. Any dilution in the requirement in Article N, E.U. (formerly Article 236, EEC) of unanimous ratification by the Member States, each in accordance with its own constitutional requirements, of amendments to the Treaties, must also require a constitutional referendum in Ireland (see *e.g.* Article 47, draft Constitution of the European Union presented to the European Parliament in 1994, which would come into force upon ratification by a majority of the Member States representing four-fifths of the total population of the present Union). One can also speculate on whether amendment of the unanimity requirement in Article 235 E.C. would require an Irish constitutional amendment. Article 235 E.C. authorises the taking of measures for which the necessary powers are not expressly provided in the Treaty of Rome but which are necessary to the attainment of Community objectives in the course of the operation of the common market. This provision allows, in effect, *ex post facto* extension of the activities of the Community in the light of its very ambitious objectives; the unanimity rule is designed to prevent its abuse or to ensure the agreement of all the Member States to what may be *in effect* a disguised Treaty amendment. A Treaty amendment that permitted rolling expansion of powers by the Council over the objections of some Member States might invoke the disapproval of the Supreme Court if not constitutionally authorised.

It was, however, the provisions of Title III which were found to be constitutionally objectionable by the majority in *Crotty*. The procedures of European Political Co-operation were established in reports agreed at Luxembourg (1970), Copenhagen (1973) and London (1981) and in the Solemn Declaration on European Union of Stuttgart (1983) (see further the discussion in Chapter 7 below of the extension of Article 29.4.5 to the European Union). Title III seemed at first sight simply to provide for the codification of this existing informal practice of foreign policy co-operation, and for the establishment of a secretariat in Brussels which was designed to assist the Member State holding the Presidency of the Council of Ministers in preparing and organising the activities of European Political Co-operation. The Commission was to be fully associated with E.P.C. and the European Parliament was to be consulted to ensure that its views were taken into consideration. However, each Contracting Party now formally undertook "to jointly formulate [*sic*] and implement a European foreign policy" (Article 30(1) S.E.A.); to inform and consult the other Parties on foreign policy matters of general interest (Article 30(2)(a) S.E.A.); to take full account of the positions of the other Contracting Parties in adopting its positions and its national measures (Article 30(2)(b)); to ensure that common principles and objectives were gradually developed and defined, in order that the determination of common positions would constitute a point of reference for the policies of the High Contracting Parties (Article 30(2)(c)). Article 1 of the Single European Act indicated that Title III was designed to confirm *and to supplement* the rules of practice in relation to European Political Co-operation which had been observed by the Member States since 1970.

The issue was, as Hederman J. put it, whether the State

"can by any act on the part of its various organs of Government enter into binding agreements with other States, or groups of States, to subordinate, or to submit, the exercise of the powers bestowed by the Constitution, to the advice or interests of other States, as distinct from electing from time to time to pursuing its own particular policies in union or in concert with other States in their pursuit of their own similar or even identical policies. The State's organs cannot contract to exercise in a particular way or by a particular procedure, their policy-making roles or in any way to fetter powers bestowed unfettered by the Constitution."

In the judgment of the Court on the 1986 Act, it was stated that "the essential nature of sovereignty is the right to say yes or to say no". Finlay C.J. and Griffin J. in dissent did not, as such, take issue with the majority's premise that sovereign powers could not be alienated at will. However, in their view, the provisions of Title III did not, as Griffin J. put it, "impose any obligations to cede any sovereignty or national interest in the field of foreign policy, nor do they allow a decision of the State on any issue of foreign policy to be overridden or vetoed". Finlay C.J. summarised the obligations of Title III as "an obligation to listen and consult" and "a right to be heard and consulted". Griffin J. laid emphasis on the terms such as "endeavour", "consultations", "endeavour to avoid" and "as far as possible". However, Henchy J. preferred to stress phrases such as "take full account", "ensure" and "shall", which indicated in his view that each State would immediately cede part of its sovereignty and freedom of action in foreign policy. Both Henchy and Walsh JJ. asserted the need for foreign policy powers to be exercised for the common good, which could not be displaced as a primary consideration by the imperative that Member States endeavour to formulate a European foreign policy. Walsh J. said:

"In enacting the Constitution the People conferred full freedom of action upon the Government to decide matters of foreign policy and to act as it thinks fit on any particular issue or issues so far as policy is concerned and as, in the opinion of the Government, the occasion requires. In my view, this freedom does not carry with it the power to abdicate that freedom or to enter into binding agreements with other States to exercise that power in a particular way or to refrain from exercising it save by particular procedures and so to bind the State in its freedom of action in its foreign policy. The freedom to formulate foreign policy is just as much a mark of sovereignty as the freedom to form economic policy and the freedom to legislate. The latter two have now been curtailed by the consent of the People to the amendment of the Constitution which is contained in Article 29.4.3. If it is now desired to qualify, curtail or inhibit the existing sovereign power to formulate and pursue such foreign policies as from time to time to the Government may seem proper, it is not within the power of the Government itself to do so."

While Walsh J. opined that the European Economic Community could be seen as a group or league of nations with which the State is associated for the purpose of international co-operation in matters of common concern, he also excluded the use of Article 29.4.2 of the Constitution to save Title III:

"[T]he limitations [of Article 29.4.2] are clear. This provision relates solely to the exercise of the executive functions of the State in its external relations and is subject to such conditions, if any, as may be determined by law. Furthermore, it simply provides for the adoption of any organ or instrument or method of procedure for the exercise of the executive functions of the State. It does not require prior consultation with any other State as to the policy itself.... The framers of the Constitution, and the People in enacting it ... clearly refrained from granting to the Government the power to bind the State by agreement with such groups of nations as to the manner or under what conditions that executive function of the State would be exercised."

The minority was of opinion that the courts could only interfere with the exercise of the executive power where there has been an "actual or threatened infringement of [a citizen's constitutional] rights". While the Court, in the judgment of Finlay C.J., had taken an expansive view of *locus standi* in respect of the challenge to the 1986 Act (thus creating an apparent exception to the principles formulated in *Cahill v. Sutton* [1980] I. R. 269), the minority stated that because Title III was not part of domestic law, the plaintiff could not point to any actual or possible invasion of his rights. The majority view, on the other hand, was that judicial intervention was possible even in respect of the State's treaty-making power, because of the courts' function of upholding the primacy of the Constitution. (See generally, on the *locus standi* and justiciability questions raised in *Crotty*, Sherlock, "Sovereignty, the Constitution and the Single European Act" (1987) 9 D.U.L.J. 101, at 109-113 (hereinafter Sherlock, Sovereignty).)

Although the decision opened up the possibility that various other international agreements touching on the conduct of foreign affairs by the State might be unconstitutional, the Government elected to put forward a simple amendment to Article 29.4.3 which merely authorised the State to ratify the Single European Act. After approval by the People in a referendum on May 25, 1987 (by 755,423 votes to 324,977), the Irish instrument of ratification was duly deposited in Rome, and the Single European Act came into force on July 1, 1987. (See further the annotation of the Tenth Amendment of the Constitution Act, 1987 below.)

Crotty v. An Taoiseach: "necessitated" measures

The immunity granted by Article 29.4.5 of the Constitution extends to "laws enacted, acts done and measures adopted by the State necessitated by the obligations of membership of the Communities". This seems to mean that it is only measures that the State is legally obliged to adopt as a result of Community membership that can enjoy this complete immunity. The Supreme Court was certainly of the view that ratification of the Single European Act was not such an obligation: this, Finlay C.J. said for the court, was "clear and was not otherwise contended". The court was then free to examine the constitutionality of the proposed ratification of the S.E.A. as it did not enjoy any immunity from such challenge.

This suggests that the test is whether the measure in question is a legal obligation of membership. This is also the view expressed extra-judicially by Walsh J. ("Reflections on the Effects of Membership of the European Communities in Irish Law" in Capotorti *et al* eds., *Du Droit International au Droit de l'Integration: Liber Amicorum Pierre Pescatore* (1987) p. 805, at 813 (hereinafter Walsh, Reflections)). Temple Lang has also observed that the "necessitated" clause must refer to State actions "necessitated objectively by the obligations of membership as determined by Community law" and could not mean those "necessitated by the obligations of membership of the Communities as ultimately judged subjectively by the Irish courts". Thus, Temple Lang has observed ("The Widening Scope of Constitutional Law" in Curtin & O'Keeffe eds., *Constitutional Adjudication in European Community and National Law* (1992), p. 229, at 231 (hereinafter Temple Lang, Scope)):

> "Article 29.4.3 [as it then was] is a *renvoi* from the Constitution of Ireland to the constitutional law of the Community, and in particular to Article 5 [E.C.]. To interpret Article 29.4.3, a reference to Luxembourg under Article 177 [E.C.] might be necessary."

The constitutionality of national action taken to comply with a Community regulation or an order of the Court of Justice is not ordinarily open to question, as compliance in each case is legally required under Community law. But this is not true of other cases. Article N, E.U. (formerly Article 236 EEC) provides that any amendment to the Union or Community Treaties shall only enter into force "after being ratified by all the Member States in accordance with their respective constitutional requirements". This presupposes that, from a Community or Union law point of view, there is no legal obligation to ratify any proposed amendment to the Treaty. As there is no such obligation, the constitutionality of any domestic legislation designed to give effect to such an amendment can be examined on its merits in advance of ratification.

Moreover, the "legal obligation" test adopted by the Supreme Court appears to be in harmony with the views of the Oireachtas at the time of the adoption of the Third Amendment. The Third Amendment of the Constitution Bill, 1972 as originally drafted gave legal protection to all measures which were "consequent on" membership of the Communities. This, however, was amended at the behest of Fine Gael (then in opposition), and the phrase "necessitated by the obligations of" was inserted in its place. Dr Garret Fitzgerald T.D. (then Opposition Spokesman on Foreign Affairs) explained the reasons for this change (258 *Dáil Debates*, Col. 402; see further the annotation of the Third Amendment of the Constitution Act, 1972 below):

> "[This] amendment does no more than the minimum necessary to secure membership. It ensures that any law passed here which can be shown legally to be necessitated by the obligations of Community membership, to be required by membership, will, to that extent, take precedence over the Constitution, but unless that can be shown and if the law is simply consequential on membership but not necessitated by it, it does not override the Constitution."

This drafting change had the inevitable result that measures (such as proposed amendments to the Treaties) which are consequent upon Community membership but which are not necessitated by it can be exposed to constitutional attack. Indeed, such proposed amendments, when shorn of constitutional immunity, may be peculiarly vulnerable to such an attack, given that any changes to the Treaties almost invariably trench on some aspect of the separation of powers, fundamental rights or State sovereignty protected by the Constitution.

What is the position of Community or Union Treaty amendments once ratified? In the Divisional High Court in *Crotty*, Barrington J. said that the second sentence of Article 29.4.3 (as it then was) only applied to "legislative and administrative measures taken in the day-to-day running of the Community", and he indicated that he had Community regulations and directives in mind. Thus, the Irish courts could examine the validity of a treaty ratification after the event, even though this might lead to "a breach of [the State's] international obligations"; it was not necessary to grant the plaintiff at that stage the extraordinary relief that he claimed. This seems an extraordinarily narrow reading of the relevant constitutional provision.

Walsh J. in the Supreme Court laid greater emphasis on the State's duties under international law:

> "If some part or all of the Treaty was subsequently translated into domestic legislation and found to be unconstitutional it would avail the State nothing in its obligations to its fellow members. It would still be bound by the Treaty. Therefore if the ratification of this Treaty under the Irish Constitution requires a referendum to amend the Constitution to give effect to it, the fact that the State did not hold a referendum would not prevent a State from being bound in international law by the Treaty.... It is not for the other States to the Treaty to satisfy themselves that the Government of Ireland observed its own constitutional requirements. This is solely a matter for the Government of Ireland and if it fails to take the necessary steps, the State cannot afterwards be heard to plead that it is not bound by the Treaty."

This position reflects the international law principle that a State cannot invoke provisions of its internal law as a ground of avoiding a treaty. The principle is set out in Article 46 of the Vienna Convention on the Law of Treaties. Ireland has not ratified the Convention, but Barrington J. described it in the High Court as an attempt to codify general principles of international law:

> "1. A State may not invoke the fact that its consent to be bound by a treaty has been expressed in violation of a provision of its internal law regarding competence to conclude treaties as invalidating its consent unless that violation is manifest and concerned a rule of its internal law of fundamental importance.
>
> 2. A violation is manifest if it would be objectively evident to any State conducting itself in the matter in accordance with normal practice and good faith."

Article 46 was intended to embody the strictest possible test for the invocation of domestic impediments to treaty-making competence in order to invalidate a treaty (Sinclair, *The Vienna Convention on the Law of Treaties* (2nd. ed., 1984) p. 171). Judged by this standard, it would appear that the constitutional transgression ultimately disclosed in *Crotty* would not have been "objectively evident". However, the concern with adherence to international law requirements which was expressed by Walsh J. has not prevented the Supreme Court from reviewing the constitutionality of the State's adherence to international treaties, *post*-ratification, on at least two occasions. In *State (Gilliland) v. Governor of Mountjoy Prison* [1987] I.R. 201, the Supreme Court declared unconstitutional the extension of the terms of Part II of the Extradition Act, 1965 to the United States pursuant to an agreement which imposed certain costs on the State but which had not been approved by Dáil Éireann as is required by Article 29.5.2 of the Constitution. In *McGimpsey v. Ireland* [1990] 1 I.R. 110, the Supreme Court examined the constitutionality of the Anglo-Irish Agreement, 1985. While it ultimately found it valid, in large part by distinguishing *Crotty* in respect of the alleged fettering of the State's foreign policy powers by the Agreement (see below), the Court did not feel formally constrained in its analysis by the breach of international law that would be caused by a contrary ruling. Moreover, it has long been clear that the Irish courts will not enforce the terms of international agreements in Ireland, however necessary this is for their efficacy, in the absence of incorporation under Article 29.6 (see *O Laighléis* [1960] I.R. 93; *E. v. E.* [1982] I.L.R.M. 497; *Norris v. Attorney-General* [1984] I.R. 436; *O'B. v. S.* [1984] I.R. 316, but cf. *Fakih v. Minister for Justice* [1993] 2 I.R. 406).

Our concern here must be with the special status of the Community and Union Treaties under the Constitution, however, and not just with the general position taken by the courts in respect of international agreements. Let us assume that an agreement amending the European Community Treaties is ratified without an amendment to the Constitution authorising such ratification first having been secured. The amendments include provisions contrary to the Constitution, which patently go beyond the scope of the existing Treaties. Relevant additions are made to the list of Community Treaties in the European Communities Act, 1972. Would the courts then have jurisdiction to entertain a challenge to the constitutionality of the State's ratification of that agreement, or of the amended Act, or of acts either of the State or of the Communities done pursuant to the amended terms of the Treaties? Barrington J. appears to have taken the view that the courts would have such a jurisdiction. Walsh J.'s remark that the State would continue to be bound by an unconstitutional agreement is as true of an ordinary international treaty as it is of one governing the European Communities or the European Union, and does not indicate expressly that the agreement or the incorporating legislation would be any the less unconstitutional or unenforceable in the domestic courts for that reason. This is, however, probably too close a reading of Walsh J.'s remarks, which indicate that he would discountenance any review of a Community Treaty after ratification having regard to the provisions of the Constitution. He stated extra-judicially, at about the same time, that "only matters which can be made the subject of a regulation or a directive, *apart from the express provisions of the Treaties*, can be regarded as laws, acts or measures necessitated by membership of the Communities" (Walsh, "Reflections on the Effects of Membership of the European Communities in Irish Law" in Capotorti *et al* eds., *Du Droit International au Droit de l'Integration: Liber Amicorum Pierre Pescatore* (1987) p. 805, at 813; authors' italics (hereinafter Walsh, Reflections)). In *S.P.U.C. (Ireland) Ltd v. Grogan* [1989] I.R. 753, at 770, McCarthy J. intimated that enforcement of the Treaty of Rome was necessitated by the obligations of membership of the Communities. Furthermore, in *Meagher v. Minister for Agriculture* [1994] 1 I.R. 329 (discussed in detail in Chapter 4 below), Finlay C.J. remarked, for the Supreme Court, that the "major or fundamental obligation necessitated by membership of the Community" was "the application of Community law ... subject to the conditions laid down in the Treaty, ... including its primacy". The test of legal obligation that emerges from *Crotty*, as developed in *Meagher v. Minister for Agriculture*, must therefore apply to the Treaties (as amended) as well as to derived obligations.

It is therefore submitted (as it was submitted by Mr Crotty) that ratification of an agreement amending the Community or Union Treaties will ordinarily deprive the Irish courts, as a matter of Irish constitutional law as well as of international and Community law, of jurisdiction to review the constitutionality of adherence by the State to such an agreement. Even in the absence of a constitutional amendment expressly authorising such ratification, this is the apparent effect of Article 29.4.5 of the Constitution, as interpreted in *Crotty* and subsequently. Upon ratification by all the Member States in accordance with Article N, E.U., the terms of such an agreement enter into force as part of the "constitutional" law of the Communities and the Union. (It has been argued that the Court of Justice may review Treaty amendments for compliance with fundamental principles of Community law, but this very remote possibility will not be considered here; see Curtin, "The Constitutional Structure of the Union: A Europe of Bits and Pieces" (1993) 30 C.M.L.Rev. 17, at 62-5 (hereinafter Curtin, Union; see further Chapter 9 below.) These new terms are thus part of the "legal order". They are part of the Treaties pursuant to which the Union and the Communities, and their institutions and competent bodies, act, and which impose obligations on the State by virtue of its membership of the Communities and the Union.

Article N, E.U., provides that ratification by Member States of an amendment to the constitutional Treaties must be "in accordance with their respective constitutional requirements". If Ireland's constitutional requirements were not complied with by the Government when ratifying such an amendment, could not an Irish court in theory declare that a ratification was unconstitutional with the potential result that the amendment never properly entered into force? The interpretation of Community law is peculiarly a matter for the European Court of Justice. While the Court of Justice has been excluded from such a role in respect of certain parts of the E.U. Treaty, it has full jurisdiction to interpret Article N, E.U., and thus to pronounce on the validity of any amendment of the Union as well as of the Community Treaties (see Article L(c), E.U.). The Court of Justice could very well say (as Walsh J. appears to have expected it would) that it is for each Member State to ensure compliance with its constitutional requirements in advance of ratification, and that it will not look behind a ratification after the event. That likelihood emerges very clearly from the decision in *Acciaierie San Michele SpA. v. High Authority*, Cases 9 & 58/65, [1967] E.C.R. 1, on which Mr Crotty relied to argue for an injunction restraining ratification of the Single Act until after a decision was reached on his application. In *San Michele*, an Italian company sought in the *Corte Constituzionale* to question the validity of Italy's accession to the European Coal and Steel Community. In refusing interim relief pending the Italian court's decision, the Court of Justice stated that it could take into consideration only the instrument of ratification, whereby the Member States bound themselves in an identical manner to adhere to the Treaty on the same conditions, so that any claim by a national of a Member State questioning such adherence would be contrary to the system of Community law. The Court of First Instance refused to review the entry into force of the Maastricht Treaty on European Union on somewhat more technical grounds, in Case T-584/93 *Roujansky v. Council* [1994] II E.C.R. 587. It stated (at para. 15) that the Treaty on European Union is not an act of a Community institution within the meaning of Articles 4 and 173 E.C., and it consequently had no jurisdiction to review its provisions. (See also Case T-179/94 *Bonnamy*, January 11, 1995).

Even if the Court of Justice were prepared to entertain a challenge after ratification to the validity of a constitutional Treaty, it is for the Court to say definitively what is meant by the phrase "constitutional requirements" in Article N. It would be unlikely to take a view less stringent than that expressed in Article 46 of the Vienna Convention. After all, the Court generally construes the Treaties "in a constitutional mode rather than employing the traditional international law methodology. Proceeding from its fragile jurisdictional base, the Court has arrogated to itself the ultimate authority to draw the line between Community law and national law" (Stein, "Lawyers, Judges and the Making of a Transnational Constitution" (1981) 75 A.J.I.L. 1). The Court would presumably take Article N, E.U. to require no more than compliance with the appropriate procedures, such as approval by Parliament, where necessary, in a Member State. This is the most plausible reading, given the Court's resistance to claims that substantive national constitutional rules can impede the application and supremacy of Community law (see, *e.g.* Case 11/70, *Internationale Handelsgesellschaft GmbH. v. Einfuhr- und Vorratsstelle für Getreide und Futtermittel* [1970] II E.C.R. 1125).

If the Supreme Court were to apply a strict *Crotty* test of legal obligation, a preliminary ruling of the Court of Justice would be determinative in deciding on the validity *as a matter of Union law* of an amendment of a Community or Union Treaty, even for the purposes of an Irish constitutional controversy and even if the alleged ground of invalidity were the failure to observe an Irish constitutional condition precedent to ratification. It is therefore contended that the Supreme Court of Ireland would be under an obligation to make a reference to the European Court of Justice (under Article 177 E.C., Article 41 ECSC; Article 150 Euratom; as extended to Article N, E.U. by Article L E.U.; *cf.* Phelan, "Necessitated by the Obligations of Membership? Article 29.4.5 of the Constitution" [1993] 11 I.L.T. 272 (hereinafter Phelan, Membership), considered in Chapter 8 below). It is not clear whether the Court of Justice would feel obliged to pronounce finally upon the question of validity, or would simply give guidance in its ruling on the interpretation of Article N, E.U., to be applied by the Irish court in dealing with the case before it. (The requirement in Case 314/85, *Foto-Frost v. Hauptzollamt Lübeck-Ost* [1987] E.C.R. 4199 that the Court of Justice itself pronounce on the validity of E.C. measures might be overcome in such a case by the contingency of such a determination on a question of national law; in any event, as was pointed out in *Roujansky*, the Treaty is not an E.C. measure as such. Furthermore, the reference would be "necessary to enable [the national court] to give judgment" in *national* litigation; it would not constitute a *direct* challenge to the validity of the Treaty. The decision in *Acciaierie San Michele* arose in a case brought directly before the Court.)

Even were the Court of Justice to adopt in its preliminary ruling the narrow interpretation of "constitutional requirements" canvassed above, the Supreme Court could counter that the requisite procedure for ratification by Ireland of a Union or Community Treaty which was in breach of the Constitution and which went beyond the essential scope and objectives of the existing Union and Community Treaties entailed passage of an Amendment of the Constitution Bill by the Oireachtas, popular referendum and signature by the President, approval of the Treaty by Dáil Éireann where it involved a charge on public funds, and deposit of the instrument of ratification by the Government. (It is implicit in Walsh J.'s judgment in *Crotty* that he considered a constitutional referendum to be part of Ireland's "constitutional requirements", where a proposed amendment to the Treaties would otherwise be inconsistent with the Constitution; this would be a matter only of Irish law.) This might seem rather disingenuous, and a deliberate misinterpretation of the ruling of the Court of Justice: it would leave all such amending agreements open to later renunciation, contrary to the requirements of Community law (and thus contrary to Article 29.4.5 of the Constitution), as it is difficult to know whether an agreement breaches the Constitution and exceeds the scope and objectives of the existing Treaties in advance of a judicial determination of the point. Such a condition might cause the Government to seek a constitutional amendment as a matter of course in advance of ratifying amending agreements; but that is hardly a development to be recommended in respect of all such changes in the constitutional Treaties. It is much more probable that the Court of Justice would give a ruling leaving the Irish court in no doubt that the validity of ratification could be challenged as a matter of Union law, if at all, only in cases of the most patent breach of normal procedures.

The State would remain theoretically subject in the event of non-compliance or renunciation to enforcement action for failure to comply with one of the Community Treaties (Articles 169, 170 E.C.; Articles 141, 142 Euratom). Were the Commission or a Member State to bring such an action in respect of Ireland's non-observance of a purportedly unconstitutional Treaty provision, the Court of Justice alone would decide whether Article N, E.U. had been properly complied with. While it would certainly be respectful of the findings of a national court about the observance of the necessary conditions for ratification by that Member State, it could conclude in a scenario such as that painted above that the Supreme Court's reading of the Court of Justice's interpretation of Article N had been too liberal; and that in Ireland's case (and in the light of the general international law principle expressed in Article 46 of the Vienna Convention), only an overt breach of the requirements of Article 29.4.1-2 and 29.5-6 could nullify the instrument of ratification and thus the impugned amendment to the Community Treaties. If the Court of Justice reached such a conclusion, contrary to a decision of the Supreme Court, its decision (as an act of an institution of the Communities) would be part of the law of the State under the conditions laid down in the Treaties (second clause, Article 29.4.5; European Communities Act, 1972, s.2(1)); and the Treaties themselves would require that the impugned Treaty amendment, duly found to be valid by the Court of Justice, should be observed in an appropriate fashion by the State, constitutional problems notwithstanding.

It is inconceivable that such judicial activity would not result in a political crisis that would then fall to be resolved at a political level (see the options described by Phelan, Membership, at 274); and it is scarcely conceivable that so great a rift could occur in the first place between the Supreme Court and the European Court of Justice. (It has been suggested that, at the very least, all kinds of public policy considerations, such as those advanced to justify the decision in *Murphy v. Attorney-General* [1982] I.R. 241, would argue against a retroactive application of a finding of invalidity; Hogan & Whyte eds.,

Kelly, *The Irish Constitution* (3rd. ed., 1994) p. 284, n. 14 (hereinafter Kelly, *Constitution*).) Nonetheless, this extreme scenario serves to illustrate a point that can have many more mundane applications: that the test of legal obligation which was intended by the drafters of what is now Article 29.4.5 of the Constitution, and which was endorsed by the Supreme Court in *Crotty*, will ordinarily prevent constitutional review of amendments to Community or Union Treaties after they enter into force. Their validity (*i.e.* their proper entry into force) can as a matter of Union law only be tested, if at all, for compliance with Article N, E.U.; and while the circumstances in which such a challenge might arise may give an influential fact-finding role to the Irish courts, this is a question to be decided ultimately either by the European Court of Justice or in accordance with its interpretation of Union law.

The meaning of the phrase "necessitated by the obligations of membership of the Communities" is also relevant to whether the State is constitutionally competent to ratify conventions negotiated under the rubric of Article 220 E.C, as well as other conventions among the Member States. The Brussels Convention on Jurisdiction and the Enforcement of Judgments in Civil and Commercial Matters 1968 grants an additional interpretative jurisdiction to the European Court of Justice, but appears to be necessitated, as Article 3(2) of the Accession Treaty obliges the State to ratify it (Hogan, "The Tenth Amendment of the Constitution Act, 1987" (1987) I.C.L.S.A. 87-01, at 87-04). However, other conventions concluded under Article 220 E.C. may not benefit from the protection of Article 29.4.5 of the Constitution, as Article 220 E.C. merely states that Member States should enter into negotiations in order to secure for their nationals the benefits of such conventions. The same must be true, *a fortiori*, of conventions negotiated outwith the scope of Article 220. Thus, a problem has arisen in respect of the Brussels Protocol to the Rome Convention on Contractual Obligations, which gives the Court of Justice an interpretative jurisdiction. Ray Burke T.D., Minister for Justice, made the following remarks in the Dáil (407 *Dáil Debates*, Col. 1936):

> "Since the Protocol would empower the Court of Justice to give rulings which would be binding on the courts of contracting States it is not possible under the Constitution of Ireland to ratify this Protocol. Accession to the 1980 Convention or Protocol is not necessitated by the obligations of membership of the European Communities and therefore is not covered by the terms of Article 29.4.3 of the Constitution."

Ireland ultimately felt able to legislate to enable ratification of the Convention, but has not acceded to the Protocol (see the Contractual Obligations (Applicable Law) Act, 1991, and annotation by Hogan, (1991) I.C.L.S.A. 8-01).

The Community Patent Convention is not based on Article 220 E.C. either. It gives an additional interpretative jurisdiction to the Court of Justice, and also (under Articles 69 and 70) to the courts of the Federal Republic of Germany, in apparent violation of Article 34.1 of the Constitution (see the comments of Michael McDowell T.D., 371 *Dáil Debates*, Cols. 2306-7, and Senator Mary Robinson, 116 *Seanad Debates*, Cols. 78-9; see further Robinson, "The Constitutional Problem in Ratifying the Community Patent Convention" in Robinson ed., *Intellectual Property* (1989) p. 69 (hereinafter Robinson, Convention)). The Preamble to the Patent Convention states that its conclusion is "necessary to facilitate the achievement of the tasks of the European Economic Community", and its signature by the representatives of the Member States was accompanied by a Council Resolution concurring in this statement, and recording the opinion of the Council that the Convention was an appropriate measure to ensure fulfilment of Community obligations (December 15, 1975) but Walsh J., writing extra-judicially, did not find the preambular recital persuasive, but seems not to have been aware of the Council Resolution (Reflections, at 813):

> "These are no more than expressions of the opinions and hopes of the High Contracting Parties, but not declarations of any Community institution. It is not a Convention envisaged by Article 220 of the Treaty of Rome."

Robinson suggested that the Convention might have been adopted as a Community regulation, like the Trademark Regulation, on the basis of Article 235 E.C., which would of course have benefited from the terms of Article 29.4.5 of the Constitution; but did not feel that the existence of this alternative could permit ratification of the Convention as a treaty, a measure which the State was under no legal obligation to ratify (Robinson, Convention, at 75; her view that the Patent Convention could have been adopted by regulation or other E.C. measure is confirmed by Advocate General Jacobs in Case C-350/92 *Spain v. Council*, at paras. 24–26; see also Opinion 1/94 *G.A.T.T.* [1994] I E.C.R., at para. 59; Case C-9/93 *Ideal Standard* [1994] I E.C.R. 2789, at para. 58; Council Regulation (E.C.) 40/94 of December 20, 1993, [1994] O.J. L11/1.). Temple Lang asserted, on the contrary, and in the light of the Council Resolution, that "[i]t seems highly unlikely that the Court of Justice, which has interpreted Article 5 [EEC] widely on a number of occasions, would rule that ratification was not legally necessary" ("The Draft Treaty establishing the European Union and the Member States: Ireland" in Bieber *et al* eds., *An Ever Closer Union* (1985) p. 241, at 243). This position is referrable to Temple Lang's more general opinion that "Article 5 can impose a duty to ratify conventions negotiated … under Community auspices. … This duty arises when it is sufficiently clear, from the circumstances in which the convention in question was negotiated or otherwise, that it is Community policy that all Member States should ratify it" (Article 5, at 658; see also Case 71/76, *Thieffry v. Conseil de l'Ordre des Advocats* [1977] E.C.R. 765). However, in many instances where the Member States have negotiated a convention in order to achieve Community objectives, they may wish to argue that they have a continuing discretion in advance of ratification as to whether the draft convention is the most appropriate means of action. Such an argument may be more plausible in cases where urgent action is not required (as was the case in Case 32/79, *Commission v. United Kingdom* [1980] E.C.R. 2403) although the Council Resolution in respect of the Patent Convention does have a tone of finality. An alternative argument from Article 5 E.C. is that a Council resolution can sometimes have obligatory effect, "when it makes specific the duties of co-operation which the Member States assumed under Article 5 of the E.E.C. Treaty" (Case 141/78, *France v. United Kingdom* [1979] E.C.R. 2923; Temple Lang, Article 5, at 668-9). This discussion is now moot, as Article 29.4.6 was adopted under the Eleventh Amendment of the Constitution Act, 1992 to permit ratification of the Community Patent Convention; but it may be of significance in other cases. The possibility of conventions between the Member States within the framework of Judicial and Home Affairs Co-operation is introduced by the Treaty on European union, and may raise similar problems (see Chapter 7 below).

The possibility that such conventions, even if not necessitated, might be within the scope and objectives of Community membership does not appear to have been canvassed. It is true that the Court in *Crotty* was concerned with the constitutionality of amendments to the Community Treaties, otherwise unconstitutional (as a matter of Irish law), that could be considered nonetheless to be within their essential scope and objectives and thus saved by the specific authorising clauses now contained in Article 29.4.3-4. However, it is not difficult to apply that reasoning also to other acts of the Member States which, though neither necessitated by membership nor issued by the Communities or their institutions, are expressly envisaged by the Treaties. Even then, however, while the adoption of such conventions might be thought generally to be within the essential scope and objectives of Community membership, the courts might not take the same view of a (limited) concession of plenary jurisdiction to the courts of another Member State as they would of a concession of a further interpretative jurisdiction (analogous to Article 177 E.C.) to the European Court of Justice.

It is probably a decisive argument against any such extension of the licence in Article 29.4.3 of the Constitution to accede to the Community Treaties to secondary measures envisaged in the Treaties (and thus within their scope and objectives) that this would deprive Article 29.4.5 of any distinct effect. Moreover, it would make irrelevant the debate over whether only acts "necessitated by" or also those "consequent upon" Community membership were immune from invalidation having regard to the provisions of the Constitution, as any secondary measure adopted by the Communities, or by the Member States within the framework of the Communities, could very likely be said to be within the essential scope and objectives of the Treaties, irrespective of the binding quality of the act or of the existence of a legal obligation to adopt it. This would appear to be contrary to the intention which it was sought to express in the relevant constitutional provisions.

It does not follow that there should be a strict division between the relevant provisions of the Constitution, with Article 29.4.3-4 applying to the constitutional Treaties, and Article 29.4.5 to secondary legislation (*pace* Barrington J. in *Crotty*). Article 29.4.5 should still apply to the constitutional Treaties, because many State acts are necessitated directly by the Treaties, which can be relied upon in national courts to justify such action (or to compel it). Furthermore, it is possible that the Irish courts could rely upon the "scope and objectives" test as a negative test of secondary obligations. Collins and O'Reilly observe, for example, that "[i]t would be possible for a litigant to argue in an Irish court that a measure adopted by the Communities was not protected from review by the second sentence of Article 29.4.3 [now Article 29.4.5] of the Constitution on the ground of conflict therewith on the basis that the measure at issue purported to deal with matters outside the scope of the original treaties" ("The Application of Community Law in Ireland 1973-1989" (1990) 27 C.M.L.Rev. 315, at 319-20). The authors do not suggest that the Irish courts question the *vires* of the secondary legislation of the Communities, which task is entrusted to the Court of Justice by Community law and by the test of legal obligation under Article 29.4.5. However, where the jurisdiction of the Court of Justice is excluded, and Article 29.4.5 nonetheless applies, in respect of the obligations of membership of the Union and of laws, acts and measures of the Union, Irish courts may wish to question *vires* under the E.U. Treaty, and may have recourse to the "essential scope and objectives" test under Article 29.4.4 of the Constitution (see further Chapter 7 below).

A further argument can be ventured in respect of conventions adopted under Article 220 E.C. or otherwise in pursuance of Community objectives. Even if Article 5 E.C. cannot be relied upon to compel ratification once such conventions are negotiated and declared by the Council (as in the case of the Patent Convention) to be necessary to the achievement of the tasks of the Community, compliance with their terms may be an obligation under Article 5 E.C. once they are ratified. The State could not at that point oppose such an obligation with a continuing discretion as to the most appropriate measures to be taken in the absence of Community action. This would preclude constitutional challenge to any acts necessitated by observance by the State of the terms of such conventions. There is insufficient authority from the Court of Justice, however, to pronounce determinatively on this point.

Does every amendment of the Community and Union Treaties require a separate constitutional amendment?

It is clear that only amendments to the Treaties which "alter the essential scope or objectives of the Communities" or of the Union and which contravene the Constitution require a separate constitutional amendment. Each member of the Supreme Court agreed in *Crotty* that Ireland could not participate in a form of European political union without a further amendment of the Constitution. Such an amendment took place to authorise ratification of the Maastricht Treaty on European Union, with its prescriptions for monetary union, political union in the foreign policy sphere, co-operation in justice and home affairs, and the creation of an over-arching European Union (see Article 29.4.4, inserted by the Eleventh Amendment of the Constitution Act, 1992, which is discussed further below). On the other hand, the validity of national legislation allowing for the entry of new Member States to the Union is scarcely in doubt, as the Supreme Court itself said that the entry of new members was an "in-built and clearly expressed aim of the Community". But other issues might not be so clear-cut. For example, in a contemporary comment, Murphy treated *Crotty* as having removed any doubts about the constitutionality of the 1975 Budgetary Treaty, which established the Court of Auditors and which greatly increased the budgetary powers of the European Parliament (Murphy, "The European Communities (Amendment) Act, 1986" (1986) I.C.L.S.A. 37-01 at 37-09 (hereinafter Murphy, 1986 Act)). At about the same time, Hogan argued that measures like the European Communities (Amendment) Act, 1977, which introduced the 1975 Treaty into Irish law, might in the future be exposed to constitutional attack (Hogan, "The Tenth Amendment of the Constitution Act, 1987" (1987) I.C.L.S.A. 87-03 at 87-03 to 87-04; for an annotation of the 1977 Act, see further below).

It is difficult to say what is encompassed by "the essential scope and objectives" of the Communities and the Union. For example, the Preamble to the Single European Act expressed the will of the High Contracting Parties "to transform relations as a whole among their States into a European Union, in accordance with the Solemn Declaration of Stuttgart of June 19, 1983"; to implement this Union on the basis of the Communities and of European Political Cooperation; "and to invest this Union with the necessary means of action"; and referred to the approval by the Heads of State or Government of the objective of the progressive realisation of economic and monetary union at their Paris Conference of October 19-21, 1972. If such were taken as the essential scope and objectives of the Communities after ratification of the Single Act was authorised by the Tenth Amendment to the Constitution, a further constitutional amendment would hardly have been necessary in respect of the Maastricht Treaty. As Henchy J. said that the Single Act would lead to a European political union in the sphere of foreign policy, it has been suggested that the enactment of the Tenth Amendment implied that no further constitutional amendment was necessary in respect of further steps towards that essential objective (see Temple Lang, *Crotty*, at 716). On the other hand, the machinery provided by the Member States in the S.E.A. for the building of the European Union was a good deal less impressive. The former Article 102a EEC (inserted by Article 20, S.E.A.) only contemplated "the convergence of economic and monetary policies". The provision made at Maastricht in 1992 for establishment of a European Central Bank and the locking of currency exchange rates preparatory to the introduction of a single currency represents more than an incidental improvement in the machinery for the pursuit of monetary union. It must be seen as a qualitative transformation, and as going beyond the concrete scope if not the ambitious objectives of the Single Act. The French *Conseil Constitutionnel* remarked that these provisions would mean that a Member State would have "no powers of its own in a field where the essential conditions for exercising national sover-

eignty are in question" (*Re Ratification of the Treaty on European Union*
[1993] 3 C.M.L.R. 345 at 356), which can hardly be said of the pre-existing
regime.

A general test can be suggested. Where an earlier Treaty was merely a
stepping stone rather than a means sufficient in itself in the attainment of
certain stated objectives, a later Treaty designed actually to achieve those
objectives will require further constitutional authorisation if it would otherwise be in breach of the Constitution. However, where the earlier Treaty
substantially provided the necessary machinery for the pursuit of its objectives, even quite far-reaching improvements and extensions of the machinery
(such as those contained in the S.E.A. in respect of the Treaty of Rome) will
nonetheless remain within its essential scope and objectives.

It appears then (subject to some possible *caveats*, such as the doubts
expressed above about changes to Article 235 E.C.) that there is some constitutional latitude to expand and improve upon the original Communities,
given the considerable powers and fields of competence granted to them at
the outset. Is the same now true of the European Union, subsequent to the
express authorisation granted to the State in Article 29.4.4 to become a member of the Union? One must again distinguish between objectives in the
achievement of which the Union is seen only as a transitional stage, and those
to which the provisions of the Treaty on European Union are immediately
relevant. Thus, alterations in the procedure for the achievement of monetary
union would probably be constitutionally unobjectionable, given the considerable transfer of national monetary sovereignty already agreed to. Even
there, however, changes greatly to the detriment of the influence of the State
(*e.g.* exclusion from the Board of the European Central Bank even if a par-
ticipant in monetary union) could be viewed as being akin to those exceptional cases where the Supreme Court would not countenance an end to
unanimous voting, thus requiring a fresh popular mandate.

The E.U. Treaty is unusual in that it expressly envisages its own alteration,
in order better to pursue its objectives. Article B, E.U. states (echoing the
Preamble) that the Union shall have among its objectives "to assert its identity on the international scene, in particular through the implementation of a
common foreign and security policy including the eventual framing of a common defence policy, which might in time lead to a common defence". Article
J.4.1 E.U. defines the common foreign and security policy in the same terms,
and Article J.4.6 E.U. states:

> "With a view to furthering the objective of this Treaty, and having in
> view the date of 1998 in the context of Article XII of the Brussels Treaty
> [expiry of the Treaty establishing the Western European Union], the
> provisions of this Article may be revised as provided for in Article N(2)
> on the basis of a report to be presented in 1996 by the Council to the
> European Council, which shall include an evaluation of the progress
> made and the experience gained until then."

In one sense, Article J.4.6 E.U. does not establish very much, as Article N,
E.U. is sufficient in itself to permit any desired amendment of Article J or of
any other provision of the Treaty. Note, however, the express connection of
an envisaged Treaty amendment with the lapse of the Western European
Union (which is an integral part of the development of the Union and of the
elaboration and implementation of decisions and actions of the Union which
have defence implications, *per* Article J.4.2, E.U.) and with Treaty objectives
that contemplate the implementation, in time, of a common defence. Could
the future implementation of a common defence, *i.e.* the creation of common
Union armed forces, be taken to be within the essential scope and objectives
of the Maastricht Treaty, and thus authorised by Article 29.4.4 despite what
would otherwise be a clear breach of Article 15.6.2 of the Constitution ("No

military or armed force, or at least of a Union integrated command, other than a military or armed force raised and maintained by the Oireachtas, shall be raised and maintained for any purpose whatsoever")? In the light of the test suggested above, the answer must be in the negative. The request in Article J.4.2 E.U. that the Western European Union act on its behalf in matters having defence implications, and the exclusion by Article J.4.3 E.U. of such matters from the procedures in Article J.3 E.U. for the adoption of joint actions of the Union, implies that the present machinery does not embrace practical defence issues.

What of a common defence policy, *i.e.* coordination of national defence policies and mutual defence commitments? Article J.4.1 states that the common foreign and security policy ("C.F.S.P.," which is "established" by Article J) "shall include all questions related to the security of the Union, including the eventual framing of a common defence policy, which might in time lead to a common defence". There is a considerable difference in the treatment of a common defence (which might arise in time) and of a common defence policy (which is included in the remit of C.F.S.P., even if it is not thought likely to be agreed for a considerable period). A binding commitment to participate in a military alliance would probably contravene Article 28.3.1 ("War shall not be declared and the State shall not participate in any war save with the assent of Dáil Éireann"). We must distinguish here between substantive outcomes and altered procedures. An unanimous agreement to amend the present framework of the common foreign and security policy in Title V of the Treaty on European Union to provide expressly for mutual defence commitments among the Member States would quite arguably be within the essential scope and objectives of the Treaty, and therefore saved by Article 29.4.4 of the Constitution. Alteration of the procedures set out in Title V, E.U., in order to accelerate the adoption of a common defence policy, might on the other hand fall foul of the Supreme Court's reservations about any dilution of the unanimity rule in certain sensitive areas. These questions may happily be moot, however, as the then Taoiseach, Mr. Albert Reynolds T.D., stated in a speech to the Institute of European Affairs in Dublin in advance of the referendum on the Eleventh Amendment of the Constitution Bill that any further agreement after 1996 with defence implications would also be put to the People (*The Irish Times*, May 19, 1992).

Similar difficult questions arise in respect of citizenship of the European Union. The Member States resolved in the Preamble to the Treaty on European Union to establish a citizenship common to nationals of their countries, and provided the means for its establishment in the amended Part II of the European Community Treaty (Article 8-8e E.C.). Part II establishes Union citizenship for all Member State nationals, and provides for legislation on the right of residence, the right to vote in municipal and European Parliament and the right to petition to European Parliament or to apply to an Ombudsman about grievances, and for agreement among the Member States on the protection of Union citizens by their diplomatic and consular representatives in third countries. Article 8e E.C. then provides (in part) that "the Council, acting unanimously on a proposal from the Commission and after consulting the European Parliament, may adopt provisions to strengthen or to add to the rights laid down in this Part, which it shall recommend to the Member States for adoption in accordance with their respective constitutional requirements". Let us assume that a proposal is made that Union citizens should have the right to vote in all national elections, which gains the unanimous approval of the Member States in the Council (itself rather an unlikely eventuality), but which a concerned person in Ireland asserts is unconstitutional. Article 16.2.ii (inserted by the Ninth Amendment of the Constitution Act, 1984) permits persons who are not Irish citizens to vote in Dáil elections, and the Electoral (Amendment) Act, 1985 permits the grant of such a right to vote to all European Community nationals, but the presidential electorate is confined to Irish citizens, *per* Article 12.2.2 of the Constitution.

If Ireland, along with the other Member States, were to ratify such a recommendation in accordance with its normal constitutional procedures under Article 29.5-6, the primary question relating to its constitutionality would be whether observance of the measure was necessitated by the obligations of membership of the Communities. The jurisprudence on Article 5 E.C. indicates that it would be. In the light of the clear wish of the Member States that a high degree of discretion be maintained in this area (expressed in their choice of a highly exceptional procedure), it is difficult to say whether Article 5 E.C. can be deemed to *require* ratification once the measure in question is unanimously recommended by the Council. If this were the case, ratification could be held to be necessitated even at that point, and would thus be immune even from prior restraint by the Irish courts. If, in the alternative, ratification were not necessitated, the courts could then decide *before ratification* whether such a measure could be saved from unconstitutionality by Article 29.4.4 of the Constitution, which authorised ratification of the E.U. Treaty. The mode of adoption of new citizenship rights under Article 8e E.C. is so similar to the procedure provided for Treaty amendment in Article N, E.U. that it makes the argument for extension to such measures of the *Crotty* "essential scope or objectives" test much more compelling than for ordinary secondary legislation.

However, it is open to doubt whether voting rights in national elections are within the scope of the present Treaty. It is well known that certain Member States vehemently opposed the inclusion of national voting rights in Article 8b E.C. because of their perceived implications for the relations of the sovereign State with its own nationals. The possibility of derogations from legislation under Article 8b.1 E.C. on municipal voting rights "where warranted by problems specific to a Member State" was introduced, *inter alia*, to permit France to ensure that non-French Union citizens elected to municipal authorities could not exercise State power (through the office of mayor) or contribute to the election of a national parliamentary body, *viz.* the French Senate (*Conseil Constitutionnel, Re Ratification of the Treaty on European Union* [1993] 3 C.M.L.R. 345; Oliver, "The French Constitution and the Treaty of Maastricht" (1994) 43 I.C.L.Q. 1; O'Keeffe, "Union Citizenship" in O'Keeffe & Twomey eds., *Legal Issues of the Maastricht Treaty* (1994) p. 87, at 96-7; Draft Directive on Voting Rights for Community Nationals in Local Elections in their Member State of Residence, [1988] O.J. C 246/3; Council Directive on participation in municipal elections, December 20, 1994). On the other hand, Article 8e E.C. appears to correspond to the Supreme Court's conception in *Crotty* of the Communities as "a developing organism with diverse and changing methods for making decisions and an inbuilt and clearly expressed objective of expansion and progress". It is impossible to predict the response of the Irish courts to such a constitutional question. The example serves to illustrate the degree to which the abandonment in many instances in the Maastricht Treaty of the normal methods of Community legislation can cause constitutional confusion at the national as well as at the Community level (see further below the annotation of Article 8e E.C., and the discussion in Chapter 7 of the Union provisions of Article 29.4.5 of the Constitution; see also Article K.3.2(c) E.U. and Article K.9 E.U.).

Crotty v. An Taoiseach: freedom to conduct foreign policy

All the members of the Supreme Court in *Crotty* accepted that decisions of the executive in the sphere of foreign policy are subject to review. The majority, however, insisted that the executive must, in the absence of a constitutional authorisation to the contrary, retain a complete freedom of action to conduct foreign policy. It was one thing to participate in European Political

Cooperation meetings on an informal basis; it was quite another (*per* Henchy J.) to enter into "a solemnly covenanted commitment to the conduct of foreign policy in a way that will lead to European Political Union, at least in the sphere of foreign policy". They viewed Title III as unduly fettering by treaty such freedom of action and ruled accordingly that it would be unconstitutional for the State to ratify the Single Act without a referendum.

The majority reasoning has an attractive symmetry to it. It is a fundamental principle of administrative law that the donee of a discretionary power cannot unduly fetter that discretion, whether by contract or otherwise (Hogan & Morgan, *Administrative Law in Ireland* (2nd. ed., 1991), pp. 503-551). The Supreme Court majority seems to have tested the exercise of the executive power in foreign policy matters by reference to analogous principles; this emerges most clearly from the *dictum* of Walsh J. quoted at length above. However, this part of the decision in *Crotty* has been strongly criticised by both political and academic commentators, largely because it was thought in its own way to fetter unduly, and to subject to unwarranted judicial interference, the power of the State to engage in foreign relations and to undertake binding treaty commitments to other States, in the name of a barely articulated conception of State sovereignty. (See, *e.g.* the comments of Deputies O'Malley, Fitzgerald, Dukes and Kemmy, 371 *Dáil Debates*, Cols. 2224-30, 2283-94, 2442-4, and 2457 respectively; Hogan, S.E.A., at 65; Murphy, 1986 Act, 37-10; Sherlock, Sovereignty, at 108-9; Temple Lang, "The Irish Court Case which delayed the Single European Act: *Crotty v. An Taoiseach and others*" (1987) 24 C.M.L.Rev. 709, at 715 (hereinafter Temple Lang, *Crotty*); Bradley, "The Referendum on the Single European Act" [1987] E.L.Rev. 301, at 306-7.)

A number of decisions of foreign and international courts has concerned subject matter similar to that in *Crotty*. A recent example, also in the context of European integration, can be found in *R. v. Secretary of State for Foreign and Commonwealth Affairs, ex. p. Rees-Mogg* [1993] 3 C.M.L.R. 101; see further Rawlings, "Legal Politics: The United Kingdom and Ratification of the Treaty on European Union", Parts I and II [1994] P.L. 254, 367). Lord Rees-Mogg challenged the proposed ratification of the Maastricht Treaty by the United Kingdom on a number of grounds, *inter alia*, that the Crown could not transfer its prerogative powers in the areas of foreign and defence policy without statutory enactment. His counsel contended that the United Kingdom could not ratify Title V (Article J) of the Treaty of European Union, concerning common foreign and security policy, because the U.K. European Communities (Amendment) Act 1993 did not authorise the inevitable loss of sovereign power. For the purposes of the case, the Queen's Bench Division of the English High Court assumed that the issues raised were justiciable and that it would indeed be unlawful for the Crown to alienate any of its prerogative powers without statutory enactment. The court decided that ratification of Title V of the E.U. Treaty would constitute an exercise of the United Kingdom's prerogative powers in relation to foreign policy and not a transfer of these powers. Prerogative powers exercised within an inter-governmental framework are not lost, but are merely being exercised in a different manner. Lloyd L.J. concluded for the Court ([1993] 3 C.M.L.R. 101, at 116):

> "So far as we know, nobody has ever suggested that the Charter of the United Nations, for example, or of the North Atlantic Treaty Organisation, involves a transfer of prerogative power. Title V should be read in the same light. In the last resort, ... it would presumably be open to the government to denounce the Treaty, or at least to fail to comply with its international obligations under Title V."

It is foolish to draw too simple a comparison between decisions reached in different constitutional contexts; the High Court in *Rees-Mogg* expressly distinguished *Crotty* because the domestic constitutional questions involved were very different. Furthermore, the court indicated that the United Kingdom retained the "escape hatch" (as a matter of domestic law) of denunciation of the Treaty; while this may indicate that ultimate sovereignty remains vested in the Member States, it is hardly a realistic option for a State which in all other respects wishes to continue as a member of the Union. Nonetheless, the attitude of the English High Court to the exercise of sovereign State power was certainly very different to that of the Supreme Court majority in *Crotty*.

The German *Bundesverfassungsgericht* addressed similar questions in *Brunner* [1994] 1 C.M.L.R. 57, at 89-91; see further Foster, "The German Constitution and E.C. Membership" [1994] P.L. 392; Herdegen, "Maastricht and the German Constitutional Court: Constitutional Restraints on 'Ever Closer Union'" (1994) 31 C.M.L.Rev. 235). It remarked that the Treaty on European Union "establishes a federation of States [*Staatenverbund*] for the purpose of realising an ever closer union of the peoples of Europe (organised as States) and not a State based on the people of one European nation". (*Staatenverbund* may be better translated as a *confederation* of States.)

> "The Member States have established the European Union in order to exercise a part of their functions in common and to that extent to exercise their sovereignty in common. ... Accordingly the Union Treaty takes account of the independence and sovereignty of the Member States, since it obliges the Union to respect the national identities of its Member States. ... [T]he term 'European Union' may indicate a concern for further integration, but as regards the intended objective the question is ultimately open."

The Court referred as well to the new Article 88(1) of the French Constitution, adopted after the decision of the *Conseil Constitutionnel* quoted above, which speaks in similar vein of Member States which exercise some of their competences in common within the European Union and the European Communities. Like the English High Court in *Rees-Mogg*, the *Bundesverfassungsgericht* also opined that Germany could ultimately revoke its adherence to the Treaty by a contrary act, as it would remain a sovereign State as defined in Article 2(1) of the United Nations Charter. The whole tone of the Court's judgment seems out of sympathy with the majority view in *Crotty*.

It is as well, however, to remember the context in which the *Bundesverfassungsgericht* reached its decision. It was not concerned with the need for a constitutional amendment (which had already been secured), but with whether such an amendment was in itself valid and sufficient to authorise ratification, as the Treaty on European Union was alleged to contravene the unamendable constitutional guarantees of the democratic and federal character of the German State (Articles 20, 38 and 79, German Constitution). The guarantee of democratic legitimation of State power was in turn found to be bound up with the sovereignty of the State ([1994] 1 C.M.L.R. 57, at 84-5). The Court therefore had to establish only that the essential nature of the German State and its constitutional order would be preserved notwithstanding Union membership. This is not the same as having to ascertain whether an aspect of sovereign power has been alienated, irrespective of whether sufficient sovereignty is retained by the alienating State either to retain the status of a sovereign State within the meaning of the United Nations Charter, or to employ its residual power to breach international obligations. The Supreme Court in *Crotty* was engaged in the latter enquiry. (On whether certain features of the Irish constitutional order are unamendable, see the discussion below of Article 29.4.5 and natural law; see further Whelan, "Constitutional Amendments in Ireland: The Competing Claims of Democracy" in Quinn *et al* eds., *Justice and Legal Theory in Ireland* (1995); and Phelan, *Revolution*, at 396–410.)

A problem closer to that in *Crotty* was presented to the Permanent Court of International Justice (the predecessor of the International Court of Justice) in its *Advisory Opinion on the Austro-German Customs Union* ([1931] P.C.I.J. Series A/B, No. 41). That case was also concerned with what might only have been a partial cession of sovereign authority. Article 88 of the Treaty of St. Germain, 1919, stated:

> "The independence of Austria is inalienable otherwise than with the consent of the Council of the League of Nations. Consequently, Austria undertakes in the absence of the consent of the said Council to abstain from any act which might directly or indirectly or by any means whatever compromise her independence."

A protocol of 1922 guaranteed the economic independence of Austria in similar terms. The Permanent Court advised by a majority of eight votes to seven that a proposed customs union between Austria and Germany (which might have been followed by a political union, *per* Borchard, [1931] A.J.I.L. 711, at 715) would be incompatible with the Treaty of St. Germain. In his separate concurring opinion, Anzilotti J. remarked (at page 58 of the Report):

> "[T]he restrictions upon a State's liberty, whether arising out of ordinary international law or contractual arrangements, do not as such in the least affect its independence. As long as those restrictions do not place the State under the legal authority of another State, the former remains an independent State however extensive and burdensome those obligations may be."

In other words, the power to negotiate treaties—even treaties which severely circumscribe the State's freedom to act—represents the very essence of sovereignty, provided that any such treaty may not place the contracting State under the authority of another State. A similar point was made by the Permanent Court in its judgment in *The Wimbledon* ([1923] P.C.I.J. Series A, No. 1, at 25).

It has been remarked that the principle espoused by the *Crotty* majority, namely, that a State loses part of its sovereignty if it alienates or unduly fetters by treaty its right to conduct foreign relations, is consistent with the jurisprudence of the Permanent Court of International Justice, but that it ascribed a far greater significance than was warranted to Title III of the Single Act (Hogan, S.E.A., at 67). Title III did not formally place Ireland in a position of subordination to other States; and there is evidence that in practice it has greatly increased Ireland's influence abroad (see Tonra, "Ireland and E.P.C.: A Victory of Substance over Form" (1994) Ir. Pol. Studies). It was also argued that the non-justiciability of Title III before the European Court of Justice indicated that it was an intrinsically political arrangement between the Member States (McMahon & Murphy, *European Community Law in the Republic of Ireland* (1989) p. 298; Hogan, S.E.A., at 67). It must be countered that the issues of the binding quality and the justiciability of international treaties are logically distinct (see Müller-Graff, "The Legal Bases of the Third Pillar and its Position in the Framework of the Union Treaty" in Monar & Morgan eds., *The Third Pillar of the European Union* (1994) p. 21, at 24; Eaton, "Common Foreign and Security Policy" in O'Keeffe & Twomey eds., *Legal Issues of the Maastricht Treaty* (1994), p. 215, at 222). Furthermore, the British Prime Minister, John Major M.P., has asserted that any dispute in the fields of common foreign and security policy and of justice and home affairs co-operation under the Maastricht Treaty could be brought to the International Court of Justice. While not a politically realistic prospect, the same option was nominally available in respect of Title III of the Single

European Act (*Hansard*, H.C. Vol. 208, col. 267; *cf.* Everling, "Reflections on the Structure of the European Union" (1992) 29 C.M.L.Rev. 1053, at 1064).

The *Crotty* decision was followed by speculation about the constitutionality of Irish membership of the United Nations Organisation (Hogan, S.E.A., at 69; Heffernan & Whelan, "Ireland, the United Nations and the Gulf Conflict: Legal Aspects" (1991) 3 Irish Studies in International Affairs 115), the Anglo-Irish Agreement (Hogan, "The Tenth Amendment to the Constitution Act, 1987" (1987) I.C.L.S.A. 87-03 at 87-05) and even the European Convention on Human Rights (Casey, *Constitutional Law in Ireland* (2nd. ed., 1992) p. 175 (hereinafter Casey, *Constitution*)).

In the case of the United Nations, the present effective powers of the Security Council appear to contravene even the "compromise" rationale suggested for the *Crotty* decision in *McGimpsey v. Ireland* (discussed immediately below; H. Ct., [1988] I.R. 567; S. Ct., [1990] 1 I.R. 110). The Security Council's power to order economic or other measures short of the use of force seems irrefutable. Whatever about Article 42 of the U.N. Charter (on military enforcement action), there is no doubt about Security Council authority to give binding decisions imposing non-military sanctions under Article 41. That it could impose such obligations was expressly recognised by the Taoiseach Mr. de Valera in the Dáil debate on the Charter in 1946, in which statement he also noted Ireland's relative inability to influence Security Council decisions (102 *Dáil Debates*, Col. 1315):

"Under Article 25 [of the Charter], we would agree to accept and carry out the decisions of the Security Council made in accordance with the Charter. That is an obligation of very wide scope, and the point to remember is that, in accepting it, we would be undertaking to carry out the decisions of a body of which we ourselves would not ordinarily be a member."

The constitutionality of the Anglo-Irish Agreement, 1985 was challenged in *McGimpsey v. Ireland* (H. Ct., [1988] I.R. 567; S. Ct., [1990] 1 I.R. 110). The plaintiffs argued *inter alia* that the agreement fettered the power of the Government to conduct foreign relations in the same manner as Title III of the Single European Act did. In the Agreement, the Irish and British Governments affirmed that any change in the status of Northern Ireland would only come about with the consent of the people of Northern Ireland (Article 1(a)). The two Governments agreed to establish an Inter-Governmental Conference concerned with Northern Ireland and with relations between the two parts of the island of Ireland (Article 2(a)). The British Government accepted that the Irish Government would put forward views and proposals on matters relating to Northern Ireland within the field of activity of the Conference (*viz.* political matters; security and related matters; legal matters, including the administration of justice; and the promotion of cross-border co-operation). It was agreed that "[i]n the interests of promoting peace and stability, determined efforts shall be made through the Conference to resolve any differences"; and it was further declared that there was no derogation from the sovereignty of either Government, and that each retained responsibility for the decisions and administration of government within its own jurisdiction (Article 2(b)).

Barrington J. rejected the challenge in the High Court. He remarked that the Inter-Governmental Conference was only a forum "in which the representatives of the two Governments find it convenient to meet on a regular basis to discuss matters of common interest relating to Northern Ireland". The express exclusion of any derogation from sovereignty was also important. The question being dealt with was therefore totally different from that at issue in *Crotty*:

> "We are not dealing with a multilateral treaty conferring powers on supranational authorities. We are dealing with a bilateral treaty between two sovereign Governments. The clear implication of Article 29.5 [of the Constitution] is that the State may commit itself to deal with some aspect of foreign policy in one way rather than in another. But this is something quite different from purporting to transfer the conduct of the foreign policy of the State to some supranational authority or even to some other State."

While Barrington J.'s judgment is four-square with the principles expressed by Anzilotti J. in 1931, it has been properly criticised for misrepresenting the *Crotty* majority's decision, which on its face turned neither on the multilateral quality of the Single European Act, nor on the powers of a supranational authority (which was in fact absent from the terms of Title III (Hogan, S.E.A., at 69). It was the binding commitment to exercise State power in a particular way or by particular procedures and to particular ends which motivated their condemnation of the Treaty.

Finlay C.J. gave the judgment for the Supreme Court on appeal (Walsh, Griffin, Hederman and McCarthy JJ. concurring in relevant part), and it is perhaps closer to *Crotty* in reasoning although it ultimately distinguishes that decision. Finlay C.J. invoked Article 29.1 of the Constitution, asserting that "[a] procedure which is likely to lead to peacable and friendly co-operation at any given time must surely be consistent with the constitutional position of a State that affirms its devotion not only to the ideal of peace and friendly co-operation but to that ideal founded on international justice and morality". This provision was mentioned, but not relied upon, by Walsh J. in *Crotty*, although Walsh J. did remark that Article 29.4.2 of the Constitution, permitting association with international organisations for the purpose of international co-operation in matters of common concern, could not save Title III of the S.E.A. (see above).

The essential point of distinction, however, was expressed as follows:

> "The Government of Ireland at any time carrying out the functions which have been agreed under the Anglo-Irish Agreement is entirely free to do so in the maner in which it, and it alone, thinks most conducive to the achieving of the aims to which it is committed. ... The basis of the decision of this Court in *Crotty v. An Taoiseach* was that the terms of the Single European Act could oblige the Government in carrying out the foreign policy of the State, to a greater or lesser extent, subservient to the national interests of other Member States. I have no doubt that there is a vast and determining difference between the provisions of this Agreement and the provisions of the Single European Act as interpreted in *Crotty v. An Taoiseach*."

The *crux* of *Crotty* (for the purpose of deciding *McGimpsey*) was not that the State would be made subject to other States, but that the State would be bound by Title III of the Single Act to consider and accommodate the interests of other States when exercising its own power within the framework of European Political Cooperation. On the other hand, while the State committed itself to make determined efforts though the Anglo-Irish Inter-Governmental Conference to resolve any differences, these efforts did not require the State to take full account of the position of the United Kingdom (although this must be a practical requirement of the resolution of differences), to seek to develop common principles and objectives, to ensure that the determination of common positions should constitute a point of reference for its policies, or to refrain as far as possible from impeding the formation of consensus; the State instead retained full sovereignty, and responsibility for the decisions and administration of government within its own jurisdiction (Article 2(b), Anglo-Irish Agreement).

One cannot help suspecting that another crucial factual difference between Title III of the S.E.A. and the Anglo-Irish Agreement was that while the former Treaty appeared to place the formal freedom of action of the State under certain constraints, the latter secured for the State a new and privileged consultative role in respect of a problem of pressing and immediate national interest. Finlay C.J. concluded that "there is, looking at the Anglo-Irish Agreement in its totality and looking at the entire scheme and thrust of the Constitution of Ireland a high improbability that a clear attempt to resolve the position with regard to the re-integration of the national territory and the position of Northern Ireland by a process of consultation, discussion and reasoned argument structured by constant communication between servants of each of the two States concerned could ever be inconsistent with a Constitution devoted to the ideals of ordered, peaceful international relations."

It was argued after Barrington J.'s decision in *McGimpsey* that the collective reasoning of Walsh, Henchy and Hederman JJ. in *Crotty* should have emphasised the unique features of the Single European Act rather than appearing to cast doubt on the Government's general treaty-making powers (Hogan, S.E.A., at 69). It is clear, however, that the decision is in this respect likely to be narrowly interpreted in future. Barrington J. observed in *McGimpsey* that "the conduct of the foreign policy of the State is not a matter which readily lends itself to judicial review and if there is any area where judicial restraint is appropriate, this is it".

However, one can argue (perhaps more plausibly in the light of the *McGimpsey* decision) that *Crotty* was an exceptional case, linked to the special qualities of the process of European integration, in which the majority simply applied the corollary of the theory of organic growth which was employed by the Court to justify the European Communities (Amendment) Act, 1986. Temple Lang remarked that "few people in Europe would consider [Henchy J.'s] judgment a balanced description of the *present effects* of Title III, or of its correct legal interpretation, as distinct from *its possible future development*" (Temple Lang, *Crotty*, at 714; authors' emphasis). But while Griffin J. found that the language of Title III preserved for the Contracting Parties "the utmost freedom of action in the sphere of foreign policy, and is in stark contrast to that used in Title II", Henchy J. distinguished between the then existing political practice of E.P.C. and a treaty commitment to confirm and supplement such a practice over time: "as a treaty, Title III is not designed in static terms.... If Ireland were to ratify the [Single Act] it would be bound in international law to engage actively in a programme which would tranch *progressively* on Ireland's independence and sovereignty in the conduct of foreign relations" (authors' italics; for an expression of sympathy with this view, see Robinson, "Tendencies towards a European Foreign Policy" in Schwarze *et al* eds., *Structure and Dimensions of European Community Policy-making* (1988), p. 65). Henchy J. was concerned to establish "the scope and objective of Title III", and remarked (authors' italics):

> "[C]ommitments expressed in Title III make manifest that, although the ultimate aim of European Union is to be reached by a pathway of gradualism, each Member State will immediately cede a portion of its sovereignty and freedom of action in matters of foreign policy. National objectives and ideological positions must defer to the aims and decisions of an institution known as European Political Cooperation. A purely national approach to foreign policy is incompatible with accession to this treaty. ... Title III is *the threshold* leading from what has been an essentially economic Community to what will now also be a political Community."

It may have been the progressive, dynamic manner in which a European Union could develop from the S.E.A. (which had under Article 1 the "objective to contribute to making concrete progress towards European unity", and which has been taken further both by practice under Title III and by the Maastricht Treaty) that persuaded the majority that a new constitutional licence was required from the outset for such commitments. (Bradley remarks that none of the Supreme Court judges mentioned Article 1 S.E.A., which he says confirms that European unity was not just a "possible ultimate objective"; "The Referendum on the Single European Act" [1987] E.L.Rev. 301, at 306.) If the scope and objectives of the original European Community Treaties could embrace the considerable institutional changes introduced by Title II of the Single European Act, so too might Title III sanction further incremental changes more intrusive on State sovereignty than its own provisions might suggest. (Without conceding this point, Temple Lang did observe that "*if* the Single Act *had* been regarded as constitutional, and if it *were* to evolve as its terms envisage, it would not be clear at what point a referendum in Ireland would become necessary"; *Crotty*, at 715 (italics in original).) In effect, the organic principle expressed in the judgment of the Supreme Court on the 1986 Act may have precluded the court from taking the view expressed above by the *Bundesverfassungsgericht*, that "as regards the intended objective the question is ultimately open".

CHAPTER FOUR

MEAGHER V. MINISTER FOR AGRICULTURE AND THE IMPLEMENTATION OF
COMMUNITY LAW

The post-*Crotty* interpretation Article 29.4.5 of the Constitution must be reconsidered in the light of the decision of the Supreme Court in *Meagher v. Minister for Agriculture* [1994] 1 I.R. 329. The decision resolves a perennial controversy about the "necessity" of implementing E.C. directives in Irish law by ministerial regulations, and has implications for the manner in which E.C. obligations of all types are received in our domestic legal system. However, in contrast with the seeming over-protectiveness in *Crotty* of the majority's conception of Irish sovereignty, *Meagher* is open to criticism for overriding Irish constitutional values, such as the principle of the separation of powers, in a way which it is contended is not necessary, and may be inappropriate, as a matter of Community law.

Section 2 of the European Communities Act, 1972 makes binding on the State and part of domestic law "the Treaties governing the European Communities and the existing and future acts adopted by the institutions of those Communities under the conditions laid down in [the] Treaties" (see the discussion below pp.171–175 of section 2 of the 1972 Act, as amended). Thus, the section requires those elements of Community law which are directly applicable (*e.g.* E.C. regulations, some Treaty provisions) or directly effective (as can transpire in the case of directives) to be enforced in Irish courts on terms dictated by the Treaties as interpreted by the Court of Justice. Such "laws enacted, acts done or measures adopted by the Communities, or institutions thereof" are free from constitutional scrutiny, according to the second clause of Article 29.4.5 of the Constitution.

Section 3 of the Act provides for the implementation in Ireland of Community measures which are not ordinarily directly enforceable in the domestic law of the Member States, such as directives. Article 189(3) E.C. provides: "A directive shall be binding, as to the result to be achieved, but shall leave to the national authorities the choice of form and methods", so that most directives require transposition into national law. While the possibility of implementation by means of an Act of the Oireachtas is left open, and is sometimes resorted to, extensive law-making power is delegated to Ministers in the section:

> (1) A Minister of State may make regulations for enabling section 2 of this Act to have full effect [*i.e.* introducing E.C. acts into domestic law under the conditions laid down in the Treaties].
> (2) Regulations under this section may contain such incidental, supplementary and consequential provisions as appear to the Minister making the regulations to be necessary for the purposes of the regulations (including provisions repealing, amending or applying, with or without modification, other law, exclusive of this Act).

This very considerable power would certainly seem at first sight to contravene Article 15.2 of the Constitution, which states that "the sole and exclusive power of making laws for the State" is vested in the Oireachtas. This provision has been interpreted to require that delegated legislation be no more than "a mere giving effect to principles and policies contained in the [parent] statute" (O'Higgins C.J. in *City View Press Ltd v. AnC.O.* [1980] I.R. 381, at 399). A similar principle is found in Community law, (see *e.g.* Case 230/78, *Eridania v. Minister of Agriculture and Forestry* [1979] E.C.R. 2749 at paragraphs 9–13). A delegation by the Oireachtas to the Government, in a statute which does not contain on its face any principles or policies, of power to amend legislation, and to decide all fundamental questions in respect of the statute's subject matter, is likely in the ordinary course to be struck down by the courts, unless it is later confirmed by the Oireachtas (Blayney J. in *McDaid v. Sheehy* [1989] I.L.R.M. 342, at 346; and the decision of the Supreme Court [1991] 1 I.R. 1). That the draftsman of the 1972 Act relied on Article 29.4.3 of the Constitution (as it then was) to protect implementing orders from such a result is evident both from the breadth of section 3(2) of the Act (which could not otherwise be defended) and from the inclusion of a (subjective) notion of necessity to justify the extreme steps that Ministers are purportedly authorised to take.

The questions raised about present practice are very important. The Community's law-making process is heavily biased in favour of its executive (the Commision) and of a body composed of representatives of the Member States' executives (the Council)—hence the oft-lamented "democratic deficit" (see, *e.g.* Moxon-Browne, 'The Legitimacy of the Union', in Keatinge ed., *Political Union* I.E.A. (1991) p.61, at 81–94; Weiler, "Eurocracy and Distrust" (1986) 61 Washington L. Rev. 1103). This is the case even after the coming into force of the Maastricht Treaty on European Union (see the annotation below of Article 189b E.C.). When many of the measures so adopted are introduced into Irish domestic law by the executive (the Government), the separation of powers enshrined in Article 6 of the Constitution is eroded. Even if Government control in the past has been such that the Oireachtas merely "legitimates bills by conducting a formalised debate on their merits climaxed by a division along predictable, party lines" (Morgan, *Constitutional Law of Ireland* (2nd ed., 1990) p.94), the legislative process is at least a public one, in which grievances and misgivings can be expressed, and some injustices may be pre-empted. In any event, the less confrontational and more considered proceedings of Oireachtas joint committees (discussed below) could lead to quite constructive discussion. Furthermore, given the enthusiasm now expressed for the involvement of national parliaments in the preparation of Community legislative initiatives, one would also expect those parliaments to have the greatest role possible in implementing Community legislation. (See Declarations 12 and 13 in the Final Act of the Maastricht Intergovernmental Conference, on the role of national Parliaments in the European Union, and on the Conference of Parliaments; the remarks of the Minister for Foreign Affairs during the second reading of the European Communities (Amendment) Bill, 1992, 424 *Dáil Debates* Cols. 1824–5; and the consensus in favour of such prior scrutiny of draft measures in the debate on the European Communities (Amendment) Bill, 1993, 433 *Dáil Debates* Cols. 1766–85.) The Maastricht Treaty affords further examples of the need for openness and public debate, as not all decisions on the implementation of Community law are simply technical. Such was the concern of the United Kingdom and Danish governments at the implications for sovereignty of an automatic move to full economic and monetary union that both secured exceptional derogations in Protocols 11 and 12 to the Treaty. It is a chastening thought that the same step can be accomplished in Ireland by ministerial order.

It appeared from the decision of the Supreme Court in *Crotty* that the notion of necessity in Article 29.4.5 was an objective one, of legal obligation, implying that the courts might not be deterred by a Minister's subjective claims of necessity under section 3(2) of the 1972 Act. The Supreme Court had already given some cause to suspect that it would look behind the claims of the legislature or executive in cases involving the suspension of the application of the Constitution. In 1976, it considered briefly the efficacy of a resolution of national emergency under Article 28.3.3 of the Constitution, which shielded the Emergency Powers Bill from judicial review (*In re Article 26 and the Emergency Powers Bill 1976* [1977] I.R. 159). The presumption that the facts stated in the relevant resolution were correct was deemed not to have been rebutted, but the question of whether the court had jurisdiction to review such a resolution was "expressly reserved for future consideration"

([1977] I.R. 159, at 176). Article 28.3.3 seems to permit a subjective assessment by the Oireachtas of the existence of a state of national emergency, or of war. (On the interpretation of Article 28.3.3, see further Morgan, "The Emergency Powers Bill Reference—II", (1979) 14 Ir. Jur. 252.) Thus, the possibility of judicial scrutiny of assertions of entitlement to constitutional immunity seemed to apply *a fortiori* in respect of claims of necessity under Article 29.4.5 of the Constitution, which appears to set an objective criterion.

There followed a long academic debate about the implementation of directives. (The arguments that follow are of a constitutional order; further policy considerations are introduced in the annotation of the European Communities Act, 1972 below.) Hogan and Morgan suggested that because Article 189 of the Treaty of Rome expressly leaves open to States the method of implementing directives, their implementation by ministerial order is not "necessitated" by Community membership. Therefore, in their view, Article 29.4.5 could not be relied upon to permit a derogation from Article 15.2 of the Constitution (Hogan & Morgan, *Administrative Law in Ireland* (2nd ed., 1991) pp. 17–18). The requirements outlined above for the validity of delegated legislation would then apply.

Professor Curtin responded to this argument by questioning whether the State has any *real* choice in respect of its mode of implementation of E.C. directives. She cited Article 5 E.E.C. and the obligation to implement directives in time, as setting the limits of the Member States' discretion and as affording sufficient "necessity" for the present arrangements to be constitutionally protected (Curtin, "Some Reflections on European Community Law in Ireland" (1989) 11 D.U.L.J. (*n.s.*) 207, at 212 (hereinafter Curtin, Reflections); see also Curtin, "Directives: the Effectiveness of Judicial Protection of Individual Rights" (1990) 27 C.M.L.Rev. 709, at 714–8 (hereinafter Curtin, Directives); and Collins & O'Reilly, Ireland, at 325):

> "Member States must recognise the consequences, in their internal legal order, of their adherence to the Community and, if necessary, adapt their procedures in such a way that they do not form an obstacle to the implementation, within the prescribed time limits, of their obligations within the framework of the Treaty."

However, Curtin acknowledges that the Court of Justice does not necessarily require legislative action in each Member State, as long as it is guaranteed that national authorities apply directives fully (Reflections, at 212). Once that can be achieved, the Court of Justice should be agnostic as to whether legislative or ministerial implementation is to be preferred. This was certainly the view of Temple Lang in 1972, in a statement which can be applied as well to implementing procedure as to the substantive content of an implementing measure ("Constitutional Aspects of Irish Membership of the E.E.C." (1972) 9 C.M.L.Rev. 167, at 175–6):

> "The constitutional rule under the Third Amendment to the Constitution is clear: if the Irish authorities have a discretion as to how to implement a directive, it must be implemented in a manner consistent with the Constitution, unless it cannot be so implemented."

That no objection would be taken to this stance by the Court of Justice can be deduced from its views in *Deutsche Milchkontor GmbH v. Germany* (Joined Cases 205–215/82, [1983] E.C.R. 2633, at 2665–6). That case involved national measures required to give effect to E.C. regulations, and the comments of the Court should apply also to directives:

> "[I]t is for the Member States, by virtue of Article 5 of the Treaty, to ensure that Community regulations, particularly those concerning the common agricultural policy, are implemented within their territory. Insofar as Community law, including its general principles, does not include common rules to this effect, the national authorities when

implementing Community regulations act in accordance with the procedural and substantive rules of their own national law."

Thus, Member States are given a certain amount of discretion about the means, procedural and substantive, by which they fulfil the obligations of result imposed by a directive, so long as they are given full legal effect in the domestic legal system (see Curtin, Directives, at 717; Case 102/79, *Commission v. Belgium* [1980] E.C.R. 1473; Case 145/82, *Commission v. Italy* [1983] E.C.R. 711; Case 236/85, *Commission v. Netherlands* [1987] E.C.R. 3989; *Browne v. An Bórd Pleanála* [1989] I.L.R.M. 865; Hogan, "The Legal Status of Administrative Rules and Circulars" (1987) 22 Ir. Jur. (*n.s.*) 194). There is therefore no reason to suppose that, from the standpoint of Community law, the Court of Justice would baulk at implementing measures being made subject to additional State requirements designed to protect national sensitivities, values or norms. By giving Member States a choice, the Treaty implicitly acknowledges the possibility that national authorities may lay down rules which govern the exercise of that choice—or may continue to be subject to local constitutional stipulations while fulfilling the Community obligation expressed in a directive. That the Communities seek as far as possible to respect the integrity of national legislative procedures is also evidenced by the Declaration appended to the Single European Act in respect of the then new Article 100a EEC, which commits the Commission to giving precedence to the use of the instrument of a directive in its proposals pursuant to the Article if harmonisation involves the amendment of legislative provisions in one or more Member States.

The Joint Committee on the Secondary Legislation of the European Communities was of a similar view (11th Report of the Joint Committee (Prl. 4669) at 5; see also Robinson, "Irish Parliamentary Scrutiny of European Communities Legislation" (1979) 16 C.M.L.Rev. 9, at 12 (hereinafter Robinson, Scrutiny)):

> "The Joint Committee believes that the Houses of the Oireachtas, as the sole legislative body in the State, is curtailed only to the minimum extent necessary to meet the Treaty obligations."

Central to Professor Curtin's argument are her doubts about the existence of any viable alternative to the present system, due to the sluggishness of the Irish legislative process (Reflections, at 212):

> "In Ireland, where an average of 36 Acts manage to become law every year and where well over 500 statutory instruments have been adopted on the basis of the European Communities Act alone, it does not require any great mathematical ability to calculate that, at the pace the Oireachtas currently operates, it would not be an appropriate form and method of ensuring the timely entry into force of directives to provide in each and every case for their approval by Parliament."

This analysis does assume, however, that directives would have to be implemented individually by the Oireachtas, and at its present tortuous pace (which has improved somewhat since 1989). One beneficial result of a great increase in Oireachtas business might be a more business-like attitude. Furthermore, omnibus bills could incorporate the terms of numerous implementing measures, which would under present practice be adopted as ministerial orders. Italian experience may give grounds for optimism on this front (Gaja, "New Developments in a Continuing Story: The Relationship between EEC Law and Italian Law" (1991) 28 C.M.L.Rev. 83, at 89; for the position in the other Member States, see Newman, "The Impact of National Parliaments on the Development of Community Law" in Capotorti *et al* eds., *Du Droit International au Droit de l'Integration: Liber Amicorum Pierre Pescatore* (1987)). Travers has remarked that omnibus bills were not a success in Ireland in the past, and refers to "the fiasco of the single confirmation measure enacted under section 4 of the original European Communities Act, 1972" (Travers, "Necessity and Chaos: How Constitutionally to Implement an E.C. Directive into Irish Law" (1993) 87, 7 *Gazette of the Incorporated Law Society of Ireland* 258, at 259 (hereinafter Travers, Chaos)). While this fiasco is attributable in some degree to a failure (avoidable in future) to circulate in advance the text of the 22 regulations which were to be confirmed by the European Communities (Confirmation of Regulations) Act, 1973, it could also be blamed in large part on the lack of interest of members of the two Houses (Travers, Chaos, at n. 16, citing Robinson, "The Irish European Communities Act, 1972" (1973) 10 C.M.L.Rev. 467). Section 4 of the European Communities Act, 1972 was amended the following year to provide simply for annulment of ministerial regulations by resolution of both Houses on the recommendation of the Joint Committee on the Secondary Legislation of the European Communities, ostensibly in order to give the Oireachtas a more effective role in supervising regulations (see further the annotation of the section below).

The Joint Committee certainly had a better record of scrutiny than the full Houses in the 1972–3 period, but failed to have its reports ever debated in the Dáil. (On the work of the Joint Committee, see Murphy, "The European Communities and the Irish Legal System" in Coombes ed. *Ireland and the European Communities* (1983), p. 29.) However, its role has now been assumed by the Joint Committee on European Affairs, which unlike the earlier Committee also has a legislative role (see paragraph 8, Terms of Reference of the Oireachtas Joint Committee on European Affairs, 142 *Seanad Debates*, Cols. 794–800.) Thus, it would be possible for much of the work on an omnibus annual bill to be done at the third (committee) stage by the Joint Committee in its *legislative* capacity (rather than as mere *ex post facto* supervisor of *executive* activity), without any real change in its work. See now s.1 of European Communities (Amendment) Act, 1995. The creation of a separate European Affairs Committee makes this all the more feasible. The second stage of an implementing bill might be attenuated, as the necessity of legislative action in accordance with the terms of the directives in question would not be in dispute. A return to the use of omnibus bills (to implement directives rather than simply to confirm ministerial orders), when a specialist committee of the Oireachtas with a good record in the scrutiny of such measures is in possession of partial legislative competence, would promise greater success than the original experiment in 1973 (see further on the role of the Joint Committee the annotation below of section 4 of the 1972 Act, as amended). Of course, the usefulness of the exercise would remain contingent on the amount of time spent debating proposed measures, as Travers correctly points out (Chaos, at n. 15.)

In any event, Curtin's argument operated on the assumption that if Hogan and Morgan's analysis were accepted, the Oireachtas would have to become involved in the implementation of *all* directives. One can argue for an alternative view of the effect of section 2 of the European Communities Act, 1972. The section clearly incorporates the Treaty of Rome and E.C. regulations into the domestic system, with the latter being automatically directly applicable by virtue of Article 189 E.C. Therefore, as part of the parent statute (as if appended to it, as the Treaties are), ministerial orders can be made pursuant to principles and policies contained in either the Treaties, or any existing E.C. regulation. But what about directives? Directives are emanations of the E.C. Treaty. It can be argued, especially as Article 189 E.C. requires that effect be given to the principles and policies contained therein by domestic authorities, that "existing and future" directives were incorporated, prospectively, into Irish domestic law by section 2 of the 1972 Act. This accords with the text of the section, and has been endorsed by at least one eminent constitutional commentator (see Casey, *Constitution*, at 166); Robinson remarked at the time of enactment of the Act that section 2 was ambiguous on the status of directives in Irish law ("The Irish European Communities Act, 1972" (1973) 10 C.M.L.Rev. 352, at 352). Such incorporation of directives into national law via Treaty and statute would not give those directives direct applicability in Irish law, as that is not a condition laid down in the Treaty, and is not in any case the norm for domestically incorporated treaty law (including parts of the E.C. Treaties themselves). While not directly applicable, they could be deemed, read with the 1972 Act itself, to constitute a parent statute, complete with policies and principles to be activated and effectuated through delegated legislation. If such an approach were adopted, many directives could presumably be introduced into Irish law by means of ministerial orders, without any question of infringing Article 15.2 of the Constitution. The exception would be those which effected a change in directly applicable Irish statute law.

Travers has also raised an objection of principle to this approach (Chaos, at 259). Both he and the authors acknowledge the flexibility which the legal instrument of the directive is designed to secure for national authorities at the implementation stage. However, Travers concludes from this that such flexibility is an inherent part of the Community law imperative embodied in the directive, that is, that flexibility is as it were obligatory upon the Member State authorities, so that ministerial choice of implementation method is protected by the provisions of Article 29.4.5 even when it is at variance with ordinary constitutional norms. The decisions of Murphy J. in *Lawlor v. Minister for Agriculture* [1988] I.L.R.M. 400 and *Greene v. Minister for Agriculture* [1990] I.L.R.M. 364 are cited as authority for this approach. In those cases (discussed in more detail below), Murphy J. opted to take a rather expansive view of the meaning of necessity, treating it as extending to the content of any measure adopted consequent upon the terms of a directive which does not depart too radically from the requirements of those terms. It should be borne in mind, however, that these decisions concern the content of Irish implementing measures rather than the implementing procedure adopted—in fact, Murphy J. ignored in *Greene* the inadequacy inherent in the implementation of the directive in question by administrative circular. It will be argued below that the questions of constitutional scrutiny, respectively, of the content of implementing measures, and of the implementing mechanism adopted, are logically distinct, and should be approached differently. The decision on appropriate instruments for the implementation of a directive is a decision in the field of the separation of powers which the courts are peculiarly well-qualified to review. For that reason (quite apart from other criticisms offered below), it is disputed whether the test set out by Murphy J. should be applied to the problem of implementation procedures. In addition, it is difficult to accept that the national flexibility granted by E.C. law in the implementation of directives should translate automatically into a requirement, as a matter of Community law, of constitutional tolerance of the Government's choice of implementing instruments. After all, the idea behind directives is that they should intrude as little as possible on the domestic norms which govern the legislative process. The flexibility granted to national authorities should not be equated invariably with executive freedom in the matter of implementation, given that the body primarily responsible for legislation in the State is the Oireachtas. The *Milchkontor* decision of the Court of Justice referred to above stands four square with this submission.

We must consider one final possible objection to the invalidation having regard to the terms of the Constitution of section 3(2) of the European Communities Act, 1972 or of regulations made thereunder. It is important even after the *Meagher* decision because the Supreme Court expressly left open the (remote) possibility, which was also implicit in the separate review by the court of the ministerial regulations at issue in the case, that delegated implementing measures could be struck down in certain circumstances. This potential problem also presents itself in relation to the constitutional review of the substantive content of national implementing measures (discussed below). A vast amount of delegated legislation has been adopted on the basis of the 1972 Act consequent upon the obligations of membership of the Communities. Even if an Irish court concludes that the mode of implementation of an E.C. directive is, within the bounds of the discretion afforded by its terms and by the Treaty, constitutionally defective, an order striking down either the parent legislation or an implementing measure (whether a separate Act of the Oireachtas or a ministerial regulation) after the date for implementation of the directive has passed would leave the State in breach of its Community obligation as to the result to be achieved by the directive. Gallagher comments that "the exercise by an Irish court of its power of judicial review under the Constitution could result in the State being in breach of its Treaty obligations and also in its being held liable to Irish citizens and to citizens of any other country affected by the non-implementation of a directive and who meet the criteria enunciated in the *Francovich* case" ("The Constitution and the Community" (1993) 1 I.J.E.L. 129, at 133; see Joined Cases C-6 & C-9/90, *Francovich & Bonifaci v. Italy* [1991] E.C.R. I 5357). This problem may seem analogous to the criticism of section 4, European Communities Act, 1972 (as amended), that annulment by the Houses of the Oireachtas of ministerial regulations would presumably leave the State in breach of its Treaty obligations (Louis, *The Community Legal Order* (2nd. ed., 1990) p. 172). Louis' comment is legitimate, but the analogy with the instant issue is not perfect. There is a difference between one organ of State overriding measures adopted by another, thereby leaving a gap in the law, and a finding by the judicial organ that a purported implementing measure was unsound from the outset. As will emerge further in the discussion below, any argument for the continued observance of national measures the offending element of which (procedural or substantive) was not necessitated by the obligations of the membership of the Communities can be countered with the Community requirement that implementing measures be appropriate and legally effective. A national measure which is constitutionally invalid (for reasons other than its compliance with a Community requirement which conflicts with a national constitutional rule) is *ipso facto* inappropriate and legally ineffective.

Of course, one could enter into a "chicken and egg" argument, by responding in turn that Community law requires that the otherwise invalid national measure must be maintained in force in order to secure the objectives of the directive, even if that measure could have been struck down by the national courts before the expiry of the implementation period on the understanding that it could be promptly and constitutionally replaced without breaching Community law. However, this would extend (illogically) to national implementing measures the reasoning which has already been applied to amendments of the Community Treaties, *viz.* that the courts may inquire into the constitutional validity of (proposed) ratification by the State of such amendments only before they enter into force as part of the Community "constitution". Implementing measures are not Community law in the same sense as the Treaties, the validity of which as a matter of Community law is within the exclusive jurisdiction of the Court of Justice; implementing measures are national law operating within the scope of Community law. They derive their legal effectiveness from national law, upon which Community law is dependent in this case for its effectiveness. To reiterate the above-quoted *dictum* from *Deutsche Milchkontor*, "the national authorities when implementing Community regulations act in accordance with the procedural and substantive rules of their own national law". It is submitted that Community law *requires*, in its own interest, the invalidation and replacement of purported implementing measures which breach such national procedural and substantive rules (other than those which must inevitably be breached because they conflict with the requirements of the directive in question). The breach by the State of its obligation to implement the directive is continuing, from the date of purported implementation, rather than arising only upon the invalidation of the legally defective measure. While it is likely never to occur, it can be argued consistently with this position that enforcement proceedings could even be taken against the State under Articles 169 and 170 E.C. in respect of the failure on its part to take proper measures to fulfil its duty of transposition.

Article 5 E.C. will require that any national lacuna in the corpus of Community law resulting from the invalidation of an implementing measure be minimised. Timely action to replace the measure is naturally expected. The order of the court seised of the issue may also require to be confined in its effects to the parties to the case and others who had initiated similar litigation (see Case 43/75, *Defrenne v. S.A.B.E.N.A. (No. 2)* [1976] E.C.R. 455; *Murphy v. Attorney-General* [1982] I.R. 241). There may also be scope, pursuant to the *Campus Oil* principle of the adjustment of constitutional rules to the imperatives of Community law, for the Irish courts to develop a jurisdiction to declare acts incompatible with the Constitution, but not void, thereby requiring the State within a specified period to rectify matters. (See the discussion in Kommers, *The Constitutional Jurisprudence of the Federal Republic of Germany* (Duke, 1989) pp. 60–1, of the development by the *Bundesverfassungsgericht* of the "admonitory decision" (*Appellentscheidung*); however, the adversarial rather than consultative context of constitutional judicial review in Ireland may make this a less attractive option, unless expressly required by the Court of Justice.) In the context of the action for annulment under the Art. 173 E.C. the Court of Justice has a similar jurisdiction. Art. 174 E.C. permits the Court to consider which of the effects of a Regulation which it has declared void shall be considered as definitive, in the interests (one supposes) of legal certainty and the settled expectations of individuals. In the case of Directives, the Court has developed an analagous power to rule that the annulment of a Directive should not take effect until a new Directive has been adopted on the correct legal basis or with full observance of the appropriate legislative procedure (see *e.g.* Case C-295/90 *Parliament v. Council* [1992] E.C.R. I 4193. Finally, the State may indeed be liable in damages to those thereby deprived of the expected benefits of an improperly implemented directive; but it should be remembered that the breach of its obligations on the part of the State giving rise to such an action for damages is constituted by the improper implementation, and not by the later invalidation.

Meagher v. Minister for Agriculture: The High Court

Meagher v. Minister for Agriculture concerned the constitutionality of section 3(2) of the European Communities Act, 1972 and of provisions of two sets of ministerial regulations under that Act: the European Communities (Control of Oestrogenic, Andogenic, Gestagenic and Thyrostatic Substances) Regulations (S.I. 1988 No. 218) and the European Communities (Control of Veterinary Medicinal Products and their Residues) Regulations (S.I. 1990 No. 171). (For a discussion of some procedural aspects of these Regulations, see Whelan, "Angel Dust and Fair Procedures—an Inquiry into Direct Effect" (1992) 10, 1 I.L.T. (*n.s.*) 17.), the criticisms in which have since been addressed by section 9, Animal Remedies Act, 1993.) The Regulations were adopted pursuant to a series of E.C. directives which have as their object the elimination of the use of certain hormonal products in the raising of livestock (Council Directives 81/602/EEC; 81/851/EEC; 85/358/EEC; 86/469/EEC; 88/146/EEC and 88/299/EEC). The specific objects of the applicant's grievance were article 16 of the 1988 Regulations, authorising the issue of search warrants by the District Court, and articles 32(8) and 11(4) of the 1988 and 1990 Regulations respectively, which provide a two year time limit for the issuing of summonses. (The time limit in respect of summary offences is ordinarily six months, under section 10(4), Petty Sessions (Ireland) Act 1851.) The applicant sought a number of reliefs by way of judicial review, chief of which was a declaration that section 3(1) and (2) of the 1972 Act was unconstitutional and void, and a declaration that the 1988 and 1990 Regulations were *ultra vires* and void. The main legal contention of the applicant was that amendment of the law by statutory instrument was not necessitated by the obligations of membership of the European Communities, even in order to implement E.C. directives, so that the instruments in question were not protected from the consequences of their otherwise patent unconstitutionality by Article 29.4.5 of the Constitution.

It was admitted by the State in the High Court in *Meagher* that section 3(2) of the Act of 1972 would be unconstitutional were it not for the operation of Article 29.4.5 of the Constitution in the manner contended for. Thus, encroachment upon the power of the Oireachtas by Ministers could only be saved from unconstitutionality where this was "necessitated" by Community membership.

Johnson J. first concluded that the impugned ministerial regulations had not been given any form of statutory endorsement, such as had saved the impugned regulations in the Supreme Court decision in *McDaid v. Sheehy* [1991] 1 I.R. 1—mere failure by the two Houses of the Oireachtas to annul by resolution a regulation (as provided for under section 4 of the 1972 Act, as amended in 1973) did not have the same effect as positive affirmation and confirmation of a regulation by an Act of the Oireachtas. The purported amendment of existing law by the Regulations had therefore to be subjected to further constitutional scrutiny.

He further considered that Article 29.4.5 of the Constitution gave the State three individual means of implementing directives—laws, acts and measures. In determining which means to employ, the Minister did not have unfettered discretion; the decision on the proper means of implementation should have regard to the whole of the Constitution:

> "[W]here it is appropriate for the purposes of the Directives and their implementation that, in regard to Article 15 of the Constitution, legislation be introduced and Acts enacted, then that should be done, and, in my view, any power given to a Minister to make regulations for the purposes of amending or repealing laws is unconstitutional."

Implicit in Johnson J.'s analysis is a presumption that E.C. law does not require any particular means of implementation so long as implementation is effective. It is this fact which deprives the Minister of any argument of necessity which could entitle him to ignore the ordinary dictates of the Constitution, and forces him to read Article 29.4.5 in harmony with the Constitution's other provisions. His idea of what is an appropriate implementation of E.C. law is built upon an appreciation of the Irish constitutional context; and the status of national implementing measures can hardly be divorced from that context.

Travers criticises the decision of Johnson J. on the basis that "it is not altogether clear where the logic of the *Meagher* case would stop" (Chaos, at n. 12.). He suggests that Irish courts might be invited to disagree with a finding of the Court of Justice that an E.C. regulation was valid and to adopt its own view on its status in the light of the principle of subsidiarity which now governs the non-exclusive competences of the European Community (Article 3b E.C.). This is clearly untenable: first, because E.C. regulations fall under section 2 of the European Communities Act, 1972; and secondly, because Johnson J. nowhere suggested that Irish courts could look behind and question the necessitated obligations of membership of the Community. Quite the contrary; he is concerned at all times with the proper exercise of "powers granted by the Constitution for the purposes of effectively implementing obligations of membership of the Communities". Only after a Minister had ascertained the substance of the measure required to implement a directive should he, in Johnson J.'s view, have considered the legislative method to be employed, which consideration should in turn have regard to the whole of the Constitution.

Meagher v. Minister for Agriculture: The Supreme Court

The Supreme Court overruled the decision of the High Court. A number of judgments were given: a single judgment of the Court on the constitutionality of the 1972 Act, as is required by Article 34.4.5 of the Constitution, delivered by Finlay C.J., and two separate judgments of Blayney and Denham JJ. (with both of which Finlay C.J. and Egan and O'Flaherty JJ. concurred) on the lawfulness of the ministerial regulations in question.

The Supreme Court took a purposive approach to the interpretation of Article 29.4.5 of the Constitution. The view taken by the Supreme Court was that some implementing machinery was necessary in order for Ireland to comply with her Community obligations. "[T]he major or fundamental obligation necessitated by membership of the Community" is that contained in section 2 of the European Communities Act, 1972, "which provides for the application of the Community law and acts as binding on the State and as part of the domestic law subject to the conditions laid down in the Treaty" (judgment of the court (Finlay C.J.)). However, the court treated this necessity as sufficient in itself to justify the actual machinery chosen in 1972 (as amended in 1973). The ministerial power in section 3 "is *prima facie* a power which is part of the necessary machinery which became a duty of the State upon its joining the Community and therefore necessitated by that membership". Having regard to the very great number of Community measures generated every year, the court emphasised the need to facilitate their direct application, or their implementation into the law of the State, thus echoing the plea by counsel for the respondent that full, efficient and timely action was required of the State in this regard.

With respect, it is submitted that such an approach is deficient for a number of reasons. In respect of the need for efficiency and expedition, the reader is directed to the discussion above, and to the fact that the discussion at the hearing in the Supreme Court of the needs generated by the flow of Community legislation was cursory to say the least.

More important, however, is the issue of principle. The patent necessity of *some* machinery for applying and implementing Community law in Ireland can hardly mean that *any* machinery will do. The Supreme Court appears to employ no qualitative criterion in assessing our machinery other than that of administrative facility. That criterion alone would leave the State free to comply with the obligations of membership of the Communities by recognising some fantastic implementing authority in Irish law, such as edicts of the Irish Permanent Representative to the Communities (whose staff would, after all, be among the best informed in the State's service about the Community measures involved). More realistically, it could permit the State to confer binding authority on instruments which at present lack that quality, such as administrative circulars, for the purposes solely of implementing Community law. One imagines that neither of these was countenanced by the Supreme Court, but the judgment of the court does not reveal why such unsatisfactory implementing devices should not be permitted. In short, the Supreme Court's test of necessity fails because it does not tell us all we need to know.

One might counter this criticism by asserting that the grounds for the court's decision subject it to some inherent limitations in point of subject matter. The court appears to have been strongly influenced by the contention of counsel for the State that at least two types of circumstances could justify amendment of the law by ministerial order under the 1972 Act:

(i) where "minor administrative regulations may be necessary to facilitate the entry of [directly applicable Community law] into the legal structure of the State" so that "the repeal, amendment or modification of any existing law by a simple ministerial regulation would be a strict necessity arising from the obligations of the State as a member of the Community and Union"; and

(ii) where "the terms of ... directives may be sufficiently specific and clear to require simple administrative application, something which would be, again, appropriately done by regulation". In effect, a test based on these grounds would be a test of appropriateness. Appropriate implementation is a requirement of Community law much relied upon by Professor Curtin, and it certainly sounds very *communautaire* to find that it is more appropriate to act by way of ministerial order where the required changes in Irish law are so mundane, so intimately attached to the direct applicability of a Community measure, or dictated to such a degree of specificity by the terms of a directive, that the deliberative role of the Oireachtas is not called for. In her subsequent judgment on the validity of the regulations, Denham J. spoke of the sterility of Oireachtas involvement in the legislative process in such cases.

It is submitted that the employment of the Community law doctrine of appropriateness in this fashion is unsustainable, for reasons which are outlined below. Nonetheless, such a compromise approach, while not ideal in the authors' view, would have something to recommend it as a balancing of the competing values of Articles 15.2 and 29.4.5 of the Constitution (as advocated in the subsequent judgment of Denham J.), not least because it might preserve the role of the Oireachtas in cases where policy questions about how a measure should be implemented remain to be decided at national level. However, when Finlay C.J. moved from summarising the State's case to announcing the decision of the court, many of the subtleties of that case were abandoned, *viz.* those relating to the *minor* administrative character of action to facilitate directly applicable Community law, and to the *specific* and *clear* character of the obligations imposed by the *terms* of a directive. Even at this point, the court sees ministerial implementation as being appropriate (and therefore "necessitated") "in some instances at least, and possibly in a great majority of instances". Two paragraphs later, the court is wary of admitting that hypothetical instances might ever occur of Community measures the implementation or application of which might not be necessarily carried out by ministerial regulation. The only limitation envisaged by the Court on the kinds of measures which can be implemented by ministerial regulation is one "having regard to the nature of the content of such regulation". This is the vaguest of standards: it might be thought to be simply a shorthand reference to the test earlier advocated by the State (which referred to the clear and specific terms of directives, etc.). However, it quickly becomes clear from the later judgments that what is meant here is that it is only where the content of a ministerial regulation has nothing remotely to do with the obligation of result contained in an E.C. directive or with the smoothing of a path for a directly applicable E.C. regulation that it will be subject to the normal rules on the relationship of delegated legislation to statute law. In effect, the class of ministerial regulations permitted under section 3(2) of the 1972 Act widens before our eyes throughout the course of the judgment of the Court and of the judgments which follow. (See also the remarks of Carroll J. in *Agra Meat Packers Ltd v. Minister for Agriculture and Food*, High Court, December 14, 1994.)

Having found the machinery of section 3(2) of the 1972 Act to be necessitated by the obligations of membership of the Communities, and thus constitutional, the Court invoked the double construction rule in *East Donegal Cooperative Livestock Marts Ltd v. Attorney-General* [1970] I.R. 317 which assumes that the Oireachtas intends delegated regulatory power to be exercised in accordance with constitutional justice. Thus, any challenge to an Irish regulation "having regard to the absence of necessity for [implementation of the parent Community measure] to be carried out by regulation instead of legislation and having regard to the nature of the content of such regulation" must be on the basis that it is an unconstitutional and *ultra vires* exercise of ministerial power. Having decided (without reference to earlier case-law) that regulations do not constitute laws within the meaning of Article 34.4.5 of the Constitution, separate judgments on this issue followed (*cf. The State (Gilliland) v. Governor of Mountjoy Prison* [1987] I.R. 201).

Blayney and Denham JJ. gave judgments on the validity of the ministerial regulations, with both of which the three other judges of the Supreme Court agreed. Blayney J. adopts the most permissive test identifiable from the judgment of the court. The power of the Minister is stated to be "a very wide one"; in the context of section 2 of the 1972 Act, it is in the present case "to ensure that the EEC directives referred to in the two [impugned] statutory instruments are part of our domestic law under the conditions laid down in the Treaties". It quickly emerges that the Minister had full power to insert a term in a regulation "provided that it was necessary for the purpose of giving effect to the directives".

This point is well substantiated by reference to the search provisions of the Irish Regulations. Directive 85/358/EEC contains in its recitals, and in Articles 1, 3 and 6, copious references to the taking of samples, to the conduct of random controls, and to the identification and investigation of the farm of origin of an animal in which traces of hormone residues are found, all of which can be taken to require some kind of authorised searches.

There is no express provision in the directives about a time limit for prosecutions. No objection was taken, however, to the fact that a number of offences was created pursuant to the directives; it followed, therefore, that such offences should be effectively prosecuted, and, Blayney J. concluded, "if it was necessary for this purpose to allow a period of two years the Minister clearly had power to allow such a period". There was evidence that the sophisticated analytical procedures required and the occasional need to conduct investigations in more than one Member State would prevent in many cases the institution of proceedings within six months:

> "Accordingly, the implementation of the directive required that the regulation should provide for an adequate time for the preparation of the prosecutions. It was not necessary that the directive should itself fix a time. It was a matter for the State to decide on the length of time required to enable the prosecution to be brought and that is what the Minister has done in providing for a period of two years."

Blayney J. himself admits that some kind of choice was open to the State in these circumstances. While the directive requires effective implementation, the State has some discretion as to how to secure this. It was open to the State, for example, to opt for an indictable offence which would not be subject to the limitation period contained in the Petty Sessions (Ireland) Act 1851. It is ironic that in the aftermath of the High Court decision in *Meagher*, the Government introduced in the Oireachtas an Animal Remedies Bill, sections 20–22 of which make it an indictable as well as a summary offence to contravene the ministerial regulations challenged in the case, with maximum penalties of £250,000 fine or 10 years' imprisonment or both. Of course, this could not be done by regulation, which indicates that even the draftsman of section 3(3) of the 1972 Act recognised that ministerial action would in at least some cases be inappropriate.

Patent as the need may be to secure effective prosecution of offences created pursuant to a directive, this clearly is not a case where the terms of the relevant directives are so clear and specific that little is left for the national authorities but to transpose them practically *verbatim* (with due regard for local drafting style and the existing legal context) into the domestic law. Substantial policy decisions about how to prosecute angel dust offences remained to be made, and Community law does not require that those decisions necessarily be made exclusively by the executive. This point is highlighted by Hogan "The Implementation of European Union Law in Ireland: The *Meagher* Case and the Democratic Deficit" (1994) 2 I.J.E.L. 190, at 197 (hereinafter Hogan, Democratic Deficit):

> "Suppose, for instance, that it was the Oireachtas rather than the European [Community] which had taken action on 'angel dust' and that in such new legislation the general policy of the Oireachtas was made clear. Let us also suppose that this new legislation was silent on the issue of time limits, but that the Minister had decided that in order to give full effect to the statute a two year time limit was necessary. In such a case it would require a brave advocate who would be prepared to argue that such an order was *intra vires* the statute on the ground that the general "policy" of the legislation was in favour of effective sanctions. In the present case the Directives in question deliberately abstained from prescribing detailed rules regarding time limits in the expectation that this matter would be regulated by national law."

The contrary view taken by Blayney J. casts light on matters left unclear in the judgment of the court:

> "[T]he State is not free. It is obliged to implement the directive and so is obliged to choose a method of implementation and, provided the method it chooses is appropriate for the purpose of satisfying the obligation of the State and the measures it incorporates do not go beyond what is required to implement the directive, it is correctly categorised as being necessitated by the directive."

As was surmised above, the Supreme Court has seized upon the Community law concept of appropriateness. It is submitted, however, that the court has assigned to it a burden which it cannot bear. Necessity under Article 29.4.5 is a requirement of Irish constitutional law the interpretation of which must be informed by the objective requirements of Community law. The Supreme Court in *Meagher* has deemed that constitutional requirement to be in some way co-terminous with a requirement of Community law, appropriateness of national measures, and has treated that Community requirement as one which in any case can be satisfied in only one way. In most cases, however, there can be more than one appropriate form of national implementation of Community obligations. The question of the type of hormone offences created—indictable or summary—is a case in point; more fundamentally, Community law expresses no view on the relative desirability of legislative or executive implementation of measures which are not immediately capable of direct applicability, so long as some legally binding method is employed and is employed in time. Accepting at all times the objective requirement that the obligations of membership of the Communities and the Union must be fulfilled, it is nonetheless disingenuous to suggest that a domestic measure which is contended to be appropriate *as a matter of Community law* to implement a directive is therefore necessitated *as a matter of Irish law* in a way which allows it to trump alternative national methods of implementation which are equally appropriate in Community law terms and which have the advantage of complying as well with important domestic constitutional norms.

Denham J. reaches a similar conclusion to Blayney J., although she approaches the case slightly differently, in a manner which ostensibly takes greater account of national constitutional sensibilities and appears somewhat less accommodating of the Government (see Travers, "The Constitutionality of the Implementation of E.C. Directives into Irish Law

Revisited" (1994) 88 *Gazette of the Incorporated Law Society of Ireland* 99, at 100). "The issue to be determined", she says, "is the balance within the national forum of sections 2 and 3 of the 1972 Act, Article 15.2 and Article 29.4.5 of Bunreacht na hÉireann and Articles 5 and 189 of the Treaty of Rome. Thus, the kernel is the word 'necessitated' in Article 29.4.5 and the 'choice' afforded in Article 189." The combination of these provisions makes it clear "that in balancing the two, the mere fact that the substance in laws enacted, acts done or measures adopted is necessary to be incorporated into domestic Irish law is not the end of the matter". In this respect, Denham J. appears to part ways with Blayney J.; but she ultimately rejoins him by a more circuitous route.

Denham J. treats an E.C. directive as being equivalent to a parent domestic statute containing principles and policies under which regulatory authority is delegated to a Minister or other body. The authors agree with her, although for divergent reasons. Denham J. draws her conclusion from the fact that the State is bound by the directive, while it is contended above that it arises from the terms of section 2 of the Act of 1972; it will be indicated below why this distinction is thought to be important. Where a matter of principle or policy is not set out in the parent directive, then the Minister cannot act pursuant to his own policy choice; he requires Oireachtas legislation. *City View Press* is relied upon to support this uncontroversial conclusion. However, "where there is in fact no choice on a policy or principle, it is a matter appropriate for delegated legislation". Such ministerial measures, even when they purport to amend statute law, do not constitute legislation of the type with which Article 15.2.1 of the Constitution is concerned. "Here what is at issue in essence is subordinate legislation as delegated under Community law."

On this point, Denham J. is *ad idem* with Blayney J., who remarked that a ministerial implementing measure which impliedly amended an existing statute would prevail over the statute "because it was in substance a measure of Community law". He continued, "[i]t is only in form that it is part of the domestic law. It derives its force from the directive which is binding on the State as to the results to be achieved." This approach puts a new and interesting "spin" on the doctrine of the primacy of Community law. It treats measures which implement, or facilitate the application of Community law as relying for their validity and binding effect, not on the national rules about legislation and so on, but on the inherent force of the parent Community measure. But it is clear that Community law itself does not support such a view. In fact, it condemns it. Time and again, the Court of Justice has denounced the purported implementation of E.C. directives by methods which as a matter of the relevant domestic law are not legally binding. It deplores with almost tedious regularity the failure by Member States to implement certain directives in time or at all. The reason for this is that a directive does not have sufficient inherent force, as a matter of Community law, to give binding effect to a domestic measure which otherwise does not have that effect; or to implement itself in the absence of any domestic measure. The Court of Justice has developed palliatives to secure for individuals the entitlements which are supposed to be bestowed upon them by E.C. directives which have not been implemented properly or at all: direct effect, the possibility of damages, the interpretative obligations of national courts. (See Case 41/74, *Van Duyn v. Home Office*: [1974] E.C.R. 137; Cases C-6 & C-9/90, *Francovich and Bonifaci v. Italy*: [1991] E.C.R. I 5357; Case C-106/89, *Marleasing S.A. v. La Commercial Internacional de Alimentacion S.A.*: [1990] E.C.R. I 4135. The latter two decisions were expressly relied upon by Blayney J.) These do not add up, however, to give directives such an independent presence in the domestic law of the Member States that the method of their adoption becomes almost immaterial.

The authors' strongest misgivings about the Supreme Court decision in *Meagher* arise in this context. Criticism has already been offered of the court's assumption that the apparent appropriateness of executive implementation of directives is exclusive, thereby failing to advert to the possibility of other legislative methods which are appropriate as a matter of both Community law and Irish constitutional law. It is now proposed (resuming a point made above) to criticise the fundamental assumption of the Supreme Court, and to question whether ministerial regulations are an appropriate method of implementation at all, *as a matter of Community law*, where it is sought to employ such regulations to amend statute law.

As a matter of domestic constitutional law, absent Article 29.4.5, ministerial regulations are not effective to amend Acts of the Oireachtas or the enactments of its predecessor parliaments which are still in force. They are comparable to administrative circulars and other *ad hoc* devices of the executive in this respect. The Court of Justice makes clear that Community law is not properly and appropriately implemented by such means, even if administrative practice actually changes as a result, because they constitute a sandy foundation for the building up of uniform obligations and entitlements throughout the Union. *Ultra vires* regulations are obviously of even less utility.

We find ourselves in a type of circular argument, as a consequence of the Supreme Court's test of appropriateness. The Court of Justice says that a measure must be legally effective to be appropriate; the Supreme Court that such measure need only be appropriate to be legally effective. There is only one way of escaping what is otherwise a vicious circle (like the "chicken and egg" problem mentioned above), and it is to abandon the Supreme Court test in favour of a strict test of necessity by reference to the objective requirements of Community law. We should ask, whether implementation of directives by ministerial order is positively required by E.C. law even where this entails the otherwise *ultra vires* power to amend law? If it is so required, then such implementation must also satisfy Article 29.4.5, and should therefore be deemed both valid and appropriate. If it is not so required, then it can hardly satisfy Article 29.4.5, and should therefore be deemed both invalid and inappropriate. It need hardly be added in the light of comments above that the authors are firmly of the latter view.

Disappointed as one may be with the result in *Meagher*, one must nonetheless recognise that a unanimous decision of the Supreme Court is not lightly overturned, and that the test set out therein will now have to be applied. Of course, it may be that it will operate simply to validate all ministerial regulations other than those provisions which are patently unrelated to an E.C. directive or other measure. Both Denham and Blayney JJ. deemed ministerial implementation to be appropriate in respect of anything which could be said to be for the purpose of satisfying an obligation arising expressly or by implication from a directive. Denham J. states that where a directive must be implemented, there is no principle or policy which can be altered by the Oireachtas. "[T]he role of the Oireachtas in such a situation would be sterile. To require the Oireachtas to legislate would be artificial." It is not a role envisaged for the National Parliament in the Constitution to "act as a window on Community directives for the members of the Oireachtas and the nation". A number of comments can be made about this conclusion. First, it would appear that Dáil and Seanad time has been foolishly wasted on "sterile debate" on those occasions when the Houses of the Oireachtas have been sufficiently privileged to be permitted to legislate for certain isolated Community obligations. (For example, and for no apparent reason, Council Directive 75/129/EEC on Collective Redundancies was implemented by the Protection of Employment Act, 1977, while Directive 77/187/EEC was implemented by the European Communities (Safeguarding of Employees Rights on Transfer of Ownership) Regulations, 1980 (S.I. No. 306).) Secondly, Denham J. appears to define as sterile any Oireachtas deliberation on modes of implementation other than those favoured by the executive. While it is trite to observe that the Oireachtas is massively deferential towards the Government which it elects, it is not unknown for Ministers to accept amendments to draft legislation in the course of debate. It has already been pointed out that there was nothing inevitable or self-evidently good about enforcement of the hormones legislation through summary offences with a two year prosecution period (as opposed to, say, summary offences with a three year prosecution period, or indictable offences subject only to general principles about unconscionable delay), which point is illustrated by the recent passage of the Animal Remedies Act, 1993. Thirdly, Denham J.'s assumption that Oireachtas is only valuably employed when legislating without constraint is contradicted by the statement of O'Flaherty J. in *Attorney-General v. Hamilton (No. 2)* [1993] I.L.R.M. 821, at 874 that deputies "are also representatives of those who elect them". As Hogan points out, "[i]f Denham J. were correct, a whole range of practices currently engaged in by the Dáil—ranging from motions condemning aspects of Government policy to debates on purely executive matters such as the Downing Street Declaration—would have to be abandoned" (Democratic Deficit, at 199). Fourthly, the Supreme Court's view can be contrasted with that of the *Bundesverfassungsgericht* in *Brunner* [1994] 1 C.M.L.R. 57 on the importance of national parliamentary debate in securing legitimacy for the activities of the Communities and the Union. While it accepted that the construction of the Communities on the basis of existing sovereign States must entail the vesting of legislative power in an institution (the Council) "composed of representatives of the Member States' governments, that is to say, on an executive basis, to a greater extent than would be constitutionally acceptable at national level", it added that "sufficiently important spheres of activity" must be reserved "in which the people of each [Member State] can develop and articulate itself in a process of will-formation which it legitimates and controls", *i.e.* that "functions and powers of substantial importance must remain for the German *Bundestag*", and by implication for the other national parliaments [1994] 1 C.M.L.R. 57, at 88; see further Hogan, Democratic Deficit, at 199–200.

The significance of the Supreme Court decision in *Meagher* is difficult to overstate. The court has indicated itself to be more *communautaire* even than the Court of Justice, but at some cost to its domestic constitutional role. The authors believe that Article 29.4.5 of the Constitution favours acceptance of the supremacy of Community law and an accommodating approach to its implementation in Ireland. However, the domestic courts should also be careful, it is submitted, to subject Irish measures to such continued constitutional scrutiny as is consistent with adherence to Community requirements. There remains a role for domestic courts, which is endorsed by Articles 5 and 189 E.C. and by the Court of Justice, to require continued compliance by national implementing measures with constitutional norms so long as such constitutional requirements are supplementary to rather than subversive of the obligations imposed by the Community legal order.

How are the decisions in *Meagher v. Minister for Agriculture* and in *Crotty v. An Taoiseach* to be read together? It was argued above that *Crotty* set out a test of strict legal obligation, as a matter of Community law, based on a literal reading of the terms of the first clause of Article 29.4.5, which is in turn consistent with the intention of the drafters. The Supreme Court in *Meagher* adopted a more teleological approach. It identified "the major or fundamental obligation necessitated by membership of the Community" as being the implementation of European Community law "under the conditions laid down in the Treaty, ... including its primacy". Machinery designed for that purpose was therefore *prima facie* necessary, and in light of the perceived circumstances, appropriate. This precluded virtually any enquiry as to whether the particular machinery employed by the State to comply with its major obligation was strictly necessary as a matter of Community law. This approach has been strongly criticised above, but it qualifies rather than over-rules *Crotty*. It is clearly the case that the *Meagher* approach to the consti-tutionality of national laws, acts or measures can only apply where there exists a legal obligation under Community law; and the tenor of the judg-ments makes clear that that is a question on which the Supreme Court sought to defer to the European Court of Justice. Thus, the Supreme Court would presumably feel free still to question the constitutionality of an unratified Community or Union Treaty; and would, in ordinary circumstances, accept the obligatory nature of a ratified Community or Union Treaty, as well as of obligations incurred under its terms. Indeed, as will be argued below, it may be possible to confine *Meagher* to its facts as they were perceived by the Supreme Court, *viz.* that there was no realistic alternative to ministerial regulations under section 3(2) of the European Communities Act, 1972 to ensure the expeditious implementation of Community directives in Ireland; and to preserve in other respects a strict test of legal obligation in ascertain-ing whether national measures pursuant to Community obligations are immune from constitutional challenge.

CHAPTER FIVE

REVIEW OF THE CONTENT OF IMPLEMENTING MEASURES

The test set out by the Supreme Court in *Meagher v. Minister for Agriculture* [1994] 1 I.R. 329, as to when ministerial implementation of directives is appropriate (and thus "necessitated" under Article 29.4.5), and when legislation must be enacted by the Oireachtas, is contingent on "the nature of the content" of the measure in question. This vital (but unhelpfully vague) linkage of procedure with substance does not exhaust the potential for constitutional scrutiny of the content of Irish implementing measures, whatever the implementing procedure employed. It is submitted that any national scheme designed to achieve the results specified by a directive should also be required, where possible, to comply with the terms of the Constitution. The pragmatic arguments used by the Supreme Court in *Meagher* to reject such a contention with regard to implementing procedure need not prevail in this instance, as it should take no more time to devise an implementing scheme that is respectful of substantive constitutional values than to devise one that is not. Thus, a strict test of necessity such as that disclosed in *Crotty v. An Taoiseach* [1987] I.R. 713, can be more easily operated under the rubric of Article 29.4.5 of the Constitution. The fact that many domestic constitutional norms are replicated at E.C. level, and apply as such to domestic measures implementing E.C. law, means that such matters must be considered in any event by the legislature or executive (Case 77/81, *Zuckerfabrik Franken GmbH v. Federal Republic of Germany* [1982] E.C.R. 681, at 694–5; Case 202/85, *Marthe Klensch and Others v. Secrétaire d'État à l'Agriculture et à la Viticulture* [1986] E.C.R. 3477 at 3508; Case C-260/89, *Elliniki Radiophonio Tileorassi* [1991] E.C.R. I 2925). It is conceded that the development of Community protection of fundamental rights by the European Court of Justice since 1970 may weaken the practical case for continued domestic constitutional scrutiny of such implementing measures, but it does not defeat it. While national courts are empowered to disapply national implementing measures that are in breach of the fundamental rights guaranteed by the Communities, it remains the case that this scheme of fundamental rights protection is under-developed, that its content is in many respects uncertain, and that its guarantees are not identical to those of the Constitution of Ireland or of any Member State (see Phelan, "Right to Life of the Unborn v. Promotion of Trade in Services: The European Court of Justice and the Normative Shaping of the European Union" (1992) 55 M.L.R. 670; Coppell & O'Neill, "The European Court of Justice: Taking Rights Seriously" (1992) 29 C.M.L.Rev. 669; Reid, *Constitution*, at 92; O'Higgins, "The Constitution and the Communities: Scope for Stress?" in O'Reilly ed., *Human Rights and Constitutional Law* (1992) 227, at 238–41). This position is also strenuously asserted by Weiler and Lockhart (" 'Taking Rights Seriously' Seriously: The European Court of Justice and its Fundamental Rights Jurisprudence—Part I" (1995) 32 C.M.L.Rev. 51, at 79–80). They argue for the existence of a double scrutiny: "[N]ational courts may review the measure not only by reference to E.C. standards, but, it is submitted, also by reference to their own standards which might be 'higher'. . . . It would always be open to the Member State courts, rather than the European Court, to strike down themselves an implementing measure for violation of human rights, even of the home-made variety, if there exists an alternative non-violative mode of implementing the Community rule." In Germany, even the acceptance of the equivalence of Community fundamental rights guarantees with those of the German Constitution has not prevented the maintenance of such scrutiny within the bounds permitted by Community law. Furthermore, as has already been remarked, the chief justification for the use of directives is that they permit Community legislation to be given effect in a manner which is to the greatest possible extent consonant with the main features and sensibilities of the national legal orders. This position now appears to be gaining acceptance in the European Court of Justice, as will be seen below.

If domestic constitutional scrutiny is permitted of national measures implementing Community law, how is one to proceed to reconcile the demands of two distinct legal systems: the Communities' and the Irish? We suggest a test akin to the "double construction" rule, which derives from the presumption of constitutionality of legislation. Where there exists a real choice between different methods of implementing a directive, the scheme which does not conflict, or conflicts least, with the provisions of the Constitution should be chosen. Walsh J. formulated what we call the double construction rule of interpretation in *McDonald v. Bord na gCon* [1965] I.R. 217:

> "[I]f in respect of any provision or provisions of the Act two or more constructions are reasonably open, one of which is constitutional and the other or others are unconstitutional, it must be presumed that the Oireachtas intended only the constitutional construction and a court called upon to adjudicate upon the constitutionality of the statutory provision should uphold the constitutional construction. It is only where there is no construction reasonably open which is not repugnant to the Constitution that the provision should be held to be repugnant."

The proposed test would operate rather differently, and would be more difficult in application. Where only one implementing scheme is open to the Government or Oireachtas, it would have the protection of Article 29.4.5, even if otherwise unconstitutional. Were more than one option available, one of them constitutional and the others not, the courts would have to strike down any scheme adopted which infringed any term of the Constitution, because it was not "necessitated" by Community membership. Such an approach is compatible with the view taken by Temple Lang in 1972 ("Constitutional Aspects of Irish Membership of the E.E.C." (1972) 9 C.M.L.Rev. 167, at 176):

> "If the Irish measure is inconsistent with the Constitution, and can be validated only under the Third Amendment, the Irish courts must look at the terms of the directive to see whether it obliged the Irish authorities to adopt a measure in precisely the terms in fact used. If not, the Irish court must decide if the directive could have been implemented by a measure compatible with the Constitution."

Such a test might be problematic simply because it assumes that the courts are qualified to know and assess the options, constitutional or otherwise, which are available to Ministers and legislators in implementing directives. It is relatively easy for courts to choose between competing interpretations of a piece of legislation—that is, after all, the basis of the judicial function. To apply a test such as that just outlined to measures implementing directives must involve straying into the more dangerous territory of executive policy choices and legislative responsibility.

This does not mean that the courts should foreswear such a line of enquiry; nor, as will be seen, would it be entirely unprecedented. But they should proceed with some caution, and with a certain deference to the decisions of the other branches of government—one must, after all, be mindful of "the comity that ought to exist between the great organs of State" (Henchy J. in *State (Woods) v. Attorney-General* [1969] I.R. 385). Kenny J. remarked in *Ryan v. Attorney-General* [1965] I.R. 294 that the presumption of constitutionality applies with particular force to legislation in which the Oireachtas seeks to reconcile personal rights with the claims of the common good. A similarly protective view should arguably be taken of efforts taken by the Oireachtas or, more commonly, by the Government, to reconcile the obligations of E.C. membership with those imposed by the Constitution—but equally, efforts should be taken to ensure that it is sought by those great organs of State to effect such a reconciliation.

Though he did not adopt the test proposed above, Murphy J. adopted in two cases, already mentioned above, an attitude that has some features in common with that just recommended. In *Lawlor v. Minister for Agriculture* [1988] I.L.R.M. 400, Murphy J. rejected a challenge to the European Communities (Milk Levy) Regulations, 1985 pursuant to Articles 40.3 and 43 of the Constitution. Interestingly, he dealt first with the substance of the plaintiff's constitutional claim, and found it wanting, and only then pointed out that the Regulations came under the protection of Article 29.4.3 (as it then was) in any event:

> "It seems to me that the word 'necessitated' in that sub-article could not be limited in its construction to laws, acts or measures all of which are in all their parts required to be enacted, done or adopted by the obligations of membership of the Community. It seems to me that the word 'necessitated' in this context must extend to and include all acts or measures which are consequent upon membership of the Community, and even where there may be a choice or degree of discretion vested in the State as to the particular manner in which it would meet the general spirit of its obligations of membership. ([1988] I.L.R.M. 400 at 418.)"

Murphy J.'s choice of words was unfortunate; as Hogan pointed out, the phrase "consequent on" was in fact replaced in the draft of the Third Amendment of the Constitution Bill in 1972 by the term "necessitated" in order to establish a strict test of legal obligation (see Hogan, S.E.A., at 61; see further the discussion above of the adoption of the wording of the Third Amendment). Binchy and Byrne have suggested that Murphy J.'s attitude might have been different had he been aware of this, as he applied the teleological method of interpretation to the measure in question in the same case (Binchy & Byrne, *Annual Review of Irish Law, 1989* (1990), p. 101). The definition of necessity offered by Murphy J. also appears to conflict with that in *Crotty*, although it has much of the flavour of the Supreme Court approach in *Meagher*. It will be remembered that the test proposed above is founded on a strict idea of necessity, *i.e.* the absence of choice. It is in deciding whether such a choice really existed that caution such as that evidenced by the attitude of Murphy J. is more appropriate. The State clearly could choose whether or not to ratify the Single European Act; its range of choices, if any, about how to implement a directive is less certain. In the latter case, a certain presumption in favour of the necessity of the scheme actually adopted is probably warranted.

The decision of Murphy J. in *Greene v. Minister for Agriculture* [1990] I.L.R.M. 364 serves to illustrate the point further. Directive 75/268/EEC requires Member States to introduce mechanisms for the purpose of maintaining reasonable farm incomes and promoting conservation in disadvantaged mountain and hill areas. Article 6 expressly gives Member States a discretion to impose additional or restrictive conditions for granting the payments over and above those specified in the Directive. Murphy J. reiterated his *dictum* from *Lawlor*. He stated that some scheme was "necessitated" by the Directive in order to implement it, and that some flexibility was to be allowed to the State, but that there was a point when a discretion conferred by a directive and exercised by a Member State was so far-reaching that it could not be said to be necessitated. The Minister's scheme passed that point in this case. While means-testing was permissible, there was nothing in the Directive about the impugned feature of the scheme, the testing of farmers' incomes by reference to the income of their spouses. This was struck down as being contrary to Article 41 of the Constitution. The case is of interest because of the degree of discretion expressly allowed by the parent Directive. (Many directives are now so detailed that they must be implemented almost *verbatim*.) Therefore, one could claim more easily, under the more accommodating approach of Murphy J. as well as under the *Crotty* "legal obligation" test, that no particular scheme was necessitated, and that a scheme had to be adopted, if possible, which was consistent with the provisions of the Constitution.

Of course, no such choice may be possible in fact. The obligation to ensure that the result enjoined by a directive is achieved may require a particular course of action, no matter what the discretion ostensibly conferred either by a provision of the directive (such as Article 6 in the instant case) or by Article 189 E.C. itself. It is not suggested that the result in *Greene* was wrong, or that the Minister had no choice but to test the total income of farming households; but there are probably cases where the room for manoeuvre of the Government or Oireachtas is quite constrained.

A rather different decision was handed down by Lynch J. in *Condon v. Minister for Agriculture*, High Court, October 12, 1990; [1993] I.J.E.L. 151. Council Regulation EEC/857/84 concerns, *inter alia*, the passing of milk quotas when land to which they are attached is sold or leased. Article 7(1) of the Regulation states that all or part of the quota would be transferred with the land in such circumstances, "according to procedures to be determined". Article 7(3) allows Member States to provide that part of the quota concerned will not pass with the land but will be added to a reserve from which quotas are distributed to deserving farmers. The Minister for Agriculture introduced a scheme whereby such a clawback would occur, of between 10 per cent and 25 per cent of the quota, where a lessee already had a quota of over 50,000 gallons. This was challenged by the applicant, a lessor, as a breach of her property rights, as she could only let her land with its quota intact to farmers with an existing quota of less than 50,000 gallons. She submitted that as the clawback scheme authorised by the E.C. Regulation was optional, it was not necessitated by membership of the European Communities.

On its face, this situation was not dissimilar to that in *Greene*—the Minister was given an express discretion, arguably so far-reaching that its exercise could not be said to be necessitated. Lynch J. approached the issue rather differently, however, in a manner worth quoting at some length (at page 9 of the judgment):

> "The fact that a scheme under Article 7(3) of Regulation 857 is optional and not mandatory does not mean that it must remain a dead letter. It is for the competent authority to decide if it should be activated and implemented and once the competent authority so decides then that necessitates details of how the scheme should work. These details are determined by the Minister as competent authority not directly by the European Community and therefore their constitutional validity arises for consideration under the first part of [Article 29.4.5]. Insofar as such details of implementation are reasonable they must be regarded as necessitated by the obligations of membership of the Communities and cannot therefore be unconstitutional. If however the details were unreasonable or unfair then they could hardly be said to be necessitated by the obligations of membership of the Communities and they would be open to constitutional challenge."

In the event, the scheme was found to be a reasonable one; and in the alternative, it was found that it did not infringe Article 43 of the Constitution in any case. However, it is very difficult to make sense of the *dictum* just quoted. Lynch J. seems to betray confusion about the Minister's capacity, his own judicial role and the meaning of necessity. The Minister acts as intervention agent in the State for the purposes of the Common Agricultural Policy of the E.C., and thus as competent authority. The competent authority (the Minister) decided to adopt an optional clawback scheme, and this, *per* Lynch J., does not appear to be open to question—perhaps because the Minister was acting in his capacity as E.C. agent. The details of such a scheme were also determined by the Minister "as competent authority", yet their necessity fell to be considered under Article 29.4.5. This apparent distinction between the capacity in which the Minister acted (a) in deciding to activate a claw-back scheme; and (b) in determining the details of such a scheme, is contradicted by Lynch J.'s description of the Minister as competent authority in both instances. Nor does it seem to be borne out by the text of Article 7(3), which speaks only of Member States (though Article 7(1) of the Regulation does not specify who is to determine the procedures of which it speaks). If the distinction is ill-founded, or was not intended, then Lynch J. can be said to have confused authority with necessity. If the Minister (*qua* Minister) is authorised to act by the Regulation, and is therefore given a choice, it is submitted that this cannot confer his decision with the trappings of necessity. Certainly, Murphy J. did not think so in *Greene*.

The question of whether the detailed scheme, adopted by the Minister *qua* Minister, was necessitated by the obligations of membership of the Communities is then deemed by Lynch J. to hinge on the reasonableness and fairness of the scheme. However, Article 29.4.5 presumably requires the Irish courts to accept State laws, acts and measures without questioning their merits, to the degree to which they are necessitated by Community membership—that must be the purpose of the immunity conferred by the subsection. To question the reasonableness of necessary measures would be to question the supremacy of Community law itself. Thus, Lynch J.'s test must not be taken to mean that Article 29.4.5 prevents any provision of the Constitution from invalidating any *reasonable* law, act or measure necessitated by Community membership—that would be reading a very considerable qualification into the text of the sub-section. He presumably means instead that Community law itself will not permit unreasonable measures, so that an unfair scheme could not validly be required to be implemented by Member States. If this is Lynch J.'s view, it is probably correct, but it leaves some questions unanswered. An Irish High Court judge may pronounce on the validity of E.C. measures, in certain limited circumstances. (The national judge may not, however, declare Community acts to be invalid. It is only where there is no doubt as to their validity that he may make a declaration to this effect—otherwise, an Article 177 reference to the Court of Justice is called for. See Case 314/85, *Foto-Frost v. Hauptzollamt Lübeck-Ost*, [1987] E.C.R. 1499.) The national judge may, and should, also question the validity, *as a matter of Community law*, of national measures adopted pursuant to Community obligations, though a preliminary reference to the the Court of Justice might be advisable (Temple Lang, Article 5, at 654–6). In either case, however, he decides what Community law *authorises*, rather than what it *requires*. That a national measure in pursuance of a discretion conferred by an E.C. directive or regulation is *intra vires* the national authority, in the eyes of Community law, does not mean that that *particular* measure is necessitated by Community law. The requirement that domestic implementing measures be reasonable is similar to the requirement that they achieve the obligation of result contained in a parent directive—it can still leave the State with a choice of reasonable methods. It is contended that it is the existence (or absence) of such a choice which determines, under Article 29.4.5, whether the *vires* of the national measure can be tested, as a matter of Irish constitutional law.

Of course, that which is reasonable in the eyes of Community law may very well be constitutional for the same reason. That which is a reasonable implementation of a milk quota clawback scheme, in the light of the objectives of the Common Agricultural Policy, may also be a reasonable delimitation of the exercise of property rights with a view to reconciling their exercise with the exigencies of the common good. One should not forget, however, that one is engaging in two qualitatively different judicial inquiries, with different aims. The assessment under principles of Community law arises from Article 5 E.C., which "obliges every national judge to be a Community law judge" (Temple Lang, Article 5, at 646; see also Temple Lang, "The Duties of National Courts under the Constitutional Law of the European Community" (1987) pp. 18–25, and the conclusions of the Advocate General in Case 237/82, *Jongeneel Kaas v. The State (Netherlands) and Stichting Centraal Orgaan Zuivelcontrole* [1984] E.C.R. 4893). The latter inquiry should arise under the Constitution of Ireland, when the former is complete, and then only if the State is left with some real choice between possible methods of achievement of an obligation imposed by membership of the E.C. For this reason, it is submitted that Lynch J.'s decision is misleading. It is possible nonetheless to sympathise with Lynch J.'s concerns, but it is hoped that the approach outlined below accommodates them.

The decision of Murphy J. in *Duff v. Minister for Agriculture*, [1993] 2 C.M.L.R. 969 is fully consistent with the foregoing analysis. The case concerned Regulation 857/84/EEC, which sets out general rules for the application of the "milk quota" or levy system established by Regulation 804/68/EEC as amended by Regulation 856/84/EEC. Article 3 of Regulation 856/84/EEC gave to Member States a discretion as to whether to grant special reference quantities (*i.e.* additional quota) to farmers who were still implementing a milk production development plan. It was decided not to do this in Ireland. The aggrieved plaintiffs sought to rely both on the general principles of Community law, *viz.* the doctrine of legitimate expectation, and on the domestic administrative law principle of reasonableness. While he rejected these arguments because of his assessment of the facts of the case (following the case-law of the Court of Justice in respect of the Community law argument), Murphy J. made clear that "the Minister's discretion was not unfettered and was not capable of being exercised in an arbitrary fashion" and would be reviewable if "the policy infringes the constitutional rights of the citizen or is shown to involve the abuse of a fiduciary function" [1994] I.J.E.L. 247, at 261–2. He implicitly accepted the dual protection afforded to citizens in relation to national implementing measures: protection pursuant to the general principles of Community law; and, protection under national standards to the extent that these are applicable consistently with Community law (which will arise where Member States are left with discretion as to how to give effect to a Community obligation).

In *Mallon v. Minister for Agriculture* (High Court, *The Irish Times*, July 29, 1994), Costello J. struck down as unconstitutional the two year maximum period of imprisonment in the same ministerial regulations as were at issue in *Meagher v. Minister for Agriculture*, on the ground that it breached the guarantee of jury trial for non-minor offences under Article 38.5 of the Constitution. It does not appear from the report of his *ex tempore* judgment that the State argued that a combination of such penalties with summary trial was necessary for the effective enforcement of the Directives, as might have been done by analogy with the Supreme Court's position in *Meagher*: this aspect of the decision has not been appealed by the State. Too much significance should not be attached to the decision, but it serves to highlight the distinct issues of implementing procedure and the content of implementing measures. Even if a Minister would have been entitled in the view of the Supreme Court in *Meagher* to amend by regulation a statute that provided that summary offences should in all cases have a maximum penalty of one year's imprisonment, this would not require that such the ministerial regulation should be free from judicial scrutiny of its terms and of their compatibility with the provisions of the Constitution.

A general, two-tier test is proposed for such judicial scrutiny. It follows the "legal obligation" approach of the Supreme Court in *Crotty*. It is consistent with the decision of Murphy J. in *Duff*. It therefore rejects the stated approach of Murphy J. in *Lawlor* and *Greene*, and any extension of *Meagher*.

Nonetheless, it is motivated by sympathy with the evident deference towards State action in those decisions, and by an interest in the reasonableness of domestic measures adopted in pursuance of Community obligations. In *Greene*, Murphy J. remarked that while membership of the Communities undoubtedly required Ireland to implement a scheme complying with Directive 75/268/EEC, "it does not follow that any and every scheme drafted in pursuance of that directive and meeting its purposes is necessarily required by our membership of the Community" [1990] I.L.R.M. 365, at 371. It is suggested that this statement should underlie the approach of the courts to the question of the constitutionality of measures adopted to implement directives in *all* cases where it arises. Clearly the introduction of provisions other than those enjoined by a directive (or by an E.C. regulation) can be an exercise of real discretion. That discretion may be expressly allowed for (as it was in *Greene*, and in *Condon*) or implicitly permitted; and in such cases, its exercise should be subject to constitutional scrutiny. But equally, the means employed to implement the terms of the directive itself can be the object of discretion, and *to that extent*, should be subject to the same measure of scrutiny. On the operation of such scrutiny, and the task of the legislator in such cases, the following comments of Barrington J. in *Hyland v. Minister for Social Welfare* are apposite [1989] I.R. 624, at 631:

> "One can therefore have great sympathy with the legislator attempting to enact social welfare legislation. The legislation is of its nature difficult and complex. The financial restraints may be pressing. He must be careful that the legislation contains no element of sexual discrimination such as might violate the equality directive. But he must also guard the institution of marriage [which Article 41 of the Constitution pledges the State to guard with special care]."

The suggested two-tier test is as follows:

> (i) Was there a *legal obligation* under Community law to adopt or enforce the measure in question? This is relatively easily answered in the case of regulations (yes, unless some element of discretion is expressly granted) and of new constitutional Treaties (no). Difficulty arises in the case of directives. There is an obligation to adopt *some* measure that can achieve the required result in conformity to the terms of the directive; but the particular measure adopted may be one of only several options available. This leads to the second question:
>
> (ii) Did there exist in fact a *real choice* in the means adopted by the Government or the Oireachtas to secure the implementation of the obligation in question? Was there *actual* as well as legal obligation? If the course pursued was in reality the only one available, then the impugned measure is one necessitated by membership. If other options existed, all of them of doubtful constitutionality, the supposed discretion of the State would also be vitiated, and the measure adopted safe from scrutiny. Only if there existed another possible course of action, of undoubted constitutionality, which was capable of fulfilling satisfactorily the terms of the relevant E.C. directive, could the measure adopted be said not to have been necessitated, actually as well as legally, by the obligations of membership of the Communities, and thus be exposed to enquiries into its compliance with the terms and guarantees of the Constitution.

It will be remarked that such a test could involve the courts in hypothetical queries about matters of executive or legislative responsibility. However, the burden of establishing the validity of such hypotheses will rest heavily on those who seek to challenge implementing measures. They would have to establish clearly, to a court wary of engaging in such enquiries, that there existed a feasible alternative to the impugned measure; that this would have constituted an adequate implementation of the relevant directive; and that it was free from the taint of unconstitutionality. In legislative fields where the courts see the reconciliation of various considerations as being peculiarly a matter for the Oireachtas, the plaintiffs' task would be far from easy. They would probably be required to substantiate such a claim with detailed submissions. Furthermore, the questions of actual and legal obligation can merge somewhat. The European Court of Justice has ruled that States are obliged to use their discretion by choosing the most appropriate forms and methods to ensure the effectiveness of directives (*Procureur du Roi v. Royer*, Case 48/75 [1976] E.C.R. 497, at 518). Thus, the plaintiff would have to satisfy the court not only of the existence of a feasible and constitutional alternative, but also that that alternative was as appropriate as the measure in question to ensure the proper fulfilment of the obligation of result imposed by the European Communities. That done, they would still have to establish that the measure actually adopted was contrary to the Constitution, in the face of a presumption of the opposite. In the case of taxation and social welfare measures, this presumption is peculiarly difficult to overturn (*Brennan v. Attorney-General* [1984] I.L.R.M. 355; *Hyland v. Minister for Social Welfare* [1989] I.R. 624.

The application of the principle of proportionality by the European Court of Justice, and by a number of national European jurisdictions, affords a precedent for this type of judicial enquiry. The principle of proportionality requires that a public authority not impose obligations on a citizen except to the extent to which they are strictly necessary in the public interest to attain the purpose of the measure (Advocate General Dutheillet de Lamothe in *Internationale Handelsgesellschaft GmbH v. Einfuhr- und Vorratsstelle für Getreide und Futtermittel*, Case 11/70, [1970] E.C.R. 1125, at 1146). The principle now appears in Article 3b E.C., alongside justiciable principles of subsidiarity, and of the limitation of the exercise of E.C. competences to the achievement of the objectives set out in the Treaty (see further the annotation below of Article 3b E.C.). This provision poses questions about necessity similar to those already discussed in an Irish context. It expressly embodies requirements of both legal and actual obligation. In certain circumstances, the Community may be obliged to act as a matter of *legal* necessity, and is exposed to possible proceedings under Article 175 E.C. for failure so to act. In areas where the Community is not conferred with exclusive competence by the Treaty, and where it has not already pre-empted Member State action by occupying the field in question, so that there is an apparent choice between Community and national measures to achieve a desired result, the *actual* necessity of Community action must be established, by reference both to the objectives of the Community and to the scale and effects of the proposed action. The necessity of the action to achieve some Treaty objective must be proved, as must the insufficiency of any alternative national or less restrictive Community measure with the same goal. (The justiciability of the subsidiarity principle in Article 3b E.C. has been a matter of debate, but will be addressed by the Court of Justice in Case 84/94, *United Kingdom v. Council*.)

The requirement of actual necessity commits the Court of Justice to asking hypothetical questions. The court must ascertain whether alternatives to the impugned E.C. action were open to the national authorities. Were there less restrictive alternatives open to the Community itself? Would they have achieved sufficiently the relevant objects? It has been answering similar questions for over 20 years, ever since it chose to enforce the principle of proportionality as part of Community law.

In *Internationale Handelsgesellschaft*, E.C. agricultural regulations required import and export licences involving the licensees in giving an undertaking to effect the proposed transactions under the guarantee of a deposit. This mechanism was claimed to be necessary to guarantee that the imports and exports for which licences were requested were actually effected, and to ensure both for the Community and for Member States precise knowledge of the intended transactions. Such knowledge, it was asserted, was essential to enable the competent authorities to make judicious use of the instruments of intervention, both ordinary and exceptional, which were at their disposal for guaranteeing the functioning of the system of prices instituted by the regulations [1970] E.C.R. 1125, at 1134–5.

The plaintiff in the case put forward an alternative scheme, of mere declaration of exports effected and of unused licences [1970] E.C.R. 1125, at 1128–9. This was rejected by the Court of Justice, as it "would, by reason of its retrospective nature and lack of any guarantee of application, be incapable of providing the competent authorities with sure data on trends in the movement of goods". The court also considered, and dismissed, another possible approach: "a system of fines imposed *a posteriori* would involve considerable administrative and legal complications at the stage of decision and execution, aggravated by the fact that the traders concerned may be beyond the reach of the intervention agencies by reason of their residence in another Member State." The court concluded that the deposit/undertaking system "has the dual advantage over other possible systems of simplicity and efficacy", and was both necessary and appropriate to enable the competent authorities to determine cereals market interventions [1970] E.C.R. 1125, at 1135–6.

The proportionality jurisdiction leaves a great deal to the judgment of the court. It is not anticipated that the subsidiarity jurisdiction, which is even more difficult of application, will be used by the court to strike down any but the most egregious of alleged breaches. However, if such questions can be answered adequately by the Court of Justice, it is reasonable to suppose that the Irish courts are also capable of doing so. To do so would permit Irish courts, to the greatest extent consistent with Community law, to observe their duties both as Community and as national constitutional courts. This appears to be the approach in Germany. The German influence on the development of the principle of proportionality by the Court of Justice is widely acknowledged (see, *e.g.* Schwarze, *European Administrative Law* (1992) pp. 64–6; Hartley, *Foundations*, at 155; Nolte, "General Principles of German and European Administrative Law—A Comparison in Historical Perspective" (1994) 57 M.L.R. 191, at 191–3). The principle of proportionality (*Verhältnismässigkeit*) includes the requirement of necessity (*Erforderlichkeit*), that the least restrictive of several possible means be used by public authorities for the achievement of public ends. The principle of proportionality is applicable in constitutional adjudication, as the measure of acceptable legislative or other restrictions on the exercise of fundamental rights (see Kommers, *The Constitutional Jurisprudence of the Federal Republic of Germany* (1989) p. 59), and its strict requirements have in turn influenced the development in Germany of the principle of double construction (*verfassungskonforme Auslegung*). While the German courts expect the Court of Justice to review E.C. directives if necessary, it is not surprising that judicial review should be possible in respect of national measures implementing E.C. directives, in so far as the manner of implementation is within the discretion of the German authorities. The *Bundesverfassungsgericht* made this clear in *M. GmbH. v. Bundesregierung* (BVerfG, May 12, 1989; [1990] 1 C.M.L.R. 570, at 574; authors' italics):

> "In the process of implementation the national legislation is subject to the restrictions imposed by the Constitution. The question whether the applicants' constitutional or equivalent rights are infringed in the implementation of the directive *within the scope for choice as to formulation allowed to the legislature by the directive* is one which is open to constitutional judicial review in all respects."

The exercise of a similar supervisory jurisdiction is recommended on the part of the Irish courts, on the lines outlined above. Considerable support for a domestic supplementary supervisory jurisdiction has recently been provided in Case C-63/93 *Duff v. Minister for Agriculture*, which arose from an Art. 177 reference by the Supreme Court on appeal from the decision of Murphy J. discussed above. In his Opinion of June 8, 1995, Advocate General Cosmas found (at paragraphs 58–59) that the Minister had not acted in breach of the general principles of Community law in deciding not to provide for the grant of special reference quantities to producers with incomplete farm development plans (as he could have done under the Regulation), but added that "there is nothing to prevent such a requirement from being founded on principles of national law which, in an appropriate case, may ensure greater protection in this respect than that afforded by the general principles applicable in the Community legal order". He stressed (at paragraph 60) that the application of such national principles "must not lead to any substantive alteration of the rules governing the additional levy scheme on milk, jeopardize the effectiveness of the scheme or compromise the successful attainment of its objectives".

It is perfectly possible, of course, for the *Meagher* test to be extended to the question of constitutional scrutiny of the content of national implementing measures. The "major or fundamental obligation necessitated by membership of the Community", *viz.* the creation of "necessary machinery" to ensure "the application of the Community law and acts binding on the State and as part of the domestic law subject to the conditions laid down in the Treaty" (Judgment of the Supreme Court (Finlay C.J.), [1994] 1 I.R. 329, at 351), might be taken also to require that the smooth operation of that implementing machinery not be obstructed by substantive domestic constitutional concerns. It is submitted, however, as it was above in respect of implementing procedure, that European Community law itself does not demand such a degree of constitutional abnegation, and that where discretion exists as to the precise content of national implementing measures, that that discretion should be exercised subject to relevant national constitutional norms. This is in keeping with the objective requirements of Community membership, with the terms and legislative history of Article 29.4.5 of the Constitution, and with the general interest in preserving to the greatest degree possible the protection of constitutional rights, freedoms and principles of governance.

CHAPTER SIX

COMMUNITY COMPETENCE AND MEMBER STATE OBLIGATION:
MIXED AGREEMENTS

Article 29.4.5 of the Constitution may be invoked to guarantee the reception into Irish law under European Communities Act, 1972, s.2 of international agreements concluded by the Communities, and to justify State acts necessitated by the obligation of the Member States to observe the terms of such agreements. Despite having their origins outside the Community legal order, and being in part the acts of non-member States, Community agreements are "an integral part of Community law" (Case 181/73, *Haegemann v. Belgium* [1974] E.C.R. 449, para. 5), and are capable of direct applicability (Case 104/81, *Hauptzollamt Mainz v. Kupferberg* [1982] E.C.R. 3641).

Community competence to conclude treaties with third countries arises expressly from the Treaties (*e.g.* in the case of the common commercial policy, or association agreements), or by implication through the doctrine of parallelism. This doctrine derives Community external competence from the existence of internal competence. This competence will be exclusive where the internal Community competence is exclusive, or where the international agreement relates to matters already the subject of internal Community measures; it will otherwise be concurrent with the Member States. In such cases, the Communities rarely act alone. It is much more common to conclude a mixed agreement, an international agreement to which both the Communities and the individual Member States are parties on one side. In such cases, the Community and the Member States will be jointly responsible to third countries for implementation of the agreement, in the absence of a restrictive clause to the contrary. Internally, the Community may implement, or the Member States will be under an E.C. obligation to do so under Article 228 E.C. There are also certain competences which are exclusive to the Member States, chief of which in practical terms is the grant by them of financial aid. The Member States alone are competent to conclude agreements on such matters with third countries, although they may also be concluded within the framework of a more extensive mixed agreement. (This is relatively rare.) Only the Member States will be competent to take internal action to implement clauses of such a mixed agreement relating to their exclusive competence; the allocation of international responsibility for their implementation may depend on the terms of the agreement. (This introductory statement on external competence is expanded upon below.)

One can test the degree to which Article 29.4.5 of the constitution commits the State to the integrity of the Community legal order by posing some questions about mixed agreements:

> (i) to what extent is a mixed agreement a Community agreement, and therefore binding on the Member States as a matter of Community law (under Article 228(7) E.C.)?

As will be seen, an agreement concerned only with matters entirely within Community competence (exclusive or concurrent) will be a Community agreement, in the absence of a restrictive clause on Community participation. The position is different where Member State exclusive competences are also involved. In that case, one reaches a second question:

> (ii) To the extent (if any) that a mixed agreement is not a Community agreement, are the Member States obliged *as a matter of Community law* to comply with the agreement?

The answer to the second question will depend largely on the responsibility of the Communities under public international law for breaches of the agreement by the Member States, and also on the obstacle presented by the

Member State breach to the Communities in the achievement of their objectives under the Treaties through the exercise of their external competences.

It is the obligatory quality of mixed agreements as a matter of Community law that is important. It has already been seen that the Irish courts are willing to review the State's participation in international agreements having regard to the provisions of the Constitution (*The State (Gilliland) v. Governor of Mountjoy Prison* [1987] I.R. 201; *McGimpsey v. Ireland* [1990] 1 I.R. 110). The first clause of Article 29.4.5 of the Constitution should operate to prevent judicial review of State acts necessitated by the observance of mixed agreements to the extent that the State is obliged as a matter of Community law to observe such agreements. The second clause, combined with section 2(1), European Communities Act, 1972, should enable the provisions of mixed agreements which are binding on the Communities to be directly applicable in the State where their terms so require. The chief object of speculation in this Chapter is whether part of a mixed agreement which is not Community law pursuant to Article 228 E.C., as considered in the first question above, can, by a positive response to the second question nonetheless incur the special protection in Irish law of Article 29.4.5 of the Constitution.

(i) MIXED AGREEMENTS AND COMMUNITY LAW

The device of the mixed agreement is specifically provided for by Article 102 Euratom, but was developed in practice under the EEC Treaty, with the approval of the Court of Justice (Opinion 1/78, *Natural Rubber Agreement* [1978] E.C.R. 2871). They will be discussed hereafter only as they arise under the European Community Treaty. Mixed agreements are usually employed "where the Community has exclusive competence over part of the subject matter of the agreement and non-exclusive or concurrent competence over the rest of the subject matter. However, the phrase "mixed agreements" is also used to describe the much rarer situations in which either part of the subject matter of the agreement is outside the competence, even the concurrent competence, of the Community, or the Community becomes a party even though it has no exclusive competence over any part of the subject matter" (Temple Lang, "The Ozone Layer Convention: A New Solution to the Question of Community Participation in 'Mixed' International Agreements" (1986) 23 C.M.L.Rev. 157, at 157–8 (hereinafter Temple Lang, Ozone); see further Hartley, *Foundations*, at 165–76; Case 22/70, *Commission v. Council (E.R.T.A.)* [1971] E.C.R. 263; Opinion 1/94, *G.A.T.T.* [1994] E.C.R. I-1). The realm of human activities is not, in the case of the Community, neatly divided into those subject to exclusive national or to exclusive Community regulation. There also exists a third category (vaster than the two exclusive spheres combined), areas of the non-exclusive or concurrent competence of the Community (*pace* the rather semantic argument of Toth, "The Principle of Subsidiarity in the Maastricht Treaty" (1992) 29 C.M.L.Rev. 1079, that all such powers are exclusive to the Community; Article 3b E.C. applies the principle of subsidiarity to "areas which do not fall within [the Community's] exclusive competence"). This is not true concurrence; rather, the term is normally used to describe sectors where the Member States retain competence only until the Community has acted to replace them in that sphere in pursuance of its objectives. Accordingly, as the Community intervenes in these areas of non-exclusive competence, the borderline between exclusive and non-exclusive (concurrent) Community competence, internal and external, shifts in favour of the former—either because the Community intervention is exhaustive, or because Member States are precluded from adopting any measure which might affect the scope or operation of Community measures, even where these are not exhaustive (see Case 22/70, *Commission v. Council (E.R.T.A.)* [1971] E.C.R. 263; clarified in Opinion 2/91, *I.L.O. Convention No. 170* [1993] 3 C.M.L.R. 800, paras. 25–6). This process is known as pre-emption. It is, therefore, possible for the subject matter of a mixed agreement (where it involves matters of concurrent competence, as most do) to become over time, more properly the subject matter of a pure Community treaty with third States (as the Community's exclusive external competences expand to match those it exercises internally).

The Community is fully competent to conclude international agreements without the participation of the Member States in respect of any subject matter which falls within its non-exclusive as well as its exclusive competence, where such external action is necessary to achieve the objectives of the Treaty. (A possible exception arises where the Member States have to undertake heavy financial commitments as a result of the agreement: Opinion 1/78, *Natural Rubber Agreement* [1979] E.C.R. 2871; *cf.* Opinion 1/94, *G.A.T.T.* [1994] E.C.R. I-1, paras. 19–21. It is suggested in Opinion 1/94 (at para. 85) that the Community should conclude international agreements in the absence of existing internal legislation only where the relevant treaty objectives cannot be attained by the adoption of autonomous (*i.e.* internal) rules; see also Opinion 2/92, March 24, 1995 at para. 32.) However, the Member States often seek to avoid pre-emption of their competences by preventing the Community agreeing Community treaties with third States in respect of matters within its non-exclusive competence, which would then carry consequences for the distribution of legislative competence (Ehlermann, "Mixed Agreements—A List of Problems" and Groux, "Mixed Negotiations" in O'Keeffe & Schermers eds., *Mixed Agreements* (1983) 3, 87, at 5–6, 90 respectively; see Opinion 1/76, *Rhine Laying-up Fund*: [1977] E.C.R. 741). However, when an agreement involves subject matter within the Community's exclusive as well as its non-exclusive competence, the Community cannot be excluded in this manner. The expedient of the mixed agreement will usually be employed in such cases.

But when a mixed agreement is signed which covers areas of exclusive Community competence and of concurrent competence, is the Community signature deemed to extend to the clauses in the concurrent sphere, or to only those of the Member States, or both? Unless it is otherwise indicated (see below), a treaty party is presumed in public international law to be a party to the whole of the treaty concerned (Tomuschat, "Liability for Mixed Agreements" in O'Keeffe & Schermers eds., *Mixed Agreements* (1983) p. 125 at 130). Similarly, "[t]o the extent that no reservations are made according to the appropriate procedure, the act of the Council by which the Community concludes the agreement is an indication that the entire agreement is meant to be binding *under Community law*" (Neuwahl, "Joint Participation in International Treaties and the Exercise of Power by the EEC and its Member States: Mixed Agreements" (1991) 28 C.M.L.Rev. 717, at 734, n. 27; authors' italics (hereinafter Neuwahl, Mixed Agreements)). This is reflective of the jurisprudence of the Court of Justice. The Yaoundé (mixed) Convention, 1963 "was concluded not only in the name of the Member States but also of the Community which, in consequence, are bound by virtue of Article 228" (Case 87/75, *Bresciani v. Amministrazione Italiana delle Finanze*: [1976] E.C.R. 129). Once a mixed agreement is concluded, it "will form an integral part of Community law" (Ruling 1/78, *Physical Protection of Nuclear Materials*: [1978] E.C.R. 2151, para. 36). Having confirmed this point in respect of the Association Agreement with Turkey, 1963, the Court extended to mixed agreements the principle first stated in respect of "pure" Community agreements in *Hauptzollamt Mainz v. Kupferberg* (Case 104/81, [1982] E.C.R. 3641) that "in ensuring respect for commitments arising from an agreement concluded by the Community institutions the Member States fulfil, within the Community system, an obligation in relation to the Community, which has assumed responsibility for the due performance of the agreement" (Case 12/86, *Demirel v. Stadt Schwäbisch Gmünd*: [1987] E.C.R. 3719, para. 11; discussed further below).

Temple Lang remarks that "[i]t seems to be believed [by the Member States] that if both the Community and the Member States become parties to a treaty, to the extent that the treaty is implemented by national measures rather than Community measures, there will be no change in the sphere of exclusive Community powers" ("European Community Constitutional Law: The Division of Power between the Community and the Member States" (1988) 39 N.I.L.Q. 209, at 226, n. 35). He counters that this view ignores the fact, which he asserts, that the Community is bound (in the absence of special circumstances, *i.e.* reservations) by the whole treaty, not merely by those provisions which it is agreed within the Community should be implemented by Community measures; and that treaties binding on the Community also bind the Member States, however they may be implemented. If the Community is deemed by Community law to be a party to the clauses within its concurrent competence, then the commitments contained therein must be Community commitments which the Member States are obliged to observe *as a matter of Community law* (under Article 228(7) E.C.). "The fact that a Member State ceased to be a party to a [mixed] treaty by which the Community was bound would not entitle the Member State to enact legislation inconsistent with the treaty." Temple Lang's position is shared, at least in part, by Neuwahl. While she doubts whether conclusion of a mixed agreement can cause pre-emption of Member State legislative competence in favour of the Community (Mixed Agreements, at 731), she nonetheless believes that the Community is a party to the entirety of a mixed agreement, to the extent that its competences permit and in the absence of any contrary provision of the agreement; and as will be seen, this imposes limits on the Member States' freedom to legislate.

Mixed agreements come in a variety of forms, some of which may result in the restriction of normal (*i.e.* full) Community participation. The situation must be different where the participation of the Community is expressly confined by the terms of the agreement to certain provisions (see, *e.g.* the Second Lomé Convention, [1979] O.J.: L347). In the alternative, it is occasionally requested by other parties to a mixed agreement that the Community side set out clearly which matters are within Member State competence, and which are within the Community's, but this is comparatively rare and is not favoured by the Community side (Groux & Manin, *The European Communities in the International Order* (1984) pp. 83–4 (hereinafter Groux & Manin, *International Order*)). It may or may not be attempted to employ such an indicative declaration to determine the degree of participation by the Community in a mixed agreement. Any such attempted linkage is faced with two problems: it usually ignores the possibility of concurrent competences; and the list of competences may not correlate very precisely with the various provisions of the mixed agreement (see Temple Lang, Ozone, at 160–1). Where it is not attempted to make such a connection between a declaration of competence and the extent of Community participation (see, *e.g.* Article 13 Vienna Convention for the Protection of the Ozone Layer, 1985; Cmnd. No. 9652 [Misc. No. 13]; discussed by Temple Lang, Ozone, at 166–8), the declaration can hardly determine as a matter of Community law, the extent to which the agreement is a Community agreement. The Court of Justice will not accept that practice on the part of the other institutions can dictate the interpretation of the Treaties as to Community competence (Opinion 1/94, *G.A.T.T.*: [1994] E.C.R. I-1, para. 52; Case 68/86, *United Kingdom v. Council*: [1988] E.C.R. 855); and in the absence of any provision confining Community participation in the agreement to the areas set out in the list of competences, Community participation will extend to all matters covered by the agreement that are within the exclusive or non-exclusive competence of the Community.

On the other hand, a link was made between participation and the declaration of competence required of the Community as a condition of accession to the United Nations Convention on the Law of the Sea, 1982 ((1982) 21, 6 I.L.M. 1261):

> "An international organisation shall be a Party to this Convention to the extent that it has competence in accordance with the declarations, communications of information or notifications [specifying the matters governed by this Convention in respect of which competence has been transferred to the organisation by its Member States, and the nature and extent of the competence transferred]" (Article 4(2), Annex IX, U.N.C.L.O.S., 1982).

This provision must make the extent of participation of the Community in the Convention contingent under international law on the declaration of competence, even if that statement is inaccurate as a matter of Community law. The conclusion of the agreement by the Council on behalf of the Community must be read to be limited by this provision, so that the obligation incurred by the Community as a matter of Community law (and extended to the Member States by Article 228(7) E.C.) is similarly limited. (However, there will be a breach of Community law if the declaration of competences leads to the Member States undertaking obligations which are within the Community's *exclusive* competence, or *vice versa*.)

A different problem arises when the Community is defined as a party only to part of a mixed agreement, but the relevant part is not specified. For example, Article 2(c) of the European Economic Area Agreement states that for the purposes of the Agreement, "the term 'Contracting Parties' means, concerning the Community and the E.C. Member States, the Community and the E.C. Member States, or the Community, or the E.C. Member States. The meaning to be attributed to this expression in each case is to be deduced from the relevant provisions of this Agreement and from the respective competences of the Community and the E.C. Member States as they follow from the [Treaties]". (The same clause is employed in, *e.g.* the declarations annexed to the Final Acts of the Association Agreement with Yugoslavia, [1983] O.J.: L41; and the Association Agreement with Turkey, [1963] O.J.: C113). While the position in respect of international responsibility may again be different, the agreement must, as above, be a Community agreement, as a matter of Community law, to the extent that it addresses matters within the exclusive and non-exclusive competence of the Community. This will ultimately fall to be decided by the Court of Justice in the event of an internal dispute between the Community and the Member States, or in national litigation (see, *e.g.* Case 65/77, *Razanatsimba* [1977] E.C.R. 2229; Case 12/86, *Demirel v. Stadt Schwäbisch Gmünd* [1987] E.C.R. 3747). The fact that participation in respect of non-exclusive competences is shared with the Member States does not negate the Community's involvement, and an obligation is incurred by the Member States under Article 228(7) E.C. which is supplementary to the international obligation undertaken directly by them. The exclusion by the terms of the agreement of Community participation in respect of matters within the Member States' exclusive competence does not add anything to the normal position under Community law, as such participation would be *ultra vires* the Community if it were attempted.

Thus, obligations under a mixed agreement relating to matters within the exclusive and non-exclusive competence of the Community constitute, within the Community legal order, obligations binding on the Member States by virtue of Article 228(7) E.C. This must activate, in the case of Ireland, the provisions of Article 29.4.5 of the Constitution to protect from constitutional scrutiny State acts entailed by such international obligations of the Community. An exception is made only where the Community is specifically excepted from participation in respect of matters within its non-exclusive competence. Where the Community is excluded from participation in an agreement concerning matters within its exclusive competence, the Member States may participate only as agents of the Community, and the agreement will constitute a Community agreement, as a matter of Community law (Case 22/70, *Commission v. Council (E.R.T.A.)* [1971] E.C.R. 263; Case 804/79, *Commission v. United Kingdom* [1981] E.C.R. 1045). Provisions of a mixed agreement concerning matters within the Member States' exclusive competence cannot form part of a Community agreement, as a matter of Community law.

(ii) MIXED AGREEMENTS AND COMMUNITY RESPONSIBILITY

It has been seen that a mixed agreement is a Community agreement, binding on the Member States under Article 228(7) E.C., to the extent that it concerns the exclusive and non-exclusive competence of the Community, and in the absence of any provision to the contrary. It cannot as a matter of Community law encroach on the exclusive competences of the Member States. Is it nonetheless possible that Member States can be obliged as a matter of Community law to observe the provisions of a mixed agreement to which the Community is not deemed, by Community law, to be a party? It is contended that this is possible, through the operation of the principle of responsibility under public international law, but there is no direct authority on the point. The question is posed in order to divine whether Article 29.4.5 of the Constitution commits the State to constitutional immunity not just for the terms of mixed agreements that constitute Community law, but also for commitments in mixed agreements within the State's exclusive competence which are nonetheless linked in fact, with the obligations incurred *inter se* by the Community and third countries.

A mixed agreement may provide for the allocation of responsibility in the event of a dispute with a third State over the performance of obligations under the agreement. For example, the Convention on Protection of the Rhine against Chemical Pollution, 1976 includes a very general statement that for the purposes of applying the Convention, the Community and its Member States shall act in their respective areas of competence. It then specifies that if a third party seeks arbitration, the Community and the Member States must jointly notify the other party whether the Member States, the Community or the Community and the Member States are parties to the dispute (Paragraph 8, Annex B, [1977] O.J.: L240). The Community often volunteers to do this in the event of a dispute instead of having to list its competences at the point when the agreement is concluded (Groux & Manin, *International Order*, p. 83). The United Nations Convention on the Law of the Sea, 1982 has a similar clause, providing that if an international organisation and its Member States fail to make such a notification within reasonable time, or provide contradictory information, they will be held jointly and severally liable (Article 5(5), Annex IX, U.N.C.L.O.S., 1982; this amounts to the United Nations having its cake and eating it, as Community participation was limited from the outset by reference to its declaration of competences: see Groux & Manin, *International Order*, p. 145, n. 2). In some cases, a notification requirement may be eschewed, in favour of a stipulation that the Community and its Member States be treated as a single party for the purpose of resolving disputes by arbitration (as in the case of the Cooperation Agreements with Algeria, Morocco, Tunisia, Egypt, Lebanon, Syria and Jordan, [1978] O.J. 263/9.)

In the absence of such a stipulation or of a joint notification, should the arbitrator or other dispute settlement forum seek to ascertain the respective competences of the Community and the Member States, or should matters proceed on the basis that in such cases, they are jointly liable for breach of any provision? The ruling of the Court of Justice on the compatibility with the EAEC Treaty of the I.A.E.A. draft Convention on the Physical Protection of Nuclear Materials may indicate acceptance of the joint responsibility of the Community and the Member States under international law for the performance of a mixed agreement (Ruling 1/78, [1978] E.C.R. 2151, para. 35; authors' italics):

> "[I]t is not necessary to set out and determine, as regards the parties to the convention, the division of powers in this respect between the Community and the Member States, particularly as it may change in the course of time. It is sufficient to state to the other contracting parties that the matter gives rise to a division of powers within the Community, *it being understood that the exact nature of that division is a domestic question in which third parties have no need to intervene.*"

A number of commentators have endorsed the view that the Community and the Member States should be jointly responsible for any breach on their side in the absence of a clause in the agreement limiting the participation of the Community or the Member States, or specifying their respective competences. In such cases, "the division of powers between the Community and its Member States cannot be invoked against third parties" (Groux & Manin, *International Order*, p. 128). Gaja adds: "When the agreement does not provide directly or indirectly for a distinction between the Community's and the Member States' rights and obligations, *or when the criteria set out for the distinction cannot lead to a solution*, the Community's and the Member States' obligations and rights must be taken with regard to the non-member States as an undivided whole" ("The European Community's Rights and Obligations under Mixed Agreements" in O'Keeffe & Schermers eds., *Mixed Agreements* (1983) p. 133, at 137; authors' italics). The criteria set out for the distinction may be unhelpful, for example, in cases where a declaration like that annexed to the Turkish and Yugoslavian Association Agreements provides that the Community is not a party to the agreement in respect of matters within exclusive Member State competence, but does not identify such matters. (For arguments in favour of joint responsibility, see also Hartley, *Foundations*, at 186; Tomuschat "Liability for Mixed Agreements" in O'Keeffe & Schermers eds., *Mixed Agreements* (1983) p. 125, at 130–1; Allott speaks in the same volume, to apparently similar effect, of the "composite participation" of the Community and the Member States: "Adherence to and Withdrawal from Mixed Agreements", p. 97, at 119; for a contrary argument, see in the same volume Balekjian, "Mixed Agreements: Complementary and Concurrent Competences?", p. 141, at 143–5). It is implicit in this approach that it can lead to the imposition of joint liability on the Member States for breach of provisions of a mixed agreement within the Community's exclusive competence and, more importantly for present purposes, liability on the part of the Community in respect of matters within the exclusive competence of the Member States. Both Tomuschat and Gaja add however that this sharing of international *responsibility* need not affect the internal distribution of *competences* in the Community legal order.

In the alternative, it can hardly be asserted that an arbitrator employed to resolve a dispute between the Community and/or the Member States, on the one hand, and a third party, on the other, is not free under international law to interpret a clause of the agreement which defines the contracting parties on the Community side differently for different purposes but fails to give further details on the allocation of obligations. However, an external assessment of the distribution of exclusive Member State and Community competences, and of concurrent competences, may differ from the view taken by the Court of Justice. In that case, the Community may also be found to be responsible under international law for matters which, as a matter of Community law, are within the exclusive competence of the Member States. Thus, to the extent of the divergence and of any accompanying finding of responsibility, the effect will be the same, from the perspective of Community law, as if the Community and the Member States had been found jointly responsible for the agreement in question.

It can be seen, therefore, that in the absence of a provision expressly confining Community participation in a mixed agreement to only certain parts thereof, or of a notification in the event of a dispute, of the division of responsibility between the Community and the Member States in respect of the subject matter of the dispute, the Community may incur international responsibility for breach of any provision of the agreement, whether it falls as a matter of Community law within the Community's exclusive or non-exclusive competences, or within the exclusive competence of the Member States. This may occur either because there is an express commitment in the agreement to joint and several liability (as in the Mediterranean Co-operation agreements mentioned above), or by operation of law in such cases, the requirement under Articles 5 and 228 E.C. that Member States do nothing that would cause the Community to be in breach of its obligations under any treaty to which it is a party (Case 104/81, *Kupferberg v. Hauptzollamt Mainz* [1982] E.C.R. 3641) should probably extend to an obligation under Article 5 E.C. to ensure that the Community is not held responsible for breach of obligations under a mixed agreement which as a matter of Community law it is not competent to undertake.

Some support for this argument can possibly be drawn from the decision of the Court of Justice in *Demirel v. Stadt Schwäbisch Gmünd* (Case 12/86, [1987] E.C.R. 3747), which concerned the Association Agreement with Turkey, of which the declaration on the extent of participation by the Community and the Member States has already been mentioned. The Court stated that the Community had a very extensive competence in an association agreement under Article 238 E.E.C. to guarantee commitments to non-member States in all fields covered by the Treaty, even if the Member States made the rules necessary to give effect to such commitments in their territory. The court reserved the question whether it had jurisdiction to rule on the interpretation of a provision in a mixed agreement containing a commitment which only the Member States could enter into in the sphere of their own powers, but stated, following *Hauptzollamt Mainz v. Kupferberg* (Case 104/81, [1982] E.C.R. 3641), that in ensuring respect for commitments arising from an agreement concluded by the Community institutions, the Member States fulfil, within the Community system, an obligation in relation to the Community, which has assumed responsibility for the due performance of the agreement. It would be unwise to attribute too much significance to the use of the term "responsibility", but the latter statement may permit the decoupling, as a matter of Community law, of the issues of Community competence and Member State obligation. If the Community can be held internationally responsible for the due performance of all the provisions of a mixed agreement, including those outside its competence, the Member States may fulfil an obligation in relation to the Community in ensuring respect for all the commitments arising from such an agreement, even those within their exclusive competence.

Such an obligation could even be asserted to exist where the respective obligations of the Community and the Member States are clearly distinguished in a mixed agreement. Third States will, for their part, have committed themselves to a single package, the advantages and disadvantages of which are unlikely to follow precisely the contours of the division of competences between the Community and the Member States (which unlikely event would permit the convenient severance of Community and Member State obligations and the termination or suspension of the third State's commitments only in respect of the latter where a Member State is in breach). Where the separate Member State and Community obligations are complementary, and third States would not have agreed to one set of commitments without agreement to the other, material breach of one of its undertakings by a Member State may lead a third State party to terminate the agreement or suspend its operation, in whole or in part, which can in turn affect the Community and its rights under the agreement (see Article 60, Vienna Convention on the Law of Treaties, 1967). This would jeopardize the attainment of the objectives of the Community Treaty, to which the conclusion of the agreement by the Community was designed to contribute. This might even occur in the case of what are known as *bi-cephalous* agreements—agreements partly within Community competence (exclusive and/or concurrent) and partly within the exclusive competence of the Member States to conclude treaties in the field of European Political Co-operation/Common Foreign and Security Policy (on which see Chapter 7 below) which may be concluded as two separate (but functionally linked) agreements. The Court of Justice opined in the *Physical Protection of Nuclear Materials Case* (Ruling 1/78, [1978] E.C.R. 2151, para. 34) that the draft Convention concerned matters, some of them within the (exclusive) competence of the Community, and some within that of the Member States, and that it could only be implemented "by means of a close association between the institutions of the Community and the Member States both in the process of negotiation and conclusion and *in the fulfilment of the obligations entered into*" (authors' italics).

Such obligations under Article 5 E.C., to the extent that they are found to exist, must affect the application of Article 29.4.5 of the Constitution. If the analysis just outlined is correct, the obligations of membership of the Communities will necessitate action by the State to ensure compliance even with those provisions of a mixed agreement which fall as a matter of Community law within the exclusive competence of the State. This could even be the case where the agreement specifically provides that the Community is not a party to the provisions in question (although it is conceded that this is a somewhat more remote prospect). This obligation would arise *irrespective* of whether such mixed agreements were deemed under Community law to be Community agreements, and thus (under European Communities Act, 1972, s.2(1)) part of the domestic law of the State under the conditions laid down in the constitutional Treaties. The obligation is conveyed into the Irish domestic legal order by the operation of Article 5 E.C., which is part of Irish law. This possible obligation may also have consequences for the status of the European Economic Area Agreement in Irish law, which is discussed below in the annotation of section 2(2) of the European Communities Act, 1972.

CHAPTER SEVEN

THE ELEVENTH AMENDMENT AND THE EUROPEAN UNION

The endorsement of the proposed Eleventh Amendment to the Constitution by the People in a referendum held on 18 June, 1992 was remarkable both for the apparent continuity that was maintained in Ireland's constitutional accommodation of European integration, and for the ambitious attitude to the results to date of that process which this approach seems to entail. The Amendment was designed in large part to enable Ireland to ratify the Maastricht Treaty on European Union. (The new Article 29.4.6 is a response to perceived constitutional problems in ratifying the unrelated Community Patent Convention, 1989; see further the discussion in Chapter 3, above.) Article 29.4.4 contains an express licence to ratify the Treaty on European Union. The new Article 29.4.5 of the Constitution is an elaboration on the former third sentence of Article 29.4.3. As has been seen, this provided for the enforcement and supremacy of Community law, and Article 29.4.5 extends its familiar formula of constitutional immunity to laws, acts and measures of the State necessitated by the obligations of membership of the Union, and to laws, acts and measures of the Union itself, and of bodies competent under the Treaties establishing the Communities. (For a comprehensive summary of the Irish ratification process, see Murphy, "Maastricht: Implementation in Ireland" (1994) 19 E.L.Rev. 94).

The European Union is founded on the European Communities, supplemented by the policies and forms of co-operation established by the Treaty on European Union (Article A, E.U.). In so far as Article 29.4.5 continues to refer to the Communities, nothing has changed. As Barrington J. pointed out in *Crotty v. An Taoiseach* [1987] I.R. 713, at 756, the Communities remain the same legal persons after amendment of the founding Treaties. The new reference to the laws, acts or measures of bodies competent under the Treaties establishing the Communities relates to the new bodies that will administer monetary union. The legislative powers of such bodies are discussed below in the annotation of the E.C. Treaty. Suffice it to say at this point that the reference to competent bodies cannot relate to some as yet undefined military wing of the Union, as was suggested in some quarters during the referendum campaign, as military activities would not come within Community competence in the new Union structure (and are probably not within Union competence at all).

The European Union is also composed of two other elements, or pillars: common foreign and security policy (C.F.S.P.) under Title V of the Treaty on European Union (Articles J–J.11); and co-operation in judicial and home affairs (C.J.H.A.) under Title VI (Articles K–K.9). As will be seen, these pillars are strongly inter-governmental in practice. While they employ the institutions of the Communities, the roles of the more supra-national institutions (the Commission, Parliament and court) are meagre relative to that of the Council. The three pillars (the Communities, C.F.S.P. and C.J.H.A.) are bound together by the Common Provisions of the Treaty on European Union, which also set out objectives for the Union, give it a single institutional framework, and provide for the exercise of attributed powers by the institutions and for respect for national identities and fundamental rights. The European Council is the sole body established by the Treaty on European Union, the other institutions being "borrowed" from the Communities. Provision is also made for amendment of all the Treaties, and for the accession of new Member States.

As a new stage in the process of creating an ever closer union among the peoples of Europe (Article A, E.U.), the insertion in the Constitution of references to the Union similar to those to the Communities might appear both natural and innocuous. In fact, it was the occasion of a minor controversy during the referendum debate. Paul Callan S.C. wrote:

> "[W]e are asked in effect whether we wish to waive the protection of the Constitution, weaken the powers of the Oireachtas and remove the jurisdiction of the courts in respect of the domestic effects of all acts of the European Union, even of those which lie outside the extended powers of the Community and the Court of Justice. ... [N]o such act, protected by the immunity, could be declared invalid by an Irish Court even if it would otherwise have been repugnant to the Constitution. ... [N]o court would be empowered to hear complaint about the effects of the laws or acts of the Union in Ireland. (Callan, "Citizens could lose right of recourse to the Courts", *The Sunday Tribune*, May 10, 1992; see also Boland, "A referendum to end others?", *The Irish Times*, May 28, 1992.")

Article 29.4.5 appears to be revolutionary in three respects.

> (i) It appears to envisage a Union which, quite outside the Community field of competence, can act in its own right. Whether the Union will be capable of such action is dependent largely on how the Treaty on European Union is applied and developed in the practice of the Member States. It is interesting that Ireland has prepared herself, constitutionally, for a relatively ambitious Union competence.
> (ii) It extends immunity from constitutional scrutiny to acts which are not subject to such scrutiny from the European Court of Justice. The jurisdiction of the European Court of Justice will not extend to the non-Community pillars of the European Union or to the Common Provisions of the Treaty (Article L, E.U.). This is in contrast to the position in respect of the Communities, where the Court of Justice has evolved an extensive human rights jurisprudence, at least in part to persuade national courts to refrain from reviewing Community acts on such grounds.
> (iii) It posits a test based on the law of the Union; but unlike the situation in respect of the Communities, the assistance of a Union body like the European Court of Justice is not available to Irish courts in interpreting that law.

These three notable features of the Amendment will now be considered in turn.

(i) UNION ACTS AND OBLIGATIONS

Article 29.4.5 of the Constitution and the European Union: Preliminary Issues

A number of issues must initially be raised about the reading of Article 29.4.5. First, the second clause of Article 29.4.5 of the Constitution appears to assume that the Union is a distinct actor with its own powers to adopt laws, acts or measures capable of having the force of law in the State, that is, that it is a legal subject independent of its Member States, with legal personality, and capacity commensurate with its attributed powers. This is not the only possible reading of the clause, as will be seen below, but it is certainly *prima facie* the most compelling one, as the clause addresses the Union in precisely the same terms as it does the Communities. The Communities have extensive legislative and other powers; and they have legal personality and any necessary capacity within the Community legal order, within the domestic legal orders of the Member States, and to a certain extent on the international plane (see, *e.g.* Articles 210, 211 E.C.). Much of the discussion that follows will concentrate on whether any such personality can be imputed to the Union.

Secondly, the apparent assumption of the legal personality of the Union need not underlie the first clause of Article 29.4.5, as the obligations of membership of the Union can be deemed to arise simply by operation of the Treaty rather than through the law-making powers of the institutions of a distinct Union. Thus, State laws, acts or measures can be justified by the necessity of adherence to the results of an inter-governmental process set out in the Treaty, just as much as by the necessity of adherence to the decisions or legislation of a supra-national entity. The question of the existence of an autonomous supra-national entity need not be addressed.

Thirdly, the role of the Irish courts in ensuring compliance by the State with many of the obligations of membership of the Communities and of the Union must be mentioned again (see also the discussion above). The courts have a variety of Community law duties: *e.g.* to enforce directly applicable and directly effective Community legislative measures; to award damages to individuals injured by non-implementation of certain Community legislative measures; to interpret national law in the light of Community legislative measures; to ensure that Community executive measures are not impeded by domestic legal obstacles.

It was suggested above that if such national judicial acts are all protected from constitutional invalidation by the first clause of Article 29.4.5, the second clause of that Article can be seen as merely supplementary to the first. In that case, and notwithstanding remaining doubts about whether "the force of law in the State" has the same meaning as the Community law concept of direct applicability, the difficult question of whether the European Union has legal personality and legal powers under the Union Treaty sufficient to adopt laws, acts or measures capable of having the force of law in the State can be avoided. As has just been pointed out, the application of the first clause of Article 29.4.5 does not require us to answer such questions about the nature of the Union.

However, until there is a judicial pronouncement on the scope and relationship of the two clauses of Article 29.4.5, it is as well to assume that the second clause may have some independent effect, and to seek to elucidate the conditions for its application. Furthermore, even the application of the first clause of Article 29.4.5 to all Union activity must require us to ascertain the extent and nature of the obligations imposed by Union membership. Thus, whatever the nature of the Union, we must know whether binding secondary obligations can be imposed pursuant to the Treaty on European Union, and whether such obligations are capable of direct applicability or other legal force in the State.

The provisions of Title VI (C.J.H.A.) and Title V (C.F.S.P.), and the Common and Final Provisions of the Treaty on European Union will now be examined, with a view to ascertaining:

(a) whether their operation can generate secondary obligations binding upon the Member States (as distinct from the primary obligation to operate the Treaty in good faith);

(b) whether such obligations are attributable to the Union as such or simply to the Member States acting in common according to procedures set out in the Treaty; and

(c) whether such obligations are capable of direct applicability or other legal force in the State.

(a) Secondary obligations under the Treaty on European Union

Co-operation in the fields of judicial and home affairs

Under Title VI, the Member States shall inform and consult one another within the Council with a view to co-ordinating their action in respect of the matters of common interest listed in Article K.1 (Article K.3.1). The Council may (a) adopt joint positions and promote any co-operation contributing to the pursuit of the objectives of the Union; (b) adopt joint action in so far as the objectives of the Union can be attained better by joint action than by the Member States acting individually; and (c) draw up conventions which it shall recommend to the Member States for adoption in accordance with their respective constitutional requirements (Article K.3.2). Measures implementing joint actions or conventions may be adopted within the Council. The Council may also decide unanimously to apply Article 100c E.C. to certain fields, and to recommend Member States to adopt that decision in accordance with their respective constitutional requirements (Article K.9).

Müller-Graff has assessed the legal effect of the exercise of the competences under Title VI ("The Legal Bases of the Third Pillar and its Position in the Framework of the Union Treaty" in Monar & Morgan eds., *The Third Pillar of the European Union* (1994) p. 21, at 33–6 (hereinafter Müller-Graff, Third Pillar)). He suggests that a joint position has to be understood as a joint declaration or recommendation without a legally binding effect on Member States (although he adds that a question of the protection of confidence in a published joint position in favour of an individual might arise in a particular case, *i.e.* an estoppel or legitimate expectation; for a possible example, see *Fakih v. Minister for Justice* [1993] 2 I.R. 406, discussed below). A joint action, he sees as being more problematic. While the same term is used in Title V, there is no provision in Title VI akin to Article J.3.4 by which joint actions commit the Member States in the positions they adopt and in the conduct of their activity. He therefore doubts the general binding quality of joint action in C.J.H.A., but says that this cannot be entirely excluded in all cases. "This will depend very much upon the concrete type of joint action and upon a concrete measure implementing joint action in a particular case. Here, it may well be that the political necessity will quickly arise to create and to establish different defined types of instruments" (Müller-Graff, Third Pillar, at 36). However, while obligations may conceivably be imposed on Member States to adhere to joint actions, it is very difficult to conceive of the development of directly applicable legal instruments under the present Treaty regime. Müller-Graff does not believe the Member States to be bound either by a decision to apply Article 100c E.C. to an area of common interest or by a convention until such time as the decision or convention is adopted in accordance with constitutional requirements.

Müller-Graff concludes that in general the measures provided for in Title VI "belong first of all to the important efforts to create acts of a politically persuasive authority for the concerted conduct of all Member States of the Union" (Third Pillar, at 36). Title VI speaks of establishing *co-operation* in this field, rather than the presumably more demanding *common policy* of Title V. While the Supreme Court majority in *Crotty v. An Taoiseach* [1987] I.R. 713 attributed considerable significance to the commitments in Title III of the Single European Act to endeavour jointly to formulate and implement a European foreign policy, it does not follow that they would have considered the State to be *bound* by common positions or joint actions adopted in European Political Co-operation, as it appears that a later expression of dissent in the Council would have robbed a common position or joint action of its status. (It was the primary obligation to endeavour to achieve a European foreign policy, rather than any secondary obligatory quality of the results of such endeavours, which concerned the Supreme Court majority.) This is a material point of distinction both from the legal order of the Communities, and from the C.F.S.P. regime (at least in respect of joint actions). The position in C.J.H.A. appears much more like that in E.P.C. If States are free, after the adoption of a position or action, to resile from it simply by indicating the withdrawal of their consent, no real obligation could be said to have arisen from which the State could not lawfully escape merely by uttering *non placet*. On the other hand, Article A, E.U. states that the task of the Union shall be to organise relations between the Member States and between their peoples in a manner demonstrating consistency and solidarity. An implied obligation of solidarity like that set out expressly in Article 5 E.C. might be seen to bind the State to positions undertaken in the Council if such had been deemed necessary to the achievement of the objectives of the Union (and where, in the case of joint action, it has been decided by the Council that those objectives can be attained better by such action than by the Member States acting individually).

Such an obligation of solidarity might also be seen to oblige Member States to adopt conventions drawn up under Article K.3.2(c), as Temple Lang suggested was the case under Article 5 E.C. in respect of the Patent Convention. It seems unlikely that an Irish court would take this view, however, as the Treaty implies a formal element of choice, on foot of the Council's recommendation, in advance of adoption of a convention under Title V. It may seem futile to debate whether the Member States acting unanimously in Council can oblige the Member States severally to take a particular action, but it must be remembered that Member State institutions other than the executive (which is represented in Council) may have interests and competences which would be prejudiced if the distinction were not maintained (see, *e.g.* the powers of the Dáil in respect of treaties imposing a charge on public funds, in Article 29.5.2 of the Constitution). Thus, the courts, if alerted, could very possibly seek at the suit of a concerned party prevent the State from acceding to such an international commitment if it was inconsistent with domestic constitutional values, as happened in *Crotty* in respect of the Single European Act.

Does Union law, as distinct from general international law, require the observance of such conventions once they came into force? As has been seen, the Irish courts are willing to review the constitutionality of State accession to treaties even after ratification (*McGimpsey v. Ireland* [1990] 1 IR 110). Such conventions are quite unlike amendments to the Community Treaties, which after being ratified become part of the superstructure of the Community itself, and thus became an element of the obligations of membership inseparable from those which had existed before. They would be separate treaties negotiated under the aegis of the Union, not unlike the Patent Convention or a convention under Article 220 E.C. (to which reference is made in Article K.3.2(c)). Observance *after ratification* of conventions promoted by the Union might nonetheless be considered to be necessitated by the obligations of membership, as a matter of good faith or solidarity. Unfortunately, here, as in a number of other areas, the exclusion of the jurisdiction of the Court of Justice ensures that the requirements of the Union Treaty in this respect can never definitively be stated. In the alternative, an Irish court could take the position that an Article K.3.2(c) convention was within the essential scope and objectives of the E.U. Treaty, and was thus protected by the licence to join the Union under Article 29.4.4, even if compliance with the Convention was not seen as necessitated by the obligations of Union membership. However, the logical problem with this approach has already been noted above in respect of conventions under Article 220 E.C.

Common Foreign and Security Policy

Under Title V, the Union and the Member States shall define and implement a common foreign and security policy (Article J.1.1). The Council shall take the decisions necessary for defining and implementing the common foreign and security policy on the basis of the general guidelines adopted by the European Council (Article J.8.1-2). The Union shall pursue the objectives set out in Article J.1.2 by (i) establishing systematic co-operation between Member States in the conduct of policy, in accordance with Article J.2; and (ii) by gradually implementing joint action, in accordance with Article J.3 (Article J.1.3). Co-operation under Article J.2 can lead to the definition by the Council of a common position, to which Member States shall ensure that their national policies conform (Article J.2.3). When the Council decides to implement joint action, it shall lay down the specific scope, the Union's general and specific objectives, if necessary its duration, and the means, procedures and conditions for its implementation (Article J.3.1); joint actions shall commit the Member States in the positions they adopt and in the conduct of their activity (Article J.3.4); and as long as the Council has not acted, the joint action shall stand (Article J.3.3).

For practical purposes, implementation of the policy will be secured in large part through the separate foreign and security policy apparatus of the Member States: through participation in international organisations and conferences (Article J.5.4); through their diplomatic and consular missions (Article J.6); through the national transposition of Council decisions (Article J.3.5); and more generally in their national policies (Article J.2.2) and in the positions they adopt and in the conduct of their activity (Article J.3.4). Operational expenditure may be charged either to the Member States or to the budget of the European Communities (Article J.11). It is this combination of Union and Member State roles that must underlie the statement in Article J.1 that *the Union and its Member States* shall define and implement a common foreign and security policy.

It is clear that measures adopted by the Council in C.F.S.P. can bind the Member States (Everling "Reflections on the Structure of the European Union" (1992) 29 C.M.L.Rev. 1053, at 1061 (hereinafter Everling, Structure)). Eaton has remarked that "[f]rom the legal point of view, the most obvious and significant change [from the S.E.A.] is from the language of endeavour, in E.P.C., to the language of obligation, in C.F.S.P." ("Common Foreign and Security Policy" in O'Keeffe & Twomey eds., *Legal Issues of the Maastricht Treaty* (1994) p. 215, at 220 (hereinafter Eaton, C.F.S.P.)). Member States shall ensure that their national policies conform to the common positions defined by the Council (Article J.2.2), and joint actions commit the Member States in the positions they adopt and in the conduct of their activity (Article J.3.4). Furthermore, as long as the Council has not acted, a joint action shall stand (Article J.3.3). This means that Member States cannot revoke a joint action at pleasure, although they may take necessary measures as a matter of urgency in cases of imperative need, having regard to the general objectives of the joint action (Article J.3.6). In order to reverse or abandon a joint action, a further unanimous decision of the Council is required. A desire to emphasise the obligatory nature of common positions and joint actions is evident in the terminology used by the Council; they are in both cases described as decisions of the Council, and listed as such in series L of the *Official Journal*.

The power of the Council in both pillars to charge the operational expenditure of the Union to the Member States is also probably obligatory in nature (see Articles J.11.2; K.8.2 E.U.). No condition is prescribed for compliance with national constitutional requirements regarding expenditure of public funds, a point of contrast both with the preservation of Member State discretion in Articles K.3.2(c) and K.9, and with the subjection to the Community budgetary procedure of a decision under Articles J.11.2 and K.8.2 to charge Union operational expenditure to the Communities. If operational expenditure in C.F.S.P. or C.J.H.A. were classified as non-compulsory, the Parliament could exercise considerable influence over the non-Community pillars through the power of the purse, which power would be denied to national parliaments by the apparently compulsory quality of a decision to distribute such costs among the Member States. (See Neuwahl, "Foreign and Security Policy and the Implementation of the Requirement of 'Consistency' under the Treaty on European Union" in O'Keeffe & Twomey eds., *Legal Issues of the Maastricht Treaty* (1994) p. 227, at 243; and Jacobs, Corbett &

Shackleton, *The European Parliament* (2nd. ed., 1992), pp. 213 *et seq.*) The Council has prepared guidelines on the financing of C.F.S.P., setting out a G.N.P. scale for Member State funding of operational expenditure (where applicable), and recommending talks between the Presidents of the Council and of the European parliament on Community financing of such expenditure (E.U. Bull. 6-94, 1.3.2).

The Common and Final Provisions

The Common Provisions of the E.U. Treaty disclose little that could be construed as the legal basis for binding secondary measures. Two provisions do bear further consideration, however: Articles F(3) and D, E.U.

Article F(3) E.U. states that "[t]he Union shall provide itself with the means necessary to attain its objectives and carry through its policies". In *Brunner* [1994] 1 C.M.L.R. 57, at 94–97, the *Bundesverfassungsgericht* considered the allegation that Article F(3) empowered the Union to provide itself, by its own authority, with the legislative and other means for the fulfilment of its objectives. It rejected this argument, *inter alia* because:

—it did not believe that the Union was a legal person or the holder of its own powers;

—this would breach the principle of specific empowerment or attributed competence which had marked the European integration process from the outset;

—it would contradict the exclusion by Article M, E.U. of any implied amendment of the Community Treaties;

—it would be inconsistent with the specific scheme of the Union Treaty, in which certain matters had been intentionally excluded from the supranational decision-making structure; and

—Article F(3) lacked the necessary procedural provisions allocating the alleged power to specific institutions and making it subject to specified voting requirements and decision-making procedures, including provision for the participation of other institutions. With the exception of the finding in respect of legal personality (as it will be considered further below), this reasoning can be immediately accepted as compelling. It does not appear that unenumerated powers to generate secondary obligations can arise under Article F(3), E.U.

Article D states that "[t]he European Council shall provide the Union with the necessary impetus for its development and shall define the general political guidelines thereof". Everling has argued that guidelines of the European Council are not decisions in the sense of the E.C. Treaty and (with the exception of recommendations on economic policies under Article 103(2) E.C.) cannot bind organs that are independent under Community law, such as follows from the nature of the European Parliament and is explicitly stipulated for the Commission in Article 157(2) E.C. and for the Court of Justice in Article 167 E.C. While the Council probably is not formally bound either, its composition suggests that in practice it will always concur with the European Council (Everling, Structure, at 1062). It does appear, on the other hand, that the Council is bound by European Council decisions under Articles J.3 and J.8 E.U. (Curtin & van Ooik, "Denmark and the Edinburgh Summit: Maastricht without Tears" in O'Keeffe & Twomey eds., *Legal Issues of the Maastricht Treaty* (1994) p. 349, at 355 (hereinafter Curtin & van Ooik, Edinburgh)), and this may also extend by implication to C.J.H.A. (Everling, Structure, at 1061–2).

It was not generally accepted prior to the coming into force of the Maastricht Treaty that the European Council summit meetings could result in binding commitments. Since the establishment of the Union, it is still open to question whether the European Council can even be described as an institution, in the absence of a provision describing it as such (*cf.* Article 4 E.C.), and in the light of its evasive language ("The European Council *shall bring together* the Heads of State or Government of the Member States and the President of the Commission"; *cf.* Article 146 E.C.). Nor is there anything in Article D, E.U. to suggest that legal obligations can result from the European Council's deliberations otherwise than through the operation of Titles V and VI, or through action within their competences by the Communities. This conclusion is drawn from the wording of Article D, E.U., which speaks of the European Council setting *political* guidelines for the Union. It is bolstered by the numerous reasons given by the *Bundesverfassungsgericht* for rejecting Article F(3) E.U. as a legal basis for competences other than those specified elsewhere in the constitutional Treaties, all of which apply equally in this instance.

The European Council summit in Edinburgh in December 1992 resulted in an exceptional document being included in its conclusions (see generally Curtin & van Ooik, Edinburgh; Howarth "The Compromise on Denmark and the Treaty on European Union: A Legal and Political Analysis" (1994) 31 C.M.L.Rev. 765). In response to the initial rejection of ratification of the Maastricht Treaty in the Danish referendum in June of that year, the European Council sought to address the voters' concerns, *inter alia*, in a "Decision of the Heads of State and Government, meeting within the European Council, concerning certain problems raised by Denmark on the Treaty on European Union", accompanied by a number of declarations of the European Council, and by further Danish unilateral declarations ([1992] O.J. C348). It appears from its title (a "decision") and content (see section E), and from the clearly indicated intentions of the Member States, that it is meant to be legally binding (Curtin & van Ooik, Edinburgh, at 352). However, it does not purport to be a decision of the European Council as such, but of the Heads of State and Government, using the summit meeting as a convenient platform to adopt an international agreement concluded in simplified form (Curtin, Edinburgh, at 355–6). Curtin and van Ooik compare it to decisions of the representatives of the Member States taken within the Council (discussed further below). The impression that the decision is not an act of the European Council is reinforced by the exclusion of the President of the Commission.

The decision addresses citizenship, economic and monetary union, defence policy and justice and home affairs. Curtin and van Ooik argue convincingly (Edinburgh, at 358–64) that it does not alter the rights and obligations of Denmark under the E.U. Treaty in any of these areas, although it emphasises certain matters that are clear from the Treaty (*e.g.* that Union citizenship does not affect Danish nationality law), clarifies others that were possibly less clear (*e.g.* that nothing in the Treaty commits Denmark to become a member of the Western European Union), and notes the exercise by Denmark of certain rights under the Treaty (to opt out of the third stage of E.M.U.). The decision is stated to be in conformity with the Treaty on European Union, and of course would not have been competent to amend that Treaty. It seems that the Member States intended the decision to constitute a type of "implementation agreement" of the Treaty, which would not require further ratification (Curtin & van Ooik, Edinburgh, at 357).

Nonetheless, the decision purports to be a legally binding "interpretation" of provisions of the E.U. Treaty under public international law (Curtin & van Ooik, Edinburgh, at 365). It is difficult to say whether it therefore creates obligations arising from membership of the Union. One must first distinguish between the Community and non-Community aspects of the decision. In so far as it addresses provisions of the European Community Treaty (on citizenship, and on economic and monetary union), the decision in the European Council may influence the interpretation of those provisions by the European Court of Justice in the same way as any interpretative declaration (see further the discussion in Chapter 9 below of interpretative declarations). However, the adoption of a particular interpretative stance by the Member States in the form of a "decision" cannot displace the Court of Justice from its ultimate monopoly of interpretative authority, nor can it cause a decision by that Court on the interpretation of the European Community Treaty to be reversed. It could not amend that Treaty otherwise than in accordance with the then requirements of Article 236 E.E.C. (see now Article N, E.U.). The purportedly *binding* quality of the decision, with regard to the European Community Treaty, is therefore either superfluous (where the decision conforms to the opinion of the Court of Justice) or invalid (where it does not).

The position is very different outside the Community pillar. Here the interpretation of the Treaty by the Court of Justice is largely excluded (see Article L, E.U.). In the absence of recourse to the International Court of Justice (which option is resisted by some commentators in respect of an integration treaty; see *e.g.* Everling, Structure, at 1064), no body has exclusive authority to interpret and enforce the Treaty (although see Article J.1.4 on the role of the Council in C.F.S.P.). It is remarked below that this raises the possibility of competing interpretations of the Treaty by national courts. It also permits the Member States to enter the interpretative field in a superior position. As Curtin and van Ooik suggest (Edinburgh, at 365), the Edinburgh decision does indeed aggravate problems of democratic accountability and of separation of powers. Parliamentary and judicial input is excluded. Nonetheless, one advantage of such "binding" interpretative decisions is that they can maintain a uniform approach to the E.U. Treaty. Of course, such interpretations may be driven more by political factors than by considerations of a judicial character, and the extension of the jurisdiction of the Court of Justice must constitute the better response to the problem of incoherence in the application of the Treaty. In the meantime, however, international agreements by the Member States, in the European Council or elsewhere, on the interpretation of the Treaty on European Union may be deemed to be authoritative statements of the obligations of the Member States in the absence of evidence of bad faith or of patent inconsistency with the terms of the Treaty. Such decisions would not constitute secondary obligations so much as amplifications of the primary obligations imposed by Union membership, but could fall within the terms of the first clause of Article 29.4.5 for all that.

Nothing in the Final Provisions of the E.U. Treaty appears to provide a legal basis for the imposition of secondary legal obligations on the Member States of the Union. There is scope for alteration of their primary obligations. Article N, E.U. sets out the procedure for the adoption of further amendments to the constitutional Treaties, and Article O, E.U. establishes the conditions for admission of new Member States. Article O illustrates the difficulty of insulating the inter-governmental pillars of the Union from the supra-national qualities of the Communities on which the Union is founded. Accession to the Union and to the Communities is simultaneous, and the continuation of the procedure formerly prescribed by Article 237 EEC (as amended by the Single European Act) gives the European Parliament control of access by other States to the activities of C.F.S.P. and C.J.H.A. as well as to the Communities. This negative power, entrusted to a supra-national institution which is independent of the Member States, should be borne in mind when the legal nature of the Union is considered below.

As asserted above, observance of Treaty amendments and of the legal consequences of new accessions is an obligation of membership of the Communities and of the Union once the relevant agreements enter into force. The Supreme Court made clear in *Crotty* that certain proposed amendments to the constitutional Treaties could be in excess of the constitutional licence granted to join the Communities (and by extension, the Union), and that such proposed amendments might therefore be unconstitutional. However, properly ratified Treaty amendments and accessions will have an immediate effect in the Community legal order in so far as they affect it, so that State measures necessitated by any consequent obligations of membership of the Communities will have constitutional immunity. Nevertheless, as the obligatory quality of properly ratified Treaty amendments and accessions emerges in the first instance from Articles N and O, E.U., it may be as well that the constitutional protection of State measures extends to those necessitated by the obligations of membership of the Union as well as of the Communities. For example, these Articles prescribe that such changes in the legal order of the Communities and the Union be ratified by the Member States in accordance with their respective constitutional requirements. The obligation (discussed above) to comply with the interpretation of the Court of Justice of the phrase "constitutional requirements" therefore arises under the Union Treaty rather than under any of the Community Treaties. A decision of the Court of Justice interpreting Articles N or O, E.U. may constitute an act of the Union for the purposes of the second clause of Article 29.4.5 of the Constitution. The same may be true of a decision of the Council under Article O, E.U.

(b) Acts of the Union or of the Member States in Common?

Particular attention must be paid to the varying attribution of competence for measures or activities in the E.U. Treaty to the Council, the Union, the Member States, or the Union and the Member States. The distinction in practice between the Member States and the institutions of the Union also bears close scrutiny. As has already been stated, the pillars established by Title V and Title VI, E.U. are highly inter-governmental. Pure inter-governmentalism is maintained in some respects, in that the Member States as such are expressly stated to perform certain functions, either in their domestic jurisdictions, *e.g.* the observance of their respective constitutional requirements in the adoption of conventions (Article K.3.2(c)); or *within* the Council, *e.g.* informing and consulting each other on foreign and security policy (Article J.2.1) or with a view to co-ordinating action in the fields of judicial and home affairs (Article K.3.1), or adoption of implementing measures under Article K.3.2(c) conventions. The latter type of Member State action is reminiscent of discussion of E.P.C. matters "on the occasion of meetings of the Council of the European Communities" (Article 30(3)(a), S.E.A.), and of the adoption of acts of the representatives of the Member States *meeting within the Council* in respect of matters outside E.C. competence (see Kapteyn & Verloren van Themaat, *Introduction to the Law of the European Communities* (1990), pp. 204–8), which activities remain attributable to the Member States. (See also the discussion above of decisions in the European Council; see further Cases 181 and 248/91 *Parliament v. Council and Commission* [1993] I E.C.R. 3685 on the difficulty in separating Community acts from certain acts of the Member States acting in common.)

In other instances, it is the Council as such which acts under the Union Treaty. Muller-Graff contrasts Titles V and VI, in that the provisions of the latter do not even mention the Union as a separate acting subject in areas within C.J.H.A. (Third Pillar, at 33). But even in C.J.H.A., the role given to the Council is prominent. Under Title V, the Council adopts common positions, and decides on the principle and the modalities of joint action (Articles J.2.2; J.3.1) and the Council is responsible for ensuring that the Member States comply with their commitment to support the Union's external and security policy in a spirit of loyalty and mutual solidarity (Article J.1.4); under Title VI, the Council adopts joint positions and joint actions, and appears to adopt measures implementing joint action (Article K.3.2 (a)–(b)). In both pillars, the Council allocates operational expenditure to the budget of the Communities or among the Member States (Articles J.11.2; K.8.2).

However, when Member States have a right of initiative, and voting by unanimity is the norm, the Council is in practical terms a vehicle of inter-governmentalism. Even in the Community context, where the Commission has sole right of initiative, and much voting is other than by unanimity, Advocate General Dutheillet de Lamothe remarked on the perennial difficulty in distinguishing the Council's dual functions as Community institution and as forum for the expression of the national concerns of the Member States (Case 22/70, *Commission v. Council (E.R.T.A.)* [1971] E.C.R. 263, at 297–8). This problem is exacerbated in the other Union pillars.

Under Community law, even acts of the Council which require unanimity are not attributable to the Member States, but to an institution of a distinct Community. Similarly, Article E, E.U. indicates that the Council as such exercises such powers as are provided for it by the provisions of the E.U. Treaty. If the measures ascribed to the Council are capable of binding the Member States, are binding measures adopted by the Council therefore Union measures, as opposed to measures simply adopted in common by the Member States, like simplified separate treaties?

The question whether there is a distinct Union decision-making power, exercised through the Council, can be restated in terms of legal personality and legal capacity. Does the Union have legal personality separate from its Member States *for the purpose of making decisions binding upon them*? The term "legal personality" must be used with great caution, because of its varying meaning. The International Court of Justice established in the *Reparations for Injuries Case* [1949] I.C.J. Rep. 174, at 180 that the legal rights and duties of an international organisation must depend on its purposes and functions, as specified or implied in its constituent documents and developed in practice. Thus, the silence of the Charter of the United Nations Organisation on international legal personality was not determinative. The question of international capacity could only be answered by analysis of its functions, and it was concluded that the United Nations needed international personality because of its dealings with States. In the absence of such legal personality in the general international order, or even in international relations with smaller groups of third States, the structure and functions of an organisation may nonetheless cause acts to be imputed to it as a distinct entity in its relations with its Member States.

Commentators are united in concluding that the European Union does not have international legal personality or capacity relative to third States or the international community in general. The Council does not appear to have competence under Titles V or VI, E.U. to adopt any legal act (most notably a treaty) which could be attributed *by third States* to the Union rather than to the Member States acting in common. Depending on the subject matter, treaty-making is undertaken by the European Community (under Article 228a E.C.) or by the Member States (see Everling, Structure, at 1061; Curtin, Union, at 27; Eaton, "Common Foreign and Security Policy" in O'Keeffe & Twomey eds., *Legal Issues of the Maastricht Treaty* (1994) p. 215, at 224 (hereinafter Eaton, C.F.S.P.); Neuwahl, "Foreign and Security Policy and the Implementation of the Requirement of 'Consistency' under the Treaty on European Union" in O'Keeffe & Twomey eds., *Legal Issues of the Maastricht Treaty* (1994) p. 227, at 237; Dehousse, "From Community to Union" in Dehousse ed., *Europe after Maastricht: An Ever Closer Union?* (1994) p. 5, at 8 (hereinafter Dehousse, Union)). One could suggest very tentatively that statements by the Presidency expressing the position of the Union pursuant to Article J.5.2 could in very limited circumstances be capable of having legal effects (see the *Eastern Greenland Case* [1933] P.C.I.J. Series A/B, No. 53; the *North Sea Continental Shelf Case* [1969] I.C.J. Rep. 4, at 25; the *Nuclear Tests Case (Australia v. France)* [1974] I.C.J. Rep. 253, at 267–71). Although its functions are performed by a particular Member State, the Presidency is an office of the Council (Article 146 E.C.). However, as the Presidency is unlikely to be represented as having the authority legally to bind the Member States by such statements, this issue is unlikely to arise.

Timmermans has pointed out some of the difficulties with the absence of international legal personality (*L'Union Européenne après Maastricht* (1992), p. 51; trans. Dehousse, Union, at 8–9): "[I]magine that damages are caused by an observer mission sent to a third country by some Member States, on the basis of a decision of the Council of Ministers of the E.C., taken within the framework of C.F.S.P. but financed in part by the Community budget. Who would be internationally responsible?" A less complex example is afforded by the possibility of injury being incurred or caused by a member of a Commission Delegation in a third country while acting pursuant to Article J.6 E.U. (See below on the privileges and immunities in the territory of the Member States of Community servants acting on Union business.)

Commentators have tended to combine their views excluding the international legal personality of the Union relative to third countries with the conclusion that the Union has no legal personality at all, even apparently within the limited international legal order—the Union legal order—created among the Member States by the Maastricht Treaty (Everling, Structure, at 1061; Curtin, Union, at 27; Eaton, C.F.S.P., at 224). However, the terms of the Treaty are rather ambivalent. On the one hand, no provision expressly confers legal personality. This can be contrasted with the European Community Treaty (Article 210), and the European Parliament's draft Union Treaty of 1984 (Article 6) and tentative draft Union Constitution of 1994 (Article 1.3). On the other hand, the parties are referred to throughout (save in Article A) as Member States, rather than as High Contracting Parties as in Title III, S.E.A. Article C states that the Union shall be served by "a single institutional framework". Article F reinforces the impression of juristic identity: "[t]he Union shall respect the national identities of its Member States ...; [t]he Union shall respect fundamental rights ...; [t]he Union shall provide itself with the means necessary to attain its objectives and carry through its policies". Provision is made for a citizenship of the Union, although this is done, significantly, in the E.C. Treaty (Articles 8-8e).

Article A presents a picture of a Union which may have some institutional identity *vis-a-vis* its Member States (though not *erga omnes*). The first sentence employs a formula also used in Article 1 E.C.:

> "By this Treaty, the High Contracting Parties establish among themselves a European Union .... The Union shall be founded on the European Communities, supplemented by the policies and forms of co-operation established by this Treaty. Its task shall be to organise ... relations between the Member States and between their peoples."

Everling remarks that while at first sight Article A gives the impression that a new entity is created, further analysis shows it simply to be an intermediate phase in the longer-term *process* of European integration, "the expression of a *political* unity of which the form and shape are to a large extent open", which will crystallise only gradually (Everling, Structure, at 1059–60). He continues (at 1063): "It can be understood as an organisational framework within which the legal persons of the Communities and the fields of co-operation of the C.F.S.P. and the C.J.H.A. are comprehended. Together with these members, it forms a unified integrative body of singular nature, aiming at an ever closer unity." Curtin describes the Union as only "a notional entity", "a *trompe l'oeil*" (Curtin, Union, at 24). Eaton states: "The Union will be *sui generis* .... It can best be described as an association of Member States which, for certain purposes and in certain ways described in the Treaty, act in common. It acts through its components, namely the Community on the one hand and the Member States acting inter-governmentally ... on the other."

Eaton gives three reasons why the Union should not be considered to have legal personality:

(i) there is no express provision for it;

(ii) functions that would require legal personality are to be exercised by the Community, *e.g.* treaty-making (where it is within E.C. competence) or development of citizenship rights (which point is also made in Curtin, Union, at 27); and

(iii) the unpublished *travaux préparatoires* contain statements by the Dutch Presidency and by the Commission and Council Legal Services that the Treaty would not confer legal personality (Eaton, C.F.S.P., at 224).

However, if the functional approach to international legal personality adopted by the International Court of Justice can be extended (as logically it can) to the issue of legal personality relative to the Member States of an international organisation, one must at least question the *certitude* with which this conclusion is pronounced. One cannot ignore the varying reference to acts of the Council and activities within the Council, in a Treaty which draws on a constitutional tradition in which the distinction between these terms is highly significant.

Article C, E.U. states that "[t]he Union shall be served by a single institutional framework" that shall respect and build upon the *acquis communautaire*. Article E, E.U. states that "[t]he European Parliament, the Council, the Commission and the Court of Justice shall exercise their powers under the conditions and for the purposes provided for, on the one hand, by the provisions of the [Community] Treaties ... and, on the other hand, by the other provisions of this [Union] Treaty". Article C has been rightly criticised, as being more "an institutional *géometrie variable*' than a single framework" (Editorial, "Post-Maastricht" (1992) 29 C.M.L.Rev. 199, at 202), as "a hybrid construction that is more singular than single" (Wellenstein, "Unity, Community, Union—What's in a Name?" (1992) 29 C.M.L.Rev. 205, at 209 (hereinafter Wellenstein, Unity)), as "mere lip-service to an ideal" (Curtin, Union, at 28). Both Curtin and Everling speak quite dismissively of the Community institutions being "borrowed" by the Union (Curtin, Union, at 27; Everling, Structure, at 1061). It is true that the Council is established not by the Union Treaty, but by Article 1 of the Merger Treaty, as the Council of the European Communities. It has since been re-named the Council of the European Union (Council Decision 93/591 of November 8, 1993, [1993] O.J. L281/18), but that in itself, as a secondary measure, cannot determine conclusively the interpretation of the primary Treaty texts: if the instant discussion demonstrates anything, it is that titles need not dictate the nature of their bearers (see Wellenstein, Unity). Curtin continues (Union, at 28):

> "[The 'single institutional framework'] is single only in the sense that the intergovernmental pillars do not have institutions of their own. The only truly Union institution is the European Council. Apart from that some of the E.C. institutions (Council, Commission, Parliament but, explicitly, not the Court of Justice) have been generously put at the disposal of the Union but in a manner different from their classic Treaty functions."

Everling states that in the two non-Community pillars, "the institutions act on the whole as instruments of inter-governmental co-operation" (Structure, at 1061). One might add to these perfectly justifiable criticisms that the reference to a single institutional *framework* may suggest that the Council in particular is simply a *forum* for the exercise of sovereign power by the Member States rather than the *institution* of the Union to which such powers have been transferred by the Member States. Furthermore, it is difficult in practice to distinguish the Council, released from the considerable constraints imposed in the Community context by its own voting rules and by the powers of the other institutions, from the Member States meeting within or on the

occasion of meetings of the Council (although that will be true of any international organisation that operates on the basis of unanimity). Nonetheless,
that distinction is made in the Treaty itself, representing a development from
the terms of Title III of the Single European Act.

Because the Union acts through institutions "borrowed" from the Communities, does this mean that the Union does not need for the performance
of its functions a legal personality supplementary to that of the Communities
on which it is founded? Can the Union be a parasite on the legal personality
and capacity of the Communities? A positive response to this question is
prompted by Eaton's observation (quoted above; C.F.S.P. at 224) that everything that would require personality is done through the Community. It is
true that the Communities provide for the administrative expenditure of the
Union, and may provide for its operational expenditure (Articles J.11.2,
K.8.2 E.U.), and enjoy legal capacity under the laws of the Member States,
e.g. to acquire or dispose of movable and immovable property which is at the
disposal of the institutions through which both the Union and the Communities act.

The matter of privileges and immunities raises more difficult questions.
The International Court of Justice attached significance in the *Reparations
Case* to the extension of privileges and immunities in the territory of the
Member States to the United Nations Organisation and to its officials (Article 105, United Nations Charter) in reaching the conclusion "that the Organisation has the capacity to bring an international claim against one of its
Members which has caused injury to it by a breach of its international obligations towards it.... The obligations entered into by States to enable the
agents of the Organisation to perform their duties are undertaken not in the
interest of the agents, but in that of the Organisation. When it claims redress
for a breach of these obligations, the Organisation is invoking its own right,
the right that the obligations due to it should be respected" ([1949] I.C.J.
Rep. 174, at 180, 182). Article 12 of the Protocol on the Privileges and Immunities of the European Communities, 1965, states that "[i]n the territory of
each Member State and whatever their nationality, officials and other servants of the Communities shall ... be immune from legal proceedings in
respect of acts performed by them in their official capacity, including their
words spoken or written". A Council or Commission official (a servant of the
Communities) whom it is sought to sue in respect of acts performed consequent on the operation of the non-Community pillars of the Union can claim
to have been acting in an official capacity, but that capacity does not arise
under the Community Treaties. That is clear both from the limited attribution of competences to the Communities, and from the terms of Article E,
E.U. It arises from the activities of the institutions as organs of the Union. If
immunity under the domestic law of the Member States were to be extended
to a Community official in such circumstances, it must surely arise from the
capacity of the Union under the Union legal order. Similarly, if an injury
were done to an official in such circumstances, any claim for reparations can
only arise in respect of the Union. It is virtually impossible to say how these
issues will be dealt with if they arise, but greater consequences than have
been predicted by others may follow from the common institutional framework of the Union.

It has been attempted to state as fairly as possible the competing evidence
for and against a Union personality distinct from that of the Member States
under the Union legal order. An argument can now be ventured on the following lines. The Council can be deemed to be the Council of the Union
pursuant to Articles C and E, E.U. and because it is granted powers in Titles
V and VI, E.U. which are clearly outside the competences of the European
Communities. Measures adopted by the Council are therefore attributable
to the Union as such. Officials of the institutions act under the aegis of the
Union when they perform their duties under these Titles. The Union there-

fore has legal personality, relative to its Member States, and capacity sufficient for the exercise of its powers, and deriving from their existence. That that personality is very limited follows from the very limited nature of the powers of the Council. It is essential that the argument just made should not be overstated. It does not follow from the attribution to the Union of personality commensurate with limited competence to make decisions binding on the Member States that it also has the other attributes of legal personality that are available to international organisations. The International Court of Justice indicated in the *Reparations Case* that there can be varying degrees of legal personality: "The subjects of the law in any legal system are not necessarily identical in their nature or extent of their rights, and their nature depends on the needs of the [international] Community" ([1949] I.C.J. Rep. 174, at 178). Many such rights are consequent upon more general international legal personality, and therefore are not relevant in this instance (see, *e.g.* Brownlie, *Principles of Public International Law* (4th ed. 1990) pp. 683–9). Legal personality within the domestic legal order of the Member States does not arise automatically. The rights to acquire or to dispose of property or to be a party to legal proceedings will be contingent on whether these rights are necessary to enable the Union effectively to discharge the functions entrusted to it by the Member States (see *Reparations for Injuries* [1949] I.C.J. Rep. 174, at 179; *cf.* the express grant of such rights in Article 211 E.C.).

It may seem futile to seek to establish whether the Union has legal personality so limited (to the Union legal order) that it cannot be a legal subject in either the general international legal order nor in the domestic legal orders of its Member States. The question is important, however, if the Union is capable of generating within the legal regime established by its founding Treaty measures having some legal force within the domestic legal order of a Member State that recognises in its Constitution the primacy of such measures. The enquiry is necessary for the limited domestic purpose of ascertaining the meaning and scope of the terms of Article 29.4.5 of the Constitution of Ireland.

It must be stressed that the argument for the limited legal personality of the Union within the legal order established by the Maastricht Treaty is made very tentatively, merely as a possible alternative to an orthodoxy that is not unpersuasive, and on the basis of often opaque Treaty provisions adopted in order to satisfy the competing objects of the Member States in the Inter-Governmental Conference. It is conceded that the argument is highly formalist, despite its functionalist premise, and that in real terms, there may be little to distinguish the Council of Titles V and VI, E.U. from a diplomatic conference. A *de minimis* requirement that the institutions of an international organisation should have some degree of independence of their Member States may preclude reliance on the distinction between acts of and within the Council. Yet if we ask whether the activities of C.F.S.P. and C.J.H.A. constitute simply a highly structured form of international relations, it is difficult to concur. Some qualitative change appears to have occurred in the relations of the Member States, now organised by the Union, which prevents one from dismissing the role of the Council in the Union as a mere legal fiction. The limited scope for adoption of certain implementing measures by the Council other than by unanimity reinforces this impression (see Articles J.3.2; K.3.2(b); see also Article K.3.2(c), although this provides for a two-thirds majority of Member States acting *within* the Council). Furthermore, the role of the European Parliament in the admission of new Member States to the Union distinguishes the Union from any other process of co-operation and common decision-making in which the Member States might become involved, no matter how similarly structured to C.F.S.P. and C.J.H.A.

The views of other academic commentators have been reinforced by the decision of the *Bundesverfassungsgericht* in *Brunner* [1994] 1 C.M.L.R. 57. The court opined that the E.U. Treaty established "a federation of States (*Staatenverbund*) for the purpose of realising an ever closer union of the peoples of Europe (organised as States) and not a State based on the people of one European nation" [1994] 1 C.M.L.R. 57, at 89. The powers of the Union as such derived from the Communities; all other powers, it implied, were retained by the Member States: "The competences and powers which are granted to the European Union and the Communities belonging to it remain essentially the activities of an economic union in so far as they are exercised through the implementation of sovereign rights.... Outside the European Communities, co-operation stays on an inter-governmental basis." [1994] 1 C.M.L.R. 57, at 90–91. The court later addressed directly the question of legal personality [1994] 1 C.M.L.R. 57, at 94–5:

> "[T]he Union Treaty at no point gives any evidence of an agreed intention of the Contracting Parties to establish an independent legal subject through the Union, which would be the holder of its own powers. In the view of the Federal Government the Union possesses no separate legal personality either in relation to the European Communities or to the Member States. That view was confirmed by Director-General Dewost [of the Commission Legal Service] in the oral hearing.... [T]he Union Treaty does not understand the Union here as being an independent legal subject, but as the designation for the Member States acting jointly; it is they who provide the Union with objectives and means under the Treaty."

As will be discussed further below, the consequence of Article L, E.U. is that there is no supra-national court with jurisdiction to contradict the interpretation by the *Bundesverfassungsgericht* of the terms of the E.U. Treaty. The national courts of other Member States remain free to agree or disagree, of course, for the purpose of their own legal systems; but the combination of the *travaux préparatoires* (if made available) and the views of academic commentators, the Commission and Council Legal Services, and the *Bundesverfassungsgericht* must be very persuasive for an Irish court.

As has already been stated, the wording of the second clause of Article 29.4.5 of the Constitution suggests a different approach. Nonetheless, a secondary reading of the clause is possible, which would be consistent with the judicial, academic and institutional views just cited. The Union could be construed, not as a distinct legal person as is the case with the Communities, but as the Member States acting in common in the decision-making forum prescribed by the E.U. Treaty. The second clause of Article 29.4.5 could be deemed to refer to the Union as a *process*, not an entity (see Everling, Structure, at 1059–60). The *Bundesverfassungsgericht* could speak, for example, of "[t]he functions of the European Union and the powers granted for their implementation", and state that "the Union carries out sovereign tasks and exercises sovereign powers", while holding that "the Union Treaty does not understand the Union as being an independent legal subject, but as the designation for the Member States acting jointly" [1994] 1 C.M.L.R. 57, at 84, 86 and 94–5 respectively. What then would be the possible effect of the second clause of Article 29.4.5?

One question that must arise in such a situation is whether acts expressly attributed to the Member States, to be taken *within* the Council, are to be treated as acts of the Union (as process) as well as acts attributed by the Union Treaty to the Council itself. In *Brunner*, the *Bundesverfassungsgericht* spoke of "measures of the European Union" only in relation to decisions of the Council, under Articles J.2.2, J.3, J.8.2, K.3.2(a)-(b) [1994] 1 C.M.L.R. 57, at 79–80. Implementation of common measures under Title VI (implicitly under Article K.3.2(b)-(c)) is attributed to the Member States themselves

[1994] 1 C.M.L.R. 57, at 81. This analysis makes sense of the distinction in Titles V and VI between the respective roles of the Council and the Member States, and will be followed in the discussion that follows. It means that decisions *within* the Council, and more importantly State action pursuant to such implementing decisions, would fall under the first clause of Article 29.4.5, which also seems sensible.

When the State exercises its sovereign powers in common with other States, legal obligations will normally be expressed in the form of a treaty or international agreement. Treaty-making can be conducted in highly simplified form, within the terms of Article 11 of the Vienna Convention on the Law of Treaties ("The consent of a State to be bound by a treaty may be expressed by signature ... acceptance, approval ... or by any other means if so agreed"). Decisions within the European Council or within the Council should be considered to be simplified treaties. This description may be extended to binding acts of the Council in the non-Community pillars of the Union if these are seen merely as exercises in common of the still distinct sovereignty of the Member States.

Article 29.5-6 of the Constitution sets out what are ordinarily the constitutional requirements in respect of adherence by the State to international agreements. Article 29.5.1 provides that "[e]very international agreement [other than those of a technical and administrative character] to which the State becomes a party shall be laid before Dáil Éireann". As this is an *ex post facto* requirement (see *Hutchinson v. Minister for Justice* [1993] I.L.R.M. 602) it appears to have no significance for the validity of agreements which are not so laid before the Dáil. As there is no requirement in the E.U. Treaty that decisions in C.F.S.P. and C.J.H.A. be published, the sub-section could however be used to counteract any tendency towards secretiveness in those pillars. In practice, such decisions are published in the *Official Journal*.

Article 29.5.2 of the Constitution is more significant: "The State shall not be bound by any international agreement [other than those of a technical and administrative character] involving a charge upon public funds unless the terms of the agreement shall have been approved by Dáil Éireann". If we assume that decisions on Member State financing of Union operational expenditure are not technical and administrative in character, the adoption of such decisions by the Council, without the prior approval of Dáil Éireann, would not bind the State, as a matter of Irish constitutional law (and possibly as a matter of public international law, under Article 46 of the Vienna Convention on the Law of Treaties) if such decisions were not saved by Article 29.4.5 of the Constitution. As will be seen, such decisions do not appear, on any construction, to have the force of law in the State, which might enable them to benefit from the second clause of Article 29.4.5. On the other hand, State action necessitated by such decisions (including any necessary appropriations) would probably be protected by the first clause of Article 29.4.5. However, while compliance with binding decisions *after adoption* must be an obligation of membership of the Union, the courts might be asked in advance to prevent approval by the State of such a decision if the approval of Dáil Éireann had not been secured (see the discussion below of "prior restraint"). The case for judicial intervention at that stage would be especially compelling, as Dáil approval is a *condition precedent* to the State becoming bound by an agreement imposing a charge upon public funds. (The position might be different in respect of anticipated approval by the State in the Council of a measure which might undermine constitutional principles only subsequent to its adoption.)

If a decision of the Council were designed to be directly applicable, or to be incorporated *by its own terms* in the domestic legal order of the Member States, this would ordinarily constitute a breach of Article 29.6 of the Constitution, which states that "[n]o international agreement shall be part of the domestic law of the State save as may be determined by the Oireachtas". (It is worth reiterating the point made in Chapter 4 above, that domestic incorporation does not necessarily entail direct applicability.) Article 29.6 is consistent with Article 15.2.1 of the Constitution, which states that "[t]he sole and exclusive power of making laws for the State is hereby vested in the Oireachtas: no other legislative authority has power to make laws for the State". As a matter of Irish law, incorporation in the domestic legal order could not be secured to Union measures by the operation of the Union Treaty in any event unless the relevant provisions of the Union Treaty were incorporated in the same manner as are the Community Treaties, *i.e.* accompanied by a provision like section 2(1), European Communities Act, 1972 making the existing and future acts of the institutions of the Union part of the domestic law of the State. There has been no such act of domestic incorporation of the Union Treaty.

Such a provision might overcome the hurdle posed by Article 29.6 to the automatic domestic incorporation of agreements among the Member States adopted as decisions of the Council pursuant to the E.U. Treaty, but would not remedy the patent conflict with Article 15.2.1 of the Constitution. For this purpose, the application of the second clause of Article 29.4.5 would be necessary.

This in turn begs the question whether the E.U. Treaty envisages any acts of the Council capable of having the force of law in the State, or which require (if the terms are not synonymous) that they be part of the domestic law of the State. (It is worth remarking in passing that the European Communities Act, 1972, s.2(1) and (2) as amended, use the terms to the same apparent purpose: the Community Treaties and derived acts are to be part of the domestic law of the State, while certain provisions of European Economic Area Agreement and derived acts are to have the force of law in the State. See further the annotation of the Act below.)

(c) Direct applicability and the force of law in the State

One must reiterate at the outset that as a matter of Irish law direct applicability cannot be secured for Union measures by Treaty provisions alone, even in conjunction with the terms of Article 29.4.5 of the Constitution. Article 29.4.5 is apparently negative in effect, preventing the provisions of the Constitution from impeding compliance with Community law. Positive provision must still be made for any directly applicable Union acts to take effect in the domestic legal order. This was not done by the European Communities (Amendment) Act, 1992, which added to the list of Community Treaties in the Act of 1972 only those parts of the Maastricht Treaty amending the Community Treaties as well as Articles L. M and P and the other Final Provisions in so far as they relate to the Community Treaties. However, the Minister for Foreign Affairs, Mr David Andrews T.D., did hint that the rest of the Treaty might not always be excluded from the law of the State, although he did not give reasons for this qualification (424 *Dáil Debates*, Col. 1818):

> "There is no provision in this legislation to cover Title V or Title VI of the Treaty on European Union. Title V concerns provisions on a common foreign and security policy where no requirement for domestic legislation is envisaged. Title VI concerns provisions on co-operation in the fields of justice and home affairs. Legislation may be required at some stage in the future to cover some of the Articles in this Title."

It seems very unlikely that the Council can adopt directly applicable laws, acts or measures as part of either co-operation in the fields of judicial and home affairs or the common foreign and security policy. The same con-

106

clusion is reached by the *Bundesverfassungsgericht* in *Brunner* [1994] 1 C.M.L.R. 57, at 79–80:

> "Article L only excludes the European Court's jurisdiction in respect of provisions of the Union Treaty which do not confer powers on the Union to take measures which have direct effect on holders of constitutional rights within the territory of the Member States.... Regardless of the binding effect on the Member States in international law of ... Council decisions ... no law may be passed by them which is directly applicable in Member States and can claim precedence."

Even if the Council can decide on measures implementing joint action in C.J.H.A., these are unlikely to be legislative in nature. Funding for drug rehabilitation programmes, police and customs co-operation or information systems, studies into cross-border fraud, measures to facilitate accommodation and integration of refugees are possible examples of joint actions, the operational expenditure for which could be charged to the budget of the Communities under Article K.8.2 (see, *e.g.* Commission Communication on a European Action Plan on Drugs, COM (94) 234). The first Council decision in the field concerns the facilitation of travel by school parties [1994] O.J. L327/1. Conventions under Article K.3.2(c) are likely to be the vehicle for rule-making, *e.g.* governing the crossing by persons of the external borders of the Member States and the exercise of controls thereon (Article K.1(2); on this topic, see the Dublin Convention, 1990, which pre-dates the Treaty on European Union); or creating new criminal offences (see Commission Proposal for a Council Act establishing a Convention for the Protection of the Communities' Financial Interests, COM (94) 214). Measures implementing conventions could be legislative in nature, if a convention so provided, but such measures are adopted within the Council by the High Contracting Parties. (Provision in a convention for implementation by the Member States in the Council by directly applicable legislative measures would however conflict with Article 15.2.1 of the Constitution, and brings us again to the question whether compliance with such conventions is an obligation of membership of the Union.)

The common foreign and security policy does not appear to be fertile ground either for directly applicable measures, given that it concerns consistent and united policy formulation rather than legislation, and is oriented towards third countries rather than towards the domestic legal orders of the Member States. When coercive economic instruments are sought to be used to secure foreign policy ends, this is done through the European Community (Article 228a E.C.; see, *e.g.* Council Decision 94/366/C.F.S.P. prohibiting satisfaction of claims by the Federal Republic of Yugoslavia [1994] O.J. L165).

We must, however, return, to the possibility that Union measures may be capable of having the force of law in the State in some sense otherwise than that of direct applicability. For example, the French *Conseil d'Etat* has remarked on the apparently obligatory quality of certain "declarations of the Twelve" within the framework of European Political Co-operation, and on the tendency of the executive authorities to take refuge behind such acts in the event of contentious domestic proceedings (*Conseil d'Etat, sur le droit Communautaire* (Paris, 1992; Do. no. 49) at 24); see also Gautier *Le Conseil d'Etat français et les actes 'Lor nomenclature' de la Communauté europééne* (1995) 31 Rev. trim. dr eur. 23, at 27).

Let us suppose, for example, that the Council adopted a joint position that the political offence exception to extradition should not extend to any relative political offences committed or allegedly committed in another Member State. Only purely political offences such as treason, sedition and espionage would continue to benefit from the exception. Would an Irish court be giving the force of law in the State to that joint position if it interpreted sections 11 or 50 of the Extradition Act, 1965 to conform to it (and in spite of the much broader ambit of the exception in the Council of Europe Convention on Extradition, 1957 on which section 11 and, by extension, section 50 are based: see *Bourke v. Attorney General* [1972] I.R. 36)? Such a conclusion would be possible if the Irish court felt *bound* to construe the Irish Act consistently with the joint position. The Irish courts have in the past given a degree of legal effect to unincorporated international agreements through the operation of a presumption of compatibility of domestic legislation with international obligations. This was suggested by Henchy J. in *O Domhnaill v. Merrick* [1985] I.L.R.M. 40, although that case concerned the interpretation of a statute (the Statute of Limitations, 1957) which was enacted *after* the adoption of the relevant international agreement (the European Convention on Human Rights). A general presumption of conformity of Irish law with the Convention on Human Rights was expressed by Henchy J. in *The State (Director of Public Prosecutions) v. Walsh* [1981] I.R. 412, which was relied upon by O'Hanlon J. in *Desmond v. Glackin (No. 1)* [1993] 3 I.R. 1. However, it is not clear whether this amounts to a grant of special status to the Convention *vis-a-vis* other treaties. If this jurisprudence gives rise to a general principle of the construction of domestic law to conform, where possible, to international obligations, and is not confined to reference to treaties pursuant to which a law was enacted, or to treaties pre-dating the law in question, it could indeed permit Union measures to have indirect legal effect through the process of statutory interpretation—a phenomenon which is of course familiar from the Community sphere (see Case 14/83, *von Colson & Kamann v. Land Nordrhein-Westfalen* [1984] E.C.R. 1891; and Case C-106/89, *Marleasing S.A. v. La Commercial Internacional de Alimentacion S.A.* [1990] E.C.R. I 4135).

It is also possible for actions of the executive to result in an unincorporated agreement having indirect legal effect in domestic law. Ireland is a party to the United Nations Convention on the Status of Refugees, 1951, as amended by the Protocol on the Status of Refugees, 1967. It was not incorporated into Irish domestic law, but the Minister for Justice undertook in a letter to a representative of the United Nations High Commissioner for Refugees to consider applications for asylum in Ireland in accordance with the Convention. In *Fakih v. Minister for Justice* [1993] 2 I.R. 406, O'Hanlon J. held that this letter bound the Minister because of the legitimate expectation to which it gave rise. In *Gutrani v. Minister for Justice* [1993] 2 I.R. 427, the Supreme Court reached the same conclusion. The court purported to act, not on the basis of legitimate expectation, but simply as a result to the undertaking given by the Minister, but the decision is difficult to understand save in terms of legitimate expectation (see also *Kajli v. Minister for Justice*, Barr J., High Court, August 21, 1992). It is perhaps too early to predict how this jurisprudence will develop. It should operate only in favour of the individual, and never in order to permit the State to impose obligations otherwise than by legislation. It does not seem probable that it could generate rights for individuals enforceable against other private parties who are strangers to the Minister's undertaking on any topic. As a result, and given the kinds of obligations which are likely to arise under Titles V and VI, E.U., it may not be of great relevance to our present enquiry. The examples just given do nonetheless indicate the uncertainty surrounding the concept of "the force of law in the State" in Article 29.4.5 of the Constitution.

One must conclude this section by stating that, with the possible exception of the need to protect decisions of the Court of Justice taken pursuant to Article L, E.U., and decisions of the Parliament and Council under Article O, E.U., the extension of the second clause of Article 29.4.5 to laws, acts and measures of the European Union seems largely otiose. To the extent that it has some effect, it is probably unwelcome, having regard to the problem of lack of judicial supervision of Union activities adumbrated above, and now to be addressed more fully.

(ii) THE UNION AND FUNDAMENTAL RIGHTS

The E.U. Treaty commits the Union to the observance of fundamental human rights. Article F(2) E.U. states: "The Union shall respect fundamental rights, as guaranteed by the European Convention for the Protection of Human Rights and Fundamental Freedoms signed in Rome on November 4, 1950 and as they result from the constitutional traditions common to the Member States, as general principles of Community law". This object is also implicit in Article C, which pledges the Union to achieving its objectives "while respecting and building upon the *acquis communautaire*". Article J.1.2 E.U. states that it shall be one of the objectives of the common foreign and security policy "to develop and consolidate democracy and the rule of law, and respect for human rights and fundamental freedoms". Article K.2.1 E.U. states: "The matters [of common interest] referred to in Article K.1 shall be dealt with in compliance with the European Convention for the Protection of Human Rights and Fundamental Freedoms of November 4, 1950 and the Convention relating to the Status of Refugees of July 28, 1951 and having regard to the protection afforded by Member States to persons persecuted on political grounds". However, no judicial machinery is provided for the enforcement of these obligations against the institutions of the Union and/or the Member States. As has already been remarked, Article L, E.U. excludes the jurisdiction of the European Court of Justice from virtually all of the non-Community elements of the Union legal order. (The Court of Justice may have occasion in limited circumstances to comment on or draw conclusions from matters apparently excluded by Article L, E.U., but this must be seen as exceptional; see further Eaton, C.F.S.P., at 221; Neuwahl, "Foreign and Security Policy and the Implementation of the Requirement of 'Consistency' under the Treaty on European Union" in O'Keeffe & Twomey eds., *Legal Issues of the Maastricht Treaty* (1994), 227, at 244–6; Curtin, Union, at 62–3; Dehousse, Union, at 11; European Parliament Legal Service contribution to a symposium of the Legal Affairs Committee of the European Parliament, has relations *entre le droit international public, le droit communautaire et le droit constitutionnel des Etats Membres* (Brussels, 1995, Pt 213.411) at 13–14.)

It therefore falls to other judicial organs to enforce fundamental rights' guarantees in respect of Union and Member State activities under Titles V and VI, E.U., whether those guarantees are those stated in the Treaty itself, or are derived exclusively either from national constitutional standards or from the European Convention on Human Rights. In *Brunner* [1994] 1 C.M.L.R. 57, at 81), the *Bundesverfassungsgericht* found that the exclusion by Article L, E.U. of the jurisdiction of the European Court of Justice over much of the E.U. Treaty did not leave a gap in the legal protection of fundamental rights because no provision was made therein for directly applicable measures, and "[i]f common actions or measures under Titles V and VI of the Union Treaty impose obligations, binding in international law, on Member States to make encroachments which are of constitutional relevance, all such encroachments, if they occur in Germany, will be subject to review in full by the German courts". The court relied in part upon the statement by the Federal Government "that it is the unanimous intention of the Member States that Article L will not lead to any gaps in legal protection" [1994] 1 C.M.L.R. 57, at 80. However, this does not appear to be true in the Irish case under Article 29.4.5 of the Constitution. Irrespective of whether the obligations are attributable to the Union or to the Member States acting in common, or whether they are directly applicable, indirectly effective, or implemented by the Government or Oireachtas, obligations incurred through the operation of the Treaty on European Union are apparently outwith the scope of Irish judicial protection of fundamental rights and of other constitutional interests.

This section addresses the remaining possible avenues of judicial protection. Two questions will be considered:

(a) whether the State can be restrained from voting for proposals in the Council which, if adopted, will lead to Union measures or (much more likely) State measures and which, though otherwise unconstitutional, will benefit from the immunity conferred by Article 29.4.5 of the Constitution; and

(b) whether Union measures, or State measures necessitated by Union membership, which benefit from constitutional immunity, will be subject to the supervision of the European Court of Human Rights.

(a) "Prior restraint" of the Government

Can the State be constrained from committing itself to a policy and to Union or State action which, though *prima facie* unconstitutional, would benefit (we will assume) from an immunity once adopted? *Crotty v. An Taoiseach* [1987] I.R. 713 illustrates clearly that proposed adherence to a treaty in such circumstances will be subject to judicial control. On the other hand, the decision of the Supreme Court in *Boland v. An Taoiseach* [1971] I.R. 371 suggests that a mere Government policy declaration (as the "Sunningdale Agreement" or communiqué was stated to be) is subject to review by the Dáil rather than by the courts (see generally Symmons, "International Treaty Obligations and the Irish Constitution: The *McGimpsey Case*" (1992) 41 I.C.L.Q. 311). It is submitted that votes by the Government in the Council in the sphere of the common foreign and security policy, and in respect of joint actions in justice and home affairs co-operation, should be governed by the former rather than the latter principle. Such a vote constitutes agreement by the State to a particular policy, within a system of mutual obligation, rather than a mere declaration of policy from which the State can depart at any time without compunction.

This conclusion is echoed by Collins. He points out that the State has the option under Title VI, E.U. of acting by way of a convention, which Article K.3.2(c) provides can be made subject to the jurisdiction of the European Court of Justice. While such a convention would not be part of Community law, the Court of Justice would probably protect fundamental rights by reference to, *inter alia*, Article K.2.1 E.U. The Irish courts might therefore require that that option be chosen by the State over any other (Collins, "The Eleventh Amendment—Problems and Perspectives" (1992) 10 I.L.T. 209, at 211 (hereinafter Collins, 11th Amendment)). A collateral effect of such a development could be the adoption by the Irish courts of a position similar to that taken in the German "*Solange II*" decision (*Wünsche Handelsgesellschaft* [1987] 3 C.M.L.R. 225), and now expressed in Article 23(1) of the German Constitution: an acceptance that the Court of Justice "guarantees a protection of fundamental rights which is essentially comparable with this Constitution". In the alternative, however, the Irish courts might simply view judicial protection by the Court of Justice as better than nothing, without conceding its equivalence to national constitutional protection. One could counter Collins' suggestion by asserting that a Member State insisting on using only one of the three policy options permitted by the Treaty, irrespective of the circumstances, would be in breach of the spirit of the Treaty, and of the commitment to solidarity in Article A, E.U.; but it is difficult to predict whether such an argument would appeal to an Irish court.

The issue of injunctive or prohibitory power in respect of Government action in the Council of Ministers has parallels in German constitutional jurisprudence (see Casey, "*Crotty v. An Taoiseach*: a Comparative Perspective" in O'Reilly ed., *Human Rights and Constitutional Law* (1992) p. 189, at 192). In two cases, *M. GmbH. v. Bundesregierung* [1990] 1 C.M.L.R. 570 and *Freistaat Bayern v. Bundesregierung* [1990] 1 C.M.L.R. 649, the *Bundeverfassungsgericht* seemed to recognise that where a Council measure could take effect without separate domestic implementation, the vote of the German executive authority could be reviewed, as it would be the final act of co-operation in the production of that measure which might possibly infringe constitutional rights. The reason that votes for Council measures requiring further domestic implementation were exempted from such scrutiny was that the implementing national measure would be subject to the restrictions imposed by the German Constitution (*M. GmbH. v. Bundesregierung* [1990] 1 C.M.L.R. 570, at 574; see also the remarks quoted immediately above from *Brunner* [1994] 1 C.M.L.R. 57, at 81). One can argue for such prior judicial review in all cases, however, because *ex post facto* review of national measures must take place subject to the constraints imposed by the Community measure in question (see Chapter 5 above). Thus, there is a case for review of all votes leading to some sort of obligation, whether it be imposed by a directly applicable act of the Union (or other act having the force of law in the State) or through the medium of "necessitated" State action. (On prior restraint in a common law context, see the decision of the Court of Appeal in *R. v. H.M. Treasury, ex p. Smedley* [1985] Q.B. 657, in which it was decided that Parliament could be "restrained" in advance (though only by a declaration), on grounds of convenience, from giving its approval to a draft Order in Council which would be *ultra vires*.)

Nonetheless, the interim decision in *Freistaat Bayern v. Bundesregierung* [1990] 1 C.M.L.R. 649 illustrates that there may in practice be decisive circumstantial constraints on a pre-emptive judicial role. On the balance of convenience, the *Bundesverfassungsgericht* refused an interim injunction against approval by the German Federal Government in the Council of a common position on a proposed E.C. directive. The subject matter of the draft directive (trans-frontier television) fell within the exclusive competence of the *Länder* (states) under the German federal division of competences, and it was opposed even in diluted form by the *Länder*. The Bavarian Government sought a declaration that approval by the Government of the draft directive in any form would breach the constitutional division of competences, and sought an interim injunction until the main action could be heard. The Court held that if an injunction were granted, the Federal Government would lose all opportunity of influencing the shape of the directive, which might be passed (by majority vote) in spite of its opposition. On the other hand, if the interim injunction were refused, but the main action ultimately succeeded, although the Federal Government would have trenched on the power of the *Länder*, nevertheless it would have used its consequent freedom of manoeuvre in the Council to bring the final text as close as possible to the desires and interests of the *Länder*. This reasoning could not be extended *verbatim* to the non-Community pillars of the Union, as voting is almost exclusively by unanimity. However, one should not perhaps place too much reliance on the power of the State in all cases to say no, as Member States which are perceived as obstructive may in practice suffer a decline in influence in all spheres of activity. The *Bundesverfassungsgericht* was willing to accept that the Federal Government would do all in its power to advance the views of the *Länder* and thus to preserve to the greatest possible extent the constitutional position. The Irish courts would probably adopt a similar presumption that the Government would take pains to protect Irish constitutional principles, following the general presumption of constitutionality. (Judgment was handed down in the Friestaat Bayern Case on 22

March 1995 relating to German measures implementing the "Television sans frontières" directive solely by reference to the division of implementing power under German constitutional law.)

Thus, judicial scrutiny of Government positions seems generally to be inappropriate in advance of often tortuous negotiations, when compromises may need to be reached, and when the Government is considered to be doing its best to safeguard constitutional rights and principles; injunctions would presumably be refused in many cases on balance of convenience grounds. The courts would not in most cases have the benefit, as they did in *Crotty*, of having before them the final negotiated document to which the State proposed to adhere. While the Irish courts might not have the same difficulty restraining Government action which ignores preliminary procedural rules (such as Article 29.5.2 of the Constitution, where applicable), they would very likely be reluctant to intervene to prevent an anticipated commitment by the State to policies or measures which it is possible (but not certain) will breach constitutional rights or principles of governance. On the other hand, the Supreme Court decision in *Society for the Protection of Unborn Children (Ireland) Ltd v. Grogan* [1989] I.R. 753 suggests that the Irish courts might be more willing than the *Bundesverfassungsgericht* to grant injunctive relief where an irrevocable and serious encroachment on constitutional rights is threatened. However, even liberal judicial recourse to such a jurisdiction would be inadequate to protect constitutional rights. Given the notorious lack of transparency of the Union's activities, the secrecy in which Council discussions take place, and the exorbitant level of legal costs, it would be difficult for interested persons to seek a court remedy in time, or at all. Furthermore, the threat to fundamental constitutional rights and principles may not always be apparent on the face of a measure, and may emerge only in practice.

If it were accepted, despite these problems, that the Irish courts could restrain the Government on constitutional grounds from approving decisions in or of the Council under Titles V and VI of the E.U. Treaty, even in very limited circumstances, an argument could also be made for the extension of that jurisdiction to decision-making in the Community pillar. This is, after all, the context in which the issue first arose in Germany. The Irish courts could distinguish between the Community and non-Community pillars by reference to the lack of judicial protection in the latter (except perhaps pursuant to Article K.3.2(c) E.U.). For example, Gallagher comments (in the context of the Communities) that Article 29.4.5 of the Constitution has the effect "of identifying the system of law (*i.e.* Irish or European) which provides the relevant fundamental rights protection" ("The Constitution and the Community" (1993) 1 I.J.E.L. 129, at 139). However, this would again entail the adoption of a "*Solange II*" position on the equivalence in content and scope of application of Irish and Community fundamental rights, and of judicial protection in the constitutional and Community legal orders. The implicit readiness of the *Bundesverfassungsgericht* to consider such an injunctive power in respect of Council decisions on the directly applicable legislation of the Communities sits ill with its acceptance of the essential equivalence of the fundamental rights protection afforded by the Community legal order with that under the German Constitution. Even their willingness in *M. GmbH. v. Bundesregierung* to review the content of national implementing measures with regard to the provisions of the Constitution seems to be out of keeping with "*Solange II*", as such measures are also subject to the fundamental rights jurisdiction of the European Court of Justice. In reality, of course, national courts are more directly accessible to individuals than the Court of Justice and may feel more comfortable applying domestic constitutional principles than the unenumerated general principles of Community law. The German courts may also wish to ensure observance of constitutional guarantees other than those of fundamental rights (as was the case in *Freistaat*

Bayern v. Bundesregierung). All of these factors could carry weight in an appropriate case with an Irish court as well. Furthermore, it is by no means clear that the Irish courts are willing to accept the "*Solange II*" view that fundamental rights protection by the European Court of Justice mirrors sufficiently that under the Constitution; certain *dicta* in *Society for the Protection of Unborn Children (Ireland) Ltd v. Grogan* [1989] I.R. 753, discussed below, indicate quite the contrary view in at least one controversial area. In the absence of such a view being taken, the Irish courts might reserve, at least in principle, the right to restrain approval by the Government of any "unconstitutional" decision in the Council, irrespective of its legal basis in the Community or Union Treaties.

In the alternative, a national "prior restraint" jurisdiction in respect of Council decisions in the Community sphere might be discountenanced by the Irish courts (or condemned by the European Court of Justice) pursuant to Article 5 E.C., on the grounds that limitations placed by reference to domestic legal standards on the authority of Ministers in the Council to approve whatever measures seem appropriate or necessary to realise the objectives of the Treaty would be a breach of the obligation of solidarity and co-operation. It might also be construed as a technical breach of Article 146 E.C., which states that the representatives of each Member State in the Council should be "authorised to commit the government of that Member State"; however, the mandatory nature of instructions to Danish Ministers by the Market Relations Committee of the *Folketing* affords a counter-example from present practice (see Newman, "The Impact of National Parliaments on the Development of Community Law" in Capotorti *et al* eds., *Du Droit International au Droit de l'Integration: Liber Amicorum Pierre Pescatore* (1987) p. 481, at 487-8). One can also counter this argument by reference to a new departure in the interpretation of Article 5 E.C. on the part of the Court of Justice—that it also imposes an obligation of co-operation on the Community with regard to the Member States (see Case C-234/89, *Delimitis* [1990] I E.C.R. 35, at paragraph 53). The Commission Legal Service has commented that this interpretation of Article 5 E.C. reflects a practice in the Council of not causing constitutional problems to Member States through use of qualified majority voting (in the contribution to a symposium organised by the Legal Affairs Committee of the European Parliament, *Les relations entre le droit international publice, le droit communautaire et le droit constitutionnel des Etats membres* (Brussels, 1995; PE 213.411), at paragraph 3.2).

(b) Supervision by the European Court of Human Rights

If judicial review by the Irish courts of measures in the fields governed by the Union's two non-Community pillars is as limited as is suggested above, one must ask whether any other body can protect human rights from encroachment by the executive acting with its Union partners. The European Court of Human Rights may be able to provide such protection.

It seems clear that the system of judicial supervision established under the European Convention on Human Rights (E.C.H.R.) cannot be automatically extended to the European Communities, or to the European Union (if it has a separate existence). The argument was once put that Article 234 EEC had the effect of substituting the European Economic Community as a whole for the E.C.H.R. obligations of the Member States, in those areas in which those States had given it competence. (Article 234 E.C. states, *inter alia*: "The rights and obligations arising from agreements concluded before the entry into force of this Treaty between one or more Member States on the one hand, and one or more third countries on the other, shall not be affected by the provisions of this Treaty".) This was always an unlikely proposition, not least because the obligations of the various States under the Convention are not uniform, due to national reservations, varying levels of acceptance of later protocols, *etc.* (see, *e.g.* Mendelson, "The Impact of E.C. Law on the Implementation of the E.C.H.R." (1983) 3 Y.E.L. 99, at 104 (hereinafter Mendelson, Convention)). In any event, Article 234 E.C. does not apply to the two new Union pillars. In *C.F.D.T. v. E.C., E.C. States collectively and E.C. States individually* [1979] 2 C.M.L.R. 299, the European Commission on Human Rights declined to exercise jurisdiction over a Community organ, the Council, because the Community was not a party to the Convention. It also declined to hold the Member States liable individually for their participation in the decisions of the Council. The *C.F.D.T.* decision was followed by the Commission on Human Rights in *Re the European School in Brussels: D. v. Belgium and the E.C.* Case 11055/84, [1987] 2 C.M.L.R. 57. The European School in Brussels was established by a convention of 1957 and a protocol of 1962 among the E.C. Member States, and was alleged to be in breach of Article 13 E.C.H.R. and Article 2, E.C.H.R. Protocol No. 1 (on the right to education). However, the Commission on Human Rights held that the school was not within Belgian jurisdiction because its activities were governed by an international convention, and that the European Communities were outwith the jurisdiction *ratione personae* of the Commission and Court of Human Rights as the Communities were not parties to the E.C.H.R. The Council has since sought an Opinion from the European Court of Justice on the compatibility with the constitutional Treaties of Accession by the Communities to the European Convention on Human Rights [1993] 4 E.U. Bull., 1.1.4. This does not arise in respect of the Union as it does not have the competence or capacity to conclude treaties.

In the absence of such accession by the Communities, the Commission on Human Rights did leave open in *C.F.D.T.* the question of the *collective* liability of the Member States under the Convention for the acts of Community organs [1979] 2 C.M.L.R. 229, at 233. At that time, one of the nine—France, which was primarily responsible for the infraction alleged by C.F.D.T.—had not accepted the right of individual petition, so that such collective liability was not thought possible. All the Member States now permit individual petition to the European Court of Human Rights. If the Court of Human Rights did not have jurisdiction in such cases, States could avoid the strictures of the Convention by delegating their responsibilities to other international organisations which they control collectively (and to some extent individually, where recourse to a veto is possible). To the extent that the *C.F.D.T.* decision might have countenanced such a lacuna, the E.C. Commission was of the opinion that it would not be followed (see Doc SJ/229/79-Def-EN, 14; see also Mendelson, Convention, at 116). Indeed, the Commission on Human Rights suggested more recently that it may accept applications against Community organs where this could be said to invoke the responsibility of each of the (then) 12 Member States, in *Dufay v. E.C., E.C. States collectively and E.C. States individually* (Application No. 13539/88, January 19, 1989; see generally Clapham, *Human Rights and the European Community: A Critical Overview* (1991) pp. 55–57).

The difficulty with liability of the Communities under the E.C.H.R., or of the Member States for the acts of the Communities, is resolved in practice because the Member States remain subject to the Convention when implementing Community obligations at the domestic level. This was established by the Commission on Human Rights in *M. v. Germany* (Application No. 13258/87, Decision of February, 1990). The case concerned alleged procedural improprieties in the imposition by the European Commission of a fine under Regulation 17/62 for breach of Article 85(1) E.C. The European Court of Justice refused to set aside the decision, finding no breach of fundamental rights. A claim that the Court of Justice had in turn violated fundamental rights protected by the German Constitution (*inter alia* the right of the managing partners to be heard personally) was rejected by the *Bundes-*

verfassungsgericht on *"Solange II"* grounds. An application was subsequently filed against Germany under the Convention. The Commission on Human Rights recalled that although it could not examine the proceedings and decisions of Community organs, "this does not mean that by granting executory power to a judgment of the European Court of Justice the competent German authorities acted *qua* Community organs and are to that extent beyond the scope of control exercised by the Convention organs" (at p. 7 of the decision).

The decision of the Commission on Human Rights effectively extends its jurisdiction *ratione materiae* over much of Community law. *M. v. Germany* did not concern a Community measure, such as a directive, which as a matter of Community law would require transposition into the domestic legal order by the Member State authorities for it to have effect. As has been seen, the German courts are willing to review the constitutionality of such national implementing measures in so far as the directive gives "scope for choice as to formulation" (*M. GmbH. v. Bundesregierung* [1990] 1 C.M.L.R. 570, at 574). *M. v. Germany* concerned a Community measure which as a matter of Community law was directly applicable, and which was required by Article 192 E.C., as a decision of the Commission imposing a pecuniary obligation on a person other than a State, to be enforceable in the territory of the Member States by a competent national authority "without other formality than verification of the authenticity of the decision". Furthermore, it was not the *national* rules of civil procedure in respect of enforcement that were the subject of the application (which rules are stated by Article 192 E.C. to govern the enforcement of Commission decisions), but certain alleged defects in the decision of the Court of Justice, a body which is outside the jurisdiction *ratione personae* of the Commission on Human Rights. However, once action was required to be taken by national authorities pursuant to the court's decision, the matter became justiciable. The willingness of the European Commission on Human Rights to consider the compatibility with the E.C.H.R. of Member State acts which as a matter of Community law result automatically from acts of the Community organs must in practice bring most of the Community legal order within its jurisdiction, because of the decentralised nature of the administration of Community law. (The European Commission's first Annual Report on Subsidiarity is the most recent confirmation that the administrative implementation of Community law is in principle to be entrusted to the Member States, without prejudice to the supervisory role of the Commission; see *Agence Europe*, No. 6376, 11 December 1994.) Some acts with patent human rights implications are performed directly by the Community institutions, *e.g.* Commission investigations under Article 14, Regulation 17/62. Even in these cases, however, the Member States maintain a monopoly of coercive power in their territories, and will ultimately have to become involved if there is resistance to the measures taken by the Community organ in question (see *e.g.* Article 14(6), Regulation 17/62).

Having made clear that a State cannot transfer powers in order to avoid responsibility under the Convention, the Commission added, however, that "the transfer of powers to an international organisation is not incompatible with the Convention provided that within that organisation fundamental rights will receive an equivalent protection" (p. 8 of the decision). This statement is reminiscent of Germany's own accommodation of its constitutional rights guarantees to the supremacy of Community law in *"Solange II"* *(Wünsche Handelsgesellschaft)* [1987] 3 C.M.L.R. 225). As the Parliament, Council and Commission had pledged to respect fundamental rights in a Joint Declaration of 1977 and the European Court of Justice had developed a human rights jurisdiction based in large part on the Convention's guarantees, and had concluded in the instant case that there had been no breach of human rights, the Commission of Human Rights declined to enquire further into the matter. In circumstances where such protection was afforded, "it would be contrary to the very idea of transferring powers to an international organisation to hold the Member States responsible for examining, in each individual case before issuing a writ of execution for a judgment of the European Court of Justice, whether Article 6 of the Convention was respected in the underlying proceedings" (p. 8 of the decision). The Commission on Human Rights therefore refrained from an interventionist stance that could have caused Member States to question the supremacy of Community law by reference not to domestic constitutional standards but to their potential liability for breach of the European Convention on Human Rights. By asserting its formal jurisdiction, however, the Commission on Human Rights preserved the possibility of such a conflict of obligations were the Communities to be accused of a particularly egregious contravention of the standards prescribed by the Convention.

Two points can be made about the common foreign and security policy and the co-operation in the fields of judicial and home affairs of the Union, in the light of the decision in *M. v. Germany* (Application No. 13258/87, Decision of February, 1990). First, it is in the nature of the subject-matter and competences set out in Titles V and VI, E.U. that decisions and policies must always, or virtually always, be given effect through national action. Such action by Member State authorities can be made subject to review by the Court of Human Rights. Secondly, while the E.U. Treaty expresses sentiments similar to those in the Joint Declaration of 1977, the exclusion of jurisdiction by the Court of Justice over the two non-Community pillars of the Union means that the Court of Human Rights will have no reason to decline to exercise its jurisdiction in respect of actions by the Member States pursuant to Union obligations. The statements of respect for the Convention and for human rights and fundamental freedoms in Articles F(2), J.1.2, and K.2.1 E.U. are unlikely to assuage the Court of Human Rights in the absence of provision for their judicial enforcement. Twomey suggests, however, that extension of the jurisdiction of the European Court of Justice to conventions adopted under Article K.3.2(c) E.U. could lead to the Commission on Human Rights declining jurisdiction in such instances ("Title VI of the Union Treaty: 'Matters of Common Interest' as a Question of Human Rights" in Monar & Morgan eds., *The Third Pillar of the European Union* (1994) p. 49, at 56).

It thus appears that the Irish government will be subject to binding human rights constraints on its actions pursuant to common policies in the fields of foreign and security policy, and justice and home affairs, even if one concludes that constitutional review of such actions by Irish courts is precluded by the terms of Article 29.4.5 of the Constitution. Whether the Convention offers sufficient guarantees is another question, given both the wide margin of appreciation that is accorded to States, and Ireland's often lackadaisical attitude to compliance with decisions of the Court of Human Rights. A further drawback is the unavailability of interlocutory relief, so that irremediable damage may be suffered, *e.g.* in a refugee case, before an application can be heard or a decision reached (Collins, 11th Amendment, at 210).

(iii) The Exclusion of the European Court of Justice

The exclusion by Article L, E.U. of the jurisdiction of the European Court of Justice over the two non-Community pillars of the Union, and over the Common Provisions in Title I (Articles A-F) of the E.U. Treaty has a number of consequences both for the Union, and for the Irish constitutional order. Foremost of these is the fact, already adverted to, that the human rights jurisprudence developed by the Court of Justice over more than two decades cannot be extended to Union action, or to State action at the instance of the

Union, in the fields of common foreign and security policy or of judicial and home-affairs co-operation. The discussion in section (ii) above is concerned largely with assessing and allaying the ill effects of this omission, which are exacerbated by the exclusion of such acts from Irish constitutional review. One of the reasons for the confinement of judicial supervision by the Court of Justice to the Community pillar must be that the other two fields were thought still to be the subject of national sensitivities about sovereignty, and to national judicial supervision (see the remarks of the German Federal Government quoted in *Brunner* [1994] 1 C.M.L.R. 57, at 80, discountenancing any lacuna in judicial protection). In a State where popular sovereignty is deemed to be expressed through a Constitution enforceable against the organs of government by the courts, the exclusion of domestic judicial review is disconcerting in areas allegedly of such peculiar national interest as to be removed from the purview of a supra-national court.

The problem of the exclusion of national fundamental rights supervision of the activity of the Union and the Member States is not likely to have been replicated in other Member States where such a jurisdiction exists. Yet in those States, the exercise of judicial supervision by the domestic courts rather than by the European Court of Justice will lead to a problem which, ironically, will also be experienced in Ireland: lack of uniformity in the obligations of the Member States.

In Ireland, the problem of lack of uniformity in the obligations of Member States of the Union may arise as follows. Temple Lang has remarked that "[t]he juxtaposition of Community law and Irish law has ... created a situation in which the interpretation of the Irish Constitution may be a matter of Community law, and not purely of Irish law" (Temple Lang, Scope, at 231). The "necessitated" clause of Article 29.4.3 (as it then was) must refer to State actions "necessitated objectively by the obligations of membership as determined by Community law", and could not mean those "necessitated by the obligations of membership of the Communities as ultimately judged subjectively by the Irish courts". This was the only way to avoid conflict between the two systems (and also to ensure the uniformity of application of Community law throughout the Member States). "Article 29.4.3 is a *renvoi* from the Constitution of Ireland to the constitutional law of the Community .... To interpret Article 29.4.3, a reference to Luxembourg under Article 177 [EEC] might be necessary" (Temple Lang, Scope, at 231). Furthermore, this approach is also implicit in the second clause of Article 29.4.5, as the *vires* of the laws, acts and measures are judged by the European Court of Justice.

But even if Ireland now subscribes to what Casey terms "an external constitution" (*Constitution*, at 164), or, in Henchy's words, "a second and transcendent constitution" ("The Irish Constitution and the E.E.C." (1977) 1 D.U.L.J. 20, at 23), it will be impossible to maintain a uniform interpretation of the Treaty on European Union among its 15 High Contracting Parties if there is no system of *renvoi* such as that described by Temple Lang. The Treaty on European Union nowhere provides that it shall be interpreted by national courts, but national courts will (and must) exercise such a jurisdiction within their domestic legal orders when the terms of the Treaty are relevant to domestic litigation. How can an Irish court decide what is "necessitated objectively by the obligations of membership as determined by [Union] law" when there is no court to determine the objective requirements of Union law? Should a law, act or measure of the State in the field of common foreign and security policy, or judicial and home affairs co-operation be challenged having regard to the provisions of the Constitution, there is little option but to decide the case according to what is "necessitated by the obligations of membership of the [Union] as ultimately judged subjectively by the Irish courts". This can even prompt arguments that the *renvoi* or strict legal obligation approach should not apply in the Community sphere either (see Phelan, "'Necessitated' by the Obligations of Membership? Article

29.4.5 of the Constitution" (1993) 11 I.L.T. 272; see generally the discussion below of the interpretative role of the Irish courts).

If the Irish courts are called upon to review the constitutionality of State measures taken to comply with a decision of the Council in the non-Community pillars, or to deny the force of law in the State to such a decision of the Council, the immunity conferred by Article 29.4.5 of the Constitution may force them to decide whether the decisions in question were *intra vires* the Council, or the Member States acting within the Council, or whether the legal basis of the decision in question in the Union Treaty gives it binding or merely recommendatory effect. National courts are not permitted to pronounce the invalidity of Community acts; this is the prerogative of the Court of Justice (Case 314/85 *Foto-Frost v. Hauptzollamt Lübeck-Ost* [1987] E.C.R. 4199). However, this is not possible in respect of decisions of or within the Council outside the Community pillar. The International Court of Justice will hardly be resorted to either, even though the E.U. Treaty is binding in international law, because a Member State government is unlikely to bring an action challenging the *vires* of a decision which has the unanimous backing of the executives of the Member States, but which may encroach on the domestic powers and competences of other organs of State, such as the legislature or judiciary, or on the rights or freedoms of individuals. (Everling argues in any event that because the E.U. Treaty is an integration treaty, sanctions under international law should not be contemplated in case of alleged infringement, despite the lack of jurisdiction of the Court of Justice; Structure, at 1064; *cf.* Eaton, C.F.S.P., at 222.) Article 29.4.5 of the Constitution notwithstanding, this leaves as the only possible forum the Irish courts, which must exercise some control, if only *in extremis*, in order to ensure that the Government does not subvert domestic constitutional norms by channelling through the Union controversial measures which are (or can be asserted to be) outside Union competence. The fact that the relevant parts of the E.U. Treaty have not been incorporated into Irish law will hardly prevent the exercise of such a jurisdiction. Even in dualist States, domestic courts "may not only be empowered but required to adjudicate on the meaning and scope of the terms of an international treaty ... where domestic legislation, though not incorporating the treaty, nevertheless requires either expressly or by necessary implication, resort to be had to its terms for the purpose of construing the legislation" (Lord Oliver, *Maclaine Watson & Co. Ltd v. Department of Trade and Industry* [1989] 3 All E.R. 523, at 545d). This statement is clearly applicable to Article 29.4.5 of the Constitution. (On the application of this principle to domestic adjudication of questions of *vires* or authority under an unincorporated international treaty, see Ralph Gibson L.J. in the Court of Appeal, in the same case, [1988] 3 All E.R. 257, at 349f-g.)

The question of *vires*, or of the obligatory effect of decisions taken at Union level, is not so significant in those Member States (such as Germany) where it is clear that the national courts will review the constitutionality of State measures even if they are adopted pursuant to such decisions. However, such constitutional review might sometimes turn on questions of *vires* under the Union Treaty, *e.g.* if German federal legislation on a topic normally within the exclusive competence of the *Länder* were asserted to be required in order to fulfil obligations incurred by virtue of Union membership. Furthermore, the *Bundesverfassungsgericht* has indicated that it will ensure that German sovereignty is not usurped through acts of Union institutions which in its view are not provided for in the Union Treaty (such as directly applicable laws); the court stated (in *Brunner* [1994] 1 C.M.L.R. 57, at 89) that it "will review legal instruments of European institutions and agencies to see whether they remain within the limits of the sovereign rights conferred on them [by the Union Treaty] or transgress them". (If the *Bundesverfassungsgericht* includes the Court of Justice among the institutions the acts of which it will review, this position could be highly subversive of the Community legal order as well; but the context of the statement quoted leaves it unclear whether this was intended.)

Thus, we may find that the German and Irish courts take different views of the extent and proper subject matter of the powers conferred on the Council by Titles V and VI, E.U. In any given set of circumstances, the German courts may strike down a State measure adopted pursuant to a Council decision, and the Irish courts may not. Other, differing approaches may be found in the other Member States.

One cannot pretend that a different formulation of the Eleventh Amendment could have done much to cure this defect in the Union's legal order. While the judicial protection of constitutional rights outside the Community pillar was too casually curtailed in Article 29.4.5, a different approach would simply have compounded the proliferation of differing standards of protection in the Member States, and thus the obstacles to a common set of obligations of membership of the Union. The drafters of Article 29.4.5 may, however, be accused of a certain sleight of hand. The extension to Union affairs of the old Article 29.4.3 immunity, which attached to Community activity, masks through the use of a familiar formula the fragmentation of the European legal order, and works to carve out zones of governmental activity (provided that the governments of the Member States act in unison) which, in Ireland's case, purport to be free of any judicial supervision. Judicial supervision of some sort there will be, however, if only because the exclusion of a Union-wide jurisdiction will place in the hands of the Irish courts the task of policing the borders of the zone of Union activity (*i.e.* by deciding questions of *vires*). The breakdown of the *renvoi* to the Court of Justice must be fatal to the proper working of the formula in Article 29.4.5 of the Constitution. It makes a mockery of the deferential references to Union acts, and to acts necessitated by the obligations of membership of the Union, that the ultimate decision on the legitimate content of these "objective" categories will lie in cases originating in Ireland, not with a Union court, but, *de facto*, with the Irish courts, the jurisdiction of which is supposed to have been excluded.

Conclusion

Article 29.4.5 of the Constitution appears to conceive, if only through the convenient extension of an old formula, of a distinct Union, to which responsibility for certain acts can be attributed. It is by no means clear that such a Union exists, or that any of its acts is capable of the force of law in the State. However, just as in the physical sciences, one cannot presume that the observer (or the mere act of observation) has no effect on the thing or process observed, so it may prove difficult neatly to separate the domestic constitutional provision from the matter of which it speaks. The Union is to a large extent an empty vessel the content of which will, over time, be determined by the attitude to it of its Member States. By anticipating a particular kind of European Union, the Eleventh Amendment itself contributes, in a very small way, to the creation of a Union in that image. By referring to the European Union, the Constitution may affect the entity or process referred to. It may contribute to our understanding of the Union (outside the Community pillar) either as an identifiable actor and entity, or as a mere inter-governmental process. It remains the case, however, that the non-Community pillars of the Union are unlikely to generate directly applicable rights and obligations, and that the extension to the Union as a whole of a formula designed for the European Communities must generate a rather false picture of its ultimate role.

The combination of Article 29.4.5 of the Constitution and the exclusion of almost any role for the European Court of Justice in the non-Community pillars of the Union will very likely have a number of effects. It may lead to prior restraint by Irish courts of Government votes in the Council on common positions, etc. which would be subject neither to national nor to Union human rights requirements. It may lead to the active use of its jurisdiction by the European Court of Human Rights, due to the unenforceability of guarantees other than those found in the European Convention on Human Rights. Neither of these is a fully satisfactory option for the protection of fundamental rights from co-ordinated encroachment by the governments of the Member States acting through the Union. The Article 29.4.5 formula also disguises another unwelcome consequence of the restriction of the jurisdiction of the European Court of Justice: the effective disavowal of the uniformity of Union law, outside the Community sphere. Despite all the fanfare surrounding the founding of a Union which "marks a new stage in the process creating an ever closer union among the peoples of Europe" (Article A, E.U.), the failure to create a Union court must leave ultimate judicial power in the Union in the hands of the national courts of the Member States.

CHAPTER EIGHT

"THE MIRROR CRACK'D FROM SIDE TO SIDE"
NORMATIVE CONFLICT AND CONSTITUTIONAL INTERPRETATION

The preceding discussion of the constitutional reception of Community law in Ireland has proceeded on the basis of an interpretation of Article 29.4.3-6 drawn from the case law to date of the Irish courts and from the stated views of the drafters of those provisions. This must follow from the task which it is sought to accomplish in this commentary, being the elaboration of the degree of faithfulness to the dictates of the "constitution" of the Communities of its reception in the Irish legal order established by the Constitution. The very existence of Article 29.4.5 of the Constitution, and of sections 1 and 2 of the European Communities Act, 1972 may belie the "constitutional" claim that Community law takes effect of its own motion and by virtue of its inherent authority throughout the territories of the Member States; but the terms of those Irish constitutional and legislative provisions, as interpreted by the Irish courts, have been or can be expected to be remarkably accommodating of the practical obligations which the European Court of Justice derives from the "constitution" of the Communities. This is the reason, in the final analysis, why the extension of the terms of Article 29.4.5 of the Constitution to the very different legal order of the Union was so sharply criticised in the previous Chapter.

In this chapter, it is proposed to review the interpretative options available to the Irish courts, which are more extensive than those thus far discussed. This review will be undertaken in the hypothetical context of a profound normative conflict between Irish constitutional values and those of the Communities, over abortion, such as that which loomed in 1989–91, but was averted, and has since been addressed by constitutional change in both legal orders. It is not sought to resolve the normative conflict in favour of one or the other source of foundational values, national or *communautaire*. That would be an exercise in political and legal philosophy beyond the scope of this work. Instead, the implications and possible interpretations of Article 29.4.3-6 will be considered from the perspective of the Irish judge who is philosophically inclined towards the vindication of the substantive Irish constitutional norm in a situation of fundamental conflict, but who is concerned also with the preservation of constitutional processes and institutions. Can such a judge constitutionally (*i.e.* as a matter of Irish constitutional law) favour the Irish norm over the competing "constitutional" requirements of the Communities? Community law does not countenance such conflicts, as Community law knows no "external constitution" (Casey, *Constitution*, at 164), no "second and transcendent constitution" (Henchy, "The Irish Constitution and the EEC" (1977) 1 D.U.L.J. 20, at 23). This question can only be asked as a matter of Irish constitutional law, as the final test of the Third, Tenth and Eleventh Amendments as the constitutional vehicles for the reception, on its own terms, of European Community law in Ireland.

The Principles of Constitutional Interpretation

Article 29.4.3-6 of the Constitution is a constitutional text, and thus falls to be interpreted by the High Court and the Supreme Court. Various forays of those courts into this difficult territory have already been analysed. These have yielded examples of the literal, the teleological and the harmonious approaches to constitutional interpretation (in *Crotty v. An Taoiseach* [1987] I.R. 713; *Meagher v. Minister for Agriculture* [1994] 1 I.R. 329; and *Campus Oil Ltd v. Minister for Industry and Energy* [1983] I.R. 82 respectively). These are three of six approaches to constitutional interpretation identified by Hogan and Whyte:

(i) the literal;
(ii) the "broad" (or teleological);
(iii) the harmonious;
(iv) the historical;
(v) the originalist or intentionalist; and
(vi) the natural law approaches (Kelly, *Constitution*, at xcviii–cxviii; see also Casey, *Constitution*, at 298–305; Forde, *Constitutional Law of Ireland* (1987) pp. 73–86, 260–66; Morgan, "Constitutional Interpretation: Three Cautionary Tales" (1988) 10 D.U.L.J. 24; Hogan, "Constitutional Interpretation", and Kelly, "Law and Manifesto", in Litton ed., *The Constitution of Ireland, 1937–1987* (1987); Barrington, "Some Problems of Constitutional Interpretation" in Curtin & O'Keeffe eds. *Constitutional Adjudication in European Community Law and National Law* (1992); Quinn, "The Nature and Significance of Critical Legal Studies" (1989) 7 I.L.T. 282; Quinn, "Reflections on the Legitimacy of Judicial Activism in the Field of Constitutional Law" (1991) Dlí 29; Whyte, "Constitutional Adjudication, Ideology and Access to the Courts" in Whelan ed., *Law and Liberty in Ireland* (1993); Whelan, "Constitutional Amendments in Ireland: The Competing Claims of Democracy" and O'Dowd, "Human Dignity under the Constitution" in Quinn *et al* eds. *Justice and Legal Theory in Ireland* (1995); Humphreys, "Constitutional Interpretation" (1993) 15 D.U.L.J. 59 (hereinafter Humphreys, Interpretation); Twomey, *Irish Constitutional Jurisprudence and Catholic Social Teaching*, M.Litt. Thesis, Trinity College, Dublin (1994); Hogan, "Unenumerated Personal Rights: Ryan's Case Re-evaluated" (1990–2) 25–7 Ir. Jur. 95; Phelan, *Revolution*, at 304–356). Hogan and Whyte remark that "the courts have shown no consistency with regard to any particular approach.... At present, however, the 'broad' and 'harmonious interpretation' approaches are probably in the ascendancy, although contemporary examples may be found in respect of all these distinct approaches". They suggest that this eclecticism allows judges to use "any such approach as will offer adventitious support for conclusions they have already reached" (Kelly, *Constitution*, at xcviii). In order to reach a conclusion about the correct interpretation and application of Article 29.4.3-6 of the Constitution, it is therefore necessary to review these interpretative theories, and the arguments that can be made on foot of them.

(i) The Literal Approach
   The literal approach to constitutional interpretation is best represented by the *dictum* of O'Higgins C.J. in *The People (Director of Public Prosecutions) v. O'Shea* [1982] I. R. 384:

> "The Constitution, as the fundamental law of the State, must be accepted, interpreted and construed according to the words which are used; and these words, where the meaning is plain and unambiguous, must be given their literal meaning."

It is plain that the *Crotty* test of legal obligation in ascertaining what is necessitated by the obligations of membership of the Communities is the product of a literal interpretation. While this approach is rightly criticised for introducing arid principles of statutory interpretation to the construction of a constitutional document which in many respects is drafted in broad terms, it is clearly more suited to the systemic or institutional provisions of the Constitution, where certainty is most desirable, than to those that employ broad conceptual terms to guarantee fundamental rights to equality, liberty, property and so on. One might add that at common law, literalism requires terms to be read in their statutory context; in constitutional terms, this can cause all but the most dictionary-bound literalism to merge with the harmonious approach so as to qualify apparently unambiguous provisions. This was acknowledged by O'Higgins C.J., although he restricted it to situations of ambiguity: "Of course, the Constitution must be construed as a whole, and not merely in parts and, where doubts or ambiguity exists, regard may be had to other provisions of the Constitution".

However, even strict literalism is not an antidote to all constitutional controversy, as will be made evident in three examples below, of the distinction between legal and political obligations, of the possible application of the doctrine of implied repeal, and of the disputed status of the Preamble to the Constitution.

(ii) The Teleological Approach

The teleological approach seeks the objective purpose of the law-maker, as it is evidenced in the legal text. This can be found in a formal list of objectives, or from examining the general scheme or thrust of the text in question. An early example of the "broad" or teleological approach can be found in the *dictum* of O'Byrne J. in *Sullivan v. Robinson* [1954] I.R. 151: "A Constitution is to be liberally construed so as to carry into effect the intentions of the people *as embodied therein*" (authors' italics). Costello J. made a similar statement in *Attorney-General v. Paperlink Ltd* [1984] I.L.R.M. 348:

> "A purposive, rather than a strictly literal approach to the interpretation of the sub-paragraphs is appropriate."

The interpretation by the Supreme Court in *Crotty* of the effect of the first sentence of Article 29.4.3 (as it then was) typifies this approach. It is also evident that the Supreme Court sought to employ such an approach in *Meagher* when it identified the major or fundamental obligation of membership of the Communities, which Article 29.4.5 was inserted to secure, and refused to allow what were perceived as sterile constitutional niceties to impede its operation. The teleological, the literal and the harmonious approaches can sometimes produce the same result, when a provision is sufficiently well-drafted that its terms express the subjective intention of the law-maker in a manner that is consistent with the objective (*i.e.* apparent) purpose of the law in question. It was essentially contended above that a purposive reading of Article 29.4.5 in *Meagher* should have read its purpose as ensuring the observance of the obligations of Community membership in the manner least intrusive on the domestic constitutional order—an objective purpose, expressed in the literal terms of the provision, that is consistent with the express subjective intention of the drafters. As will be seen below, however, the purposive approach can be employed to many different effects.

(iii) The Harmonious Approach

The doctrine of harmonious interpretation requires that constitutional provisions should not be construed in isolation from all other parts of the Constitution among which they are embedded, but should be so construed as to harmonise with the other parts (Kelly, *Constitution*, at ci). Henchy J. expressed the doctrine thus in *The People (Director of Public Prosecutions) v. O'Shea* [1982] I. R. 384:

> "Any single constitutional right or power is but a component in an ensemble of interconnected and interacting provisions which must be brought into play as part of a larger composition, and which must be given such an integrated interpretation as will fit it harmoniously into the general constitutional order and modulation. It may be said of a constitution, more than of any other legal instrument, that 'the letter killeth, but the spirit giveth life'."

Two related doctrines can also be identified: the hierarchy of constitutional guarantees, and the doctrine of abuse of rights. Although neither has the same level of support as the general doctrine of harmonious interpretation, both are of interest in interpreting Article 29.4.5 of the Constitution.

Griffin J. expressed the idea of a hierarchy of constitutional rules and rights in *People v. Shaw* [1982] I.R. 1:

"[Where a harmonious application of constitutional rules is not possible] the hierarchy or priority of the conflicting rights must be examined, both as between themselves and in relation to the general welfare of society."

Such a hierarchy was also identified by Hamilton P. in *Attorney-General (S.P.U.C. Ltd) v. Open Door Counselling Ltd* [1988] I.R. 593, and by Finlay C.J. and Egan J. in *Attorney-General v. X* [1992] 1 I.R. 1: both cases involved (as *Shaw* did) the right to life. Hogan and Whyte suggest that the chief shortcoming of the hierarchical approach is that an "*a priori* ranking of such rights (*e.g.* life over liberty, liberty over free speech, etc.) focuses on philosophical abstractions which, if inflexibly employed, would tend to lead to the predetermination of the outcome of particular litigation, at the expense of the flexibility which is desirable in any judicial appraisal of the relevant facts of each case and the competing merits of particular arguments" (Kelly, *Constitution*, at cvii). A further problem arises in identifying the place of abstract rights and freedoms in such a hierarchy. Nonetheless, it is difficult to object to a presumptive privileging of the right to life, even if the presumption can be reversed in some cases.

One potentially relevant aspect of the "abuse of rights" doctrine requires that the Constitution should not be construed as giving immunity or protection to activities or acts which are subversive of the Constitution itself. Such a doctrine underlies the German concept of "militant democracy" (*streitbare Demokratie*), which requires that the Constitution be interpreted "in a manner consistent with [its] fundamental principles and its system of values ... that does not submit to abuse of basic rights or an attack on the liberal order of the State" (*Bundesverfassungsgericht, Klass* (1970) 30 BVergGE 1; Article 18, German Constitution quoted in Kelly, *Constitution*, at cviii, n. 39; see further Kommers, *The Constitutional Jurisprudence of the Federal Republic of Germany* (Duke, 1989) pp. 43–4). This doctrine has been deemed applicable in a number of Irish cases, with varying degrees of rigour, where the offence specified in an extradition warrant is perceived to undermine the Irish constitutional order as well as that of the requesting State, and is thus ineligible for the benefit of the political offence exception under section 50 of the Extradition Act, 1965 (*Quinn v. Wren* [1985] I.R. 322; *Russell v. Fanning* [1988] I.R. 505; considerably reduced in scope in *Finucane v. McMahon* [1990] 1 I.R. 156). Such a doctrine could have far-reaching effects on the interpretation of Article 29.4.5 if obligations incurred under Community or Union law were considered to be subversive of the entire constitutional order.

(iv) The Historical Approach

The historical approach to constitutional interpretation has a number of strands. It can purport to seek the subjective intention or understanding of the legislator, or the objective meaning of the document at the time of enactment. Bork summarises the more appealing objective doctrine in its American "original understanding" guise (*The Tempting of America: The Political Seduction of the Law* (1990)):

"The search is not for subjective intention. If someone found a letter from George Washington to Martha telling her that what he meant by the power to lay taxes was not what other people meant, this would not change our reading of the Constitution in the slightest. Nor would the subjective intention of all the members of a ratifying convention alter anything.... All that counts is how the words used in the Constitution would have been understood at the time."

Of course, George Washington's hypothetical letter, or the debates of a constitutional convention, would be evidence of the understanding of 1789; but they would be no more determinative evidence than other contemporary sources of the meaning of the terms in question. If it is evident that the stated intention of a framer was widely accepted as being fully expressed in the text of a constitutional provision, then that subjective source becomes powerful evidence of objective meaning at the time. This can, of course, be contended for the Dáil debates on the amended text of the Third Amendment. The absence of such primary sources is not fatal, however, as the subjective intention of the framers is not in point as such (*pace* Kelly, *Constitution*, at cxvi–cxvii; *cf.* Whyte, "Constitutional Adjudication, Ideology and Access to the Courts" in Whelan ed. *Law and Liberty in Ireland* (1993) p. 149, at 156). Greater difficulties are caused for the "original understanding" approach in Ireland by the problems of evidence of understandings in 1937, and by the contingency of certain constitutional objectives and guarantees on progressive realisation in accordance with changing social circumstances (Humphreys, Interpretation, at 64).

The objective historical or "original understanding" approach is simply an adjunct to a literal or teleological approach, in seeking the meaning or purpose of the Constitution. It differs from the ordinary application of those approaches, however, in that it is the objective meaning or purpose of 1937 that is supposed to emerge; this may differ significantly from the construction that might be placed on an identically expressed clause or list of objectives in 1995, which is what is normally sought to be done when the Constitution is interpreted (see *e.g.* Walsh J. in *McGee v. Attorney-General* [1974] I.R. 287).

One example of the historical approach in Irish constitutional jurisprudence is the use of the state of the law in 1937 to shed light on the Constitution itself. Such a historical approach is generally disparaged for the purpose of interpreting the broad guarantees of individual rights and freedoms in the Constitution. (It also puts the cart before the horse, as laws were continued in force subject to the Constitution and only to the extent that they were not inconsistent therewith, *per* Article 50.) However, an understanding of the state of the law in 1937 can be of some utility "where some law-based system is at issue ... [*e.g.* in *Attorney-General v. Hamilton (No. 1)* [1993] 2 I.R. 250 on Cabinet confidentiality; and in *Attorney-General v. Hamilton (No. 2)* [1993] I.L.R.M. 821 on parliamentary privilege]. Thus, it may be said that where the Constitution carefully defines certain powers, rights, privileges and procedures (as is the case, for example, of the powers of the President, the scope of parliamentary privilege, the regulation of Dáil and Seanad elections and definition of a money bill) the courts must follow the text carefully, aided, where necessary, by a historical understanding of what the framers sought to achieve" (Kelly, *Constitution*, pp. cxii–cxiii; see also Kelly, "Law and Manifesto" in Litton ed., *The Constitution of Ireland, 1937–1987* (1987)).

Article 29.4.3-6 is, of course, a set of procedural provisions in this sense, listing a set of Treaties and how obligations under them are to take effect in Irish law. Two qualifications need, however, to be ventured. First, the operation of Article 29.4.5 affects all provisions of the Constitution, including the broad and constantly developing guarantees of fundamental rights. Secondly, the historical, like the literal approach, must be defeated where a provision makes it clear that it is not to be interpreted in this fashion (see Humphreys, *Interpretation*, p. 67). The Community legal order, like the domestic protection of fundamental rights, is painted in broad strokes in the Treaties, the details being filled in over time through the acts of the various institutions, including the Court of Justice. Provision for this is made in the text of Article 29.4.5 of the Constitution, so that it is difficult to view Article

29.4.3-6 as simply a licence to join the Communities and the Union, and to accept the obligations of membership and the acts of the institutions thereof, as they stood in 1972, 1987 and 1992 (see the decision of the Supreme Court on the European Communities (Amendment) Act, 1986, *Crotty v. An Taoiseach* [1987] I.R. 713).

Use of the purported state of public opinion in 1937 in interpreting the Constitution can be even more unreal than referring to the state of the law, not least because "[i]t would plainly be impossible to identify with the necessary degree of accuracy of description the standards or mores of the Irish people in 1937" (*per* McCarthy J., dissenting, in *Norris v. Attorney-General* [1984] I.R. 36). Hogan and Whyte suggest, however, "that there are contexts in which the exercise would seem not unreal, but an antidote to unreality: for instance, in trying to decide whether the kind of literal interpretation of the Constitution which has now become common produces a sense which can really be imputed to the people (or the Dáil, or the draftsmen) of 1937" (Kelly, *Constitution*, p. cxv). An example of this "negative" historical approach can be found in the judgment of Henchy J. in *The People (Director of Public Prosecutions) v. O'Shea* [1982] I.R. 384. Dissenting on the question whether the general words of Article 34.4.3 of the Constitution meant that appeals could be brought to the Supreme Court against a verdict of acquittal in the High Court (sitting as the Central Criminal Court), he stated that "it is arguably to be contended that if such opinion had been expressed by any reputable person or body, the Constitution would never have been enacted by the people". Such arguments should however be used with caution (not least because they lay claim to a *conditional* insight into the *subjective* intention of the people). It would of course be possible to argue in respect of any piece of Community legislation, or decision of the Court of Justice, that had the people known that Community membership entailed such obligations, they would never have voted for the Third, Tenth or Eleventh Amendments (depending on whichever Treaty provision is the legal basis of the offending item), and Article 29.4.3-6 should be construed accordingly. Such an argument is only defensible, if at all, in the case of a patent abuse of power by the Community or Union institutions (see further the *dicta* of the *Bundesverfassungsgericht* in *Brunner* [1994] 1 C.M.L.R. 57, at 84, 88–9, 92, discussed below).

(v) The Natural Law Approach

The existence of natural law is expressly acknowledged in a number of provisions of the Constitution (in particular, in Articles 41, 42 and 43 on the family, education and property respectively). The development of the doctrine of unenumerated rights under Article 40.3 of the Constitution is attributable in large part to the natural law approach to constitutional interpretation (Kelly, *Constitution*, p. cxviii; Hogan, "Unenumerated Personal Rights: *Ryan's Case* Re-evaluated" (1990–2) 25–7 Ir. Jur. 95; Whelan, "Constitutional Amendments in Ireland: The Competing Claims of Democracy" in Quinn *et al* eds., *Justice and Legal Theory in Ireland* (1995)). While an overt invocation of natural law in judicial reasoning has waned somewhat over the past decade reaching its nadir in the Supreme Court decision in *Re Article 26 and the Regulation of Information (Services outside the State for Termination of Pregnancies) Bill, 1995,* [1995] 2 I.L.R.M. 81 (discussed below), not least because of the seemingly diffuse and subjective quality of such standards, it will probably continue to be employed "as a mechanism of avoiding an unpalatable result in any case where this might be produced by a stark, literalist interpretation of the Constitution" (Kelly, *Constitution*, p. cxviii). Moreover, a broad teleological approach to constitutional interpretation, invoking preambular objectives like the assurance of the dignity and freedom of the individual, the attainment of true social order, and the promotion of the common good (not to mention the democratic nature of the State under Article 5), will tend to merge in practice with a secular form of natural law.

The *locus classicus* of the natural law approach in modern Irish constitutional jurisprudence is the judgment of Walsh J. in *McGee v. Attorney-General* [1974] I.R. 284:

> "Articles 41, 42 and 43 emphatically reject the theory that there are no rights without laws, no rights contrary to the law and no rights anterior to the law. They indicate that justice is placed above the law and acknowledge that natural rights, or human rights, are not created by law but that the Constitution confirms their existence and gives them protection.... In this country, it falls finally upon the judges to interpret the Constitution and in doing so to determine, where necessary, the rights which are superior or antecedent to positive law, or which are imprescriptible or inalienable.... The very structure and content of the Articles dealing with fundamental rights clearly indicate that justice is not subordinate to the law. In particular, the terms of Article 40.3 expressly subordinate the law to justice."

Perhaps the most common indictment of natural law reasoning is that it is alleged to be hopelessly open-ended and uncertain. Even if we accept that the Irish courts subscribe to a theologically derived natural law as "the law of God discovered by human reason" (see Walsh, "The Constitution and Constitutional Rights" in Litton ed., *The Constitution of Ireland 1937–1987* (Dublin, 1987) p. 86 at 94; O'Hanlon, "Natural Rights and the Irish Constitution" (1993) 11 I.L.T. 8; *cf.* Humphreys, Interpretation, at 71–3), that tradition is itself a good deal more complex than is admitted by the judges (see Clarke, "The Role of Natural Law in Irish Constitutional Law" (1982) 17 Ir. Jur. 187; Kelly, *Constitution*, p. 678). The claim of *exclusive* judicial authority to expound the requirements of a natural law discoverable by the exercise of human reason has also been criticised (see Duncan, "Can Natural Law be used in Constitutional Interpretation?" in Treacy & Whyte eds., *Religion, Morality and Public Policy* (1995) p. 125).

Despite its alleged shortcomings, protection by natural law of rights which are "antecedent and superior to all positive law" (Article 41.1.1) poses problems for an immunity clause such as Article 29.4.5 of the Constitution. Hogan and Whyte observe (Kelly, *Constitution*, pp. 682–3):

> "This inconsistency does not appear to have been adverted to in the caselaw to date and, given the constitutional recognition of the 'higher law', can presumably be resolved only by qualifying the immunities from judicial review conferred by [Article 29.4.5]."

Phelan has argued cogently that natural law and natural rights are the foundational values of the Irish Constitution and are fundamental to its legitimacy (in *Revolt or Revolution: The Constitutional Boundaries of the European Community* (1995)). This view is supported, for example, by the judgment of Costello J. in *Murray v. Ireland* [1985] I.R. 532, 538–9, in which *all* constitutional fundamental rights are stated to be antecedent and superior to positive law, *i.e.* natural rights. Phelan considers as the basis of natural law the application of the permanently relevant principles of practical reason to the fundamental commitments of Irish constitutional law which appear, upon reflection, to be self-evidently good (*Revolution*, at 313). Central to this process is the realisation of the common good: "an abstract term for the set of conditions in society which enables persons best to pursue in their lives the fundamental commitments and values espoused by the Constitution. The conditions of the common good act as a counterweight to the uncontrolled pursuit of the good of an individual but at the same time facilitate an individual in the securing of his or her good in life within society" (*Revolution*, at 340).

On this view, the principles of natural law are (or should be) operative whenever the Irish courts engage in the interpretation or application of the Constitution, irrespective of whether natural law is expressly invoked; and abandonment of the judicial task of securing the rights of the individual within the constitutional common good in favour of an externally-imposed and differently legitimated conception of rights and the general interest must amount to a sort of constitutional revolution. This thesis runs contrary to at least one other analysis of the sources of legitimacy of the Constitution, which identifies competing ideologies at work in the text, *viz.* liberalism and theocracy (Quinn, "Reflections on the Legitimacy of Judicial Activism in the Field of Constitutional Law" (1991) Dh-29; Whyte prefers the terms liberalism and communitarianism: "Constitutional Adjudication, Ideology, and Access to the Courts" in Whelan ed., *Law and Liberty in Ireland* (1993)). One does not have to embrace entirely the latter analysis in order to entertain misgivings about a unitary conception of Irish constitutional values; one can also argue, on the contrary, that it is possible to accept Phelan's unitary conception solely because it is expressed in terms too general to invite dissent, or to facilitate consensual analysis beyond the simple observation that the Irish conception of individual rights and the common good, and of the balance between them, is different from that current in other States, or in the Community legal order. It is nonetheless important to appreciate that the favouring of one such external conception over that indigenous to Ireland (however subjectively applied by Irish judges on a case by case basis) represents, from Phelan's perspective, a veritable subversion of the Irish constitutional order rather than simply an (extensive) accommodation of a supranational legal order chosen as the vehicle for the advancement of the general interest.

Normative Conflict and the Interpretative Role of the Irish Courts: Article 29.4.5 Redux?

It was stated at the beginning of the foregoing section that controversies concerning the interpretation of Article 29.4.3-5 of the Constitution fall to be resolved by the High Court and the Supreme Court, as is the case in respect of all provisions of the Constitution. This uncontroversial position was expressed rather controversially (because of the perceived implication that Irish courts might differ with the Court of Justice as to the obligations of membership of the Communities) in some extra-curial remarks of T.F. O'Higgins, former Chief Justice and Judge of the European Court of Justice ("The Constitution and the Communities—Scope for Stress?" in O'Reilly ed., *Human Rights and Constitutional Law: Essays in Honour of Brian Walsh* (1992), 227, at 229):

> "Should a question arise as to whether a particular measure is ... 'necessitated' it would seem to me to be one exclusively for the High Court under the provisions of Article 34.3.2 of the Constitution. I cannot see on what basis jurisdiction to decide what is, essentially, a question as to the validity of a law having regard to the Constitution, can be conferred on or exercised by any other court."

McCarthy J. stated in the Supreme Court in *S.P.U.C. (Ireland) Ltd v. Grogan* [1989] I.R. 753 that "[t]he sole authority for the construction of the Constitution lies in the Irish courts, the final authority being this court" [1989] I.R. 753, at 770. McCarthy J.'s judgment also illustrates, however, that the questions of interpretative authority and normative authority are distinct, and that Irish constitutional provisions, subject to authoritative construction only by Irish courts, may nonetheless be construed to defer to competing norms. McCarthy J. continued:

"Article 29.4.3 [as it then was] may exclude from constitutional invalidation some provisions of the Treaty of Rome the enforcement of which is necessitated by the obligations of membership of the European Communities; it may be that in enacting the Eighth Amendment to the Constitution as explained by this court in the *Open Door Counselling* case, the people of Ireland did so in breach of the Treaty to which Ireland had acceded in 1973."

Walsh J., on the other hand, indicated the potential significance of the retention of domestic interpretative authority over the provision by which, as a matter of Irish constitutional law, Community law ("including its primacy", *per* the Supreme Court in *Meagher v. Minister for Agriculture* [1994] 1 I.R. 329, 351) is received in Ireland. It has already been argued above that his judgment in *Campus Oil Ltd v. Minister for Industry and Energy* [1983] I.R. 82 was not nearly so *communautaire* in its reasoning as its result might suggest. This point is amplified by Walsh J.'s judgment in *Grogan*, in which he stated pointedly [1989] I.R. 753, 768–9:

"It was sought to be argued in the present case that the effect of [the Third Amendment] ... is to qualify all rights, including fundamental rights, guaranteed by the Constitution .... Any answer to the reference from the Court of Justice will have to be considered in the light of our own constitutional provisions. In the last analysis only this court can decide finally what are the effects of the interaction of the Eighth Amendment [Article 40.3.3] and the Third Amendment of the Constitution."

In *S.P.U.C. (Ireland) Ltd v. Grogan*, the Society for the Protection of Unborn Children sought an injunction prohibiting the provision of abortion information in Ireland by university students' unions, in handbooks distributed annually to students. This information included specific information on the identity, location and means of communication with abortion clinics in Great Britain. Distribution of such abortion information by non-directive counsellors had already been prohibited by the Supreme Court pursuant to Article 40.3.3 of the Constitution because it was deemed to be assistance in obtaining an abortion outside the jurisdiction (*Attorney-General, ex rel. S.P.U.C. (Ireland) Ltd v. Open Door Counselling* [1988] I.R. 593). While procuring an abortion outside the jurisdiction of Ireland was not a crime, the court in *Open Door* felt obliged to prevent activity which threatened the constitutionally protected right to life of the unborn; this right was deemed to be superior to the competing rights of privacy and of association, freedom of expression and right to disseminate information.

In the High Court in *Grogan*, Carroll J. felt that an interpretation of Community law was necessary for her to reach judgment, and made a reference to the Court of Justice for a preliminary ruling under Article 177 EEC. The Community law point at issue was whether the performance of abortions for gain constituted a service within the meaning of the EEC Treaty, and whether there was, by corollary, a right to distribute in one Member State information relating to the provision of that service in another Member State. In the meantime, Carroll J. made no express order refusing or adjourning the application for an injunction. On appeal against this failure to grant an interlocutory injunction pending receipt of the preliminary ruling of the Court of Justice, the Supreme Court balanced the clear constitutional prohibition on the dissemination of abortion information of the type involved, against what was seen as merely "a possible or putative right which might exist in European law as a corollary to a right to travel so as to avail of services" (*per* Finlay C.J. [1989] I. R. 753, at 765), and granted an injunction. The above-quoted *obiter* remarks of McCarthy and Walsh JJ. concerned the possibility of the Court of Justice ruling that the defendant students' unions were entitled under Community law to disseminate abortion information, and the clear conflict that this would occasion with the requirements of Article 40.3.3 of the Constitution as interpreted by the Supreme Court.

The ruling of the Court of Justice did not directly assist the defendant students' unions. The court held that the performance of abortions for gain was a service within the meaning of Article 60 EEC, but that the students' unions could not avail of any rights under the Treaty because they were not in a commercial relationship with the providers of the service (Case 159/90, *S.P.U.C. (Ireland) Ltd v. Grogan* [1991] E.C.R. I 4685). The clear implication was that agencies having a commercial relationship with abortion clinics in another Member State, or indeed the clinics themselves, would be entitled as a matter of Community law to distribute information in Ireland about the service provided and on how to avail of it. An exception could be permitted to Ireland on grounds of public policy, public security or public health, under Article 56 EEC, but such derogations by Member States from Community law are subject to the supervision of the Court of Justice. In exercising this supervisory jurisdiction, the Court of Justice ensures that derogations serve genuine public policy aims that are compatible with the Treaty, that the restriction on Community rights is proportionate to the public policy interest served, and is consistent with the general principles of Community law, which include the protection of fundamental rights, as guaranteed by the European Convention on Human Rights, and as they result from the constitutional traditions common to the Member States. In his Opinion in *Grogan*, Advocate General van Gerven concluded that a ban on travel outside Ireland to avail of abortion services would be disproportionate, but that a ban on information constituting assistance in procuring an abortion was neither a disproportionate restriction of Community rights in respect of services nor an unacceptable restriction on freedom of expression. However, the European Court of Human Rights decided in *Open Door Counselling Ltd v. Ireland* (Series A, No. 246; (1993) 15 E.H.R.R. 244) that the prohibitory injunction granted against the counselling centres by the Supreme Court was a disproportionate restriction on free expression, guaranteed under Article 10 of the Convention on Human Rights. This increases the likelihood that the Court of Justice, in an appropriate case, would take the same view. On the other hand, Costello J. concluded in the High Court in *Attorney-General v. X* [1992] 1 I.R. 1 that the imposition of a travel ban on a girl who wished to travel to England for an abortion would not be disproportionate. (For a full account of these developments, see Kelly, *Constitution*, pp. 792–806; Phelan, "Right to Life of the Unborn v. Promotion of Trade in Services: The European Court of Justice and the Normative Shaping of the European Union" (1992) 55 M.L.R. 647 (hereinafter Phelan, Union); Curtin, Casenote on *S.P.U.C. (Ireland) Ltd v. Grogan* (1992) 29 C.M.L.Rev. 585; de Búrca "Fundamental Human Rights and the Reach of European Community Law" (1993) 13 O.J.L.S. 283; Kingston & Whelan, "The Protection of the Unborn in Three Legal Orders" (1992) 10 I.L.T. 93, 104, 166, 189.)

There thus existed the potential for a conflict, in respect of extremely controversial subject-matter, between the substantive guarantees and requirements of European Community law and Irish constitutional law—the kind of conflict which Article 29.4.5 was designed to resolve. The comments of the judges of the Supreme Court in *Grogan* on the interpretation of this provision of the Constitution therefore went to the heart of the matter. Pains have since been taken both at the Irish and the European level to resolve the perceived substantive conflict, through Protocol No. 17 to the Maastricht Treaty (discussed in Chapter 9 below), and through the Thirteenth and Fourteenth Amendments to the Constitution of Ireland regarding travel and information. Notwithstanding these efforts (which are not guaranteed to be perfectly successful; see Whelan, "Some Aspects of the Twelfth and Thirteenth Amendments of the Constitution", unpublished manuscript, Trinity College Dublin Library (1994) (hereinafter Whelan, Amendments); see also the discussion in Chapter 2 above of the possible problems with sections 6 and 7 of the Regulation of Information (services outside the State for Termination of Pregnancies) Bill, 1995), this potentially explosive conflict between the Irish and Community legal orders can serve to illustrate in the discussion that follows the interpretative debate about Article 29.4.5 of the Constitution.

Phelan has expounded a detailed argument for the exclusivity of the role of the Irish courts in interpreting Article 29.4.5 of the Constitution (Phelan, Membership, at 272–5; a version of this argument also appears in Phelan, *Revolution*, at 376 *et seq.*). Gallagher has asserted that where the constitutional validity of a national law, act or measure (otherwise unconstitutional) turns on whether it is necessitated by the obligations of membership of the Communities, a party in the Supreme Court can demand as of right that a reference be made to the Court of Justice under Article 177 E.C. because a decision on a question of Community law is necessary to enable the court to give judgment (Gallagher, "The Constitution and the Community" (1993) I.J.E.L. 129, at 130–2; see also Casey, *Constitution*, p. 171; Temple Lang, Scope, at 231; see also the discussion in Chapter 2 above of the possible obligation to make a reference in such circumstances even in the context of an Article 26 Reference by the President to the Supreme Court). Phelan takes issue with this assertion in respect of a challenge to such a measure where the court does not believe it is "necessitated by the obligations of membership" (as that constitutional formula is interpreted by the court), and that it is unconstitutional and void. Leaving aside the *acte clair* doctrine (Case 283/81, *CILFIT v. Minister for Health* [1982] E.C.R. 3415), the preliminary ruling will only be necessary to enable the Supreme Court to give judgment on the constitutionality of the impugned Irish measure if it is obliged to follow and to give effect to the ruling once it is made. "That is, must the interpretation of Article 29.4.5 follow European Community law? If yes, then the reference would be necessary, and therefore as of right. If no, then the [party] would have no right to a reference, and [the impugned measure] would remain void" (Phelan, Membership, at 231).

Phelan gives as an example of the interpretation of Article 29.4.5 not following Community law the decision of the Supreme Court in *Meagher v. Minister for Agriculture* [1994] 1 I.R. 329 discussed above, "because the machinery in section 3(2) [of the European Communities Act, 1972] is not, as a matter of Community law, necessitated as an obligation of membership. Community law has no rules on what the domestic machinery should be, so long as the result complies with Community law". (The decision in *Campus Oil Ltd v. Minister for Industry and Energy* [1983] I.R. 82 could also be employed in favour of this argument, no matter which of the possible interpretations of that decision is favoured.) Phelan continues:

> "Therefore, the Supreme Court decision turns on giving a different meaning to 'necessitated by the obligations of membership' than that given by Community law. It is a constitutional law meaning, albeit one which in this case is more *communautaire* than Community law itself."

Phelan acknowledges, however, that this does not give an answer to the question posed by the converse situation, *viz.* where Community law *does* require a particular national measure, must the Irish courts follow the Court of Justice ruling that such a measure is "necessitated"? As a matter of Irish constitutional law, are the Irish courts free, in their interpretation of Article 29.4.5, to be less *communautaire* than the European Court of Justice as well as more so? He suggests a number of circumstances where this might be possible:

"[L]et us suppose that the constitutional rule (Z) which [the impugned measure] X violates is particularly important (for example, a basic principle on the separation of the judicial and other powers of government, on the people's right to be consulted in a referendum, a human right, etc.).... It is perfectly legitimate as a matter of constitutional construction to apply any of the following methods of interpretation. First, a historical interpretation of Article 29.4.5 along these lines: in amending the Constitution the people did not intend to allow the rendering inapplicable of Z by a measure such as X. Second, an interpretation of Article 29.4.5 in the light of the Constitution as a whole holding (this phrase is not meant to be disparaging) that the tail cannot wag the dog. Third, that Article 29.4.5 must be read in the light of the goals of the Constitution, which precludes the overriding of Z by X. Fourth, an interpretation of Article 29.4.5 in the light of its interaction with a particular Article.... Furthermore, the protection afforded by Article 29.4.5 may be limited because it is a shield solely against provisions of the Constitution, not against natural law."

Phelan adds a different possible literal interpretation of the provisions of Article 29.4.5. He suggests a distinction "between what is necessitated by European Community law and what is necessitated by European Community membership. The latter is partly a political question, and one of which the Court of Justice is not necessarily the authoritative interpreter". This implies that the scope of political obligations of membership could be narrower than that of legal obligations, thus permitting the court, as a matter of Irish constitutional law, to evade certain of the requirements of Community law that are not, in political terms, enforceable.

By taking any one of these interpretative paths to strike down a national measure required of the State as a matter of European Community law, Phelan concedes that the Supreme Court could cause the State to be found in breach of its obligations under the Treaty. A resulting decision of the Court of Justice in enforcement proceedings that the Treaty obligation (or regulation or directive) in question was directly applicable would mean that it would fall to be considered under the second clause of Article 29.4.5 as a law, act or measure of the Communities (assuming that decisions of the Court of Justice are among the laws, acts and measures of the institutions of the Communities). This, it is suggested, would require it to be enforced after all (see also O'Higgins, "The Constitution and the Communities—Scope for Stress?" in O'Reilly ed., *Human Rights and Constitutional Law* (1992) p. 227, at 229), although Phelan expressly refrains in his article from considering further interpretative arguments against such an eventuality. (See the discussion in Chapter 1 above of the interpretation of the second clause of Article 29.4.5 of the Constitution.) In his view, however, any such conclusion would not, however, disturb Phelan's central point about the first sentence of Article 29.4.5, and his rejection of any automatic right to an Article 177 E.C. reference to the Court of Justice where the constitutionality of a national measure is challenged. One can counter, however, that any such effect of the second clause of Article 29.4.5. must constitute an argument for a complementary (and therefore *communautaire*) interpretation of the first clause.

Phelan employs one further argument to make his case. Article 29.4.5 also governs national measures necessitated by the obligations of membership of the European Union. As was observed above, obligations under the Common Provisions of the E.U. Treaty, and in the fields of common foreign and security policy and of judicial and home affairs co-operation are outside the jurisdiction of the European Court of Justice. The Irish courts are therefore unable to follow the Court of Justice in deciding what obligations arise from these provisions. This, he says, implies that Articles 29.4.5 of the Constitution cannot be interpreted to refer to measures necessitated by the obligations of membership of the Union *or the Communities* as construed by the Court of Justice. Before returning to the general point made by Phelan, one must counter that the exclusion of the jurisdiction of the Court of Justice in some areas should not undermine its role in those areas where it exercises jurisdiction (which point is reinforced by Article M, E.U., although that need not in itself affect the Irish constitutional position). Secondly, while the very fact that such an argument can be made is another cause for criticism of the terms of the Eleventh Amendment, it is an argument which only became possible with its enactment in 1992, and need not affect as a matter of course the judicial construction of the constitutional concept of measures "necessitated by the obligations of membership of the Communities", which predates it by 20 years and which has already generated an interpretative jurisprudence.

For the purpose of analysing the various interpretative options canvassed by Phelan, it may be useful to give them a little more hypothetical flesh. Suppose that the Thirteenth and Fourteenth Amendments of the Constitution of Ireland have not been enacted, nor has Protocol No. 17 to the Maastricht Treaty been adopted. (This hypothesis is employed because the conflict between the two legal orders is clearer and more fundamental than any surmised still to exist after the adoption of these provisions.) Legislation is enacted in Ireland permitting abortion clinics established in another Member State to disseminate information about their services in private non-directive counselling sessions with pregnant women. (This is still unlawful under sections 6 and 7 of the Regulation of Information (Services outside the State for Termination of Pregnancies) Act, 1995.) The constitutionality of the Act is challenged by an interested party. Article 40.3.3 of the Constitution is interpreted by the High Court to prohibit in all circumstances (save where there is a real and substantial risk to the life of the mother which can only be avoided by the termination of her pregnancy, as in *Attorney-General v. X* [1992] 1 I.R. 1) the distribution by abortion clinics of information constituting assistance in procuring an abortion abroad; the European Court of Justice rules in a preliminary reference in the same case that the clinics are entitled under Community law to distribute such information, and, that so complete a prohibition as that imposed by the High Court would be a disproportionate restriction of that entitlement, and impermissible as a public policy derogation under the Treaty. It is clear that the Act is the most restrictive measure that will be tolerated by the Court of Justice (thus complying with the test suggested in Chapter 5 above for constitutional review of the content of national measures giving effect to Community law obligations).

A simple application by the High Court of the literal *Crotty* test of legal obligation would speedily resolve the conflict. The Act would be deemed to be necessitated by the obligations of membership of the Communities; the provisions of Article 40.3.3 would therefore be precluded from invalidating it, and it would stand. Through the operation of the first sentence of Article 29.4.5, the contention before the Court of Justice of the defendants in *Grogan* would be realised, *viz.* that "the principle of the primacy of Community law ... requires national courts to apply Community law in its entirety and so construe any new provision which uses a phrase such as 'as far as practicable' as meaning 'in so far as is compatible with obligations under Community law'" ([1991] E.C.R. I 4685, I 4697). It should be noted, however, that the hypothetical examples given in Chapter 3 above of the possible operation of the legal obligation test all described, advisedly, what the Irish judge would *ordinarily* do. A conflict such as that now under discussion would involve national constitutional principles that are, as Advocate General van Gerven observed in *Grogan*, "regarded in that Member State as forming part of the basic principles of society", involving "a value judgment as to the necessity to protect unborn human life which is regarded as fundamental in the Member State concerned" [1991] E.C.R. I 4685, I 4719–20. It would be an extraordinary situation, and one in which the Irish judge might well seek "adventitious support" from the various interpretative theories to take a different path. One must assume, however, that the court would seek to establish a test capable of consistent application in future cases as well as in the case in hand.

There are some possible literal readings of the Constitution that would achieve a different result to that described immediately above. First, Phelan suggests a difference between the obligations imposed by European Community law, and the political obligations of Community membership. He does not develop the distinction, but some problems are immediately apparent. A test of political obligation would speedily collapse into a test of how much the State could get away with. Furthermore, while the European Court of Justice would not necessarily be the authoritative interpreter of political obligation, it would also be invidious for the Irish courts to have to engage in such a task (although the employment of such a test in a constitutional context would require it). One might conclude that the test of political obligation could in some cases have a broader rather than a narrower scope than that of legal obligation: it is difficult to deny, after all, the political imperative that was felt in many quarters for Ireland to ratify the Single European Act. (The Danish experience with the Maastricht Treaty is also illustrative of this point.) However, while a test of political obligation might give constitutional immunity to more rather than fewer measures than one of legal obligation, it clearly would be employed in the instant case to narrow the immunity granted by Article 29.4.5 of the Constitution. A test of political obligation could speedily collapse into a test of how much the State could get away with. Furthermore, while the European Court of Justice would not necessarily be the authoritative interpreter of *political* obligation, it could also be invidious for the Irish courts to have to engage in such a task, although the employment of such a test in a constitutional context would require it. (On the general reluctance of the Irish courts to engage in political questions, see *McKenna v. An Taoiseach*, Costello J., High Court, June 8, 1992; *Duff v. Minister for Agriculture* [1993] 2 C.M.L.R. 969; [1994] I.J.E.L. 247.) Nonetheless, the test of political obligation could be recast in terms of expectation and therefore of intention and of objectives. If Ireland expected to join, and was politically committed to a certain type of Community which it is contended was disclosed by the terms of the Treaty, the purported obligations of a judicially and legislatively developed Community with more extensive competences, more ambitious objectives and more alien fundamental norms could be said to be outwith both the intention of the drafters, and the objectives, of the Third and subsequent related Amendments. This argument could run into problems in respect of both the presence in the Treaty in 1972 of Article 235 EEC, and the development to that point of the "constitutional" jurisprudence of the Court of Justice, but will be considered further below.

A literal argument based on the principles of statutory interpretation has been offered by Walsh J., writing extra-judicially (Walsh, Reflections, at 820):

> "In view of the fact that the 'anti-abortion' amendment to the Constitution was enacted many years after Ireland joined the European Communities, the question of the effect of an *'acte postérieur'* in the field of human rights may fall to be considered."

This question amplifies an apparent invocation of the doctrine of harmonious interpretation by Walsh J. in *Grogan*, asking "whether or not the Eighth Amendment itself qualifies the amendment to Article 29" ([1989] I.R. 753, at 768); this statement should possibly be recast as a suggestion of implied amendment. Bennion defines the principle of implied amendment as follows (*Statutory Interpretation* (1992) p. 192):

> "Where a later enactment does not expressly amend (whether textually or indirectly) an earlier enactment which it has power to override, but

the provisions of the later enactment are inconsistent with those of the earlier, the later by implication amends the earlier so far as is necessary to remove the inconsistency between them."

However, the problem with a conflict between the Third and the Eighth Amendments is that the inconsistency is not apparent. Article 29.4.5 of the Constitution is a procedural provision, conceding primacy to obligations incurred under another legal order. It does not on its face conflict with a substantive provision such as Aricle 40.3.3 of the Constitution. The conflict arises instead between a Community obligation to which Article 29.4.5 refers, and the requirements of Article 40.3.3. There is no necessary implication from the enactment of the Eighth Amendment that conflicts between its provisions and those of Community law should be resolved in a manner different to that in which other such conflicts with the terms of the Constitution are dealt with. (The repeal of the third sentence of Article 29.4.3 and its re-enactment with additional references to the obligations of membership of the European Union as Article 29.4.5, by the Eleventh Amendment of the Constitution Act, 1992, also robs this argument of some of its formal force; on the other hand, this occurred after the adoption of Protocol No. 17 to the Maastricht Treaty.)

A final, very narrow literal argument arises from a close reading of the terms of Article 29.4.5. It has been suggested that the Preamble is not a "provision" of the Constitution, and is therefore not subject to amendment under the terms of Article 46 of the Constitution (Kelly, *Constitution*, p. 9; a similar argument is made in Phelan, *Revolution*, p. 389). It would follow from this that the statement in Article 29.4.5 that "[n]o provision of this Constitution invalidates laws enacted, acts done or measures adopted by the State which are necessitated by the obligations of membership of the European Union or of the Communities" would not prevent the invalidation of a national measure pursuant to the Preamble. (A similar argument can be made in respect of the second clause of Article 29.4.5.) The Preamble has often been invoked to assist in the interpretation of particular provisions of the Constitution (see the numerous cases discussed in Kelly, *Constitution*, pp. 3-9). But it is not clear that the Preamble contains constitutional obligations, enforceable as such without reference to any other provision of the Constitution (if only Article 40.3 and the doctrine of unenumerated rights). However, Hederman J. suggested that the Preamble could give rise to binding constitutional norms in his dissenting judgment in *Russell v. Fanning* [1988] I.R. 505, stating that the re-integration of the national territory is:

> "by the provisions [*sic*] of the Preamble to the Constitution and of Article 3 of the Constitution a constitutional imperative and not one the pursuit or non-pursuit of which is within the discretion of the Government or any other organ of State."

This statement was endorsed by the Supreme Court in *McGimpsey v. Ireland* [1990] 1 I.R. 110. Finlay C.J., speaking for the Court, said that Articles 2 and 3 of the Constitution should be read with the Preamble. Even in these two cases, however, it is not clear that the Preamble alone can have legal effects. It probably is not profitable to continue to speculate on the enforceability of the Preamble as such. However, such a highly literalist reading of Article 29.4.5 could give added strength to teleological or harmonious interpretations of Article 29.4.5, which will be considered further below.

The first possibility considered by Phelan is an historical approach: "in amending the Constitution, the people did not intend to allow the rendering inapplicable of Z by a measure such as X". He cites in support the dissenting judgment of Henchy J. in *The People (Director of Public Prosecutions) v. O'Shea* [1982] I.R. 384. It was contended above that Henchy J. employed a *subjective* historical test in that case, an approach which is very vulnerable both to the practical problem of lack of evidence, and to the theoretical problems inherent in any attempt to conflate the views of over a million voters into a single intention (as well as in attempting to identify the subjective intention of even a single person).

An objective historical approach might be more sustainable. The people, in approving the Third Amendment, thereby authorised the ratification of the Treaty provisions on services which are central to the pronouncements of the European Court of Justice on the matter in hand. The extension by the Court of Justice of Treaty prohibitions on discriminatory national rules to rules which are not formally discriminatory but which are in practice more burdensome on persons providing or receiving services across Member State frontiers underlies the Community interest in Irish rules relating to abortion information. This extension is not uncontroversial as a matter of Community law, based as it is on a teleological interpretation of the Treaties that goes significantly beyond the text (see Article 60, E.C.; Marenco, "Restrictions on Freedom to Provide Services"(1991) 11 Y.E.L. 111; Phelan, Union, at 675–6). It could be asserted that while the decisions of the European Court of Justice are normally determinative of the legal obligations to which the State subscribed when it ratified the Treaties, the Irish courts retain the right, as a matter of Irish law, to review an obligation arising from an alleged abuse of competence by the Court of Justice. (This very point is made elsewhere by Phelan, *Revolution*, at 445–6; see also at 368–9, 373.) This right could be claimed even though Treaty ratification entailed acceptance of the primacy of a legal order the obligations of which are interpreted in the light the objectives of the constitutional Treaties, where a particular decision of the Court of Justice is perceived *by the Irish court* to go beyond the essential scope and objectives of the Treaties as ratified and thus to fall outside the terms of the authorisation given in the first sentence of Article 29.4.3 in 1972. Therefore, as a matter of Irish law, it would not be considered to be a legal obligation of membership, *pace* the view of the European Court of Justice. (This represents the re-packaging of the political obligation argument discussed above.)

It was remarked above that Collins and O'Reilly suggested the rudiments of such an approach ("The Application of Community Law in Ireland, 1973–89" (1990) 27 C.M.L.Rev. 315, at 319). So too did Walsh J. in *Grogan* [1989] I.R. 753, at 769:

> "The fact that particular activities, even grossly immoral ones, may be permitted to a greater or lesser extent in some Member States does not mean that they are considered to be within the objectives of the treaties of the European Communities, particularly the Treaty of Rome.... *A fortiori* it cannot be one of the objectives of the European Communities that a Member State should be obliged to permit activities which are clearly designed to set at nought the constitutional guarantees for the protection within the State of a fundamental human right."

This approach is also suggested by the decision of the *Bundesverfassungsgericht* in *Brunner* [1994] 1 C.M.L.R. 57, at 84, 88–9, 94. Article 23(1) of the German Constitution permits the transfer of sovereign powers in order to co-operate in the development of the European Union, which is subject to, *inter alia*, the principles of democracy and of the rule of law. The German elector exercises his right under Article 38 of the Constitution to participate in the democratic legitimation of the sovereign power transferred to the European Communities through the decision of the *Bundestag* on the Act of Accession [1994] 1 C.M.L.R. 57, at 88–9:

> "There is accordingly a breach of Article 38 of the Constitution if an Act that opens up the German legal system to the direct validity and appli-

cation of the law of the (supra-national) European Communities does not establish with sufficient certainty the powers that are transferred and the intended programme of integration.... In view of the fact that the text of an international treaty must be worked out between the parties, the same requirements cannot be set for the certainty and tightness of the rules of a treaty as are imposed in the case of an Act.... What is decisive is that Germany's membership and the rights and duties that follow therefrom (and especially the immediately binding legal effect within the national sphere of the Communities' actions) have been defined in the Treaty so as to be predictable for the legislature and are enacted by it in the Act of Accession with sufficient certainty.... Thus, if European institutions or agencies were to treat or develop the Union Treaty in a way that was no longer covered by the Treaty in the form that is the basis for the Act of Accession, the resultant legislative instruments would not be legally binding within the sphere of German sovereignty.... Accordingly the Federal Constitutional Court will review legal instruments of European institutions and agencies to see whether they remain within the limits of the sovereign rights conferred on them or transgress them."

Two remarks should be made about the decision of the *Bundesverfassungsgericht*. First, its primary concern was with an allegation that Article F(3) E.U. gave the Union power to determine its own powers. Article F(3) states: "The Union shall provide itself with the means necessary to attain its objectives and carry through its policies". The Court concluded, however, that "Article F(3) merely makes a statement of intent in the context of policies and programmes to the effect that the Member States (which form the Union) wish to provide it with adequate resources under whichever particular procedure is necessary for that purpose" [1994] 1 C.M.L.R. 57, at 94; and that the Community institutions remained subject to the principle of limited competence, which principle had been strengthened by Article 3b E.C. (see annotation below). Secondly, the Court showed itself to be satisfied that the development of Community law to date had remained within the bounds of the Treaties. It must therefore require a very considerable departure from the text of the Treaties for the *Bundesverfassungsgericht* to intervene.

Article 235 E.C. is also relevant. The requirement of unanimity under Article 235 E.C. implicates every Member State in the decision taken, but the measure remains one of the Council, a Community institution. If the Council, acting on a Commission proposal and after consulting the Parliament, can take such action as is necessary to attain one of the objectives of the E.C. Treaty even where the Treaty has not provided the requisite powers, it is only the combination of practical circumstances (requiring certain action) and the very extensive Treaty objectives which ultimately defines the legislative competence of the Community (see, *e.g.* Temple Lang, "The Draft Treaty establishing the European Union and the Member States: Ireland" in Bieber *et al* eds., *An Ever Closer Union* (1985) p. 241, at 246, where he describes the EEC Treaty as "a *traité-cadre*, a constitutional framework, not a static *traité-loi*"). Of course, a national court could object to legislation adopted under Article 235 E.C., alleging that it was not necessary to achieve the objectives of the Treaty, or not appropriate; the principle of subsidiarity in Article 3b E.C. must make this more tempting. However, the privileging of the Treaty objectives in the Treaty itself must make it difficult in any but the most patently abusive case for a national court to review the compatibility of a legislative or judicial decision of the Communities with the Treaty as ratified by that Member State. An Irish court could nonetheless take the historical approach described above to interpret Article 29.4.3–5 as precluding reliance on Community rules deemed by that court to be in excess of competence in order to save from invalidity an otherwise unconstitutional national measure.

Phelan's second and third suggested interpretations can be taken together. These are "[s]econd, an interpretation of Article 29.4.5 in the light of the Constitution as a whole; . . . [and t]hird, that Article 29.4.5 must be read in the light of the goals of the Constitution, which precludes the overriding of Z by X". The Supreme Court decision in *Campus Oil Ltd v. Minister for Industry and Energy* [1983] I.R. 82 provides some support for such an approach, although it is not clear that it was intended to permit Article 29.4.5 to be trumped as a matter of Irish constitutional law by other provisions of the Constitution, rather than *vice versa*. An all-embracing harmonious reading of the Constitution will tend to correspond to a teleological reading, because the general scheme of the Constitution is best identified in terms of its goals. These can emerge from detailed provisions, *e.g.* Articles 12, 15–16 and 28 indicate that the State is intended to be democratic; but general programmatic statements, *e.g.* in Articles 1, 5 and 6, and in the Preamble, are also of great assistance. Any provision can be interpreted to conform as well as possible to the objectives of democracy, sovereignty, human dignity, social order, national re-unification and international peace which emerge both from other specific prescriptions and from such general statements.

In this context, a narrow literal reading of the reference to provisions of the Constitution in Article 29.4.5 would permit the Preamble to be employed in ascertaining its meaning. In particular, any legal obligation of European Community membership that was perceived fatally to undermine the preambular objective of assuring the dignity of the individual could be deemed to be outside the scope of the immunity conferred by Article 29.4.5. As respect for the right to life of the unborn is guaranteed, on a footing of equality with born persons, such a doctrine could be applied to an obligation to permit certain forms of assistance in procuring an abortion such as the distribution of information about abortion clinics.

It would also be possible to refer to the rest of the Constitution when interpreting Article 29.4.5, its apparently exclusory words notwithstanding, as the object of the exercise would be to ascertain the meaning of those words. Again, an obligation that was seen totally to contravene the principles of the primacy of the individual and the family on which the entire system of the protection of fundamental rights is built might run foul of the Irish courts. The Court of Justice developed a fundamental rights jurisdiction in part to counter similar threats from the German and Italian Constitutional Courts (*Bundesverfassungsgericht: Internationale Handelsgesellschaft mbH v. Einfuhr-und Vorratsstelle für Getreide und Futtermittel* [1974] 2 C.M.L.R. 540; *Wünsche Handelsgesellschaft* [1987] 3 C.M.L.R. 225; *Corte Constituzionale: Frontini v. Ministero delle Finanze* [1973] Giur. Cost. 2041; *Spa. Granital v. Amministrazione Finanziaria* [1984] Giur. Cost. 1098; E.C.J.: Case 11/70, *Internationale Handelsgesellschaft mbH v. Einfuhr-und Vorratsstelle für Getreide und Futtermittel* [1970] E.C.R. 1125; Case 4/73, *J. Nold K.G. v. Commission* [1974] E.C.R. 49; Article F(2) E.U.). Article 23(1) of the German Constitution can be read, in the light of the jurisprudence of the *Bundesverfassungsgericht*, as a recognition of fact but also, exceptionally, as a condition: "[T]he Federal Republic of Germany will co-operate in the development of the European Union, which . . . guarantees a protection of fundamental rights *which is essentially comparable with this Constitution*" (authors' italics).

Walsh J. has contended extra-judicially that the Court of Justice, by having recourse to common constitutional traditions and to the European Convention on Human Rights, has ignored "the possibility of mutual inconsistencies or contradictions lurking in these sources" (Walsh, Reflections, at 818; for criticism of the manner in which the Court of Justice has developed Community fundamental rights, see Phelan, Union; Coppell & O'Neill, "The

European Court of Justice: Taking Rights Seriously?" (1992) 29 C.M.L.Rev. 669; for a defence, see de Búrca, "Fundamental Human Rights and the Reach of European Community Law" (1993) 13 O.J.L.S. 283; and Weiler and Lockhart "'Taking Rights Seriously' Seriously", Parts I and II (1995) 32 C.M.L.Rev.). It is ironic that the Community fundamental rights jurisdiction developed in response to national constitutional rebellion, and founded largely upon the apparently common standards of the European Convention on Human Rights, should itself be the potential occasion of national constitutional rebellion as it is employed to limit the right of a Member State *under the Treaty* to derogate from Community law in order to protect national fundamental rights (see generally Phelan, *Union*; see also Reid, *Constitution*, p. 92).

If the Irish court concluded that the prohibition of abortion information was fundamental to the protection of unborn life and to the constitutional order, and that the fundamental rights guarantees of the Court of Justice were insufficient to protect that fundamental interest from the operation of Community rules, it could apply the abuse of rights doctrine described above. Article 29.4.5 could be deemed ineffective to undermine the constitutional order.

There is a problem with this approach. Article 29.4.5 is clearly designed to protect from invalidation national measures that would otherwise be unconstitutional, and to permit enforcement of Community laws that would otherwise be unenforceable. Unless Article 29.4.5 is to be deprived of all effect, the interpretation outlined immediately above would require the Irish courts to distinguish, from case to case, between those constitutional guarantees that are fundamental to the constitutional order and those which, in the circumstances of a given case, are "expendable". It is not inconceivable that the courts would undertake such a task. Phelan has provided some guidance with a draft Treaty provision which would effectively turn the tables in the instant hypothetical normative conflict. He suggests that the privileging of more fundamental national constitutional principles be guaranteed *within the Community legal order* as follows (Union, at 688):

> "The special types of rights embedded in national constitutions which are considered by the national courts (a) to express basic principles concerning life, liberty, religion and the family; (b) to have as their interpretative teleology a national vision of personhood and morality; and (c) to be fundamental to the legitimacy of the national legal system and the preservation of its concept of law; take precedence over European Community law within their fields of application.

Such a provision would create a *renvoi* in the opposite direction to that from Irish to Community constitutional law described by Temple Lang (as it is suggested below is true in a limited sense of Protocol No. 17 to the Maastricht Treaty). However, whether such a provision is inserted in the constitutional Treaties of the Communities, or in the alternative "the incompatibility ... between competing conceptions of rational justification which are embedded in different traditions" (Phelan, Union, at 687) is addressed at the point of reception of Community law in Ireland, the inherent subjectivity with which the task would be performed by the national courts would be a major target of criticism, as it is of the hierarchical approach to the protection of fundamental rights. Indeed, one of the reasons given by the then Taoiseach, Jack Lynch T.D. for rejecting the Labour Party proposal that the Third Amendment should contain a list of constitutional provisions expressly qualified in favour of Community law was that it would give an impression that some (unqualified) provisions were more fundamental than others (257 *Dáil Debates* Col. 1727).

This brings us to Phelan's fourth option, "an interpretation of Article 29.4.5 in the light of its interaction with a particular Article". Many of the teleological and harmonious interpretative arguments deployed in the foregoing discussion could also be employed under this rubric, were a court so minded. It is the interaction of Article 29.4.5 with Article 40.3.3 of the Constitution that is most apposite to our hypothetical conflict of norms. This has already been considered above, from a literal viewpoint. The doctrine of the hierarchy of rights has never seemed stronger than when it has been applied to the right to life, and a telling argument can be made for the superiority of a constitutional guarantee of life over any competing obligation, legal or political. (Critics of the Irish abortion information jurisprudence contend that there are some circumstances, when the threat to life is remote or indirect, and the restriction placed on other rights very great, when the hierarchical approach is counter-productive; and this viewpoint is inherent in Hogan and Whyte's above-quoted criticism of the inflexibility of this approach. This should not determine our principled analysis of the effect of the doctrine on the interpretation of Article 29.4.5, however, as it will always be possible to devise a hypothetical conflict of norms where the threat to unborn life is more direct or immediate than that from abortion information.)

However, the interaction of constitutional provisions could just as plausibly have a different outcome. The Irish courts have in the past found the threat posed to constitutionally protected unborn life by the dissemination of certain types of information to outweigh the restriction on the rights of privacy, association and expression inherent in a prohibition of such information. The introduction of the very strongly worded constitutional interest in and authorisation of membership of the Communities and the Union to this balancing process could change the outcome, and cause Article 40.3.3 (which guarantees respect for unborn life "as far as practicable") to give way, in this instance, to the obligations of membership. This, after all, was the result in *Campus Oil Ltd v. Minister for Industry and Energy* [1983] I.R. 82, although the constitutional rule involved there was probably not of foundational importance, and was made the subject of a very limited exception.

Finally, Phelan suggests (with an argument similar to that used above in respect of the Preamble) that "the protection afforded by Article 29.4.5 may be limited because it is a shield solely against provisions of the Constitution, not natural law rules recognised under it". The right to life of the unborn was considered to be constitutionally protected even before the enactment of the Eighth Amendment (*per* Walsh J., *McGee v. Attorney-General* [1974] I.R. 284; Walsh J. in *G v. an Bórd Uchtála* [1980] I.R. 32; Barrington J. in *Finn v. Attorney General* [1983] I.R. 154; McCarthy J. in *Norris v. Attorney-General* [1984] I.R. 36). This protection was attributable at least in part to the operation of natural law principles (O'Hanlon, "Natural Rights and the Irish Constitution" (1993) 11 I.L.T. 8). Should Article 40.3.3 be disabled in any way, it could be argued that these principles would continue to operate. An Irish court that wished to adopt this reasoning would have a number of precedents available to it to support its decision. Unless Article 29.4.5 is seen as disabling reference to natural law principles by organs of State established under the Constitution (a literal reading not likely to recommend itself to a court intent on relying upon natural law), there is nothing in the Constitution that need stop a court taking this course. This is recognised by Hogan and Whyte, although they comment that in practical terms, the rejection of the apparent requirements of the text of the Constitution pursuant to natural law reasoning is difficult to reconcile with democratic principles (Kelly, *Constitution*, p. 683). Humphreys has argued for a secular natural law approach, informed in particular by the European tradition to which such a strong commitment is expressed in the Third, Tenth and Eleventh Amendments: the decision of O'Hanlon J. in *Desmond v. Glackin* [1993] 3 I.R. 1, is cited to support this argument (Humphreys, Interpretation, at 72–3; see also Gallagher, "The Constitution and the Community" [1993] 1 I.J.E.L. 129, at 141). Such a natural law perspective could well have the opposite effect to that contended for by Phelan, although it is not the strongest in the Irish natural law tradition. The chief practical obstacle to a natural law based argument must be the recent decision of the Supreme Court in *Re Article 26 and the Regulation of Information (Services outside the State for Termination of Pregnancies) Bill*, 1995, [1995] 2 I.L.R.M. 81. It was argued by counsel appointed by the Court to represent the rights of the unborn that the Fourteenth Amendment (on the freedom to obtain or make available in the State abortion information in certain circumstances) had been invalidly adopted, because it was contrary to natural law on which the Constitution was founded. (For a similar argument, see Phelan, *Revolution*, at 396–410; *cf.* Whelan, "Constitutional Amendments in Ireland: the competing claims of democracy" in Quinn *et al* eds., *Justice and Legal Theory in Ireland* (1995). The Supreme Court responded that in no case in which the Irish Courts had developed the corpus of unenumerated personal rights had they identified rights which could not be reasonably implied from the provisions of the Constitution, interpreted in accordance with the judges' ideas of prudence, justice and charity. It continued:

> "The Courts, as they were and are bound to, recognised the Constitution as the fundamental law of the State to which the organs of the State were subject and at no stage recognised the provisions of natural law as superior to the Constitution. The people were entitled to amend the Constitution in accordance with the provisions of Article 46 of the Constitution and the Constitution as so amended ... is the fundamental and supreme law of the State representing as it does the will of the people."

One may remark that the Supreme Court created a false distinction between the Constitution and the natural law, not least because one of the chief avenues for the introduction of natural law thinking into Irish Constitutional law is the preambular commitment to the concepts of prudence, justice and charity. It follows from this (and is in no way excluded by the Court's decision) that natural law can retain a collateral or interpretative significance under the Constitution. For example, Doyle J. stated in *Murphy v. P.M.P.A. Insurance Co.* [1978] I.R.L.M. 725 that natural law existed side by side with the Constitution. It remains the case that the Supreme Court's judgment is positivist in tone, with its emphasis on the popular will, and suggests a lack of sympathy with use of natural law arguments to attempt to deflect the courts from less value-orientated readings of the constitutional text. (See also the judgment of Murphy J. in *F v. F and Ireland* [1994] I.L.R.M. 401).

CONCLUSION

One must conclude that an Irish court could build a case on any of the existing principles of constitutional interpretation to permit the invalidation of a national measure which, as a matter of Community law, is necessitated by the obligations of membership of the Communities. Phelan's logic is impeccable. In a case where the conflict between the respective requirements of Irish substantive constitutional law and of Community law is extremely grave, it is impossible to predict with certainty that an Irish court would not choose one of the options just discussed to favour the application of the Irish constitutional norm.

However (and Phelan does not seek to contend otherwise), it must also be concluded that none of these options represents the test to which the Irish courts subscribe at present. The judge who wishes to use them must face the additional task of justifying a departure from Supreme Court precedent.

Whether the continued observance of Supreme Court precedent would constitute, in a case of grave normative conflict, a constitutional revolution is difficult to judge, as it must be in any case where substantive rather than procedural subversion is alleged, and where the alleged subversive is not an avowedly political body, but the judicial body entrusted with the interpret-

141

ation of the Constitutional text purportedly violated. If the foundation of constitutional legitimacy is a *judicially articulated* conception of the protection of the individual in society, how does one gain say the integration, by judicial interpretation of a text adopted by the People and couched in absolutist terms, of the Irish Constitutional order into a greater Community legal order founded upon the ideal of a supranational general interest? If one can speak of a revolution (and the effects, actual and potential, of European legal integration are profound), it took place most likely, in 1972.

The current domestic constitutional test for the reception of Community law obligations in Ireland is that which emerges from the decision of the Supreme Court in *Crotty v. An Taoiseach*, as developed (with somewhat excessive zeal) in *Meagher v. Minister for Agriculture*. It is supported by *dicta* of Henchy J. in *Doyle v. An Taoiseach* [1986] I.L.R.M. 693, who spoke of Community law as having "the paramount force and effect of constitutional provisions", and of Costello J. in *Pigs and Bacon Commission v. McCarron* (High Court, June 30, 1978 (1979) J.I.S.E.L.); and by the outcome and (possibly) the reasoning in *Campus Oil Ltd v. Minister for Industry and Energy*. The decisions of Murphy J. in *Lawlor v. Minister for Agriculture* [1990] 1 I.R. 356 and *Greene v. Minister for Agriculture* [1990] 2 I.R. 17 provide partial support, despite the criticisms voiced above. Compliance with the Treaties, and with E.C. regulations, directives and decisions, is the legal duty, as a matter of Community law, of Member States. They must give direct applicability in their domestic law to those elements of Community law that require it, and must take appropriate steps to implement in their domestic law elements of Community law that require implementation. Article 29.4.5 of the Constitution has been interpreted by the Irish courts (which have sole jurisdiction to interpret it) to free from constitutional scrutiny national measures that comply with these obligations, as defined in Community law. While the fact-finding and reasoning of the Supreme Court in *Meagher* were criticised above, the decision was consistent with *Crotty* in upholding the primacy of Community law, and of making compliance with its obligations the fundamental object of the first clause of Article 29.4.5. (One can almost imagine judicial questioning of the constitutionality of such obligations being described as "sterile".) That those obligations were arguably misconstrued in *Meagher* does not defeat the point; nor does the debatable factual conclusion of the Court that there was no realistic alternative method of implementation of Community obligations to that in section 3(2) of the European Communities Act, 1972. Had the Supreme Court made an Article 177 E.C. reference to the European Court of Justice, posing the question, "where there is only one effective method of implementing Community obligations in time, is it an obligation of Community law to employ such a method?", the Court of Justice could only answer in the affirmative. It was in posing this flawed question to itself that the Supreme Court can ultimately be said to have erred in *Meagher*. Its decision does not prevent us from seeking to ensure that national measures effect the least possible intrusion on constitutional norms that is consistent with compliance with the obligations of Community law.

Article 29.4.5 has been found to date to constitute a *renvoi* from the Constitution of Ireland to the constitutional law of the Community (Temple Lang, Scope, at p. 231). Neither *Crotty* nor *Meagher*, nor the other authorities just mentioned, suggests that the Irish courts countenance any reading of Article 29.4.5 which would cause the State to be in breach of its obligations under Community law. The rumblings in the Supreme Court in *Grogan* were too moot to affect this conclusion although *cf.* Phelan, *Revolution*, 495–6. While an interpretative *volte face* is always possible, one cannot at this juncture predict its contours, or gauge with any confidence how persuasive will be the arguments in its favour.

CHAPTER NINE

RENVOI IN REVERSE? PROTOCOL NO. 17 TO THE MAASTRICHT TREATY

A chapter of this commentary is devoted to Protocol No. 17 to the Maastricht Treaty, which is not a provision of the Constitution of Ireland, because it appears to reverse the process of reception of law from one legal order by another under Article 29.4.5 that has been discussed so far. Irish constitutional law is "received" by Community law in a limited and negative sense: limited both in subject matter and in scope, negative because no fresh positive obligation is thereby created in the Community legal order—the Protocol simply sets a limit to the ordinary application of Community law. It is as well to make clear that the Protocol has the same status as a provision of the Treaty, as a matter of international law (see Article 2(1), Vienna Convention on the Law of Treaties, 1969) or more importantly in this context, of Community law (see Article 239 E.C.).

An account has already been given of the jurisprudence in the Irish courts, the European Court of Human Rights, and the European Court of Justice, arising from the application of Article 40.3.3 of the Constitution of Ireland to the provision of abortion information in Ireland. The insertion of Protocol No. 17 in the Maastricht Treaty on European Union must be seen primarily as a response to the possibility, raised by the decision of the European Court of Justice in *S.P.U.C. (Ireland) Ltd v. Grogan* [1991] E.C.R. I 4685 and discussed above, that the prohibition imposed by the Irish courts on certain forms of abortion information might in certain circumstances be contary to Community law. It may also have been intended to counteract the more remote possibility that the classification as a service of the provision of abortions for gain might lead to conflicts between Irish and Community law in respect of the (apparent) prohibition of abortion in Ireland. The Protocol states that nothing in the constitutional Treaties "shall affect the application in Ireland of Article 40.3.3 of the Constitution of Ireland". The Protocol is stated to be annexed to the Treaty on European Union and to the Treaties establishing the European Communities.

Before considering the import of the Protocol, it is necessary to add some brief observations on the decision of the Supreme Court in *Attorney General v. X* [1992]. The *X Case* commenced with an application to the High Court by the Attorney General on February 6, 1992 to restrain a pregnant girl from leaving the State because she sought an abortion in the United Kingdom. A majority in the Supreme Court (Finlay C.J., Egan, McCarthy and O'Flaherty JJ.; Hederman J. dissenting) overruled the decision of Costello J. in the High Court to impose an injunction prohibiting her from leaving the State. They found that the mother's suicidal state constituted a real and substantial threat to her life that could be countered only by terminating the pregnancy, and that this entitled her under Article 40.3.3 of the Constitution to obtain an abortion, either in the State or elsewhere. Nonetheless, three judges (Finlay C.J., O'Flaherty J. and the dissenting Hederman J.) were of the view that in the absence of such circumstances, mothers could be restrained from travelling abroad to obtain abortions. Thus, travel restrictions, which had been hypothetically considered and dismissed by Advocate General van Gerven in *S.P.U.C. (Ireland) Ltd v. Grogan* [1991] E.C.R. I-4685 were expressly approved, on somewhat differing conditions, by both the High Court and (*obiter*) by the Supreme Court.

The decisions of both the High Court and the Supreme Court were the objects of intense public debate, in respect of both the "substantive issue" of abortion in Ireland, and that of travel restrictions. This in turn triggered renewed debate on the information question. It appeared, further, that Protocol No. 17 would prevent the reversal of the information decisions of the Irish courts, and of the travel *dicta*, by the requirements of Community law (although this was the subject of considerable debate in the popular media among academic and other lawyers, as will be seen). The success of the referendum on the Eleventh Amendment to the Constitution, which was required in order to ratify the E.U. Treaty, appeared to be threatened by the opposition of various groups to this perceived effect of the Protocol. The Government's efforts to obtain an amendment to the Protocol, excluding any effect on travel or information, were unavailing, as the other Member States were reluctant to open the Treaty to re-negotiation. Instead, the expedient was adopted of a Declaration of 1 May 1992 by the High Contracting Parties to the E.U. Treaty, "[t]hat it was and is their intention that the Protocol shall not limit freedom to travel between Member States or, in accordance with conditions which may be laid down, in conformity with Community law, by Irish legislation, to obtain or make available in Ireland information relating to services lawfully available in Member States". This statement was described as a "legal interpretation". The significance of the Declaration will be considered below, after a review of the *prima facie* effect of the Protocol. In the discussion that follows, it will be presumed that even after the enactment of the Twelfth and Thirteenth Amendments to the Constitution (on travel and information) in December 1992, and the decision of the Supreme Court of *Re Article 26 of the Constitution and the Regulation of Information (Services outside the State for Termination of Pregnancies) Bill*, 1995, [1995] 2 I.L.R.M. 81, conflict is still possible between Irish constitutional law and substantive Community law (see Whelan, Amendments), which conflict the Protocol might be expected to resolve. (One possible point of conflict is the prohibition of commercial links between providers of abortion information in Ireland and providers of abortion services in other Member States by the Irish information legislation.)

Protocol No. 17 and Community Law

The Protocol appears as a matter of Community law to have instituted a "*renvoi* in reverse" because it makes the operation of the constitutional Treaties of the Communities contingent in certain circumstances on the objective requirements of a provision of the Constitution of Ireland as determined by the Irish courts (*cf.* Temple Lang, Scope, at 231). It directs the European Court of Justice to defer to Irish law in so far as there may be a conflict between Community law and the application in Ireland of Article 40.3.3 of the Constitution. However, this *renvoi* may be distinguishable from that which is asserted ordinarily to exist from Irish constitutional law to the objective requirements of Community law as determined by the Court of Justice. The Irish *renvoi* has two elements: first, the acceptance that the European Court of Justice is the authoritative arbiter of the obligations of membership of the Communities, and of the validity of the laws, acts and measures of the Communities, to which Article 29.4.5 of the Constitution refers; and secondly, the establishment by Article 29.4.5 of an unconditional derogation from the normal supremacy of the Constitution in favour of Community law, so determined. Both of these elements can be challenged pursuant to plausible constitutional arguments, *e.g.* by reference to the scope and objectives of the Community Treaties, as perceived by the Irish courts, in respect of the first element, or by reference to the superior norms of natural law, in respect of the second; but the Irish courts have yet to act on such arguments. However, similar limiting arguments are available to the Court of Justice in respect of the *renvoi* effected by the Protocol.

First, the Protocol is specific rather than general in scope. Article 29.4.5 of the Constitution can be understood to conceive of the obligations of membership of the Communities, and of the laws, acts and measures of the Communities, as being all those determined to be such by the Court of Justice, because the reference to the Communities in that Article is general and open-ended in nature. Any other position would put the Irish courts in the position of competing interpreters of the Treaties. The Protocol, on the other hand, is specific and exceptional. Even if the Court of Justice is obliged to accept unquestioningly the decisions of the Irish courts on the meaning of Article 40.3.3 of the Constitution, that obligation only arises where those decisions relate to "the application in Ireland" of Article 40.3.3. Thus, the *renvoi* to Irish constitutional law is circumscribed by a condition expressed in the Protocol itself, and therefore a part of Community law to be interpreted by the Court of Justice. It is open to the Court of Justice to determine the extent of the *renvoi* without in any way second-guessing the Irish courts as authoritative arbiters of the requirements of the Irish Constitution. (The Irish courts are similarly free as a matter of constitutional law to set conditions to the reception in Ireland of Community law, as interpreted authoritatively by the Court of Justice, by their construction of terms such as "necessitated" or "the force of law" in Article 29.4.5, but have to date adopted an approach which has not caused conflict with the requirements of the Community legal order.)

It is also possible for the Court of Justice, again without questioning the interpretative authority of the Irish courts in respect of Article 40.3.3 of the Constitution, to hold that the Protocol institutes a conditional rather than an absolute *renvoi* to Irish constitutional law. The limited scope of the *renvoi*, as a specific exception to the general norm of the supremacy of Community law, could make such a finding seem more plausible. It can be argued that the Protocol is a derogation from the Community Treaties akin to those based on public policy, public health, etc. If the Court of Justice favours such an approach, it would subject an Irish claim under the Protocol to the same strict scrutiny as other derogations, requiring that the Irish measure be consistently and uniformly applied, that there be legal certainty about its scope, that it not be disproportionate, that it not breach the fundamental human rights guaranteed by the Communities. Even if "application in Ireland" were given a broad construction, the setting of such conditions would lead to precisely the same situation as already existed under Article 56 EEC, in which it was likely that an Irish claim that restrictions on travel and commercially-provided information were justified by Irish public policy would be rejected by the Court of Justice as disproportionate.

It is always difficult for a court to assert that a newly-adopted and hard-won provision is simply declaratory of the existing law, when the evidence is that it was sought thereby to change it. (A similar problem faced those who argued that the Thirteenth Amendment to the Constitution should be read in the light of the pre-existing abortion information jurisprudence of the Supreme Court; see Whelan, Amendments and now the decision of the Supreme Court in the *Regulation of Information Bill Reference Case*.) Furthermore, the wording of the Protocol is on its face unconditional: *nothing* in the Treaties shall affect the application in Ireland of Article 40.3.3. The alternative construction of the Protocol is that it takes measures contributing to the application in Ireland of Article 40.3.3 out of the remit of the Community legal order altogether. Thus, principles of Community law could not be invoked to challenge such Irish measures, on this reasoning: Member States have transferred their sovereignty to the Communities in certain areas; the Protocol constitutes a limitation by Ireland, in agreement with the other Member States, on its transfer of powers; Ireland has reserved full rights in respect of matters governed by Article 40.3.3, so that such matters cannot be said to be within the sphere of Community law at all (to the extent that Article 40.3.3 is applied in Ireland); the Irish courts have exclusive power to determine the ambit of Article 40.3.3 of the Constitution of Ireland, with the Court of Justice merely concurring in this exceptional jurisdiction, and supervising its effect on Community law (see Hyland, *The Sunday Tribune*, February 23, 1992; Whelan, *The Irish Times*, February 26, 1992); one can also borrow an argument from Phelan, *Revolution*, at 238, that the Community should be as free as the Court of Justice deems the Member States to have been to transfer or limit its pre-existing sovereignty in defined fields.

Such an unconditional derogation from the application of the general principles of Community law could raise a different problem. While it may appear, *e.g.* from Article N, E.U., that the Member States have full original power to alter the "constitution" of the European Communities (the constitutional Treaties), arguments are increasingly being made that Protocols and Treaty amendments may be reviewed by the European Court of Justice "on grounds either that they putatively breach fundamental human rights as protected in the Community legal order or violate certain fundamental constitutional principles with mandatory (and hence superior) status in the Community legal order such as the supremacy of Community law over all provisions of national law" (Curtin, Union, at 63). Support is sought for this view from considerations 46 and 71–2 of Opinion 1/91 (on the draft European Economic Area Agreement [1991] E.C.R. 1), which refer to the "foundations of the Community". This language can be traced back to the decision in *Amministrazione delle Finanze dello Stato v. Simmenthal S.p.A.* (Case 106/77, [1978] E.C.R. 629), in which the Court of Justice stated that a denial of the supremacy of Community law would be "a corresponding denial of the effectiveness of obligations undertaken unconditionally and *irrevocably* by Member States pursuant to the Treaty and would thus imperil *the very foundations of the Community*" (authors' italics). The statement in consideration 72 of Opinion 1/91 that the amendment of the Treaty of Rome proposed by the European Commission could not cure the incompatibility with Article 164 EEC "and, more generally, with the very foundations of the Community", of the court system envisaged by the E.E.A. Agreement has been stated to furnish some "supportive guidance" (Curtin, Union, at 64; see also the Explanatory Statement to the Draft Constitution presented to the European Parliament in 1994, p. 10); but the Court of Justice seems in fact to have been careful to restrict itself simply to stating that the particular amendment suggested was insufficient to resolve the conflict. It is virtually certain that the assumption of any such jurisdiction to review Treaty amendments would provoke rebellion by at least some Member State courts (and by other organs of the Member States as well). The *Bundesverfassungsgericht* asserted in *Brunner* [1994] 1 C.M.L.R. 57 that the Member States remained sovereign "Masters of the Treaties" (*Herren der Verträge*), the very status questioned by Curtin (Union, at 63). It is not clear in any event that the Protocol, in either a broad or narrow interpretation, undermines the very foundations of the legal order—this is especially so if one accepts the premise that sovereignty or competence is inherently alienable.

If the Court of Justice does not wish unnecessarily to invoke Member State wrath, either by subjecting the operation of the Protocol to the general principles of Community law, or by subjecting the Protocol itself to judicial review, it is likely to seek to limit the *renvoi* required by the Protocol through a restrictive reading of "the application in Ireland of Article 40.3.3 of the Constitution of Ireland". It can derive support for such a strategy from ambiguity of this phrase, and from the subsequent Declaration. The important question is whether the imposition by the Irish courts of restrictions on travel abroad, and on the distribution of information in Ireland on how to obtain an abortion abroad, should be deemed by the Court of Justice to be applications in Ireland of Article 40.3.3 of the Constitution.

In the academic debate on the topic in 1992, Professors Binchy and Curtin answered this question in the negative, with Whyte inclining tentatively to their view (Binchy, *The Irish Times*, February 25, 1992; Curtin, *The Irish Times*, March 2, 1992; Whyte, "Abortion and the Law" (1992) 42 Doctrine & Life 253, at 272 (hereinafter Whyte, Abortion)). Hogan, Hyland, Kingston and Whelan questioned this conclusion (Hogan, "Protocol 17" in Keatinge ed. *Maastricht and Ireland* (1992) 109 (hereinafter Hogan, Protocol); Hyland, *The Sunday Tribune*, February 23, 1992; Whelan, *The Irish Times*, February 26, 1992; Kingston & Whelan, "The Protection of the Unborn in Three Legal Orders—Part III" (1992) 10 I.L.T. 166). It should be noted that some of these positions were taken before the adoption of the Declaration of May 1, 1992 and of the travel and information amendments to the Constitution of November 1992; while some of the factual hypotheses (*e.g.* in relation to travel prohibitions) are unlikely as a matter of *Irish* constitutional law, they remain useful in casting light on the possible readings of the Protocol in any remaining potential areas of conflict.

Binchy asserted that the Protocol makes a "crucial distinction between application *in Ireland* and application *in Irish constitutional law*. The former application is one of specific territorial delimitation; the latter contains no such delimitation." The Protocol involves, in his view, a subtraction from and modification of the potential territorial remit of Article 40.3.3 in its application outside Ireland in any other Member State. Thus, if an injunction were sought in Ireland against a proposed abortion in Britain, the court would have to proceed on the basis that the contemplated act was one which was subject to Community law.

Binchy's argument that the Protocol does not affect travel may be inconsistent with his view that it protects any ban or restrictions (of which some remain) on counselling and provision of abortion information in Ireland. Prohibition of the entry or circulation of something in the State (abortion information) is, logically, the exercise of a similar *territorial* jurisdiction by the Irish courts to prohibition of a person's exit from the State (see Whelan, *The Irish Times*, February 26, 1992). On the other hand, a distinction can be drawn between the two: control of the entry and circulation of informational matter is designed to prevent the occurrence of certain prohibited activites in Irish territory, *viz.* the provision of assistance in the obtaining of abortions abroad; control of exit of persons, while exercisable only if they are in Irish territory, is designed to prevent the occurrence of certain activities, discountenanced but not as such prohibited by Irish law, outside Irish territory, *viz.* the actual obtaining of an abortion abroad. This distinction can be countered with another drawn from the jurisprudence of the Irish courts. While the courts have in the past taken steps, or indicated their willingness to take steps, to prevent the distribution of abortion information that amounts to assistance in obtaining an abortion abroad, and to prohibit pregnant women from leaving the State in order to obtain an abortion abroad, they never sought to prohibit obtaining an abortion abroad, either by injunction or by an extension of the extra-territorial criminal jurisdiction of the State. Indeed, it was felt by Hederman J. in the *X Case* that the limitation of the terms of a prohibitory injunction to travel for the purpose of the obtaining of an abortion abroad would be insufficient to protect the right to life of the unborn, because it could so easily be evaded. (This issue was not addressed directly by Finlay C.J. or Egan J.) This must indicate a consciousness on the part of Hederman J. of the territorial bounds to the court's effective power, whatever of its jurisdiction; yet he included the imposition of a general injunction against travel outside the State among the measures the court could impose that could be effective in the territory of the State (despite some doubts on the part of Finlay C.J. and Egan J. as to the efficacy even of this measure).

Hogan also took issue with at least some of Binchy's analysis. He distinguished between an action seeking an injunction against someone still in Ireland preventing them from leaving the jurisdiction, and an action against a woman who has already travelled from Dublin to, say, Amsterdam for the purpose of securing an abortion there. (While it was not the subject of much judicial comment because the family returned to Ireland for the hearing, the *X Case* could have been of the latter type.) In the latter case, any injunction granted to enforce Article 40.3.3 would have to be applied not in Ireland but *in the Netherlands*—which application would not benefit from the protection afforded by the Protocol, and would almost certainly be contrary to Community law. In the former case, the Protocol probably would operate, "since an injunction would not be extra-territorial in either its operation or effect (being directed to an Irish woman within Ireland)" (Hogan, Protocol, at 115–116). The nationality of the woman does not in fact seem to be determinative in such cases, although it can be anticipated that the effect of an injunction restraining a Dutch woman from returning to the Netherlands for an abortion would be politically even more explosive than the *X Case*.

Curtin took the view that the Court of Justice would not permit the Protocol to be relied upon by the Irish courts to restrict either travel or information (Curtin, *The Irish Times*, March 2, March 7, April 24, 1992; Union, at 48, n. 129):

> "The [European Court of Justice] will not allow the precise and limited scope of the wording used in the Protocol to be interpreted in a manner that would result in a significant derogation for Ireland from existing well-established tenets of Community law such as the supremacy of Community law over national law. It follows that the Court [of Justice] will not allow the Protocol to be used by the Irish State to protect injunctions preventing pregnant women from travelling abroad from Community law scrutiny (*The Irish Times*, March 2, 1992)."

Curtin adds that "as a matter of Community law the words 'application in Ireland' will be interpreted (ultimately by the Court of Justice) so as to limit the derogation to purely internal matters. At which point, of course, it is no longer a derogation from the court's case law" (Union, at 48, n. 129). This would again leave us in the situation of the Protocol being construed as making no change in the law. While there is some evidence that the Council Legal Service was satisfied that the Protocol did not cut across the existing rights of Community citizens (Flynn, *The Irish Times*, March 25, 1992), even Curtin has conceded that this interpretation would be inconsistent with the apparent intentions of the Member States in adopting the Protocol (Union, at 49; italics in original):

> "Whereas I believe it is true that none of the Member States intended to allow Ireland to restrict the right to travel itself, it is submitted that the whole purpose of including the Protocol in the first place was to close the door that seemed to be left ajar (with regard to the—commercial—provision of *information* in Ireland concerning abortion services in other Member States) by the Court of Justice in *S.P.U.C. v. Grogan*. That was precisely the reason, it is suggested, for choosing the words 'the application *in Ireland*' in the first place."

If we accept this very credible account of the intention underlying the adoption of the Protocol, what are we to make of the Declaration by the High Contracting Parties that "it was and is their intention" that the Protocol should limit neither travel or information? Article 31 of the Vienna Convention on the Law of Treaties, 1969, has been prayed in aid by Fitzsimons (*The Irish Times*, May 6, 1992). Article 31(3) of the Convention states that interpreting a treaty, "[t]here shall be taken into account, together with the context, [*inter alia*] any subsequent agreement between the parties regarding the interpretation of the treaty or the application of its provisions". While not described as such, the Declaration can be deemed to be such an agreement. However, two arguments can be proffered against reliance upon the Declaration, the second a good deal more compelling than the first.

The first argument is an extension of that made by Toth in respect of the Declarations that were annexed to the Final Act adopted at the conclusion of the Single European Act ("The Legal Status of the Declarations Annexed to the Single European Act" (1986) 23 C.M.L.Rev. 803 (hereinafter Toth, Declarations). On this topic, see also Schermers (1991) 28 C.M.L.Rev. 275, Case C-445/93 *Parliament v. Commission*; C-292/89 *Antonissen*, at paragraph 18; Case C-297/92 *Pogglieri*). Toth considered that the Declarations were part of the context of the S.E.A., as Article 31(2) of the Vienna Convention defines the context for the purpose of the interpretation of a treaty as including "any agreement relating to the treaty which was made between all the parties in connexion with the conclusion of the treaty". He continued (Declarations, at 810):

> "There is, however, an absolute bar which prevents the European Court of Justice from taking any of the Declarations into account as part of the 'context' in which to interpret the Act. This arises from Article 31 of the Act itself, which stipulates that the provisions of the three original Community Treaties concerning the powers of the court and the exercise of those powers 'shall apply only to the provisions of Title II and to Article 32'. Since the court's jurisdiction has not been explicitly extended to the Final Act and to the annexed Declarations, the court ... could only interpret those Declarations if they could be regarded as forming an "integral part" of Title II or Article 32. However, [pursuant to a convincing preceding argument], they cannot be so regarded and therefore the court cannot consider them even as the 'context' of the Act."

This argument could be extended by analogy, by invoking Article L, E.U., to preclude reliance on the Declaration of 1 May 1992 in interpreting Protocol 17 of the Maastricht Treaty. With respect, however, Toth's original argument is not convincing, and this is equally true of the mooted extension. The primary power (and duty) of the Court of Justice under the Treaty of Rome is to "ensure that in the interpretation and application of this Treaty the law is observed". This object is served by the various procedures and forms of action set out in the subsequent Articles. The Court of Justice was precluded by Article 31 S.E.A. and by Article L, E.U. from interpreting and applying parts of those Treaties other than those specified in those Articles. This cannot prevent the court looking to the excluded parts for guidance, where relevant, in the interpretation of those parts of the Community Treaty that may be affected by them. For example, the court could not interpret Article 228a E.C. if it were not able to take judicial notice of the terms of Title V of the E.U. Treaty. To seek such interpetative guidance from Treaty provisions outside the court's jurisdiction is not thereby to extend its jurisdiction to them. Similarly, national private law rules are not within the court's jurisdiction; but it cannot be asserted that the court interprets and applies those rules (in the sense meant by Article 164 E.C.) when it seeks to ascertain the general principles common to the laws of the Member States in respect of non-contractual liability for the purposes of Article 215 E.C. By the same token, the court should be able to have recourse to the Declaration of 1 May 1992, not in order to interpret or apply that Declaration as part of Community law, but to assist it in interpreting and applying the Protocol, which is an integral part of the Community Treaties. (See also the remarks of Lord Oliver, quoted above, on the interpretation of unincorporated treaties by domestic courts of a dualist State, which may be in point: *Maclaine Watson & Co. Ltd v. Department of Trade and Industry and the International Tin Council* [1989] 3 All E.R. 523, at 545d.)

The second argument against reliance on the Declaration is founded upon its implausibility. Article 31 of the Vienna Convention on the Law of Treaties has as its fundamental interpretative principle the statement that "[a] treaty shall be interpreted in good faith in accordance with the ordinary meaning to be given to the terms of the treaty in their context and in the light of its object and purpose". One can at least doubt that the Declaration is a *bona fide* statement of the intention of the High Contracting Parties at the time of the adoption of the Protocol. Curtin's comments on the Member States' real intentions have already been quoted. Phelan asserts that the Declaration and the Protocol conflict (Union, at 687). Handoll describes the Declaration as "a change of heart" ("The Protection of National Interests in the European Union" (1994) 3 I.J.E.L. 221, at 232). It has been observed that if travel was not meant to be affected by the Protocol (as is asserted in the Declaration), the action of the Attorney General in commencing the *X Case* on the day immediately preceding the signing of the Maastricht Treaty (February 7, 1992) flew in the face of the Government's understanding of Community law (McDowell, *The Irish Times*, April 17–18, 1992; Whyte, Abortion, at n. 33; although the Attorney General acted in his role as *parens patriae* and not as legal adviser to the Government). Whyte is also sceptical about the Government's actions after the decision of the Supreme Court in *Attorney-General v. X* (Abortion, at 266):

> "The Government's position ... would appear to be inconsistent inasmuch as the attempt to persuade the other Member States to accept a modification of the Protocol was arguably premised on the belief that the Protocol, as it stood, did affect rights to travel and to receive and obtain information. However, in the aftermath of the failure of that attempt, the Government now suggests that the Protocol actually confirms the right to travel for Irish women."

The characterisation of the Declaration as a "retrospective claim" (Hogan, Protocol 17, at 119), at odds with the evident intention of the parties, may go to its very validity. If the Declaration is so inconsistent with the original meaning of the Protocol as to amount to an attempted modification or variation of its terms, it might be better classified as an attempted amendment of the Treaties, which by virtue of Article N, E.U. is ineffective. (For an example of an interpretative agreement which clearly amends the treaty in question in so far as there is a conflict between them, see the Agreement relating to the Implementation of Part XI of the United Nations Convention on the Law of the Sea, 1982, of July 29, 1994; see further Anderson, "Further Efforts to ensure Universal Participation in the United Nations Convention on the Law of the Sea" (1994) 43 I.C.L.Q. 886, at 892.) With regard to interpretative agreements, Sinclair has stated that "[i]t follows naturally from the proposition that the parties to a treaty are legally entitled to modify the treaty or indeed to terminate it that they are empowered to interpret it"; and the following comments on the role of subsequent practice in the application of a treaty in establishing the agreement of the parties as to its interpretation are equally applicable to formal interpretative agreements (*The Vienna Convention on the Law of Treaties* (2nd. ed., 1984), pp. 136, 138):

> "It will be apparent that the subsequent practice of the parties may operate as a tacit or implicit modification of the terms of the treaty. It is inevitably difficult, if not impossible, to fix the dividing line between interpretation properly so called and modification effected under the pretext of interpretation. There is therefore a close link between the concept that subsequent practice is an element to be taken into account in the interpretation of a treaty and the concept that a treaty may be modified by subsequent practice of the parties."

While the European Court of Justice may be happy to draw upon international law as a source of interpretative guidance in construing the Treaties, it seems very unlikely that it would adopt this approach to the interpretation of the "constitution" of the Community legal order. A procedure for amendment of the constitutional Treaties by the Member States is specified therein, but ultimate interpretative authority is vested in the Court of Justice. The freedom of the Member States to modify the Treaties can be exercised only in accordance with Article N, E.U. The Court of Justice has stated, in the context of the choice of legal basis for Community measures, that "a mere practice of the Council cannot derogate from the rules laid down in the Treaty and cannot, therefore, create a precedent binding on Community institutions with regard to the correct legal basis" (Opinion 1/94 *G.A.T.T.* [1994] E.C.R. I 1, para. 52; see also Case 68/86, *United Kingdom v. Council* [1988] E.C.R. 855). Difficult as it may be, the court must insist on distinguishing between modifications of the Treaties, and practice or agreement among the Member States which is in conformity with the Treaties as interpreted by the Court of Justice.

The fact remains that the statement in the Declaration of the Member States' intentions, however disingenuous, is probably consistent with the preferences of the Court of Justice. However, the court must also be mindful of the possibility of judicial rebellion in Ireland, the potential ammunition for which was outlined in the discussion of constitutional interpretation above. By following the Declaration, the Court of Justice could preserve entirely intact the corpus of Community law in this difficult and controversial area. But extension of the Protocol to abortion information, at the least, (and thus to such remaining points of possible conflict between Community law and Irish law as exist) would allow the court, which is dependent on the co-operation of national courts, to avoid encroaching on an area of such obvious sensitivity, and to rely on the Protocol as an excuse for restraint in its otherwise vigorous enforcement of the principles of Community law. It is difficult to predict in advance the course the Court of Justice might take in the difficult circumstances of a controversial case.

Protocol No. 17 and the Treaty on European Union

One must first ask whether the Protocol is part of Union law (as distinct from Community law). It is stated both in the text of the Protocol and in the Final Act of the Inter-Governmental Conferences to be annexed to the E.U. Treaty as well as to the Community Treaties. However, there is no provision in the Union Treaty itself equivalent to Article 239 E.C., which states that "[t]he protocols annexed to this Treaty by common accord of the Member States shall form an integral part thereof" (see also Article 207 Euratom and Article 84 ECSC) In *Groupement des Industries Sidérurgiques Luxembourgeoises v. High Authority* (Cases 7 & 9/54, [1956] E.C.R. 175, at 194), the Court of Justice held that certain annexes and protocols to the Treaty establishing the European Coal and Steel Community were "equally binding" only by virtue of the fact that they were expressly incorporated in this way (see further Toth, Declarations, at 810–11). However, an argument from omission is not entirely convincing, and the Queen's Bench Division of the English High Court offered counter-arguments from the text of the Treaty in *R. v. Secretary of State for Foreign and Commonwealth Affairs, ex p. Rees-Mogg* [1993] 3 C.M.L.R. 101, at 108-9. Counsel for Lord Rees-Mogg did not adduce the argument just mentioned, but did argue (in respect of the Protocol on Social Policy) that the Final Act of the Inter-Governmental Conferences "identifies three separate texts, (i) the Treaty on European Union, (ii) the Protocols and (iii) the Declarations", to indicate that that Protocol in question was not part of the Treaty. The High Court was reluctant to reach such a conclusion on such evidence:

> "The arguments the other way are much stronger. For example, the only provision relating to ratification is Article R of Title VII. There is no separate provision calling for ratification of the Protocols or the Declarations. It is inconceivable that the High Contracting Parties did not intend Article R to cover ratification of the Protocols as well as ratification of the Treaty. If so, it follows they were using the word 'Treaty' to include the Protocols."

The Court continued that the instruments of ratification already lodged, by France, Spain, Portugal, Ireland, the Netherlands and Denmark contained no references to the Protocols, but simply ratified the Treaty. Satow's *Guide to Diplomatic Practice* (5th ed., at para. 29.27) was also relied upon, to show that ratification of a treaty or convention "will normally *ipso facto* involve ratification of any supplementary or additional protocol [drawn up by the same negotiators, and dealing with ancillary or incidental matters such as the interpretation of particular articles of the main treaty or convention or any supplementary provision of a minor character]". The Court could also have relied upon the decision of the International Court of Justice in the *Ambatielos Case (First Phase)* to dispel any remaining doubts [1952] I.C.J. Rep. 30. The court attributed considerable significance to the ratification by both parties by a single instrument, and registration with the League of Nations as a single document, of an Anglo-Greek treaty and accompanying declaration. The declaration was signed contemporaneously with, but separately from, the treaty, and dealt with a matter which, though also separate, had a certain connection with it, as it concerned claims under a previous treaty now superseded by the treaty in question. The Court found that the declaration formed an integral part of the treaty, in the nature of an interpretation clause, so that any dispute concerning the interpretation or application of the declaration would be governed by the adjudication clause of the treaty, providing for a reference to the Court. This conclusion was criticised for attributing too much significance to the routine formalities of ratification (by a number of dissenting judges, and, *e.g.* by Fitzmaurice, "The Law and Procedure of the International Court of Justice 1951–4: Treaty Interpretation and other Treaty Points" (1957) 33 B.Y.I.L. 203, at 255–62). However, this was in part because on the actual language of the declaration, there was much to suggest that it was not part of the treaty, as the Court itself pointed out ([1952] I.C.J. Rep. 30 at 41-2). For example, it referred to the Anglo-Greek Treaty by its full name, as though it were quite a separate instrument. Protocol No. 17, on the other hand, states specifically that it "shall be annexed to the Treaty on European Union and to the Treaties establishing the European Communities". Thus, the manner of ratification of the E.U. Treaty, on which the English High Court relied in *Rees-Mogg*, appears in the case of Protocol No. 17 to have been consistent with the intentions of the parties as expressed in the text of the Protocol.

More difficult questions are raised by the interpretation of the Protocol in so far as it relates to the E.U. Treaty rather than to the Community Treaties. Article L, E.U. does not include the Protocol among the provisions of the Treaty on European Union to which the powers of the Court of Justice are extended. In the absence of such an authoritative interpreter, the Protocol must fall to be interpreted by the Member States, and thus by their courts (and in particular the Irish courts) in any domestic litigation, *to the extent that it relates to the non-Community pillars of the Union*. Article M, E.U. states that nothing in the Treaty shall affect the Community Treaties (other than the specific amendments thereof in Titles II-IV), so that the Protocol annexed to the Union Treaty cannot be interpreted to encroach on Community law on travel and information, which is instead subject to the Protocol annexed to the Community Treaties as interpreted by the Court of Justice (see above).

It is difficult to conceive of measures that might be adopted under Titles V or VI, E.U. that could affect the application in Ireland of Article 40.3.3 of the Constitution of Ireland. However, it must be remembered that the Irish courts could take a much more expansive view than the Court of Justice of what is meant by application in Ireland. Even if it were known, the interpretation of the Court of Justice in the Community context need not be determinative of the meaning of the same words in the different context of the E.U. Treaty. The Court of Justice has itself acknowledged that the same legal provision can be differently construed in different treaties or other instruments; this lay at the heart of the court's first Opinion on the draft European Economic Area Agreement (see Opinion 1/91, *E.E.A. (No. 1)* [1991] E.C.R. I 1; see also Case 270/80, *Polydor and R.S.O. Records Inc v. Harlequin Record Shops and Simons Records* [1982] E.C.R. 329; Case 104/81, *Hauptzollamt Mainz v. C.A. Kupferberg & Cie. KG a.A.* [1982] E.C.R. 3641). The Court of Justice could counter that the integrative objectives of the E.U. Treaty are sufficiently close to those of the Community Treaties (compare, *e.g.* Article B, E.U. and Article 2 E.C.) that the same meaning should be attributed to the Protocol in both contexts, but might not have the opportunity of expressing this view in national litigation arising from the operation of Titles V or VI, E.U. Therefore, unlike the position in Community law, the *renvoi* effected by the Protocol from Union law to Irish constitutional law may be effectively controlled by the Irish courts. This would be highly subversive of the Union legal order save for the fact, already discussed above, that the interpretation of the Treaty on European Union is effectively nationalised in any event.

The Council has already adopted a joint action under Title V, E.U. on the negotiation of a Stability Pact for Europe with a number of formerly Communist States in central and eastern Europe, with a view to cultural co-operation, language training, economic co-operation, judicial co-operation, environmental protection, guarantees of borders and protection of minority rights (Council Decisions 93/728/C.F.S.P.; 94/315/C.F.S.P.) Let us suppose that a decision is reached by the Council under Article J.3 E.U. that the Member States shall conclude Stability Pacts with these third States offering certain "soft" security assistance (as defence matters proper are excluded from the scope of joint action by Article J.4.3 E.U.) and financial and expert assistance with democratisation and legal reform, in return for the adoption and enforcement by the beneficiary States of certain fundamental rights and minority rights guarantees. The catalogue of guarantees includes rights of privacy and of reproductive freedom which entail, patently or latently, a freedom of access to abortion greatly in excess of that permitted by Article 40.3.3 of the Constitution of Ireland. By a decision of the Council under Article J.11.2 E.U., operational expenditure to which the implementation of the joint action gives rise is to be charged to the Member States. (It is interesting, in the context of this hypothesis, to note the adoption by the Court on 29 May 1995 of a uniform clause making Community agreements with third countries subject to their observance of democratic principles and fundamental human rights, as set out in the Universal Declaration of Human Rights, the final Helsinki Act and the Paris Charter for a new Europe (Agence Europe No. 6490 (n.s.), 29/30 May 1995).)

After the ratification of the Stability Pacts by all parties, suppose a constitutional challenge is mounted in Ireland to the appropriation of monies for the purpose of Stability Pact expenditure, on the basis that participation by the State in the Pact is contrary to the guarantee of the right to life of the unborn in Article 40.3.3 of the Constitution. The Irish court concludes that the challenge should ordinarily succeed, as the appropriation constitutes assistance in Ireland in the provision of abortion abroad. (It is conceded that this conclusion does not by any means flow automatically from the jurisprudence to date, but it is hoped that it seems sufficiently plausible to proceed with this speculation.) Article 29.4.5 of the Constitution is pleaded in defence of the impugned appropriation. Presuming that the E.U. Treaty can require the conclusion of treaties by the Member States with third countries pursuant to joint actions of the Council in C.F.S.P., action by the State to implement the Pact must be necessitated by the obligations of membership of the Union. (See the discussion in Chapter 7 above.) However, any such obligation can be defeated by the Protocol. It would require a very expansive interpretation of the terms of the Protocol to attempt to apply it to the conclusion by the State of a treaty the execution of which takes place entirely outside Ireland. However, the imposition of an injunction by the Irish courts prohibiting the necessary appropriations from Irish revenues for the purposes of the Pact can be more credibly construed as an "application in Ireland of Article 40.3.3 of the Constitution of Ireland". One is reminded of the decision in *The State (Gilliland) v. Governor of Mountjoy Prison* [1987] I.R. 201, in which it was the extension by order to the United States of the provisions of Part II of the Extradition Act, 1965 which was declared unconstitutional by the Supreme Court, and not the extradition treaty with the United States.

Let us suppose in the alternative that combined Association Agreements and Stability Pacts are concluded with the States of central and eastern Europe by way of mixed agreement by both the Communities, within their competences, and the Member States, pursuant to a joint action in C.F.S.P. The agreement again contains the offending provision on privacy and reproductive rights. Certain expenditures are again charged to the Member States, but the mixed agreement does not contain a clause attributing the various obligations under the agreement to the Communities or to the Member States, as the case may be. A constitutional challenge is again brought in the Irish courts to the necessary appropriation. However, it is now pleaded in defence of the impugned measure that it is necessitated by the obligations of membership of the Communities *and* of the Union. The argument from the obligations of membership of the Union has already been rehearsed, and the Protocol could very possibly be invoked by the Irish courts to reject it. The argument from Community membership arises from the discussion above of the possible obligation of Member States under Article 5 E.C. to observe their side of mixed agreements even in respect of matters within the exclusive jurisdiction of the Member States, at the very least where the Member States and the Community could be jointly liable for any breach. The Irish court could again invoke the Protocol, but could be pressed to make an Article 177 E.C. reference to the Court of Justice on its interpretation as a part of the Community Treaty. The Court of Justice might in turn rule that restraint of the State from observing a Community obligation to honour an international agreement which is executed entirely outside Ireland did not constitute "the application in Ireland of Article 40.3.3 of the Constitution of Ireland".

The likelihood of the occurrence of litigation such as that just outlined must be very small. Nonetheless, these speculations do illustrate the additional complexity that has been introduced into the relationship of Irish and Community/Union law by three developments: the addition of the Protocol to the constitutional Treaties, the extension to the Union of Article 29.4.5 of the Constitution, and the exclusion of the Court of Justice from the interpretation and application of much of the E.U. Treaty.

THIRD AMENDMENT OF THE CONSTITUTION ACT, 1972

ARRANGEMENT OF SECTIONS

SECT.
1. Amendment of Article 29 of the Constitution.
2. Citation.

SCHEDULE

PART I

PART II

Citation

This Act may be cited as the Third Amendment of the Constitution Act: see section 2(2).

Commencement

This Act was approved by the electorate at a referendum in May, 1972. 1,041,890 voted for the proposed amendment (82.4 per cent) and 211,891 (27.6 per cent) against. The Act was signed by the President on June 8, 1972.

Parliamentary Debates

257 *Dáil Debates*, Cols. 1069–1142; 1285–1388; 1497–1555; 1720–1734 (Second Stage);
258 *Dáil Debates*, Cols. 393–484; 519–623 (Third and Final Stages);
72 *Seanad Debates*, Cols. 509–554 (Second Stage);
72 *Seanad Debates*, Cols. 558–616 (Third and Final Stages).

An Act to amend the Constitution.   [June 8, 1972]

WHEREAS by virtue of Article 46 of the Constitution any provision of the Constitution may be amended in the manner provided by that Article:

AND WHEREAS it is proposed to amend Article 29 of the Constitution:

Be it therefore enacted by the Oireachtas as follows:

Amendment of Article 29 of the Constitution

1.—Article 29 of the Constitution is hereby amended as follows:

(a) the subsection set out in *Part I* of the Schedule to this Act shall be added to section 4 of the Irish text.

(b) the subsection set out in *Part II* of the Schedule to this Act shall be added to section 4 of the English text.

Citation

2.—(1) The amendment of the Constitution effected by this Act shall be called the Third Amendment of the Constitution.

(2) This Act may be cited as the Third Amendment of the Constitution Act, 1972.

GENERAL NOTE

Much of the effect of the Third Amendment of the Constitution Act has already been described above in the discussion of the terms of Art. 29.4.3-6 of the Constitution. The referendum on the Bill was used by the Government as the political measure of the willingness of the people to join the Communities as well as to secure popular approval of the constitutional change required by such a step. This was criticised by Justin Keating T.D. (Labour). He advocated instead a referendum under Art. 27 of the Constitution to approve the general principle of Community membership, followed by a constitutional referendum in respect of specific amendments prepared by the Oireachtas on foot of such a political mandate (257 *Dáil Debates*, cols. 1074–5).

It has remained the practice of Irish Governments to use a constitutional referendum on new treaties on European integration for this broader political purpose. This has prevented the precise legal significance of proposed constitutional amendments from becoming central to the referendum debate. Thus, it is normally in the Oireachtas that such legal concerns are addressed. As has been seen, this was the case in respect of the Third Amendment, with the acceptance by the Government of the Fine Gael amendment to the wording of the second sentence of the proposed Article 29.4.3 of the Constitution, substituting "necessitated by" for "consequent upon" (258 *Dáil Debates*, col. 402; Dr. Garret Fitzgerald T.D.). That committee stage amendment was signposted at the second stage by Liam Cosgrave T.D., who viewed the original wording as "unnecessarily wide and in fact dangerous" (257 *Dáil Debates*, col. 1112); and by Deputy Richard Ryan, also of Fine Gael, who cited to indicate the danger posed by the term the *Oxford English Dictionary* definition of "consequent" as describing something following another in order "without implication of causal connection" (257 *Dáil Debates*, col. 1286).

The Government and Fine Gael were in agreement, however, about the need for a general amendment, confined to the objective requirements of Community law. The Taoiseach remarked, when introducing the Bill, that it was not practical to undertake a line by line amendment of the Constitution. Conflicts could readily be foreseen with organic arrangements laid down by the Constitution: the legislative, executive and judicial powers set out in Articles 15, 28 and 34 of the Constitution. Other, less foreseeable conflicts might only emerge in the course of future litigation, when it might be too late to resolve them. "The Government, accordingly, decided that the most appropriate approach would be to achieve the desired result by means of an amendment which would remove the incompatibilities in a general way while ensuring at the same time that the amendment was confined to the specific obligations arising from membership of the Communities." (257 *Dáil Debates*, col. 1073.)

The Labour Party objected to this approach, describing it as a scrapping of the Constitution by stealth (Justin Keating T.D., 257 *Dáil Debates*, cols. 1074–5). He argued that Article 46 of the Constitution requires specific amendment of relevant articles, "and not a buckshot amendment fired off in the general direction of the Constitution" (257 *Dáil Debates*, cols. 1082–3). Deputy Keating also objected to the express mention of the E.C. Treaties in the text of the Constitution, asserting that it would be more in keeping with the dignity of such a document to relegate such details to an appendix. Deputy Keating proceeded to list a number of provisions of the Constitution that might be adversely affected by E.C. membership, from Article 5 on the sovereign and democratic nature of the State to Article 10 on the ownership of natural resources. This list was the undoing of the Deputy's argument, as Garret Fitzgerald T.D. countered that it was so speculative as to strengthen the case for a general provision such as that proposed.

The debate on the Third Amendment also prefigured some of the issues raised in *Crotty v. An Taoiseach* [1987] I.R. 713. The Taoiseach remarked when introducing the Third Amendment: "It is not the Government's intention, nor is the proposed amendment designed to cover, any possible incompatibility with the present Constitution which might arise as a result of obligations which it might be necessary to assume if we wished to become a member of any political community in Europe which may eventually be created and evolving from the present Communities [which] … depending on the form and nature of the political community proposed, might well require a separate constitutional amendment" (257 *Dáil Debates*, cols. 1073–4). While one may differ (as the minority did) with the finding of the Supreme Court majority in *Crotty* that European Political Co-operation under the Single European Act entailed a significant limitation on the powers of the State in external political relations, the conclusion they drew from that finding was perfectly in keeping with the original intention of the drafters of the Third Amendment.

The passage of the Third Amendment was supplemented by the enactment of the European Communities Act, 1972, section 1 of which incorporated the E.C. Treaties and the body of E.C. law into the law of the State (see further the annotation of the Act below). A statute complying with Article 29.6 of the Constitution was seen as useful to dispel any doubts about such incorporation, even though the Third Amendment seemed to make this unnecessary (Robinson, "The Irish European Communities Act, 1972" (1973) 10 C.M.L.Rev. 352). In *Crotty v. An Taoiseach* [1987] I.R. 713, Barrington J. stated that the European Communities Act was necessary in order to incorporate the Treaties, thus confirming the wisdom of this course [1987] I.R. 713, at 757.

SCHEDULE

3° Tig leis an Stát do bheith ina chomhalta den Chomhphobal Eorpach do Ghual agus Cruach (do bunuigheadh le Connradh do sínigheadh i bPáras an 18adh lá d'Aibreán, 1951), de Chomhphobal Eacnamaíochta na hEorpa (do bunuigheadh le Connradh do sínigheadh insan Róimh an 25adh lá de Mhárta, 1957) agus den Chomhphobal Eorpach do Fhuinneamh Adamhach (do bunuigheadh le Connradh do sínigheadh insan Róimh an 25adh lá de Mhárta, 1957). Ní dhéanann aon fhoráileamh atá insan Bhunreacht so aon dlighthe d'achtuigh, gníomhartha do rinne nó bearta le n-ar ghlac an Stát, de bhíthin riachtanais na n-oibleagáidí mar chomhalta de na Comhphobail, do chur ó bhail dlighidh ná cosc do chur le dlighthe d'achtuigh, gníomhartha do rinne nó bearta le n-ar ghlac na Comhphobail, nó institiúidí de na Comhphobail, ó fheidhm dlighidh do bheith acu sa Stát.

3° The State may become a member of the European Coal and Steel Community (established by Treaty signed at Paris on the 18th day of April, 1951), the European Economic Community (established by Treaty signed at Rome on the 25th Day of March, 1957) and the European Atomic Energy Community (established by Treaty signed at Rome on the 25th day of March, 1957). No provision of this Constitution invalidates laws enacted, acts done or measures adopted by the State necessitated by the obligations of membership of the Communities or prevents laws enacted, acts done or measures adopted by the Communities, or institutions thereof, from having the force of law in the State.

TENTH AMENDMENT OF THE CONSTITUTION ACT, 1987

ARRANGEMENT OF SECTIONS

SECT.
1. Amendment of Article 29 of the Constitution.
2. Citation.

SCHEDULE

PART I

PART II

Citation

This Act may be cited as the Tenth Amendment of the Constitution Act: see section 2(2) below.

Commencement

This Act was approved by the electorate at a referendum on May 25, 1987. 755,423 voted for the proposed amendment (70 per cent) and 324,977 (30 per cent) against. The Act was signed by the President on June 22, 1987.

Parliamentary Debates

371 *Dáil Debates*, Cols. 2187–2485 (Second Stage);
371 *Dáil Debates*, Cols. 2497–2601 (Committee and Final Stages);
116 *Seanad Debates*, Cols. 28–53; 61–233 (Second Stage);
116 *Seanad Debates*, Cols. 234–272 (Committee and Final Stages).

An Act to amend the Constitution. [June 22, 1987]

WHEREAS by virtue of Article 46 of the Constitution any provision of the Constitution may be amended in the manner provided by that Article:

AND WHEREAS it is proposed to amend Article 29 of the Constitution:

Be it therefore enacted by the Oireachtas as follows:

Amendment of Article 29 of the Constitution

1.—Article 29 of the Constitution is hereby amended as follows:

(a) the sentence set out in *Part I* of the Schedule to this Act shall be inserted in subsection 3° of section 4 of the Irish text after the first sentence.

(b) the sentence set out in *Part II* of the Schedule to this Act shall be inserted in subsection 3° of section 4 of the English text after the first sentence.

GENERAL NOTE

This constitutional amendment was passed in the wake of the decision of the Supreme Court in *Crotty v. An Taoiseach* on 9 April, 1987 [1987] I.R. 713. In *Crotty*, the Court had held that it would be unconstitutional for the State to ratify the Single European Act (see the analysis above of the *Crotty* decision). As all the other Member States had ratified the Single European Act by 1 January, 1987 (the agreed deadline for ratification), it was necessary to secure as quickly as possible a constitutional amendment that would permit ratification by the State. The Government therefore elected to promote a "narrow" amendment to Article 29.4.3 of the Constitution. While various Ministers recognised the other constitutional difficulties thrown up by *Crotty*, it was felt that these matters would have to await a more detailed examination by the Attorney-General's office (see, *e.g.* comments by Brian Lenihan T.D., Minister for Foreign Affairs, 371 *Dáil Debates*, Cols. 2509–2514). The amendment was carried by 755,423 votes to 324,977 (*Iris Oigifiúil*, May 29, 1987). This left unresolved two issues discussed above:

(i) the power of the Government to negotiate and enter binding treaties concerning foreign affairs; and

(ii) the vexed question of the interpretation of the term "necessitated" in Art. 29.4.3 of the Constitution.

The Irish instrument of ratification was deposited in Rome on 24 June, 1987, accompanied by a declaration on neutrality outside military alliances, and the Single European Act came into force on 1 July, 1987. The European Communities (Amendment) Act, 1986 had survived the constitutional challenge in *Crotty*, but its entry into force was contingent upon successful ratification, and it also came into force on 1 July, 1987 (European Communities (Amendment) Act, 1986 (Commencement) Order, 1987 (S.I. No. 170); see further the discussion of the Act below).

Citation

2.—(1) The amendment of the Constitution effected by this Act shall be called the Tenth Amendment of the Constitution.

(2) This Act may be cited as the Tenth Amendment of the Constitution Act, 1987.

SCHEDULE

PART I

Tig leis an Stát an Ionstraim Eorpach Aonair (do sínigheadh tar ceann Bhallstáit na gComhphobal i Lucsamburg an 17adh lá d'Fheabhra, 1986, agus insan Háig an 28adh lá d'Fheabhra, 1986) do dhaingniú.

PART II

The State may ratify the Single European Act (signed on behalf of the Member States of the Communities at Luxembourg on the 17th day of February, 1986, and at The Hague on the 28th day of February, 1986).

ELEVENTH AMENDMENT OF THE CONSTITUTION ACT, 1992

ARRANGEMENT OF SECTIONS

SECT.
1. Amendment of Article 29 of the Constitution.
2. Citation.

SCHEDULE

PART I

PART II

An Act to amend the Constitution.   [July 16, 1992]

Citation

This Act may be cited as the Elventh Amendment of the Constitution Act: see section 2(2) below.

Commencement

This Act was approved by the electorate at a referendum on 18 June, 1992. 1,001,076 voted for the proposed amendment (68.7 per cent) and 448,655 (30.8 per cent) against. The Act was signed by the President on 3 August, 1992.

Statutory Instrument

Referendum (Special Difficulty) Order 1992 (S.I. No. 128).

Parliamentary Debates

419 *Dáil Debates* Cols. 155–234; 263–308; 631–700 (Second Stage);
419 *Dáil Debates* Cols. 790–818 (Committee and Final Stages);
132 *Seanad Debates* Cols. 956–1075; 1101–1176 (Second Stage);
132 *Seanad Debates* Cols. 1177–1215 (Committee and Final Stages).

WHEREAS by virtue of Article 46 of the Constitution any provision of the Constitution may be amended in the manner provided by that Article:

AND WHEREAS it is proposed to amend Article 29 of the Constitution:

Be it therefore enacted by the Oireachtas as follows:

Amendment of Article 29 of the Constitution

1.—Article 29.4 of the Constitution is hereby amended as follows:
(a) by the repeal of the third sentence in subsection 3° of section 4 of the Irish text and by the insertion of the text set out in *Part I* of the Schedule to this Act;
(b) by the repeal of the third sentence in subsection 3° of section 4 of the English text and by the insertion of the text set out in *Part II* of the Schedule to this Act.

GENERAL NOTE

Much of the effect of the Eleventh Amendment of the Constitution Act has already been described above in the discussion of the terms of Article 29.4.3–6 of the Constitution. The primary purpose of the adoption of the Amendment was to facilitate ratification by the State of the Maastricht Treaty on European Union. The opportunity was also taken to allay doubts about the constitutionality of ratification of the Community Patents Convention, 1989.

The Amendment also reorganised the constitutional provisions dealing with membership of the European Communities and now of the European Union.

The original Art. 29.4.3 of the Constitution (inserted by the Third Amendment of the Constitution Act, 1972) consisted of two sentences: the first authorising membership of the three European Communities; the second providing for the constitutional immunity and domestic enforceability of E.C. law and of domestic measures necessitated by membership of the Communities. The Tenth Amendment of the Constitution Act, 1987, inserted, between these two sentences, a further sentence authorising ratification of the Single European Act. The European Communities (Amendment) Act, 1986, incorporating into Irish law the provisions of the S.E.A. which amended the E.C. Treaties, had already been found to be constitutional in *Crotty v. An Taoiseach* [1987] I.R. 713; thus, the Tenth Amendment simply served to authorise participation in formalised European Political Co-operation under Title III of the Single European Act. These authorising clauses remain in Article 29.4.3 of the Constitution.

Article 29.4.4 comprises a similar sentence authorising ratification of the Maastricht Treaty on European Union and membership of the Union. By analogy with the reasoning of the Supreme Court in *Crotty*, this was necessary because elements of the E.U. Treaty could reasonably be asserted not to have been encompassed by the existing scheme and objectives of the E.C. Treaties (or by the non-Community E.P.C. element of the Single European Act). While economic and monetary union had been an objective of the Communities at least since 1970, the provisions on achievement of that objective in the Maastricht Treaty constituted such a leap forward from that political aspiration as to require a new mandate. Union citizenship has little practical consequence for Ireland as its chief domestic result, *viz.* certain voting rights for other E.C. nationals, had already been secured at a constitutional level; but its conceptual implications are considerable. The provisions on a Common Foreign and Security Policy arguably represent a considerable development from E.P.C., and the inclusion of Co-operation in the fields of Judicial and Home Affairs in a treaty, while in large part only a formalisation of existing practice, might also have been subject to objection as leading to a qualitative change in the position of a sovereign Member State. Possibly most significant of all was the creation of the European Union. While the exact juridical status of the Union is unclear (as was outlined above), it was wise to secure fresh authorisation before attempting to ratify the Treaty.

Article 29.4.5 now contains what was originally the second sentence of Article 29.4.3, amended to ensure the force of law for Union as well as E.C. measures, and to grant constitutional immunity to national measures necessitated by the obligations of Union as well as E.C. membership.

The problems with this amended formula have already been outlined above. The reference to E.C. institutions is extended to include competent bodies, as the monetary authorities envisaged for economic and monetary union will have certain legislative competences, but do not have the status of E.C. institutions.

The new Art. 29.4.6 authorises ratification of the Community Patents Convention, 1989. Unlike, for example, the Brussels Convention on Jurisdiction and the Enforcement of Judgments in Civil and Commercial Matters, 1968, ratification of the Patents Convention could not be a condition of membership. The *Crotty* decision, and the additional role granted to the European Court of Justice in the Convention, suggested that it would be unconstitutional to ratify without express authorisation, which this section provides (see further Robinson, "The Constitutional Problem in Ratifying the Community Patents Convention" in Robinson ed., *Intellectual Property* (Dublin 1989) p. 69).

Citation

2.—(1) The amendment of the Constitution effected by this Act shall be called the Eleventh Amendment of the Constitution.

(2) This Act may be cited as the Eleventh Amendment of the Constitution Act, 1992.

SCHEDULE

Part I

4° Tig leis an Stát an Connradh ar an Aontas Eorpach a sínigheadh i Maastricht ar an 7adh lá d'Fheabhra, 1992, do dhaingniú agus tig leis do bheith ina chomhalta den Aontas san.

5° Ní dhéanann aon fhoráileamh atá insan Bhunreacht so aon dlighthe d'achtuigh, gníomhartha do rinne nó bearta le n-ar ghlac an Stát, de bhíthin riachtanais na n-oibleagáidí mar chomhalta den Aontas Eorpach nó de na Comhphobail do chur ó bhail dlighidh ná cosc do chur le dlighthe d'achtuigh, gníomhartha do rinne nó bearta le n-ar ghlac an tAontas Eorpach nó na Comhphobail nó institiúidí díobh, nó comhluchtaí atá inneamhail fá na Connarthaí ag bunú na gComhphobal, ó fheidhm dlighidh do bheith aca sa Stát.

6° Tig leis an Stát an Comhaontú maidir le Paitinní Comhphobail a tarrainguigheadh suas idir Ballstáit na gComhphobal agus a rinneadh i Lucsamburg ar an 15adh lá de Nollaig, 1989, do dhaingniú.

Part II

4° The State may ratify the Treaty on European Union signed at Maastricht on the 7th day of February, 1992, and may become a member of that Union.

5° No provision of this Constitution invalidates laws enacted, acts done or measures adopted by the State which are necessitated by the obligations of membership of the European Union or of the Communities, or prevents laws enacted, acts done or measures adopted by the European Union or by the Communities or by institutions thereof, or by bodies competent under the Treaties establishing the Communities, from having the force of law in the State.

6° The State may ratify the Agreement relating to Community Patents drawn up between the Member States of the Communities and done at Luxembourg on the 15th day of December, 1989.

PART 2: IRISH STATUTORY MATERIAL AND THE TREATY ON EUROPEAN UNION

INTRODUCTION

EUROPEAN COMMUNITIES ACTS, 1972–1995

While the Third, Tenth and Eleventh Amendments of the Constitution were necessary to enable Ireland to accede to the European Communities and European Union and to provide a bulwark of constitutional immunity for all acts, decisions and measures taken or enacted by the institutions of the Community and Union, further domestic legislation was necessary by virtue of Article 29.6 of the Constitution to enable the Treaty of Rome and the other E.C. constitutional treaties to have the force of law in the domestic law of the State. The provisions of Article 29.4.3–6 are not self-executing, but are merely enabling in character.

The principal legislation is still the European Communities Act, 1972. Section 1 of that Act defines the phrase "the treaties governing the European Communities" and this phrase has been subsequently amended by legislation on eight occasions to cater for the development and expansion of the Treaties governing the European Communities. Sections 3 and 4 of this Act are also of fundamental importance, dealing as they do with the conditions under which the Treaties will form part of the domestic law of the State and the transposition of directives by ministerial regulation into domestic law. This method of transposition has itself been amended by the European Communities (Amendment) Act, 1977.

The domestic legislation between 1977 and 1985 which amended the 1972 Act was of a more routine (if nonetheless important) character. The European Communities (Amendment) Act, 1977 gave effect in Irish law to the terms of the Second Budgetary Treaty, 1974. There then followed the European Communities (Amendment) Act, 1979 (which allowed for the accession of the Hellenic Republic (Greece)) and the European Communities (Amendment) Act, 1985 allowed for the withdrawal of Greenland. The European Communities (Amendment) (No. 2) Act, 1986 allowed for the accession of Spain and Portugal to the Communities.

The European Communities (Amendment) Act, 1986 was the single most important item of European legislation to have been enacted since 1972. The 1986 Act was the vehicle whereby the Single European Act ("S.E.A.") or, more accurately, certain parts of it were made part of Irish domestic law. Those parts of the S.E.A.—notably Title III dealing with European Political Co-operation—which did not amend the Treaty of Rome (and the other constitutional treaties) were not incorporated into domestic law. The amendments to the Treaty of Rome effected by the S.E.A. had the objective of removing all existing barriers to the creation of one internal market for goods, services, capital and labour by December 31, 1992 and this would be done, in part, by extending the circumstances in which qualified majority voting would suffice at Council level.

There then followed the European Communities (Amendment) Act, 1992. This measure was of immense importance, since it provided for the incorporation into domestic law of certain provisions of the Maastricht Treaty on European Union. The European Communities (Amendment) Act, 1993 added to the list of treaties in this section which are part of the domestic law of the State, two agreements amending the Protocol on the Statute of the European Investment Bank. The 1993 Act also dealt with the accession of the State to the European Economic Area and certain issues which were raised in the High Court judgment in *Meagher v. Minister for Agriculture* [1994] 1 I.R. 329.

Finally, the European Communities (Amendment) Act, 1994 gave effect to the provisions of the 1994 Corfu Treaty which allowed for the accession of Austria, Finland and Sweden to the European Union, while the European Communities (Amendment) Act, 1995 transferred the supervisory statutory functions hitherto exercised by the Joint Committee on Foreign Affairs to the newly created Joint Committee on European Affairs.

EUROPEAN COMMUNITIES ACT, 1972

(1972, No. 27)

ARRANGEMENT OF SECTIONS

SECT.
1. Definitions.
2. General Provision.
3. Power to make regulations.
4. Effect and confirmation of regulations.
5. Report to Houses of Oireachtas.
6. Short title.

An Act to make provision with respect of the membership of the State of the European Communities   [December 6, 1972]

GENERAL NOTE

If Article 29.4.3 was the constitutional vehicle which enabled the State to join the European Communities, further legislation was necessary, by virtue of Article 29.6, to enable the Treaty of Rome and the other constitutional Community Treaties to have the force of law in the State. This was accomplished by the European Communities Act, 1972. The 1972 Act is remarkably short, consisting only of six sections (the final section contains the short title), but it continues to provide the basis for the transposition of Community law into the Irish legal system.

Section 1 defines the phrase "the treaties governing the European Communities" and this phrase has been subsequently amended on eight occasions (1977, 1979, 1985 (twice), 1986, 1992, 1993 and 1994) to cater for the development and expansion of the European Communities. The constitutional treaties of the Communities as they existed in 1972 consisted of the following:

    a. the ECSC Treaty (1951);
    b. the EEC Treaty (1957);
    c. the Euratom Treaty (1957);
    d. the Conventions on Institutions Common to the Communities (1957);
    e. the Merger Treaty (1965);
    f. the first Budgetary Treaty (1970);
    g. the Treaty of Accession of Ireland to the EEC and Euratom (1972) and
    h. the Decision of the Council on the Accession of Ireland to the ECSC (1972).

Section 2 makes these Treaties and the "existing and future acts adopted by the institutions of those Communities" part of the domestic law of the State "under the conditions laid down in those treaties." Sections 3 and 4 deal with a Minister's power to make regulations and this is discussed below. Section 5 obliges the Government to make a twice-yearly report to each House of the Oireachtas on developments in the European Communities.

Citation

This Act may be cited as the European Communities Act, 1972: see section 6 of the 1972 Act.

Commencement

The 1972 Act came into force on the day Ireland acceded to the European Communities, *viz.*, January 1, 1973.

European Communities Act, 1972

Parliamentary Debates

263 *Dáil Debates* Cols. 90–259 (Second Stage); Cols. 924–969; 1011–1057; 1102–1122; 1125–1246 (Committee Stage); Cols. 1684–1751 (Report and Final Stages)
73 *Seanad Debates* Cols. 829–910; 925–952 (Second stage); 999–1026 (Committee and Final Stages)

Be it enacted by the Oireachtas as follows:

Definitions

1.—(1) In this Act—
"the European Communities" means the European Economic Community, the European Coal and Steel Community and the European Atomic Energy Community;
"the treaties governing the European Communities" means—
(a) "the ECSC Treaty", that is to say, the Treaty establishing the European Coal and Steel Community, signed at Paris on the 18th day of April, 1951,
(b) "the EEC Treaty", that is to say, the Treaty establishing the European Economic Community, signed at Rome on the 25th day of March, 1957,
(c) "the Euratom Treaty", that is to say, the Treaty establishing the European Atomic Energy Community, signed at Rome on the 25th day of March, 1957,
(d) the Convention on certain Institutions common to European Communities, signed at Rome on the 25th day of March 1957,
(e) the Treaty establishing a single Council and a single Commission of the European Communities, signed at Brussels on the 8th day of April, 1965.
(f) the Treaty amending certain Budgetary Provisions of the Treaties establishing the European Communities and of the Treaty establishing a single Council and a single Commission of the European Communities. signed at Luxembourg on the 22nd day of April, 1970.
(g) the Treaty relating to the accession of Ireland to the European Economic Community and to the European Atomic Energy Community, signed at Brussels on the 22nd day of January, 1972,
(h) the decision, of the 22nd day of January, 1972, of the Council of the European Communities relating to the accession of Ireland to the European Coal and Steel Community, as supplemented or amended by treaties or other acts of which the dates of entry into force are dates not later than the 1st day of January, 1973, and:
(i) the Treaty amending certain financial provisions of the treaties establishing the European Communities and of the Treaty establishing a single Council and a single Commission of the European Communities, signed at Brussels on the 22nd day of July, 1975[1], and
(j) the Treaty relating to the accession of the Hellenic Republic to the European Economic Community and to the European Atomic Energy Community, signed at Athens on the 28th day of May, 1979, and
(k) the decision, of the 24th day of May, 1979, of the Council of the European Communities relating to the accession of the Hellenic Republic to the European Coal and Steel Community[2], and
(l) the Treaty amending, with regard to Greenland, the Treaties establishing the European Communities, signed at Brussels on the 13th day of March, 1984[3], and
(m) the Treaty concerning the accession of the Kingdom of Spain and the Portuguese Republic to the European Economic Community and to the

---

[1] Subsection (i) was inserted by s.1 of the European Communities (Amendment) Act, 1977.
[2] Subsections (j) and (k) were inserted by s.1 of the European Communities (Amendment) Act, 1979.
[3] Subsection (l) was inserted by s.1 of the European Communities (Amendment) Act, 1983.

European Atomic Energy Community, signed at Lisbon and Madrid on the 12th day of June, 1985, and

(n) the decision, of the 11th day of June, 1985, of the Council of the European Communities relating to the accession of the Kingdom of Spain and the Portuguese Republic to the European Coal and Steel Community[4], and

(o) the following provisions of the Single European Act (done at Luxembourg on the 17th day of February, 1986, and at The Hague on the 28th day of February, 1986), namely, Art, 3.1; Title II; Arts. 31 and 32; and, in so far as they relate to the said Art. 3.1, the said Title II and the said Arts. 31 and 32, Arts. 33 and 34[5], and

(p) the following provisions of the Treaty on European Union, namely, Titles II, III and IV; in Title VII, Arts. L, M and P, and the other provisions of that Title in so far as they relate to any of the treaties governing the European Communities as defined by this subsection; together with the Protocols (whether expressed to be annexed to the Treaty establishing the European Community, or to the said Treaty on European Union and the Treaties establishing the European Communities), done at Maastricht on the 7th day of February, 1992[6], and

(q) the Act amending the Protocol on the Statute of the European Investment Bank, empowering the Board of Governors to establish a European Investment Fund, signed at Brussels on the 25th day of March, 1993, together with the Treaty amending certain provisions of the Protocol on the Statute of the European Investment Bank, signed at Brussels on the 10th day of July, 1975[7], and

(r) the Treaty concerning the accession of the Kingdom of Norway, the Republic of Austria, the Republic of Finland and the Kingdom of Sweden to the European Union signed at Corfu on the 24th day of June, 1994 in so far as that Treaty relates to the European Communities[8].

(2) (a) In the foregoing subsection "treaties or other acts of which the dates of entry into force are dates not later than the 1st day of January, 1973" does not include a treaty or other act of which the date of entry into force is later than the 22nd day of January, 1972, unless the Government have, not later than the 1st day of January, 1973, by order declared that this section applies to it.

(b) Where an order under this section is proposed to be made, a draft thereof shall be laid before each House of the Oireachtas and the order shall not be made until a resolution approving of the draft has been passed by each such House.

GENERAL NOTE

The 1977 Act
    The 1977 Act gave effect in Irish law to the terms of the Second Budgetary Treaty, 1974. This Treaty amended the Treaty of Rome in a number of respects. First, it established the Court of Auditors. This body roughly approximates in terms of membership to the Court of Justice, save that its principal functions lies in the examination of the Community accounts and the submission of an annual report concerning the management of the Community finances. The court has been given enhanced functions in the wake of the Maastricht Treaty: see Art. 188 a–c E.C. The 1974 Treaty also gave the European Parliament a role for the first time in the supervision of the Community budget. These powers have now been further amended by the Maastricht Treaty and are now to be found in Art. 206 E.C.

---

[4] Subsections (m) and (n) were inserted by s.1 of the European Communities (No. 2) Act, 1985.
[5] Subsection (o) was inserted by s.1(1) of the European Communities (Amendment) Act, 1986.
[6] Subsection (p) was inserted by s.1(1) of the European Communities (Amendment) Act, 1992.
[7] Subsection (q) was inserted by s.2(1)(b) of the European Communities (Amendment) Act, 1993.
[8] Subsection (r) was inserted by s.1(1) of the European Communities (Amendment) Act, 1994.

The 1979 Act and the accession of the Hellenic Republic (Greece)

This legislation gave effect to the May 1979 Treaty allowing for the accession of the Hellenic Republic (Greece) to the European Communities. This legislation came into force on January 1, 1981 with the formal accession of Greece to the European Communities.

The 1985 Act and the withdrawal of Greenland from the European Communities

When Denmark joined the Communities in 1973, Greenland did so as well by virtue of its status within the Danish realm. Following the grant of home rule status within the Danish realm in 1979, Greenland held a referendum in February 1982 on continued Community membership. At that referendum 53 per cent of the population voted to withdraw from the Communities—their main grievance was the belief that the fishing fleets of the other Member States had exceeded their fish quotas in Greenlandic waters. This led to the Brussels Treaty of 1984 whereby the withdrawal of Greeland was agreed, subject to the ratification of all 10 Member States in accordance with their constitutional requirements.

In the case of Ireland, this required the amendment of the 1972 Act and, in particular, the definition therein of the phrase "the treaties governing the European Communities". It had been intended that the Treaty would have been ratified by all Member States by January 1, 1985 but due to an embarrassing oversight, the 1985 Act only completed its passage through the Oireachtas in January, 1985. The Treaty then duly entered into force on February 1, 1985. (See further Weiss,"Greenland's Withdrawal from the European Communities" (1985) 10 E.L.Rev. 173.)

The 1985 (No. 2) Act and the accession of Spain and Portugal

On June 11, 1985 the European Council decided to approve the accession of Spain and Portugal. The Treaty of Accession was signed on the following day in Madrid and Lisbon respectively. Article 2 of the Treaty required that it be ratified by all Member States in accordance with their own constitutional requirements. Following the enactment of the 1985 (No. 2) Act, this Treaty of Accession was duly ratified by Ireland on December 2, 1985 and Spain and Portugal duly acceded to the Community on January 1, 1986.

The 1986 Act and the Single European Act

The 1986 Act was the vehicle whereby the Single European Act (S.E.A.) or, more accurately, certain parts of it were made part of Irish domestic law. Those parts of the S.E.A.—notably Title III dealing with European Political Co-operation—which did not amend the Treaty of Rome (and the other constitutional Treaties) were not incorporated into domestic law.

The term Single Act was essentially a misnomer, since it incorporated two separate treaties. The S.E.A. was a product of the Inter-Governmental Conference which had been convened at Milan in June 1985 in order (i) to propose certain amendments to the EEC Treaties and (ii) to draft a separate Treaty on political co-operation and European security. The texts prepared by the conference were consolidated and formally adopted as the S.E.A. in February 1986. (For a further analysis of the origins and background to the SEA, see Murphy, "The Single European Act" (1985) 20 *Irish Jurist* 17, 239.)

The Single Act was essentially a response to the "Euroscleoris" which had overtaken the Communities in the early 1980s. The requirement of unanimity at Council meetings—the political compromise which had broken the "empty chair" crisis of 1965—had slowed down decision-making, with the result that insufficient progress had been made in the achievement of the Common Market which had been the objective of the original Treaty of Rome. The Inter-Governmental Conference had coincided with the publication of the Commission's seminal *White Paper* (1985) which had identified the continued obstacles to progress towards an internal market. The amendments to the Treaty of Rome effected by the S.E.A. had the objective of removing all existing barriers to the creation of one internal market for goods, services, capital and labour by December 31, 1992 and this would be done, in part, by extending the circumstances in which qualified majority voting would suffice at Council level.

The S.E.A. consisted of a Preamble, 34 Articles arranged in four Titles and a Final Act consisting of 20 declarations adopted either by the Inter-Governmental Conference or by the Commission or individual Member States.

Title I accomplished three things:

(i) it formally linked the European Communities and European Political Co-operation, their objectives concerning European unity;

(ii) it formally recognised the European Council; and

(iii) it formally changed the name of Assembly to European Parliament.

Title II effected a number of significant amendments to the Treaty of Rome. First, it allowed for the establishment of the Court of First Instance. Secondly, it increased the power of the Parliament, a process that has been further enhanced by the Maastricht Treaty (see above).

Thirdly, it established the single market programme which provided for the creation of a single market in goods, services, labour and capital by the end of December 1992. The principal means of achieving this was through the extension of majority voting at Council level, thus speeding up the process of legislating for the elimination of barriers to the achievement of the Single Market.

Title III provided for the establishment of European Political Co-operation, which was the initial formalised step of co-operation at foreign affairs level. Title III has now been repealed and replaced by Title V of the Maastricht Treaty.

The 1992 Act and Maastricht Treaty on European Union

Section 1 of the European Communities (Amendment) Act 1992 provides for the addition of certain provisions only of the Maastricht Treaty on European Union to the list in section 1 of the 1972 Act of "the treaties governing the European Communities". This is because the Treaty has a fuller agenda than the mere amendment and extension of the three basic Community treaties.

Similarly, in the European Communities (Amendment) Act, 1986, it was only provisions of the Single European Act amending these treaties (which provisions were concentrated largely in Title II of the S.E.A.) which were incorporated into Irish law. At the time, this "constitutional schizophrenia" was explained on the basis that the "Single European Act" in fact amounted to two treaties: one on the Communities and another, quite separate, on European Political Co-operation (see Murphy, 1986 Act, at 37–02, 37–05). The Maastricht Treaty combines the two (along with the hitherto informal "Trevi" process of judicial and police co-operation) as separate pillars of the new Union structure (Art. A). Nonetheless, it was thought inappropriate to incorporate the provisions on Common Foreign and Security Policy and on Judicial and Home Affairs Co-operation into Irish law. The Minister for Foreign Affairs (Mr. D. Andrews T.D.) explained this in the Dáil (424 *Dáil Debates*, col. 1818):

> "There is no provision in this legislation to cover Title V or Title VI of the Treaty on European Union. Title V concerns provisions on a common foreign and security policy where no requirement for domestic legislation is envisaged. Title VI concerns provisions on co-operation in the fields of justice and home affairs. Legislation may be required at some stage in the future to cover some of the Articles in this Title. However, no legislation is required, nor would it be appropriate, at this stage to cover the provisions of this Title."

By virtue of the omission of these Titles from the 1992 Act, neither Union legislation nor domestic delegated legislation pursuant to Union measures can be anticipated. This, it is submitted, reinforces the point made elsewhere that the extension of the constitutional immunity in Article 29.4.5 to Union acts (as distinct from those of the Communities) was probably premature.

The Maastricht amendments to the EEC Treaty (transforming it in the process into the European Community Treaty) are annotated at length below.

The 1993 Act and the European Investment Bank

The 1993 Act added to the list of treaties in this section which are part of the domestic law of the State, two agreements amending the Protocol on the Statute of the European Investment Bank. The Act of March 25, 1993 amending the Protocol on the Statute of the European Investment Bank empowers the Board of Governors to establish a European Investment Fund. The Fund is part of the Communities' growth initiative agreed at the European Council at Edinburgh in December 1992. The founder members are the European Investment Bank, the Community, and other major financial institutions. Some 40 per cent of the Funds' projected capital of two billion ECU comes from the European Investment Bank, 30 per cent from the Communities, and the remainder from other parties. The Fund is to provide financial guarantees for borrowings, assisting small and medium sized enterprises, and facilitating private financing of infrastructural projects.

The Treaty of July 10, 1975 is a purely technical agreement not requiring incorporation in Irish law, but inserted for the sake of clarity.

The 1994 Act and the accession of Austria, Finland, Sweden and Norway

The 1994 Corfu Treaty allowed for the accession of Austria, Finland, Sweden and Norway to the European Union. The major political issue raised by the accession—apart from the broader issue of the enlargement itself—was the question of qualified majority voting at the Council level. The compromise allowed the blocking minority to move after accession from 23 votes to 27. In addition, the Member States agreed to a delaying mechanism when it was clear that at least 23 votes were opposed to the proposal. A solution must then be found or a blocking minority of 27 emerge within a reasonable time, as otherwise the measure will be adopted by a qualified majority. (This compromise has since been slightly amended in the light of the non-accession of Norway.)

Following referenda in June, October and November 1994, the electorates in Austria, Finland and Sweden voted to join the European Union (with majorities of 66.6 per cent, 57.1 per cent and 52.3 per cent respectively). However, by a referendum held on November 28, 1994 the Norwegian people voted not to join the Communities (by 52.3 per cent to 47.7 per cent). Article 2 of the Accession Treaty addressed the possibility that not all of the applicant countries would be in a position to ratify the Treaty. The Accession Treaty provides that the Council, acting unanimously, is permitted to make the necessary technical adjustments as a consequence of this. The Council reached political agreement on this at the General Affairs Council of December 19–20, 1994, and gave effect to this agreement by decision dated January 1, 1995 (see E.C. Press Release 4061/95). Thus, Title I of the Accession Treaty has been adjusted to delete the reference to 15 Norwegian MEPs, to the three Norwegian votes in the Council, and to the nine Norwegian members of the Economic and Social Committee and the Committee of the Regions. The stipulations that there should be 21 Commissioners and 16 judges of the Court of Justice have also been changed.

Somewhat curiously, these adjustments did not affect the Irish ratification procedures which involved the 1994 Act, a Dáil resolution approving the terms of the Corfu Treaty of Accession in accordance with Article 29.5.2 of the Constitution and the formal ratification of the Treaty by the State. In other words, it was sufficient for Ireland to accede to a Treaty which contained an in-built mechanism allowing for its adjustment in the light of non-ratification by one of the acceding States.

In accordance with precedent, the 1994 Act gives effect in domestic law to the accession Treaty in so far as it relates to the European Communities. The reason for this was explained by the then Minister of State at the Department of Foreign Affairs (Mr. T. Kitt T.D.) speaking at the Report Stage of the Bill in the Seanad (141 *Seanad Debates*, cols. 942-943):

> "This [decision] is consistent with the fact that under the Treaty on European Union as it stands, and the three pillar structure that it established, only measures taken under the first pillar—the Communities pillar—have been made part of the domestic law of the State. The other two pillars established under the Treaty on European Union ... that make up the Union structure—justice and home affairs and common foreign and security policy—were not made part of the domestic law of the State in 1992 by the required amendment to the European Communities Act, 1972, as amended. The same policy was followed in our legislation to give effect to our obligations under the Single European Act in 1987."

General Provision

2.—(1) From the 1st day of January 1973, the treaties governing the European Communities and the existing and future acts adopted by the institutions of those Communities [and by the bodies competent under the said treaties][9] shall be binding on the State and shall be part of the domestic law thereof under the conditions laid down in those treaties.

(2) Without prejudice to subsection (1) of this section, from the coming into force of the EEA Agreement, the provisions of that Agreement and the acts to be adopted by institutions established by that Agreement which, pursuant to the treaties governing the European Communities, will be binding on the State and an integral part of the legal order of those Communities, shall have the force of law in the State on the conditions laid down in those treaties and in that Agreement[10].

GENERAL NOTE

Treaties governing the European Communities part of domestic law
Sections 1 and 2 of the 1972 Act introduce the entire corpus of E.C. law into Irish law "under the conditions laid down in [the] treaties". Thus, they require those elements of E.C. law which

---

[9] The words in brackets were inserted by s.2 of the European Communities Act, 1992.

[10] Section 2(2) was inserted by s.3 of the European Communities (Amendment) Act, 1993 and the original s.2 was re-numbered as s.2(1).

are directly applicable, (*e.g.* Community regulations and some treaty provisions) or directly effective (as can transpire in the case of directives) to be enforced in Irish courts on terms dictated by the treaties as interpreted by the Court of Justice. Such "laws enacted, acts done or measures adopted by the Communities, or institutions thereof" are free from constitutional scrutiny. In *Meagher v. Minister for Agriculture* [1994] 1 I.R. 329, 350; Finlay C.J. described section 2 in the following terms:

> "Section 2 of the Act which provides for the application of the Community law and acts binding on the State and as part of the domestic law subject to the conditions laid down in the Treaty which, of course, including its primacy, is the major or fundamental obligation necessitated by membership of the Community."

Starting from this premise, therefore, the Court went on to uphold the constitutionality of the regulation-making power contained in section 3 (see further the discussion above).

Implementation of the European Economic Area agreement

Sections 2(2) (together with sections 3 and 4 of the European Communities (Amendment) Act, 1992) concern the implementation of the European Economic Area Agreement between the E.C. and its Member States, on the one hand, and the States (excluding Switzerland) of the European Free Trade Association (EFTA) on the other. (Following a negative vote on the Swiss referendum on the EEA in December 1992, Liechtenstein voted in a referendum in 1993 to accede to the EEA and this resulted in amendment of its customs union with Switzerland. The EEA entered into force in Liechtenstein on January 1, 1994.) The Agreement was signed at Oporto on May 2, 1992, and was amended by a Protocol signed in Brussels on March 17, 1993. In some respects, the Agreement has been overtaken by events, since in the light of the accesion of Austria, Finland and Sweden to the European Union, the membership of EFTA has been reduced to four countries (Switzerland, Iceland, Norway and Liechtenstein), with Switzerland staying outside the EEA.

In essence, the Agreement is designed to extend the E.C.'s four freedoms (relating to persons, services, capital, and goods) to the territories of both the E.C. and the EFTA States, while preventing the distortion of competition and fostering closer co-operation in a number of discrete fields, (*e.g.* social policy, education, research and development, and environment). There are general guarantees of non-discrimination on grounds of nationality (without prejudice to property-ownership rules) and of the sort of co-operation in fulfilling the Agreement which in the E.C. is termed the commitment to solidarity. Many formulae familiar from the E.C. and ECSC Treaties are employed, and where they arise are to be read in accordance with previous rulings of the European Court of Justice, save where it is otherwise provided. The Agreement is to prevail over existing international agreements so far as they cover the same subject matter.

The institutional structure of the EEA is set out in Part VII of the Agreement. General political impetus is provided by the EEA Council, comprised of E.C. Commissioners, the members of the E.C. Council and a representative of each of the participating EFTA governments. There is also an EEA Joint Committee, which in composition resembles the E.C. Council; all the contracting parties are represented on it (including the Commission representing the Communities), and it is to meet regularly. Many executive and other functions are split between the E.C. Commission and the EFTA Surveillance Authority, *e.g.* in the area of competition. Also established are a Joint Parliamentary Committee, with equal representation from EFTA national parliaments and the European Parliament, and an EEA Consultative Committee in which the Community's Economic and Social Committee and the equivalent EFTA Consultative Committee are represented. Initial plans to found an EEA Court drawing some of its membership from the European Court of Justice were scotched by the latter court in its Opinion 1/91 [1992] E.C.R. 6079, on the grounds, *inter alia*, that interpretation even of identical E.C. and EEA legal provisions would be determined by the different objectives of the two organisations expressed in their founding treaties, and that this would produce an insoluble conflict of interests for the E.C. judges, as well as undermining the distinctive nature of the E.C. legal order. Instead, an EFTA Court of Justice has been established by separate agreement with certain competences relating to the application of the Agreement in or among the EFTA States. The Joint Committee is to keep under review the jurisprudence of both courts (European Court of Justice and EFTA Court of Justice). EFTA States may permit their courts to seek a ruling from the Court of Justice on the interpretation of EEA law. If the Joint Committee is unable to achieve homogenous interpretation of rulings of the two courts on the same legal provision, which provision is analogous to a provision of E.C. law, the parties to a dispute may agree after three months to refer the issue to the European Court of Justice; in the absence of such a reference, safeguard measures may be taken by parties after six months (with the possibility of rebalancing measures by other parties).

When preparing legislation in the areas covered by the Agreement, the E.C. Commission is to enter into very full consultation with EFTA States. The EEA Joint Committee can generate binding Acts which correspond in nature either to directly applicable E.C. regulations, or to E.C. directives, in respect of which there is a choice of methods of implementation. A number of annexes to the Agreement reproduce, with necessary modifications, E.C. legislation which is to be extended to the EEA—the *acquis communautaire* accepted by the EFTA States. These Annexes may be amended by the Joint Committee. Where the E.C. is to introduce new legislation in an area covered by one of the annexes to the Agreement, the Joint Committee must seek to amend the annex in harmony with this new development so that new E.C. and EEA legal provisions will ideally come into force simultaneously. Where it proves impossible to reach agreement in the Joint Committee, the ultimate solution is the suspension of the application of the Agreement in the affected sector. Decisions of the Joint Committee bind the parties once they come into force. However, this can only occur where parties which must comply with domestic constitutional requirements have done so; if ratification cannot be secured, the relevant decision is suspended, as is the operation of the Agreement in that sector where the E.C. wishes to proceed with related changes within its legal order. This arrangement differs markedly from the automatic supremacy which is insisted upon in respect of the ordinary legislative acts of the E.C.; but it must be remembered that the annexes, however technical their content, are attached to the founding treaty of the EEA, so that an analogy with Article N, E.U. (formerly Art. 236 EEC) may be more appropriate. Furthermore, the very reason for the existence of the EEA is to try to win a liberal trading relationship for the EFTA States and the E.C., which does not entail adherence of the former to a supranational political and legal order like that of the Communities (see, *e.g.* Schermers, Casenote on Opinions 1/91 and 1/92).

Part II of the Agreement concerns: (i) free movement of goods, and reproduces existing E.C. rules prohibiting customs duties and equivalent measures; (ii) quantitative restrictions and equivalent measures other than those designed to promote certain familiar objectives such as public policy, public health, conservation of national heritage, and so on, where the measures are not arbitrary or a disguised restriction; and (iii) discriminatory internal taxes. However, these guarantees apply only to certain goods originating in the contracting States (as opposed to the more extensive class of goods in free circulation therein), and detailed rules on origin (subject to GATT commitments) are outlined in a protocol. There are special rules for agricultural and fisheries products, with provision for biennial reviews in order to further liberalisation in these sectors. State commercial monopolies are required to avoid national discrimination in procurement. Provision for simplification of border controls and other procedures, and a number of other ancillary matters, *e.g.* product liability are also addressed. Anti-dumping and other countervailing measures may not be employed as between the parties.

Part III addresses the other three freedoms. Free movement of workers is provided for (with special provisions regarding public service employment). Measures are authorised, *e.g.* on mutual recognition of qualifications, and on aggregation of relevant working periods for social welfare purposes.

Establishment and services are subject to similarly liberal regimes reminiscent in virtually all respects of those already in existence in the E.C. There are special provisions on transport, subject to a general principle of non-discrimination. Movement of capital is also liberalised, largely on E.C. lines, with provision for non-discrimination in the application of domestic rules to capital movements. There are somewhat more extensive options for protective measures: in response to evasion of rules on capital transfer, disturbances of the capital market, distortion in competition due to exchange rate changes by another contracting party, or balance of payments problems.

Part IV relates to competition and other common rules. The rules contained in Arts. 85 and 86 of the E.C. Treaty on anti-competitive agreements and concerted practices, and on abuse of a dominant position, are reproduced. Cases are referred to the E.C. Commission or the EFTA Surveillance Authority, according to the States between which trade is affected or where a dominant position exists. Competence is also allocated between these two bodies (above certain thresholds) to control concentrations, to supervise public monopolies, and to review state aids. There are special provisions on procurement and on intellectual property.

Part V concerns miscellaneous matters relevant to the four freedoms: equal pay for equal work; the encouragement of better working conditions; consumer protection and environmental protection. Part VI governs co-operation in a number of other sectors: education and training; information services; research and development; social policy; tourism; civil protection and the audio-visual sector. Dialogue is to take place in the framework of the EEA Joint Committee. Co-operation can take the form of participation in E.C. framework programmes, parallel legislation, and co-ordination of activities in international fora.

173

Section 2(2) of the European Communities Act, 1972 (as inserted by section 3 of the European Communities (Amendment) Act, 1993) provides for the EEA Agreement and consequent legislative acts of its institutions to be part of the law of the State, in so far as the Agreement and the acts of its institutions are binding on the State pursuant to the E.C. Treaties, *i.e.* as a matter of E.C. law.

The EEA Agreement is a mixed agreement, that is, an agreement to which both the Community and the individual Member States of the E.C. are parties on one side. (See further the discussion above). Article 2(c) of the EEA Agreement, states that for the purposes of the Agreement, "the Term 'Contracting Parties' means: concerning the Community and the E.C. Member States, the Community and the Member States, or the Community or the E.C. Member States. The meaning to be attributed to this expression in each case is to be deduced from the relevant provisions of this Agreement and from the respective competences of the Community and the E.C. Member States as they follow from the [Treaties]". In so far, therefore, as the EEA Agreement is a Community treaty, and thus an act adopted by the institutions of the Community, it is presumably already part of Ireland's domestic legal order in accordance with the terms of section 2(1) of the European Communities Act, 1972. This is submitted to be the case even if it is not directly applicable in all respects, and is in need of further implementation by E.C. or national measures: (see the similar argument above in respect of provisions of the constitutional Treaties and directives to the extent that they are not directly applicable or directly effective). Therefore it did not need further incorporation through the new section 2(2) inserted by section 3 of the 1993 Act (although caution may have been sensible).

However, if one takes it that certain matters within the scope of the EEA Agreement may be within the exclusive jurisdiction of the Member States (although they are hard to identify), and that the Community is stated not to be a party to the EEA Agreement in respect of such matters, is it therefore the case that such provisions of the Agreement have not been made part of Irish law under section 2(2) of the 1972 Act? The Community is not competent to conclude agreements governing subject matter which is within the exclusive competence of the Member States, even if it is dealt with in a treaty with third States which also addresses matters which are within the concurrent or exclusive jurisdiction of the Community (that format being simply a convenience). There is the possibility, adverted to in the discussion above of mixed agreements, that potentially joint international liabililty for breach of a mixed agreement can impose a Community law duty on the Member States under Article 5 E.C. to observe obligations incurred within the sphere of their exclusive competence. If this speculation is well-founded, we must ask whether the operation of such an obligation would bring all of the provisions of the EEA Agreement within the terms of section 2(2) of the 1972 Act, thus making them part of Irish law.

Section 2(2) of the European Communities Act, 1972 gives the force of law in the State to the Agreement and to acts of the EEA institutions "which, pursuant to the treaties governing the European Communities, will be binding on the State and an integral part of the legal order of those Communities". The latter part of this legislative formula is borrowed from the jurisprudence of the European Court of Justice; and even in *Demirel v. Stadt Schwäbisch Gmünd* Case 12/86, [1987] E.C.R. 3719 the court did not go so far as to say that provisions of a mixed agreement within the exclusive competence of the Member States could be an integral part of the Community legal order. The question remains whether the (possible) supplementation of the Member States' international law obligation to observe such provisions by a Community law obligation under Article 5 E.C. means that the State is bound by a mixed agreement in its entirety pursuant to the Community Treaty (so that all of the EEA Agreement would then come within the terms of section 2(2)). This must depend on whether a rather scholastic distinction should be drawn between an obligation as a matter of Community law (under Article 5 E.C.) to observe the agreement's terms (in order not to expose the Community to international responsibility), and a finding that Community law is a source (under Art. 228 E.C.) of the binding power of the agreement on the Member States additional to the principles of public international law. The latter position seems inconsistent with the principle of the attribution of competence in the Community legal order, but the question must inevitably be left open. The precise status of the EEA Agreements in Irish law is therefore in doubt.

This is relevant because the regulatory power of Ministers is affected by EEA membership. Section 3 of the 1972 Act empowers Ministers to make regulations "for enabling section 2 of this Act to have full effect", which must therefore include a power to make regulations to give effect to the EEA Agreement *in so far as it has the force of law in the State*. No great problem is raised by existing regulations under the European Communities Act, 1972, or under other enactments which implemented the obligations of the State under the Community Treaties, as these are to be construed as if adapted as required by or under the EEA Agreement, by virtue of section 4(1) of the European Communities (Amendment) Act, 1993; and section 4(2) provides that in particular, references to the Member States of the Communities or to persons affected by the Community Treaties are to be construed, where necessary, to include references to the other EEA States and to persons affected by the EEA Agreement. Three things may be said here of the effect of these rather vague provisions (which are further annotated below). First, even if compliance with the EEA Agreement were not necessitated by Community membership (which it is, at least in part), the amendment by reference of all relevant enactments and ministerial regulations by *statutory* provisions gets over any constitutional problems relating to implementing procedure (although it cannot thereby remedy any constitutional problems with the content of such national measures which might arise in so far as that precise content is not dictated by Community law or, latterly, by the EEA Agreement). Secondly, while one can quibble about the wording, these provisions are designed to affect only legislation or delegated legislation adopted to comply with the obligations of Community law. (This is much clearer from the first sub-section than from the second, as references to the Member States of the Communities in national legislation need not necessarily arise consequent on such obligations, as the terms of the Electoral Act, 1992 make clear; see the annotation of Art. 8b E.C. below.) As the EEA Agreement sets out in its Annexes the Community legislation which is to be applied throughout the EEA, it is national measures implementing such Community legislation which is largely affected by section 4. On the other hand, section 4 probably does not affect provisions of national law which govern such matters within exclusive Member State competence as are affected by the EEA Agreement, which national provisions will have to be amended where necessary to comply with it. (The difficulty in identifying such national law is further evidence of the unhelpful nature of participation clauses such as Article 2(c) of the EEA Agreement, which suggests the presence of provisions of the Agreement affecting exclusive national competences when none may exist.) Thirdly, these provisions appear to be retrospective only (although this again is clearer from the first sub-section than from the second), "without prejudice to the future exercise of the powers conferred by section 3 of the Act of 1972". Thus, ministerial regulations adopted in future under the 1972 Act will presumably have to provide expressly for their application to the EEA States. Can such ministerial regulations now be made, repealing, amending or applying, with or without modification, national law which falls within exclusive national competence, to the extent (if any) that this is required by the EEA Agreement, or by acts adopted by institutions established by that Agreement, *i.e.* regulations which could not ordinarily be made pursuanat to the Community Treaties themselves? This will turn on the question discussed above, on the nature of the Member State obligation to observe a mixed agreement in its entirety. It will also turn on the interpretation of the statutory provisions in question, which must incline one towards a negative response. Whatever may be the outcome of the Community law question of obligation, it seems clear from the terms of the European Communities (Amendment) Act, 1993 (both section 4, and section 2, which inserted section 2(2) in the 1972 Act) that it was intended that the ministerial regulatory power should be available in respect of the EEA Agreement only to the extent that it is a Community agreement, the obligations of which were assumed by the Community institutions acting within their normal competences. The 1993 Act was complimented for this at the time of its enactment, which perhaps significantly came between the High Court and Supreme Court decisions in *Meagher v. Minister for Agriculture* [1994] 1 I.R. 329, for resisting the temptation to seek to envelop in the net of Community "necessity" matters not in fact the subject of Community law (see Whelan, "The European Communities (Amendment) Act, 1993" (1993) ICLSA 25–01, at 25–08; to which this note is otherwise a substantial amendment.)

Power to make regulations

3.—(1) A Minister of State may make regulations for enabling section 2 of this Act to have full effect.

(2) Regulations under this section may contain such incidental, supplementary and consequential provisions as appear to the Minister making the regulations to be necessary for the purposes of the regulations (including provisions repealing, amending or applying, with or without modification, other law, exclusive of this Act).

(3) Regulations under this section shall not create an indictable offence.

(4) Regulations under this section may be made before the 1st day of January, 1973, but regulations so made shall not come into operation before that day.

General Note

To avoid any possible confusion, it should be emphasised that the use of the word "regulations" is in its Irish (and not Community law) sense, *i.e.* statutory instruments.

Section 3: Power to make regulations, including incidental, supplementary and consequential provisions

The power to make regulations by ministerial order was described by Blayney J. in *Meagher* as "a very wide one" and the exercise of such powers will be regarded as *intra vires* provided [1994] 1 I.R. 329, 356:

> "that it was necessary for the purpose of giving effect to these Directives. Accordingly the Directives have to be looked at to see if these provisions are necessary for their implementation and when this is done it becomes quite clear that they are."

(See further the discussion above). Blayney J. thus went to on to uphold the validity of the extension of the time limit for prosecutions under the European Communities (Control of Veterinary Medicinal Products and their Residues) Regulations, 1988–1990 from six months to two years, even though such an extension had not been expressly sanctioned by the relevant directives [1994] 1 I.R. at 359:

> "It was submitted ... that there was nothing in the Directive which expressly justified a two-year time limit and for that reason it was not justified. The Directive clearly required ... that offences be created and ... it had to be possible for these offences to be effectively prosecuted. Accordingly, the implementation of the Directive required that the Regulations should provide for an adequate time for the preparation of the prosecutions. It was not necessary that the Directive should itself fix a time. It was a matter for the State to decide on the length of time required to enable a prosecution to be brought and this is what the Minister has done in providing for a period of two years."

It will be seen, therefore, that the power to make regulations which are "incidental, supplementary and consequential" includes the power to make such regulations as may be deemed necessary by the Minister to give effect to the Directive, even though the matters in question may not have been spelled out in the Directive itself. The principal limitation would appear to be that envisaged by the Supreme Court in *Meagher* itself, namely, the "hypothetical" circumstances in which the Directive should have been implemented by legislation rather than by regulation. In those circumstances, the challenge would succeed on the basis of the measure being *ultra vires* the regulation-making power in section 3(2) as opposed to the validity of the sub-section itself. It may be noted that in *Agra Meat Packers Ltd v. Minister for Agriculture and Food* (High Court, December 14, 1994), Carroll J. said that the power under section 3 enabled the Minister to pass regulations "providing the necessary administrative procedures to give full effect to the substantive provisions of [a] Directive, but that he has no authority to legislate on matters outside of or contradictory to a [a] Directive."

Section 3(3): Regulations may not create an indictable offence

Section 3(3) is, essentially, a concession to the legislative sovereignty of the Oireachtas in that by virtue of this sub-section no ministerial regulation can create an indictable offence. This is not in any sense ordained or required by Community law, but it is rather a self-imposed limitation on the Ministerial capacity to prescribe the contents of such Regulations. The words "indictable offence" would appear to mean no more than that the offence is capable of being tried on indictment: as Asquith L.J. said in *Hastings and Folkestone Glassworks Ltd v. Kalson* [1949] 1 K.B. 214, at 220: "An 'indictable offence' without any qualifying context can mean nothing else but an offence in respect of which an indictment would lie .... It is none the less indictable because if the prosecution choose it could proceed in respect of it summarily."

The vast majority of E.C. Directives are transposed into Irish law by means of statutory instrument. Since section 3(3) provides that the creation of indictable offences is precluded where a statutory instrument has been used for this purpose, the Oireachtas will occasionally resort to the use of primary legislation in order to provide for the creation of such offences. A good recent example of this is provided by the Animal Remedies Act, 1993 which replaced a number of statutory instruments made under the 1972 Act which had earlier given effect to various E.C. Directives controlling the manufacture and use of illegal growth promoters. As the then Minister of State at the Department of Agriculture, Food and Forestry (Mr. L. Hyland T.D.) explained at the Second Stage of the Bill in the Dáil (429 *Dáil Debates*, cols. 1518–1519):

> "Because of the limitations of our domestic legislation to implement these [E.C. Directives] the European Communities Act, 1972 has been utilised to provide the substantial powers of enforcement necessary to combat what, in many instances, amounts to serious criminal activity in relation to the supply and use of illegal substances. A series of very stringent legislative measures entitled the European Communities (Control of Veterinary Medicinal Products and their Residues) Regulations, 1988 to 1992, have, therefore, been introduced to prohibit the manufacture, importation, sale, possession and use of illegal substances or the abusive use of their authorised substances. Despite this, the regulations lack effective-

ness because the European Communities Act provides for summary offences only. This means that the maximum penalties which may be imposed are those applicable to summary jurisdiction, which in the context of profits to be gained from the illegal use of these substances are insufficient to have a substantial deterrent effect."

The penalties were thus increased from a maximum of two years' imprisonment and a £1,000 fine (applicable under the 1988 and 1990 Regulations) to a maximum of 10 years' imprisonment plus a £100,000 fine following conviction on indictment for offences under section 20 of the 1993 Act: see section 23(1)(b) Animal Remedies Act, 1993. The two years maximum penalty was itself held unconstitutional by Costello J. in the High Court in *Mallon v. Minister for Agriculture, The Irish Times*, July 28, 1994 on the ground that the Regulations created a penalty following summary conviction which meant that the offence in question was not a minor offence for the purposes of Article 38.2 of the Constitution.

Effect and confirmation of regulations

4.—(1)(a) Regulations under this Act shall have statutory effect.

(b) If the Joint Committee on European Affairs[11] recommends to the Houses of the Oireachtas that any regulations under this Act be annulled and a resolution annulling the regulations is passed by both such Houses within one year after the regulations are made, the regulations shall be annulled accordingly and shall cease to have statutory effect, but without prejudice to the validity of anything previously done thereunder.

(2) (a) If when regulations under this Act are made, or at any time within one year thereafter and while the regulations have statutory effect, Dáil Eireann stands adjourned for a period of more than 10 days and if, during the adjournment, at least one-third of the members of Dáil Eireann by notice in writing to the Ceann Comhairle require Dáil Eireann to be summoned, the Ceann Comhairle shall summon Dáil Eireann to meet on a day named by him being neither more than 21 days after the receipt by him of the notice nor less than 10 days after the issue of the summons.[12]

(b) If when regulations under this Act are made, or at any time within one year thereafter and while the regulations have statutory effect, Seanad Eireann stands adjourned for a period of more than 10 days and if, during the adjournment, at least one third of the members of Seanad Eireann by notice in writing to the Cathaoirleach require Seanad Eireann to be summoned, the Cathaoirleach shall summon Seanad Eireann to meet on a day named by him being neither more than 21 days after the receipt by him of the notice nor less than 10 days after the issue of the summons.

(c) Paragraphs (a) and (b) of this subsection shall not apply to regulations in relation to which a resolution for their annulment has been refused by either House of the Oireachtas.[13]

---

[11] The subsection originally referred to Joint Committee on Secondary Legislation of the European Communities, but the change to Joint Committee on Foreign Affairs was effected by s.6(1) of the European Communities (Amendment) Act, 1993. This in turn was amended by s.1 of the European Communities (Amendment) Act, 1995 so that the reference should now be to the new Joint Committee on European Affairs.

[12] This subsection does not apply to earlier regulations made under the original s.4 of the 1972 Act, as s.1(2) of the European Communities (Amendment) Act, 1973 provides that:

"This section shall have effect in relation to regulations under the European Communities Act, 1972, other than regulations confirmed by the European Communities (Confirmation of Regulations) Act, 1973, and regulations that ceased to have statutory effect before the passing of this Act."

[13] As inserted by s.1 of the European Communities (Amendment) Act, 1973.

Irish Statutory Material

GENERAL NOTE

Regulations to have statutory effect

The effect of section 4 is to give such regulations statutory effect. Such a provision would ordinarily be regarded as unconstitutional in that it usurps the exclusive legislative power of the Oireachtas, contrary to Article 15.2.1 of the Constitution. Article 29.4.5 provides constitutional cover for a provision of this kind: see the comments of Denham J. in *Meagher v. Minister for Agriculture* [1994] 1 I.R. 329, 364–365. While the utility of sections 3 and 4 of the 1972 Act as a means of efficious implementation of E.C. Directives cannot be gainsaid, there are, nevertheless, powerful policy arguments which can be marshalled against the use of this procedure.

In the first place, parliamentary scrutiny provides a valuable safeguard against executive and administrative beaurocracy. It has to be recognised that in many instances the implementing authorities will, if left to their own devices, act in the same manner as any other interest group— they will suit themselves. They will thus place a premium on measures which they consider will best promote the straightforward and effective implementation of the Directive in question, but often at the expense of other important values and interests. This can be seen in the *Meagher* case itself: the extended time limit made matters easier for the Department of Agriculture, but it is a fair guess that the civil service was not unduly troubled by the civil liberties dimension of such a far-reaching departure from the six-months norm.

Secondly, parliamentary legislation has the value of openness and "transparency". The Joint Oireachtas Committee frequently drew attention to the importance of this when criticising Ministers for excessive reliance on the use of the powers conferred by the 1972 Act. Indeed, there does not appear to have been any instance of where the Oireachtas has ever annulled a statutory instrument made pursuant to section 3 of the 1972 Act. Moreover, the use of statutory instruments is a form of "hidden law" which allows Ministers to avoid effective parliamentary scrutiny.

Thirdly, the "principles and policies" test helps to improve the drafting of legislation: rather than draft opaque, open-ended clauses, the new constitutional consciousness has forced the parliamentary draftsman to be much more precise in respect of the powers conferred on the executive.

Finally, there is the question of democratic principles itself. While it may have been true in the past to regard the Oireachtas as a law-declaring rather than a law-making body (*i.e.* that the Oireachtas essentially rubber-stamps Bills presented by the Government), this cannot detract from the constitutional principle that the right to legislate is the principal function of the Oireachtas. Besides, there is now increasing evidence that the Oireachtas takes its legislative role much more seriously and the last few years have witnessed a huge increase in the number of Dáil and Seanad amendments to legislation—as witnessed in the wholesale amendments to the such diverse recent legislation as the Animal Remedies Act, 1993 and the Criminal Justice (Public Order) Act, 1994. This opportunity is denied in the case of orders made under the 1972 Act. On this topic, see further G. Hogan, "The implementation of European Union law in Ireland: the *Meagher* Case and Democratic Deficit" (1994) 2 *Irish Journal of European Law* 190.

The Joint Committee on European Affairs

At the risk of causing confusion with the EEA Joint Committee discussed above, the term "Joint Committee" in the discussion that follows connotes a Joint Committee of the Houses of the Oireachtas. Section 6 of the 1993 Act provided that the role of the Oireachtas Joint Committee on Secondary Legislation of the European Communities under section 4 of the European Communities Act, 1972 (as amended in 1973) will be undertaken after its establishment by the new Joint Committee on Foreign Affairs, and amended the 1972 Act accordingly. In fact, the Joint Committee had been established by the time the Bill came to be debated in July 1993, but section 6(2) was left undisturbed; (see 433 *Dáil Debates* Col. 1771). The Joint Committee's powers have now been transferred to the Joint Committee on European Affairs: see the discussion below on European Communities (Amendment) Act, 1995.

This provision of the 1993 Bill was the subject of considerable debate in the Oireachtas, not least because Phil Hogan T.D. (Fine Gael) proposed its amendment by the insertion of a further sub-section (3) in the following terms: "All European Communities Directives and Regulations shall be referred to the Joint Committee on Foreign Affairs for approval before implementation". It is apparent that the term regulations here refers to E.C. regulations under Art. 189 E.C. (as opposed to regulations under section 3 of the European Communities Act, 1972).

The proposal appears to have been the victim of poor drafting. European Community regulations, once issued, are directly applicable in the Member States, and cannot be made subject to review by national parliaments. Directives, while not directly applicable, are equally binding on Member States as to the result to be achieved, and the achievement of that result cannot be made contingent on its approval by domestic parliamentarians (see the comments of J. Bruton T.D.,

433 *Dáil Debates* Col. 1781); parliamentarians may be in a position to dictate simply the manner of implementation (so long as it is effective), depending on the constitutional allocation of power in the Member State in question. The clause appears from the debate (but not from its terms) to have envisaged parliamentary surveillance of ministerial orders implementing E.C. Directives and (where the need arises) Regulations (433 *Dáil Debates* Cols. 1763–4). However, if the *Meagher* decision had been upheld, the clause might have been otiose, in that a far greater Oireachtas involvement in such implementation measures would have been warranted, at least where the amendment of existing law was involved. Johnson J.'s decision having been disapproved by the Supreme Court, it is unclear how Deputy Hogan's proposed clause would have related to sections 3(1) and 4 of the 1972 Act (as amended by the European Communities (Amendment) Act, 1973). It was argued above that the Joint Committee on European Affairs could be used in its legislative capacity to do most of the work in debating, amending and approving omnibus bills to implement directives through the Oireachtas. However, this opportunity was not taken by the Government in the aftermath of the Supreme Court reprieve in *Meagher*.

However, Deputy Hogan's clause seems also to have been intended to give the Joint Committee on Foreign Affairs a greater role in the scrutiny of draft E.C. legislation in advance of its adoption by the E.C. institutions (433 *Dáil Debates* Col. 1765—which aim is not clear from the terms of the proposed amendment either). As Deputy de Rossa pointed out, two distinct matters arose for consideration by the House: "the regulation the Government makes to implement a Directive already decided at European level in the context of Irish conditions and Irish law, and the [initial] proposal by the European Community in a global sense" (433 *Dáil Debates* Col. 1785). Such possibility of advance scrutiny of draft E.C. measures was the subject of approval from all sides of the House (see, e.g. M. McDowell T.D., 433 *Dáil Debates* Cols. 1766–8, P. de Rossa T.D., 433 *Dáil Debates* Cols. 1771–2, B. Lenihan T.D., and 433 *Dáil Debates* Cols. 1777–8; see also the initial debate on the European Communities Bill, 1972, 263 *Dáil Debates* Cols. 90–208).

In fact, the terms of reference of the (then) Joint Committee on Foreign Affairs (like those of the Joint Committee on the Secondary Legislation of the European Communities since 1977) included discussion of "such programmes and guidelines prepared by the Commission of the European Communities as a basis for possible legislative action and such drafts of Regulations, Directives, decisions, recommendations and opinions of the Council of Ministers proposed by the Commission" and "such acts of the institutions of those Communities" as it selects for scrutiny (Para. 10, Terms of Reference of the Joint Committee on Foreign Affairs, Order of April 28, 1993). This ranks Ireland, at least on paper, with such rigorous parliamentary scrutineers as the British and the Danes. However, practice leaves the Irish deputies and senators at something of a disadvantage. (The Joint Committee on European Affairs has similar terms of reference.)

The British Government has undertaken to deposit with Parliament copies of all proposals submitted to the Council for decision and not to agree to any such proposal in the Council until each House has had an opportunity to consider the proposal. Every text (912 in 1986) is deposited with Parliament within two days of its receipt in London, and the Minister responsible will submit an explanatory memorandum within two weeks, which summarises its content, objectives and legal basis, its likely impact on United Kingdom law, any material policy considerations, the legislative timetable and the relevant voting procedure and degree of involvement of the European Parliament. An updating memorandum is forwarded if the original proposals are substantially amended. Select Committees of both Houses consider these matters (the Lords Committee having somewhat wider competence to consider the merits of proposals than that of the Commons). Matters which are forwarded for debate in the Commons occasionally, but rarely (and never in the Lords) result in the passing of a resolution obliging a Minister to vote a certain way. Even where not so mandated, however, it appears that Ministers take very seriously the majority view expressed in either House (see generally Newman, "The Impact of National Parliaments on the Development of Community Law" in Capotorti, *et al.* (eds.) *Du Droit International au Droit de l'Integration: Liber Amicorum Pierre Pescatore* (1987), p. 481, at 488–493) (hereinafter Newman, Parliaments).

In Denmark, the Market Relations Committee of the *Folketing* (parliament) has to approve the line Ministers take on every Community proposal, including any changes in the Minister's stance where proposals are amended. The Government submits written memoranda of a factual nature on all the more important items on the agenda of forthcoming Council meetings (more than 200 annually). Because of its mandating function, the Committee holds discussions in secret, and reports are not published on individual texts (Newman, Parliaments, pp. 487–488).

In Ireland, Government memoranda have not in the past been automatically available on all draft E.C. proposals, and unlike its Danish and British counterparts, the Joint Committee did not succeed in securing the regular attendance of Ministers to give evidence of Government policy on draft proposals (Robinson, "Irish Parliamentary Scrutiny of European Communities legislation" (1979) 16 C.M.L.Rev. 9, at 18–9) (hereinafter Robinson, Scrutiny)). Co-operation was ultimately secured in gaining access to proposed changes in draft proposals. The Joint Committee on Foreign Affairs may not *sub poena* witnesses and Ministers retain the right to certify that certain information is confidential or that its disclosure would be prejudicial to the State's international relations (para. 14, Terms of Reference). Declaration 12 appended to the Maastricht Treaty, on the role of national Parliaments in the European Union, may lead to a greater voice for the Joint Committee in dealing with E.C. proposals. The Governments of the Member States declare that they will ensure that national Parliaments receive Commission proposals for legislation in good time for information or possible examination; and Deputy Eithne Fitzgerald, Minister for State at the Department of Foreign Affairs, stated that the Department would be glad to facilitate members of the Joint Committee's European sub-committee in this regard (433 *Dáil Debates* Col. 1773). Incidentally, the chairman of the Joint Committee on Secondary Legislation was traditionally a member of the Opposition, following the practice in the Committee on Public Accounts (Robinson, Scrutiny, p. 13); this practice appears to have lapsed in the transition to the Joint Committee on Foreign Affairs. Whether the Government or the Joint Committee will therefore be more compliant in the future is difficult to predict. The Programme for a Government of Renewal of the present Government includes a commitment to establish a separate European Affairs Committee.

The less developed machinery in other national Parliaments for the scrutiny of draft E.C. legislative proposals is often attributable to the greater role those legislative bodies play in the implementation of E.C. measures such as E.C. directives. For example, the Italian Parliament has always had a role in implementing directives which entail the amendment of existing Italian law (see Gaja, "New Developments in a Continuing Story: the Relationship between EEC Law and Italian Law" (1991) 28 C.M.L.Rev. 83. Pergola and Duca, "Community Law and the Italian Constitution" (1985) 79 A.J.I.L. 598).

Even in France, where the Government has, under Article 37 of the Constitution, the power to make law by decree in specified areas without the need for any delegation of power from the Parliament, new primary legislation is generally required to implement directives outside those areas (*Arret* of the *Conseil d'Etat*, May 20, 1964, discussed in Louis, *The Community Legal Order* (2nd. ed., 1990) p. 169).

The *Meagher* decision has meant that the Oireachtas has no such role. The terms of reference of the Joint Committee on Secondary Legislation of the European Communities, like those of the Joint Committee on European Affairs, are silent on the scrutiny of draft ministerial regulations under the European Communities Act, 1972 (or under other legislation, where the regulations aare necessitated by the obligations of membership of the Communities). Such scrutiny was, and is, permitted, only after the event, in furtherance of the functions of the Joint Committees, old and new, under section 4 of the Act of 1972, as amended. Deputies and senators will naturally be reluctant to annul domestic measures, the annulling of which would presumably leave Ireland in breach of her Treaty obligations. Thus, the section has not proved to be an effective instrument of parliamentary control of the executive, a point recognised by Johnson J. in the High Court in *Meagher* in distinguishing the case before him from the decision of the Supreme Court in *McDaid v. Sheehy* [1991] I.R. 1. It was attempted in 1973, when the European Communities (Amendment) Bill was being debated, to insert a power of the Houses of the Oireachtas to amend as well as annul ministerial regulations. This would have allowed the Houses at least to vary elements of the national implementing scheme in the regulations without undermining the State's duty to achieve the result set out in the parent directive or other E.C. measure. However, the Government refused to countenance what was seen as undue interference with the executive discretion (267 *Dáil Debates* Cols. 1339–1394).

This has not stopped the Joint Committee from expressing trenchant criticism of the handiwork of the Government from time to time. It remains to be seen whether their condemnation of unnecessary or inappropriate levels of intervention by the executive on foot of EC law will be echoed by the post-*Meagher* Supreme Court. One example is provided in the thirtieth report of the First Joint Committee on the Secondary Legislation of the European Communities (Prl. 5419, 1976, at 11).

> "The Joint Committee doubts that to secure the purposes of a directive [aimed at harmonizing national laws], it would ever be necessary for one Member State to make it an offence for persons subject to its jurisdiction to infringe the implementing legislation of another Member State. Nevertheless, regulation 5 of the Food Standards (Certain Sugars) (E.C.) Regulations 1975 (S.I. No. 118 of 1975) purports to do just that. It provides that certain products "shall not be exported to any Member State of the European Communities unless they comply with the directive as applied in that Member State". The Joint Committee regards this provision as undesirable because it makes an offence depend on proof of foreign law, and as unnecessary because an exporter cannot succeed in his purpose unless he complies with the law of the importing State."

The Fifth Joint Committee raised similar concerns about unnecessary levels of criminalisation in its Eighth Report. Directive 79/893/EEC was designed to prevent trade in and use of certain materials, and regulation 4 of the European Communities (Materials and Articles in Contact with Foodstuffs) Regulations, 1988 (S.I. No. 60) made it an offence to manufacture, sell, import or use in the course of business materials not manufactured in accordance with the Regulations. The Joint Committee questioned the need for strict liability to be imposed at all stages of the chain of distribution (on sellers and users as well as on manufacturers and importers), saying that a real discretion was vested in national authorities in this respect. Furthermore, an offence arose under reg. 4 where the prohibited materials "transfer their constituents to foodstuffs which could ... bring about an unacceptable change in the composition of the foodstuffs". The Joint Committee could not believe that a statutory offence of such vagueness would be possible if it were solely a matter for domestic legislation. While the Directive used the term "unacceptable change", the Committee thought a definition of what was "unacceptable" was necessary at the very least, which requirement might in fact be imposed by Community law, which has indicated the importance of the principle of legal certainty (Fifth Joint Oireachtas Committee on the Secondary Legislation of the European Communities, Eighth Report, at paras. 17–18).

In the same Report, the Fifth Joint Committee also condemned as unacceptable a purported power to vary the application of regulations in individual cases—a condemnation reminiscent of the facts of *East Donegal Co-operative v. Attorney-General* [1970] I.R. 317. Regulation 4 of the European Communities (Life Assurance Accounts, Statements and Valuations) Regulations, 1986 (S.I. No. 437) states:

> "(1) The Minister may, on the application or with the consent of any undertaking, issue a direction in writing that specified provisions of these Regulations shall not apply to the undertaking or shall apply to it with such modification as may be specified in the direction."

Delegated legislative power, in the Joint Committee's view, could not be regarded as enabling a Minister to assume power under Regulations to grant administratively a dispensation from an obligation to comply with them. It would have recommended the annulment of this provision, it stated, except that the one year period in which this could be done had passed (Fifth Joint Oireachtas Committee on the Secondary Legislation of the European Communities, Eighth Report, at paras. 4–5).

Differences of opinion can also exist between the Oireachtas and the Government about the maximum penalities provided for in regulations under the 1972 Act. For example, the First Joint Committee questioned in its 57th Report (Prl. 6265, 1977) whether a maximum penalty of £500 and/or six months' imprisonment was warranted for failure to supply information in response to questionnaires circulated to employers, as was provided for in the European Communities (Statistical Surveys) Regulations, 1976 (S.I. No. 223). This maximum penalty was contrasted with that of only £50 in the European Communities (Road Traffic) (Compulsory Insurance) Regulations, 1975 (S.I. No. 178).

In each of the above cases, the criticism of the Joint Committee was ultimately founded on its opinion that provisions of ministerial regulations which it thought arbitrary or extreme were not dictated by the terms of the directive which was sought to be implemented. Nonetheless, it is difficult to say that these instances fell outside the principles and policies of the directives as that notion was so broadly interpreted by the Supreme Court in *Meagher*. We must await further cases to be able with certainty to draw the line between ministerial action which is deemed to be appropriate and necessary in the implementation of directives and other Community obligations, and that which is not.

Report to Houses of Oireachtas

5.—The Government shall make a report twice yearly to each House of the Oireachtas on developments in the European Communities.

Short title

6.—This Act may be cited as the European Communities Act, 1972.

EUROPEAN COMMUNITIES (CONFIRMATION OF REGULATIONS) ACT, 1973

(1973, No. 5)

Be it enacted by the Oireachtas as follows:

ARRANGEMENT OF SECTIONS

SECT.
1. Confirmation of Regulations.
2. Short Title

An Act to confirm certain regulations made under the European Communities Act, 1972   [June 11, 1973]

GENERAL NOTE

This was the only measure ever passed under the old system of implementing directives which required the confirmation by the Oireachtas in omnibus form of a schedule of implementing regulations. While this form of parliamentary supervision was in itself inadequate, it at least required the Oireachtas to have some form of active involvement in the implementing procedures. The system was changed by the European Communities (Amendment) Act, 1973 and the negative supervisory role of the Oireachtas is now set out in section 4 of the European Communities Act, 1972, as amended.

Citation

This Act may be cited as the European Communities (Confirmation of Regulations) Act, 1973: see section 2.

Commencement

This Act came into force on the day it was signed by the President in accordance with Article 25.4.1 of the Constitution, *viz.*, June 11, 1973.

Parliamentary Debates

265 *Dáil Debates* Cols. 1779–1864 (Second and subsequent stages);
75 *Seanad Debates* Cols.15–60 (Second and subsequent stages).

Confirmation of Regulations

1.—The several Regulations mentioned in column (2) of the Schedule to this Act, and made under the European Communities Act, 1972, are hereby confirmed.

Short Title

2.—This Act may be cited as the European Communities (Confirmation of Regulations) Act, 1973.

EUROPEAN COMMUNITIES (AMENDMENT) ACT, 1973

(1973, No. 20)

ARRANGEMENT OF SECTIONS

SECT.
1. Amendment of section 4 of the 1972 Act.
2. Short Title.

An Act to amend the European Communities Act, 1972   [August 4, 1973]

GENERAL NOTE

The original section 4 had provided that regulations made by a Minister of State for the purpose of giving effect in Irish law to EC Directives required to be confirmed by legislation within six months from the date of their promulgation, the new section 4 provided that, thereafter such regulations should have immediate statutory effect. This is discussed further above.

Citation

This Act may be cited as the European Communities (Amendment) Act, 1973: see section 2.

Commencement

This Act was signed by the President and came into force on August 4, 1973 in accordance with Article 25.4.1 of the Constitution.

Parliamentary Debates

267 *Dáil Debates* Cols. 1339–1398 (Second, Committee and Final Stages);
75 *Seanad Debates* Cols. 734–787 (Second and Final Stages).

Acts referred to

European Communities Act, 1972	1972, No. 27
European Communities (Confirmation of Regulations) Act, 1973	1973, No. 5

Amendment of section 4 of the 1972 Act

1.—[Section 1 of the 1973 Act amended the 1972 Act by the substitution for the original section 4 of the present version of that section.]

Short Title

2.—This Act may be cited as the European Communities (Amendment) Act, 1973.

EUROPEAN COMMUNITIES (AMENDMENT) ACT, 1977

(1979, No. 5)

ARRANGEMENT OF SECTIONS

SECT.
1. Amendment of European Communities Act, 1972.
2. Short title and commencement etc.

An Act to amend the European Communities Act, 1972, so as to provide that the treaty amending certain financial provisions of the treaties establishing the European Communities and of the Treaty establishing a single Council and a single Commission shall be part of the domestic law of the State. [March 29, 1977]

GENERAL NOTE

This legislation amended the 1972 Act and was designed to allow the Government to ratify the Second Budgetary Treaty, 1974 and to provide that such amendments to the Treaties would form part of the domestic law of the State. This is discussed above.

Citation

This Act may be cited as the European Communities (Amendment) Act, 1979: see section 2(1).

Commencement

The Act passed into law on March 29, 1977.

Parliamentary Debates

297 *Dáil Debates* Cols. 1290–1328 (Second Stage, Committee and Final Stages);
86 *Seanad Debates* Cols. 403–442 (Second Stage, Committee and Final Stages).

Acts referred to

European Communities Act, 1972   1972, No. 27

Amendment of European Communities Act, 1972

1.—[Section 1 amended the definition of the words "the treaties governing the European Communities" in section 1(1) of the 1972 Act so as to provide for the ratification by the State of the Brussels Treaty 1975. This is discussed above.]

Short title, collective citation, construction and commencement

2.—(1) This Act may be cited as the European Communities (Amendment) Act, 1979.

(2) The European Communities Acts, 1972, the European Communities (Amendment) Act, 1977 and this Act may be cited together as the European Communities Acts, 1972 to 1979, and shall be construed together as one Act.

(3) This Act shall come into operation on such date as the Minister appoints by order.

EUROPEAN COMMUNITIES (AMENDMENT) ACT, 1979

(1979, No. 32)

ARRANGEMENT OF SECTIONS

SECT.
1. Amendment of European Communities Act, 1972.
2. Short title, collective citation, construction and commencement.

An Act to amend the European Communities Act, 1972, so as to provide that the treaty relating to the accession of the Hellenic Republic to the European Economic Community and to the European Atomic Energy Community and the decision of the Council of the European Communities relating to the accession of the Hellenic Republic to the European Coal and Steel Community shall be part of the domestic law of the State.   [December 11, 1979]

GENERAL NOTE

This Act amended the 1972 Act in order to enable the Government to ratify the Greek (Hellenic Republic) Accession Treaty and to provide that it would become part of the domestic law of the State.

Citation

This Act may be cited as the European Communities (Amendment) Act, 1979: see section 2(1).

Commencement

The Act passed into law on December 11, 1979 and came into force on January 1, 1981 by virtue of the European Communities (Amendment) Act, 1979 (Commencement) Order 1980, (S.I. No. 392).

Parliamentary Debates

317 *Dáil Debates* Cols. 255–314 (Second Stage, Committee and Final Stages);
93 *Seanad Debates* Cols. 411–457 (Second Stage, Committee and Final Stages).

Acts referred to

European Communities Act, 1972   1972, No. 27
European Communities (Amendment) Act, 1973   1973, No. 20

Amendment of European Communities Act, 1972

1.—[Section 1 amended the definition of the words "the treaties governing the European Communities" in section 1(1) of the 1972 Act so as to provide for the accession of the Hellenic Republic to the European Communities. This is discussed above.]

Short title, collective citation, construction and commencement

2.—(1) This Act may be cited as the European Communities (Amendment) Act, 1979.

(2) The European Communities Acts, 1972, the European Communities (Amendment) Act, 1977 and this Act may be cited together as the European Communities Acts, 1972 to 1979, and shall be construed together as one Act.

(3) This Act shall come into operation on such date as the Minister appoints by order.

EUROPEAN COMMUNITIES (AMENDMENT) ACT, 1985

(1985, No. 1)

ARRANGEMENT OF SECTIONS

SECT.
1. Amendment of European Communities Act, 1972.
2. Short title, collective citation, construction and commencement.

An Act to amend the European Communities Act, 1972, so as to provide that the Treaty providing that each of the treaties establishing the European Communities (within the meaning of the European Communities Act, 1972) shall cease to apply to Greenland and introducing new arrangements between the said countries and Greenland shall be part of the domestic law of the State.   [January 23, 1985]

GENERAL NOTE

This legislation amended the 1972 Act to enable the State to ratify the Brussels Treaty, 1984 (discussed above), which provided for the Greenlandic withdrawal from the European Communties, to provide that this treaty would form part of the domestic law of the State.

Citation

This Act may be cited as the European Communities (Amendment) Act, 1985: see section 2(1).

Commencement

The Act passed into law on January 23, 1985 and came into force on February 1, 1985 by virtue of the European Communities (Amendment) Act, 1985 (Commencement) Order 1985, (S.I. No. 34).

Parliamentary Debates

355 *Dáil Debates* Cols. 235–257 (Second Stage, Committee and Final Stages)
106 *Seanad Debates* Cols. 1057–1065 (Second Stage, Committee and Final Stages)

Acts referred to

European Communities Act, 1972   1972, No. 27
European Communities Act, 1979   1979. No. 32

Amendment of European Communities Act, 1972

1.—[Section 1 amended the definition of the words "the treaties governing the European Communities" in section 1(1) of the 1972 Act so as to provide for the withdrawal of Greenland from the European Communities. This is discussed above]

Short title, collective citation, construction and commencement

2.—(1) This Act may be cited as the European Communities (Amendment) Act, 1985.

(2) The European Communities Acts, 1972 to 1979, and this Act may be cited together as the European Communities Acts, 1972 to 1985, and shall be construed together as one Act.

(3) This Act shall come into operation on such date as the Minister for Foreign Affairs may appoint by order.

GENERAL NOTE

This section provides for the short title, collective citation and construction and commencement of the Act. It had been originally intended that the Brussels Treaty, 1984 (which provided for the withdrawal of Greenland) would have come into force by January 1, 1985. Through what appears to have been a legislative oversight, Ireland found itself in the embarrassing position of being the only Member State not to have adhered to the legislative timetable. The President signed the measure on January 23, 1985 and the Act came into force on February 1, 1985, the same day as the Brussels Treaty itself.

EUROPEAN COMMUNITIES (AMENDMENT) (No. 2) ACT, 1985

(1985, No. 19)

ARRANGEMENT OF SECTIONS

SECT.
1. Amendment of European Communities Act, 1972.
2. Short title, collective citation, construction and commencement.

An Act to amend the European Communities Act, 1972, so as to provide that the treaty concerning the Accession of the Kingdom of Spain and the Portuguese Republic to the European Economic Community and to the European Atomic Energy Community and the decision of the Council of the European Communities relating to the Accession of the Kingdom of Spain and the Portuguese Republic to the European Coal and Steel Community shall be part of the domestic law of the State.

[November 26, 1985]

GENERAL NOTE

Citation

This Act may be cited as the European Communities (Amendment) (No. 2) Act, 1979: see section 2(1).

Commencement

The Act passed into law on November 23, 1985 and came into force on January 1, 1986 by virtue of the European Communities (Amendment) (No. 2) Act, 1985 (Commencement) Order 1985.

Parliamentary Debates

361 *Dáil Debates* Cols. 556–583; 1037–1056; 1432–1447 (Second Stage, Committee and Final Stages);

110 *Seanad Debates* Cols. 3–49; 40–51 (Second Stage, Committee and Final Stages).

Acts referred to

European Communities Act, 1972   1972, No. 27
European Communities Acts, 1972–1985

Amendment of European Communities Act, 1972

1.—[Section 1 amended the definition of the words "the treaties governing the European Communities" in section 1(1) of the 1972 Act so as to provide for the accession of Portugal and Spain to the European Communities. Following the enactment of the 1985 (No. 2) Act the Government ratified the Spanish and Portuguese Accession Treaty on December 2, 1985 and the Act entered into force on January 1, 1986.]

Short title, collective citation, construction and commencement

2.—(1) This Act may be cited as the European Communities (Amendment)(No. 2) Act, 1985.

(2) The collective citation, the European Communities Acts, 1972 to 1985, shall include this Act.

(3) This Act shall come into operation on such date as the Minister for Foreign Affairs appoints by order.

EUROPEAN COMMUNITIES (AMENDMENT) ACT, 1986

(1986, No. 37)

ARRANGEMENT OF SECTIONS

SECT.
1. Amendment of section 1 of European Communities Act, 1972.
2. Construction of references to Assembly of European Communities.
3. Short title, collective citation, construction and commencement.

An Act to amend the European Communities Act, 1972, so as to provide that certain provisions of the Single European Act hereinafter specified shall be part of the domestic law of the State and to provide for other connected matters.   [December 23, 1986]

GENERAL NOTE

Citation

This Act may be cited as the European Communities (Amendment) Act, 1986: see section 3(1).

Commencement

The Act passed into law on December 23, 1986. It had been originally intended that the Single European Act should enter into force for all Member States on January 1, 1987. However, in *Crotty v. An Taoiseach* [1987] I.R. 713, Barrington J. granted an injunction on December 24, 1985 restraining the State from ratifying the Single Act pending the outcome of a constitutional challenge to the validity of that ratification. In judgments delivered on April 9, 1987 the Supreme Court held that ratification of Title III would be unconstitutional in the absence of a referendum. The referendum itself was held on May 22, 1987 and the ratification of the Single Act was approved by 755,423 votes to 324,977. The Tenth Amendment of Constitution Act 1987 was duly enacted on June 22, 1987. The Irish instrument of ratification was lodged in Rome with the Italian Government on June 24, 1987 and, in accordance with Article 33(2), the Single Act entered into force on July 1, 1987, *i.e.* the first day of the month following that in which the last instrument of ratification was lodged with the Italian Government. By order made by the Minister for Foreign Affairs under section 3(3) of the 1986 Act, the European Communities (Amendment) Act, 1986 (Commencement) Order, 1987 (S.I. No. 170), the 1986 Act came into force on July 1, 1987.

Parliamentary Debates

370 *Dáil Debates* Cols. 2369–2656 (Second Stage, Committee and Final Stages);
115 *Seanad Debates* Cols. 952–1051; 1118–1251 (Second Stage); 1311–1342 (Committee and Final Stages).

Acts referred to

European Communities Acts, 1972 to 1985.

Statutory Instrument

European Communities (Amendment) Act, 1986 (Commencement) Order, 1987 (S.I. No. 170)

Be it enacted by the Oireachtas as follows:

Amendment of the European Communities Act, 1972

1.—[Section 1 incorporated into Irish law those elements of the Single Act which amended the constitutional Treaties of the E.C. Only Article 3(1) in Title I (which changed the name of the Assembly to "the European Parliament"); Title II (which contained all the significant amendments, principally to the Treaty of Rome itself) and Articles 31 and 32 of Title IV (which delimited the review powers of the Court of Justice and the effects of the S.E.A. on the constitutional Treaties) became part of domestic law. This meant that the provisions on the European Council and EPC in Titles I and III and the Final Act did *not* become part of Irish law, but the State is bound to observe these provisions as part its general international treaty obligations. These provisions have in any event been largely overtaken by the Maastricht Treaty on European Union. For a further discussion of the impact of the S.E.A., see above.]

Construction of references to Assembly of European Communities

2.—References to the Assembly of the European Communities in any Act passed or statutory instrument made before the commencement of the Act shall be construed as references to the European Parliament.

GENERAL NOTE

This section required that all references in either primary or secondary legislation in which references have been made to the Assembly of the European Communities should now be construed as references to the European Parliament. This section gives effect to Article 3(1) of the S.E.A. and the legislation principally affected by this section were the European Assembly Elections Act, 1977 and the European Assembly Elections Act, 1985. See now the European Parliament Elections Act, 1993.

Short title, collective citation, construction and commencement

3.—(1) This Act may be cited as the European Communities (Amendment) Act, 1986.

(2) The European Communities Acts, 1972 to 1985, and this Act may be cited together as the European Communities Acts, 1972 to 1986, and shall be construed together as one Act.

(3) This Act shall come into operation on such date as the Minister for Foreign Affairs may appoint by order.

GENERAL NOTE

This section provides for the short title, collective citation and construction and commencement of the Act. The Act came into force on July 1, 1987.

EUROPEAN COMMUNITIES (AMENDMENT) ACT, 1992

(1992, No. 24)

ARRANGEMENT OF SECTIONS

SECT.
1. Amendment of section 1 of European Communities Act, 1972.
2. Amendment of section 2 of European Communities Act, 1972.
3. Short title, collective citation, construction and commencement.

An Act to amend the European Communities Act, 1972, and to provide for other connected matters.   [November 11, 1992]

GENERAL NOTE

This Act was designed to incorporate into Irish law those provisions of the Maastricht Treaty on European Union which affected the Community Treaties. The effect of most of those provisions is set out in the annotation below of the European Community Treaty. The effect of the excluded provisions, relating the the non-Community aspects of the European Union, is discussed in the analysis above of the Eleventh Amendment of the Constitution, and in the introduction below to the Maastricht Treaty.

Statutory Instrument

European Communities (Amendment) Act, 1992 (Commencement) Order, 1993 (S.I. No. 304)

Commencement

The 1992 Act was signed by the President on November 11, 1992. By virtue of the European Communities (Amendment) Act, 1992 (Commencement) Order, 1993 (S.I. No. 304) the 1992 Act came into force on November 1, 1993.

Parliamentary Debates

424 *Dáil Debates* Cols. 1817–1868, 2341–2352 (Second Stage);
424 *Dáil Debates* Cols. 2353–2355 (Committee and Subsequent Stages);
134 *Seanad Debates* Cols. 1035–1069 (Second and Subsequent Stages).

Acts referred to

European Communities Acts, 1972 to 1986

Be it enacted by the Oireachtas as follows:

Amendment of section 1 of European Communities Act, 1972

1.—[This section amended section 1 of the European Communities Act, 1972, by extending the definition "the treaties governing the European Communities" as to incorporate certain provisions of the Maastricht Treaty, namely, Titles II, III and IV; in Title VII, Articles L, M and P, and the other provisions of that Title "in so far as they relate to any of the treaties governing the European Communities as defined by this subsection; together with the Protocols (whether expressed to be annexed to the Treaty establishing the European Community, or to the said Treaty on European Union and the Treaties establishing the European Communities), done at Maastricht on the 7th day of February, 1992." The significance of this amendment is discussed above in the general note to section 1 of the 1972 Act].

Amendment of section 2 of European Communities Act, 1972

2.—Section 2 of the European Communities Act, 1972, is hereby amended by the insertion after "those Communities", of the words "and by bodies competent under the said treaties".

189

[This section extends the force of law in the State to acts of the competent bodies under the Community treaties. These are the monetary bodies established by Article 4 E.C., which do not have the status of Community institutions, but which will have certain law-making functions. This question is discussed further above.]

Short title, collective citation, construction and commencement

3.—(1) This Act may be cited as the European Communities (Amendment) Act, 1992.

(2) The European Communities Acts, 1972 to 1986, and this Act may be cited together as the European Communities Acts, 1972 to 1992, and shall be construed together as one Act.

(3) This Act shall come into operation on such day as may be appointed by order made by the Minister for Foreign Affairs.

GENERAL NOTE

Article R(2) of the Maastricht Treaty provided for the instruments of ratification of the Member States to be deposited with the government of the Italian Republic, and that the Treaty shall enter into force on January 1, 1993, or, failing full ratification by that date, on the first day of the month following the deposit of the instrument of ratification by the last signatory State to take this step. Following the second Danish referendum on May 18, 1993, the final enactment of the (U.K.) European Communities (Amendment) Act 1993 in July 1993 and the decision of the English High Court in *R. v. Home Secretary, ex p. Rees-Mogg* [1994] 1 All E.R. 457 the way was cleared for the ratification by Denmark and the United Kingdom. The Federal Republic of Germany finally ratified the Treaty in the wake of the decision of the Federal Constitutional Court (Bundesverfassungsgericht) in October 1993 in *Re Brunner* [1994] 1 C.M.L.R. 57 and the Treaty thus came into force on November 1, 1993. By virtue of the European Communities (Amendment) Act, 1992 (Commencement) Order, 1993 (S.I. No. 304) the 1992 Act came into force on the same day.

EUROPEAN COMMUNITIES (AMENDMENT) ACT, 1993

(1993, No. 25)

ARRANGEMENT OF SECTIONS

SECT.
1. Interpretation.
2. Amendment of section 1 of Act of 1972.
3. Amendment of section 2 of Act of 1972.
4. Adaptations to take account of EEA Agreement.
5. Regulations under Act of 1972.
6. Amendment of section 4 of Act of 1972.
7. Short title, collective citation, construction and commencement.

An Act to amend the European Communities Act, 1972, and to provide for other connected matters.

GENERAL NOTE

The European Communities (Amendment) Act, 1993 performs a number of diverse tasks. It facilitates the establishment of the European Investment Fund (section 2) and the European

Economic Area (sections 3 and 4). It addresses the consequences of the decision of Johnson J. in the High Court in *Meagher v. Minister for Agriculture and Food* [1994] 1 I.R. 329 (before that decision was reversed by the Supreme Court in November 1993) for the past and future implementation of E.C. Directives and similar measures by ministerial regulations under the European Communities Act, 1972 (section 5). Finally, it facilitates Oireachtas reform by substituting the Oireachtas Joint Committee on Foreign Affairs for the Joint Committee on the Secondary Legislation of the European Communities in section 4 of the European Communities Act, 1972, as amended (section 6).

Citation

This Act may be cited as the European Communities (Amendment) Act, 1993: see section 7(1).

Commencement

By virtue of the European Communities (Amendment) Act, 1993 (Section 3)(Commencement) Order, 1993 (S.I. No. 415) section 3 of the 1993 Act came into force on January 1, 1994. By virtue of European Communities (Amendment) Act, 1993 (Section 2)(Commencement) Order, 1994 (S.I. No. 122), section 2 came into force on May 5, 1994. By virtue of European Communities (Amendment) Act, 1993 (Section 6(1))(Commencement) Order, 1994 (S.I. No. 91), section 6(1) came into force on April 26, 1994. The rest of the Act came into force upon its enactment in accordance with Article 25.4.1 of the Constitution.

Parliamentary Debates

433 *Dáil Debates* 1696–1728 (Second Stage); 1752–1791 (Committee and Final Stages); 157 *Seanad Debates* Cols. 1038–1077 (Second and Subsequent Stages).

Acts Referred to

European Communities Act, 1972	1972, No. 27
European Communities Acts, 1972 to 1992	
European Communities (Amendment) Act, 1973	1973, No. 20
European Communities (Amendment) Act, 1992	1972, No. 24
Petty Sessions (Ireland) Act, 1851	1851 c. 93

Statutory Instruments

European Communities (Amendment) Act, 1993 (Section 2)(Commencement) Order, 1994 (S.I. No. 122)
European Communities (Amendment) Act, 1993 (Section 3)(Commencement) Order, 1993 (S.I. No. 415)
European Communities (Amendment) Act, 1993 (Section 6(1))(Commencement) Order, 1994 (S.I. No. 91)

Be it enacted by the Oireachtas as follows:

Interpretation

1.—(1) In this Act—
"the Act of 1972" means the European Communities Act, 1972;
"EEA Agreement" means the Agreement on the European Economic Area signed in Oporto on the 2nd day of May, 1992, as adjusted by the Protocol to that Agreement done at Brussels on the 17th day of March, 1993.

(2) In this Act, a reference to any enactment shall, unless the context otherwise requires, be construed as a reference to that enactment as amended, adapted or extended by or under any subsequent enactment including this Act.

Amendment of section 1 of Act of 1972

2.—[This section amends section 1 of the 1972 Act by further extending the definition of the phrase "the treaties governing the European Communities" to include the Act amending the Protocol on the Statute of the European

Investment Bank, empowering the Board of Governors to establish a European Investment Fund, signed at Brussels on the 25th day of March, 1993, together with the Treaty amending certain provisions of the Protocol on the Statute of the European Investment Bank, signed at Brussels on the 10th day of July, 1975. This matter is discussed further above.]

Amendment of section 2 of Act of 1972

3.—[This section inserts a new sub-section into section 2 of the 1972 Act whereby the provisions of the EEA Agreement and the acts to be adopted by institutions established by that Agreement which, pursuant to the treaties governing the European Communities, will be binding on the State and an integral part of the legal order of those Communities, shall have the force of law in the State on the conditions laid down in those treaties and in that Agreement. This is discussed further above.]

Adaptations to take account of EEA Agreement

4.—(1) Without prejudice to the future exercise of the powers conferred by section 3 of the Act of 1972, any regulations made under the said section 3 which are in force immediately before the coming into operation of section 3 of this Act, and any enactment, or instrument made under an enactment, which implements obligations of the State under the treaties governing the European Communities, shall, as far as practicable, be construed as if, on the coming into operation of section 3 of this Act, they were adapted as required by or under the EEA Agreement.

(2) Without prejudice to the generality of subsection (1) of this section, in any regulations made under section 3 of the Act of 1972, and in any enactment, or instrument made under an enactment, any reference to the Member States of the European Communities or to any person who is affected by the treaties governing those Communities shall, in so far as may be necessary to give effect to the obligations of the State pursuant to the EEA Agreement, be construed as including a reference to those States (not being Member States of the said Communities) which are contracting parties to the EEA Agreement and any person who is affected by the EEA Agreement.

GENERAL NOTE

This section provides that, as far as practicable, existing law and regulations adopted pursuant to E.C. obligations should be read as being adapted as required by the EEA Agreement, and references to the E.C. and its Member States and those affected by its treaties should be read, so far as may be necessary, as applying also to the EEA Agreement parties and to persons affected by that Agreement. One can appreciate the difficulty in amending appropriately all existing E.C. related law, but this blanket provision is liable to cause great difficulties to practitioners, as not all E.C. derived rights and duties are involved. They will have to refer to the annexes of the Agreement, and to the subsequent decisions of the EEA Joint Committee, to find out which E.C. measures (and thus which Irish implementing measures) are to be extended to the full territory of the EEA; or, as may arise under Articles 102–104 of the EEA Agreement, which are suspended in the EFTA portion of that territory by reason of failure to agree in the Joint Committee to adapt new developments in Community law.

Regulations under Act of 1972

5.—(1) Without prejudice to the future exercise of the powers conferred by section 3 of the Act of 1972, all regulations made under section 3 of the Act of 1972 prior to the passing of this Act as hereby confirmed as on and from the date upon which they purported to come into operation.

(2) Subsection (1) of this section shall operate to confirm regulations or any provision of any regulation to the extent only that such confirmation is in accordance with the Constitution.

(3) Nothing in subsection (1) or (2) of this section shall be construed to mean that but for this Act, any regulations or provision of regulations would

for any reason be invalid having regard to the provisions of the Constitution or otherwise.

(4) Notwithstanding section 10(4) of the Petty Sessions (Ireland) Act, 1851, proceedings in respect of offences committed after the passing of this Act under regulations (whether made before or after such passing) under the Act of 1972 may be instituted at any time within two years from the date of the commission of the offence.

(5) Subsection (1) of this section shall apply to all regulations made under section 3 of the Act of 1972 prior to the passing of this Act subject to any adaptation, amendment or revocation thereof whether by regulations made under the said section 3 or by any Act of the Oireachtas or instrument thereunder.

GENERAL NOTE

Sections 5(1) to 5(3)—the response to Meagher
The relatively modest power of the Oireachtas Joint Committees (on the Secondary Legislation of the European Communities (1973–93); and on European Affairs, from the enactment of this Act) is discussed above and forms part of the context of this section. Section 3 of the European Communities Act, 1972 purports to permit Ministers to implement E.C. measures like directives by statutory instrument, even where this involves the repeal or amendment of existing law, including Acts of the Oireachtas. Section 4 originally provided for legislative confirmation of such orders, but the following year it was amended to give such orders statutory effect. Instead of obligatory legislative confirmation, there was to be scrutiny by an Oireachtas Joint Committee, an annual report on E.C. secondary legislation (rarely debated) and a power of annulment of statutory orders under the Act by the Houses of the Oireachtas.

In *Meagher v. Minister for Agriculture* [1994] 1 I.R. 329 a ministerial regulation was challenged which purported to amend existing statute law by expanding the powers of search and seizure of the authorities, and extending the permissible period for summary prosecutions from six months to two years, in respect of the hormone use offences created by those regulations. Johnson J. declared as unconstitutional the use of ministerial orders to amend or repeal Acts of Parliament or of the Oireachtas, as a breach of Art. 15.2 of the Constitution which vests exclusive legislative power in the Oireachtas. This practice was denied constitutional immunity under Art. 29.4.3 of the Constitution, because that Article envisaged a number of different means of implementation, *i.e.* laws, acts and measures, from which the State had to choose in each instance in a constitutional fashion. Section 5 constitutes the State's interim response to Johnson J.'s decision which was, however, later overturned by the Supreme Court (see above for further discussion). Section 5(1) confirms legislatively all ministerial regulations made under section 3 of the 1972 Act up to the passing of the 1993 Act. Thus, by this parliamentary embrace, all purported amendments of statute law in such regulations are protected from invalidation under Art. 15.2 of the Constitution.

However, the State had not thereby conceded anything. Section 5(1) is stated to be without prejudice to the future exercise of ministerial powers under the 1972 Act, and s.5(3) states that nothing in the section should be taken as conceding the invalidity of the relevant ministerial regulations without such validation. If one can ignore the critical political flavour of his remarks, and add some necessary qualifications, the position is well summed up in the words of Deputy Phil Hogan: "The provision before us makes everything legal that the High Court has declared to be illegal, while at the same time insisting in its own legislation that this effort is unnecessary because in the Government's view everything the High Court found to be illegal is, in fact, legal" (433 *Dáil Debates*, Col. 1709).

Section 5(2) was open to objection inasmuch as it states that s.5(1) confirms regulations only to the extent that such confirmation is in accordance with the Constitution. A number of potential problems were raised about retrospective validation of regulations, not least the rule against retroactive criminal sanctions in Art. 15 of the Constitution (which guarantee has more recently been held to extend in some respects to the imposition of civil liability). Instead of dealing with such problems directly, citizens are left to guess what has been confirmed and what has lapsed, a type of drafting disapproved of in the strongest terms almost 70 years ago by Hanna J. in *Attorney-General v. McBride* [1928] I.R. 451. *McBride* concerned a provision (s.3) of the Public Safety Act, 1927 which was of the opposite intent to s.5(2) of the Act of 1993, but worked in a similar fashion. It provided that every provision of the Act which was found to be in contravention of any provision of the Constitution would to the extent of that contravention operate and have effect as an amendment to the Constitution, a statutory statement of the now abandoned doctrine of implied amendment of the Constitution. Hanna J. railed against such a dragnet clause, which failed to specify the Article, or part of an Article, of the Constitution which was to be amended, or whether in fact any amendment was made. The section "leaves the subjects of the State ... in the dark as to what is really altered in the Constitution, instead of enlightening them to any change in their status.... The rights of the people should not be obscured by the facile pen of the parliamentary draftsman."

In the case of the instant Act, it was the law which made way before the Constitution, and not vice versa; and it is self-evident that s.5(1) of the 1993 Act is powerless to confirm a ministerial regulation from the date on which it first purported to come into operation where that would be contrary to the Constitution. Nonetheless, it appears that the draftsman has attempted through the facile phrasing of s.5(2) to abdicate any further responsibility to tailor the confirmation process more precisely to specific requirements of the Constitution. Of course, more positive attempts to cope with constitutional difficulties might have been found by the courts to be wide of the mark, but this was hardly an excuse for leaving it entirely to the courts to decide whether or not a particular regulation had been confirmed. The principle invoked by Hanna J. in *McBride* might be described today as the principle of legal certainty or legal security. Had regulations come to be enforced in reliance on this Act, it could have been argued that legal security is a general principle of E.C. law, and that these general principles also bind the Member States when they implement E.C. law with the result that the Irish regulations might have been unenforceable against individuals as a matter of E.C. law (see generally Hartley, *Foundations of European Community Law* (3rd ed., 1994), pp. 149–54.

In the event, ss.5(1) to 5(3) have been rendered otiose in the light of the Supreme Court in the *Meagher* case. As the constitutionality of s.3 of the 1972 Act was upheld in *Meagher*, the question of validating regulations made thereunder does not really arise. The only circumstances in which s.5(1) might continue to have relevance might be to validate regulations held to be *ultra vires* the Minister's powers under s.3 on the ground that the directives in question should properly have been implemented by statute: (see [1994] 1 I.R. 329, at 352–3, *per* Finlay C.J.)

Section 5(4): the extension of the time limit to two years

Section 5(4) is a sort of "grudge" provision. It singles out s.10(4) of the Petty Sessions (Ireland) Act, 1851, the purported amendment of which had been struck down by the High Court in *Meagher*, and reinstitutes (prospectively only) the two year extended prosecution period which was at issue in that case. In other words, the effect of section 5(4) is to provide for a two year time limit in the case of all prosecutions under E.C. regulations.

The constitutionality of the extension of this time limit may be questioned. It must be recalled that in *Meagher* the two year time limit was found to have been justified in view of the logistical difficulties in assembling the necessary veterinary evidence within the six month time limit: (see [1994] 1 I.R. 329 at 358–9, *per* Blayney J.) But such an objective justification will scarcely be available in *every* instance of a prosecution under E.C. regulations, since there may well be cases where the assembly of evidence for such prosecutions would be very straight forward and could easily be achieved within the standard six months time limit.

The Supreme Court has stressed the importance of the constitutional right to an early trial (see, *e.g. Director of Public Prosecutions v. Byrne* [1994] 2 I.L.R.M. 91; *G v. Director of Public Prosecutions* [1994] 1 I.R. 374; *Cahalane v. Murphy* [1994] 2 I.L.R.M. 383) and the extension of the statutory time limit to two years on this undifferentiated basis (*i.e.* without objective proof of the necessity for the extended time limit) might be viewed either as a failure by the State to vindicate the constitutional right to early trial or, alternatively, as a disproportionate attack on this right.

Furthermore, the extended time limit is anomalous. It might mean that the six months time limit would apply to quite serious and complex offences, whereas a two year limit would apply to less serious and less complex offences simply because the offences *happened* to be ones created—fortuitously as far as the accused is concerned—by regulations made under the 1972 Act. The reasoning of the Supreme Court in *Cox v. Ireland* [1992] 2 I.R. 503 might well have some application in this context. For example, there is now a two year prosecution period for the offence of failing to answer certain statistical questionnaires, the creation of which was criticised by the First Joint Committee on the Secondary Legislation of the E.C. in its 57th Report (Prl. 6265, 1977), discussed above.

It must be conceded that there are some instances where the two year time limit has been extended in the case of summary prosecutions arising under other legislation and examples include section 22(2) of the Animal Remedies Act, 1993 (two years) and section 48 of the Road Traffic Act, 1994 (six months limit may be extended where new facts come to light). It is also true that the six months time limit does not apply at all in the case of indictable offences scheduled by section 2 of the Criminal Justice Act, 1951: (see *Director of Public Prosecutions v. Logan* [1994] 2 I.L.R.M. 229). But there is by definition a significant difference between summary and indictable offences and since only summary offences can be created under regulations made under s.3(2) of the 1972 Act (see s.3(3)) the objection here is to what might be contended is the arbitrary difference between the time limits specified for certain types of summary offences to the potential prejudice of defendants charged with summary offences created by regulations made under the 1972 Act.

Amendment of section 4 of Act of 1972

6.—[Section 6 provides that section 4 of 1972 Act shall stand amended by the substitution for "Joint Committee on Secondary Legislation of the European Communities" of "Joint Committee on Foreign Affairs". See the annotation to section 4 of the 1972 Act.]

Short title, collective citation, construction and commencement

7.—(1) This Act may be cited as the European Communities (Amendment) Act, 1993.

(2) The European Communities Acts, 1972 to 1992, and this Act may be cited together as the European Communities Acts, 1972 to 1993, and shall be construed together as one Act.

(3) Sections 2 and 3 of this Act shall come into operation on such day or days as may be appointed by order or orders made by the Minister for Foreign Affairs.

EUROPEAN COMMUNITIES (AMENDMENT) ACT, 1994

(1994, No. 30)

ARRANGEMENT OF SECTIONS

SECT.
1. Amendment of section 1 of the European Communities Act, 1972
2. Short title, collective citation, construction and commencement.

An Act to amend the European Communities Act, 1972 so as to provide that certain provisions of the Treaty concerning the Accession of the Kingdom of Norway, the Republic of Austria, the Republic of Finland and the Kingdom of Sweden to the European Union shall be part of the domestic law of the State. [December 7, 1994]

Citation

This Act may be cited as the European Communities (Amendment) Act, 1994: see section 2(1).

Commencement

By virtue of the European Communities (Amendment) Act, 1994 (Commencement) Order, 1994 (S.I. No. 455), the 1994 Act came into force on January 1, 1995.

Parliamentary Debates

446 *Dáil Debates* Cols. 299–378; 462–476; 758–779; 842–887 (Second stage)
447 *Dáil Debates* Cols. 514–515 (Report of Joint Committee and Final stages)
141 *Seanad Debates* Cols. 650–718 (Second stage)
141 *Seanad Debates* Cols. 937–959 (Report and Final Stages)

Acts referred to

European Communities Acts, 1972 to 1993

GENERAL NOTE

This Act amends the definition section of the 1972 Act so as to permit the State to ratify the provisions of the Corfu Treaty which in turn provided for the accession of Austria, Finland and Sweden to the European Union on January 1, 1995. The effect of the 1994 Act, together with the complications resulting from the Norwegian "No" vote, is discussed further above.

Statutory instrument

European Communities (Amendment) Act, 1994 (Commencement) Order, 1994 (S.I. No. 455)

Be it enacted by the Oireachtas as follows:

Amendment of section 1 of European Communities Act, 1972

2.—[This section amended section 1 of the European Communities Act, 1972, by extending the definition "the treaties governing the European Communities" so as to include the Accession Treaty for Finland, Austria, Sweden and Norway.]

Short title, collective citation, construction and commencement

2.—(1) This Act may be cited as the European Communities (Amendment) Act, 1994.

(2) The European Communities Acts, 1972 to 1993 and this Act may be cited together as the European Communities Acts, 1972 to 1994 and shall be construed together as one Act.

EUROPEAN COMMUNITIES (AMENDMENT) ACT, 1995

(1995, No. 6)

ARRANGEMENT OF SECTIONS

SECT.
1. Amendment of section 4 of European Communities Act, 1972
2. Short title, collective citation, and construction.

An Act to amend section 4 of the European Communities Act, 1972.

[23rd May, 1995]

INTRODUCTION AND GENERAL NOTE

Citation

European Communities (Amendment) Act 1995: see section 2(1) of the 1994 Act. By virtue of section 2(2), the European Communities Acts, 1972 to 1994 and this Act may be cited together as the European Communities Acts, 1972 to 1995 and may be cited together as one Act.

Commencement

By virtue of Article 25.4.1., the 1995 Act came into force on the day on which it was signed by the President, that is May 23, 1995.

Parliamentary Debates

452 *Dáil Debates* Cols. 1128–1165; 1893–1913 (Second and subsequent stages)
143 *Seanad Debates* Cols. 12–59 (Second and subsequent stages)

Acts Referred to

European Communities Act, 1972	1972 No. 27
European Communities (Amendment) Act 1973	1973 No. 20
European Communities (Amendment) Act, 1993	1993 No. 25
European Communities Acts, 1972 to 1994	

Be it enacted by the Oireachtas as follows:

Amendment of section 4 of European Communities Act, 1972

1.—Section 4 (inserted by the European Communities (Amendment) Act, 1973) of the European Communities Act, 1972, is hereby amended by the substitution for "Joint Committee on Foreign Affairs" (inserted by section 6 of the European Communities (Amendment) Act, 1993) of "Joint Committee on European Affairs".

GENERAL NOTE

The purpose of this Act is to reflect the decision to establish the Joint Committee on European Affairs by transferring the statutory functions exercised by the Joint Committee on Foreign Affairs in relation to the supervision of EC secondary legislation to the Joint Committee on European Affairs. This power had originally been vested in the Joint Committee on Secondary

Legislation of the European Communities but had been recently transferred to the Joint Committee on Foreign Affairs by s.6(1) of the European Communities (Amendment) Act, 1993.

Paragraph 8 of the Joint Committee's terms of reference (see 142 *Seanad Debates* Cols. 794–800) provides as follows:

"That the Joint Committee shall, in particular consider:
  (i) such programmes and guidelines prepared by the Commission of the European Communities as a basis for possible legislative action and such drafts of regulations, directives, decisions, recommendations, and opinions of the Council of Ministers proposed by the Commission,
  (ii) such acts of the institutions of those Communities,
  (iii) such regulations under the European Communities Acts, 1972–1994, and
  (iv) such other instruments made under statute and necessitated by the obligations of membership of those Communities
as the Committee may select and shall report thereon to both Houses of the Oireachtas".

Moreover, while the Committee has power to send for persons and papers, paragraph 11 of the terms of reference provide that such information need not be disclosed "if a member of the Government certifies in writing that such information is confidential or that its disclosure would be prejudicial to the State's international relations".

The terms of reference of the Committee thus replicate in this respect those of the former Joint Committee on Foreign Affairs. In both instances, however, the terms of reference are considerably broader than those of the former Joint Committee on the Secondary Legislation of the European Communities. There appears to have been general agreement in the Oireachtas that the former Joint Committee on Secondary Legislation was not a great success. Deputy Ferris described the former Committee as "ineffective" (452 *Dáil Debates* Col. 1145) and Deputy O'Malley was even less impressed with its work (452 *Dáil Debates* Cols. 1138–1139):

"...[it] sat for 20 years but did not really function. In so far as it examined any secondary legislation, it did so months, often years, after it had come into effect. Even if that committee unanimously disagreed with the secondary legislation ... it could not have done anything about it because most of that legislation contains a provision that it can only be set aside within 21 sitting days by a resolution of both Houses".

Several deputies adverted to the enhanced scrutiny available in some parliaments, with the position of the Danish Folketing being singled out for special praise. Deputy O'Malley thought (at Col. 1139) that:

"the ideal position and I accept that we cannot achieve it overnight—is the Danish one where draft directives are considered in advance by a similar committee of the Danish Parliament and cannot be adopted by Denmark at the Council of Ministers unless they have been cleared in advance by the appropriate committee of the Danish Parliament".

While the casual observer might deduce from the terms of reference of the Joint Committee that Irish parliamentary scrutiny of EC legislation approaches that of the Danish model, the reality, unfortunately, has, of course, been otherwise: see below at pp. 178–181. Many deputies expressed the view that parliamentary review by the Committee would, in Deputy Andrews' words (452 *Dáil Debates* Col. 1896), in future "anticipate legislation rather than receive it". Time will tell whether such an expectation can be fulfilled.

One further interesting question which is prompted by a consideration of the terms of reference is whether it is legally open to the Oireachtas to revoke a statutory instrument which has lawfully transposed a directive into national law? Even if such a revocation were feasible, it would raise the distinct possibility that the State might be exposed to damages for breach of Community law under the *Francovich* doctrine.

Short title, collective citation and construction

2.—(1) This Act may be cited at the European Communities (Amendment) Act, 1995.

(2) The European Communities Acts, 1971 to 1994, and this Act may be cited together as the European Communities Acts, 1972 to 1995, and shall be construed together as one Act.

GENERAL NOTE

This Act may be cited as the European Communities (Amendment) Act, 1995; see section 2(1). The European Communities Acts, 1972 to 1994 and this Act may be cited together as the European Communities Acts, 1972 to 1995.

THE TREATY ON EUROPEAN UNION

The negotiation process in the inter-governmental conferences on economic and monetary union and on political union (discussed below) culminated in the draft treaty agreed at the Maastricht summit of the Heads of State and Government of the European Communities of December 9–10, 1991. After finalising the text and translating it into the official languages of the Communities, the Member States signed this agreement on February 7, 1992 in Maastricht. It then took its official title of the Treaty on European Union (TEU). The TEU amends the European Economic Community (EEC) Treaty, or Treaty of Rome, of 1957 and renames it the European Community (E.C.) Treaty. This is the second major amendment to the Treaty of Rome, the first having taken place when the Single European Act (S.E.A.) came into force in 1987.

The Treaty on European Union amends the other two constituent Treaties of the European Communities: those governing the European Coal and Steel Community (ECSC) and the European Atomic Energy Community (Euratom). These sectoral Communities are of much less significance than the broad-ranging E.C. The TEU preserves in a modified form the three founding Treaties of the European Communities. In addition the TEU contains a number of free-standing provisions at the beginning and end of the Treaty (Arts. A-F and J-S). These establish two spheres of inter-governmental co-operation, a common foreign and security policy and co-operation in the fields of justice and home affairs. The European Union is often referred to as a temple made up of three pillars; the existing Communities as amended and the two spheres of inter-governmental co-operation. From a practising lawyer's perspective the E.C. pillar is much more important than the others.

The Treaty on European Union only entered into force on November 1, 1993 after it had been ratified in all 12 Member States, in accordance with their respective constitutional requirements (Art. R(1) E.U.). The target date set for the successful completion of the national ratification processes was January 1, 1993 (Art. R(2) E.U.), to coincide with the completion of the Internal Market (Art. 8a EEC, as inserted by the Single European Act: now Article 7a E.C.).

However, numerous domestic difficulties meant that the target date was not met. The German Constitutional Court only made a determinative ruling on the challenges raised to ratification in that country on October 12, 1993 (see *In re Brunner* [1994] 1 C.M.L.R. 57) and thus Germany was the last of the signatory States to complete the ratification process, despite overwhelming parliamentary support for the Treaty. In Denmark, the second Maastricht referendum on May 18, 1993 returned a positive verdict, overturning the narrow "No" vote of June 1992 (the result in the second referendum: 56.8 per cent for, 43.2 per cent against: on the first referendum and its implications see (1992) 29 C.M.L.Rev., 855–859). Part of the reason for the success of the second referendum was the adoption of the Decision Concerning Denmark at the Edinburgh Summit of Heads of State and Government (the European Council) in December 1992 (discussed above). The Danish Government's aim, prior to this meeting, was that any solution to their problems be legally binding, without necessitating any further Treaty amendment, which led to the adoption of a somewhat ingenious solution. For the first time, the European Council announced the adoption of a legally binding decision, although it does not attempt to alter the Treaty on European Union in any way; it simply clarifies its meaning in four key areas: citizenship; economic and monetary union; defence policy; and justice and home affairs. This decision would, nevertheless, appear to have been sufficient to persuade the Danish voters (see Weatherill and Beaumont, *E.C. Law*, (1993), pp. 774–779; Curtin & van Ooik, "Denmark and the Edinburgh Summit: Maastricht without Tears" in O'Keeffe & Twomey eds., *Legal Issues of the Maastricht Treaty* (1994), p. 349). The first Danish referendum had resulted in rejection of the Treaty, in June 1992; this was followed later that month by a 67 per cent vote in favour in the Irish referendum on the Eleventh Amendment of the Constitution Bill (see above), and by the barest of majorities in favour of ratification in the French referendum of September 1992 (see generally Laursen & Vanhoonacker, *The Ratification of the Maastricht Treaty* (1994)).

The United Kingdom's Bill amending the European Communities Act had a tortuous path through Parliament, followed by further difficulty in procuring a majority for a resolution on the Social Protocol (see below), which was obtained only by the Prime Minister making the adoption of the resolution a confidence issue. The actual ratification process was held up by the unsuccessful action for judicial review initiated by Lord Rees-Mogg (*R. v. Secretary of State for Foreign and Commonwealth Affairs, ex p. Rees-Mogg* [1993] 3 C.M.L.R. 101.). After Lord Rees-Mogg decided not to appeal the case, the United Kingdom ratified the Treaty on August 2, 1993. (On the British ratification process, see further Marshall, "The Maastricht Proceedings" [1993] P.L. 402; Rawlings, "Legal Politics: The United Kingdom and Ratification of the Treaty on European Union" (1994) P.L. 254, 367; Beaumont & Moir, *The European Communities (Amendment) Act, 1993* (1994), 32–16—32–26.)

The Treaty on European Union (TEU)

The TEU marks a further stage in the founding of the EEC Treaty's (the Treaty of Rome's) expressed objective of an "ever closer union among the peoples of Europe". The Treaty establishes an entirely new creature known as the European Union. This novel entity is to be founded on the European Communities, supplemented by the policies and forms of co-operation established by the new Treaty (Art. A E.U.). The bulk of the Treaty, however, consists of amendments to the founding Treaties of the European Communities. The amendments to the Treaty of Rome, which established the European Economic Community (as amended by the S.E.A.), are of the greatest practical significance and are individually annotated below. The amendments to the 1951 Treaty of Paris establishing the European Coal and Steel Community (E.C.S.C.) (Title III, E.U.) and the 1957 Treaty establishing the European Atomic Energy Community (Euratom) (Title IV, E.U.), essentially parallel the main amendments to the Treaty of Rome and generally reflect the institutional and procedural changes made therein. For this reason, and due to their relative lack of practical importance, they are not dealt with by these annotations.

Background

The decision to convene an inter-governmental conference under Art. 236 EEC which set in motion the Treaty amendment process, was initially taken at the Madrid European Council in June 1989. The deliberations of the European Council at Madrid centred around proposals for economic and monetary union and followed the examination of the issue by a committee consisting mainly of central bank governors, chaired by the President of the Commission, Jacques Delors (*Report of the Committee for the Study of Economic and Monetary Union in the European Community (Delors Report)*, (Luxembourg, Office for Official Publications of the E.C.,1989)).

The movement towards economic and monetary union can be seen as part of the momentum created by the Single European Market. The Delors committee and others were very quick to point out that a single market ultimately requires a single currency if the full benefits of market integration are to be achieved. The Commission's estimates put the economic benefits from a single currency in the European Community at about 10 per cent of the Community's real gross national product, half a per cent of which is from reduced transaction costs and the remainder from greater monetary stability and the elimination of exchange risks (E.C. Commission, Emerson and Huhne eds., *The E.C.U. Report* (1991)). Indeed, the S.E.A., effective from July 1, 1987, had been in force for less than six months when the Hanover European Council meeting of December 1987 entrusted the Delors committee with the task of investigating and putting forward proposals on economic and monetary union.

The Delors committee's recommendation of a three-stage process towards economic and monetary union was quickly taken on board by the Member States, who authorised the commencement of the first stage of the economic and monetary union process in July 1990. The first stage required no Treaty amendment, simply emphasising the underlying aims of the internal market programme for the achievement of full economic and monetary union, and encouraging the Member States to pursue the objectives laid down under the S.E.A. as well as the pursuit of currency stability within the ambit of the existing Exchange Rate Mechanism (ERM) of the European Monetary System (EMS).

Because the implementation of the second and third stages required the amendment of the founding Treaties, it was necessary to convene an inter-governmental conference to examine the matter. At the Strasbourg European Council of December 1989, it was decided to convene such a conference by the end of 1990 to map out the latter stages of economic and monetary union. The reason for the lengthy period between the decision to convene the inter-governmental conference and its start was, originally, to allow the first stage of economic and monetary union to get off the ground. In fact, this year-and-a-half proved to be a window of opportunity for all parties who felt that the Treaty revision should go beyond economic and monetary union and address a far wider agenda of political reform. It must also be emphasised that the pursuit of economic and monetary convergence is not an apolitical goal; while the projected economic benefits are undeniable, the resurgence of the drive for economic and monetary union was based on a desire to underline moves towards further European political integration.

In the early months of 1990, concrete proposals for political reform started to come through. The first set came from the European Parliament (the so-called "Martin" reports, named after the head of the institutional affairs committee, David Martin M.E.P.; see [1990] O.J. C96/114, C231/97 and C324/219) and advocated the strengthening of Community competences in the social and environmental fields, the integration of European political co-operation (Title III, S.E.A.) into the Community sphere and increased legislative powers for itself, including some form of co-decision with the Council, a limited right of legislative initiative and the extension of the assent procedure to all international agreements entered into by the Community. The main impetus, however, for the convening of a parallel conference on political union was the joint Kohl/Mitterand communiqué to the then President in office of the Council, the Taoiseach, Charles Haughey T.D. The desire of Chancellor Kohl and President Mitterand to extend the European agenda was debated seriously at the extraordinary Dublin summit of April 28, 1990, but a decision on a further inter-governmental conference was postponed due to the reluctance of certain Member States to move in the direction suggested.

It was at the Dublin European Council of June 25–26, 1990 that the decision to convene an inter-governmental conference on political union was taken. Nevertheless, the debate in Dublin revealed the existence of entirely opposing views among the Member States on virtually all aspects of further political development of the Communities. Such disagreements would mark all stages of the negotiations leading up to the final deliberations at Maastricht.

Prior to the opening of the inter-governmental conferences in Rome in December 1990, the Commission produced its own proposals for political reform (Inter-governmental Conferences: Contributions by the Commission, E.C. Bull., Supp. 2/91). Its contribution to the debate called for, *inter alia*, increased Community competences in such areas as social policy, the free movement of persons, health protection, an increase in the effectiveness of the Community's decision-making procedures through extended qualified majority voting in the Council of Ministers, and the revision of the Treaty to include a new title on a common foreign and security policy.

It was the issue of the common foreign and security policy that dominated the debate at following conference meetings (Laursen and Vanhoonacker eds., *The Inter-governmental Conference on Political Union* (1992), Chap. 1). States concerned at the lack of a coherent Community foreign policy, especially in the light of the Gulf conflict and the Yugoslav crisis, were supportive of the Commission's proposals to back up the Community's undoubted economic strength with an effective external Community influence in the political arena. However, the predominance of the debate on proposals for change to such previously inter-governmental areas left many other issues unclarified. Indeed, many of the main issues, such as the powers of the European Parliament, extension of qualified majority voting in the Council, and increased Community competences in a number of fields, were left to be hammered out at the two-day Maastricht summit itself. This was evidenced by the U.K.'s eleventh hour opt-out from the E.U. Treaty development of the Social Protocol (see Arts. 117–122 E.C. and notes thereon).

Structure of the new Union

Much of the debate prior to the Maastricht summit concerned the extent to which important exclusive national competences should be transferred to the Community sphere. This was particularly true with regard to foreign and security policy, defence, and elements of judicial and interior ministry affairs, where the Member States and Community institutions were substantially divided over the extent to which such a transfer should take place. While there was agreement on the need for some degree of co-operation on these matters, the means by which such co-operation would be achieved was a divisive issue. The ceding of national sovereignty in such areas, through their transfer to the Communities or the introduction of majority voting in the Council, proved highly sensitive.

These disagreements were mirrored in the Luxembourg Presidency's draft Treaty drawn up to provide an initial basis for negotiation. The publication of the Luxembourg Presidency's draft Treaty on Political Union on April 12, 1991 confirmed the fact that at least some Member States would not accept major areas of policy-making, *e.g.* foreign and defence issues, being brought within the framework of the Communities. The draft proposed what became known as the temple structure, whereby the three European Communities would constitute a pillar of the new European Union, while separate pillars were created to encompass, firstly, a common foreign and security policy and secondly, co-operation in the fields of justice and home affairs. Although economic and monetary union is often cited as a separate pillar, given the uniqueness of its process, it is encompassed in the body of the E.C. Treaty, so will be dealt with as part of the enlarged E.C. pillar. To complete the temple analogy, sitting atop these pillars is the inter-governmental European Council; its role being to provide the Union with the necessary impetus for development and the definition of the general political guidelines thereof (Art. D, E.U.).

Much to the surprise of the Member States, one of the first acts of the Dutch Presidency when it took over in the run-up to the Maastricht summit was to revise completely the basis for negotiations at a time when everyone considered the Luxembourg draft determinative (see *Agence Europe*, September 25, 1991). The Dutch draft was based upon an organic Community with common foreign and security policy and justice and home affairs incorporated into the body of the Community and the introduction of majority voting in the Council of Ministers in all legislative matters. The sovereignty implications of such an overtly federalist plan, christened the "tree" approach (the new competences branching out of the main Community "trunk"), proved too much for all Member States except for the Netherlands and Belgium (Buchan, "Why the temple proved stronger than the tree", *Financial Times*, December 7, 1991; and Corbett, "The Inter-governmental Conference on Political Union", *Journal of Common Market Studies*, (1992) Vol. 30, at 280). Negotiations then continued on the basis of the Luxembourg draft but with a number of amendments to appease the more federalist Member States. These included the provision that the "Union shall be served by a single institutional framework" (Art. C, E.U.). This has been described as paying mere lip service to an ideal; the Community institutions are lent to the new pillars, but with duties far removed from their classic Treaty functions. The two pillars of common foreign and security policy and justice and home affairs co-operation are essentially inter-governmental. They give no role to the European Court, very little influence to the European Parliament, the Commission has only a shared right of initiative and the Council acts predominantly by unanimity (see Curtin, "The Constitutional Structure of the Union: A Europe of Bits and Pieces" (1993) 30 C.M.L.Rev. 17, at 28; and editorial comments, "Post-Maastricht" (1992) 29 C.M.L.Rev. 199; see further the discussion above). Other amendments made to the original Luxembourg draft, apart from amendments to the E.C. provisions themselves which will be dealt with below, were the inclusion of the reference to the development of the *acquis communautaire* (the corpus of existing Community law) as one of the goals of the new Union and an explicit reference to the convening of a new inter-governmental conference in 1996 to revise the Union structure (Art. N, E.U.). On the other hand, at the U.K.'s insistence, any reference to the word "federal" in the E.U. Treaty was removed at Maastricht.

The pillars of a common foreign and security policy and co-operation in the fields of justice and home affairs

The non-Community pillars of the Union have already been considered above in the discussion of the Eleventh Amendment of the Constitution. The pillar structure of the Union is not an entirely new development. Foreign policy co-operation between the Member States in the guise of European political co-operation was given Treaty status for the first time by Title III of the S.E.A. but remained outwith the scope of the Community Treaties (see Nuttall, *European Political Co-operation* (1992); see also the discussion above of *Crotty v. An Taoiseach* [1987] I.R. 713). Meetings of the foreign ministers to discuss European political co-operation were artificially distinct from Council meetings, which involved the same people but were within the institutional scheme of the Community legal order. This artificiality has been somewhat reduced by the E.U. Treaty. The meetings of the foreign ministers will now take place under the normal guise of the Council, and the European political co-operation secretariat has been merged into the larger Council Secretariat. It remains to be seen whether or not this will mark anything more than a shift towards greater involvement of the Council and its staff in the workings of foreign policy. It is still the same people who are taking the decisions, thus much will depend on how strong the political desire is to see the development of a common European foreign policy. The overall retention of the unanimity requirement would tend to suggest that agreements will be limited (see Stein, "Foreign Policy at Maastricht: *Non in commotione Dominus*" (1992) 29 C.M.L.Rev. 663). However, the attribution of such decisions as are taken to the Council may not be without significance for the legal status of the Union, as may also be true of the justice and home affairs pillar. On the process of common foreign and security policy, see Title V, E.U.

Inter-governmental co-operation in the amorphous justice and home affairs field has also gone on between the Member States for many years. National authorities have been forced to reassess their policies in such areas over the last decade or so. Just as the drive to secure a single voice in foreign affairs necessitated the development of an embryonic common foreign and security policy, so the creation of the Single Market without internal frontiers necessitated developments in the fields of immigration and asylum policy and judicial co-operation. The EEC Treaty failed to give any clear authority to the Community instruments to deal with such matters and, as a result, co-operation at the inter-governmental level became prevalent (*cf.* Opinion of the European Parliament, [1990] O.J. C96/274, a call for Commission to initiate legislation in the fields of immigration and asylum). The bodies involved in this area were diverse including, for example, the Trevi group of ministers of the interior, established as early as 1975 to deal with international terrorism, but with a scope later covering virtually all aspects of international crime and policing. Over the years, further ad hoc bodies were created as and when a need was perceived. The Treaty on European Union gathers all these bodies and activities under one inter-governmental rubric. Once again, the requirement of unanimity for action will prove a stumbling block to effective and rapid decision making (see the annotation below of Art. 100c E.C.). This rationalisation does not fundamentally alter the basis of the process, that of inter-governmental co-operation. The provisions on justice and home affairs are set out in Title VI, E.U. This envisages certain specified areas which the Member States are to regard as matters of common interest (Art. K.1 E.U.). The nine topics for co-operation listed under Art. K.1 are: asylum; rules regarding the crossing of external borders; immigration; drugs; international fraud; judicial co-operation in civil matters and similarly in criminal matters; co-operation between customs services; and, finally, police co-operation. Of these areas, the last three must be distinguished from the others in that they are left exclusively the subject of inter-governmental co-operation; they are excluded from the process of "*passarelle*" (Art. K.9 E.U.), described below, and the Commission is precluded from initiating action in these fields.

The pillars of justice and home affairs and common foreign and security policy are not therefore new, but they are strengthened by their inclusion within the Treaty. Moreover, they are not as neatly separated from the Communities themselves as would appear to be the case from the classification of a pillar structure; as Curtin puts it: "the popular analogy coined, of the construction of a temple, implies a degree of architectural stability and aesthetic finish which is both inaccurate and pretentious" (Curtin, "The Constitutional

Structure of the Union: A Europe of Bits and Pieces" (1993) 30 C.M.L.Rev. 17, at 24). Administrative expenditure incurred by these pillars will be charged to the normal European Community budget. Operational expenditure, on the other hand, will only come under the Community budget if Member States vote unanimously for this to take place. Otherwise, it will be charged to the Member States in accordance with a scale to be decided (Arts. J.11.2 and K.8.2 E.U.; for the scale decided upon, see E.U. Bull. 6/94, point 1.3.2). Any action taken by the Union in the common foreign and security field requiring agreements with third states or international organisations must be carried out under the Community guise of Art. 228 E.C. or by agreement among all 15 Member States; the Union lacking the international legal personality to conclude such agreements itself (see Steenbergen, "Maastricht: *De Externe Betrekkingen*" (1992) S.E.W. 741; see further the discussion above of the legal personality of the Union).

Further complicating the unwieldy relationship between the existing Community and Union structures are the "passarelle" provisions, providing for the transfer of certain Union competences into the Community arena. Art. K.9 allows the Council, acting unanimously, to select any of the six areas of justice and home affairs co-operation listed under Arts. K.1(1)–1(6) E.U. for transfer and to have the provisions of Art. 100c E.C. apply to such transferred matters; co-operation in criminal matters (Arts. K1(7)–1(9) E.U.) does not fall under this provision. Any such transfer does not necessitate a Treaty revision but must be adopted by the Member States in accordance with their respective constitutional requirements (see notes on Art. 100c E.C.).

The inclusion of visa policy within the Community sphere during the inter-governmental conference negotiations (Art. 100c E.C.) means that the procedure for dealing with persons from third countries entering the Community is to be a twin track approach. For visa policy, the Council will follow the E.C. Treaty procedure by deciding unanimously, on the basis of a Commission proposal, which third countries require a visa for their nationals to enter the E.C. Qualified majority voting will apply from January 1, 1996. Other matters, such as immigration policy, will be determined at the inter-governmental level. This does not deal with the need, often expressed by many of the mainland European States dealing with the influx of refugees from Eastern Europe and further afield, for an integrated Community immigration policy dealing with both visas and asylum (for excellent summaries of the current position see Tomuschat, "A Right to Asylum in Europe" (1992) 13 Human Rights Law Review, 257; and Lambert, *Seeking Asylum: Comparative Law and Practice in Selected European Countries* (1995)).

Finally, the Union provisions rely greatly on the Community institutions for their effective implementation; the only truly Union entities being the European Council and the bodies of national civil servants set up to oversee the operation of the new pillars. While these new pillars borrow the Community institutions for certain purposes they make only minimal use of them. The inter-governmental institutions of the Council and the European Council are given the key powers. The European Parliament is to be kept regularly informed of the main aspects of the co-operation in these fields, but this does not require prior consultation nor is failure to consult enforceable before the European Court of Justice (Art. L, E.U.; *cf.* Case 139/79, *Roquette Freres S.A. v. Council* [1980] E.C.R. 3393). The Commission is to be "fully associated" with the work carried out in these fields but will find itself in direct competition with the bodies of national civil servants created under these provisions; the co-ordinating committee under Art. K.4 (justice and home affairs) and the analogous committee of political directors under Art. J.8(5) (common foreign and security policy). It will also be forced to surrender its monopoly of policy initiative; the Member States and co-ordinating committees of national civil servants are both empowered to initiate proposals in these fields. Its strength of influence in these fields will depend on the strength of the Commission itself. It will prove difficult wholly to delimit those areas falling under the justice and home affairs title from those falling under the Community sphere of action. This is especially true with regard to the implications of justice and home affairs policy on existing Member State governmental co-operation on the free movement of persons in the Community under Art. 7a E.C. (see Schütte, "Schengen: Its Meaning for the Free Movement of Persons in Europe" (1991) 28 C.M.L.Rev. 549; and O'Keeffe, "The Free Movement of Persons and the Single Market" (1992) 17 E.L.Rev. 3). This ought to give the Commission some extra degree of influence in the justice and home affairs sphere.

By virtue of Art. L, E.U., the areas of common foreign and security policy and justice and home affairs are expressly non-justiciable by the European Court of Justice, except in the very specialised situation where the Member States make express provision for such jurisdiction in relation to the provisions of a convention negotiated under the justice and home affairs pillar (Art. K.3 E.U.). The exclusion of the jurisdiction of the Court of Justice marks the inter-governmental nature of the processes under these pillars. In his second reading speech on the U.K.'s 1993 Bill giving effect to the amendments to domestic law encompassed in the Treaty, John Major asserted that in the fields of justice and home affairs and common foreign and security policy: "any dispute would go to the International Court of Justice, not to the European Court" (*Hansard*, H.C. vol. 208, col. 267; *cf.* Everling, "Reflections on the Structure of the European Union" (1992) 29 C.M.L.Rev. 1053, at 1064). Any disputes in this field would no doubt be resolved in a political rather than a judicial context. None of this, however, denies the binding effect of the Treaty on European Union as an instrument of international law under the basic rule, *pacta sunt servanda.*

Article L, E.U. also excludes European Court jurisdiction over the Common Provisions in Title I. One of the most obvious results of this exclusion is that the express reference to the European Convention on Human Rights (ECHR) in Art. F(2) E.U. adds little if anything to current practice with regard to the Community protection of human rights. Prior to the Maastricht summit, there had been many calls for the incorporation into Community law of the ECHR or the inclusion of a Community charter of fundamental rights (the Commission supports Community accession to ECHR; E.C. Bull. Supp. 2/79, repeated in E.C. Bull. 11/90 and supported by the European Parliament, [1991] O.J. C290). In the end, the only references to such protection were included in the non-justiciable Art. F(2) and in the preamble. Any protection of fundamental rights under the Community system will have to continue on an ad hoc basis as individual cases are decided by the Court of Justice (for development of Community human rights (see Weiler *et al.*, *European Union: The Human Rights Challenge*, vols. 1–3 (1991); Hartley, *The Foundations of European Community Law* (3rd. ed., 1994), pp. 139–49; Dauses, "The Protection of Fundamental Rights in the Community Legal Order", (1985) 10 E.L.Rev. 398; and Coppel and O'Neill, *The European Court of Justice: Taking Rights Seriously?* (1992) 29 C.M.L.Rev. 669). The Council has since sought the opinion of the Court of Justice on the compatibility with the Treaties of the accession of the Communities to the ECHR [1993] 4 E.U. Bull, point 1.1.4.

In common with all prior Treaty revisions, the actual negotiations were conducted in strict secrecy and no official *travaux préparatoires* (records of the intentions of the negotiators) are available on the conduct of the conferences (for commentary on the negotiations see Laursen and Vanhoonacker eds., *The International Conference on Political Union* (1992); also Corbett, "The International Conference on Political Union", *Journal of Common Market Studies* (1992) 30, at 271).

Treaty on European Union

The scheme of the Treaty on European Union

The scheme of the E.U. Treaty reflects the structure of the Union itself, with seven separate titles, each one dealing with a different aspect of the Treaty's programme. Title I (Arts. A–F) contains the Common Provisions: legal declarations of intent covering such issues as the role of the Union and of the European Council and the relationship between the Union and the Communities themselves. Title II (Art. G) contains the amendments to the EEC Treaty, constituting, as mentioned previously, by far the largest part of the TEU. Technical amendments to the ECSC and Euratom Treaties are then contained within Titles III (Art. H) and IV (Art. I) respectively. The provisions on common foreign and security policy are to be found in Title V (Arts. J.1–J.11) and on co-operation in the fields of justice and home affairs under Title VI (Arts. K–K.9). Title VII (Arts. L–S) contains the Treaty's Final Provisions.

Amendments to the Treaty of Rome establishing the European Economic Community

Article G of the E.U. Treaty contains the amendments to the EEC Treaty (the Treaty of Rome), which established the European Economic Community. It contains 86 paragraphs, which amend large parts of the EEC Treaty. The very first paragraph of Art. G stipulates that the term "European Economic Community" shall be replaced by the term "European Community". Thus references to the EEC Treaty infer the position prior to the Maastricht amendments and references to the E.C. Treaty are post-Maastricht.

Much of the opposition to the further European integration through the Communities is attributable to the way increased E.C. competences transfer sovereign powers from the Member States. One of the more bizarre manifestations of this concern was the U.K. Government's insistence that it would not ratify a Treaty incorporating the word "federal" into the text. The Luxembourg draft Treaty's reference to "a process leading gradually to a Union with a federal goal" (Art. A, Luxembourg draft) was removed at Maastricht after intense pressure from the U.K. negotiators ("U.K. Wins Battle to Drop the Federal Goal", *Financial Times*, December 4, 1991).

The dispute over the word "federal" was simply a distraction. The real concern over the Treaty was with the extent to which it would be a centralising force. Whether having a "federal" goal is synonomous with moving towards a more centralised Europe is debatable; many of today's federal States exhibit a much greater degree of decentralisation than the U.K., with its highly centralised governmental machinery. While a definitive breakdown of the Treaty in this respect is impossible, the determination of the centralising nature of the Treaty, in the E.C. context, must centre, first, on an assessment of the increased instances of qualified majority voting in the Council, and secondly, on any increase in the powers of the European Parliament at the expense of the Council. If one were to use these as indicators of the extent to which the E.U. Treaty amendments to the EEC Treaty signal a centralising tendency, the Treaty would not appear to be a major threat to Member State autonomy. The increase in the scope of qualified majority voting is negligible; there are only 11 new instances in the Treaty as amended (emergency visa requirements, Art. 100c(2); education (incentive measures and recommendations), Art. 126(4); vocational training measures (replacing simple majority voting), Art. 127(4); health (incentive measures and recommendations), Art. 129; consumer protection, Art. 129a(2); trans-European networks guidelines (inter-operability and finance), Art. 129d; research and technological development, Art. 130j–l; environment (except fiscal, land use, water and energy), Art. 130s; development policy, Art. 130w; approval of European Parliament regulations governing the Ombudsman, Art. 138e; and certain aspects of social policy among the fourteen, Art. 2(2), Protocol No. 14). In the field of economic and monetary union, the majority process is more prevalent but is tempered by the provision for "opt-outs" by Denmark (already exercised at the Edinburgh summit of the European Council) and the U.K. Unanimity is retained in the Treaty for the majority of politically sensitive matters such as the harmonisation of indirect taxes (Art. 99), approximation of laws falling within the common market but outside the internal market (Art. 100), granting of Community financial assistance to a Member State in difficulties (Art. 103a), and the general power to pass laws coming within the objectives of the Community (Art. 235). In the constitutional sphere, the vast majority of provisions continue to require the unanimous agreement of the Member States; these include decisions concerning the Community's own resources (Art. 201), the acceptance of a new Member State (Art. 237 EEC; now Art. O, E.U.), changes in the number of judges and Advocates General in the Court of Justice (Arts. 165 and 166) and the approval of a uniform procedure for the European Parliamentary elections (Art. 138(3)). All in all, the amended E.C. Treaty provides for 55 instances of unanimity voting in Council. The case that the Maastricht amendments to the EEC Treaty constitute a move towards centralisation in this respect is therefore hardly persuasive (see Weatherill and Beaumont, *E.C. Law* (1993), pp. 69–71). The Maastricht amendments make no reference to the continued existence or otherwise of the so-called Luxembourg compromise whereby a Member State is able to exercise a veto in the Council where its important interests are at stake (see Vasey, "Decision Making in the Agriculture Council and the Luxembourg Compromise" (1988) 25 C.M.L.Rev. 725). While some Member States insist that the compromise holds (see, *e.g.* John Major M.P., *Hansard*, H.C. vol. 208, col. 272), there is not a consensus among the Member States on this matter (see Hartley, *Foundations of European Community Law* (3rd. ed. 1994), pp. 21–3). It is likely that a Member State wishing actively to invoke this veto will find it increasingly difficult as its use generally diminishes (see Editorial, (1986) 23 C.M.L.Rev. 744, which discussed the relative rarity of the compromise at the ministerial level and the reluctance of the Member States to continue its application in the Committee of Permanent Representatives (COREPER)). A claim that vital national interests are at stake will be particularly difficult to make in an area where the state concerned has recently agreed to Treaty amendments permitting qualified majority voting in that area (see Weatherill and Beaumont, *EC Law* (1993), pp. 67–9).

The other factor determinative of the centralising nature of the Community process is the extent to which the European Parliament can influence the content of Community legislation. This influence, minimal prior to the passing of the S.E.A., grew with the introduction of the co-operation procedure and will do so again as a result of the Maastricht amendments to the E.C. Treaty. Nonetheless, the Council still remains the pre-eminent institution in the legislative process. Despite the calls for a power of co-decision between the European Parliament and the Council, in part to address the essentially undemocratic nature of the Council process whereby members of national governments meet in secret to pass legislative measures, the amendments agreed at Maastricht fall far short of such co-decision. The introduction of the new "conciliation and veto" procedure (known imaginatively in the E.C. Treaty as the "procedure referred to in Art. 189b E.C."), while giving the European Parliament for the first time a right of veto over legislation it does not approve of, does not allow the European Parliament to adopt legislation on which the Council has expressed a negative opinion. The Council thus maintains its power to determine the legislative make-up of the Community legal order, the European Parliament simply having a somewhat greater say in the process than before. This being so, the new procedure is complex and restricted initially to only thirteen legislative bases. These include the majority of those areas previously using the co-operation procedure, aimed at the achievement of the internal market and introduced by the S.E.A. (Art. 149(2) EEC replaced by Art. 189c E.C.), as well as the provisions under the "new" Community competences introduced into the E.C. Treaty at Maastricht (examples are education, vocational training and youth measures but excluding any harmonisation of national laws, Art. 126(4); trans-European network guidelines, Art. 129d; incentive measures in the fields of public health and culture, Articles 129(4) and 128(5) respectively). For a detailed breakdown of the procedure and its scope of application, see the note on Art. 189b E.C.

An important factor in any discussion of the centralising tendency of the E.C. Treaty is an analysis of the new competences attributed to the Community; naturally any increase in the scope of Community action means a proportionate decrease in the national sphere of action. This transfer from the Member States to the Community has been kept to the minimum by the E.U. Treaty. This would not appear to be the case from a cursory glance at Art. 3 of the E.C. Treaty, which would suggest that the increase in the Community's scope of action has been far from minimal; the list of Community activities is a good deal longer than in the Treaty of Rome, as amended by the S.E.A. That is because the list has been extended to include references to the new competence chapters included in the Maastricht Treaty for the first time. Nine additional policy areas are listed in Art. 3, but that does not mean that there are nine new areas of competence. In all these areas, competence has already been exercised under the Treaty of Rome and the S.E.A.

The "new" fields of activity include the following (laid down under the titles by which they will be known): culture; public health; consumer protection; trans-European networks; and industry and development co-operation. The E.U. Treaty also strengthens the provisions in the Titles on economic and social cohesion and the environment, which were inserted by the S.E.A. The degree of power given to the Community to adopt actions under the different titles is highly divergent. In the fields of culture and public health, the Community is empowered simply to supplement and encourage national action, with the express proviso that any measures taken at the Community level shall preclude the harmonisation of national laws. On the other hand, the powers attributed to the Community in the field of consumer protection permit the adoption of wide-ranging Community measures aimed at such harmonisation. (On this topic see Lane, "New Community Competences under the Maastricht Treaty" (1993) 30 C.M.L.Rev. 939.)

The preceding discussion has focused on the centralising tendencies of the new Treaty; it is also necessary to look at its decentralising forces. The E.U. Treaty introduces into the E.C. Treaty the principle of subsidiarity (Art. 3b E.C.) with a view to ensuring a more appropriate use of competences shared between the Member States and the Community institutions. The preamble to the E.U. Treaty highlights the brake that subsidiarity is intended to place on a centralising Europe. It provides that the Member States are "resolved to continue the process of creating an ever closer union among the peoples of Europe, in which decisions are taken as closely as possible to the citizen in accordance with the principle of subsidiarity". The principle of subsidiarity will prove very difficult to apply in the judicial context. Subsidiarity's impact will depend largely upon the degree to which it is absorbed into the institutional culture of the Community. Political rather than legal factors are likely to determine how much restraint the Community institutions exercise in the promulgation of Community legislation (see the annotation of Art. 3b E.C.).

Another small decentralising step is the removal of simple majority voting in the Council from substantive areas concerning vocational training (contrast Art. 128 EEC and Arts. 126 and 127 E.C.) and external relations (contrast Art. 228 EEC and Art. 228 E.C.). The shift to qualified majority voting and unanimity prevents the possibility of the Ministers who represent the great majority of the Community's population being out-voted in Council.

The provisions of the E.U. Treaty amending the EEC Treaty make some interesting alterations to the Community process in the field of political union; an umbrella term used to convey all areas not specifically covered by economic and monetary union. This being the case, it must be emphasised that the Maastricht amendments do not alter all of the pre-existing EEC Treaty. Many of the most utilised provisions of the Treaty remain almost wholly unaltered; this is the case with regard to the free movement of goods (Arts. 9–37 EEC), agriculture (Arts. 38–47 EEC) and competition policy (Arts. 85–94 EEC, with minor amendments in Arts. 92(3) and 94). The fundamental freedoms of establishment, services and workers are simply amended to provide for the application of a new legislative procedure; something which is quite common in the Maastricht amendments. The areas of the Treaty which have seen the most substantial amendments are the institutional provisions (Arts. 137–198e), the free movement of capital provisions (Arts. 73a–73h), and the Community competences chapter (Arts. 110–130y). Elsewhere the amendments are impossible to categorise and range from the simply inconsequential to the essential. The core of the Treaty amendments consists of the substantive provisions governing the move to the third stage of economic and monetary union, with its single currency and independent monetary authority (Arts. 102a–109). This marks a new departure for the Community; the laying down of strict timetables for movement through the three stages highlights the imperative nature of the process. Finally, the only other wholly new addition to the Treaty is a section dealing with the new Union "citizenship", a mixed bag of rights consequent on Union citizenship, something much more notable for its symbolic value than any substantive content (Arts. 8–8e).

As Curtin has identified, a striking feature of the new Union Treaty is the large number of annexed protocols and declarations (Curtin, "The Constitutional Structure of the Union: A Europe of Bits and Pieces" (1993) 30 C.M.L.Rev. 17, 44). While the use of such instruments is nothing new to the drafters of the Community Treaties, their use in the TEU is often at variance with their generally understood purpose. While such protocols are ideal instruments to prevent over-elaboration of technical or transitional matters in the body of the Treaty (as with the annexed Protocol on the Statutes of the European System of Central Banks and European Central Bank and the Protocol on the excessive deficit procedure in the field of economic and monetary union), they have also been utilised to give effect to opt-outs negotiated by the Member States from fundamental Treaty obligations. This can be seen as a manifestation of the move towards a Europe *á la carte*. Prime examples of this movement can be seen in the first Protocol annexed to the Treaty which provides for the retention by the Danes of legislation preventing the purchase by nationals of other Member States of second homes in Denmark. This marks an abrogation of the fundamental principle of Community law of free movement for the purpose of securing services and goods. The two opt-outs secured by the U.K. are encompassed in protocols appended to the E.U. Treaty. The first of these is Protocol No. 11, by which the U.K. is given the opportunity permanently to derogate from the requirements of the third stage of economic and monetary union with its single currency and independent central bank; Denmark has a similar opportunity under Protocol No. 12. The second opt-out secured by the U.K. is from the development of the social provisions agreed to by the other 11 (now 14) Member States. This aspect of the Treaty has caused a great deal of confusion due in part to the interchangeable use of confusingly similar terms. These include references to the "Social Chapter", the "Social Charter" and the "Social Protocol". It might be helpful to attempt a clarification of the different terms in use, and their origins.

209

The EEC Treaty, as it stood prior to the Maastricht amendments, contained a chapter on "social provisions" (Title III, Chap. 1, Arts. 117–122). The original "Social Chapter" provides for Member States to "agree on the need to promote improved working conditions and an improved standard of living for workers" (Art. 117 EEC) and for the Commission to promote closer co-operation in the fields of, *inter alia*, employment, labour law and working conditions, vocational training, social security, the prevention of occupational accidents, occupational hygiene and the right of association (Art. 118 EEC). Art. 118a (inserted by the S.E.A.) allows the Council, acting by qualified majority vote, to adopt directives on health and safety issues. Article 119 then lays down the principle of equal pay for equal work. These provisions have provided the base for a large number of Community-wide social measures, but the requirement of unanimity proved a stumbling block to wider developments. Nevertheless, the Commission made extensive use of Arts. 118a and 100a EEC to facilitate decision-making by taking advantage of the qualified majority voting procedure applicable to these provisions. Some of the legal bases chosen have proven controversial. A prime example is the Draft Directive on the organisation of working time (COM (89) 568 final), which the Commission initiated as a "health and safety" measure under Art. 118a. The Directive was adopted on November 23, 1993 and the U.K. Government confirmed it would seek the amendment of the measure in the Court of Justice under Art. 173 E.C. (see *The Times*, November 24, 1993). The opposition to such legislative initiatives underlines the U.K. Government's stance on what it sees as expensive social provisions which damage competitiveness. This approach has been decried as the "sweat shop" approach by many critics of the social opt-out.

In December 1989, all the Member States of the Community, except the U.K., signed the Community Charter of the Fundamental Social Rights of Workers (the Social Charter). This charter is purely declaratory in nature and amounts to a political commitment among the signatories to further progress in a number of broadly defined social spheres. Some Commission initiatives under the Action Programme (COM(89) 568 final), on certain of the proposals contained in the Social Charter, have proven successful. These include the recent Directive on the protection at work of pregnant women and on maternity provisions (Dir. 92/85/EEC) passed under Art. 118a EEC. The 11 Member States of the Community, apart from the U.K., were still keen to press on further with more concrete reforms.

The E.U. Treaty gave them this opportunity. While it does not in any significant way amend the Social Chapter in the EEC Treaty, a unique approach was taken by the 11 Member States keen to progress in more ambitious fields of social policy, in the face of outright U.K. opposition to any such development. The Protocol on Social Policy annexed to the E.U. Treaty (Protocol No. 14) records the agreement of all 12 (now 15) Member States that 11 (now 14) of them (*i.e.* with the exception of the U.K.) are authorised to utilise the existing European Community institutions to implement a Social Policy Agreement, annexed to the Protocol itself, amounts to a revised and updated Social Chapter, providing for wider areas of Community competence in the social field and more importantly an increase in the scope of qualified majority voting. These measures, originally intended by the Dutch Presidency to replace the existing Social Chapter, include qualified majority voting in the areas of workers' health and safety, working conditions, the information and consultation of workers and sexual equality in the labour market and the workplace. Unanimous agreement is required for progress in the fields of social security, protection of workers on termination of their employment, conditions of employment for legally resident non-Community nationals and financial contributions for the promotion of employment and job creation.

These increases in the power of the Community in the social sphere are undeniably modest. While the increase in qualified majority voting from just health and safety to four new areas may well expedite decision-making in these new fields, a number of the provisions merely amount to duplications of pre-existing measures, for example, health and safety measures are already covered by Art. 118a EEC while the equality provision in Art. 119 EEC is essentially rewritten in Art. 6 of the Agreement. The only addition to this Article consists of the controversial provision permitting positive discrimination for women in the labour market. Article 2(6) of the Agreement, in a provision which could well have been drafted for the U.K. Government, declares that the Agreement does not to apply to pay, the right of association, the right to strike or the right to impose lock-outs.

The convoluted legal implications of the existence of two sets of provisions concerning social policy will be dealt with later in these annotations (see the General Note on Chap. 1 of Title VIII of the E.C. Treaty).

Article 239 E.C., unrevised by the E.U. Treaty, provides that protocols annexed to the E.C. Treaty are to be considered as an "integral part" of it. The emergence of measures such as the Irish abortion Protocol, as well as the Protocols just described, has been asserted to be profoundly damaging to the legal structure of the Communities, built upon the principle of uniform supremacy over national law (see the discussion above of Protocol No. 17). The possibility of Member States selecting which areas of their laws ought to remain outwith the scope of Community influence prejudices the unique nature of the Community system, and seems inconsistent with the expressed desire in the E.U. Treaty to "maintain in full the *acquis communautaire* and build on it" (Arts. B and C, E.U.). The risk of the damaging scenario of a two-speed Community is all too apparent (Curtin, "The Constitutional Structure of the Union: A Europe of Bits and Pieces" (1993) 30 C.M.L.Rev. 17 at 44). On the other hand, a measure like Protocol No. 17 may be seen as a specific response to growing pressure to maintain the priority of certain fundamental national values even in the sphere of application of Community law, which may result in greater attempts in future to balance the imperatives of national and Community constitutional law and legitimating political philosophies (see Phelan, "Right to Life of the Unborn v. Promotion of Trade in Services: The European Court of Justice and the Normative Shaping of the European Union" (1992) 55 M.L.R. 670, at 686–9).

Institutional reform

A great number of the changes concern the institutional set-up of the European Union. The inter-governmental star has risen as regards the new Union competences, where the European Council and Council of Ministers are dominant, but these are areas which were formerly even more firmly reserved by the Member States. In the Community structure itself there has been a modest increase in the powers of the supra-national Parliament and, to a much lesser extent, the Commission.

The European Parliament (Arts. 137–143 E.C.)

The European Parliament will now exercise "the powers conferred upon it by this Treaty" (Art. 137 E.C.) as opposed to the "advisory and supervisory" (Art. 137 EEC) role it pursued prior to Maastricht. Most significantly it finds itself the recipient of a new legislative role in certain specified areas. Pressure from the more integrationist states led to the creation of this new legislative procedure, under which, for the first time, Parliament has the power to veto certain legislative proposals outright (Art. 189b E.C.). It also sees the formalisation of a number of activities previously carried out by convention, such as the creation of committees of inquiry to investigate alleged contraventions or maladministration in the implementation of Community law (Art. 138c E.C.) and the development of Parliament's role in the appointment of the Commission (Art. 158 E.C.). With the development of the European Parliament's role in the legislative procedure through the introduction of the conciliation and veto procedure and the extension of the assent procedure (single reading; positive parliamentary approval necessary), the European Parliament is now in the position to apply the brake to the Community legislative process, but cannot press the accelerator without the consent of the Council. Nevertheless, the powers of the European Parliament will be substantially increased in all areas of Community competence, thanks to the potential for cross-bargaining. In other words, the European Parliament will consent to a certain measure under the conciliation and veto or assent procedures on the explicit grounds that in another area where it exercises a great deal less formal influence, its proposals will be given effect. This will be the price for its consent. Such bargaining will be effective only if the Council is anxious to secure legislation in the area covered by the conciliation and veto or assent procedures; it always has the opportunity simply to let a proposal lapse if European Parliament agreement is not forthcoming. The Maastricht amendments also recognise a limited right of legislative initiative for the European Parliament (Art. 138b); while this falls short of the European Parliament being in a position to require the Commission to submit a legislative proposal on a specific topic, it will give the European Parliament a significant degree of informal leverage. It is quite possible that the European Parliament will select a number of its initiatives as proposals falling under this Article and call the Commission to account until there is some follow-up (Venables, *The Amendment of the Treaties* (1992), p. 74). The power of the European Parliament to secure the dismissal of the Commission by passing a motion of censure by a two-thirds majority under Art. 144 EEC is retained and in drastic circumstances could be utilised in this context. The formalisation of the European Parliament vote of confidence in the Commission prior to their taking office can be used as a platform for the European Parliament to make its legislative initiatives quite clear to the incoming Commission. This was made clear in the consultation of the Parliament in 1994 in respect of the appointment of M. Santer as President of the Commission, and in the questioning of candidate Commissioners in the Parliament in January 1995.

The Commission (Arts. 156–163 E.C.)

The major amendment as regards the Commission concerns the enhanced role of the European Parliament in the appointment of the Commission (Art. 158). Also significant is the Commission's role in the economic and monetary union process, *e.g.* its involvement in assessing the Member States' economic performances as a basis for their entering the third stage. Finally, the Commission will have the power to recommend to the Court of Justice the level of sanction it envisages for Member State non-compliance under the new Art. 171 E.C.

A declaration appended to Art. 157 E.C. declares that a review of the number of Commissioners will take place "no later than the end of 1992". The "EFTA" enlargement (by which Austria, Sweden and Finland acceded to the Union as of January 1, 1995) did not lead to any radical changes. While no determinative ruling has yet been made, there is every likelihood that the process of further enlargement to the east and in the Mediterranean region will render the current position of larger Member States having two Commissioners untenable. Even the prospect of one State, one Commissioner, with the resultant rise in the influence of the smaller Member States, may prove controversial in a Community of 20 or more Member States. While the Luxembourg draft mentioned the possibility of deputy Commissioners, this was not pursued in the final Treaty.

The European Court of Justice (Arts. 165–184 E.C.)

The most significant innovation concerning the European Court of Justice is the new procedure envisaged for enforcement actions under Arts. 169–171 E.C. It is now provided that a financial penalty may be imposed upon states which fail to comply with a judgment of the Court. This development was advocated by the U.K. which has a good record of implementation of Community legislation (see Tenth Annual Report on Commission monitoring of the Application of Community law (COM (93) 320 final)). The procedure to be followed in the application of this sanction is long and drawn out. In some cases a more immediate remedy may be available under the Courts development of the principle of State liability for non-implementation of Community legislation, enunciated in the landmark case of *Francovich and Bonifaci v. Italy* (Cases C-6, C-9/90, [1991] E.C.R. I 5359, noted by Bebr (1992) 29 C.M.L.Rev. 571). For an elaboration of this principle and of the new powers of the Court of Justice, see the annotation of Art. 171 E.C.

Another important change is the greater range of jurisdictional issues that the Council can agree to transfer from the Court of Justice to the Court of First Instance (see the annotation of Art. 168a E.C.).

The Committee of the Regions (Art. 198a–198c E.C.)

The new advisory Committee of the Regions will adopt a similar function to the pre-existing Economic and Social Committee (Arts. 193–198 E.C.). It will be consulted in the legislative process but in a very restricted number of areas, and its powers are purely advisory. While the Committee is largely impotent, its inclusion reflects the desire of certain Member States, most notably Germany with its powerful regional bodies (*Länder*), to see local governments with a much greater say in the Community legislative process; at best the Committee of the Regions marks a symbolic acceptance of this principle.

The Council of Ministers (Arts. 145–154 E.C.)

The Maastricht amendments have made very few alterations to the role of the Council in the Community, although it has seen the range of its powers increase in the fields of economic and monetary union and in the pillars of justice and home affairs co-operation and common foreign and security policy. The virtual retention of all the powers previously exercised by this body, the Community's principal legislative branch is not altogether surprising when one considers that the Treaty amendments were negotiated by the same government ministers who attend the Council.

Legislative procedures

There is no uniform procedure for the making of Community legislation, and the E.U. Treaty amendments have further added to the procedures applicable (for an overview see Weatherill and Beaumont, *E.C. Law* (1993), Chap. 5). The result is a bewildering array of legislative procedures which impedes any real understanding of the Community law making process: "Political accountability, sanctioned by universal suffrage, can indeed only be effective where the actors in the legislative process are known in advance to everyone and when their respective prerogatives and responsibilities can be identified by the public" (Lenaerts, "Some Reflections on the Separation of Powers in the European Communities" (1991) 28 C.M.L.Rev. 11, at 20).

The assent procedure introduced by the S.E.A. is retained but with an increased scope of application. This procedure, which effectively attributes to the European Parliament a right of veto, is now applicable to free movement of citizens (Art. 8a(2) E.C.), legislation increasing the European Central Bank's powers of prudential supervision (Art. 105(6) E.C.), amending certain articles of the Statute of the European System of Central Banks (Art. 106(5) E.C.), the creation of the new cohesion fund and the definition of the tasks of the structural funds (Art. 130d(1) E.C.) and the adoption of a uniform procedure for elections to the European Parliament (Art. 138(2) E.C.). It is also still applicable to the conclusion of certain international agreements (Art. 228(3) E.C.) and the accession of new Member States (Art. O, E.U.). This procedure avoids the complexities inherent in the new conciliation and veto procedure while still giving the European Parliament a veto. It does not, however, give the European Parliament an opportunity to amend proposals. In an attempt to rectify this the European Parliament has amended its Rules of Procedure to try to create a conciliation process with the Council as part of the assent procedure (see Rule 52G(3), [1993] O.J. C268/51). The parliamentary committee responsible for considering the Council's legislative proposals may make an interim report recommending modifications to them. If any of these modifications are passed by the Parliament by the same majority as is required for final assent then the President of the Parliament will request the Council to open a conciliation procedure. If the Council refuses to engage in conciliation then the implied threat is that the Parliament will refuse to give assent to a proposal in its unmodified form.

The new conciliation and veto procedure introduced by Art. 189b E.C. has certain of the elements of the co-operation procedure (Art. 149(2) EEC, now Art. 189c E.C.), such as the double reading in the European Parliament, but permits the convening of a third stage conciliation process where an equal number of members of the Council and the European Parliament meet to hammer out their differences. This procedure, permitting the European Parliament to reject legislation of which it does not approve, is of byzantine complexity and lacks legislative transparency. The European Parliament has expressed the opinion that its power to veto legislation is effectively circumscribed by the negative perception which would fall upon this body if it were seen to be blocking legislation which had already spent upwards of six months going through the early stages of the procedure. The then President of the European Parliament, Baron Crespo, was probably exaggerating the "political suicide" of the institution involved in the European Parliament being seen to be exercising such a negative role. The European Parliament's powers have increased as a result of the introduction of this procedure, despite its imperfections.

The co-operation procedure, which had, relatively effectively, enabled the European Parliament to secure amendments to the legislation enacted under it, is preserved under the E.U. Treaty amendments to the E.C. Treaty. (Up to 50 per cent of the Parliament's proposed amendments were accepted.) A number of the measures originally covered by this procedure are promoted to the conciliation and veto procedure. The co-operation procedure will apply to the adoption of social measures between the 14 and to a number of the economic and monetary union provisions.

One unwelcome aspect of the E.C. Treaty, as far as the degree of European Parliament involvement is concerned, is the retention of the consultation procedure as one of the prevalent legislative processes. The European Parliament is merely entitled to give an opinion on the measure at hand, and the Commission and Council are then entirely free to disregard this opinion if they so desire. This procedure is retained, along with unanimity in the Council, for a number of politically sensitive areas of Community competence, such as the harmonisation of indirect taxes (Art. 99 E.C.) and other constitutional matters, including the achievement of Community goals under Art. 235 E.C. One disturbing aspect of the consultation procedure is the Council practice which has grown up of adopting a political position in the Council prior to the consultation of the European Parliament, thus fettering the discretion of the Council as regards any opinion returning from the European Parliament, no matter how meritorious. Even more regrettable is the continuation of some law-making powers in the Community where there is no requirement to consult the European Parliament (see Weatherill and Beaumont, *E.C. Law* (1993), pp. 94–5, 125, 130, 796–7).

A great deal of criticism centres on the disregard which has been paid to institutional efficiency in the interests of national interests. This is of course unavoidable in a Treaty revision process which requires the unanimous agreement of all the Member States. This is manifested in the wide variety of legislative procedures now applicable to the adoption of the Community legislation. What is also unavoidable is an increase in the number of challenges being made to the legislative basis of Community law (see, *e.g.* Case C-300/89, *Commission v. Council (Titanium Dioxide)* [1991] I E.C.R. 2867). With the existence of widely divergent legislative procedures under which each institution's role varies greatly, there will undoubtedly be an increase in such litigation before the Court of Justice. This will further threaten the efficient operation of the legislative process.

Economic and monetary union (Arts. 102a–109m E.C.)

The core of the substantive amendments to the EEC Treaty is the section dealing with economic and monetary union; effectively a treaty within a treaty. Agreement upon the route towards eventual economic and monetary union was quickly reached at Maastricht. The existence of a general consensus among the Member States on the main points, as well as the availability of authoritative and influential materials prior to the summit, made the Maastricht negotiations something of a formality. The Delors committee report and the draft statute of the European System of Central Banks drawn up by the Committee of Governors of the Central Banks of the Member States, were among a corpus of materials facilitating discussion throughout.

Article 3a E.C. defines the activities of the Member States and the Community institutions in the realisation of full economic and monetary union. In the economic field, the goal is the adoption of an economic policy which is based on close co-ordination of Member State's economic policies and is conducted in accordance with the principle of an open market economy with free competition. As regards monetary policy, the aim is the irrevocable fixing of exchange rates, leading to the introduction of a single currency, the ECU, and the definition and conduct of a single monetary and exchange rate policy, the primary objective of both of which shall be to maintain price stability.

The Treaty goes on to state that the achievement of economic and monetary union shall have the following guiding principles: stable prices, sound public finances and monetary conditions and a sustainable balance of payments (Art. 3a(3) E.C.).

There is a marked difference between the means by which economic union is to be secured under the Treaty and the much stricter requirements envisaged for monetary union. This is reflected in their separate treatment in the amended E.C. Treaty. Chapter 1 of the new Title VI (Arts. 102a–104c E.C.) deals with economic policy, while Chap. 2 is dedicated to the monetary policy of the Community (Arts. 105–109 E.C.).

The movement towards the convergence of economic policies remains essentially decentralised. Article 103 E.C. highlights the extent to which the pressure for economic convergence rests upon the Member States themselves. It states that the Council shall, acting by a qualified majority on a recommendation from the Commission, formulate a draft setting out broad guidelines for the economic policies of the Member States and the Community and that it reports to the European Council. After the European Council has discussed a conclusion on the broad guidelines, the Council, acting by a qualified majority, must adopt a recommendation setting out the broad guidelines. Moreover, the Council shall, on the basis of reports from the Commission, monitor economic developments in each of the Member States, as well as the consistency of economic policies with the aforementioned broad guidelines. Should it appear to the Council that the Member States' policies are not consistent with the guidelines, then it may make the necessary recommendations to any Member State concerned, or make its recommendations public and thus apply some political pressure on the State (Art. 103(4) E.C.).

The main goal of the economic co-ordination provisions is the avoidance of excessive government deficits (Art. 104c(1) E.C. and appended Protocol No. 5). No sanctions are envisaged for non-compliance with this obligation during the second stage but, upon the coming into effect of the third stage, punitive measures may be applied in the last resort to States adjudged to have failed in the application of the guidelines (Art. 104c(11) E.C.).

In comparison with economic co-ordination, the path towards monetary union is truly deserving of the term "union". The final goal of an independent Central Bank overseeing a single currency will signal an almost absolute transfer of powers in monetary and exchange rate matters from the Member States to the European System of Central Banks and, to a lesser extent, to the Community institutions. The European Central Bank will be based in Frankfurt. It will control the money supply, interest rates and the exchange rate of the ECU. The Bank's decision-making bodies will be made up of bankers rather than politicians. The Bank's primary objective will be price stability. Politicians will not be tempted, or indeed be able, to adjust monetary policy to fit the short-term needs of the electoral cycles in the different Member States which participate in the single currency. The expectation is that low rates of inflation will be preserved more consistently than when politicians control monetary policy. The choice of Frankfurt as the seat of the Bank reflects the hope that it will retain something of the credibility of its forerunner in that city, the Bundesbank. The decision that Frankfurt would be the seat of the Bank was taken at Head of State and Government level in November 1993 (see [1993] O.J. C323/1).

The path mapped out at Maastricht towards economic and monetary union reflects the desire of at least 10 of the then 12 Member States to move rapidly towards full union, while retaining some of the flexibility of a staged process to give time to achieve the necessary economic convergence. The E.C. Treaty thus lays down a strict timetable for the achievement of economic and monetary union in three stages.

The first stage, already under way in 1991, had at its heart the pursuit of greater convergence between the economic performances of the Member States, with the aim of completing the internal market under Art. 8a EEC (now Art. 7a E.C.), thus providing the stepping stone towards the greater convergence of stage two.

The convergence in stage one of economic and monetary union was to be achieved through two inter-related initiatives. First, the liberalisation of capital flows was pursued through the dismantling of foreign exchange restrictions, largely as a result of Directive 88/361 ([1988] O.J. L178/5) implementing Article 67 EEC. Such liberalisation of the flow of capital tends to restrict the ability of national authorities to tinker with economic and monetary policy, thus making for a degree of market-led convergence.

Secondly, the Exchange Rate Mechanism (ERM) of the European Monetary System (EMS) attempted to lock exchange rates within fixed parameters, maintained by interest rate differentials in the Member States. (For a history and explanation of the EMS, established in March 1979, see Rey (1980) 17 C.M.L.Rev. 78). However, extreme pressure in the international capital markets in September 1992 led to the suspension of sterling and the lira from the ERM. It remains unclear to what extent this will affect the viability of the

ERM and planned progress towards economic and monetary union. While no provision in the Treaty expressly requires membership of the ERM as a precondition of movement to the second stage of economic and monetary union, the Treaty does make exchange rate stability a precursor of such a move. Nevertheless, the decision to alter the normal bandings of the ERM from 2.25 per cent to 15 per cent in the summer of 1993, as a result of further strains on the ERM, may well make compliance with one of the convergence criteria simpler. This states that one of the conditions for the move to the third stage is that the Member State's currency has "respected the normal fluctuation margins provided for by the ERM of the EMS without severe tensions for at least two years before the examination as to suitability for the third stage" (Art. 3 of the Protocol on the Convergence Criteria; Art. 109j E.C.).

The second stage of monetary union commenced on January 1, 1994 (Art. 109e(1) E.C.), and requires the Member States to complete the free movement of capital and payments, not only between themselves, but also between Member States and third countries (Art. 73b E.C.). Any derogations given to Greece and Portugal can continue up to December 31, 1995 at the latest (Art. 73e E.C.). Only Greece has been granted such a derogation ([1992] O.J. L409/33).

As already mentioned, during the second stage Member States are to endeavour to avoid excessive government deficits. No sanctions can be taken to enforce this until the third stage (Art. 109e (3) and (4) E.C.). Also relevant in terms of economic policy, the second stage marks the coming into force of other provisions intended to secure improved budgetary discipline in the Member States. These include a prohibition on the granting of credit facilities by the European Central Bank or any central bank, to governmental bodies or Community institutions (Art. 104) and the loss of privileged access of governmental and Community bodies to financial institutions (Art. 104a E.C.). Furthermore, the Community and Member States will be precluded from assuming the commitments of governmental bodies or public undertakings (Art. 10 4 E.C., the no-bailing out rule; see the annotation of this Art. below).

In the monetary sphere, the European Monetary Institute was established in Frankfurt at the beginning of the second stage. This body consists of the Governors of the national central banks, plus a President appointed by common accord of the Member States, from amongst persons of recognised professional experience in economic or monetary matters. The President is Professor Baron Alexandre Lamfalussy. The European Monetary Institute, itself without a great number of formal legal powers, will prepare the ground for the much more powerful European Central Bank to come into existence for the move to the third stage. The opinions and recommendations of the European Monetary Institute will have no binding force as regards the orientation of economic and monetary policy, but its role in "giving birth" to the European Central Bank will be paramount. The European Monetary Institute will, by December 31, 1996 at the latest, lay down the regulatory, organisational and logistical framework for the European Central Bank. Other functions of the European Monetary Institute will be to strengthen co-operation between the national central banks, to monitor the functioning of the EMS and to facilitate the use of the existing ECU (made up of a basket of the currencies of the Member States). Finally, as regards the second stage, each Member State is to start the process leading to the independence of its central bank (Art. 109e(5) E.C.).

The E.C. Treaty envisages that the third and final stage of economic and monetary union, with an independent Community central bank overseeing the single currency, will come into being, at the latest, on January 1, 1999 (Art. 109j(4) E.C.). Prior to this date, but not later than December 31, 1996, the Council, meeting in the composition of the Heads of Government and

217

State, can decide by a qualified majority to set an earlier date for the commencement of the third stage if a majority of the Member States achieve certain economic targets, which are the convergence criteria required for the third stage (Art. 109j(3) E.C.).

These criteria are laid down in Art. 109j E.C. and the annexed Protocol. The four targets, which may be applied with a degree of flexibility, are as follows; first, an average rate of inflation, observed over a period of one year before the examination, which does not exceed by more than 1.5 per cent the average of the three best performing States (Art. 1 of Protocol No. 6 on the Convergence Criteria); second, the avoidance of an excessive government budgetary deficit which is defined as meaning an annual budget deficit of less than 3 per cent of Gross Domestic Product and an overall public debt ratio not exceeding 60 per cent of Gross Domestic Product (Art. 1 of Protocol No. 5 on the Excessive Deficit Procedure); third, the Member State's currency must have stayed within the normal fluctuation margins in the ERM without severe tensions for at least two years prior to the period of the examination (Art. 3 of Protocol No. 6); and fourth, the Member State's average long-term interest rate, measured over a period of one year before the examination, must not exceed by more than 2 per cent the average interest rates in the three best performing States in terms of price stability (in other words, inflation rates) (Article 4 of Protocol No. 6).

The Council must determine which Member States have fulfilled the criteria by July 1, 1998. The third stage of economic and monetary union will then commence on January 1, 1999. While there is no specified minimum number of States which must have fulfilled these criteria for the move to the third stage to take place, it is unlikely that any system could function effectively without the participation of Germany and at least a core of the other Member States.

While the progress towards economic and monetary union is legally irrevocable, the U.K. and Denmark negotiated derogations or "opt-outs" at Maastricht as regards the third stage of economic and monetary union. In the U.K. this amounts to a proviso that parliamentary approval, based on a comprehensive up-to-date report on the progress of economic and monetary union, must be forthcoming before the U.K. can move towards the third stage (s.2, European Communities Act, 1993 (U.K.)). The Danish opt-out at Maastricht was essentially in the same terms, but assent is required in this case in the form of a special referendum. Nevertheless, at the Edinburgh European Council in December 1992, the Danish government committed itself to exercising its right to opt out. If the Danes were to choose to move to the third stage of economic and monetary union, however, they are still quite at liberty to apply to the Council under Art. 109k(2) E.C. for leave to enter.

1996 and enlargement

A unique feature of the TEU is that it pre-emptively convokes the next set of constitutional talks for 1996 (Art. N(2) E.U.). Art. B, E.U. declares that the purpose of this revision process will be to "maintain in full the *acquis communautaire* and build on it with a view to considering to what extent the policies and forms of co-operation introduced by this Treaty may need to be revised with the aim of ensuring the effectiveness of the mechanisms and the institutions of the Community." This wording reflects a concession to the more integrationist Member States, who wished to see the Maastricht intergovernmental conference process go beyond inter-governmental agreements in the fields of justice and home affairs and common foreign and security policy. It is also likely to be relied upon in the next inter-governmental conference as providing a basis for considering the rationalisation of the divergent legislative procedures applicable to the adoption of Community measures. Nevertheless, the inter-governmental conference in 1996 is not confined to these matters but has an open mandate. Certain areas, such as the extension of the conciliation and veto procedure (Art. 189b(8) E.C.), are expressly singled out as meriting attention, but the nature of the inter-governmental conference process precludes nothing from consideration. A Committee of Reflection is to be established under the Spanish Presidency in the later part of 1995, with nominees of each of the Member States and two nominees of the European Parliament, to consider possible avenues for constitutional development.

Prior even to the Treaty revision process envisaged for 1996, there was a real possibility that the accession of new States to the Community would provide an earlier opportunity for substantial amendment of the Treaties. This opportunity was not taken on the occasion of the EFTA enlargement, although the negotiation of Accession Agreements with Austria, Finland, Norway and Sweden was the occasion of a (largely unsuccessful) attempt by the U.K. to dilute the operation of qualified majority voting (see the annotation above of the European Communities Amendment Act, 1994; Norway later declined to join after a negative referendum result).

As of May 1993, the E.C. had received eight formal applications for membership: the four listed EFTA and Switzerland (also an EFTA State), Turkey, Cyprus (see COM(93) 312 final) and Malta (COM(93) 31 3 final). At least as many again have announced their intention of applying in the future, with the most obvious applicants being some of the Central and Eastern European and Baltic States. The Central and Eastern European states are envisaged as the second wave of new applicants, but accession is unlikely until after the end of the century. The fundamental problems that will be faced by any such enlargement have been well documented elsewhere. In the next stage of constitutional talks, the institutional challenges which enlargement will create, as well as the language and other difficulties, will have to be addressed. One of the primary discussions will concern the feasibility of maintaining the requirement of unanimity in the Council, this being difficult enough to secure in a Community of 12 or 15 far less 20, and possible adjustments to the number of votes required in the Council to achieve a qualified majority. (See E.C. Commission, *Europe and the Challenge of Enlargement*, E.C. Bull. Supplement 3/92; Ungerer, "Institutional Consequences of Broadening and Deepening the Community: The Consequences for the Decision-Making Process" (1993) 30 C.M.L.Rev. 71; European Parliament draft Constitution of the European Union, 1994 (Herman Report); Lamers, *Deutschlands außenpolitische Verantwortung und seine Interessen* (Bonn, 1993); Europäische Strukturkommission, *Reformbericht "Europa 96" zur Europäischen Union* (Mainz, 1994); Lamoussure, *Le Monde*, May 31, 1994).

On the TEU in general see O'Keeffe & Twomey eds., *Legal Issues of the Maastricht Treaty* (1993); Church and Phinnemore, *European Union and European Community* (1994); Dehousse ed., *Europe after Maastricht: An Ever Closer Union?* (1994); Holland, *European Integration: From Community to Union* (1994); Monar *et al* eds., *The Maastricht Treaty on European Union: Legal Complexity and Political Dynamic* (1993).

ABBREVIATIONS

COREPER	: Committee of Permanent Representatives
E.C.	: European Community
EEC	: European Economic Community
ECHR	: European Convention on Human Rights
ECOFIN	: Council of Finance Ministers
ECOSOC	: Economic and Social Committee
ECSC	: European Coal and Steel Community
EMS	: European Monetary System
ERM	: Exchange Rate Mechanism
Euratom	: European Atomic Energy Community
S.E.A.	: Single European Act
TEU	: Treaty on European Union

Treaty on European Union

TREATY ON EUROPEAN UNION

ADOPTED BY THE E.C. MEMBER STATES

(Done at Maastricht)   February 7, 1992

Entry into force: November 1, 1993
Territorial application: E.C. Member States

TABLE OF CONTENTS

Arrangement of Articles
Text of the Treaty

Arrangement of Articles

ARTICLE

TITLE I—*Common Provisions*

A   Establishment of European Union.
B   Objectives of Union.
C   Consistency and continuity of Union activities.
D   European Council.
E   Institutions governed by provisions in E.C. Treaty etc.
F   Respect for national identities of Member States and for fundamental rights.

TITLE II—*Provisions amending the EEC Treaty with a view to establishing the European Community*

G   Amendments to EEC Treaty, including change of name to E.C. Treaty [for content of amendments see E.C. Treaty above]

TITLE III—*Provisions amending the ECSC Treaty*

H   Amendments to ECSC Treaty [not included here]

TITLE IV—*Provisions amending the Euratom Treaty*

I   Amendments to Euratom Treaty [not included here]

TITLE V—*Provisions on a Common Foreign and Security Policy*

J   Establishment of a common foreign and security policy.
      J.1   Objectives; support by Member States.
      J.2   Co-ordination of Member States' action.
      J.3   Procedure for joint action.
      J.4   Defence; involvement of WEU.
      J.5   Representation of Union by the Presidency; responsibilities of Member States in international organisations of which only some Member States are members.

J.6   Co-operation by diplomatic and consular missions.
J.7   Consultation of European Parliament.
J.8   Role of European Council.
J.9   Involvement of E.C. Commission.
J.10   Review of security provisions.
J.11   Application of E.C. Treaty provisions on Parliament, Council & Commission; budget.

TITLE VI—*Provisions on Co-operation in the Fields of Justice and Home Affairs*

K   Introduction of co-operation in administration of civil, criminal & administrative justice and police.
K.1   Fields of co-operation.
K.2   Compliance with European Convention on Human Rights & Convention on Status of Refugees; Member States' responsibility for law and order.
K.3   Consultation between Member States; joint action by Council.
K.4   Co-ordinating Committee; involvement of Commission; voting in Council.
K.5   Member States' duties in international organisations.
K.6   Involvement of European Parliament.
K.7   Permissibility of closer co-operation between some Member States.
K.8   Application of E.C. Treaty provisions on Parliament, Council & Commission; budget.
K.9   Application of Article 100c of E.C. Treaty.

TITLE VII—*Final Provisions*

L   Limitation of extent of application of European Court's powers to this Treaty.
M   Saving of provisions of the Basic Treaties (E.C., ECSC, Euratom).
N   Treaty amendment.
O   Applications for new membership.
P   Repeal of certain provisions in Merger Treaty and Single European Act.
Q   Unlimited period of Treaty.
R   Ratification and entry into force.
S   Languages of authentic text.

PROTOCOLS
(All but Protocol 17 are appended in this book to the E.C. Treaty)

[1]   Danish law on acquisition of second homes.
[2]   Prospective effect of *Barber* ruling of the European Court re. Art. 119 E.C.
[3]   Statute of the European System of Central Banks (ESCB) and of the European Central Bank (ECB).

CHAPTER I: *Constitution of the ECSB*

1. The European System of Central Banks.

CHAPTER II: *Objectives and Tasks of the ECSB*

2. Objectives.
3. Tasks.
4. Advisory functions.
5. Collection of statistical information.
6. International co-operation.

CHAPTER III: *Organisation of the ECSB*

7. Independence.
8. General principle.
9. The European Central Bank.
10. The Governing Council.
11. The Executive Board.
12. Responsibilities of the decision-making bodies.
13. The President.
14. National central banks.
15. Reporting commitments.
16. Bank notes.

CHAPTER IV: *Monetary Functions and Operations of the ECSB*

17. Accounts with the ECB and the national central banks.
18. Open market and credit operations.
19. Minimum reserves.
20. Other instruments of monetary control.
21. Operations with public entities.
22. Clearing and payment systems.
23. External operations.
24. Other operations.

CHAPTER V: *Prudential supervision*

25. Prudential supervision.

CHAPTER VI: *Financial Provisions of the ESCB*

26. Financial accounts.
27. Auditing.
28. Capital of the ECB.
29. Key for capital subscription.
30. Transfer of foreign reserve assets to the ECB.
31. Foreign reserve assets held by national central banks.
32. Allocation of monetary income of national central banks.
33. Allocation of net profits and losses of the ECB.

CHAPTER VII: *General Provisions*

34. Legal acts.
35. Judicial control and related matters.
36. Staff.
37. Seat.
38. Professional secrecy.
39. Signatories.
40. Privileges and immunities.

CHAPTER VIII: *Amendment of the Statute and complementary legislation*

   41. Simplified amendment procedure.
   42. Complementary legislation.

CHAPTER IX: *Transitional and Other Provisions for the ECSB*

   43. General provisions.
   44. Transitional tasks of the ECB.
   45. The General Council of the ECB.
   46. Rules of procedure of the General Council.
   47. Responsibilities of the General Council.
   48. Transitional provisions for the capital of the ECB.
   49. Deferred payment of capital, reserves and provisions of the ECB.
   50. Initial appointment of the members of the Executive Board.
   51. Derogation from Article 32.
   52. Exchange of bank notes in Community currencies.
   53. Applicability of the transitional provisions.
[4]   Statute of the European Monetary Institute (EMI)
   1. Constitution and name.
   2. Objectives.
   3. General principles.
   4. Primary tasks.
   5. Advisory functions.
   6. Operational and technical functions.
   7. Other tasks.
   8. Independence.
   9. Administration.
   10. Meetings of the Council of the EMI and voting procedures.
   11. Interinstitutional co-operation and reporting requirements.
   12. Currency denomination.
   13. Seat.
   14. Legal capacity.
   15. Legal acts.
   16. Financial resources.
   17. Annual accounts and auditing.
   18. Staff.
   19. Judicial control and related matters.
   20. Professional secrecy.
   21. Privileges and immunities.
   22. Signatories.
   23. Liquidation of the EMI.
[5]   Excessive deficit procedure.
   1. Reference values under Article 104c of the E.C. Treaty.
   2. Definitions in Article 104c of the E.C. Treaty.
   3. Responsibility of Member States for deficits of general government.
   4. Statistical data.
[6]   Convergence criteria referred to in Article 109j of the E.C. Treaty.
   1. Criterion on price stability.
   2. Criterion on the government budgetary position.
   3. Criterion on participation in the Exchange Rate Mechanism.
   4. Criterion on the convergence of interest rates.
   5. Statistical data.
   6. Council's powers to legislate.

[7]   Amendment of Protocol on Privileges and Immunities.
[8]   Powers of the National Bank of Denmark regarding non-Community Danish territories.
[9]   Continuance of interest-free credit facility with Banco de Portugal for Azores and Madeira.
[10] Transition to Third Stage of Economic & Monetary Union.
[11] Special position of United Kingdom regarding Third Stage of EMU.
[12] Special position of Denmark regarding Third Stage of EMU.
[13] French privilege of monetary emission in its overseas territories.
[14] Adoption of Agreement on Social Policy between 11 Member States (excluding U.K.).
      1. Social objectives.
      2. Community powers.
      3. Commission powers.
      4. Collective agreements between management and labour; homologation by Council decisions.
      5. Co-operation between Member States.
      6. Equal pay for equal work.
      7. Annual progress report.
Declaration on Article 2(2).
Declaration on Article 4(2).
[15] Economic and Social Cohesion.
[16] Economic & Social Committee and Committee of the Regions to have common organisational structure.
[17] Saving of Article 40.3.3. (anti-abortion amendment) of the Irish Constitution.

DECLARATIONS
(Declarations 1–26 are appended in this book to the E.C. Treaty)

(1)   Civil protection, energy and tourism.
(2)   Nationality of a Member State.
(3)   Part 3, Titles III & VI of the E.C. Treaty (meeting of Finance Council).
(4)   Part 3, Title VI of the E.C. Treaty (attendance of Finance Ministers at meetings of European Council when discussing EMU matters).
(5)   Monetary co-operation with non-Community countries.
(6)   Monetary relations with San Marino, Vatican City & Monaco.
(7)   Art. 73d E.C. Treaty: standstill for certain national tax laws.
(8)   Art. 109 E.C. Treaty: use of term 'formal agreements.'
(9)   Part 3, Title XVI of the E.C. Treaty (nature conservation).
(10) Arts. 109, 130r & 130y E.C. Treaty: saving of the rules laid down by the European Court in the *E.R.T.A.* case.
(11) Maintenance of derogations to Spain & Portugal under the Emissions Directive 88/609.
(12) Financing of European Development Fund.
(13) Role of national Parliaments in the European Union.
(14) Conference of the Parliaments.
(15) Number of members of the Commission and European Parliament.
(16) Hierarchy of Community acts.
(17) Right of access to information.
(18) Estimated costs to be included in Commission proposals.
(19) Implementation of Community law by Member States.
(20) Environmental impact assessment statement to be included in Commission proposals.

(21) Court of Auditors.
(22) Economic & Social Committee budget and staff management.
(23) Co-operation with charitable associations.
(24) Protection of animals.
(25) Representation of the interests of overseas countries & territories.
(26) The outermost regions of the Community (French overseas departments, Azores, Madeira, Canary Is.).
(27) Voting in the field of the common foreign & security policy.
(28) Practical arrangements in the field of the common foreign & security policy.
(29) Use of languages in the field of the common foreign & security policy.
(30) Western European Union I & II.
(31) Asylum.
(32) Police co-operation.
(33) Disputes between the ECB & the EMI and their servants.

THE TREATY

[The Heads of State of Belgium, Denmark, Germany, Greece, Spain, France, Ireland, Italy, Luxembourg, the Netherlands, Portugal and the United Kingdom]

RESOLVED to mark a new stage in the process of European integration undertaken with the establishment of the European Communities,

RECALLING the historic importance of the ending of the division of the European continent and the need to create firm bases for the construction of the future Europe,

CONFIRMING their attachment to the principles of liberty, democracy and respect for human rights and fundamental freedoms and of the rule of law,

DESIRING to deepen the solidarity between their peoples while respecting their history, their culture and their traditions,

DESIRING to enhance further the democratic and efficient functioning of the institutions so as to enable them better to carry out, within a single institutional framework, the tasks entrusted to them,

RESOLVED to achieve the strengthening and the convergence of their economies and to establish an economic and monetary union including, in accordance with the provisions of this Treaty, a single and stable currency,

DETERMINED to promote economic and social progress for their peoples, within the context of the accomplishment of the internal market and of reinforced cohesion and environmental protection, and to implement policies ensuring that advances in economic integration are accompanied by parallel progress in other fields,

RESOLVED to establish a citizenship common to nationals of their countries,

RESOLVED to implement a common foreign and security policy including the eventual framing of a common defence policy, which might in time lead to a common defence, thereby reinforcing the European identity and its independence in order to promote peace, security and progress in Europe and in the world,

REAFFIRMING their objective to facilitate the free movement of persons, while ensuring the safety and security of their peoples, by including provisions on justice and home affairs in this Treaty,

RESOLVED to continue the process of creating an ever closer union among the peoples of Europe, in which decisions are taken as closely as possible to the citizen in accordance with the principle of subsidiarity,

IN VIEW of further steps to be taken in order to advance European integration,

HAVE DECIDED to establish a European Union and to this end have designated [their plenipotentiaries]

WHO, having exchanged their full powers, found in good and due form, have agreed as follows:

TITLE I

Common Provisions

Article A

By this Treaty, the High Contracting Parties establish among themselves a European Union, hereinafter called "the Union."

This Treaty marks a new stage in the process of creating an ever closer union among the peoples of Europe, in which decisions are taken as closely as possible to the citizen.

The Union shall be founded on the European Communities, supplemented by the policies and forms of co-operation established by this Treaty. Its task shall be to organise, in a manner demonstrating consistency and solidarity, relations between the Member States and between their peoples.

Article B

The Union shall set itself the following objectives:
— to promote economic and social progress which is balanced and sustainable, in particular through the creation of an area without internal frontiers, through the strengthening of economic and social cohesion and through the establishment of economic and monetary union, ultimately including a single currency in accordance with the provisions of this Treaty;
— to assert its identity on the international scene, in particular through the implementation of a common foreign and security policy including the eventual framing of a common defence policy, which might in time lead to a common defence;
— to strengthen the protection of the rights and interests of the nationals of its Member States through the introduction of a citizenship of the Union;
— to develop close co-operation on justice and home affairs;
— to maintain in full the "*acquis communautaire*" and build on it with a view to considering, through the procedure referred to in Article N(2), to what extent the policies and forms of co-operation introduced by this Treaty may need to be revised with the aim of ensuring the effectiveness of the mechanisms and the institutions of the Community.

The objectives of the Union shall be achieved as provided in this Treaty and in accordance with the conditions and the timetable set out therein while respecting the principle of subsidiarity as defined in Article 3b of the Treaty establishing the European Community.

Article C

The Union shall be served by a single institutional framework which shall ensure the consistency and the continuity of the activities carried out in order to attain its objectives while respecting and building upon the "*acquis communautaire*."

The Union shall in particular ensure the consistency of its external activities as a whole in the context of its external relations, security, economic and development policies. The Council and the Commission shall be responsible for ensuring such consistency. They shall ensure the implementation of these policies, each in accordance with its respective powers.

Article D

The European Council shall provide the Union with the necessary impetus for its development and shall define the general political guidelines thereof.

The European Council shall bring together the Heads of State or of Government of the Member States and the President of the Commission.

They shall be assisted by the Ministers for Foreign Affairs of the Member States and by a Member of the Commission. The European Council shall meet at least twice a year, under the chairmanship of the Head of State or of Government of the Member State which holds the Presidency of the Council.

The European Council shall submit to the European Parliament a report after each of its meetings and a yearly written report on the progress achieved by the Union.

Article E

The European Parliament, the Council, the Commission and the Court of Justice shall exercise their powers under the conditions and for the purposes provided for, on the one hand, by the provisions of the Treaties establishing the European Communities and of the subsequent Treaties and Acts modifying and supplementing them and, on the other hand, by the other provisions of this Treaty.

Article F

1. The Union shall respect the national identities of its Member States, whose systems of government are founded on the principles of democracy.

2. The Union shall respect fundamental rights, as guaranteed by the European Convention for the Protection of Human Rights and Fundamental Freedoms signed in Rome on November 4, 1950 and as they result from the constitutional traditions common to the Member States, as general principles of Community law.

3. The Union shall provide itself with the means necessary to attain its objectives and carry through its policies.

GENERAL NOTE

The jurisprudence of the Court of Justice in the field of human rights may demonstrate that there is something which may well assume relevance in the context of the review of the Maastricht Treaty by the Inter-Governmental conference next year. There is now a very considerable literature on this topic. For fuller treatments of this complex theme, see generally, Dauses, "The Protection of Fundamental Rights in the Community Legal Order" (1985) 10 E.L.R. 398; Shermers, "The Scales in the Balance: National Constitutional Court v. Court of Justice" (1990) 27 C.M.L.Rev. 669; Lenaerts, "Fundamental Rights to be Included in a Community Catalogue" (1991) 16 E.L.R. 367; Coppel and O'Neil, "The European Court of Justice: Taking Rights Seriously?" (1992) 29 C.M.L.Rev. 669; Jacobs, "The Protection of Human Rights in the Member States of the E.C.: the impact of the case law of the Court of Justice in O'Reilly" ed., *Human Rights and Constitutional Law: Essays in Honour of Brian Walsh* (Dublin, 1992) p.243; de Burca "Fundamental Human Rights and the Reach of Community Law" (1993) 13 *Oxford Journal of Legal Studies* 283; Twomey, "The European Union: Three Pillars without a Human Rights Foundation" in O'Keeffe and Twomey eds., *Legal Issues of the Maastricht Treaty* (London, 1939), p.121; van Hamme, "Human Rights and the Treaty of Rome" in Heffernan ed., *Human Rights: A European Perspective* (Dublin, 1994) p.70; Weiler and Lockhart, "'Taking Rights Seriously' seriously: the European Court and its Fundamental Rights Jurisprudence" (1995) 32 C.M.L.Rev. 51; O'Leary, "The Relationship between Community Citizenship and the Protection of Fundamental Rights in Community Law" (1995) 32 C.M.L.Rev. 519.

The precise legal source of the Court of Justice's authority to protect those fundamental rights is somewhat obscure. Some commentators point to Art. 164:

> "The Court of Justice shall ensure that in the interpretation and application of this Treaty the law is observed."

Thus, in *R. v. Ministry of Agriculture, ex p. Bostock*, Advocate General Gulmann appeared to suggest that Art. 164 was the foundation of the Court of Justice's fundamental rights jurisprudence: see [1994] E.C.R. I-955, 971. As one distinguished Advocate General has put it:

> "The Court has based its case law ... on the very general provision of Article 164 ... which requires the Court to ensure that in the interpretation and application of the Treaty the law is observed. 'The law' here is taken to refer to the common legal heritage of the Member States including the general principles recognised in the national legal systems."

(See Jacobs, "The Protection of Human Rights in the Member States of the European Community" in O'Reilly ed., *Human Rights and Constitutional Law* (Dublin, 1992) p.243). This however, seems a rather dubious basis for such a wide-ranging jurisprudence. At best the phrase "the law is observed" is a reference to the general principle of legality and not—as it is increasingly becoming—to the indirect incorporation of the ECHR in cases involving discretionary national administrative acts which impact on Community law rights. Had the drafters of the Treaty intended that the Court of Justice should protect certain unenumerated fundamental rights, then one would have expected that phrases such as "general principles of law are observed and the fundamental human rights are protected" would have been used instead of the present language of Article 164.

There have been political developments at Community level which, it might be argued, have given implicit sanction to these judicial developments. First, in April 1989 the European Parliament adopted a further Declaration of Fundamental Rights and Freedoms: [1989] O.J. C 120/51. This Declaration is, like the earlier 1977 Declaration, largely aspirational in character and symbolic in its effect. Nevertheless, such a Declaration clearly adds further momentum to this process. More importantly, Article F(2) of the Maastrich Treaty now attempts to re-state, albeit in a non-justiciable form, the principles governing the protection of fundamental rights by the Court of Justice. There is thus the remarkable situation whereby the Court of Justice has assumed a human rights jurisdiction which has no self-evident legal basis. It is true that Article F(2) re-states in codified form the actual pronouncements of the Court of Justice in the Human rights area, but the drafters of the Maastricht Treaty expressly refrained from conferring such a jurisdiction on the Court. Why, therefore, should the Court now seek to read an unwritten bill of rights into Community law when the drafters of Europe's constitutional treaties expressly refrained from conferring such a jurisdiction on the Court? What is equally extraordinary is that few of the commentators have stopped to query the legitimacy of this entire jurisprudence. The commentators are divided on the question of whether the Court of Justice is simply using the human rights issue defensively and as a strategy to safeguard its own supremacy doctrine or whether the Court is genuinely committed to the development and protection of human rights. See in this regard the views of Coppel and O'Neill, "The European Court of Justice: Taking Rights Seriously?" (1992) 29 C.M.L.Rev. 669 and the response of Weiler and Lockhart, " 'Taking Rights Seriously': the European Court and its Fundamental Rights Jurisprudence" (1995) 32 C.M.L.Rev. 51, 579.

As far as future developments are concerned, there is at present a proposal from the European Council that the E.C. itself should become a member of the ECHR and the Court of Justice has been asked to give an opinion under Art. 228 of the Treaty of Rome. There would seem to be at least two legal difficulties with this proposal. First, the E.C. is not a "State" in the manner originally understood by the ECHR. Secondly, the judicial autonomy of the Court of Justice as final arbiter of all decisions of E.C. law might be compromised if its decisions could effectively be reviewed by the European Court of Human Rights. There are direct analogies here with the Court of Justice's decision in Opinion 1/91 *Opinion on the Draft Agreement on a European Economic Area* [1992] E.C.R. I-6079. In this case the Court of Justice held that a proposal to create a new E.C.-EFTA Court (composed of judges drawn from the Court of Justice and the EFTA states) which would have had jurisdiction to adjudicate on trade and competition issues arising out of the Economic Area Agreement between the E.C. and EFTA would be contrary to fundamental principles of Community law, since it jeopardised the institutional autonomy of the Court of Justice as the final judicial arbiter within the Community on such issues. Nevertheless, the Court's opinion contains a passage which suggests that ratification of the ECHR by the Community would not, in principle, at least, be contrary to E.C. Law:

> "Where, however, an international agreement provides for its own system of courts, including a court with jurisdiction to settle disputes between the Contracting Parties to the agreement, and, as a result, to interpret its provisions, the decisions of that Court will be binding

on the Community institutions, including the Court of Justice … An international agreement providing for such a system of courts is in principle compatible with Community law. The Community's competence in the field of international relations and its capacity to conclude international agreements necessarily entails the power to submit to the decisions of a court which is created or designed by such an agreement as regards the interpretation and application of its provisions."

And while it is true that Article 230 of the Treaty of Rome provides that the Community "shall establish all appropriate forms of co-operation with the Council of Europe", this provision of itself would not appear to be sufficient to overcome these difficulties.

Perhaps the best solution would be for the E.C. to adopt its own Bill of Rights. This, however, would certainly meet with political objections from the United Kingdom and, perhaps, from some other Member States. The present U.K. Government believes that the Court of Justice already has too much power and they would almost certainly object to a proposal, the practical effect of which would be to make the ECHR (or some E.C. variant thereof) part of a revised version of the Maastricht Treaty. And while this may be happening in part in practice anyhow—given that the Court of Justice's jurisprudence has, in effect, sanctioned the indirect incorporation of the ECHR in those cases where national legislation inter-acts with Community law—the political obstacles are formidable. The "Euro-sceptics" in the United Kindom would doubtless see the adoption of such a Bill of Rights as a further step in the direction of a European super-state.

TITLE II

Provisions Amending the Treaty Establishing the European Economic Community with a View to Establishing The European Community

Article G

The Treaty establishing the European Economic Community shall be amended in accordance with the provisions of this Article, in order to establish a European Community.

GENERAL NOTE

The amendments to the E.E.C. Treaty transforming it into the E.C. Treaty are incorporated into the text of the E.C. Treaty or set out above and are explained in the annotations.

TITLE III

Provisions Amending the Treaty Establishing The European Coal and Steel Community

Article H

The Treaty establishing the European Coal and Steel Community shall be amended in accordance with the provisions of this Article.

GENERAL NOTE

The amendments to this Treaty are not reproduced or commented upon here due to the relatively narrow scope of their applicability.

TITLE IV

Provisions Amending the Treaty Establishing The European Atomic Energy Community

Article I

The Treaty establishing the European Atomic Energy Community shall be amended in accordance with the provisions of this Article.

GENERAL NOTE

The amendments to this Treaty are not reproduced or commented upon here due to the relatively narrow scope of their applicability.

TITLE V

Provisions on a Common Foreign and Security Policy

Article J

A common foreign and security policy is hereby established which shall be governed by the following provisions.

Article J.1

1. The Union and its Member States shall define and implement a common foreign and security policy, governed by the provisions of this Title and covering all areas of foreign and security policy.
2. The objectives of the common foreign and security policy shall be:
   — to safeguard the common values, fundamental interests and independence of the Union;
   — to strengthen the security of the Union and its Member States in all ways;
   — to preserve peace and strengthen international security, in accordance with the principles of the United Nations Charter as well as the principles of the Helsinki Final Act and the objectives of the Paris Charter;
   — to promote international co-operation;
   — to develop and consolidate democracy and the rule of law, and respect for human rights and fundamental freedoms.
3. The Union shall pursue these objectives:
   — by establishing systematic co-operation between Member States in the conduct of policy, in accordance with Article J.2;
   — by gradually implementing, in accordance with Article J.3, joint action in the areas in which the Member States have important interests in common.
4. The Member States shall support the Union's external and security policy actively and unreservedly in a spirit of loyalty and mutual solidarity. They shall refrain from any action which is contrary to the interests of the Union or likely to impair its effectiveness as a cohesive force in international relations. The Council shall ensure that these principles are complied with.

Article J.2

1. Member States shall inform and consult one another within the Council on any matter of foreign and security policy of general interest in order to ensure that their combined influence is exerted as effectively as possible by means of concerted and convergent action.
2. Whenever it deems it necessary, the Council shall define a common position.
Member States shall ensure that their national policies conform to the common positions.
3. Member States shall co-ordinate their action in international organisations and at international conferences. They shall uphold the common positions in such fora.
In international organisations and at international conferences where not all the Member States participate, those which do take part shall uphold the common positions.

Article J.3

The procedure for adopting joint action in matters covered by the foreign and security policy shall be the following:
1. The Council shall decide, on the basis of general guidelines from the European Council, that a matter should be the subject of joint action.
   Whenever the Council decides on the principle of joint action, it

shall lay down the specific scope, the Union's general and specific objectives in carrying out such action, if necessary its duration, and the means, procedures and conditions for its implementation.

2. The Council shall, when adopting the joint action and at any stage during its development, define those matters on which decisions are to be taken by a qualified majority.

[Where the Council is required to act by a qualified majority pursuant to the preceding subparagraph, the votes of its members shall be weighted in accordance with Article 148(2) of the Treaty establishing the European Community, and, for their adoption, acts of the Council shall require at least 62 votes in favour, cast by at least 10 members.]

3. If there is a change in circumstances having a substantial effect on a question subject to joint action, the Council shall review the principles and objectives of that action and take the necessary decisions. As long as the Council has not acted, the joint action shall stand.

4. Joint actions shall commit the Member States in the positions they adopt and in the conduct of their activity.

5. Whenever there is any plan to adopt a national position or take national action pursuant to a joint action, information shall be provided in time to allow, if necessary, for prior consultations within the Council. The obligation to provide prior information shall not apply to measures which are merely a national transposition of Council decisions.

6. In cases of imperative need arising from changes in the situation and failing a Council decision, Member States may take the necessary measures as a matter of urgency having regard to the general objectives of the joint action. The Member State concerned shall inform the Council immediately of any such measures.

7. Should there be any major difficulties in implementing a joint action, a Member State shall refer them to the Council which shall discuss them and seek appropriate solutions. Such solutions shall not run counter to the objectives of the joint action or impair its effectiveness.

GENERAL NOTE

The amendments in paragraph 2 were made by the Act of Accession [1994] O.J. C241/08.

Article J.4

1. The common foreign and security policy shall include all questions related to the security of the Union, including the eventual framing of a common defence policy, which might in time lead to a common defence.

2. The Union requests the Western European Union (WEU), which is an integral part of the development of the Union, to elaborate and implement decisions and actions of the Union which have defence implications. The Council shall, in agreement with the institutions of the WEU, adopt the necessary practical arrangements.

3. Issues having defence implications dealt with under this Article shall not be subject to the procedures set out in Article J.3.

4. The policy of the Union in accordance with this Article shall not prejudice the specific character of the security and defence policy of certain Member States and shall respect the obligations of certain Member States under the North Atlantic Treaty and be compatible with the common security and defence policy established within that framework.

5. The provisions of this Article shall not prevent the development of closer co-operation between two or more Member States on a bilateral level, in the framework of the WEU and the Atlantic Alliance, provided such co-operation does not run counter to or impede that provided for in this Title.

6. With a view to furthering the objective of this Treaty, and having in view the date of 1998 in the context of Article XII of the Brussels Treaty, the provisions of this Article may be revised as provided for in Article N(2) on the basis of a report to be presented in 1996 by the Council to the European Council, which shall include an evaluation of the progress made and the experience gained until then.

Article J.5

1. The Presidency shall represent the Union in matters coming within the common foreign and security policy.

2. The Presidency shall be responsible for the implementation of common measures; in that capacity it shall in principle express the position of the Union in international organisations and international conferences.

3. In the tasks referred to in paragraphs 1 and 2, the Presidency shall be assisted if need be by the previous and next Member States to hold the Presidency. The Commission shall be fully associated in these tasks.

4. Without prejudice to Article J.2(3) and Article J.3(4), Member States represented in international organisations or international conferences where not all the Member States participate shall keep the latter informed of any matter of common interest.

Member States which are also members of the United Nations Security Council will concert and keep the other Member States fully informed. Member States which are permanent members of the Security Council will, in the execution of their functions, ensure the defence of the positions and the interests of the Union, without prejudice to their responsibilities under the provisions of the United Nations Charter.

Article J.6

The diplomatic and consular missions of the Member States and the Commission Delegations in third countries and international conferences, and their representations to international organisations, shall co-operate in ensuring that the common positions and common measures adopted by the Council are complied with and implemented.

They shall step up co-operation by exchanging information, carrying out joint assessments and contributing to the implementation of the provisions referred to in Article 8c of the Treaty establishing the European Community.

Article J.7

The Presidency shall consult the European Parliament on the main aspects and the basic choices of the common foreign and security policy and shall ensure that the views of the European Parliament are duly taken into consideration. The European Parliament shall be kept regularly informed by the Presidency and the Commission of the development of the Union's foreign and security policy.

The European Parliament may ask questions of the Council or make recommendations to it. It shall hold an annual debate on progress in implementing the common foreign and security policy.

Article J.8

1. The European Council shall define the principles of and general guidelines for the common foreign and security policy.

2. The Council shall take the decisions necessary for defining and implementing the common foreign and security policy on the basis of the general guidelines adopted by the European Council. It shall ensure the unity, consistency and effectiveness of action by the Union.

The Council shall act unanimously, except for procedural questions and in the case referred to in Article J.3(2).

3. Any Member State or the Commission may refer to the Council any question relating to the common foreign and security policy and may submit proposals to the Council.

4. In cases requiring a rapid decision, the Presidency, of its own motion, or at the request of the Commission or a Member State, shall convene an extraordinary council meeting within 48 hours or, in an emergency, within a shorter period.

5. Without prejudice to Article 151 of the Treaty establishing the European Community, a Political Committee consisting of Political Directors shall monitor the international situation in the areas covered by common foreign and security policy and contribute to the definition of policies by delivering opinions to the Council at the request of the Council or on its own initiative. It shall also monitor the implementation of agreed policies, without prejudice to the responsibility of the Presidency and the Commission.

Article J.9

The Commission shall be fully associated with the work carried out in the common foreign and security policy field.

Article J.10

On the occasion of any review of the security provisions under Article J.4, the conference which is convened to that effect shall also examine whether any other amendments need to be made to provisions relating to the common foreign and security policy.

Article J.11

1. The provisions referred to in Articles 137, 138, 139 to 142, 146, 147, 150 to 153, 157 to 163 and 217 of the Treaty establishing the European Community shall apply to the provisions relating to the areas referred to in this Title.

2. Administrative expenditure which the provisions relating to the areas referred to in this Title entail for the institutions shall be charged to the budget of the European Communities.

The Council may also:

— either decide unanimously that operating expenditure to which the implementation of those provisions gives rise is to be charged to the budget of the European Communities; in that event, the budgetary procedure laid down in the Treaty establishing the European Community shall be applicable;

— or determine that such expenditure shall be charged to the Member States, where appropriate in accordance with a scale to be decided.

TITLE VI

Provisions on Co-operation
in the Fields of Justice and Home Affairs

Article K

Co-operation in the fields of justice and home affairs shall be governed by the following provisions.

Article K.1

For the purposes of achieving the objectives of the Union, in particular the free movement of persons, and without prejudice to the powers of the European Community, Member States shall regard the following areas as matters of common interest:

1. asylum policy;
2. rules governing the crossing by persons of the external borders of the Member States and the exercise of controls thereon;
3. immigration policy and policy regarding nationals of third countries:
    (a) conditions of entry and movement by nationals of third countries to the territory of Member States;
    (b) conditions of residence by nationals of third countries on the territory of Member States, including family reunion and access to employment;
    (c) combating unauthorised immigration, residence and work by nationals of third countries on the territory of Member States;
4. combating drug addiction in so far as this is not covered by 7 to 9.
5. combating fraud on an international scale in so far as this is not covered by 7 to 9;
6. judicial co-operation in civil matters;
7. judicial co-operation in criminal matters;
8. customs co-operation;
9. police co-operation for the purposes of preventing and combating terrorism, unlawful drug trafficking and other serious forms of international crime, including if necessary certain aspects of customs co-operation, in connection with the organisation of a Union-wide system for exchanging information within a European Police Office (Europol).

Article K.2

1. The matters referred to in Article K.1 shall be dealt with in compliance with the European Convention for the Protection of Human Rights and Fundamental Freedoms of November 4, 1950 and the Convention relating to the Status of Refugees of July 28, 1951 and having regard to the protection afforded by Member States to persons persecuted on political grounds.

2. This Title shall not affect the exercise of the responsibilities incumbent upon Member States with regard to the maintenance of law and order and the safeguarding of internal security.

Article K.3

1. In the areas referred to in Article K.1, Member States shall inform and consult one another within the Council with a view to co-ordinating their action. To that end, they shall establish collaboration between the relevant departments of their administrations.

2. The Council may:
    — on the initiative of any Member State or of the Commission, in the areas referred to in Article K.1(1) to (6);
    — on the initiative of any Member State, in the areas referred to in Article K.1(7) to (9):
    (a) adopt joint positions and promote, using the appropriate form and procedures, any co-operation contributing to the pursuit of the objectives of the Union;
    (b) adopt joint action in so far as the objectives of the Union can be attained better by joint action than by the Member States acting individually on account of the scale or effects of the action envisaged; it may decide that measures implementing joint action are to be adopted by a qualified majority;
    (c) without prejudice to Article 220 of the Treaty establishing the European Community, draw up conventions which it shall recommend to the Member States for adoption in accordance with their respective constitutional requirements.

234

Unless otherwise provided by such conventions, measures implementing them shall be adopted within the Council by a majority of two-thirds of the High Contracting Parties.

Such conventions may stipulate that the Court of Justice shall have jurisdiction to interpret their provisions and to rule on any disputes regarding their application, in accordance with such arrangements as they may lay down.

Article K.4

1. A Co-ordinating Committee shall be set up consisting of senior officials. In addition to its co-ordinating role, it shall be the task of the Committee to:
— give opinions for the attention of the Council, either at the Council's request or on its own initiative;
— contribute, without prejudice to Article 151 of the Treaty establishing the European Community, to the preparation of the Council's discussions in the areas referred to in Article K.1 and, in accordance with the conditions laid down in Article 100d of the Treaty establishing the European Community, in the areas referred to in Article 100c of that Treaty.

2. The Commission shall be fully associated with the work in the areas referred to in this Title.

3. The Council shall act unanimously, except on matters of procedure and in cases where Article K.3 expressly provides for other voting rules.

[Where the Council is required to act by a qualified majority, the votes of its members shall be weighted as laid down in Article 148(2) of the Treaty establishing the European Community, and, for their adoption, acts of the Council shall require at least 62 votes in favour, cast by at least 10 members.]

GENERAL NOTE

The amendments in paragraph 3 were made by the Act of Accession [1994] O.J. C241/08; [1995] O.J. L1/1.

Article K.5

Within international organisations and at international conferences in which they take part, Member States shall defend the common positions adopted under the provisions of this Title.

Article K.6

The Presidency and the Commission shall regularly inform the European Parliament of discussions in the areas covered by this Title.

The Presidency shall consult the European Parliament on the principal aspects of activities in the areas referred to in this Title and shall ensure that the views of the European Parliament are duly taken into consideration.

The European Parliament may ask questions of the Council or make recommendations to it. Each year, it shall hold a debate on the progress made in implementation of the areas referred to in this Title.

Article K.7

The provisions of this Title shall not prevent the establishment or development of closer co-operation between two or more Member States in so far as such co-operation does not conflict with, or impede, that provided for in this Title.

Article K.8

1. The provisions referred to in Articles 137, 138, 139 to 142, 146, 147, 150 to 153, 157 to 163 and 217 of the Treaty establishing the European Com-

munity shall apply to the provisions relating to the areas referred to in this Title.

2. Administrative expenditure which the provisions relating to the areas referred to in this Title entail for the institutions shall be charged to the budget of the European Communities.

The Council may also:

— either decide unanimously that operating expenditure to which the implementation of those provisions gives rise is to be charged to the budget of the European Communities; in that event, the budgetary procedure laid down in the Treaty establishing the European Community shall be applicable;

— or determine that such expenditure shall be charged to the Member States, where appropriate in accordance with a scale to be decided.

Article K.9

The Council, acting unanimously on the initiative of the Commission or a Member State, may decide to apply Article 100c of the Treaty establishing the European Community to action in areas referred to in Article K.1(1) to (6), and at the same time determine the relevant voting conditions relating to it. It shall recommend the Member States to adopt that decision in accordance with their respective constitutional requirements.

TITLE VII

Final Provisions

Article L

The provisions of the Treaty establishing the European Community, the Treaty establishing the European Coal and Steel Community and the Treaty establishing the European Atomic Energy Community concerning the powers of the Court of Justice of the European Communities and the exercise of those powers shall apply only to the following provisions of this Treaty:

(a) provisions amending the Treaty establishing the European Economic Community with a view to establishing the European Community, the Treaty establishing the European Coal and Steel Community and the Treaty establishing the European Atomic Energy Community;

(b) the third subparagraph of Article K.3(2)(c);

(c) Articles L to S.

Article M

Subject to the provisions amending the Treaty establishing the European Economic Community with a view to establishing the European Community, the Treaty establishing the European Coal and Steel Community and the Treaty establishing the European Atomic Energy Community, and to these final provisions, nothing in this Treaty shall affect the Treaties establishing the European Communities or the subsequent Treaties and Acts modifying or supplementing them.

Article N

1. The government of any Member State or the Commission may submit to the Council proposals for the amendment of the Treaties on which the Union is founded.

If the Council, after consulting the European Parliament and, where appropriate, the Commission, delivers an opinion in favour of calling a conference of representatives of the governments of the Member States, the conference shall be convened by the President of the Council for the purpose of determining by common accord the amendments to be made to those

Treaties. The European Central Bank shall also be consulted in the case of institutional changes in the monetary area.

The amendments shall enter into force after being ratified by all the Member States in accordance with their respective constitutional requirements.

2. A conference of representatives of the governments of the Member States shall be convened in 1996 to examine those provisions of this Treaty for which revision is provided, in accordance with the objectives set out in Articles A and B.

Article O

Any European State may apply to become a Member of the Union. It shall address its application to the Council, which shall act unanimously after consulting the Commission and after receiving the assent of the European Parliament, which shall act by an absolute majority of its component members.

The conditions of admission and the adjustments to the Treaties on which the Union is founded which such admission entails shall be the subject of an agreement between the Member States and the applicant State. This agreement shall be submitted for ratification by all the Contracting States in accordance with their respective constitutional requirements.

GENERAL NOTE

Articles N and O of the TEU are considered below in the General Note on the repealed Arts. 236 and 237 of the E.E.C. Treaty.

Article P

1. Articles 2 to 7 and 10 to 19 of the Treaty establishing a single Council and a single Commission of the European Communities, signed in Brussels on 8 April 1965, are hereby repealed.

2. Article 2, Article 3(2) and Title III of the Single European Act signed in Luxembourg on February 17, 1986 and in The Hague on February 28, 1986 are hereby repealed.

Article Q

This Treaty is concluded for an unlimited period.

Article R

1. This Treaty shall be ratified by the High Contracting Parties in accordance with their respective constitutional requirements. The instruments of ratification shall be deposited with the government of the Italian Republic.

2. This Treaty shall enter into force on January 1, 1993, provided that all the instruments of ratification have been deposited, or, failing that, on the first day of the month following the deposit of the instrument of ratification by the last signatory State to take this step.

Article S

This Treaty, drawn up in a single original in the Danish, Dutch, English, French, German, Greek, Irish, Italian, Portuguese and Spanish languages, the texts in each of these languages being equally authentic, shall be deposited in the archives of the government of the Italian Republic, which will transmit a certified copy to each of the governments of the other signatory States.

PROTOCOL ANNEXED TO THE TREATY ON EUROPEAN UNION AND TO THE TREATIES ESTABLISHING THE EUROPEAN COMMUNITIES

Nothing in the Treaty on European Union, or in the Treaties establishing the European Communites, or in the Treaties or Acts modifying or supplementing those Treaties, shall affect the application in Ireland of Article 40.3.3. of the Constitution of Ireland.

On May 1, 1992, in Guimaräes (Portugal), the High Contracting Parties to the Treaty on European Union adopted the following Declaration:

DECLARATION OF THE HIGH CONTRACTING PARTIES TO THE TREATY ON EUROPEAN UNION

The High Contracting Parties to the Treaty on European Union signed at Maastricht on the seventh day of February 1992.

Having considered the terms of Protocol No. 17 to the said Treaty on European Union which is annexed to that Treaty and to the Treaties establishing the European Communities,

Hereby give the following legal interpretation:

That it was and is their intention that the Protocol shall not limit freedom to travel between Member States or, in accordance with conditions which may be laid down, in conformity with Community law, by Irish legislation, to obtain or make available in Ireland information relating to services lawfully available in Member States.

At the same time the High Contracting Parties solemnly declare that, in the event of a future constitutional amendment in Ireland which concerns the subject matter of Article 40.3.3 of the Constitution of Ireland and which does not conflict with the intention of the High Contracting Parties hereinbefore expressed, they will, following the entry into force of the Treaty on European Union, be favourably disposed to amending the said Protocol so as to extend its application to such constitutional amendment if Ireland so requests.

DECLARATIONS 27–32 OF THE TREATY ON EUROPEAN UNION

DECLARATION ON VOTING IN THE FIELD OF THE COMMON FOREIGN AND SECURITY POLICY

The Conference agrees that, with regard to Council decisions requiring unanimity, Member States will, to the extent possible, avoid preventing a unanimous decision where a qualified majority exists in favour of that decision.

DECLARATION ON PRACTICAL ARRANGEMENTS IN THE FIELD OF THE COMMON FOREIGN AND SECURITY POLICY

The Conference agrees that the division of work between the Political Committee and the Permanent Representatives Committee will be examined at a later stage, as will the practical arrangements for merging the Political Co-operation Secretariat with the General Secretariat at the Council and for co-operation between the latter and the Commission.

DECLARATION ON THE USE OF LANGUAGES IN THE FIELD OF THE COMMON FOREIGN AND SECURITY POLICY

The Conference agrees that the use of languages shall be in accordance with the rules of the European Communities.

For COREU communications, the current practice of European Political Co-operation will serve as a guide for the time being.

All common foreign and security policy texts which are submitted to or adopted at meetings of the European Council and of the Council as well as all texts which are to be published are immediately and simultaneously translated into all the official Community languages.

DECLARATIONS ON WESTERN EUROPEAN UNION

of Belgium, Germany, Spain, France, Italy, Luxembourg, the Netherlands, Portugal and the United Kingdom of Great Britain and Northern Ireland, which are members of the Western European Union and also members of the European Union on

DECLARATION I

THE ROLE OF THE WESTERN EUROPEAN UNION AND ITS RELATIONS WITH THE EUROPEAN UNION AND WITH THE ATLANTIC ALLIANCE

Introduction

1. WEU Member States agree on the need to develop a genuine European security and defence identity and a greater European responsibility on defence matters. This identity will be pursued through a gradual process involving successive phases. WEU will form an integral part of the process of the development of the European Union and will enhance its contribution to solidarity within the Atlantic Alliance.

WEU Member States agree to strengthen the role of WEU, in the longer term perspective of a common defence policy within the European Union which might in time lead to a common defence, compatible with that of the Atlantic Alliance.

2. WEU will be developed as the defence component of the European Union and as the means to strengthen the European pillar of the Atlantic Alliance. To this end, it will formulate common European defence policy and carry forward its concrete implementation through the further development of its own operational role.

WEU Member States take note of Article J.4 relating to the common foreign and security policy of the Treaty of European Union which reads as follows:

[*see pp. 40–49 above*]

A. *WEU's relations with European Union*

3. The objective is to build up WEU in stages as the defence component of the European Union. To this end, WEU is prepared, at the request of the European Union, to elaborate and implement decisions and actions of the Union which have defence implications.

To this end, WEU will take the following measures to develop a close working relationship with the Union:

    — as appropriate, synchronisation of the dates and venues of meetings and harmonisation of working methods;

— establishment of close co-operation between the Council and Secretariat-General of WEU on the one hand, and the Council of the Union and General Secretariat of the Council on the other;
— consideration of the harmonisation of the sequence and duration of the respective Presidencies;
— arranging for appropriate modalities so as to ensure that the Commission of the European Communities is regularly informed and, as appropriate, consulted on WEU activities in accordance with the role of the Commission in the common foreign and security policy as defined in the Treaty on European Union;
— encouragement of closer co-operation between the Parliamentary Assembly of WEU and the European Parliament.

The WEU Council shall, in agreement with the competent bodies of the European Union, adopt the necessary practical arrangements.

B. *WEU's relations with the Atlantic Alliance*

4. The objective is to develop WEU as a means to strengthen the European pillar of the Atlantic Alliance. Accordingly WEU is prepared to develop further the close working links between WEU and the Alliance and to strengthen the role, responsibilities and contributions of WEU Member States in the Alliance. This will be undertaken on the basis of the necessary transparency and complementarity between the emerging European security and defence identity and the Alliance. WEU will act in conformity with the positions adopted in the Atlantic Alliance.

— WEU Member States will intensify the co-ordination on Alliance issues which represent an important common interest with the aim of introducing joint positions agreed in WEU into the process of consultation in the Alliance which will remain the essential forum for consultation among its members and the venue for agreement on policies bearing on the security and defence commitments of Allies under the North Atlantic Treaty.
— Where necessary, dates and venues of meetings will be synchronised and working methods harmonised.
— Close co-operation will be established between the Secretariats-General of WEU and NATO.

C. *Operational role of WEU*

5. WEU's operational role will be strengthened by examining and defining appropriate missions, structures and means, covering in particular:
— WEU planning cell;
— closer military co-operation complementary to the Alliance in particular in the fields of logistics, transport, training and strategic surveillance;
— meetings of WEU Chiefs of Defence Staff;
— military units answerable to WEU.

Other proposals will be examined further, including:
— enhanced co-operation in the field of armaments with the aim of creating a European armaments agency;
— development of the WEU Institute into a European Security and Defence Academy. Arrangements aimed at giving WEU a stronger operational role will be fully compatible with the military dispositions necessary to ensure the collective defence of all Allies.

D. *Other measures*

6. As a consequence of the measures set out above, and in order to facilitate the strengthening of WEU's role, the seat of the WEU Council and Secretariat will be transferred to Brussels.

7. Representation on the WEU Council must be such that the Council is able to exercise its functions continuously in accordance with Article VIII of the modified Brussels Treaty. Member-States may draw on a double-hatting formula, to be worked out, consisting of their representatives to the Alliance and to the European Union.

8. WEU notes that, in accordance with the provisions of Article J.4(6) concerning the common foreign and security policy of the Treaty on European Union, the Union will decide to review the provisions of this Article with a view to furthering the objective to be set by it in accordance with the procedure defined. The WEU will re-examine the present provisions in 1996. This re-examination will take account of the progress and experience acquired and will extend to relations between WEU and the Atlantic Alliance.

DECLARATION II

The Member States of WEU welcome the development of the European security and defence identity. They are determined, taking into account the role of WEU as the defence component of the European Union and as the means to strengthen the European pillar of the Atlantic Alliance, to put the relationship between WEU and the other European States on a new basis for the sake of stability and security in Europe. In this spirit, they propose the following.

States which are members of the European Union are invited to accede to WEU on conditions to be agreed in accordance with Article XI of the modified Brussels Treaty, or to become observers if they so wish. Simultaneously, other European Member States of NATO are invited to become associate members of WEU in a way which will give them the possibility of participating fully in the activities of WEU.

The Member States of WEU assume that treaties and agreements corresponding with the above proposals will be concluded before December 31, 1992.

DECLARATION ON ASYLUM

1. The Conference agrees that, in the context of the proceedings provided for in Articles K.1 and K.3 of the provisions on co-operation in the fields of justice and home affairs, the Council will consider as a matter of priority questions concerning Member States' asylum policies, with the aim of adopting, by the beginning of 1993, common action to harmonise aspects of them, in the light of the work programme and timetable contained in the report on asylum drawn up at the request of the European Council meeting in Luxembourg on June 28 and 29, 1991.

2. In this connection, the Council will also consider, by the end of 1993, on the basis of a report, the possibility of applying Article K.9 to such matters.

DECLARATION ON POLICE CO-OPERATION

The Conference confirms the agreement of the Member States on the objectives underlying the German delegation's proposals at the European Council meeting in Luxembourg on June 28 and 29, 1991.

For the present, the Member States agree to examine as a matter of priority the drafts submitted to them, on the basis of the work programme and timetable agreed upon in the report drawn up at the request of the Luxembourg European Council, and they are willing to envisage the adoption of practical measures in areas such as those suggested by the German delegation, relating to the following functions in the exchange of information and experience:

— support for national criminal investigation and security authorities, in particular in the co-ordination of investigations and search operations;
— creation of data bases;
— central analysis and assessment of information in order to take stock of the situation and identify investigative approaches;
— collection and analysis of national prevention programmes for forwarding to Member States and for drawing up Europe-wide prevention strategies;
— measures relating to further training, research, forensic matters and criminal records departments.

Member States agree to consider on the basis of a report, during 1994 at the latest, whether the scope of such co-operation should be extended.

DECLARATION ON DISPUTES BETWEEN THE ECB AND THE EMI AND THEIR SERVANTS

The Conference considers it proper that the Court of First Instance should hear this class of action in accordance with Article 168a of the Treaty establishing the European Community. The Conference therefore invites the institutions to adapt the relevant rules accordingly.

PART 3: THE E.C. TREATY

TREATY ESTABLISHING THE EUROPEAN COMMUNITY
(previously the European Economic Community)

ADOPTED BY THE E.C. MEMBER-STATES

(Done at Rome)   March 25, 1957

(as amended, most recently at Maastricht by the Treaty on European Union)   February 7, 1992

GENERAL NOTE
   Entry into force (in amended form): November 1, 1993
   Territorial application: E.C. Member States

ARRANGEMENT OF ARTICLES

ARTICLE

PART ONE (PRINCIPLES)

1.   Establishment of the European Community.
2.   Tasks of the Community.
3.   Activities of the Community.
3a.   Economic policy.
3b.   Community powers; subsidiarity principle.
4.   Institutions of the Community.
4a.   Establishment of European System of Central Banks.
4b.   Establishment of European Investment Bank.
5.   Obligations of the Member States.
6.   Prohibition on nationality discrimination.
7.   Establishment of the common market.
7a.   Establishment of the internal market.
7b.   Progress reports and guidelines for balanced progress.
7c.   Derogations from citizens' right to freedom of movement and residence.

PART TWO (CITIZENSHIP OF THE UNION)

8.   Establishment of Union citizenship.
8a.   Right to freedom of movement and residence.
8b.   Right to stand for political office and voting rights.
8c.   Right to diplomatic representation.
8d.   Right to petition the European Parliament and the Ombudsman.
8e.   Development of citizens' rights.

PART THREE (COMMUNITY POLICIES)

TITLE I: FREE MOVEMENT OF GOODS

9.   Customs Union.
10.   Goods in free circulation.
11.   Implementation by Member States.

CHAPTER 1 (CUSTOMS UNION)

SECTION 1: ELIMINATION OF CUSTOMS DUTIES BETWEEN MEMBER STATES

12.   Prohibition on new duties and charges of equivalent effect.
13.   Abolition of existing duties and charges with equivalent effect.
14.   Base duty and timetable for reductions; levels of reductions; calculation of customs receipts; settlement of special problems; progress reports; Article amendment.
15.   Power of Member States to suspend the collection of duties during the transitional period; declaration of will to reduce duties more rapidly, economic situation permitting.
16.   Time limit for the abolition of all duties.
17.   Duties of a fiscal nature.

SECTION 2: SETTING UP OF THE COMMON CUSTOMS TARIFF

18. Declaration on free trade.
19. Levels of duties in the common customs tariff.
20. List G products.
21. Resolution of technical difficulties in applying Articles 19 and 20.
22. Duties of a fiscal nature.
23. Timetable for Member States to amend tariffs applicable to third countries; time limit for complete application of the common customs tariff.
24. Power of Member States to change duties more rapidly than provided for in Article 23.
25. Conditions for granting a Member State tariff quotas at a reduced rate of duty.
26. Conditions authorising a Member State to postpone the lowering or raising of duties.
27. Approximation of laws as regards customs matters.
28. Autonomous alteration or suspension of duties.
29. Guidelines for setting up the common customs tariff.

CHAPTER 2 (ELIMINATION OF QUANTITATIVE RESTRICTIONS BETWEEN MEMBER STATES)

30. Prohibition on quantitative restrictions and measures of equivalent effect between Member States.
31. Prohibition on introducing new quantitative restrictions or measures of equivalent effect.
32. Prohibition on making existing quotas and measures more restrictive and time limit for their abolition.
33. Timetable for converting bilateral quotas into global quotas and for increasing global quotas.
34. Prohibition on and abolition of existing export restrictions and measures of equivalent effect.
35. Declaration of good intent as regards abolition of quantitative restrictions.
36. Derogations permitted.
37. Liberalisation of public procurement.

TITLE II: AGRICULTURE

38. Inclusion of agriculture in the common market and definition of agricultural products to include fisheries.
39. Objectives of the common agricultural policy and criteria for forming it.
40. Timetable for development of the common agricultural policy; establishment of a common organisation of agricultural markets and agricultural guidance and guarantee funds.
41. Co-ordination of research and training and joint measures to promote consumption.
42. Delimination of the application of the competition rules to agriculture.
43. Preparation for working out and implementing the common agricultural policy; replacement of national marketing organisations by the common organisation.
44. Minimum price systems for imports during the transitional period.
45. Regulation of trade where national producers have a guaranteed market or imports are needed.
46. Countervailing charges on state-aided products.
47. Functions of the Economic and Social Committee.

TITLE III: FREE MOVEMENT OF PERSONS, SERVICES AND CAPITAL

CHAPTER 1 (WORKERS)

48. Time limit for establishing freedom of movement for workers, the rights involved and derogations.
49. Legislative procedures and priorities.
50. Encouragement for the exchange of young workers.
51. Social security arrangements for migrant workers.

Chapter 2 (Right of Establishment)

52. Abolition of restrictions to the right of establishment and the rights involved.
53. Prohibition on introducing new restrictions on the right of establishment.
54. Programme for abolishing existing restrictions; sectoral liberalisation; legislative priorities.
55. Derogation for official activity; power to derogate in specific areas.
56. Derogation for national laws relating to public policy, public security or public health and co-ordination of those laws.
57. Mutual recognition of diplomas and the co-ordination of laws relating to the self-employed.
58. Right of establishment of corporate entities.

Chapter 3 (Services)

59. Abolition of restrictions on freedom to provide services; power to extend rights to third-country nationals established within the Community.
60. Definition of services and non-discrimination.
61. Transport, banking and insurance services.
62. Prohibition on introducing new restrictions on providing services.
63. Programme for abolishing all existing restrictions; sectoral liberalisation; priority services.
64. Declaration of good intent as regards liberalisation.
65. Non-discriminatory application of existing restrictions.
66. Application of Articles 55–58 to this chapter.

Chapter 4 (Capital and Payments)

67. Abolition of restrictions on the movement of capital.
68. Liberalisation of exchange authorisations; non-discriminatory application of domestic law governing the capital market and credit system; prohibition on cross border loans financing a Member State or its local authorities without agreement.
69. Legislative procedure.
70. Co-ordination of exchange policies *vis-à-vis* third countries.
71. Avoidance of new exchange restrictions within the Community; declaration of good intent as regards liberalisation.
72. Capital movements to and from third countries.
73. Protective measures in the event of difficulties on national capital markets.
73a. Replacement of Articles 67–73 by Articles 73b–73g after 1993.
73b. Prohibition on all restrictions on the movement of capital and payments.
73c. Restrictions with respect to third countries existing on 31 December 1993; power of the Council to legislate on the movement of capital to or from third countries; unanimity required if retrogressive.
73d. Derogations permitted.
73e. Maintenance of derogations existing at 31 December 1993 until 31 December 1995.
73f. Safeguard measures with regard to third countries.
73g. Interruption of economic relations with third countries by the Council and Member States.
73h. Transitional measures applicable until 1 January 1994.

Title IV: Transport

74. Common transport policy.
75. Ambit of Community action and legislative procedures.
76. Non-discriminatory application of existing rules.
77. Permissible aids.
78. Measures on transport rates and conditions.
79. Abolition of pricing discrimination.
80. Prohibition on unauthorised support for particular undertakings.
81. Additional charges imposed for crossing frontiers.
82. Division of Germany.
83. Establishment of Advisory Committee for transport.
84. Application of the provisions to transport by rail, road and inland waterway; power of Council to decide on Community action for air and sea transport.

TITLE V: COMMON RULES ON COMPETITION, TAXATION AND APPROXIMATION OF LAWS

CHAPTER 1 (RULES ON COMPETITION)

SECTION 1: RULES APPLYING TO UNDERTAKINGS

85.   Prohibited agreements and concerted practices; conditions for exemption.
86.   Prohibition of abuse of a dominant position.
87.   Legislative priorities and procedures.
88.   Transitional enforcement powers of national authorities.
89.   Transitional enforcement powers of the Commission.
90.   Public undertakings.

SECTION 2: DUMPING

91.   Protective measures within the Community; free reimportation of goods in free circulation.

SECTION 3: AIDS GRANTED BY STATES

92.   Prohibited and permissible State aids.
93.   Policing and enforcement powers of the Commission; referral to the Council; obligation on Member States to notify aids.
94.   Legislative powers and procedures.

CHAPTER 2 (TAX PROVISIONS)

95.   Prohibition on discriminatory taxation; cessation of existing discrimination.
96.   Prohibition on excessive export refunds.
97.   Establishment of average rates for turnover taxes.
98.   Prohibition on unauthorised export refunds or countervailing import charges.
99.   Harmonisation of legislation for indirect taxes.

CHAPTER 3 (APPROXIMATION OF LAWS)

100.   Legislative powers and procedure; unanimity.
100a.   Alternative legislative powers and procedure for completing the internal market; majority voting; laws relating to fiscal matters or those relating to the free movement of person and workers' rights excepted; notification of post-harmonisation national protectionist measures.
100b.   Inventory of national laws not harmonised.
100c.   Visa requirements for non-Community nationals; uniform format for visas.
100d.   Role of the Co-ordinating Committee set up under Article K.4 of the European Union Treaty.
101.   Elimination of distortions of competition in the common market caused by differing national laws.
102.   Consultation on national legislative proposals likely to distort competition in the common market.

TITLE VI: ECONOMIC AND MONETARY POLICY

CHAPTER 1 (ECONOMIC POLICY)

102a.   Economic policies of the Member States.
103.   Co-ordination of economic policies; establishment of guidelines for economic policies; monitoring of developments in the Member States; action on diverging policies.
103a.   Power of the Council to adapt to the economic situation; Community financial assistance to Member States.
104.   Prohibition on any public entity having credit facilities with the European Central Bank (ECB) or any national central bank.
104a.   Prohibition on any public entity having favoured access to financial institutions.
104b.   Prohibition on Community liability for the commitments of national public entities and on one Member State being liable for the commitments of public entities in another.
104c.   Avoidance of excessive government deficits; monitoring of budgetary discipline; enforcement by the Council.

248

CHAPTER 2 (MONETARY POLICY)

105.   Objectives and tasks of the European System of Central Banks (ESCB); consultation with the ECB.
105a.   Authorisation for issuing bank notes and coins; harmonisation of denominations and specifications of coins.
106.   Composition and control of the ESCB; adoption and amendment of the Statute of the ESCB; legal personality of the ECB.
107.   Independence of the ECB and national central banks.
108.   Compatibility of national legislation with the Treaty and the Statute of the ESCB.
108a.   Legislative and enforcement powers of the ECB.
109.   Powers of the Council as regards monetary and foreign exchange matters; treaty-making powers; adjustment of ECU central rates; competence of Member States.

CHAPTER 3 (INSTITUTIONAL PROVISIONS)

109a.   Composition of the governing council and executive board of the ECB.
109b.   Right of representation to the Council and the ECB; ESCB annual report.
109c.   Establishment of a Monetary Committee; establishment of an Economic and Financial Committee and liquidation of the Monetary Committee.
109d.   Consultation with the Commission.

CHAPTER 4 (TRANSITIONAL PROVISIONS)

109e.   Second stage of economic and monetary union.
109f.   Establishment of the European Monetary Institute.
109g.   Composition of the ECU.
109h.   Authorisation of protective measures for balance of payments difficulties.
109i.   Independent protective measures.
109j.   Progress reports on economic and monetary union.
109k.   Member States with a derogation.
109l.   Third stage of economic and monetary union; establishment of the ESCB and the ECB; liquidation of the EMI; introduction of the ECU as single currency.
109m.   Exchange rate policy of Member States with a derogation.

TITLE VII: COMMON COMMERCIAL POLICY

110.   World trade and the competitive strength of Community undertakings.
111.   [*repealed at Maastricht*]
112.   Aid for exports to third countries.
113.   Implementation of the common commercial policy; treaties.
114.   [*repealed at Maastricht*]
115.   Protective measures.
116.   [*repealed at Maastricht*]

TITLE VIII: SOCIAL POLICY, EDUCATION, VOCATIONAL TRAINING AND YOUTH

CHAPTER 1 (SOCIAL PROVISIONS)

117.   Need to improve working conditions.
118.   Promotion of inter-State co-operation in specified areas.
118a.   Power to legislate on labour matters.
118b.   Dialogue between the social partners.
119.   Equal pay for equal work.
120.   Paid holiday schemes.
121.   Implementation of common measures, particularly on social security.
122.   Chapter on social developments in Commission's annual report to the European Parliament.

CHAPTER 2 (THE EUROPEAN SOCIAL FUND)

123.   Establishment of European Social Fund.
124.   Administration of Fund.
125.   Implementing decisions relating to the Fund.

CHAPTER 3 (EDUCATION, VOCATIONAL TRAINING AND YOUTH)

126.   Education.
127.   Vocational training.

TITLE IX: CULTURE

128.   Cultural action.

TITLE X: PUBLIC HEALTH

129.   Public health.

TITLE XI: CONSUMER PROTECTION

129a.   Consumer protection.

TITLE XII: TRANS-EUROPEAN NETWORKS

129b.   Trans-European networks in transport, telecommunications and energy infrastructure.
129c.   Action to promote such networks.
129d.   Powers to adopt guidelines and other measures.

TITLE XIII: INDUSTRY

130.   Industrial policy.

TITLE XIV: ECONOMIC AND SOCIAL COHESION

130a.   Reducing economic disparities between regions.
130b.   National and Community economic policies to take cohesion into account; action through the structural funds.
130c.   European Regional Development Fund.
130d.   Powers of the Council to control structural funds and set up a Cohesion Fund.
130e.   Implementing decisions relating to the European Regional Development Fund.

TITLE XV: RESEARCH AND TECHNOLOGICAL DEVELOPMENT

130f.   Support for research and technological development.
130g.   Action in pursuit of these objectives.
130h.   Co-ordination of national R & D activities.
130i.   Multiannual framework programme.
130j.   Implementation of multiannual framework programme.
130k.   Supplementary programmes.
130l.   Multi-State R & D programmes.
130m.   Co-operation in Community R & D with non-member countries and international organisations.
130n.   Joint undertakings etc. for Community R & D.
130o.   Powers of the Council.
130p.   Commission annual report on R & D to European Parliament.
130q.   [*Repealed at Maastricht*]

TITLE XVI: ENVIRONMENT

130r.   Community environment policy.
130s.   Powers of the Council.
130t.   Powers of the Member States.

TITLE XVII: DEVELOPMENT CO-OPERATION

130u.   Community policy in the sphere of development co-operation.
130v.   Consideration for development co-operation in policies likely to affect developing countries.
130w.   Powers of the Council.
130x.   Co-ordination of Member States and Community policies.
130y.   Co-operation with non-member countries and international organisations.

PART FOUR (ASSOCIATION OF THE OVERSEAS COUNTRIES AND TERRITORIES)

131.   Association of former dependent territories.
132.   Objectives of association.
133.   Customs duties.
134.   Remedial action when customs duties cause deflections of trade.
135.   Freedom of movement of migrant workers.
136.   Procedural role of annexed Implementing Convention.
136a. Application to Greenland.

PART FIVE (INSTITUTIONS OF THE COMMUNITY)

TITLE I: PROVISIONS GOVERNING THE INSTITUTIONS

CHAPTER 1 (THE INSTITUTIONS)

SECTION 1: THE EUROPEAN PARLIAMENT

137.   European Parliament.
138.   Direct elections.
138a. Political parties.
138b. Legislative powers.
138c. Committee of Inquiry.
138d. Right of petition.
138e. Ombudsman.
139.   Annual and extraordinary sessions.
140.   President and officers; attendance of Commissioners at meetings; hearing of Council
          representatives.
141.   Voting; quorum.
142.   Rules of procedure.
143.   Discussion of Commission's annual report.
144.   Motion of censure.

SECTION 2: THE COUNCIL

145.   Functions of Council.
146.   Composition of Council.
147.   Convening of meetings.
148.   Voting.
149.   [*Repealed at Maastricht*]
150.   Proxy votes.
151.   Coreper; Secretary General and Secretariat; rules of procedure.
152.   Power to request Commission to undertake studies.
153.   Committees.
154.   Determination of remuneration of Commissioners and Judges.

SECTION 3: THE COMMISSION

155.   Functions of Commission.
156.   Annual report.
157.   Composition of Commission.
158.   Appointment of members.
159.   Retirement of members.
160.   Dismissal of members.
161.   Vice-Presidents.
162.   Co-operation between Commission and Council; rules of procedure.
163.   Voting and quorum.

SECTION 4: THE COURT OF JUSTICE

164. Function.
165. Judges.
166. Advocates General.
167. Appointment of Judges and Advocates General.
168. Registrar.
168a. Court of First Instance.
169. Actions by Commission against Member State.
170. Actions by Member States against Member States.
171. Compliance by Member State with Court's judgment.
172. Jurisdiction as regards penalties.
173. Judicial review of acts of Community institutions.
174. Court's power to annul.
175. Action for failure to act.
176. Compliance by institution with Court's judgment.
177. Reference for preliminary ruling.
178. Jurisdiction in actions against the Community for damages.
179. Jurisdiction in staff disputes.
180. Jurisdiction in cases involving the European Investment Bank, the European Central Bank & the ESCB.
181. Judgment pursuant to arbitration clauses.
182. Jurisdiction by special agreement.
183. Jurisdiction of national courts in cases involving the Community.
184. Plea of invalidity of Community act.
185. Interim suspension of disputed Community act.
186. Interim measures.
187. Enforcement of Court judgments.
188. Statute of the Court; rules of procedure.

SECTION 5: THE COURT OF AUDITORS

188a. Function.
188b. Composition of the Court of Auditors.
188c. Auditing procedure.

CHAPTER 2 (PROVISIONS COMMON TO SEVERAL INSTITUTIONS)

189.   Forms of Community act.
189a. Amendment of draft Commission proposal.
189b. Conciliation and Veto Procedure.
189c. Co-operation Procedure.
190.   Statement of reasons in regulations, directives and decisions.
191.   Publication and entry into force.
192.   Enforcement of decisions imposing pecuniary obligations.

CHAPTER 3 (THE ECONOMIC AND SOCIAL COMMITTEE)

193.   Establishment and composition of Economic and Social Committee.
194.   Nationality, appointment and independence of members.
195.   Appointment procedure.
196.   Officers; rules of procedure; convening of meetings.
197.   Specialised sections and sub-committees.
198.   Consultation of the Committee.

CHAPTER 4 (THE COMMITTEE OF THE REGIONS)

198a. Establishment and composition of Committee; members.
198b. Officers; rules of procedure; convening of meetings.
198c. Consultation of the Committee.

CHAPTER 5 (EUROPEAN INVESTMENT BANK)

198d. Establishment and composition.
198e. Task of the Bank.

TITLE II: FINANCIAL PROVISIONS

199.   Financial estimates.
200.   [*Repealed at Maastricht*]
201.   Budget to be financed from own resources.
201a.   Budgetary discipline.
202.   Appropriations for expenditure.
203.   Financial year; budget.
204.   Interim budget if budget proposals not adopted in time.
205.   Implementation of budget.
205a.   Submission of annual accounts.
206.   Budgetary discharge given by European Parliament.
206a.   [*Repealed at Maastricht*]
206b.   [*Repealed at Maastricht*]
207.   Accounting currency for the budget.
208.   Currency switching by Commission.
209.   Power of Council to make Financial Regulations and lay down rules and procedures.
209a.   Action to counter fraud affecting the financial interests of the Community.

PART SIX (GENERAL AND FINAL PROVISIONS)

210.   Community's legal personality.
211.   Community's legal capacity in Member States.
212.   Staff of the institutions; staff regulations.
213.   Commission's powers to collect information and carry out checks.
214.   Official secrets.
215.   Contractual and non-contractual liability of the Community.
216.   Seat of the institutions.
217.   Languages of the institutions.
218.   Privileges and immunities.
219.   Non-justiciability of disputes relating to the E.C. Treaty outside the bounds of the Treaty.
220.   Intention to adopt treaty laws on equal protection, abolition of double taxation, mutual recognition of companies, cross-border company mergers, recognition and enforcement of foreign judgments and arbitral awards.
221.   Abolition of nationality discrimination as regards participation in capital of companies.
222.   Saving of national legislative power over property ownership.
223.   Preservation by Member States of their state secrets; Member State measures to protect security.
224.   Inter-State consultation in cases of serious internal disturbances, war, serious international tension and international peace obligations.
225.   Distorting effect of security measures under Articles 223 and 224; remedies for misuse of such measures.
226.   Authorisation to take protective measures to meet serious economic difficulties during transitional period.
227.   Territorial application of the Treaty.
228.   Treaty-making power and procedure.
228a.   Procedure for international joint economic boycotts.
229.   Relations with United Nations, U.N. specialised agencies, GATT and other international organisations.
230.   Co-operation with Council of Europe.
231.   Co-operation with OECD.
232.   Avoidance of overlap with ECSC and Euratom Treaties.
233.   Saving for Belgo-Luxembourg Economic Union and Benelux.
234.   Status of Member States' pre-entry or pre-accession treaty obligations.
235.   General residual legislative power clause.
236.   [*Repealed at Maastricht*]
237.   [*Repealed at Maastricht*]
238.   Conclusion of association agreements between Community and other States or organisations.
239.   Protocols annexed to Treaty to form integral part of it. [*Only the Protocols annexed by the TEU are reproduced here*]
240.   Treaty concluded for unlimited period.

SETTING UP OF THE INSTITUTIONS

241.   First meeting of Council.
242.   Council to set up the Economic and Social Committee.
243.   First meeting of Assembly.
244.   Establishment of the Court of Justice and starting work.
245.   Establishment of the Commission and starting work.
246.   First financial year and first budget.

FINAL PROVISIONS

247.   Ratification and entry into force.
248.   Authentic texts and depositary.

THE AMENDED E.C. TREATY

PREAMBLE

[THE HEADS OF STATE]

DETERMINED to lay the foundations of an ever closer union among the peoples of Europe,

RESOLVED to ensure the economic and social progress of their countries by common action to eliminate the barriers which divide Europe,

AFFIRMING as the essential objective of their efforts the constant improvement of the living and working conditions of their peoples,

RECOGNISING that the removal of existing obstacles calls for concerted action in order to guarantee steady expansion, balanced trade and fair competition,

ANXIOUS to strengthen the unity of their economies and to ensure their harmonious development by reducing the differences existing between the various regions and the backwardness of the less favoured regions,

DESIRING to contribute, by means of a common commercial policy, to the progressive abolition of restrictions on international trade,

INTENDING to confirm the solidarity which binds Europe and the overseas countries and desiring to ensure the development of their prosperity, in accordance with the principles of the Charter of the United Nations, peace and liberty, and calling upon the other peoples of Europe who share their ideal to join in their efforts,

HAVE DECIDED to create a European Community and to this end . . . have agreed as follows.

GENERAL NOTE

Articles which have been altered (other than mere renumbering) have the heading italicised (*e.g. Article 3*). In some cases (*e.g.* new *Art. 128*) the whole text of the Article is new; in others there are only minor drafting changes.

PART ONE (PRINCIPLES)

Article 1

By this Treaty, the HIGH CONTRACTING PARTIES establish among themselves a EUROPEAN COMMUNITY.

GENERAL NOTE

The changed nomenclature from the European Economic Community to the more general European Community is not entirely symbolic. It marks a significant realisation by the Member States that the Community is now more than a strictly economic entity. This is highlighted by the expansion of Art. 3 E.C. to cover 20 different areas of Community interest; including some which are far from being specifically economic in nature. This is reflected in the amendment of

Art. 3, below, to include a policy in the sphere of the environment, in the promotion of research and technological development and a policy in the social sphere. Also indicative of the broader scope of the new Community is the inclusion of new legislative bases in the fields of education, culture, public health, consumer protection and development co-operation.

The change in name increases the scope for European Court of Justice rulings supporting disputed Community action in spheres without an obvious economic flavour, in, for example, Art. 235 cases. The Court of Justice has not seen the E.C. in the past as an exclusively economic entity (Case 43/75, *Defrenne v. SABENA* [1976] E.C.R. 455, at 472), and has often stressed its broader political purpose (Opinion 1/91, *European Economic Area (No. 1)* [1991] E.C.R.-6079). As a result, it is not clear to what extent, if any, the change in name will affect its jurisprudence. What is clear is that the Court of Justice has always given Art. 235 EEC a very broad interpretation and has not shied away from ruling in favour of legislation purportedly based on Art. 235 EEC but with, at best, tenuous links with the fulfilment of the then Treaty objectives (see the note on Art. 235 E.C.). On the other hand, it can be contended that the preclusion of harmonising legislation under certain new provisions (*e.g.* Art. 126 E.C. on education) also precludes action under Art. 235 E.C. in these spheres.

One result of the name change may be increased confusion regarding the different Community bodies: in the past, the combined European Coal and Steel Community, Euratom and EEC were collectively known as the European Community or Communities.

Article 2

The Community shall have as its task, by establishing a common market and an economic and monetary union and by implementing the common policies or activities referred to in Articles 3 and 3a, to promote throughout the Community a harmonious and balanced development of economic activities, sustainable and non-inflationary growth respecting the environment, a high degree of convergence of economic performance, a high level of employment and of social protection, the raising of the standard of living and quality of life, and economic and social cohesion and solidarity among Member States.

GENERAL NOTE

Article 2 is a broadly phrased declaration of the Community's intent. The original provision, drawn up in 1957, was in need of revision to take account of the Community's developing role; not least in the light of the further evolution of the Community agreed at Maastricht. Article 2 EEC provided for the promotion throughout the Community of "a harmonious development of economic activities, a continuous and balanced expansion, an increase in stability, an accelerated standard of living and closer relations between the States belonging to it". The amended version of Art. 2, to take account of the new, more diverse Community activities, makes reference to the broadened Art. 3 and the new Art. 3a on economic and monetary union, as well as setting out a number of less specific and more politically oriented declarations of intent.

The existence of such mixed, and possibly even contradictory, declarations will mean a great deal rests on the interpretation of the provisions, and on the political will to see them implemented. The Court of Justice, in interpreting an individual Article of the Treaty or provision of Community law will often set it in its context in the Treaty and construe it in the light of the objectives set out in the preamble and Arts. 2 and 3 E.C. The task of the Court in "reconciling and prioritising these objectives" will not be made any easier by the amendments enunciated in the new Art. 2 E.C. (Plender (1982) 2 Y.E.L. 57, at 75). The Court will have to make the determinative rulings on the application of these provisions. It has not shrunk from this task in the past. Its approach was summarised in Case 28/66 *Netherlands v. Commission* [1968] E.C.R. 1, 12–13: "Although the general objectives of the Treaty, set out in Arts. 2 and 3, cannot always be pursued simultaneously in their totality, the Community must continuously reconcile these objectives when considered individually and, when conflict arises, must grant such priority to certain general objectives as appear necessary, having regard to the economic facts or circumstances in the light of which it adopts its decisions". Subjective application of the new Art. 2 would appear to be unavoidable.

Nevertheless, Member States are required to conduct their economic policies with a view to contributing to the achievement of the objectives of the Community as defined in Art. 2 (Art. 102a E.C.). This will not be made any easier by the fact that, in this sphere, the objectives of the Treaty are argued to be contradictory. Article 2 requires "a high level of employment and of social protection" yet the U.K. government has repeatedly asserted that the adoption of a high level of social protection makes for uncompetitiveness and thus leads to higher unemployment.

On the other hand, some politicians on the left have argued that "non-inflationary growth with the essential goal of price stability" (Art. 3a E.C.) is incompatible with a high level of employment and the provision of wide-ranging social services by the State.

Article 2 also forms the basis for the application of the law-making power of Art. 235 E.C. It could be argued that the expanded Art. 2 provides the Community with a much broader law-making power, but this is questionable in two respects. First, the potentially unlimited legislative power of Art. 235 is constrained by the requirement of unanimity in Council for any legislative measure under that Art. and this will tend to prevent agreement on any development of the politically sensitive generalities espoused in the new Art. 2. Secondly, the wording of the original Art. 2 that the Community should seek to promote "closer relations between the States belonging to it" justified the propagation of legislation in a very wide number of areas not specifically covered by the Treaty (see notes on Art. 235 E.C.). Whether or not the more specific provisions in the new Art. 2 permit action under Art. 235 will depend more on political pressures than legal justification.

The statement of the principle of proportionality in Art. 3b, that "any action by the Community must not go beyond what is necessary to achieve the objectives of this Treaty", must also be read in the light of Art. 2.

Article 3

For the purposes set out in Article 2, the activities of the Community shall include, as provided in this Treaty and in accordance with the timetable set out therein:

(a) the elimination, as between Member States, of customs duties and of quantitative restrictions on the import and export of goods, and of all other measures having equivalent effect;

(b) a common commercial policy;

(c) an internal market characterised by the abolition, as between Member States, of obstacles to the free movement of goods, persons, services and capital;

(d) measures concerning the entry and movement of persons in the internal market as provided for in Article 100c;

(e) a common policy in the sphere of agriculture and fisheries;

(f) a common policy in the sphere of transport;

(g) a system of ensuring that competition in the internal market is not distorted;

(h) the approximation of the laws of Member States to the extent required for the proper functioning of the common market;

(i) a policy in the social sphere comprising a European Social Fund;

(j) the strengthening of economic and social cohesion;

(k) a policy in the sphere of the environment;

(l) the strengthening of the competitiveness of Community industry;

(m) the promotion of research and technological development;

(n) encouragement for the establishment and development of trans-European networks;

(o) a contribution to the attainment of a high level of health protection;

(p) a contribution to education and training of quality and to the flowering of the cultures of the Member States;

(q) a policy in the sphere of development co-operation;

(r) the association of the overseas countries and territories in order to increase trade and promote jointly economic and social development;

(s) a contribution to the strengthening of consumer protection;

(t) measures in the spheres of energy, civil protection and tourism.

GENERAL NOTE

This Article, setting out in detail the scope of the Community's activities, highlights the development of the Community. Numerically, the 11 areas of Community competence in the original EEC Treaty have been expanded to 20 diverse Community concerns. The jurisprudence of the Court of Justice on the Art. 5 "fidelity" clause means that the Member States are committed to "facilitate the achievement of the Community's tasks" (Art. 5 E.C., unamended) and in this respect the existence of a common policy at Community level requires the Member States to participate in the furtherance of that policy (Case 805/79, *Commission v. United Kingdom* [1981] E.C.R. 1045, at 1047). However, as Weatherill has pointed out: "the jurisprudence dealing with the use of Art. 5 to commit Member States to act in accordance with Community policies is rather underdeveloped" (Research Paper, 1993, No. 6, University of Nottingham).

The objectives of the Treaty laid down here must still be read in the light of the developing Art. 5 jurisprudence of the Court of Justice (see Temple Lang (1990) 27 C.M.L.Rev. 645). The Court is increasingly using Art. 5 to draw different agencies into the shaping of the Community. This has been particularly shown in the obligations imposed on the Member State courts to ensure the effective application of Community law, which reached new lengths in the case of Cases C–6 & C–9/90, *Francovich and Boniface v. Italy* ([1991] E.C.R. 5359; see notes on Art. 171). The Court has also ruled that the duty imposed by Art. 5 is applicable to the Community institutions (Case 2/88, *Zwartveld*, [1990] I E.C.R. 3365). This duty was found to require the Commission to take action to support the enforcement of Community law at the national level. It is highly unlikely that the Court of Justice would utilise similar reasoning to force the Commission to adopt legislation in one of the listed policy fields of the Community, unless of course there existed a specific time-frame for the adoption of any such measures. For the Court to intervene in any other situation would amount to an implicit breach of the "separation of powers in the Community", especially in the light of the Commission's right of legislative initiative.

Nevertheless, a number of the additions to the list of Community activities in this Article are flattered by a cursory glance. The provisions on culture, education, and public health leave little scope for Community activity, with the emphasis on action at national level. In the majority of these fields, harmonisation is specifically excluded and the Community is simply to support Member State initiatives. These matters will be dealt with in the notes on the relevant Articles.

In terms of amendments to existing provisions of the section, Arts. 3(a) and (h) E.C. on the functioning of the common market remain unchanged. The variation in the usage of the terms "common" and "internal" markets is worthy of mention here. The amended version of Art. 3(c) contains a specific reference to the creation of an internal market and might give some indication of the scope of the "internal market" in so far as the achievement of the four freedoms of goods, persons, services and capital is to "characterise" the internal market. The concept is defined in similar terms in Art. 7a E.C. (formerly Art. 8a EEC). It was possible to argue that the wording of this provision and its express reference to the abolition, *between Member States*, of these restrictions to trade implied that the internal market was wholly concerned with intra-Community matters and could not impinge on external affairs. This view could be countered by reference to the view of the Court of Justice of the external competence of the Community under Art. 238 EEC in Case 12/86, *Demirel v. Stadt Schwäbisch Gmünd*: [1987] E.C.R. 3719, and was implicitly rejected in Opinion 1/94, *G.A.T.T.*: [1994] I E.C.R. 1, at para. 88 in which the Court recognised a non-exclusive Community external competence under Art. 100a E.C. Nowhere in the Treaty is the notion of the "common market" actually defined but, as Wyatt and Dashwood point out, its primary meaning can be gathered from Art. 2 EEC where it is one of the two means by which the Community is to achieve the objectives laid out in the rest of that Article, the other now being the achievement of economic and monetary union (Wyatt and Dashwood, *European Community Law* (3rd. ed., 1993), pp. 357-8). They surmise that the common market covers the whole range of Community activities other than those concerned with the approximation of economic policies. One might venture that the term "internal market" has a more *laissez-faire* deregulatory tone than "common market" (with its inclusion of the common organisation of various markets), an impression reinforced by its association with the 1992 programme. Any possible distinction is interesting, because the amended Art. 3(g) E.C. (previously Art. 3(h) EEC) now speaks of the distortion of competition in the *internal* market; Art. 3(h) EEC referred formerly to the *common* market. The reason for this alteration is unclear, but on the hypothesis just stated, it could be intended to indicate a more liberal market-led approach to competition.

Article 3(b) E.C. reflects the new stage in the development of the Community. The wording, which previously referred to the "establishment of a common customs tariff and a common commercial policy" is altered to reflect the continuing progress of the commercial policy. The reference to the common customs tariff is dropped, presumably because it is an acknowledged part of the common commercial policy and no longer requires an explicit reference in the Treaty.

Similar amendments are made to Arts. 3(e), (f) and (g). Article 3(e) is also amended to provide the first mention of fisheries as part of a common Community policy. This is long overdue. The original definition of agriculture in the EEC Treaty included fisheries as an element of the agriculture sector, covered by Arts. 38–46 (see Annex II to the Treaty). The importance of fisheries to the Community led to the building up of a detailed body of law covering this area. This took place through many Community initiatives and the developing Court of Justice jurisprudence in the field (*e.g.* Case 32/79, *Commission v. United Kingdom (Fishery Conservation Measures)*: [1980] E.C.R. 2403, and Case 804/79, *Commission v. United Kingdom (Fishery Conservation Measures (No. 2)*): [1981] E.C.R. 1045). The inclusion of the reference to fisheries as an autonomous Community policy merely confirms current practice. Regulation 3760/92 sets out the principal provisions of the Common Fisheries Policy ([1992] O.J. L389/1; see now the Commission Communication on the fisheries crisis, COM (94) 335; for earlier developments of that policy see Mathijsen, *A Guide to European Community Law* (6th ed., 1995), pp. 283–8).

Article 3(d), inserted by the E.U. Treaty, gives the status of a Community objective to the controversial Art. 100c E.C., which establishes a new procedure for the adoption of measures regarding visas for persons crossing the external borders of the Community. Article 3(d) also elevates to the level of a Community objective the adoption of a common format for visas. Prior to January 1996, decisions as to which third countries' nationals will require visas can be taken by the Council only by unanimity (Art. 100c(1) E.C.), but temporary measures not lasting more than six months can be taken by qualified majority (Art. 100c(2) E.C.). After January 1, 1996 all decisions in this area will be taken by qualified majority.

The old Art. 3(g) EEC on the "co-ordination of the economic policies of the Member States" is removed, having been rendered obsolete by the new provisions on economic and monetary union.

Article 3(i) is updated to cover a social policy and not just the European Social Fund, as was the case following the S.E.A. amendments. The specific provisions in the original Art. 3(i) on the "improved employment opportunities" and the raising of workers' standards of living are removed. Although social policy is elevated to an activity of the Community, the substantive provisions on social policy in the E.C. Treaty were not widened at Maastricht because the U.K. refused to permit any such changes. Instead, the Social Protocol provides for all the Member States except the U.K. to make some modest changes in the social field.

Article 3(j) EEC, inserted by the S.E.A., simply made reference to the European Investment Bank and its role in the economic expansion of the Community, whereas the new provision is much broader, referring to the strengthening of economic and social cohesion. The latter concept was introduced into the Treaty by the S.E.A. in Arts. 130a to 130e. It refers to the Structural Funds in the Community, which seek to lessen the disparities between the levels of development in the various regions of the Community. The TEU introduced provision for a new Structural Fund, the so-called Cohesion Fund (Art. 130d E.C.), to aid the four poorest States in the Community (Greece, Ireland, Portugal and Spain). Further details are given in the note on Art. 130d.

Articles 3(k) and (m) E.C. on the environment and research and development respectively are additions to Art. 3. Nevertheless, both spheres have been included in the Treaty since the S.E.A. amendments. The environment has been elevated from an area of Community action to a Community policy, to reflect its slightly more dynamic role. One of the changes to its set-up is the recognition that "environmental protection requirements must be integrated into the definition and implementation of other Community policies" (Art. 130r(2) E.C.). While the old Art. 130r(2) EEC stated that "environmental protection requirements shall be a component of the Community's other policies", this was a less rigorous guarantee that environmental issues would be an important part of the Community's policies in areas such as transport and agriculture.

The addition of new objectives to the Treaty may appear impressive in strict numerical terms but the substance is not quite so grand. Many of the areas covered by this article, and dealt with in new provisions in the Treaty itself, are essentially codifying measures. A prime example of a "new" area that was, in fact, already being dealt with, admittedly on a more ad hoc basis, is development co-operation (Art. 3(q) E.C.). Its inclusion in the policy sphere of the Community is, however, indicative of the new general Community competence in this field under the new Title XVII of the amended Treaty. This also marks some progress away from the old development regime under Art. 3(r) E.C. (previously Art. 3(k) EEC), whereby special relationships were envisaged with overseas countries and territories of the Member States (Arts. 131–136a E.C., unamended). The Community has used its powers under Art. 113 EEC to conclude international agreements as part of the common commercial policy; often with development co-operation as a key element (see Case 45/86, *Commission v. Council (Generalised Tariff Preferences)*: [1987] E.C.R. 1493, 1522). Such measures have naturally not been restricted to the strict geographical boundaries laid down in Arts. 131 to 136a EEC. Article 3(q) E.C. codifies this application of the development provisions.

Articles 3(n), (o) and (p) E.C. on trans-European networks, health protection and education, and training and culture respectively, while marking the inclusion of these spheres as part of the Community policies laid down in Part Three of the Treaty, do not create a great deal of scope for Community action. This is reflected in the wording of Art. 3; Community activity in these areas is confined to "encouragement" and "contribution" rather than the harmonisation of the laws and regulations of Member States (except to ensure the inter-operability of trans-European networks in transport, telecommunications and energy infrastructure; see Art. 129c(1)). The inclusion of these areas in Art. 3 is somewhat ambiguous at this stage of the Community's development, given that they remain essentially national competences.

The new Art. 3(1) E.C. on the strengthening of the competitiveness of Community industry (see also Art. 130 E.C.) is an enigmatic provision and could give scope for considerable Community expenditure on measures currently financed by Member States (U.K. Select Committee on European Legislation, 15th Report, Session 1991–92, 24, pp. xxxix–lx at xlvii). Whether or not this will be the case is dependent on the achievement of unanimity in the Council (Art. 130(3)) and on budgetary constraints.

The final list of Community policies as espoused in the E.U. Treaty marks something of a watering down of the original Luxembourg draft Treaty. In particular, the Luxembourg proposal included consumer protection, energy, civil protection, and tourism. While consumer protection was retained in the negotiations (see Art. 3s E.C. and Art. 129a E.C.), energy, civil protection and tourism are left in the anomalous position of being included in the list of Community objectives (Art. 3(t) E.C.) without corresponding operative provisions in the Treaty itself. Declaration No. 1 on civil protection, tourism and energy appended to the Treaty, provides that these matters will be examined in the 1996 round of Treaty negotiations, to decide upon their potential inclusion as Titles within the Treaty. It remains to be seen whether the political difficulties that prevented their inclusion at Maastricht will be resolved by then.

Article 3a

1. For the purposes set out in Article 2, the activities of the Member States and the Community shall include, as provided in this Treaty and in accordance with the timetable set out therein, the adoption of an economic policy which is based on the close co-ordination of Member States' economic policies, on the internal market and on the definition of common objectives, and conducted in accordance with the principle of an open market economy with free competition.

2. Concurrently with the foregoing, and as provided in this Treaty and in accordance with the timetable and the procedures set out therein, these activities shall include the irrevocable fixing of exchange rates leading to the introduction of a single currency, the ECU, and the definition and conduct of a single monetary policy and exchange rate policy the primary objective of both of which shall be to maintain price stability and, without prejudice to this objective, to support the general economic policies in the Community, in accordance with the principle of an open market economy with free competition.

3. These activities of the Member States and the Community shall entail compliance with the following guiding principles: stable prices, sound public finances and monetary conditions and a sustainable balance of payments.

GENERAL NOTE

The centre-piece of the E.U. Treaty amendments is the establishment of a timetable for the progress towards economic and monetary union. This timetable was subsequently called into question by recessionary pressures in the European economy and the fluctuations in the ERM of the EMS (see Introduction and General Note above and the General Note on Title VI below). However, there now appears to be renewed optimism that a limited "hard core" monetary union can take place in 1999, even if its achievement in 1997 by a majority of Member States seems unlikely.

Article 3a sets out the broad goals of the progress envisaged towards economic and monetary union. It lays down the principles and tasks of the Community in pursuit of the specific provisions in Arts. 102a–109m E.C.

Article 3a(1) lays down the principles underlying the economic aspect of the union. The wording of this provision reflects the essentially decentralised nature of the progress towards economic union. The Community economic policy is to be based on the co-ordination of the Member States' own policies rather than on a single policy applicable to all Member States.

Article 3a(2) sets out the more specific and definite proposals underlying the achievement of the monetary side of the union process. The wording "irrevocable" and "single" highlight the nature of this process.

As with Art. 3a(1), this process is to take place in accordance with the timetable set out in the Treaty. It is possible that that timetable may be altered at the inter-governmental conference in

1996, despite the renewed optimism just mentioned. Whatever happens to the specific details of the economic and monetary union process, including the convergence criteria or the timetable itself, the fundamental principles of the process laid down in this Article are likely to remain. The ideas of an open market economy and stable prices, sound public finances, and a sustainable balance of payments are essential prerequisites of any effective convergence of the Member State economies.

Article 3b

The Community shall act within the limits of the powers conferred upon it by this Treaty and of the objectives assigned to it therein.

In areas which do not fall within its exclusive competence, the Community shall take action, in accordance with the principle of subsidiarity, only if and in so far as the objectives of the proposed action cannot be sufficiently achieved by the Member States and can therefore, by reason of the scale or effects of the proposed action, be better achieved by the Community.

Any action by the Community shall not go beyond what is necessary to achieve the objectives of this Treaty.

GENERAL NOTE

This marks the latest stage in the ongoing debate on the allocation of regulatory competences in the Community. The extension of the Community in the E.U. Treaty provided a forum for the rehashing of the old and unsettled problems of who should do what within the Community, an issue that has been present since the very inception of the EEC. The second paragraph of Art. 3b, encompassing the principle of subsidiarity, is the most significant attempt to date, and aims to lay down a guiding framework for the effective exercise of regulatory competences (see on this topic, Wilke and Wallace, *Approaches to Subsidiarity and Power Sharing in the European Community*, R.I.I.A. Discussion Papers No. 27, London, Royal Institute of International Affairs, 1990).

The principle of subsidiarity is implicit in Art. A of the E.U. Treaty, where it is stated that "This Treaty marks a new stage in the process of creating an ever closer union among the peoples of Europe, *in which decisions are taken as closely as possible to the citizen*" (emphasis added). The inclusion of the principle in its current format was particularly championed by the U.K. which tends to perceive it as a means of renationalising, and reclaiming competences currently exercised by the Community or, more graphically, as a "prophylactic against the contagion of Brussels" (Mackenzie Stuart, "Subsidiarity: A Busted Flush?" in Curtin & O'Keeffe eds., *Constitutional Adjudication in European Community and National Law* (1992), p. 21).

Attempts to attach a date to the emergence of the principle have been taken *ad absurdia*; most commentators distinguish the first explicit reference in the encyclical *Quadragesimo Anno* of Pope Pius XI in 1931: "Let the public authority leave to the lower groupings the care of lesser matters where it would expend an inordinate effort. It will thus be able to carry out more freely and more effectively those functions which belong only to it because it alone can perform them."

Whatever the minutiae of its origins it is a basic tenet of a democratic system that the decision-making process be carried out as close to the citizen as is viable. In so far as it relates to a layered decision-making process, there is little doubt that the principle of subsidiarity is the expression of a particular type of political culture—that of federal states ((1990) R.T.D.E. 441, esp. at p. 453). The division of competences between the *Länder* and the federal authority in Germany is an example of "subsidiarity" in action in a federal context (Santer in *Subsidiarity: The Challenge of Change, Proceedings of Jacques Delors Colloquium*, EIPA, (1991), p. 19). It has been remarked, however, that the principle of subsidiarity set out in Art. 79 of the German Constitution has not been effective (Everling, "Reflections on the Structure of the Union" (1992) 29 C.M.L.Rev. 1053).

The second paragraph of this Article, containing the Community definition of subsidiarity is an attempt to rationalise the division of competences in the Community. It is widely asserted that subsidiarity is best understood as a political or constitutional convention, rather than as a legal principle. It is capable of judicial application, but in a necessarily highly subjective fashion, which may lead to judicial restraint. Questions on the topic will hinge as much on the political practice of the Community institutions and of the Member States as upon the interpretation of the principle by the Court of Justice.

Para. 1

This paragraph would seem to be an express formulation of the *ultra vires* rule, based on the fundamental premise that the Community does not have *compétence de la compétence*, but only *compétence d'attribution.* The first clause: "the Community shall act within the limits of the powers conferred under this Treaty", reiterates the first ground of review under Art. 173 E.C. that the Community shall act only in those areas where it is competent to do so. The reason for the inclusion of the phrase "and of the objectives assigned to it therein" is, as Hartley points out, somewhat more ambiguous. He reasons that it marks another reformulation of an Art. 173 ground of review, that of the misuse of powers (42 I.C.L.Q. 213, at 215). Where the Community is acting within the powers assigned to it, it must use those powers only to attain the objectives assigned to it. As the Court puts it "a decision may amount to a misuse of powers if it appears to have been taken for purposes other than those stated" (Cases 18, 35/65, *Gutmann v. Commission* [1966] E.C.R. 103).

The paragraph, taken as a whole, may not be particularly significant in legal terms. Its inclusion, however, symbolises the desire of certain Member States to be reassured of the specific and limited nature of the Community's sphere of action.

Para. 2

The ambiguities surrounding the Community concept of subsidiarity found in this paragraph make the subsequent examination necessarily subjective. Reference must thus be made to the plethora of literature on the subject: Emiliou, "Subsidiarity: An Effective Barrier against the Enterprises of Ambition?" (1992) 17 E.L.Rev. 383; Toth, "The Principle of Subsidiarity in the Maastricht Treaty" (1992) 29 C.M.L.Rev. 1107; Lasok, (1992) 142 New L.J. 1228; U.K. Foreign Affairs Committee, *Europe after Maastricht*, Interim Report, Session 1992–93; *Subsidiarity: the Challenge of Change, Proceedings of Jacques Delors Colloquium*, EIPA, (1991); Mackenzie-Stuart, "Subsidiarity: A Busted Flush?" in Curtin & O'Keeffe eds., *Constitutional Adjudication in European Community and National Law* (1992); Walker, *Subsidiarity: Its Application in Practice*, I.E.A. (1994); de Groof ed., *Subsidiarity and Education* (1994); and Cass, "The Word that saves Maastricht? The Principle of Subsidiarity and the Division of Powers within the European Community" (1992) 29 C.M.L.Rev. 1107.

The first sentence of this paragraph indicates that the subsidiarity principle is not applicable to areas "within the exclusive competence of the Community". The dichotomy between areas of exclusive and concurrent jurisdiction is one well known to students of federalism. Matters within the former category are to be exempt from the application of subsidiarity. They are to be carried out by the Community and there will be no burden on the Community institutions to justify any exercise of their regulatory competences in these areas. Unfortunately, nowhere in the Treaty is any explicit recognition given to the categorisation of particular areas into either exclusive or concurrent competences. This has led some commentators to assert that the result will be that the subsidiarity test will be utilised only in a very restricted number of areas. This viewpoint, which is essentially based on pre-Maastricht European Court of Justice jurisprudence, involves two main predicates.

First, there is the doctrine of supremacy of Community law, whereby the enactment of Community legislation in a specified area automatically precludes the application of any conflicting provisions of national law. This need not lead to exclusive competence, however, as there are myriad areas where both the Community and the Member States exercise complementary competences; conflicting legislation is a special case.

More cogently, opponents of an unquantified "exclusive competences" exception, point to the Court's practice in declaring "Community exclusive jurisdiction" in fields where the Community has exercised the right conferred by the Treaty to take binding measures in that area. As Toth makes clear, once the Community has "occupied the field" by taking legislative action in certain areas, any national measure not expressly authorised by the Community or which exceeds the limits of the powers delegated back to the Member State is illegal. The concern is that the continued utilisation of such jurisprudence in the application of Art. 3b will mean that subsidiarity would be applicable only when the Community legislated for the first time in a new field. The current practice of the Community would tend to suggest that the notion of the Community "occupying the field" is becoming dated. More and more the Community is moving towards minimum harmonisation, which specifically leaves the Member States with the power to adopt stricter laws or set higher standards, provided they satisfy the minimum laid down by the Community (see, *e.g.* Mortelmans, "Minimum Harmonisation and Consumer Protection" [1988] E.C.L.J. 2). A great deal of the internal market operates on this principle; a tacit acknowledgement of the impossibility of legislating for every eventuality and also the need to permit differences in Member States with different attitudes and traditions. The decision of the Court of Justice in Opinion 2/91 I.L.O. *Convention No. 170* ([1993] C.M.L.R.) indicates that the principle of minimum harmonisation will effectively prevent the acquisition of exclusive competence by the Community in policy areas so harmonised.

It is certainly inconvenient that no exhaustive list of measures coming within the exclusive jurisdiction of the Community is laid down by the Treaty; however, any such list would be liable to extension over time in respect of areas where the Community acts definitively; and the scope of listed policy fields would remain the subject of disputes (see, *e.g.* Opinion 1/94 *GATT* [1994] I E.C.R. 1 on the scope of the common commercial policy). A draft on subsidiarity submitted to the European Parliament by Giscard D'Estaing followed the German Constitution and set out defined areas of Community and Member State competence. The Commission, in its Communication to the Council and Parliament (SEC (92) 1990 final, CONS DOC 9649/92), admitted that the Maastricht Treaty had confused the Member States by drawing a distinction between exclusive competences and concurrent competences shared with the Member States without clarifying the content of each category. In response, the Commission laid down a list of measures it considered fell within the exclusive competence of the Community. These measures centre on the four fundamental freedoms, and other common policies essential for the completion of the internal market, including: the removal of barriers to the free movement of goods, persons, services and capital (Art. 8a EEC, now Art. 7a E.C.); the common commercial policy (Art. 113 E.C.); the general rules on competition; the common organisation of agricultural markets (Art. 39); the conservation of fishery resources (Art. 102) and organisation of fishery markets; the essential elements of transport policy (Art. 75); and measures necessitated by the third stage of economic and monetary union (CONS DOC 9649/92, at 7). This list is not "fixed indefinitely" but will have to change as "European integration progresses". To this list of exclusive competences must be added specific Community obligations, including, *inter alia*, competition policy, enforcement of Community law and Community expenditure (conclusions of the Presidency, Edinburgh Summit 12/10/92, SN 456/92).

The opinions of the Commission on the matter, while certainly indicative of its intended future practice, are not binding. Opinion 1/94 of the Court of Justice (*GATT* [1994] E.C.R. I–1) certainly indicates, in the field of external relations, that the Commission's prescriptions need not be determinative.

Turning now to the subsidiarity principle proper, it will apply to all areas in which regulatory competence is to be shared between the Community and Member States. The burden of proof appears to rest on the Community institutions to demonstrate the need to legislate at the Community level, rather than at the national level. The Article appears to posit a two-tier test, with requirements that the Community demonstrate that national action cannot achieve the relevant objectives, and also, that the measures it takes will be a better response to the requirements of the situation than national action. However, these requirements must be conflated in practice (as is indicated by the term "therefore" which connects the two requirements): it is the insufficiency of Member State action, by reason of the scale and effects of the action required, which will indicate that the objective can be better achieved by the Community.

The Commission has laid down draft guidelines on the assessment of the fulfilment of these tests, while acknowledging "an inevitable lack of precision" and the need to treat each case on an individual basis. More helpfully, the Commission suggested a number of *indicia* of the need for action at the Community level. These include: the cross-border implications of the proposed action; the consequences of failure to act within the Community; and the need to avoid the distortion of competition within the Community. The influence of "cross-border implications" on the assessment of the competent regulatory body was recognised in the Spinelli Draft Treaty on European Union of 1984 ([1984] 2 E.C. Bull.). Given today's highly market-integrated Community, it is very difficult for measures to pertain to one Member State alone.

It is unlikely to be in the judicial application of nebulous tests of efficiency and necessity that the principle of subsidiarity will prove its worth. In the political sphere it may make the Commission more restrained in the measures it proposes and the Council more cautious in the measures it adopts. Subsidiarity depends for its political effectiveness on its acceptance into the "institutional culture" of the Community. The European Parliament has committed itself to paying particular attention to whether a legislative proposal respects the principle of subsidiarity (see Rule 36E of the European Parliament's Rules of Procedure as amended subsequent to the E.U. Treaty in [1993] O.J. C268/51).

There are already examples of such acceptance. The application of a *de minimis* attitude to regulatory measures is implicit in both the Edinburgh summit conclusions and the Commission Communication. Where possible, the imposition of legislative harmonisation is to be avoided and replaced by the least obtrusive alternative, for example, mutual recognition, the adoption of recommendations, the provision of financial support or the promotion of co-operation between Member States. Moreover, the withdrawal of proposed legislative measures at the Edinburgh summit and similar subsequent action(see, *e.g.* [1993] 11 E.C. Bull., 2.2.1 and [1994] 6 E.U. Bull., 1.1.1), while not dealing with any matters of great substance, would tend to suggest that at least the principle is being noted by the institutions (see Weatherill and Beaumont, *E.C. Law*, (1993) pp. 779–82). On the other hand, many of the policy options just mentioned run contrary to the recommendations of the Sutherland Report on the Internal Market, which suggested that there was a failure to realise the promise of the internal market because of diverse implementation practices in the Member States.

In legal terms, the major question as regards the subsidiarity principle is the role of the Court of Justice in its application. Despite many protestations that the essentially political nature of the concept ought to preclude judicial consideration of what will be little more than political value judgments, the inclusion of subsidiarity as one of the principles of the Community means that it is the duty of the court under Art. 164 E.C. to rule on its application and interpretation. Subsidiarity is a legal principle; it is merely very difficult to interpret. The existence of so many imponderables makes it impossible to predict the approach of the court. Much discussion has of course centred on the court's past predilection for the expansion of the Community's power and of its own jurisdiction.

It would seem that it will be very difficult to succeed in any action for the annulment of a piece of Community legislation on the grounds of infringement of the subsidiarity principle. This is particularly so for individuals, who would need to fulfil the strict *locus standi* requirements of Art. 173 E.C.

The Commission reported to the December 1993 European Council on a review of certain Community rules with a view to adapting them to the subsidiarity principle. An inter-institutional declaration on the principles of democracy, transparency and subsidiarity has been adopted (E.C. Bull. 10–93, 1.6.2 & 2.2.1), as well as an inter-institutional agreement on the implementation of the principle ([1993] 10 E.C. Bull., 1.6.3 & 2.2.1).

Another very important aspect of the subsidiarity principle concerns the number of levels to which the principle will be applicable. A literal reading of the Article suggests that the lowest level at which the matter might be dealt with efficiently is the correct one. This has led to a great deal of debate about the future role of the regions and other such bodies in the regulation of the Community. However, the Article speaks only of the achievement of the objects of action by the Member States, thus apparently leaving it to each State to decide how these competences should be distributed within its own political system.

Para. 3

The third paragraph of this Article is an expression of the general Community law principle of proportionality and thus is an extension of the *vires* condition in the first paragraph. The Court of Justice applies the proportionality test to any Community action (see Weatherill and Beaumont, *E.C. Law* (1993), pp. 225–226; Hartley, *Foundations of European Community Law*, (3rd. ed., 1994), pp. 155–6; see further the discussion above of proportionality in Community and German law, and the authorities cited there).

Article 4

1. The tasks entrusted to the Community shall be carried out by the following institutions:
    a European Parliament,
    a Council,
    a Commission,
    a Court of Justice,
    a Court of Auditors.
Each institution shall act within the limits of the powers conferred upon it by this Treaty.
2. The Council and the Commission shall be assisted by an Economic and Social Committee and a Committee of the Regions acting in an advisory capacity.

General Note

Para. 1

This article has been amended to take account of the elevation of the Court of Auditors to the status of a fully fledged Community institution. The court was set up by the Financial Provisions Treaty in 1975 and held its first session in 1977. The membership of the court is roughly equivalent to that of the Court of Justice. Its main responsibility lies in the examination of the Community accounts and the submission of an annual report on the sound management of the Community finances.

The upgrading of the court will not affect its duties, which are now laid down in Arts. 188a–c. The provisions governing the court have been moved to Part V of the amended Treaty, dealing with the institutions. The original Art. 206 E.C. which contained essentially similar provisions, is now dedicated to the budgetary procedure in general.

The goal of stricter and more effective financial controls in the Community is highlighted by the insertion of Art. 209a E.C. on the combating of the fraudulent use of Community funds. See generally, *The Legal Protection of the Financial Interests of the Community* (1994).

Para. 2

This paragraph has been amended to take account of the creation of the new Committee of the Regions (Art. 198a–c E.C.). Its inclusion alongside the Economic and Social Committee reflects the two bodies' similar tasks and make-up. Moreover, Protocol No. 16, appended to the Treaty, states that the two Committees are to have a common institutional structure.

Article 4a

A European System of Central Banks (hereinafter referred to as "ESCB") and a European Central Bank (hereinafter referred to as "ECB") shall be established in accordance with the procedures laid down in this Treaty; they shall act within the limits of the powers conferred upon them by this Treaty and by the Statute of the ESCB and of the ECB (hereinafter referred to as "Statute of the ESCB") annexed thereto.

GENERAL NOTE

This Article gives effective institutional status to the new monetary organs of the Community. The start of the third stage of economic and monetary union will bring into being the European System of Central Banks and the European Central Bank to carry out the tasks entrusted to them, in particular the definition and implementation of a Community monetary policy.

The governing Statute of the European Central Bank and the European System of Central Banks is laid down in the Protocol on the Statute of the European System of Central Banks and the European Central Bank (Protocol No. 3), supplementing the institutional provisions in the Treaty itself (Arts. 109a–d E.C.).

The failure to include the European Central Bank and the European System of Central Banks in Art. 4 E.C. (institutions of the Community) would appear to be due to the fact that these bodies will not come into being until a later date. Nevertheless, the European Central Bank and European System of Central Banks are for all practical purposes Community institutions. The European Central Bank will have legal personality (Art. 9 of Protocol No. 3) and may be a party to legal proceedings in Member State courts. Moreover, European Central Bank legislation will be subject to the usual procedures for judicial review under Art. 173 E.C. Such legislation is permitted to have the force of law in Ireland by virtue of the extension of the second clause of Art. 29.4.5 of the Constitution to "bodies competent under the Treaties establishing the Communities" (see above).

Article 4b

A European Investment Bank is hereby established, which shall act within the limits of the powers conferred upon it by this Treaty and the Statute annexed thereto.

GENERAL NOTE

Under the EEC Treaty, the European Investment Bank was given the task of facilitating the economic expansion of the Community by opening up new resources (Art. 3(j) EEC, repealed). Reflecting the European Investment Bank's position as an element of Community policy, the provisions governing the organisation, tasks and working methods of the European Investment Bank were located in Arts. 129 and 130 EEC. The Maastricht amendments have moved these provisions into the institutional title at Arts. 198d and 198e E.C. They remain largely unaltered and the Protocol on the Statute of the European Investment Bank annexed to the Treaty is untouched.

The establishment of the European Investment Bank by the Community Treaty itself is merely an acknowledgement of its *de facto* institutional status prior to the Maastricht amendments. The European Investment Bank has enjoyed legal personality under Art. 129 EEC and, under Art. 180 EEC (unamended in relation to European Investment Bank), the Court of Justice has jurisdiction in disputes concerning the fulfilment of the Member States' obligations under the Statute of the European Investment Bank or regarding any measures adopted by the Governors of the European Investment Bank.

Article 5

Member States shall take all appropriate measures, whether general or particular, to ensure fulfilment of the obligations arising out of this Treaty or resulting from action taken by the institutions of the Community. They shall facilitate the achievement of the Community's tasks.

They shall abstain from any measure which could jeopardise the attainment of the objectives of this Treaty.

Article 6

Within the scope of application of this Treaty, and without prejudice to any special provisions contained therein, any discrimination on grounds of nationality shall be prohibited.

The Council, acting in accordance with the procedure referred to in Article 189c, may adopt rules designed to prohibit such discrimination.

GENERAL NOTE

This Article, previously Art. 7 EEC, replaces the obsolete Art. 6 EEC on economic policy co-ordination. The content of the original Art. 7 EEC is preserved, continuing the application of the co-operation procedure to measures in this area (as introduced by the S.E.A.). The only alteration is to take account of the changed nomenclature for this procedure (the simple terminology "co-operation" has been replaced by the "procedure referred to in Art. 189c E.C.").

In pursuing measures under this Article, the Community institutions are permitted to enact regulations, directives and recommendations at their discretion. However, the actual promulgation of measures under this provision is rare. Measures under the more specific provisions on the four freedoms are much more common.

However, in *European Parliament v. Council* (Case C-295/90, [1992] I E.C.R. 4193), the European Court of Justice found that the adoption of a Directive under Art. 235 EEC, on the right of residence of students, was invalid and the Council ought to have relied instead on Art. 7 EEC. The court went on to record that "measures adopted under the second paragraph of Art. 7 EEC (now Art. 6 E.C.) did not necessarily have to be limited to regulating the rights derived from the first paragraph of that Article, but could also deal with aspects where regulation appeared necessary to enable those rights to be exercised effectively". This ruling would seem to open up further the potential for Art. 6 E.C. to be utilised as a legislative basis (see O'Leary, (1992) 30 C.M.L.Rev. 639 for analysis of the implications of this case).

More important than the enactment of Community legislation, is the potential this Article affords those alleging discrimination to take their cases before the relevant national court. Such actions are common, but rest on the alleged discrimination not falling under one of the more specific anti-discriminatory Articles such as the provisions on the four freedoms, competition rules, or special anti-discrimination rules in the fields of agriculture or transport. The case law in this field is vast. For an overview see Kapteyn & Verloren van Themaat, *Introduction to the Law of the European Communities* (2nd ed., 1989) pp. 92–7.

In the interests of clarity, it is to be regretted that such an important and well known Article has been renumbered. The inclusion of the new provisions which reputedly necessitated such alterations could have been carried out much less clumsily.

Article 7

1. The common market shall be progressively established during a transitional period of 12 years.

This transitional period shall be divided into three stages of four years each; the length of each stage may be altered in accordance with the provisions set out below.

2. To each stage there shall be assigned a set of actions to be initiated and carried through concurrently.

3. Transition from the first to the second stage shall be conditional upon a finding that the objectives specifically laid down in this Treaty for the first stage have in fact been attained in substance and that, subject to the exceptions and procedures provided for in this Treaty, the obligations have been fulfilled.

This finding shall be made at the end of the fourth year by the Council, acting unanimously on a report from the Commission. A Member State may not, however, prevent unanimity by relying upon the non-fulfilment of its own obligations. Failing unanimity, the first stage shall automatically be extended for one year.

At the end of the fifth year, the Council shall make its finding under the same conditions. Failing unanimity, the first stage shall automatically be extended for a further year.

At the end of the sixth year, the Council shall make its finding, acting by a qualified majority on a report from the Commission.

4. Within one month of the last-mentioned vote any Member State which voted with the minority or, if the required majority was not obtained, any Member State shall be entitled to call upon the Council to appoint an arbitration board whose decision shall be binding upon all Member States and upon the institutions of the Community. The arbitration board shall consist of three members appointed by the Council acting unanimously on a proposal from the Commission.

If the Council has not appointed the members of the arbitration board within one month of being called upon to do so, they shall be appointed by the Court of Justice within a further period of one month.

The arbitration board shall elect its own Chairman.

The board shall make its award within six months of the date of the Council vote referred to in the last subparagraph of paragraph 3.

5. The second and third stages may not be extended or curtailed except by a decision of the Council, acting unanimously on a proposal from the Commission.

6. Nothing in the preceding paragraphs shall cause the transitional period to last more than 15 years after the entry into force of this Treaty.

7. Save for the exceptions or derogations provided for in this Treaty, the expiry of the transitional period shall constitute the latest date by which all the rules laid down must enter into force and all the measures required for establishing the common market must be implemented.

GENERAL NOTE

Again, this Article represents a renumbering of an existing provision rather than a substantive amendment to the Community Treaties. This Article, previously Art. 8 EEC, deals with the transitional period to the original goal of a common market as set out by the EEC Treaty. The reason for its continued inclusion in the Treaty is unclear, given that its provisions are universally obsolete.

Article 7a

The Community shall adopt measures with the aim of progressively establishing the internal market over a period expiring on December 31, 1992, in accordance with the provisions of this Article and of Articles 7b, 7c, 28, 57(2), 59, 70(1), 84, 99, 100a and 100b and without prejudice to the other provisions of this Treaty.

The internal market shall comprise an area without internal frontiers in which the free movement of goods, persons, services and capital is ensured in accordance with the provisions of this Treaty.

Article 7b

The Commission shall report to the Council before December 31, 1988 and again before December 31, 1990 on the progress made towards achieving the internal market within the time limit fixed in Article 7a.

The Council, acting by a qualified majority on a proposal from the Commission, shall determine the guidelines and conditions necessary to ensure balanced progress in all the sectors concerned.

Article 7c

When drawing up its proposals with a view to achieving the objectives set out in Article 7a, the Commission shall take into account the extent of the effort that certain economies showing differences in development will have to sustain during the period of establishment of the internal market and it may propose appropriate provisions.

If these provisions take the form of derogations, they must be of a temporary nature and must cause the least possible disturbance to the functioning of the common market.

GENERAL NOTE

Articles 7a–7c originally introduced by the SEA, are unchanged but have been renumbered from Arts. 8a–c EEC to their current titles.

PART TWO (CITIZENSHIP OF THE UNION)

GENERAL NOTE

Part Two of the E.C. Treaty is now concerned exclusively with the new provisions on the citizenship of the Union. Article 8 E.C. lays down the fundamental basis of this concept, while the specific rights attached to the status of Community citizenship are laid down in Arts. 8a–d E.C. The rights included in Part Two of the Treaty and related Articles are restrictive and far from the wide scope envisaged by some of the Member States in the run-up to the Maastricht summit. Nevertheless, the mere inclusion of such a politically sensitive topic within the Community structure itself is important, not least in terms of the symbolism for the new Union. (For a general analysis of this part of the Treaty see Hyland, Loftus & Whelan, *Citizenship of the European Union* I.E.A. (1995); Closa, "The Concept of Citizenship in the Treaty on European Union" (1992) 29 C.M.L.Rev. 1137).

As an inherently political concept, the Member States were significantly divided over the nature and scope of any notion of Union citizenship. The conferral of rights and duties on persons as citizens of the Union was seen by many national parliaments as a challenge to national sovereignty. The inclusion of political, social, economic and human rights were all mooted in the subsequent negotiations.

The first reference to the inclusion of a concept of citizenship in the inter-governmental negotiations came from the Spanish Prime Minister Felipe Gonzalez (*Agence Europe* No. 5252, May 11, 1990).

The basis for his assertion was the political determination to see the creation of the new Union structure backed up by a proper definition of the rights and duties of the citizens of this new entity. In pursuit of this goal he sought, *inter alia*, unlimited freedom of movement and the right to vote and stand for election regardless of country of residence.

The European Parliament, in its contribution on the matter, called for a comprehensive catalogue of fundamental rights and freedoms attributable to Union citizens. This catalogue, essentially based on the Council of Europe's European Convention on Human Rights, contained rights specific to the Community process, including the right to move freely as well as certain social rights (See European Parliament Resolution of November 22, 1990, *Rapporteur* D. Martin). The Commission, having already recorded its desire to see the Community accede to the European Convention on Human Rights, requested the consideration of broader issues such as a specific right to equal opportunities and equal enjoyment of social rights.

Human rights do not appear to have been specifically dealt with by the European Council in its deliberations on citizenship. The only reference to the European Convention on Human Rights is contained in the expressly non-justiciable Art. F of the Common Provisions of the E.U. Treaty; any development of Community human rights will continue instead through Court of

Justice jurisprudence. It is not desirable to restrict fundamental human rights to those who are citizens of the Union but rather, on the model of the European Convention on Human Rights, to apply those rights to all who are present within the Union. The Council has now sought the opinion of the Court of Justice on the compatibility with the Treaties of accession by the Communities to the Convention ([1993] 4 E.U. Bull., 1.1.4).

The final enunciation of the concept of Union citizenship in the TEU falls far short of many expectations, and not just in terms of human rights. The European Council's conclusions from the Rome summit called for the development of citizenship rights in a number of areas. First, civic rights, including the participation of non-nationals in municipal and European Parliamentary elections. Secondly, social and economic rights, such as the freedom of movement and equality of opportunities and treatment for all Union citizens. Thirdly, the Council looked to Union co-operation in the protection of citizens outwith the Community. Fourthly, it raised the possibility of the development of the defence of citizen's rights through some form of administrative officer in the Community. These areas are all reflected in the new provisions.

Two fundamental points must be made. First, the majority of the rights set out in Part Two of the Treaty are simply additional to existing rights already found elsewhere in the Treaty; they are supplementing current protections rather than creating new ones. This is especially true as regards Art. 8a where the free movement of citizens is reiterated. This adds very little to the situation under current Community law, as developed by the residence directives. Secondly, as Hartley is keen to point out ("Constitutional and Institutional Implications of the Maastricht Agreement" (1993) 42 I.C.L.Q. 213, at 219–220), those provisions which do seem to create new citizenship rights, such as the minor foray into political issues in Art. 8b, are subject to subsequent unanimous agreement by the Council as to their content. This is equally true of Art. 8c, where negotiations will be required with third countries as well as intra-Member State agreements.

Article 8

1. Citizenship of the Union is hereby established.
Every person holding the nationality of a Member State shall be a citizen of the Union.
2. Citizens of the Union shall enjoy the rights conferred by this Treaty and shall be subject to the duties imposed thereby.

GENERAL NOTE

Para. (1)

This paragraph, duplicating the wording of the Commission draft, establishes the principle of Union citizenship. The second sentence however is the operative provision. This lays down the basic principle for the conferral of Union citizenship that "every person holding the nationality of a Member State shall be a citizen of the Union". Thus the nationality laws of the Member States will implicitly decree those persons who are eligible for Union citizenship. While this will generally attribute the rights of citizenship to all Member State nationals there is nothing to stop Member States from making declarations defining those persons who qualify as their nationals for Community law purposes. The U.K. have such a declaration in force, laid down after the passing of the British Nationality Act 1981 (see [1983] O.J. C23/1). It is a moot point as to whether or not the Court of Justice could overrule the nationality provisions of a Member State for failure to comply with Treaty obligations. The fact that the vast majority of Community rights fall to be conferred on individuals solely by virtue of their status as Community nationals (with some exceptions, *e.g.* Arts. 30 and 95 E.C.) makes these nationality provisions very important. Declaration No. 2 to the Treaty on the nationality of a Member State states that: "the question whether an individual possesses the nationality of a Member State shall be settled solely by reference to the national law of the Member State concerned". This view has been accepted by the Court of Justice in *Micheletti v. Delegación del Gobierno en Cantabria* (Case C–369/90, [1992] E.C.R. I–4239). While the Court stated that the definition of nationality was within the competence of Member States, it stated that this competence must be exercised in compliance with Community law; it is not anticipated, however, that this qualification will cause the Court to intervene in national decisions on this sensitive topic. (See also Evans, "Nationality Law and European Integration", (1991) 16 E.L.Rev. 192).

The prospect for any harmonisation of the European rules for decreeing nationality is remote for three reasons. First, the conferral of the status of citizen is entwined with that of nationality for international law purposes, and thus relates to the basic principles of state sovereignty; it is therefore unlikely to be given up to the Community institutions. Secondly, the pressure to give up such powers is unlikely to be forthcoming. If the Member States' rules on the conferral of citizenship were divergent, then those states with stricter conditions might well press for tighter Community-wide controls. The reality is that, although the Member States do exercise different tests for conferring citizenship, they tend in general to be quite strict. Thirdly, any codification of the law on acquisition of citizenship is unlikely unless the rights exercisable by virtue of this status become much more important and, as a result, the Member States find it necessary to reach an agreement on exactly who should be a citizen and thus benefit from these rights.

Para. (2)

This seemingly innocuous section has created a great deal of controversy as well as highlighting the nature of citizenship. The Article makes it quite clear that the rights and duties of the Union are to be additional to the national rights and responsibilities stemming from the citizenship of a Member State, and additional to the Community rights and responsibilities stemming from the Community Treaties. The interplay of these different rights and duties will be a matter for the Court of Justice. It is unlikely, even in the event of the Court conferring direct applicability on Art. 8, that the resultant litigation would have any determinative effect on current practice. This is a direct result of the fact that many of the Union citizenship provisions add little to existing rights in the Community sphere. Litigation is most likely to assert the right of free movement within the Member States, under Art. 8a(1), but the wording of that provision specifically retains the exceptions to the principle found in existing Community law (see note on that Article). Litigation on free movement of persons probably has a better chance of success under Art. 7a E.C.

The controversy on this Article surrounds the inclusion of the reference to the obligation of Union citizen to comply with the "duties imposed" as a result of such citizenship. The current provisions on citizenship confer only rights and entitlements so this reference to indistinct future duties caused concern in many of the Member States (including Ireland) prior to ratification, not least due to scare-mongering over the potential of conscription as one of the potential duties to be imposed on Union citizens. Such fears are essentially ungrounded, given that any development of the citizenship provisions requires unanimity in Council and their adoption by the Member States in accordance with their respective constitutional practice (Art. 8e E.C.). Thus nothing can be added without the effective equivalent of an inter-governmental conference on the subject, with no legal potential for the imposition on a Member State of an undesired Treaty addition. Section A of the Decision Concerning Denmark adopted at the Edinburgh European Council makes it clear that any addition to the citizenship provisions in that country will require, as well as unanimity in Council, either a majority of five-sixths of the Parliament or a majority in Parliament and in a popular referendum ([1992] 12 E.C. Bull., I.5). This adds nothing new to the provisions of Article 8e but was felt necessary by the Danish government to quell concerns in that country over potentially unwelcome developments in the field of citizenship being forced on the Danes.

Article 8a

1. Every citizen of the Union shall have the right to move and reside freely within the territory of the Member States, subject to the limitations and conditions laid down in this Treaty and by the measures adopted to give it effect.

2. The Council may adopt provisions with a view to facilitating the exercise of the rights referred to in paragraph 1; save as otherwise provided in this Treaty, the Council shall act unanimously on a proposal from the Commission and after obtaining the assent of the European Parliament.

GENERAL NOTE

Para. (1)

This Article deals with the principle of free movement of citizens in the Union. The original Treaty, in particular Arts. 48–52 EEC, enshrined the rights of freedom of movement and residence for Community nationals. This did not, however, lead to the creation of a systematic regime of freedom of movement for all Community nationals. This position is continued by the new Article which, while seeming to create a generalised right to free movement for Union (as opposed to Community) citizens, must be read in terms of the pre-existing exceptions to that freedom as embodied in the secondary legislation on the subject.

Prior to June 30, 1992, the exercise of the freedom of movement and residence was dependent on the person's economic status. Under the old provisions, Member State nationals who were workers or dependants of workers, enjoyed a right to live in any Member State and to claim State benefits on the same conditions as nationals of the host State. The specifics of this general right were laid down in a number of regulations and directives (*e.g.* Reg. 1612/68 on the eligibility of nationals of Member States to take employment in another State "with the same priority as nationals of that state" and to be joined by their families; Regulation 1251/70 on the right to remain in the State after the period of employment has terminated; Dir. 68/369 on the abolition of restrictions on free movement and residence in the Community and Dirs. 75/34 and 75/35 extending similar rights to self-employed persons).

The three new Directives which took effect from June 30, 1992 still do not create a general right of free movement and residence as desired by the Commission. They certainly extended the net to new categories of Community nationals, attributing such rights to students (Dir. 90/366/EEC, [1990] O.J. L180/30), retired workers (Dir. 90/365/EEC, [1990] O.J. L180/28) and all "non-economically active persons" (Dir. 90/364/EEC, [1990] O.J. L180/26). Directive 90/366/EEC on student residence was annulled by the Court of Justice in *European Parliament v. Council* (Case C–295/90, [1992] I E.C.R. 4193) but was replaced on the appropriate legal basis by Dir. 93/96/EEC ([1993] O.J. L317/59). Directive 90/364/EEC, which attributes the right of residence to all those nationals of Member States (now Union citizens) who do not already enjoy that right under an existing provision of Community law means that virtually all Community nationals are now covered. Thus it has been argued, quite credibly, that little is added by the new Art. 8a (Hartley, (1993) 42 I.C.L.Q. 213, at 219). However, the exceptions laid down in the secondary legislation outlined above will continue to apply under the new Art. 8a. Thus the application of Art. 8a will be open only to those with sufficient resources, who will not become a burden on the Member State, and who have sickness insurance where relevant. These requirements apply to both nationals and dependants alike and aim to prevent nationals "shopping" for the most generous social security provisions in the Community. The citizenship freedoms in Art. 8a are also subject to derogations on the grounds of public policy, public security and health, probably to be applied in accordance with the jurisprudence built up around the existing Dir. 64/221 EEC.

Para. (2)

This Article permits the adoption of measures facilitating the exercise of these rights by Council adoption of a Commission proposal. While this procedure is less arduous than that laid down in Art. 8e E.C. it still requires Council unanimity and the Parliament is given a power of veto over any measure by virtue of the assent procedure.

Article 8b

1. Every citizen of the Union residing in a Member State of which he is not a national shall have the right to vote and to stand as a candidate at municipal elections in the Member State in which he resides, under the same conditions as nationals of that State. This right shall be exercised subject to detailed arrangements to be adopted before December 31, 1994 by the Council, acting unanimously on a proposal from the Commission and after consulting the European Parliament; these arrangements may provide for derogations where warranted by problems specific to a Member State.

2. Without prejudice to Article 138(3) and to the provisions adopted for its implementation, every citizen of the Union residing in a Member State of which he is not a national shall have the right to vote and to stand as a candidate in elections to the European Parliament in the Member State in which he resides, under the same conditions as nationals of that State. This right shall be exercised subject to detailed arrangements to be adopted before December 31, 1993 by the Council, acting unanimously on a proposal from the Commission and after consulting the European Parliament; these arrangements may provide for derogations where warranted by problems specific to a Member State.

General Note

This Article recognises the right of every citizen of the Union to vote and stand for election in the European Parliament and municipal elections in the Member State in which he resides. This is a large symbolic step for the Community, the first time that political rights as such have been laid down in the Treaty. The attribution of such rights to all citizens of the Union means that factors external to the Member State will determine eligibility to vote and stand for election. However, the reference to the potential for Member State derogations is indicative of the difficulties which were envisaged, and derogations have been secured by a number of Member States.

Treaty Establishing the European Community

Para. (1)

Under this Article, citizens of the Union are to be eligible to vote in municipal elections in the Member State in which they are resident "under the same conditions as the nationals of that state". This right is to be exercised subject to detailed arrangements adopted before December 31, 1994. (Closa "The Concept of Citizenship in the Treaty on European Union" (1992) 29 C.M.L.Rev. 1137, 1163).

The Council has now adopted a directive on participation in municipal elections (see E.C. Press Release 11871/94, recording the decisions of the Council of December 19–20, 1994). The requirement of unanimity in Council for the adoption of these detailed arrangements meant that derogations from the rules were probably unavoidable. The wording "where warranted by the problems specific to a Member State" was generally taken as a reference to Luxembourg, where over 25 per cent of the resident population consists of non-Luxembourg national Union citizens. Thus the attribution of voting rights to these persons would have significantly altered the make-up of the Luxembourg electorate and was opposed by the Luxembourg Government. However, the specific reference to the potential of derogations may have encouraged other Member States to assert their own national problems as grounds for special treatment, thus threatening the degree of uniformity necessary to ensure the effective operation of this right. This has happened in the case of Belgium, which has won the right for communes where the linguistic balance may be tipped by a large foreign population to provide particularly stringent residence requirements before other Union citizens may vote. France has placed checks on the entitlement of non-French local representatives to vote for the Senate or to hold the offices of mayor or deputy mayor (which have substantial police powers). Ireland, which grants local suffrage to all residents for a certain period irrespective of nationality, has not felt the need for similar restrictions; while the powers of local authorities are limited, they do have a role in electing members of Seanad Éireann. The right of other Community nationals to vote at local elections has never been as problematic in Ireland as it has been in jurisdictions such as France. This may reflect an element of national tolerance, but probably also reflects the fact that Ireland has a relatively low percentage of non-nationals residing in the State in comparison with other jurisdictions.

Non-citizens who are resident in the State were first given the right to vote at local elections by s.1 of the Local Elections Act, 1972. This section has now been replaced by the combined provisions of s.10 of the Electoral Act, 1992 and s.23 of the Local Government Act, 1994. The right of non-nationals resident in the State to stand as candidates in local elections is now recognised for the first time by s.5 of the 1994 Act. Article 8b E.C. acknowledges that restrictions can be placed on the eligibility of potential candidates, provided these conditions apply equally to citizens and non-nationals. Section 6 imposes certain disqualifications (*e.g.* persons serving a prison sentence for longer than six months), but these disqualifications apply equally to nationals and non-nationals alike. It may be noted that these provisions apply to all resident non-nationals and not simply to citizens of other Community countries.

Para. (2)

Similar provisions are envisaged as regards the conferral of electoral rights for the European Parliamentary elections. The provision was subject to the adoption by unanimity of detailed arrangements by December 31, 1993. This was a year earlier than the timetable envisaged under Art. 8b(1) because of the desire to see the rules in force prior to the 1994 European Parliamentary elections.

The Council passed a Directive (93/109/E.C.) in December 1993 to provide for the right to vote and stand for the European Parliament, to be implemented by February 1994 and in good time for the elections in June 1994. It provides for a derogation in respect of problems specific to a Member State, where Union citizens from other Member States form over 20 per cent of the voting age population; in that case, a residence requirement is permitted (five years for suffrage, 10 years for candidacy). However, derogations are subject to review, and the residence requirement is not applicable to Union citizens who by reason of residence outside their own Member State have lost their entitlement to vote or stand there. This derogation was designed for Luxembourg. Ireland has long adopted a *communautaire* attitude in the case of elections to the European Parliament. Thus, ever since the first direct elections in 1979, all Community citizens resident in Ireland have been given the right to vote at such elections, under s.3 of the European Assembly Elections Act, 1977. By virtue of s.7 of the 1977 Act, Community nationals resident in Ireland may stand for elections to the European Parliament on the same basis as Irish citizens. Section 3 of the 1977 Act has now been replaced by section 9 of the Electoral Act, 1992, which provides that:

> "A person shall be entitled to be registered as a European elector in a constituency if he has reached the age of eighteen years and if, on the qualifying date, he was ordinarily resident in that constituency and was either—

(a) a citizen of Ireland, or
(b) a national of a Member State other than the State."

Unlike the case of local elections, this right is—understandably—confined to Community nationals. Directive 93/109/E.C. was implemented in Ireland by the European Parliament Elections (Voting and Candidature) Regulations, 1994 (S.I. No. 14), which has primacy over the European Parliament Election Acts, 1977 to 1993.

Article 8b E.C. does not address the question of voting rights for non-nationals in other nationals elections, such as Dáil elections, Presidential elections and referenda. The Electoral (Amendment) Bill, 1983 proposed to extend the franchise to British citizens for all three such elections, but this Bill was declared unconstitutional by the Supreme Court, in *Re The Electoral (Amendment) Bill, 1983* [1984] I.R. 268. Article 16.2 of the Constitution was amended by the Ninth Amendment of the Constitution Act, 1984 to allow for the extension of the franchise to non-nationals by Act of the Oireachtas (see Hogan & Whyte eds., Kelly, *The Irish Constitution* (3rd ed., 1994) pp. 149–159). This was first done in 1986 and section 8(2)(a) of the Electoral Act, 1992 grants the right to vote in Dáil elections (but not presidential elections or referenda) to British citizens. The same section enables the right to vote in Dáil elections to be extended to citizens of other Community Member States by ministerial order. Section 8(3) specifies the criteria on which such order might be made, namely, if the Minister is satisfied that voting rights are accorded to Irish citizens in that State, then a reciprocal gesture will be made in favour of the citizens of that other Community Member State. No such order has yet been made.

Initiatives on voting and candidacy for the European Parliament are expressed to be without prejudice to Art. 138(3) E.C., which gives the Parliament the right to propose a uniform electoral procedure. Its proposal was rejected by the Council in 1982. The de Gucht Report of the Parliament's Committee on Institutional Affairs was adopted in 1991, which suggested a much less rigid uniformity, preferring simply a harmonization of the main elements of electoral procedure in accordance with the principle of proportional representation. A formal proposal on these lines has not yet been presented to the Council.

Article 8c

Every citizen of the Union shall, in the territory of a third country in which the Member State of which he is a national is not represented, be entitled to protection by the diplomatic or consular authorities of any Member State, on the same conditions as the nationals of that State.

Before December 31, 1993, Member States shall establish the necessary rules among themselves and start the international negotiations required to secure this protection.

GENERAL NOTE

This Article projects the principle of Union citizenship to situations outwith the Community borders. The citizens of the Union are to be entitled to diplomatic protection in the territory of a third country by another Member States' external authorities "on the same conditions as the nationals of that State".

The scope of this Article is narrower than envisaged in the Commission draft Treaty (Art. X8, [1991] E.C. Bull. Supp. 2, at 85), where the national could have relied on the protection of any Member State and this was not conditional on his/her own Member State being represented in the third country. The final draft as contained in this Article marks the continuation of national concerns in this area. The protection of another Member State is afforded solely where the national's own Member State is not represented in the third country. This derogates from the spirit of a true Union and fails to take account of the situation where a national is in one part of a large country, a vast distance from his own Member States' diplomatic facilities but legally excluded from having reliance on a more conveniently located diplomatic authority of another Member State. This is particularly relevant as regards the smaller Member States, who do not have the resources to maintain a diplomatic presence throughout the world; even the larger states are consistently cutting back on their external representation. Furthermore, while the Commission delegations in third countries are to co-operate in expressing the common foreign and security policy of the Union (Art. J.6 E.U.), they are not promoted to the status of Union or even Community missions, and the opportunity to involve them in the protection of Community citizens was not taken. This highlights the distinction between the internal status of citizen, and the external status of national of a sovereign State. Although this Article on diplomatic protection is unusually located in the Community Treaty, its mechanisms are reminiscent of the inter-governmental co-operation of the other Union pillars, with its attempt to preserve State sovereignty.

A great deal will rest on actual governmental practice in the setting up of the rules between the Member States and the negotiation of the international agreements which will be necessary to secure the effective implementation of this right. Issues that will have to be addressed include the determination of which Member State will represent the citizen of the Union if more than one Member State has a diplomatic presence in that country. Will this depend on the existence of a bilateral agreement between the unrepresented national's Member State and the diplomatic authority he seeks to rely on or will it be governed by an agreement among all of the Member States? An agreement on the implementation of Art. 8c in practice was concluded before the Treaty came into force, in March 1993, in the framework of European political co-operation. These rules came into force on July 1, 1993. These rules have been acknowledged to exist by the Minister for Foreign Affairs in the Dáil (on October 6, 1993), but they have not been made public. This is despite a statement in the Commission's Report on Union Citizenship of 1993 (Com (93) 702) that the guidelines had ben publicised in the Member States. The Report records that the guidelines cover "assistance and possible repatriation in cases of distress such as death, accident, violent attack, severe illness or arrest". The Report also records agreement on a common format European Emergency Travel Document.

It also remains to be seen the extent to which the Court of Justice will be able to intervene in this area, given the predominance of inter-governmental agreements. Nevertheless, the jurisdiction of the Court of Justice is not explicitly excluded from any of the citizenship provisions and Art. 164 E.C. thus makes it the duty of the court to ensure the application of the law in this field.

Article 8d

Every citizen of the Union shall have the right to petition the European Parliament in accordance with Article 138d.

Every citizen of the Union may apply to the Ombudsman established in accordance with Article 138e.

GENERAL NOTE

Para. (1)

The right of every citizen of the Union to petition the European Parliament adds very little to current practice. This right has been available since 1953, under Rule 128 of the European Parliament's Rules of Procedure. Its constitutionalisation may well cause greater use to be made of what is an increasingly popular means of redress by disaffected parties. The number of petitions received grows every year, and reached 1083 in the parliamentary year 1993–94. Its inclusion among the Treaty citizenship rights is something of a misnomer, however, given that the right is not exclusive to Union citizens but is rather a general right available to all those residing within the Community. It is available to a much broader group of people than Union citizens *per se*, including, as well as resident natural persons, legal persons with a statutory seat in a Member State. The detailed provisions governing the right are laid down in the new Art. 138d E.C.

Although the right of petition is expressly open to all citizens of the Union; it would appear that the right has been intentionally circumscribed to exclude petitions on the inter-governmental pillars of Union competence. Article 138d E.C. restricts the area of competence of petitions to "matters within the Community's fields of activity". It may well fall upon the Court of Justice to rule on the exact scope of this right.

Para. (2)

The new office of Community ombudsman, set up by Art. 138d of the E.C. Treaty, gives Union citizens the right to address complaints concerning instances of maladministration in the Community institutions to an independent ombudsman appointed by the European Parliament. Once again the right is not exclusive to Union citizens and applies to the same categories of person as for petitioning the European Parliament.

The European Parliament adopted a Decision on the office of the Ombudsman in March 1994. He is to be completely independent, with similar terms of employment to a judge of the European Court of Justice. With the exception of judicial matters, he can inquire into the activities of the Community institutions and bodies, at the instigation of any resident in Union territory. All information, files, etc. are to be provided by the Community upon request, but provision is made for the secrecy of certain Community and Member State documents, *etc.* Community officials may be required to testify before him. Member States are required to co-operate through their Permanent Representatives, but they are not themselves subject to inquiry even in their implementation of Community law and policy. Matters from the other Union pillars are excluded from the Ombudsman's remit as well.

One of the matters to be addressed in practice will have to be the relationship between the office of ombudsman and the right of petition to the European Parliament. The latter body expressed its dismay at the relatively limited powers attributed to the Ombudsman and the clash of functions it envisaged with its Committee of Petitions (European Parliament Interim Report on European Citizenship, European Parliament Document A3-0139/91). Resolution of these problems may have to await the appointment of an Ombudsman. The Parliament deferred the appointment into 1995 due to the inability of the major political groups to agree on the allocation of the post.

Article 8e

The Commission shall report to the European Parliament, to the Council and to the Economic and Social Committee before December 31, 1993 and then every three years on the application of the provisions of this Part. This report shall take account of the development of the Union. On this basis, and without prejudice to the other provisions of this Treaty, the Council, acting unanimously on a proposal from the Commission and after consulting the European Parliament, may adopt provisions to strengthen or to add to the rights laid down in this Part, which it shall recommend to the Member States for adoption in accordance with their respective constitutional requirements.

GENERAL NOTE

This Article lays down the procedure governing the future modification of the citizenship provisions of the Treaty. The first paragraph provides for the production of a Commission report on the application of the citizenship provisions. This report is to form the basis of any legislative initiative aimed at strengthening or adding to the catalogue of citizenship rights currently laid out in the Treaty. As Closa points out, the only modifications envisaged to this part of the Treaty are positive in that they must "strengthen or add to" the existing rights. Member States might well retain the current restricted list of citizenship provisions. While the Commission has the right of initiative to put forward proposals in this field, any progress is dependent upon unanimity in the Council and furthermore any such measures must be adopted in accordance with the constitutional requirements of the respective Member States.

The E.U. Treaty entered into force much later than was originally envisaged, and as a result there was little for the Commission to report under Art. 8e. However, a report was made (COM (93) 702) in which it was stated that, due to the time constraints, it was impossible to decide "whether fresh initiatives are called for". As a result the Commission decided to submit a further report not provided for in the Treaties before the end of 1994. By that stage, it was hoped that the Commission would have some picture of the state of implementation of the provisions, and be able to assess the need for the adoption of the additional measures envisaged by Art. 8e. The 1994 Report was not available at the time of writing.

What is interesting about Art. 8e is not so much its substance but the way in which legislation adopted under its provisions is to be implemented in the Member States. The actual legislative provisions are standard enough; the Commission proposes the legislation, the European Parliament is consulted, and Council unanimously adopts it. This is, in a sense, a fairly conservative approach; the European Parliament must undoubtedly have been disappointed with only a consultative input, given that either co-operation, or the new conciliation and veto procedure (Art. 189b, E.C.), were available. Similarly, providing for unanimous as opposed to ordinary or qualified majority voting in the Council gave each Member State a potential veto over any measures proposed by the Commission.

Normally, once a legislative measure is passed, it will be implemented by each Member State in accordance with Art. 189 E.C., and if a Member State fails to implement the legislation, there is a number of different routes by which enforcement may be ensured, for example enforcement actions under Art. 169 E.C., through the concept of direct effect, and by individuals suing the Member State in question for non-enforcement under the principle laid down in the *Francovich* case.

However, under Art. 8e, it is provided that once legislation is passed, the Council "shall recommend (that legislation) for adoption in accordance with their respective constitutional requirements". This seems to mean (a) that Member States have a discretion as to whether or not they decide to adopt the legislation at all, and (b) even where they decide to do so, it must be in accordance with their "respective constitutional requirements". (This phrase also appears in respect of judicial and home affairs co-operation in Art. K.3.2.(c) E.U.) The only other place in the E.C. Treaty where the Member States' "constitutional requirements" were mentioned was in the equally anomalous Art. 138 (on a uniform electoral procedure for the European Parliament; see annotation below) and under Art. 236, which dealt with the mechanism for amending the Treaty (now replaced by the very similar Art. N, E.U.). Under the latter provision, once Treaty amendments have been agreed by common accord of the Member States the amendments enter into force after "being ratified by all the Member States in accordance with their respective constitutional requirements". This is clearly appropriate in the context of Treaty amendments, because until they enter into force, they cannot be considered to be part of Community law, and therefore doctrines such as supremacy and direct effect would not be relevant. The idea that they should have to be tested, as it were, against existing constitutional rules in the Member States before they become part of Community law is in conformity with the *acquis communautaire*.

But the situation is quite different in the case of legislation which has been adopted as Community law, such as that adopted under Art. 8e. Article 8e, as an amendment to the Treaty, has already been ratified by the Member States in acccordance with their respective constitutional requirements. Therefore there seems to be no reason legally why any legislation adopted under Art. 8e should have to go through the constitutional gamut in the Member States, particularly since this legislation can only be passed by unanimity in any case. One suspects that Art. 8e exists to preclude recourse to Art. 235 E.C. as a legal basis for enhancing citizenship rights, by providing a specific if tortuous basis for such developments. It remains to be seen whether the Court of Justice would see Art. 8e as preempting Art. 235, as the latter results in binding legislation and the former does not. As Art. 235 itself requires unanimity to take measures necessary for the attainment of an objective of the Community for which the Treaty has not provided the necessary powers, the question may never arise, if just one Member State resists citizenship legislation on that legal basis.

It may be possible to extend Temple Lang's argument in respect of conventions under Art. 220 E.C. (see the discussion above) to provisions under Art. 8e E.C., *viz.* that Art. 5 E.C. would require their adoption once agreed upon by the Council. This would however reduce such provisions to the status of directives, imposing an obligation as to the result on the Member States, which does not appear to be the intention of Art. 8e.

PART THREE (COMMUNITY POLICIES)

GENERAL NOTE

Community policies
    The addition of the new provisions establishing Union citizenship under the heading Part Two has led to a renumbering of the remaining titles. The original Parts Two and Three of the EEC Treaty on the "Foundations of the Community" and "Policy of the Community" are now regrouped under the single heading of "Community Policies" in Part Three of the E.C. Treaty (Arts. 9–130y E.C.).

TITLE I: Free Movement of Goods

Article 9

1. The Community shall be based upon a customs union which shall cover all trade in goods and which shall involve the prohibition between Member States of customs duties on imports and exports and of all charges having equivalent effect, and the adoption of a common customs tariff in their relations with third countries.

2. The provisions of Chapter 1, Section 1, and of Chapter 2 of this Title shall apply to products originating in Member States and to products coming from third countries which are in free circulation in Member States.

Article 10

1. Products coming from a third country shall be considered to be in free circulation in a Member State if the import formalities have been complied with and any customs duties or charges having equivalent effect which are payable have been levied in that Member State, and if they have not benefited from a total or partial drawback of such duties or charges.

2. The Commission shall, before the end of the first year after the entry into force of this Treaty, determine the methods of administrative co-operation

to be adopted for the purpose of applying Article 9(2), taking into account the need to reduce as much as possible formalities imposed on trade.

Before the end of the first year after the entry into force of this Treaty, the Commission shall lay down the provisions applicable, as regards trade between Member States, to goods originating in another Member State in whose manufacture products have been used on which the exporting Member State has not levied the appropriate customs duties or charges having equivalent effect, or which have benefited from a total or partial drawback of such duties or charges.

In adopting these provisions, the Commission shall take into account the rules for the elimination of customs duties within the Community and for the progressive application of the common customs tariff.

Article 11

Member States shall take all appropriate measures to enable Governments to carry out, within the periods of time laid down, the obligations with regard to customs duties which devolve upon them pursuant to this Treaty.

Chapter 1 (The Customs Union)

SECTION 1: Elimination of customs duties between Member States

Article 12

Member States shall refrain from introducing between themselves any new customs duties on imports or exports or any charges having equivalent effect, and from increasing those which they already apply in their trade with each other.

Article 13

1. Customs duties on imports in force between Member States shall be progressively abolished by them during the transitional period in accordance with Articles 14 and 15.

2. Charges having an effect equivalent to customs duties on imports, in force between Member States, shall be progressively abolished by them during the transitional period. The Commission shall determine by means of directives the timetable for such abolition. It shall be guided by the rules contained in Article 14(2) and (3) and by the directives issued by the Council pursuant to Article 14(2).

Article 14

1. For each product, the basic duty to which the successive reductions shall be applied shall be the duty applied on January 1, 1957.

2. The timetable for the reductions shall be determined as follows:
   (a) during the first stage, the first reduction shall be made one year after the date when this Treaty enters into force; the second reduction, eighteen months later; the third reduction, at the end of the fourth year after the date when this Treaty enters into force;
   (b) during the second stage, a reduction shall be made eighteen months after that stage begins; a second reduction, eighteen months after the preceding one; a third reduction, one year later;
   (c) any remaining reductions shall be made during the third stage; the Council shall, acting by a qualified majority on a proposal from the Commission, determine the timetable therefor by means of directives.

3. At the time of the first reduction, Member States shall introduce between themselves a duty on each product equal to the basic duty minus 10 per cent.

At the time of each subsequent reduction, each Member State shall reduce its customs duties as a whole in such manner as to lower by 10 per cent its total customs receipts as defined in paragraph 4 and to reduce the duty on each product by at least 5 per cent of the basic duty.

In the case, however, of products on which the duty is still in excess of 30 per cent, each reduction must be at least 10 per cent of the basic duty.

4. The total customs receipts of each Member State, as referred to in paragraph 3, shall be calculated by multiplying the value of its imports from other Member States during 1956 by the basic duties.

5. Any special problems raised in applying paragraphs 1 to 4 shall be settled by directives issued by the Council acting by a qualified majority on a proposal from the Commission.

6. Member States shall report to the Commission on the manner in which effect has been given to the preceding rules for the reduction of duties. They shall endeavour to ensure that the reduction made in the duties on each product shall amount:

— at the end of the first stage, to at least 25 per cent of the basic duty;
— at the end of the second stage, to at least 50 per cent of the basic duty.

If the Commission finds that there is a risk that the objectives laid down in Article 13, and the percentages laid down in this paragraph, cannot be attained, it shall make all appropriate recommendations to Member States.

7. The provisions of this Article may be amended by the Council, acting unanimously on a proposal from the Commission and after consulting the European Parliament.

Article 15

1. Irrespective of the provisions of Article 14, any Member State may, in the course of the transitional period, suspend in whole or in part the collection of duties applied by it to products imported from other Member States. It shall inform the other Member States and the Commission thereof.

2. The Member States declare their readiness to reduce customs duties against the other Member States more rapidly than is provided for in Article 14 if their general economic situation and the situation of the economic sector concerned so permit.

To this end, the Commission shall make recommendations to the Member States concerned.

Article 16

Member States shall abolish between themselves customs duties on exports and charges having equivalent effect by the end of the first stage at the latest.

Article 17

1. The provisions of Articles 9 to 15(1) shall also apply to customs duties of a fiscal nature. Such duties shall not, however, be taken into consideration for the purpose of calculating either total customs receipts or the reduction of customs duties as a whole as referred to in Article 14(3) and (4).

Such duties shall, at each reduction, be lowered by not less than 10 per cent of the basic duty. Member States may reduce such duties more rapidly than is provided for in Article 14.

2. Member States shall, before the end of the first year after the entry into force of this Treaty, inform the Commission of their customs duties of a fiscal nature.

3. Member States shall retain the right to substitute for these duties an internal tax which complies with the provisions of Article 95.

4. If the Commission finds that substitution for any customs duty of a fiscal nature meets with serious difficulties in a Member State, it shall authorise that State to retain the duty on condition that it shall abolish it not later than six years after the entry into force of this Treaty. Such authorisation must be applied for before the end of the first year after the entry into force of this Treaty.

SECTION 2: Setting up of the common customs tariff

Article 18

The Member States declare their readiness to contribute to the development of international trade and the lowering of barriers to trade by entering into agreements designed, on a basis of reciprocity and mutual advantage, to reduce customs duties below the general level of which they could avail themselves as a result of the establishment of a customs union between them.

Article 19

1. Subject to the conditions and within the limits provided for hereinafter, duties in the common customs tariff shall be at the level of the arithmetical average of the duties applied in the four customs territories comprised in the Community.

2. The duties taken as the basis for calculating this average shall be those applied by Member States on 1 January 1957.

In the case of the Italian tariff, however, the duty applied shall be that without the temporary 10 per cent reduction. Furthermore, with respect to items on which the Italian tariff contains a conventional duty, this duty shall be substituted for the duty applied as defined above, provided that it does not exceed that latter by more than 10 per cent. Where the conventional duty exceeds the duty applied as defined above by more than 10 per cent, the latter duty plus 10 per cent shall be taken as the basis for calculating the arithmetical average.

With regard to the tariff headings in List A, the duties shown in that List shall, for the purpose of calculating the arithmetical average, be substituted for the duties applied.

3. The duties in the common customs tariff shall not exceed:
(a) 3 per cent for products within the tariff headings in List B;
(b) 10 per cent for products within the tariff headings in List C;
(c) 15 per cent for products within the tariff headings in List D;
(d) 25 per cent for products within the tariff headings in List E;
where in respect of such products, the tariff of the Benelux countries contains a duty not exceeding 3 per cent, such duty shall, for the purpose of calculating the arithmetical average, be raised to 12 per cent.

4. List F prescribes the duties applicable to the products listed therein.

5. The Lists of tariff headings referred to in this Article and in Article 20 are set out in Annex I to this Treaty.

Article 20

The duties applicable to the products in List G shall be determined by negotiation between the Member States. Each Member State may add further products to this List to a value not exceeding 2 per cent of the total value of its imports from third countries in the course of the year 1956.

The Commission shall take all appropriate steps to ensure that such negotiations shall be undertaken before the end of the second year after the entry into force of this Treaty and be concluded before the end of the first stage.

If, for certain products, no agreement can be reached within these periods, the Council shall, on a proposal from the Commission, acting unanimously until the end of the second stage and by a qualified majority thereafter, determine the duties in the common customs tariff.

Article 21

1. Technical difficulties which may arise in applying Articles 19 and 20 shall be resolved, within two years of the entry into force of this Treaty, by directives issued by the Council acting by a qualified majority on a proposal from the Commission.

2. Before the end of the first stage, or at latest when the duties are determined, the Council shall, acting by a qualified majority on a proposal from the Commission, decide on any adjustments required in the interests of the internal consistency of the common customs tariff as a result of applying the rules set out in Articles 19 and 20, taking account in particular of the degree of processing undergone by the various goods to which the common tariff applies.

Article 22

The Commission shall, within two years of the entry into force of this Treaty, determine the extent to which the customs duties of a fiscal nature referred to in Article 17(2) shall be taken into account in calculating the arithmetical average provided for in Article 19(1). The Commission shall take account of any protective character which such duties may have.

Within six months of such determination, any Member State may request that the procedure provided for in Article 20 should be applied to the product in question, but in this event the percentage limit provided in that Article shall not be applicable to that State.

Article 23

1. For the purpose of the progressive introduction of the common customs tariff, Member States shall amend their tariffs applicable to third countries as follows:
   (a) in the case of tariff headings on which the duties applied in practice on 1 January 1957 do not differ by more than 15 per cent in either direction from the duties in the common customs tariff, the latter duties shall be applied at the end of the fourth year after the entry into force of this Treaty;
   (b) in any other case, each Member State shall, as from the same date, apply a duty reducing by 30 per cent the difference between the duty applied in practice on 1 January 1957 and the duty in the common customs tariff;
   (c) at the end of the second stage this difference shall again be reduced by 30 per cent;
   (d) in the case of tariff headings for which the duties in the common customs tariff are not yet available at the end of the first stage, each Member State shall, within six months of the Council's action in accordance with Article 20, apply such duties as would result from application of the rules contained in this paragraph.

2. Where a Member State has been granted an authorisation under Article 17(4), it need not, for as long as that authorisation remains valid, apply the preceding provisions to the tariff headings to which the authorisation applies. When such authorisation expires, the Member State concerned shall apply such duty as would have resulted from application of the rules contained in paragraph 1.

3. The common customs tariff shall be applied in its entirety by the end of the transitional period at the latest.

Article 24

Member States shall remain free to change their duties more rapidly than is provided for in Article 23 in order to bring them into line with the common customs tariff.

Article 25

1. If the Commission finds that the production in Member States of particular products contained in Lists B, C and D is insufficient to supply the demands of one of the Member States, and that such supply traditionally depends to a considerable extent on imports from third countries, the Council shall, acting by a qualified majority on a proposal from the Commission, grant the Member State concerned tariff quotas at a reduced rate of duty or duty free.

Such quotas may not exceed the limits beyond which the risk might arise of activities being transferred to the detriment of other Member States.

2. In the case of the products in List E, and of those in List G for which the rates of duty have been determined in accordance with the procedure provided for in the third paragraph of Article 20, the Commission shall, where a change in sources of supply or shortage of supplies within the Community is such as to entail harmful consequences for the processing industries of a Member State, at the request of that Member State, grant it tariff quotas at a reduced rate of duty or duty free.

Such quotas may not exceed the limits beyond which the risk might arise of activities being transferred to the detriment of other Member States.

3. In the case of the products listed in Annex II to this Treaty, the Commission may authorise any Member State to suspend, in whole or in part, collection of the duties applicable or may grant such Member State tariff quotas at a reduced rate of duty or duty free, provided that no serious disturbance of the market of the products concerned results therefrom.

4. The Commission shall periodically examine tariff quotas granted pursuant to this Article.

Article 26

The Commission may authorise any Member State encountering special difficulties to postpone the lowering or raising of duties provided for in Article 23 in respect of particular headings in its tariff.

Such authorisation may only be granted for a limited period and in respect of tariff headings which, taken together, represent for such State not more than 5 per cent of the value of its imports from third countries in the course of the latest year for which statistical data are available.

Article 27

Before the end of the first stage, Member States shall, in so far as may be necessary, take steps to approximate their provisions laid down by law, regulation or administrative action in respect of customs matters. To this end, the Commission shall make all appropriate recommendations to Member States.

Article 28

Any autonomous alteration or suspension of duties in the common customs tariff shall be decided by the Council acting by a qualified majority on a proposal from the Commission.

Article 29

In carrying out the tasks entrusted to it under this Section the Commission shall be guided by:
(a) the need to promote trade between Member States and third countries;
(b) developments in conditions of competition within the Community in so far as they lead to an improvement in the competitive capacity of undertakings;
(c) the requirements of the Community as regards the supply of raw materials and semi-finished goods; in this connection the Commission shall take care to avoid distorting conditions of competition between Member States in respect of finished goods;
(d) the need to avoid serious disturbances in the economies of Member States and to ensure rational development of production and an expansion of consumption within the Community.

Chapter 2 (Elimination of Quantitative Restrictions between Member States)

Article 30

Quantitative restrictions on imports and all measures having equivalent effect shall, without prejudice to the following provisions, be prohibited between Member States.

Article 31

Member States shall refrain from introducing between themselves any new quantitative restrictions or measures having equivalent effect.
This obligation shall, however, relate only to the degree of liberalisation attained in pursuance of the decisions of the Council of the Organisation for European Economic Co-operation of 14 January 1955. Member States shall supply the Commission, not later than six months after the entry into force of this Treaty, with lists of the products liberalised by them in pursuance of these decisions. These lists shall be consolidated between Member States.

Article 32

In their trade with one another Member States shall refrain from making more restrictive the quotas and measures having equivalent effect existing at the date of the entry into force of this Treaty.
These quotas shall be abolished by the end of the transitional period at the latest. During that period, they shall be progressively abolished in accordance with the following provisions.

Article 33

1. One year after the entry into force of this Treaty, each Member State shall convert any bilateral quotas open to any other Member States into global quotas open without discrimination to all other Member States.
On the same date, Member States shall increase the aggregate of the global quotas so established in such a manner as to bring about an increase of not less than 20 per cent in their total value as compared with the preceding year. The global quota for each product, however, shall be increased by not less than 10 per cent.
The quotas shall be increased annually in accordance with the same rules and in the same proportions in relation to the preceding year.

The fourth increase shall take place at the end of the fourth year after the entry into force of this Treaty; the fifth, one year after the beginning of the second stage.

2. Where, in the case of a product which has not been liberalised, the global quota does not amount to 3 per cent of the national production of the State concerned, a quota equal to not less than 3 per cent of such national production shall be introduced not later than one year after the entry into force of this Treaty. This quota shall be raised to 4 per cent at the end of the second year, and to 5 per cent at the end of the third. Thereafter, the Member State concerned shall increase the quota by not less than 15 per cent annually.

Where there is no such national production, the Commission shall take a decision establishing an appropriate quota.

3. At the end of the tenth year, each quota shall be equal to not less than 20 per cent of the national production.

4. If the Commission finds by means of a decision that during two successive years the imports of any product have been below the level of the quota opened, this global quota shall not be taken into account in calculating the total value of the global quotas. In such case, the Member State shall abolish quota restrictions on the product concerned.

5. In the case of quotas representing more than 20 per cent of the national production of the product concerned, the Council may, acting by a qualified majority on a proposal from the Commission, reduce the minimum percentage of 10 per cent laid down in paragraph 1. This alteration shall not, however, affect the obligation to increase the total value of global quotas by 20 per cent annually.

6. Member States which have exceeded their obligations as regards the degree of liberalisation attained in pursuance of the decisions of the Council of the Organisation for European Economic Co-operation of January 14, 1955 shall be entitled, when calculating the annual total increase of 20 per cent provided for in paragraph 1, to take into account the amount of imports liberalised by autonomous action. Such calculation shall be submitted to the Commission for its prior approval.

7. The Commission shall issue directives establishing the procedure and timetable in accordance with which Member States shall abolish, as between themselves, any measures in existence when this Treaty enters into force which have an effect equivalent to quotas.

8. If the Commission finds that the application of the provisions of this Article, and in particular of the provisions concerning percentages, makes it impossible to ensure that the abolition of quotas provided for in the second paragraph of Article 32 is carried out progressively, the Council may, on a proposal from the Commission, acting unanimously during the first stage and by a qualified majority thereafter, amend the procedure laid down in this Article and may, in particular, increase the percentages fixed.

Article 34

1. Quantitative restrictions on exports, and all measures having equivalent effect, shall be prohibited between Member States.

2. Member States shall, by the end of the first stage at the latest, abolish all quantitative restrictions on exports and any measures having equivalent effect which are in existence when this Treaty enters into force.

Article 35

The Member States declare their readiness to abolish quantitative restrictions on imports from and exports to other Member States more rapidly than is provided for in the preceding Articles, if their general economic situation and the situation of the economic sector concerned so permit.

To this end, the Commission shall make recommendations to the Member States concerned.

Article 36

The provisions of Articles 30 to 34 shall not preclude prohibitions or restrictions on imports, exports or goods in transit justified on grounds of public morality, public policy or public security; the protection of health and life of humans, animals or plants; the protection of national treasures possessing artistic, historic or archaeological value; or the protection of industrial and commercial property. Such prohibitions or restrictions shall not, however, constitute a means of arbitrary discrimination or a disguised restriction on trade between Member States.

Article 37

1. Member States shall progressively adjust any State monopolies of a commercial character so as to ensure that when the transitional period has ended no discrimination regarding the conditions under which goods are procured and marketed exists between nationals of Member States.

The provisions of this Article shall apply to any body through which a Member State, in law or in fact, either directly or indirectly supervises, determines or appreciably influences imports or exports between Member States. These provisions shall likewise apply to monopolies delegated by the State to others.

2. Member States shall refrain from introducing any new measure which is contrary to the principles laid down in paragraph 1 or which restricts the scope of the Articles dealing with the abolition of customs duties and quantitative restrictions between Member States.

3. The timetable for the measures referred to in paragraph 1 shall be harmonised with the abolition of quantitative restrictions on the same products provided for in Articles 30 to 34.

If a product is subject to a State monopoly of a commercial character in only one or some Member States, the Commission may authorise the other Member States to apply protective measures until the adjustment provided for in paragraph 1 has been effected; the Commission shall determine the conditions and details of such measures.

4. If a State monopoly of a commercial character has rules which are designed to make it easier to dispose of agricultural products or obtain for them the best return, steps should be taken in applying the rules contained in this Article to ensure equivalent safeguards for the employment and standard of living of the producers concerned, account being taken of the adjustments that will be possible and the specialisation that will be needed with the passage of time.

5. The obligations on Member States shall be binding only in so far as they are compatible with existing international agreements.

6. With effect from the first stage the Commission shall make recommendations as to the manner in which and the timetable according to which the adjustment provided for in this Article shall be carried out.

TITLE II: Agriculture

Article 38

1. The common market shall extend to agriculture and trade in agricultural products. 'Agricultural products' means the products of the soil, of stock-farming and of fisheries and products of first-stage processing directly related to these products.

2. Save as otherwise provided in Articles 39 to 46, the rules laid down for the establishment of the common market shall apply to agricultural products.

3. The products subject to the provisions of Articles 39 to 46 are listed in Annex II to this Treaty. Within two years of the entry into force of this Treaty, however, the Council shall, acting by a qualified majority on a proposal from the Commission, decide what products are to be added to this list.

4. The operation and development of the common market for agricultural products must be accompanied by the establishment of a common agricultural policy among the Member States.

Article 39

1. The objectives of the common agricultural policy shall be:
   (a) to increase agricultural productivity by promoting technical progress and by ensuring the rational development of agricultural production and the optimum utilisation of the factors of production, in particular labour;
   (b) thus to ensure a fair standard of living for the agricultural community, in particular by increasing the individual earnings of persons engaged in agriculture;
   (c) to stabilise markets;
   (d) to assure the availability of supplies;
   (e) to ensure that supplies reach consumers at reasonable prices.

2. In working out the common agricultural policy and the special methods for its application, account shall be taken of:
   (a) the particular nature of agricultural activity, which results from the social structure of agriculture and from structural and natural disparities between the various agricultural regions;
   (b) the need to effect the appropriate adjustments by degrees;
   (c) the fact that in the Member States agriculture constitutes a sector closely linked with the economy as a whole.

Article 40

1. Member-States shall develop the common agricultural policy by degrees during the transitional period and shall bring it into force by the end of that period at the latest.

2. In order to attain the objectives set out in Article 39 a common organisation of agricultural markets shall be established.

This organisation shall take one of the following forms, depending on the product concerned:
   (a) common rules on competition;
   (b) compulsory co-ordination of the various national market organisations:
   (c) a European market organisation.

3. The common organisation established in accordance with paragraph 2 may include all measures required to attain the objectives set out in Article 39, in particular regulation of prices, aids for the production and marketing of the various products, storage and carryover arrangements and common machinery for stabilising imports or exports.

The common organisation shall be limited to pursuit of the objectives set out in Article 39 and shall exclude any discrimination between producers or consumers within the Community.

Any common price policy shall be based on common criteria and uniform methods of calculation.

4. In order to enable the common organisation referred to in paragraph 2 to attain its objectives, one or more agricultural guidance and guarantee funds may be set up.

Article 41

To enable the objectives set out in Article 39 to be attained, provision may be made within the framework of the common agricultural policy for measures such as:
  (a) an effective co-ordination of efforts in the spheres of vocational training, of research and of the dissemination of agricultural knowledge; this may include joint financing of projects or institutions;
  (b) joint measures to promote consumption of certain products.

Article 42

The provisions of the Chapter relating to rules on competition shall apply to production of and trade in agricultural products only to the extent determined by the Council within the framework of Article 43(2) and (3) and in accordance with the procedure laid down therein, account being taken of the objectives set out in Article 39.
The Council may, in particular, authorise the granting of aid:
  (a) for the protection of enterprises handicapped by structural or natural conditions;
  (b) within the framework of economic development programmes.

Article 43

1. In order to evolve the broad lines of a common agricultural policy, the Commission shall, immediately this Treaty enters into force, convene a conference of the Member States with a view to making a comparison of their agricultural policies, in particular by producing a statement of their resources and needs.
2. Having taken into account the work of the conference provided for in paragraph 1, after consulting the Economic and Social Committee and within two years of the entry into force of this Treaty, the Commission shall submit proposals for working out and implementing the common agricultural policy, including the replacement of the national organisations by one of the forms of common organisation provided for in Article 40(2), and for implementing the measures specified in this Title.
These proposals shall take account of the interdependence of the agricultural matters mentioned in this Title.
The Council shall, on a proposal from the Commission and after consulting the European Parliament, acting unanimously during the first two stages and by a qualified majority thereafter, make regulations, issue directives, or take decisions, without prejudice to any recommendations it may also make.
3. The Council may, acting by a qualified majority and in accordance with paragraph 2, replace the national market organisations by the common organisation provided for in Article 40(2) if:
  (a) the common organisation offers Member States which are opposed to this measure and which have an organisation of their own for the production in question equivalent safeguards for the employment and standard of living of the producers concerned, account being taken of the adjustments that will be possible and the specialisation that will be needed with the passage of time;
  (b) such an organisation ensures conditions for trade within the Community similar to those existing in a national market.

4. If a common organisation for certain raw materials is established before a common organisation exists for the corresponding processed products, such raw materials as are used for processed products intended for export to third countries may be imported from outside the Community.

Article 44

1. In so far as progressive abolition of customs duties and quantitative restrictions between Member States may result in prices likely to jeopardise the attainment of the objectives set out in Article 39, each Member State shall, during the transitional period, be entitled to apply to particular products, in a non-discriminatory manner and in substitution for quotas and to such an extent as shall not impede the expansion of the volume of trade provided for in Article 45(2), a system of minimum prices below which imports may be either:
— temporarily suspended or reduced; or
— allowed, but subjected to the condition that they are made at a price
    higher than the minimum price for the product concerned.
In the latter case the minimum prices shall not include customs duties.
2. Minimum prices shall neither cause a reduction of the trade existing between Member States when this Treaty enters into force nor form an obstacle to progressive expansion of this trade. Minimum prices shall not be applied so as to form an obstacle to the development of a natural preference between Member States.
3. As soon as this Treaty enters into force the Council shall, on a proposal from the Commission, determine objective criteria for the establishment of minimum price systems and for the fixing of such prices.

These criteria shall in particular take account of the average national production costs in the Member State applying the minimum price, of the position of the various undertakings concerned in relation to such average production costs, and of the need to promote both the progressive improvement of agricultural practice and the adjustments and specialisation needed within the common market.

The Commission shall further propose a procedure for revising these criteria in order to allow for and speed up technical progress and to approximate prices progressively within the common market.

These criteria and the procedure for revising them shall be determined by the Council acting unanimously within three years of the entry into force of this Treaty.
4. Until the decision of the Council takes effect, Member States may fix minimum prices on condition that these are communicated beforehand to the Commission and to the other Member States so that they may submit their comments.

Once the Council has taken its decision, Member States shall fix minimum prices on the basis of the criteria determined as above.

The Council may, acting by a qualified majority on a proposal from the Commission, rectify any decisions taken by Member States which do not conform to the criteria defined above.
5. If it does not prove possible to determine the said objective criteria for certain products by the beginning of the third stage, the Council may, acting by a qualified majority on a proposal from the Commission, vary the minimum prices applied to these products.
6. At the end of the transitional period, a table of minimum prices still in force shall be drawn up. The Council shall, acting on a proposal from the Commission and by a majority of nine votes in accordance with the weighting laid down in the first subparagraph of Article 148(2), determine the system to be applied within the framework of the common agricultural policy.

Article 45

1. Until national market organisations have been replaced by one of the forms of common organisation referred to in Article 40(2), trade in products in respect of which certain Member States:
— have arrangements designed to guarantee national producers a market for their products; and
— are in need of imports,
shall be developed by the conclusion of long-term agreements or contracts between importing and exporting Member States.

These agreements or contracts shall be directed towards the progressive abolition of any discrimination in the application of these arrangements to the various producers within the Community.

Such agreements or contracts shall be concluded during the first stage; account shall be taken of the principle of reciprocity.

2. As regards quantities, these agreements or contracts shall be based on the average volume of trade between Member States in the products concerned during the three years before the entry into force of this Treaty and shall provide for an increase in the volume of trade within the limits of existing requirements, account being taken of traditional patterns of trade.

As regards prices, these agreements or contracts shall enable producers to dispose of the agreed quantities at prices which shall be progressively approximated to those paid to national producers on the domestic market of the purchasing country.

This approximation shall proceed as steadily as possible and shall be completed by the end of the transitional period at the latest.

Prices shall be negotiated between the parties concerned with the framework of directives issued by the Commission for the purpose of implementing the two preceding subparagraphs.

If the first stage is extended, these agreements or contracts shall continue to be carried out in accordance with the conditions applicable at the end of the fourth year after the entry into force of this Treaty, the obligation to increase quantities and to approximate prices being suspended until the transition to the second stage.

Member States shall avail themselves of any opportunity open to them under their legislation, particularly in respect of import policy, to ensure the conclusion and carrying out of these agreements or contracts.

3. To the extent that Member States require raw materials for the manufacture of products to be exported outside the Community in competition with products of third countries, the above agreements or contracts shall not form an obstacle to the importation of raw materials for this purpose from third countries. This provision shall not, however, apply if the Council unanimously decides to make provision for payments required to compensate for the higher price paid on goods imported for this purpose on the basis of these agreements or contracts in relation to the delivered price of the same goods purchased on the world market.

Article 46

Where in a Member State a product is subject to a national market organisation or to internal rules having equivalent effect which affect the competitive position of similar production in another Member State, a countervailing charge shall be applied by Member States to imports of this product coming from the Member State where such organisation or rules exist, unless that State applies a countervailing charge on export.

The Commission shall fix the amount of these charges at the level required to redress the balance; it may also authorise other measures, the conditions and details of which it shall determine.

Article 47

As to the functions to be performed by the Economic and Social Committee in pursuance of this Title, its agricultural section shall hold itself at the disposal of the Commission to prepare, in accordance with the provisions of Articles 197 and 198, the deliberations of the Committee.

TITLE III: Free Movement of Persons, Services and Capital

Chapter 1 (Workers)

Article 48

1. Freedom of movement for workers shall be secured within the Community by the end of the transitional period at the latest.
2. Such freedom of movement shall entail the abolition of any discrimination based on nationality between workers of the Member States as regards employment, remuneration and other conditions of work and employment.
3. It shall entail the right, subject to limitations justified on grounds of public policy, public security or public health:
   (a) to accept offers of employment actually made;
   (b) to move freely within the territory of Member States for this purpose;
   (c) to stay in a Member State for the purpose of employment in accordance with the provisions governing the employment of nationals of that State laid down by law, regulation or administrative action;
   (d) to remain in the territory of a Member State after having been employed in that State, subject to conditions which shall be embodied in implementing regulations to be drawn up by the Commission.
4. The provisions of this Article shall not apply to employment in the public service.

Article 49

As soon as this Treaty enters into force, the Council shall, acting in accordance with the procedure referred to in Article 189b and after consulting the Economic and Social Committee, issue directives or make regulations setting out the measures required to bring about, by progressive stages, freedom of movement for workers, as defined in Article 48, in particular:
   (a) by ensuring close co-operation between national employment services;
   (b) by systematically and progressively abolishing those administrative procedures and practices and those qualifying periods in respect of eligibility for available employment, whether resulting from national legislation or from agreements previously concluded between Member States, the maintenance of which would form an obstacle to liberalisation of the movement of workers;
   (c) by systematically and progressively abolishing all such qualifying periods and other restrictions provided for either under national legislation or under agreements previously concluded between Member States as imposed on workers of other Member States conditions regarding the free choice of employment other than those imposed on workers of the State concerned;
   (d) by setting up appropriate machinery to bring offers of employment into touch with applications for employment and to facilitate the achievement of a balance between supply and demand in the employment market in such a way as to avoid serious threats to the standard of living and level of employment in the various regions and industries.

GENERAL NOTE

This is the operative provision under which the majority of the secondary legislation giving effect to the freedom of movement of workers under Art. 48 has been passed. The amendment relates purely to the post-Maastricht legislative procedure applicable to the adoption of such legislation. The relevant procedure is now the conciliation and veto procedure (Art. 189b E.C.). In common with the majority of the provisions dealing with the achievement of the single market, this marks an upgrading from the co-operation procedure introduced by the S.E.A. (Art. 149(2) E.E.C., now Art. 189c E.C.).

Article 50

Member States shall, within the framework of a joint programme, encourage the exchange of young workers.

Article 51

The Council shall acting unanimously on a proposal from the Commission, adopt such measures in the field of social security as are necessary to provide freedom of movement for workers; to this end, it shall make arrangements to secure for migrant workers and their dependants:
  (a) aggregation, for the purpose of acquiring and retaining the right to benefit and of calculating the amount of benefit, of all periods taken into account under the laws of the several countries;
  (b) payment of benefits to persons resident in the territories of Member States.

Chapter 2 (Right of Establishment)

Article 52

Within the framework of the provisions set out below, restrictions on the freedom of establishment of nationals of a Member State in the territory of another Member State shall be abolished by progressive stages in the course of the transitional period. Such progressive abolition shall also apply to restrictions on the setting up of agencies, branches or subsidiaries by nationals of any Member State established in the territory of any Member State.

Freedom of establishment shall include the right to take up and pursue activities as self-employed persons and to set up and manage undertakings, in particular companies or firms within the meaning of the second paragraph of Article 58, under the conditions laid down for its own nationals by the law of the country where such establishment is effected, subject to the provisions of the Chapter relating to capital.

Article 53

Member States shall not introduce any new restrictions on the right of establishment in their territories of nationals of other Member States, save as otherwise provided in this Treaty.

Article 54

1. Before the end of the first stage, the Council shall, acting unanimously on a proposal from the Commission and after consulting the Economic and Social Committee and the European Parliament, draw up a general programme for the abolition of existing restrictions on freedom of establishment within the Community. The Commission shall submit its proposal to the Council during the first two years of the first stage.

The programme shall set out the general conditions under which freedom of establishment is to be attained in the case of each type of activity and in particular the stages by which it is to be attained.

2. In order to implement this general programme or, in the absence of such programme, in order to achieve a stage in attaining freedom of establishment as regards a particular activity, the Council, acting in accordance with the procedure referred to in Article 189b and after consulting the Economic and Social Committee, shall act by means of directives.

3. The Council and the Commission shall carry out the duties devolving upon them under the preceding provisions, in particular:

(a) by according, as a general rule, priority treatment to activities where freedom of establishment makes a particularly valuable contribution to the development of production and trade;

(b) by ensuring close co-operation between the competent authorities in the Member States in order to ascertain the particular situation within the Community of the various activities concerned;

(c) by abolishing those administrative procedures and practices, whether resulting from national legislation or from agreements previously concluded between Member States, the maintenance of which would form an obstacle to freedom of establishment;

(d) by ensuring that workers of one Member State employed in the territory of another Member State may remain in that territory for the purpose of taking up activities therein as self-employed persons, where they satisfy the conditions which they would be required to satisfy if they were entering that State at the time when they intended to take up such activities;

(e) by enabling a national of one Member State to acquire and use land and buildings situated in the territory of another Member State, in so far as this does not conflict with the principles laid down in Article 39(2);

(f) by effecting the progressive abolition of restrictions on freedom of establishment in every branch of activity under consideration, both as regards the conditions for setting up agencies, branches or subsidiaries in the territory of a Member State and as regards the subsidiaries in the territory of a Member State and as regards the conditions governing the entry of personnel belonging to the main establishment into managerial or supervisory posts in such agencies, branches or subsidiaries;

(g) by co-ordinating to the necessary extent the safeguards which, for the protection of the interests of members and others, are required by Member States of companies or firms within the meaning of the second paragraph of Article 58 with a view to making such safeguards equivalent throughout the Community;

(h) by satisfying themselves that the conditions of establishment are not distorted by aids granted by Member States.

General Note

Article 54 permits the adoption of legislation aimed at the achievement of the freedom of establishment (Art. 52 EEC/E.C.). The only change in the Article is that the co-operation procedure, operating in this field since the coming into force of the S.E.A. (Art. 149(2) EEC, now Art. 189c E.C.) is now replaced by the conciliation and veto procedure (Art. 189b E.C.).

Article 55

The provisions of this Chapter shall not apply, so far as any given Member State is concerned, to activities which in that State are connected, even occasionally, with the exercise of official authority.

The Council may, acting by a qualified majority on a proposal from the Commission, rule that the provisions of this Chapter shall not apply to certain activities.

Article 56

1. The provisions of this Chapter and measures taken in pursuance thereof shall not prejudice the applicability of provisions laid down by law, regulation or administrative action providing for special treatment for foreign nationals on grounds of public policy, public security or public health.

2. Before the end of the transitional period, the Council shall, acting unanimously on a proposal from the Commission and after consulting the European Parliament, issue directives for the co-ordination of the abovementioned provisions laid down by law, regulation or administrative action. After the end of the second stage, however, the Council shall, acting in accordance with the procedure referred to in Article 189b, issue directives for the co-ordination of such provisions as, in each Member State, are a matter for regulation or administrative action.

GENERAL NOTE

This Article is aimed at the co-ordination of the constraints within Member States on the freedom of establishment due to public policy, public health and public security. The passing of directives with this purpose is now to be carried out under the conciliation and veto procedure (Art. 189b E.C. replacing the co-operation procedure in Art. 149(2) EEC, now Art. 189c E.C.). The remainder of the Article is unamended.

Article 57

1. In order to make it easier for persons to take up and pursue activities as self-employed persons, the Council shall, acting in accordance with the procedure referred to in Article 189b, issue directives for the mutual recognition of diplomas, certificates and other evidence of formal qualifications.

2. For the same purpose, the Council shall, before the end of the transitional period, issue directives for the co-ordination of the provisions laid down by law, regulation or administrative action in Member States concerning the taking up and pursuit of activities as self-employed persons. The Council, acting unanimously on a proposal from the Commission and after consulting the European Parliament, shall decide on directives the implementation of which involves in at least one Member State amendment of the existing principles laid down by law governing the professions with respect to training and conditions of access for natural persons. In other cases the Council shall act in accordance with the procedure referred to in Article 189b.

3. In the case of the medical and allied and pharmaceutical professions, the progressive abolition of restrictions shall be dependent upon co-ordination of the conditions for their exercise in the various Member States.

GENERAL NOTE

The amendment of this Article alters the legislative procedure for the adoption of directives aimed at the mutual recognition of diplomas. The co-operation procedure is replaced by the new conciliation and veto procedure under Art. 189b E.C.

Article 57(2) provides for the co-ordination of the legislative and administrative procedures laid down by Member States concerning the taking-up and pursuit of activities by self-employed persons. The principle is retained that unanimity be required to adopt directives which, in at least one Member State, would require amendment to existing legislation on the taking-up of and access to a particular profession. The applicable process in the absence of a need for such national legislation is now the conciliation and veto procedure (Art. 189b E.C.). See Weatherill and Beaumont, *E.C. Law* (1993), pp. 526–529 and Kapteyn & Verloren van Themaat, *Introduction to the Law of European Communities*, (1989), pp. 536–540.

Article 58

Companies or firms formed in accordance with the law of a Member State and having their registered office, central administration or principal place of business within the Community shall, for the purposes of this Chapter, be treated in the same way as natural persons who are nationals of Member States.

'Companies or firms' means companies or firms constituted under civil or commercial law, including co-operative societies, and other legal persons governed by public or private law, save for those which are non-profit-making.

Chapter 3 (Services)

Article 59

Within the framework of the provisions set out below, restrictions on freedom to provide services within the Community shall be progressively abolished during the transitional period in respect of nationals of Member States who are established in a State of the Community other than that of the person for whom the services are intended.

The Council may, acting by a qualified majority on a proposal from the Commission, extend the provisions of the Chapter to nationals of a third country who provide services and who are established within the Community.

Article 60

Services shall be considered to be 'services' within the meaning of this Treaty where they are normally provided for remuneration, in so far as they are not governed by the provisions relating to freedom of movement for goods, capital and persons.

'Services' shall in particular include:
(a) activities of an industrial character;
(b) activities of a commercial character:
(c) activities of craftsmen;
(d) activities of the professions.

Without prejudice to the provisions of the Chapter relating to the right of establishment, the person providing a service may, in order to do so, temporarily pursue his activity in the State where the service is provided, under the same conditions as are imposed by that State on its own nationals.

Article 61

1. Freedom to provide services in the field of transport shall be governed by the provisions of the title relating to transport.

2. The liberalisation of banking and insurance services connected with movements of capital shall be effected in step with the progressive liberalisation of movement of capital.

Article 62

Save as otherwise provided in this Treaty, Member States shall not introduce any new restrictions on the freedom to provide services which have in fact been attained at the date of the entry into force of this Treaty.

Article 63

1. Before the end of the first stage, the Council shall, acting unanimously on a proposal from the Commission and after consulting the Economic and Social Committee and the European Parliament, draw up a general programme for the abolition of existing restrictions on freedom to provide ser-

vices within the Community. The Commission shall submit its proposal to the Council during the first two years of the first stage.

The programme shall set out the general conditions under which and the stages by which each type of service is to be liberalised.

2. In order to implement this general programme or, in the absence of such programme, in order to achieve a stage in the liberalisation of a specific service, the Council shall, on a proposal from the Commission and after consulting the Economic and Social Committee and the European Parliament, issue directives, acting unanimously until the end of the first stage and by a qualified majority thereafter.

3. As regards the proposals and decisions referred to in paragraphs 1 and 2, priority shall as a general rule be given to those services which directly affect production costs or the liberalisation of which helps to promote trade in goods.

Article 64

The Member States declare their readiness to undertake the liberalisation of services beyond the extent required by the directives issued pursuant to Article 63(2), if their general economic situation and the situation of the economic sector concerned so permit.

To this end, the Commission shall make recommendations to the Member States concerned.

Article 65

As long as restrictions on freedom to provide services have not been abolished, each Member State shall apply such restrictions without distinction on grounds of nationality or residence to all persons providing services within the meaning of the first paragraph of Article 59.

Article 66

The provisions of Articles 55 to 58 shall apply to the matters covered by this Chapter.

Chapter 4 (Capital and Payments)

GENERAL NOTE

The provisions on capital and payments in Arts. 67–73 EEC remained in force until January 1, 1994 (Art. 73a E.C.) when they were superseded by the new rules encompassed in Arts. 73b–g E.C.

The changes made to this chapter by the E.U. Treaty are designed to further liberalise free movement of capital, following the coming into force of the second stage of economic and monetary union on January 1, 1994. The overall aim is to secure the outright freedom of movement for capital and payments between the Member States and between Member States and third countries (Art. 73b E.C.).

The free movement of capital between the Member States has already been secured to a large extent thanks to Dir. 88/361/EEC, which came into force between nine of the Member States on July 1, 1990 (see below).

The free movement of capital was included in the original EEC Treaty as one of the four freedoms deemed necessary for the creation of a common European market (Arts. 67–73 EEC). The European Court in Case 203/80, *Criminal Proceedings Against Casati* [1981] E.C.R. 2595 reiterated that the free movement of capital is a key element of the market integration process.

Nevertheless, the unequivocal rules that characterise the other freedoms were long absent in this field. The movement of capital across borders causes greater implications for national economies than related provisions on the freedom of movement of workers, goods and services. Capital can be moved much more easily than people, and major outflows could take place from the relatively weak economies of the Community, adding further to their problems.

The provisions of the EEC Treaty dealing with capital reflect these qualifications. The requirement in Art. 67 EEC that capital movement be freed "only to the extent necessary to ensure the proper functioning of the common market" sets Art. 67 apart from its companion provisions in the areas of free movement of workers, goods and services. It also deprives Art. 67 EEC of direct effect, as was seen in *Casati*.

The amplification of the restricted rights included in this chapter was dependent on the promulgation of legislation by the Council under Art. 69 EEC. Developments in this area were very slow and restrictive until the passing of Dir. 88/361/E.E.C. [1988] O.J. L178/5 aimed at achievement of the internal market called for by Art. 8a EEC (now Art. 7a E.C.) inserted by the S.E.A. (for examination of pre-1988 legislation and an assessment of Directive 88/361 see Oliver and Bache, "Free Movement of Capital: Recent Developments" (1989) 26 C.M.L.Rev. 61).

The objective of Directive 88/361 is to implement Art. 67 by abolishing the remaining restrictions on movements of capital between persons resident in Member States. The Directive came into effect as regards the majority of the Member States at the start of July 1990 (Art. 6(1)). Spain, Ireland, Greece and Portugal were granted an extension until the end of 1992 before full compliance was required, and in the cases of Greece and Portugal further extensions until the end of 1995 may be granted in the event of balance of payments difficulties or the failure of their financial systems to adapt sufficiently (Art. 73e E.C.). Any such further derogations must be agreed according to the procedure laid down in Art. 69 EEC. A derogation in relation to Greece, applicable until January 1, 1995, was agreed by Council Dir. 92/122/E.E.C. ([1992] O.J. L409/33).

The Directive itself contains certain exceptions. Member States may take safeguard measures where short-term capital movements of exceptional magnitude impose serious strains on the foreign exchange markets, leading to serious disturbances in the conduct of monetary and exchange rate policies (Art. 3). The Council was due to review the continued application of this exception by the end of 1992 but no alteration was made. With the pressures being encountered in the capital markets during that year, any move to revoke the latitude afforded by Art. 3 was always going to be unlikely. The turmoil in the ERM brought the issue of currency restrictions to the fore, with huge quantities of capital flowing out of the beleaguered countries. While Ireland and Spain temporarily reintroduced limited currency controls, this did not prevent the sustained attacks on their and other ERM currencies.

Member States were also given some room for fiscal manoeuvre by the provision under Art. 108 EEC relating to serious balance of payments disequilibrium. The Member State could take restricted measures to ensure that the problems it faced would not endanger the other goals.

Article 67

1. During the transitional period and to the extent necessary to ensure the proper functioning of the common market, Member States shall progressively abolish between themselves all restrictions on the movement of capital belonging to persons resident in Member States and any discrimination based on the nationality or on the place of residence of the parties or on the place where such capital is invested.

2. Current payments connected with the movements of capital between Member States shall be freed from all restrictions by the end of the first stage at the latest.

Article 68

1. Member States shall, as regards the matters dealt with in this Chapter, be as liberal as possible in granting such exchange authorisations as are still necessary after the entry into force of this Treaty.

2. Where a Member State applies to the movements of capital liberalised in accordance with the provisions of this Chapter the domestic rules governing the capital market and the credit system, it shall do so in a non-discriminatory manner.

3. Loans for the direct or indirect financing of a Member State or its regional or local authorities shall not be issued or placed in other Member States unless the States concerned have reached agreement thereon. This provision shall not preclude the application of Article 22 of the Protocol on the Statute of the European Investment Bank.

Article 69

The Council shall, on a proposal from the Commission, which for this purpose shall consult the Monetary Committee provided for in Article 105, issue the necessary directives for the progressive implementation of the provisions of Article 67, acting unanimously during the first two stages and by a qualified majority thereafter.

Article 70

1. The Commission shall propose to the Council measures for the progressive co-ordination of the exchange policies of Member States in respect of the movement of capital between those States and third countries. For this purpose the Council shall issue directives, acting by a qualified majority. It shall endeavour to attain the highest possible degree of liberalisation. Unanimity shall be required for measures which constitute a step back as regards the liberalisation of capital movements.

2. Where the measures taken in accordance with paragraph 1 do not permit the elimination of differences between the exchange rules of Member States and where such differences could lead persons resident in one of the Member States to use the freer transfer facilities within the Community which are provided for in Article 67 in order to evade the rules of one of the Member States concerning the movement of capital to or from third countries, that State may, after consulting the other Member States and the Commission, take appropriate measures to overcome these difficulties.

Should the Council find that these measures are restricting the free movement of capital within the Community to a greater extent than is required for the purpose of overcoming the difficulties, it may, acting by a qualified majority on a proposal from the Commission, decide that the State concerned shall amend or abolish these measures.

Article 71

Member States shall endeavour to avoid introducing within the Community any new exchange restrictions on the movement of capital and current payments connected with such movements, and shall endeavour not to make existing rules more restrictive.

They declare their readiness to go beyond the degree of liberalisation of capital movements provided for in the preceding Articles in so far as their economic situation, in particular the situation of their balance of payments, so permits.

The Commission may, after consulting the Monetary Committee, make recommendations to Member States on this subject.

Article 72

Member States shall keep the Commission informed of any movements of capital to and from third countries which come to their knowledge. The Commission may deliver to Member States any opinions which it considers appropriate on this subject.

Article 73

1. If movements of capital lead to disturbances in the functioning of the capital market in any Member State, the Commission shall, after consulting the Monetary Committee, authorise that State to take protective measures in the field of capital movements, the conditions and details of which the Commission shall determine.

The Council may, acting by a qualified majority, revoke this authorisation or amend the conditions or details thereof.

2. A Member State which is in difficulties may, however, on grounds of secrecy or urgency, take the measures mentioned above, where this proves necessary, on its own initiative. The Commission and the other Member States shall be informed of such measures by the date of their entry into force at the latest. In this event the Commission may, after consulting the Monetary Committee, decide that the State concerned shall amend or abolish the measures.

GENERAL NOTE

The new provisions (Arts. 73a–h E.C.)
While the freedom of movement of capital had been largely secured under Dir. 88/361, from January 1, 1994 capital movements became subject to the unequivocally worded provisions of Art. 73b E.C. whereby all restrictions on the freedom of movement of capital and payments between Member States and between Member States and third countries are prohibited.

There is an absolute prohibition on restrictions on capital movements between Member States but there remains the possibility of restrictions between Member States and third countries. The majority of the new provisions are concerned with the conditions for such derogations as regards third countries and would seem to permit extensive exceptions to the general rule in Art. 73b E.C. Art. 73c(1) E.C. permits the continued application of national or Community law, existing prior to January 1, 1994, which restricts the movement of capital to or from third countries. There was thus nothing to stop the Community or Member States from "stocking up" protections prior to this deadline; neither Art. 71 EEC or Dir. 88/361/EEC dealt with extra-Community transfers (see Art. 1 of the Directive). Under Art. 72 EEC the Member States are simply under an obligation to keep the Commission informed of capital movements to or from third countries. Protections against capital moving to non-member States will be ineffective if capital can be moved to a Member State which has no such restrictions on capital movement and from there moved to a non-member State.

The result of the new capital provisions may be limited, at least in the short-term. As regards capital and payments movements between the Member States, little has been added to the protections afforded by Dir. 88/361. The major alteration is the removal of the potential derogations afforded by this provision including the short-term safeguard measures permitted by Art. 3 of the Directive. Also removed is the potential derogation afforded by Art. 73 EEC, whereby if movements of capital led to disturbances in the functioning of the capital market in any Member State, it could take emergency measures on its own initiative (Art. 73(2) EEC) or with the authorisation of the Commission (Art. 73(1) EEC). The removal of this protective measure from January 1, 1994 could have been unwelcome if the lack of meaningful economic and monetary convergence of the Member State economies had opened up further problems of pressures being applied on Member State currencies. This has not yet occurred, but may arise if the commitment to narrow ERM bands is reiterated. Whatever the pressures, the commitment to free movement of capital appears virtually absolute; exceptions are permitted in Arts. 73d(1) and 73d(2) concerning, *inter alia*, taxation matters and statistical analysis of capital flows but with the express proviso that these do not constitute a disguised restriction on the free movement of capital (Art. 73(d)(3) E.C.). The vexed matter of taxation could well prove one of the major stumbling blocks to the free movement of capital both intra-Community and *vis-á-vis* third countries. There is a potential contradiction between the wording of Art. 73d E.C. and the appended declaration which will require to be clarified. The current divergent interpretations on the scope of permissible tax measures with regard to Community and non-Community nationals is discussed in the note on Art. 73d.

Returning to the effects of the new provisions. The significant change from the legislation applicable prior to the E.U. Treaty coming into force is the commitment to freedom of capital and payments between the Member States and third countries. Nevertheless, this commitment is subject to a wide variety of potential derogations. As already mentioned there is the proviso that existing restrictive measures could remain in force after the January 1, 1994 deadline (Art. 73c(1) E.C.). There is also a provision permitting the Council, acting on a qualified majority, to enact safeguard measures for a maximum of six months where capital movements to or from third countries threaten or cause serious difficulties for the operation of economic and monetary union (Art. 73f E.C.). Other potential restrictions which may be applied by the Member States are included in Art. 73g(2) E.C., which permits the imposition of unilateral measures against a third country for serious political reasons or on the grounds of urgency. The Community is likewise permitted to take such measures as are agreed under the common foreign and security policy pillar (Art. 73g(1) E.C.).

Nowhere in these new provisions is there any provision for the formal involvement of the European Parliament in the legislative process. (Art. 73g merely makes it necessary for the European Parliament to be informed after the event, should the Council vote for the abolition or amendment of any Member State's economic sanction in force against a third State.)

Article 73a

As from 1 January 1994, Articles 67 to 73 shall be replaced by Articles 73b, c, d, e, f and g.

GENERAL NOTE

This article sets the time-scale for the coming into force of the new provisions on the freedom of movement of capital and payments. Arts. 73(b)–(g) are the operative provisions which have dictated the policy governing this area since January 1, 1994. Prior to that date, the existing legislation in the field, primarily Dir. 88/361, had to be read in the light of the new Art. 73h E.C. The intermediate provisions contained in this Article took effect on the coming into force of the Treaty (on November 1, 1993) and lapsed two months later on January 1, 1994. The Treaty thus provided for a transitional phase during which the liberalisation of capital movements and payments would continue to be tied to the liberalisation of the other freedoms enshrined in the E.C. Treaty; it cannot have been anticipated that the transitional period would be so short.

1. Within the framework of the provisions set out in this Chapter, all restrictions on the movement of capital between Member States and between Member States and third countries shall be prohibited.

Article 73b

1. Within the framework of the provisions set out in this Chapter, all restrictions on the movement of capital between Member States and between Member States and third countries shall be prohibited.

2. Within the framework of the provisions set out in this Chapter, all restrictions on payments between Member States and between Member States and third countries shall be prohibited.

GENERAL NOTE

The division of this section into two sub-paragraphs reflects the practice under the existing Treaty provisions of dealing with the freedom of movement of capital and payments separately (Art. 67(1) EEC on capital and 67(2) EEC on payments). This dichotomy has only now been expressly recognised in the Titles of the Treaty, whereby the new heading to Chapter 4 reads "capital and payments" as opposed to its old single word title of "capital". Nevertheless, this change is purely cosmetic. The Court of Justice, in the few cases on this topic, developed a distinction between the free movement of capital and the free movement of payments. The court accepted that capital movements are not the only transactions that involve transfers of currency. Currency may be transferred in order to invest the funds themselves or it may be transferred to make a specific purchase. In the latter case, currency movement is a precondition for the exercise of other freedoms, such as those relating to goods, persons and services (see Cases 203/80, *Casati* [1981] E.C.R. 2 595; 308/86, *Ministère Public v. Lambert* [1988] E.C.R. 4369; and 286/82, 26/83, *Luisi and Carbone v. Ministero del Tesoro* [1984] E.C.R. 377). The result was protection for the free movement of payments analogous to the protection afforded to the other freedoms.

With the gradual removal of restrictions on the free movement of capital, any distinction between the treatment of capital and payments has been steadily removed. Article 73b E.C. would seem to have taken this to its logical conclusion with the prohibition of any restrictions to the free movement of capital ensured by para. 1 and with regard to payments in para. 2. In both cases this prohibition is absolute, but with regard to the freedom of movement of capital with third countries it is crucial to note the qualifying phrase: "within the framework of the provisions set out in this chapter". Due to the potentially more "injurious" effects of capital transfers, several of the restrictions do not apply to payments: Articles 73c(1) and (2) and 73f E.C. make reference only to "capital". It is difficult to regard the omission of any reference to "payments" in these Articles as an oversight, in so far as Art. 73g E.C. makes express allusion to the potential restriction of both capital and payments. It would therefore seem that the distinction drawn by the European Court between capital and payments in Community matters will continue to be applicable, but only in cases with an external third country element.

The wording of this Article and the prohibitions which it enunciates ought to be capable of direct applicability and thus permit the enforcement of its obligations before the national courts. Those Member States which maintain restrictions on this freedom, not justified under any other heading, will probably find themselves the subject of Art. 169 E.C. proceedings.

Article 73c

1. The provisions of Article 73b shall be without prejudice to the application to third countries of any restrictions which exist on 31 December 1993 under national or Community law adopted in respect of the movement of capital to or from third countries involving direct investment (including investment in real estate), establishment, the provision of financial services or the admission of securities to capital markets.

2. Whilst endeavouring to achieve the objective of free movement of capital between Member States and third countries to the greatest extent possible and without prejudice to the other Chapters of this Treaty, the Council may, acting by a qualified majority on a proposal from the Commission, adopt measures on the movement of capital to or from third countries involving direct investment (including investment in real estate), establishment, the provision of financial services or the admission of securities to capital markets.

Unanimity shall be required for measures under this paragraph which constitute a step back in Community law as regards the liberalisation of the movement of capital to or from third countries.

GENERAL NOTE

Para. (1)

This Article permits measures restricting the flow of capital to or from third countries, in existence on December 31, 1993, to remain applicable after the deadline for the abolition of restrictions on capital movements has come into being. As already mentioned, this seems to render the supposed prohibition on measures preventing the free movement of capital between third States and the Community somewhat otiose. The scope of areas in which national or Community legislation derogating from the free movement of capital to or from third countries is permissible is large, including any form of direct investment, establishment, the provision of financial services or the admission of securities to the capital markets. The majority of these appear to be aimed at preventing extra-Community competition in these fields, notably as regards the provision of financial services. Moreover, the Article concerns both the inflow and outflow of capital, thus permitting national laws preventing internal investment, as well as permitting rules aimed at preventing the outflow of capital from a Member State to a third country. Moreover, there is no deadline set by the Treaty for the abolition of such restrictions. So long as they were in existence on December 31, 1993, then they may continue, *ad infinitum*, unless the Community adopts legislation on the matter under Art. 73(2) E.C.

Para. (2)

This paragraph lays down the legislative procedure applicable to the promulgation of measures dealing with the movement of capital to and from third countries in the four areas listed, encompassing direct investment, establishment, the provision of financial services or the admission of securities to capital markets. Those measures which "constitute a step back in Community law" as regards the liberalisation of the movement of capital must be approved by a unanimous Council, while other measures (not specifically defined but presumably all other measures apart from those already mentioned) are subject to qualified majority acceptance. This reflects the wording and purpose of Art. 70 EEC, which it superseded on January 1, 1994.

Article 73d

1. The provisions of Article 73b shall be without prejudice to the right of Member States:
   (a) to apply the relevant provisions of their tax law which distinguish between tax-payers who are not in the same situation with regard to their place of residence or with regard to the place where their capital is invested;
   (b) to take all requisite measures to prevent infringements of national law and regulations, in particular in the field of taxation and the prudential

supervision of financial institutions, or to lay down procedures for the declaration of capital movements for purposes of administrative or statistical information, or to take measures which are justified on grounds of public policy or public security.

2. The provisions of this Chapter shall be without prejudice to the applicability of restrictions on the right of establishment which are compatible with this Treaty.

3. The measures and procedures referred to in paragraphs 1 and 2 shall not constitute a means of arbitrary discrimination or a disguised restriction on the free movement of capital and payments as defined in Article 73b.

GENERAL NOTE

This Article gives some discretion to Member States to derogate from the absolute requirement of free movement of capital in Art. 73b E.C. This is achieved by setting out in paras. 1 and 2 the specific areas where this is permissible, but making them subject to the proviso contained in paragraph 3.

Para. (1)(a)

The issue of taxation is one of the most contentious as regards the influence of the Community. This Article preserves the right of the Member States to charge tax within their own boundaries at different levels, which are dependent on the residence of the tax-payer. Dassesse suggests that the wording of this Article is potentially in conflict with the appended Declaration on Art. 73d E.C. The original wording of the Declaration provided that the Member States would have the right to apply the relevant provisions of their tax laws "only with respect to the relevant provisions which existed at the end of 1993". However, the Declaration was later substantially amended by the addition of a new second clause which reads "this Declaration shall apply only to capital movements between Member States and to payments effected between Member States". Dassesse argues that while Art. 73d E.C. appears to permit the Member States to discriminate between local residents, other Member State nationals and nationals of third countries, the Declaration would seem to permit differentiation between taxpayers only as regards those measures which are in force at the end of 1993 and only for operations concerning residents of other Member States. Some Member States, reading the Declaration together with Art. 73d E.C., see this as imposing a duty on all Member States not to adopt tax measures which treat residents of other Member States more favourably than their own residents. In other words a prohibition on the adoption of measures making the Member State a "tax haven" for residents of other Member States. Other Member States have interpreted the provisions as permitting a Member State to treat residents of third countries less favourably than nationals of other Member States. This is particularly asserted with regard to the refusal to refund a withholding tax on securities held by a third country resident, even though such refunds are granted to Community residents (see Dassesse, "The Treaty on European Union: Implications for the Free Movement of Capital" [1992] 6 J.I.B.L. 38). The merit of these arguments is to a great extent contingent on the legal status of declarations appended to the Community Treaties. Toth, referring to the S.E.A., described the declarations appended to that instrument as "having no effect on the interpretation of the S.E.A. by the E.C.J." (Toth, "The Legal Status of Declarations Appended to the S.E.A." (1986) 23 C.M.L.Rev. 811.) However, his argument has already been criticised above, and does not appear very persuasive. What may be more significant is the argument ventured above about the invalidity of agreements between the Member States which effectively seek to amend the Treaty under the guise of interpreting it. The force of this argument will turn on the degree to which the Declaration is perceived to be irreconcilable with the terms of Art. 73d E.C.

Para. (1)(b)

This paragraph permits checks applied to the movement of capital to continue, for example to ensure the proper supervision of financial institutions or for the compilation of administrative or statistical information (reiteration of Art. 4 of Directive 88/361/EEC) and allows the Member States to take measures justified on the grounds of public policy or public security.

The exception in relation to "public policy" or "public security" would appear to afford a potentially wide let-out clause to the otherwise absolute prohibition on measures preventing the flow of capital and payments between Member States. While it is impossible to predict to what extent Member States might rely on this provision, it is easier to predict the tests which will have to be fulfilled in order to justify such actions. In any challenge to legislation derogating from free movement of capital or payments on any of the grounds listed in this Article, the Member State will have to prove that its actions are proportionate to the goals sought. The European Court would ultimately determine the lawfulness of any such derogations (see Case 42/82, *Commission v. France*: [1983] E.C.R. 1013, in the context of Art. 36 EEC). It has always, as regards other fundamental freedoms, refused to accept a broad definition of this exception (as regards the free movement of goods under Art. 36 EEC, see Weatherill and Beaumont, *E.C. Law* (1993), pp. 399–404).

Para. (2)

This paragraph permits the continued reliance by Member States on the existing restrictions applicable to the freedom of establishment (Arts. 52–66 E.C.). The provisions in this chapter are to have no effect on the continued reliance on such derogations. While Art. 52 E.C. makes it clear that the right of establishment must be exercised "subject to the provisions of the chapter on capital", this paragraph makes it clear that the exceptions to the freedom of establishment continue to be applicable regardless. These restrictions include the exception in the case of activities concerned with the exercise of official authority (Art. 55 E.C. and Case 2/74, *Reyners v. Belgium* [1974] E.C.R. 631), as well as the permissible restrictions laid down in Art. 56 E.C. that special measures may be taken as regards foreign nationals on the grounds of public policy, public health or public security. (See Weatherill and Beaumont, *E.C. Law*, (1993) pp. 511–513 and 517–521; Wyatt and Dashwood, *European Community Law* (3rd. ed., 1993), pp. 291–293, 307–312.) This paragraph ensured that such restrictions as still applied on January 1, 1994 would not be subject to attack on the grounds that they do not comply with the absolute freedom of capital laid down in Art. 73b E.C.

This paragraph must be read in the light of para. 3 which dictates that any measures must not constitute a means of arbitrary discrimination or a disguised restriction on the free movement of capital (see note on that paragraph).

While dealing with the free movement of services, the Court of Justice has made an important ruling, of ambiguous legal relevance to the present Article, on the permissible scope of restrictions to one of the fundamental freedoms. This occurred in *Bachmann v. Belgium* and *Commission v. Belgium* (Cases 204 and 300/90, [1992] E.C.R. I–249), in which the Court of Justice, in contrast to its previous jurisprudence on the topic, found that Member States were permitted to take measures which restrict the free provision of cross-border services where such measures are necessary to ensure "the coherence of their national tax system". It is impossible to predict the potential of the Court of Justice developing such a derogation in the establishment field and thus accruing further derogations from the free movement of capital through the present Article.

Para. (3)

This paragraph reiterates the provision common to Community law, emphasising the restricted scope within which any derogations to the fundamental freedoms in the Treaty are to be exercised. Such a test inevitably involves a delicate balancing of the derogation and its purpose. Art. 36 E.C. contains an identically worded provision as regards measures derogating from the free movement of goods. As this type of provision is new to the field of capital movement, it is likely that the jurisprudence of the European Court as regards Art. 36 E.C. will prove illuminating. The measures will only be justified where they are no more restrictive than is strictly necessary, in other words, in accordance with the principle of proportionality (see Cases 5/77 *Tedeschi (Carlo) Denkavit Commerciale SRL* [1977] E.C.R. 1556; and 251/78, *Denkavit v. Minister für Ernährung Landwirtschaft and Forsten* [1979] E.C.R. 3327, at para. 21). The requirements that the restriction be proportionate, not constitute a disguised restriction on trade nor be a means of arbitrary discrimination cannot be considered in isolation. For example, the test of proportionality may well indicate the existence of a disguised restriction on trade (see Wyatt and Dashwood, *European Community Law* (1993), p. 229). For an overview of this field as regards Art. 36, see Weatherill and Beaumont, *E.C. Law* (1993), Chap. 16.

Given that any measures are to be assessed in terms of their compliance with the free movement of capital and payments as defined in Art. 73b, it is highly likely that the Court of Justice will apply strict tests to any derogation measures.

Article 73e

By way of derogation from Article 73b, Member States which, on December 31, 1993, enjoy a derogation on the basis of existing Community law, shall be entitled to maintain, until December 31, 1995 at the latest, restrictions on movements of capital authorised by such derogations as exist on that date.

GENERAL NOTE

This Article allows those Member States who were permitted to maintain restrictions on the movement of capital on December 31, 1993 to maintain these restrictions in force until December 31, 1995 at the latest. Under Directive 88/361/EEC, transitional arrangements were made permitting four Member States (Spain, Greece, Ireland and Portugal) to continue the application of certain restrictions to the liberalised provisions until the end of 1992. Provision was also made for the possibility of further extension of the transitional arrangements by up to three years for Greece and Portugal (Art. 6(2), Dir. 88/361/EEC). Such arrangements must be subject to agreement by the Council, in accordance with the procedure laid down in Art. 69 EEC. Directive 92/122/EEC (O.J. 1992 L407/1) authorised Greece to defer the liberalisation of certain capital movements pursuant to Art. 6(2) of Dir. 88/361/EEC, until January 1, 1995.

Article 73f

Where, in exceptional circumstances, movements of capital to or from third countries cause, or threaten to cause, serious difficulties for the operation of economic and monetary union, the Council, acting by a qualified majority on a proposal from the Commission and after consulting the ECB, may take safeguard measures with regard to third countries for a period not exceeding six months if such measures are strictly necessary.

GENERAL NOTE

This Article permits the Council, acting by a qualified majority on a proposal from the Commission, to enact safeguard measures with regard to third countries, for a period not exceeding six months. The wording of this Article makes it quite clear that such measures must not be taken lightly. The words "exceptional circumstances", "serious difficulties", and "strictly necessary" make this provision appear very much a last resort measure.

Also relevant in this respect are the provisions in Arts. 109h and 109i E.C. on serious balance of payments difficulties in the Member States (see notes on those articles).

No express provision is made as to the date at which this provision is to come into effect but the reference to the consultation of the European Central Bank and to economic and monetary union makes it seem that it may not take effect until the coming into force of the third stage of economic and monetary union.

Article 73g

1. If, in the case envisaged in Article 228a, action by the Community is deemed necessary, the Council may, in accordance with the procedure provided for in Article 228a, take the necessary urgent measures on the movement of capital and on payments as regards the third countries concerned.

2. Without prejudice to Article 224 and as long as the Council has not taken measures pursuant to paragraph 1, a Member State may, for serious political reasons and on grounds of urgency, take unilateral measures against a third country with regard to capital movements and payments. The Commission and the other Member States shall be informed of such measures by the date of their entry into force at the latest.

The Council may, acting by a qualified majority on a proposal from the Commission, decide that the Member State concerned shall amend or abolish such measures. The President of the Council shall inform the European Parliament of any such decision taken by the Council.

GENERAL NOTE

This Article gives authority to further derogations from the outright freedom of capital espoused in this chapter. These derogations are based on essentially political considerations, including the imposition of economic sanctions on third countries (para. 1). It also permits unilateral derogations by Member States in their relations with third countries, but subject to Community revocation (para. 2).

Para. (1)

This paragraph gives weight to the new Art. 228a E.C. added at Maastricht. Under Art. 228a E.C., the Council is to take the necessary urgent measures required to interrupt or reduce, in part or completely, economic relations with one or more third countries. Such measures, to be adopted by qualified majority in the Council, are incorporated into Community law by virtue of Art. 228a E.C. and are based on common positions or joint actions taken under the inter-governmental foreign and security policy pillar (Title V E.U.). The political agreement to impose economic sanctions on a third country is taken under the common foreign and security policy pillar but the necessary legal measures to suspend free movement of capital or payments with that country are taken under Arts. 228a E.C. and 73g(1) of the E.C. Treaty. Article 73g(1) authorises such economic sanctions in so far as they represent a derogation from the free movement of capital. It must be observed that this Article permits the derogation from the freedom of movement of payments as well as capital, thus permitting very wide-ranging sanctions against the countries involved.

Para. (2)

This paragraph permits a Member State to take unilateral measures against a third country, with regard to capital movements and payments, for serious political reasons and on grounds of urgency. The scope of this measure is far from clear. The existence of Community action under Art. 228a E.C. precludes the application of unilateral measures. Article 73g(2) is without prejudice to Art. 224 E.C., which requires Member States to consult each other with a view to taking the steps needed to prevent the functioning of the common market being affected by certain unilateral measures being taken by a Member State due to war, terrorism or United Nations economic or military sanctions.

Whatever the scope of the Member State action, it is obviously preferable to have Community action. Any unilateral measure must be referred to the Commission and other Member States prior to its entry into force, thus permitting its discussion under the aegis of the common foreign and security policy which is based on such inter-governmental negotiations. Moreover, the Council, acting by a qualified majority, may decide to abolish or amend any such measure. This constitutes quite a significant step as regards Community oversight of the Member States' foreign policy operations. Economic sanctions by a Member State on a non-member State can be overturned by the Community, acting by qualified majority in Council. The European Parliament is to be informed of any action taken by the Council under this Article.

Article 73h

Until 1 January 1994, the following provisions shall be applicable:
(1) Each Member State undertakes to authorise, in the currency of the Member State in which the creditor or the beneficiary resides, any payments connected with the movement of goods, services or capital, and any transfers of capital and earnings, to the extent that the movement of goods, services, capital and persons between Member States has been liberalised pursuant to this Treaty.

The Member States declare their readiness to undertake the liberalisation of payments beyond the extent provided in the preceding subparagraph, in so far as their economic situation in general and the state of their balance of payments in particular so permit.
(2) In so far as movements of goods, services and capital are limited only by restrictions on payments connected therewith, these restrictions shall be progressively abolished by applying, *mutatis mutandis*, the provisions of this Chapter and the Chapters relating to the abolition of quantitative restrictions and to the liberalisation of services.
(3) Member States undertake not to introduce between themselves any new restrictions on transfers connected with the invisible transactions listed in Annex III to this Treaty.

The progressive abolition of existing restrictions shall be effected in accordance with the provisions of Articles 63 to 65, in so far as such abolition is not governed by the provisions contained in paragraphs 1 and 2 or by the other provisions of this Chapter.
(4) If need be, Member States shall consult each other on the measures to be taken to enable the payments and transfers mentioned in this Article to be effected; such measures shall not prejudice the attainment of the objectives set out in this Treaty.

GENERAL NOTE

This Article consists of transitional provisions which applied until the new Arts. 73b–g E.C. came into force on January 1, 1994. These provisions are a motley collection of declarations and measures ancillary to the on-going liberalisation of payments and capital freedoms, in essence, an exercise in spring cleaning. These provisions will not be analysed in detail.

Para. (1)

This paragraph aimed to ensure the freedom of payments by laying down that the Member States must authorise payments in the currency of the creditor where the transaction is in relation to the free movement of goods, services and capital. The Member States thus could not fetter the movement of payments on the ground that a certain currency was not acceptable for the transaction. The currency had to be that of the creditor's Member State, which excluded the application of this provision to third country residents or non-Community currencies. The last sentence indicates that this provision applied only in those areas which had already been liberalised by the Treaty, thus adding little to practice.

Para. (2)

Once again, this symbolised the desire to see the progressive removal of all restrictions on the free movement of payments, where these restrictions impeded the other market freedoms. This added little to current practice, and the only devices open to pursue such goals were those provisions of the Treaty already in existence.

Para. (3)

As regards the invisible transactions listed in Annex III to the Treaty, the Member States were to avoid the introduction of any new restrictions on such transfers.

Para. (4)

This Article simply provides for non-obligatory consultation between the Member States on the measures deemed necessary for achievement of the freedoms envisaged under Art. 73h E.C.

TITLE IV: Transport

Article 74

The objectives of this Treaty shall, in matters governed by this Title, be pursued by Member States within the framework of a common transport policy.

Article 75

1. For the purpose of implementing Article 74, and taking into account the distinctive features of transport, the Council shall, acting in accordance with the procedure referred to in Article 189c and after consulting the Economic and Social Committee, lay down:
   (a) common rules applicable to international transport to or from the territory of a Member State or passing across the territory of one or more Member States;
   (b) the conditions under which non-resident carriers may operate transport services within a Member State;
   (c) measures to improve transport safety;
   (d) any other appropriate provisions.
2. The provisions referred to in (a) and (b) of paragraph 1 shall be laid down during the transitional period.
3. By way of derogation from the procedure provided for in paragraph 1, where the application of provisions concerning the principles of the regulat-

ory system for transport would be liable to have a serious effect on the standard of living and on employment in certain areas and on the operation of transport facilities, they shall be laid down by the Council acting unanimously on a proposal from the Commission, after consulting the European Parliament and the Economic and Social Committee.

In so doing, the Council shall take into account the need for adaptation to the economic development which will result from establishing the common market.

GENERAL NOTE

Para. (1)

This Article, which constitutes the core of the transport provisions in the E.C. Treaty, is amended slightly. The legislative procedure for the promulgation of measures, as listed in sub-paragraphs (a)–(d) is altered from a requirement of qualified majority in Council, after consulting the European Parliament, to the application of the co-operation procedure (Art. 189c E.C.). This gives the European Parliament a greater say in the legislative process (see note on Art. 189c E.C.). For analysis of transport policy itself, see Mathijsen, *A Guide to European Community Law* (6th ed., 1995), pp. 288–97; see also [1993] E.C. Bull, Supp. 3, *The Future Development of the Common Transport Policy.*

The Article is also amended to include the new sub-paragraph (c) on "measures to improve transport safety". Community action, in line with the procedure outlined above, is now available in this field. This power probably existed already under the catch-all provision, previously Art. 73(1)(c) EEC, which is retitled (d) to make way for the new, specific provision (see 31st Report of the U.K. Select Committee on European Legislation, Session 1988–89 H.C. 15–xxxi, para. 11).

Para. (3)

While the adoption of transport measures under Art. 75(1) is altered from the consultation procedure to the co-operation procedure, the consultation procedure is to be applied to legislation under Art. 75(3), whereas previously the Council could act without consulting the Parliament. Unanimity in the Council is preserved.

Article 76

Until the provisions referred to in Article 75(1) have been laid down, no Member State may, without the unanimous approval of the Council, make the various provisions governing the subject when this Treaty enters into force less favourable in their direct or indirect effect on carriers of other Member States as compared with carriers who are nationals of that State.

Article 77

Aids shall be compatible with this Treaty if they meet the needs of co-ordination of transport or if they represent reimbursement for the discharge of certain obligations inherent in the concept of a public service.

Article 78

Any measures taken within the framework of this Treaty in respect of transport rates and conditions shall take account of the economic circumstances of carriers.

Article 79

1. In the case of transport within the Community, discrimination which takes the form of carriers charging different rates and imposing different conditions for the carriage of the same goods over the same transport links on grounds of the country of origin or of destination of the goods in question, shall be abolished, at the latest, before the end of the second stage.

2. Paragraph 1 shall not prevent the Council from adopting other measures in pursuance of Article 75(1).

3.Within two years of the entry into force of this Treaty, the Council shall, acting by a qualified majority on a proposal from the Commission and after consulting the Economic and Social Committee, lay down rules for implementing the provisions of paragraph 1.

The Council may in particular lay down the provisions needed to enable the institutions of the Community to secure compliance with the rule laid down in paragraph 1 and to ensure that users benefit from it to the full.

4. The Commission shall, acting on its own initiative or on application by a Member State, investigate any cases of discrimination falling within paragraph 1 and, after consulting any Member State concerned, shall take the necessary decisions within the framework of the rules laid down in accordance with the provisions of paragraph 3.

Article 80

1. The imposition by a Member State, in respect of transport operations carried out within the Community, of rates and conditions involving any element of support or protection in the interest of one or more particular undertakings or industries shall be prohibited as from the beginning of the second stage, unless authorised by the Commission.

2. The Commission shall, acting on its own initiative or on application by a Member State, examine the rates and conditions referred to in paragraph 1, taking account in particular of the requirements of an appropriate regional economic policy, the needs of underdeveloped areas and the problems of areas seriously affected by political circumstances on the one hand, and of the effects of such rates and conditions on competition between the different modes of transport on the other.

After consulting each Member State concerned, the Commission shall take the necessary decisions.

3. The prohibition provided for in paragraph 1 shall not apply to tariffs fixed to meet competition.

Article 81

Charges or dues in respect of the crossing of frontiers which are charged by a carrier in addition to the transport rates shall not exceed a reasonable level after taking the costs actually incurred thereby into account.

Member States shall endeavour to reduce these costs progressively.

The Commission may make recommendations to Member States for the application of this Article.

Article 82

The provisions of this Title shall not form an obstacle to the application of measures taken in the Federal Republic of Germany to the extent that such measures are required in order to compensate for the economic disadvantages caused by the division of Germany to the economy of certain areas of the Federal Republic affected by that division.

Article 83

An Advisory Committee consisting of experts designated by the Governments of Member States, shall be attached to the Commission. The Commission, whenever it considers it desirable, shall consult the Committee on transport matters without prejudice to the powers of the transport section of the Economic and Social Committee.

Article 84

1. The provisions of this Title shall apply to transport by rail, road and inland waterway.

2. The Council may, acting by a qualified majority, decide whether, to what extent and by what procedure appropriate provisions may be laid down for sea and air transport.

The procedural provisions of Article 75(1) and (3) shall apply.

TITLE V: Common Rules on Competition, Taxation and Approximation of Laws

GENERAL NOTE

The alteration to the heading of this section of the Treaty (previously Title I on "Common Rules" under the main heading of Part Three: "Policy of the Community") is entirely cosmetic. Where it used to read "common rules" we now have "common rules on competition, taxation and the approximation of laws"; exactly what this section had dealt with in the past, without any necessity to make this explicit in the Title. The substantive provisions under this title have changed very little.

Chapter 1 (Rules on Competition)

SECTION 1: Rules applying to undertakings

Article 85

1. The following shall be prohibited as incompatible with the common market: all agreements between undertakings, decisions by associations of undertakings and concerted practices which may affect trade between Member States and which have as their object or effect the prevention, restriction or distortion of competition within the common market, and in particular those which:
   (a) directly or indirectly fix purchase or selling prices or any other trading conditions;
   (b) limit or control production, markets, technical development, or investment;
   (c) share markets or sources of supply;
   (d) apply dissimilar conditions to equivalent transactions with other trading parties, thereby placing them at a competitive disadvantage;
   (e) make the conclusion of contracts subject to acceptance by the other parties of supplementary obligations which, by their nature or according to commercial usage, have no connection with the subject of such contracts.

2. Any agreements or decisions prohibited pursuant to this Article shall be automatically void.

3. The provisions of paragraph 1 may, however, be declared inapplicable in the case of:
   — any agreement or category of agreements between undertakings;
   — any decision or category of decisions by associations of undertakings;
   — any concerted practice or category of concerted practices;
   which contributes to improving the production or distribution of goods or to promoting technical or economic progress, while allowing consumers a fair share of the resulting benefit, and which does not :
   (a) impose on the undertakings concerned restrictions which are not indispensable to the attainment of these objectives;

(b) afford such undertakings the possibility of eliminating competition in respect of a substantial part of the products in question.

Article 86

Any abuse by one or more undertakings of a dominant position within the common market or in a substantial part of it shall be prohibited as incompatible with the common market in so far as it may affect trade between Member States.

Such abuse may, in particular, consist in:

(a) directly or indirectly imposing unfair purchase or selling prices or other unfair trading conditions;
(b) limiting production, markets or technical development to the prejudice of consumers;
(c) applying dissimilar conditions to equivalent transactions with other trading parties, thereby placing them at a competitive disadvantage;
(d) making the conclusion of contracts subject to acceptance by the other parties of supplementary obligations which, by their nature or according to commercial usage, have no connection with the subject of such contracts.

Article 87

1. Within three years of the entry into force of this Treaty the Council shall, acting unanimously on a proposal from the Commission and after consulting the European Parliament, adopt any appropriate regulations or directives to give effect to the principles set out in Articles 85 and 86.

If such provisions have not been adopted within the period mentioned, they shall be laid down by the Council, acting by a qualified majority on a proposal from the Commission and after consulting the European Parliament.

2. The regulations or directives referred to in paragraph 1 shall be designed in particular:

(a) to ensure compliance with the prohibitions laid down in Article 85(1) and in Article 86 by making provision for fines and periodic penalty payments;
(b) to lay down detailed rules for the application of Article 85(3), taking into account the need to ensure effective supervision on the one hand, and to simplify administration to the greatest possible extent on the other;
(c) to define, if need be, in the various branches of the economy, the scope of the provisions of Articles 85 and 86;
(d) to define the respective functions of the Commission and of the Court of Justice in applying the provisions laid down in this paragraph;
(e) to determine the relationship between national laws and the provisions contained in this Section or adopted pursuant to this Article.

Article 88

Until the entry into force of the provisions adopted in pursuance of Article 87, the authorities in Member States shall rule on the admissibility of agreements, decisions and concerted practices and on abuse of a dominant position in the common market in accordance with the law of their country and with the provisions of Article 85, in particular paragraph 3, and of Article 86.

Article 89

1. Without prejudice to Article 88, the Commission shall, as soon as it takes up its duties, ensure the application of the principles laid down in Articles 85

and 86. On application by a Member State or on its own initiative, and in co-operation with the competent authorities in the Member States, who shall give it their assistance, the Commission shall investigate cases of suspected infringement of these principles. If it finds that there has been an infringement, it shall propose appropriate measures to bring it to an end.

2. If the infringement is not brought to an end, the Commission shall record such infringement of the principles in a reasoned decision. The Commission may publish its decision and authorise Member States to take the measures, the conditions and details of which it shall determine, needed to remedy the situation.

Article 90

1. In the case of public undertakings and undertakings to which Member States grant special or exclusive rights, Member States shall neither enact nor maintain in force any measure contrary to the rules contained in this Treaty, in particular to those rules provided for in Article 6 and Articles 85 to 94.

2. Undertakings entrusted with the operation of services of general economic interest or having the character of a revenue-producing monopoly shall be subject to the rules contained in this Treaty, in particular to the rules on competition, in so far as the application of such rules does not obstruct the performance, in law or in fact, of the particular tasks assigned to them. The development of trade must not be affected to such an extent as would be contrary to the interests of the Community.

3. The Commission shall ensure the application of the provisions of this Article and shall, where necessary, address appropriate directives or decisions to Member States.

Section 2: Dumping

Article 91

1. If during the transitional period, the Commission, on application by a Member State or by any other interested party, finds that dumping is being practised within the common market, it shall address recommendations to the person or persons with whom such practices originate for the purpose of putting an end to them.

Should the practices continue, the Commission shall authorise the injured Member State to take protective measures, the conditions and details of which the Commission shall determine.

2. As soon as this Treaty enters into force, products which originate in or are in free circulation in one Member State and which have been exported to another Member State shall, on reimportation, be admitted into the territory of the first-mentioned State free of all customs duties, quantitative restrictions or measures having equivalent effect. The Commission shall lay down appropriate rules for the application of this paragraph.

Section 3: Aids granted by States

Article 92

1. Save as otherwise provided in this Treaty, any aid granted by a Member State or through State resources in any form whatsoever which distorts or threatens to distort competition by favouring certain undertakings or the production of certain goods shall, in so far as it affects trade between Member States, be incompatible with the common market.

2. The following shall be compatible with the common market:
   (a) aid having a social character, granted to individual consumers, provided that such aid is granted without discrimination related to the origin of the products concerned;

(b) aid to make good the damage caused by natural disasters or exceptional occurrences;

(c) aid granted to the economy of certain areas of the Federal Republic of Germany affected by the division of Germany, in so far as such aid is required in order to compensate for the economic disadvantages caused by that division.

3. The following may be considered to be compatible with the common market:

(a) aid to promote the economic development of areas where the standard of living is abnormally low or where there is serious underemployment;

(b) aid to promote the execution of an important project of common European interest or to remedy a serious disturbance in the economy of a Member State;

(c) aid to facilitate the development of certain economic activities or of certain economic areas, where such aid does not adversely affect trading conditions to an extent contrary to the common interest. However, the aids granted to shipbuilding as of January 1, 1957 shall, in so far as they serve only to compensate for the absence of customs protection, be progressively reduced under the same conditions as apply to the elimination of customs duties, subject to the provisions of this Treaty concerning common commercial policy towards third countries;

(d) aid to promote culture and heritage conservation where such aid does not affect trading conditions and competition in the Community to an extent that is contrary to the common interest;

(e) such other categories of aid as may be specified by decision of the Council acting by a qualified majority on a proposal from the Commission.

GENERAL NOTE

Para. (3)

A minor amendment is made to this Article; the new sub-paragraph (d) on the granting of State aid to promote culture and heritage conservation, subject to the provisos listed therein, has been inserted. The existing sub-paragraph (d) is therefore moved to (e). On State aid in general, see Weatherill and Beaumont, *E.C. Law* (1993), Chap. 27.

Article 93

1. The Commission shall, in co-operation with Member States, keep under constant review all systems of aid existing in those States. It shall propose to the latter any appropriate measures required by the progressive development or by the functioning of the common market.

2. If, after giving notice to the parties concerned to submit their comments, the Commission finds that aid granted by a State or through State resources is not compatible with the common market having regard to Article 92, or that such aid is being misused, it shall decide that the State concerned shall abolish or alter such aid within a period of time to be determined by the Commission.

If the State concerned does not comply with this decision within the prescribed time, the Commission or any other interested State may, in derogation from the provisions of Articles 169 and 170, refer the matter to the Court of Justice direct.

On application by a Member State, the Council, may, acting unanimously, decide that aid which that State is granting or intends to grant shall be considered to be compatible with the common market, in derogation from the provisions of Article 92 or from the regulations provided for in Article 94, if such a decision is justified by exceptional circumstances. If, as regards the aid in question, the Commission has already initiated the procedure provided for in the first subparagraph of this paragraph, the fact that the State concerned has made its application to the Council shall have the effect of suspending that procedure until the Council has made its attitude known.

If, however, the Council has not made its attitude known within three months of the said application being made, the Commission shall give its decision on the case.

3. The Commission shall be informed, in sufficient time to enable it to submit its comments, of any plans to grant or alter aid. If it considers that any such plan is not compatible with the common market having regard to Article 92, it shall without delay initiate the procedure provided for in paragraph 2. The Member State concerned shall not put its proposed measures into effect until this procedure has resulted in a final decision.

Article 94

The Council, acting by a qualified majority on a proposal from the Commission and after consulting the European Parliament, may make any appropriate regulations for the application of Articles 92 and 93 and may in particular determine the conditions in which Article 93(3) shall apply and the categories of aid exempted from this procedure.

GENERAL NOTE

This Article is amended to make provision for the consultation of the European Parliament in the adoption of measures under this head.

Chapter 2: (Tax Provisions)

Article 95

No Member State shall impose, directly or indirectly, on the products of other Member States any internal taxation of any kind in excess of that imposed directly or indirectly on similar domestic products.

Furthermore, no Member State shall impose on the products of other Member States any internal taxation of such a nature as to afford indirect protection to other products.

Member States shall, not later than at the beginning of the second stage, repeal or amend any provisions existing when this Treaty enters into force which conflict with the preceding rules.

Article 96

Where products are exported to the territory of any Member State, any repayment of internal taxation shall not exceed the internal taxation imposed on them whether directly or indirectly.

Article 97

Member States which levy a turnover tax calculated on a cumulative multi-stage tax system may, in the case of internal taxation imposed by them on imported products or of repayments allowed by them on exported products, establish average rates for products or groups of products, provided that there is no infringement of the principles laid down in Articles 95 and 96.

Where the average rates established by a Member State do not conform to these principles, the Commission shall address appropriate directives or decisions to the State concerned.

Article 98

In the case of charges other than turnover taxes, excise duties and other forms of indirect taxation, remissions and repayments in respect of exports to other Member States may not be granted and countervailing charges in respect of imports from Member States may not be imposed unless the measures contemplated have been previously approved for a limited period by the Council acting by a qualified majority on a proposal from the Commission.

Article 99

The Council shall, acting unanimously on a proposal from the Commission and after consulting the European Parliament and the Economic and Social Committee, adopt provisions for the harmonisation of legislation concerning turnover taxes, excise duties and other forms of indirect taxation to the extent that such harmonisation is necessary to ensure the establishment and the functioning of the internal market within the time-limit laid down in Article 7a.

GENERAL NOTE

This Article, on the harmonisation of indirect taxes, as befitting its nationally contentious status, remains the subject of unanimity in Council. The amendments to this Article, in keeping with those to the topic in general, are negligible. It is amended to provide for the consultation of the Economic and Social Committee (ECOSOC) but it is difficult to envisage why this change has come about at this stage in the development of the Community. Political disagreement prevented any meaningful change taking place to this Article. Article 7a is referred to, rather than Art. 8a, reflecting the fact that the latter Article was renumbered to the former by the TEU.

Chapter 3 (Approximation of Laws)

Article 100

The Council shall, acting unanimously on a proposal from the Commission and after consulting the European Parliament and the Economic and Social Committee, issue directives for the approximation of such laws, regulations or administrative provisions of the Member States as directly affect the establishment or functioning of the common market.

GENERAL NOTE

This Article, central to the approximation of the laws of the Member States for the purpose of the achievement of the common market, is updated but no significant alterations made.

The requirement of unanimity in the Council is upheld, but European Parliament and Economic and Social Committee consultation is widened to cover all matters under this Article. This rationalises an unduly complicated situation whereby consultation was necessitated only where the implementation of Community measures would have involved the amendment of one or more Member States' domestic legislation.

Article 100a

1. By way of derogation from Article 100 and save where otherwise provided in this Treaty, the following provisions shall apply for the achievement of the objectives set out in Article 7a. The Council shall, acting in accordance with the procedure referred to in Article 189b and after consulting the Economic and Social Committee, adopt the measures for the approximation of the provisions laid down by law, regulation or administrative action in Member States which have as their object the establishment and functioning of the internal market.

2. Paragraph 1 shall not apply to fiscal provisions, to those relating to the free movement of persons nor to those relating to the rights and interests of employed persons.

3. The Commission, in its proposals envisaged in paragraph 1 concerning health, safety, environmental protection and consumer protection, will take as a base a high level of protection.

4. If, after the adoption of a harmonisation measure by the Council acting by a qualified majority, a Member State deems it necessary to apply national provisions on grounds of major needs referred to in Article 36, or relating to protection of the environment or the working environment, it shall notify the Commission of these provisions.

The Commission shall confirm the provisions involved after having verified that they are not a means of arbitrary discrimination or a disguised restriction on trade between Member States.

By way of derogation from the procedure laid down in Articles 169 and 170, the Commission or any Member State may bring the matter directly before the Court of Justice if it considers that another Member State is making improper use of the powers provided for in this Article.

5. The harmonisation measures referred to above shall, in appropriate cases, include a safeguard clause authorising the Member States to take, for one or more of the non-economic reasons referred to in Article 36, provisional measures subject to a Community control procedure.

GENERAL NOTE

This Article, introduced by the S.E.A. as a base for the adoption of legislation for the achievement of the objectives set out in Art. 8a EEC (now Art. 7a E.C.), the completion of the internal market, is altered as regards the legislative procedure necessary for the promulgation of such measures. The conciliation and veto procedure (Art. 189b E.C.) is introduced to replace the co-operation procedure. Questions may be asked about the effect of altering the legislative procedure as regards a process supposed to have been completed by the end of 1992. The nature of the internal market process, however, means that the need for Community legislation is ever present. While the great majority of those measures deemed necessary for the completion of the internal market are in place, the development of technology and changing circumstances mean that legislation will continually be necessary under this heading. Moreover, the objectives laid down under what is now Art. 7a E.C. are a wide base for any further legislative action that may be deemed necessary for the proper functioning of the internal market. The granting of real legislative power to the Parliament in the area of the internal market is one of the most significant changes made by the Maastricht Treaty in the gradual evolution of that body into a genuine legislature.

Article 100b

1. During 1992, the Commission shall, together with each Member State, draw up an inventory of national laws, regulations and administrative provisions which fall under Article 100a and which have not been harmonised pursuant to that Article.

The Council, acting in accordance with the provisions of Article 100a, may decide that the provisions in force in a Member State must be recognised as being equivalent to those applied by another Member State.

2. The provisions of Article 100a(4) shall apply by analogy.

3. The Commission shall draw up the inventory referred to in the first subparagraph of paragraph 1 and shall submit appropriate proposals in good time to allow the Council to act before the end of 1992.

Article 100c

1. The Council, acting unanimously on a proposal from the Commission and after consulting the European Parliament, shall determine the third countries whose nationals must be in possession of a visa when crossing the external borders of the Member States.

2. However, in the event of an emergency situation in a third country posing a threat of a sudden inflow of nationals from that country into the Community, the Council, acting by a qualified majority on a recommendation from the Commission, may introduce, for a period not exceeding six months, a visa requirement for nationals from the country in question. The visa requirement established under this paragraph may be extended in accordance with the procedure referred to in paragraph 1.

3. From 1 January 1996, the Council shall act by a qualified majority on the decisions referred to in paragraph 1. The Council shall, before that date, acting by a qualified majority on a proposal from the Commission and after consulting the European Parliament, adopt measures relating to a uniform format for visas.

4. In the matters referred to in this Article, the Commission shall examine any request made by a Member State that it submit a proposal to the Council.

5. This Article shall be without prejudice to the exercise of the responsibilities incumbent upon the Member States with regard to the maintenance of law and order and the safeguarding of internal security.

6. This Article shall apply to other matters if so decided pursuant to Article K.9 of the provisions of the Treaty on European Union which relate to co-operation in the fields of justice and home affairs, subject to the voting conditions determined at the same time.

7. The provisions of the conventions in force between the Member States governing matters covered by this Article shall remain in force until their content has been replaced by directives or measures adopted pursuant to this Article.

GENERAL NOTE

This is a new addition to the Treaty, bringing matters of visa policy within the Community sphere of action for the first time. The inclusion of visa matters within the Community sphere marks an admission, urged by the practical experience of the Benelux countries, that the creation of an area without internal frontiers requires the creation of some form of common policy towards third country nationals. This was agreed to as regards visa policy, but the treatment of third country nationals will still take place on two levels. While visa policy will be determined at the Community level, the remainder of essential matters governing third country nationals, such as asylum and immigration policy, will continue to be dealt with at the inter-governmental level, in accordance with the procedures envisaged for the justice and home affairs pillar of the Union.

A number of relatively novel procedures is envisaged in Art. 100c, reflecting the uneasy alliance of Community and national influences, in what is a sensitive field for Member State authorities.

The scope of the areas to be dealt with under the Treaty is restricted to the determination of which third countries' nationals will be required to be in possession of a visa when crossing the external borders of the Community (Art. 100c(1) E.C.). Tied to this is the marginal issue of the creation of a uniform format for visas (Art. 100c(3) E.C.). The original process of determining which third countries' nationals require visas is to be carried out by a unanimous vote in Council (but changing to qualified majority from January 1, 1996 (Art. 100c(3) E.C.)).

The remainder of topics in this area, such as asylum policy, extradition, judicial co-operation, etc. (see the list of matters of common interest under the justice and home affairs pillar, Art. K.1 E.U.), remain in the inter-governmental arena. Nevertheless, certain of these matters (Art. K.1(1)–(6)) may be transferred into the Community sphere without the necessity of a further inter-governmental conference (Art. 100c(6) E.C.). Asylum policy is a prime candidate for such a transfer (see Declaration No.31 to the Treaty on European Union). It is not, however, a simple matter to increase the scope of Art. 100c, as the decision to do so requires unanimity in the Council and the adoption of the measures in accordance with the constitutional requirements of each Member State (Art. K.9 E.U.).

Moreover, conventions governing areas covered by this Article, in force between the Member States, will remain in force until their content has been replaced by directives or measures adopted pursuant to this Article (Art. 100c(7) E.C.).

Para. (1)

This paragraph provides for the determination of which third countries' nationals shall require visas before crossing the external borders of the Community. Such harmonisation of visa policy is deemed essential in order to permit the opening up of internal frontiers; certain Member States are reluctant to see all internal frontiers come down with no guarantee that other Member States might be operating less stringent external controls than their own indigenous policies. This is particularly true in the case of the U.K.

All decisions in this field will have to be taken by unanimous vote in Council until January 1, 1996 when qualified majority voting will take over (Art. 100c(3) E.C.). Express provision is made for the consultation of the European Parliament prior to the adoption of any measure. The Commission's proposals are at the time of writing undergoing legislative scrutiny in the Council and Parliament (see [1994] O.J. C11/15).

Para. (2)

This paragraph permits the adoption of emergency measures to impose visa requirements on third country nationals not previously covered by the visa requirement but who threaten to flood the Community. Such measures may be adopted by qualified majority vote and remain in force for a maximum of six months initially, but are subject to potentially unlimited extension under the applicable Art. 100c(1) E.C. voting procedure. Significantly, no provision is made for any consultation of the European Parliament. The latter body was a staunch opponent of this form of visa policy, viewing it as an unjustified manifestation of the "Fortress Europe" mentality. The problem envisaged by the European Parliament was that the imposition of a visa requirement on a country facing an internal emergency, requires persons who wish to leave that country to visit a Member State's diplomatic premises there to request a visa. In time of war or civil unrest, these diplomatic facilities may not be left in operation and the time taken to process such applications prevents the rapid assessment of cases deserving of a visa. In other words, the imposition of a visa requirement upon a warring state or during severe civil disturbances is an effective barrier to refugees fleeing such areas, even if they are genuine political refugees.

Para. (4)

This adds little to the current practice as regards the initiation of legislation in the Community sphere. The Commission retains its monopoly of legislative initiative but express provision is made that it must examine any request made by a Member State that it submit a proposal to the Council. In ᴄther matters the Commission would normally examine any such request, and this Article merely formalises the process. There is no duty on the Commission to submit a proposal.

Para. (5)

This paragraph highlights the sensitivity of the Community competence in relation to visas, with its close relationship to the typically jealously guarded national competence in the areas of internal security and law and order. This paragraph permits a potentially wide exception to the application of this Article in the Member States. It is impossible to predict the scope of measures which the Member States will rely on as falling under this exception. As visas are within Community competence, it is within the jurisdiction of the Court of Justice to rule on the breadth of exception allowed under this paragraph. The matter could either come before the court for a preliminary ruling under Art. 177 or in an action brought against the Member State under Arts. 169 or 170. Thus the court has an opportunity to rule on the acceptability of such measures in an area where national government discretion has largely been left unchecked.

Para. (6)

This is one of the most interesting and novel provisions of the new amended Treaty. It provides for the transfer of competences currently dealt with at the inter-governmental level, under the justice and home affairs pillar, into the Community sphere. Article K.9 E.U. lays down the procedure for this transfer, known also as *passarelle*. The process is applicable to the activities laid down in Arts. K.1(1)–(6) E.U., which are: asylum policy; rules governing the crossing by persons of the external borders of the Member States; immigration policy including conditions of entry, residence, work and movement; combating drug addiction; combating international fraud; and judicial co-operation in civil matters. Those matters not open to any transfer under this process are: judicial co-operation in criminal matters (K.1(7) E.U.); customs co-operation (K.1(8) E.U.) and international police co-operation (K.1(9) E.U.). The majority of these matters, be they in the former or latter categories, are currently covered by international conventions and multilateral agreements which have sprung up on an ad hoc basis, when and where perceived necessary (see note on Art. 100c(7) E.C.). At present, asylum policy is the prime candidate for a transfer into the Community sphere (Dec. No. 31 to the T.E.U.).

The achievement of any such transfer will prove very difficult and, while it may take place without an inter-governmental conference being convened under Art. N, E.U., it has the same requirement of unanimous agreement by government ministers from each of the Member States, followed by approval in accordance with the appropriate constitutional process in each of these States. In Denmark, a majority of five-sixths of members of the Danish Parliament or both a majority of members of the Parliament and a majority of votes in a referendum is required (see the Danish Declaration on Co-operation in the fields of justice and home affairs, published at the Edinburgh European Council in December 1992; and Weatherill and Beaumont, *E.C. Law* (1993) p. 777). The U.K. is opposed to any transfer of competences by the *passarelle* (Kenneth Clark M.P., then Home Secretary, *Hansard*, H.C. vol. 295, col. 26).

In its report of November 1993, the Commission was of opinion that it was too soon after the coming into force of the E.U. Treaty to recommend transfers of matters of common interest into the Community competence ([1993] 11 E.C. Bull., 1.5.5). The Council has indicated that it will review the matter at the end of 1995 at the latest ([1994] 6 E.U. Bull., 1.4.4).

Para. (7)

There is a plethora of multilateral agreements existing at present in this field, but co-operation at the inter-governmental level on an ad hoc basis has not been followed up by comprehensive progress in the completion of international conventions. Article 100c(7) E.C. makes provision for the continued existence of these multilateral instruments until they are replaced by directives or measures adopted pursuant to this Article. One of the most important agreements in this field is the Schengen accord. Initiated by the Benelux countries, France and Germany, this agreement provides for the gradual elimination of all border and customs formalities between the countries concerned. Nine of the Member States are now affiliated to the Schengen Convention of June 19, 1990 which elaborates on the earlier agreement (for text see (1991) 30 I.L.M. 68) and makes provision for, *inter alia*, action on visa policy, asylum seekers, police and security measures, and extradition (see Schütte, "Schengen: Its Meaning for the Free Movement of Persons in Europe", (1991) 28 C.M.L.Rev. 549). The U.K., Ireland and Denmark are the only pre-enlargement Member States which are not members of the agreement. (It appears that Austria will be a party.) A Community-wide initiative to abolish all internal borders was envisaged by the S.E.A. (Art. 8a E.E.C., now Art. 7a E.C., on the free movement of persons throughout the Community by the end of 1992), but has not materialised. The nine Schengen Member States are, however, to remove all the remaining stumbling blocks to the elimination of internal borders by March 23, 1995.

Another key agreement in this field is the draft Convention on the Crossing of External Borders which is currently being held up by the dispute between the U.K. and Spain over the status of Gibraltar (see the discussion on the Convention in *Hansard*, H.C. vol. 193, col. 242). Resolution of this problem was a central aim of the German Presidency in the latter half of 1994, but no tangible progress was recorded. National interests in these fields have proven to be a real handicap to the conclusion of any such agreements. The introduction of qualified majority voting in 1996 in the limited fields provided for under this Article will thus mark something of a watershed.

The other main prospect for international agreement in this area is the Dublin Convention, signed in 1990 (Cmnd. 1623, and (1991) 30 I.L.M. 425), which deals with the problem of determining the State responsible for examining applications for asylum lodged in one of the Member States. It provides for the controversial first stop asylum policy, whereby the country in which the asylum seeker arrived first or first made his claim is responsible for the processing of the claim. In particular it calls for the setting up of an exchange of information about applicants, thus attempting to highlight false or multiple asylum claims. The Convention has not yet entered into force, although eight Member States had ratified it by the end of 1994, and Ireland plans to do so after the enactment of the Refugee Bill. Two of the stumbling blocks are the civil liberties implications of the information exchange and, more importantly, the worries from States such as Germany with many land borders that the first stop rule will require them to consider an unduly high proportion of all asylum claims. The Convention is only a partial step towards a common asylum policy, as it does not harmonise the substantive rules on the grant of asylum by the various Member States. It has been alleged that refusal by the other Member States to consider an asylum request once it has been considered and rejected by one Member State (which is the basis of the "one stop" approach) will put them in breach of the Geneva Convention on the Status of Refugees, 1951.

Article 100d

The Co-ordinating Committee consisting of senior officials set up by Article K.4 of the Treaty on European Union shall contribute, without prejudice to the provisions of Article 151, to the preparation of the proceedings of the Council in the fields referred to in Article 100c.

This Article makes provision for the Co-ordinating Committee of senior officials, set up under the justice and home affairs pillar (Art. K.4 E.U.), to act alongside COREPER in the matters to be dealt with under Art. 100c. This body of senior civil servants active in this field in their respective Member States (known as the K.4 Committee) will prepare the ground for Council meetings. This Article is necessary to give Community effect to the actions of this body. These officials, accountable only to the national governments, are highly influential, and yet their work will be largely invisible to the scrutiny of both the national and European Parliaments. It has rapidly taken over the work of the diverse groups previously operating in this area, such as the various Trevi working groups and the Ad Hoc Group on Immigration. Both Arts. 100d E.C. and K.4 E.U. provide that the co-ordinating committee is to operate without prejudice to Art. 151 E.C., thus signalling an unclear relationship with COREPER.

Article 101

Where the Commission finds that a difference between the provisions laid down by law, regulation or administrative action in Member States is distorting the conditions of competition in the common market and that the resultant distortion needs to be eliminated, it shall consult the Member States concerned.

If such consultation does not result in an agreement eliminating the distortion in question, the Council shall, on a proposal from the Commission, acting unanimously during the first stage and by a qualified majority thereafter, issue the necessary directives. The Commission and the Council may take any other appropriate measures provided for in this Treaty.

Article 102

1. Where there is reason to fear that the adoption or amendment of a provision laid down by law, regulation or administrative action may cause distortion within the meaning of Article 101, a Member State desiring to proceed therewith shall consult the Commission. After consulting the Member States, the Commission shall recommend to the States concerned such measures as may be appropriate to avoid the distortion in question.

2. If a State desiring to introduce or amend its own provisions does not comply with the recommendation addressed to it by the Commission, other Member States shall not be required, in pursuance of Article 101, to amend their own provisions in order to eliminate such distortion. If the Member State which has ignored the recommendation of the Commission causes distortion detrimental only to itself, the provisions of Article 101 shall not apply.

TITLE VI: Economic and Monetary Policy

The section on economic and monetary union is one of the most complicated parts of the Treaty, by virtue not only of its content, but also of its lay-out. The subject matter is necessarily detailed and, in order to prevent the body of the Treaty becoming too lengthy and technical, many of the more complex provisions are included in Protocols annexed to the Treaty. The application of the Treaty Articles requires frequent cross-reference to these Protocols.

First, it is necessary to make a few points on the process towards economic and monetary union, specifically the means envisaged by this Treaty, and the Delors Committee Report (*Report on Economic and Monetary Union in the European Community*, Luxembourg, Office for Official Publications of the European Communities, 1989). In keeping with the Delors Report, the E.U. Treaty envisages a gradual progress towards the achievement of full economic and monetary union. This is deemed to consist of a single currency overseen by an independent monetary authority. Nevertheless, this should be seen as two separate unification processes. On the one hand, the achievement of economic union can be seen as a natural progression of the S.E.A.'s aim of an internal market, in which goods, services, assets and production factors are freely traded. With markets for goods already largely integrated, the completion of economic union requires the elimination of the remaining constraints on the mobility of services, capital and labour in the Community. On the other hand, the economic unification of the Community is to be tied to the achievement of a monetary union. This process was defined by the Delors Report as requiring: "a currency area in which policies are managed jointly, with the single most important condition for a monetary union being fulfilled only when the decisive step was taken to lock exchange rates irrevocably". This process will be achieved through: "a new monetary institution necessary because a single monetary policy cannot result from independent decisions and actions by different central banks" (paras. 22 and 33 of the Delors Report). In other words, the Report envisaged the introduction of a single currency and the transfer of responsibility for monetary policy from the national to the European level. The reasoning behind the decision to adopt this parallel approach of economic and monetary union is open to some debate in economic circles. It has been asserted that, while monetary union does add some value to the achievement of economic union, it is far from essential for its success. Nevertheless, the achievement of monetary union, as well as bolstering economic union, marks a very important step towards a true European Union, with its centralised decision-making structure. Thus, the achievement of full economic and monetary union has long been seen by the Commission as a vital part of the political unification of Europe.

The achievement of economic union simply envisages co-ordination of economic policies, rather than centralised control (other than to prevent excessive government deficits) and thus the Community will not take control of taxation or public spending policies in the Member States. The only "control" it will exercise is the indirect power to ensure that the Member State shall not maintain an excessive government deficit.

One of the fundamental problems in designing a strategy for economic and monetary union arose with regard to the speed of the process. The Delors Report, like the E.U. Treaty itself, envisaged a three stage process towards full economic and monetary union. The Delors Report insisted that the first stage would commence on July 1, 1990 (para. 30) but gave no further dates for the achievement of the later steps. The E.U. Treaty does not give any specific date for the start of the first stage, which is presumed to have commenced already, but it does lay down strict and irrevocable dates for the achievement of the second and third stages. The second stage was to commence on January 1, 1994 and is envisaged as the stage during which the Member States will take the steps necessary to permit the achievement of full economic and monetary union at the beginning of the third stage. The second stage is seen as a period of rapid transition, during which the Member States still make the determinative decisions but, with the common goal of full union in mind. The third stage is due to commence, at the latest, by January 1, 1999.

Not all the Member States will make the transition to the third stage by this date. Political derogations were permitted at the Maastricht summit, which saw the U.K. and Denmark obtain a right to opt out of the otherwise inevitable move towards the third stage. The other States which will not progress towards the third stage will be those which fail to fulfil the necessary economic criteria laid down in the Treaty.

The achievement of full economic and monetary union in the Community by the date envisaged is at present a matter of heated debate in Europe. One result of the gradual nature of the progress towards the third stage of economic and monetary union is that the political and practical costs of withdrawal are relatively minimal at all stages prior to the building of the common institutions (see Fratianni, Von Hagen *et al*, "The Maastricht Way to Economic and Monetary Union", *Essays in International Finance*, No. 187, 1992, Princeton University at 10–15). The key building block in the creation of the single currency was to be the ERM of the EMS. It was expected that the maintenance of relatively tight bands (2.25 per cent) would create economic convergence and act as a driving force in the securing of the Member States' commitment to full economic and monetary union. With the recent problems in the ERM, the forced withdrawal of Italy and the U.K. in 1992 and the widening of the bands to 15 per cent in 1993, that may seem more of a hope than a realistic expectation. Moreover, the achievement of economic convergence criteria as a prerequisite to the move to the third stage, permits national "discretion", through the level of effort put in by the Member State in achieving the necessary convergence. For example, a State could deliberately increase its borrowing beyond the 3 per cent ratio of Gross Domestic Product mentioned in Art. 1 of the Protocol on the Excessive Deficit Procedure if it did not wish to join the single currency. However, this would be a rather drastic and, in political terms, probably an unnecessary step. Most Member States have adopted the Maastricht criteria as the touchstone of their fiscal and monetary policies. The chief obstacle to those countries which have taken considerable efforts to comply with the Treaty (successfully in many cases) would appear now to be German insistence on a strict reading of the criteria, *viz.* that they should be shown to be achieved not at the peak of the business cycle (which Europe is approaching at the moment) but at the trough.

Returning to the structure of the economic and monetary union provisions themselves, the new Arts. 102a–104c E.C. deal with economic policy, and lay down the process for the gradual convergence of the economic policies of the Member States. This is to be achieved by the conferral of duties on the Member States and Community institutions, in a manner not wholly unfamiliar as regards other areas of the Treaty. Article 102a E.C. lays down the general guiding principles of the process, while the main means of achieving the co-ordination of economic policies, through the surveillance of the Member States' economic policies, is found in Art. 103 E.C. The Council is to exercise a general monitoring role, acting on the basis of reports from the Commission, to assess Member State compliance with the broad guidelines on economic policy laid down under Art. 103(2) E.C. Article 104–104b E.C. sets out a small number of prohibited practices in the area of public sector finance, including the favouring of public authorities in the provision of credit facilities by central banks (Art. 104 E.C.). Article 104c contains the critical duty on Member States that they "avoid excessive government deficits". It is up to the Commission to monitor the budgetary situation and government debt in Member States and to identify "gross errors" (Art. 104c(2) E.C.). The basic criteria are specified, involving the ratio of government deficit, and of government debt, to Gross Domestic Product in relation to a reference value. These reference values are set out in Art. 1 of the Protocol on the Excessive Deficit Procedure annexed to the Treaty and are defined as (a) 3 per cent for the ratio of planned or actual government deficit to Gross Domestic Product, and (b) 60 per cent for the ratio of government debt to Gross Domestic Product. Articles 104c(3)–(14) E.C. then deal with the enforcement measures applicable in this area. The scale of sanction is progressively stepped up as the process continues, but the punitive sanctions laid down in Art. 104c(11) E.C. will not be applicable until the third stage comes into force and will only apply as regards States which have made the transition to the single currency. The basis of the enforcement measures prior to the coming into force of the third stage is the adverse publicity of a negative Council report. Nevertheless, the criteria for judging the excessive deficit may not be applied in a strict fashion, as Art. 104c(2) E.C. makes clear. A judgmental element is implicit, whereby the non-compliance with the reference values in the Protocol is less important than the overall trend in the figures. There have already been sharp exchanges between the Commission and the Bundesbank on the reading of these trends.

The provisions on monetary policy laid down in Arts. 105–109m E.C. are very different from the preceding economic provisions. They introduce new bodies and structures which will come into operation progressively and in accordance with a pre-determined timetable. National competences in this field will be progressively removed into the hands of an independent monetary authority overseeing a single currency. The major problem with the Treaty provisions in this field, is that they are laid out in a manner which will appear a great deal more logical upon the coming into force of the third stage of economic and monetary union. At all stages prior to that, the governing provisions are structured in a far from coherent way. Article 105 E.C. is a prime example of this. It lays down the primary objective of the European System of Central Banks as the maintenance of price stability. It goes on to elaborate on the basic tasks of this body which include: the definition and implementation of the monetary policy of the Community; the conducting of foreign exchange operations; the holding and management of the official foreign reserves of the Member States; and the promotion of the smooth operation of payment systems. Despite the appearance of this Article at the forefront of the section on monetary policy, it will only come into force at the outset of the third stage of economic and monetary union, when the European System of Central Banks and the European Central Bank itself will take over the running of the Community monetary policy. Article 106 E.C. lays down the composition of the European System of Central Banks, as well as making reference to the governing statute of this body, which is included in the detailed Protocol on the Statute of the European System of Central Banks and of the European Central Bank, annexed to the Treaty. The remainder of this chapter of the Treaty (Arts. 107–109 E.C.) concerns the European System of Central Banks and the European Central Bank; including the enjoining of their independence from national and Community authorities (Article 107 E.C.). For an excellent comparison of the European System of Central Banks and the German *Bundesbank* see Fratianni, von Hagen *et al*, "The Maastricht Way to Economic and Monetary Union", *Essays in International Finance*, No. 187, 1992, Princeton University, at 28–42.

The chapter on "institutional provisions" under Arts. 109a–d E.C. marks a further lack of transparency in this area. Articles 109 a and b E.C. shed some light on the composition of the European Central Bank and its ruling bodies, but must be read alongside the Statute of the European System of Central Banks and European Central Bank as well as the preceding paragraphs on the Bank system. Article 109c E.C. provides for the creation of an advisory Monetary Committee, which will be superseded at the start of the third stage by an analogous body, the Economic and Financial Committee. Article 109d, mysteriously included in the institutional provisions, lays down a list of areas where the Council or a Member State may request the Commission to make a recommendation or proposal.

Articles 109e–109m contain the so-called "Transitional Provisions". Included in this section are all those Articles dealing with the first and second stages of the economic and monetary union process. The first stage gave way to the second stage on January 1, 1994 (Art. 109e(1) E.C.). The duties of each Member State in the period up to this transition were laid down in Art. 109e(2) E.C. Article 109e(3) E.C. adds to the general confusion by dictating which of the foregoing provisions on economic and monetary union are to apply from the beginning of the second stage and which from the start of the third stage; in other words it aims to unscramble the transitional from the permanent. Article 109f E.C. provides for the establishment of the European Monetary Institute as from January 1, 1994. The Statute of this body is laid down in a Protocol to the Treaty and its tasks are, *inter alia*, the strengthening of co-operation between national central banks; the monitoring of the EMS; and the easing of the development of the single currency, the ECU (see Art. 109f(2) E.C.). The central feature of the European Monetary Institute is that it performs an essentially consultative and co-ordinating role, during a stage at which policy responsibilities still generally remain at the national level. Article 109f(3) E.C. lays out the tasks of the European Monetary Institute in preparation for the third stage. The European Monetary Institute is the midwife for the birth of the much more powerful European Central Bank which is to oversee the single currency.

No set date is envisaged for the move to the third stage but it is provided that, if no date has been set by the end of 1997, then the third stage is to start on January 1, 1999 (Art. 109j(4) E.C.). Whether or not this fall back date is needed depends on the convergence of the Member States' economic performances prior to this date. The achievement of some degree of sustainable convergence is seen as essential to ensure effective and lasting union, with the minimum of economic hardship. Article 109j(1) requires the Commission and the European Monetary Institute to report to the Council on the progress made by the Member States towards economic and monetary union. This progress report is based on the achievement of the four convergence criteria laid down in this Article, and elaborated in the Protocol on the Convergence Criteria and on the Excessive Deficit Procedure. Article 109j(2) then requires the Council, by qualified majority vote, and on the basis of the reports prepared under Art. 109j(1), to assess for each Member State whether it fulfils the conditions necessary for the adoption of a single currency. If a majority of the Member States (excluding Denmark and the U.K. if they exercise their opt-outs) fulfil these four conditions then it is up to the Council, prior to December 31, 1996, to decide if it is appropriate for the Community to enter the third stage. If so, it will then set the date (Art. 109j(3) E.C.).

All those Member States who do not fulfil the conditions laid down in the Treaty are then classed as "Member States with a derogation". The status of such countries must be reviewed every two years and, in the meantime, specified Articles will apply to them. There is no specific number of countries required for the move to the third stage if the fall back date of January 1, 1999 is invoked (see Art. 109j(4) E.C.). The irrevocability of this move is highlighted by the Protocol on the transition to the third stage of economic and monetary union. It provides that no Member State shall prevent the entering into the third stage and that all states shall expedite the preparatory work aimed at this goal. It will, nevertheless, remain to be seen whether or not the Treaty timetable will be retained at the inter-governmental conference scheduled for 1996.

The specific provisions governing the U.K. opt-out from the third stage of economic and monetary union are included in the Protocol on certain provisions relating to the U.K. This provides that the U.K. shall not be obliged to move to the third stage without a separate decision by its government and parliament. The Decision concerning Denmark, passed at the Edinburgh European Council, recognised that Denmark had exercised its right under the Protocol on certain provisions relating to Denmark, not to move to the third stage. Thus, unless specific notification is given to the Council by the U.K. and Denmark they will be classed as "Member States with a derogation" on the coming into force of the third stage. The respective Protocols contain intricate details excluding the two countries from various economic and monetary union provisions.

Chapter 1 (Economic Policy)

Article 102a

Member States shall conduct their economic policies with a view to contributing to the achievement of the objectives of the Community, as defined in Article 2, and in the context of the broad guidelines referred to in Article 103(2).

The Member States and the Community shall act in accordance with the principle of an open market economy with free competition, favouring an efficient allocation of resources, and in compliance with the principles set out in Article 3a.

GENERAL NOTE

This Article amounts to little more than a broad statement of general policy, as regards the conduct of the Member States' economic policies. These policies are to be co-ordinated with a view to the achievement of the objectives of the Community, set out in Art. 2 of the Treaty, the broad guidelines referred to in Art. 103(2) E.C. and in compliance with the principles set out in Art. 3a. Article 2 E.C. has been updated to take account of the new Community competences in the pursuit of economic and monetary union and thus talks of "a high degree of convergence of economic performances", the core feature of the economic policy provisions of the Treaty. Some scepticism has been voiced about the likelihood of achievement of all of the objectives laid out in Art. 2 E.C. (see note on that Article). The co-ordination of economic policies to achieve "a high level of employment and social protection, and the raising of the standard of living" will not be easy, given the divergent economic and political opinion as to how these goals can be achieved (*e.g.* greater deregulation to provide growth and higher employment levels or regulation to ensure better social protection for workers). In other words, the pursuit of all these goals may require contradictory economic strategies. Nevertheless, Art. 2 must be taken for what it is, a statement of intent; the relevant part for the purposes of Art. 102a E.C. is the goal of "a high degree of convergence of economic performances". Article 3a E.C. duplicates the wording of this Article when it talks of "the adoption of an economic policy based on the close co-ordination of the Member States' economic policies". The most cogent and clear-cut reference in this Article as to the background factors determining the economic policy of the Community is the reference to the guidelines laid down in Art. 103(2) E.C. These broad guidelines laid down by the Council will act as the tangible basis of the Member States' economic policies (see note on that Article).

Article 103

1. Member-States shall regard their economic policies as a matter of common concern and shall co-ordinate them within the Council, in accordance with the provisions of Article 102a.

2. The Council shall, acting by a qualified majority on a recommendation from the Commission, formulate a draft for the broad guidelines of the economic policies of the Member States and of the Community, and shall report its findings to the European Council.

The European Council shall, acting on the basis of this report from the Council, discuss a conclusion on the broad guidelines of the economic policies of the Member States and of the Community.

On the basis of this conclusion, the Council shall, acting by a qualified majority, adopt a recommendation setting out these broad guidelines. The Council shall inform the European Parliament of its recommendation.

3. In order to ensure closer co-ordination of economic policies and sustained convergence of the economic performances of the Member States, the Council shall, on the basis of reports submitted by the Commission, monitor economic developments in each of the Member States and in the Community as well as the consistency of economic policies with the broad guidelines referred to in paragraph 2, and regularly carry out an overall assessment.

For the purpose of this multilateral surveillance, Member States shall forward information to the Commission about important measures taken by them in the field of their economic policy and such other information as they deem necessary.

4. Where it is established, under the procedure referred to in paragraph 3, that the economic policies of a Member State are not consistent with the broad guidelines referred to in paragraph 2 or that they risk jeopardising the proper functioning of economic and monetary union, the Council may, act-

ing by a qualified majority on a recommendation from the Commission, make the necessary recommendations to the Member State concerned.

The Council may, acting by a qualified majority on a proposal from the Commission, decide to make its recommendations public.

The President of the Council and the Commission shall report to the European Parliament on the results of multilateral surveillance. The President of the Council may be invited to appear before the competent Committee of the European Parliament if the Council has made its recommendations public.

5. The Council, acting in accordance with the procedure referred to in Article 189c, may adopt detailed rules for the multilateral surveillance procedure referred to in paragraphs 3 and 4 of this Article.

GENERAL NOTE

Para. (1)
This Article forms the core of the economic component of economic and monetary union. The Member States' economic policies are to be co-ordinated within the Council. This indicates the relatively weak nature of this process. Given the wide scope for interpretation of the meaning of Art. 102a E.C., it is difficult to predict what economic policy guidelines will be adopted by the Council, although they have been marked to date by an emphasis on budgetary prudence.

Para. (2)
This lays out the apparatus for the co-ordination of the Member States' economic policies. The Council, acting on a recommendation from the Commission, will formulate a draft of the broad guidelines of the economic policies of the Member States and the Community. This draft then passes to the European Council which prepares a conclusion on the topic. It is strange that the European Council is given a role to play under the E.C. Treaty. It would have been more consistent and institutionally appropriate to follow the pattern in Art. 109j E.C. and have the guidelines adopted by the Council in the composition of the Heads of State or Government. The conclusion of the European Council will then pass back to the Council before the latter body adopts, by a qualified majority vote, a recommendation setting out these guidelines. Being a recommendation, the Treaty is quite explicit that it has "no binding force" (Art. 189 E.C.).

One matter of some confusion is that no guidance is given as to the voting rights in the European Council in the adoption of their "conclusions". The Treaty does not indicate whether the Heads of Government and of State have to be unanimous as to the "conclusions" adopted or whether some form of majority voting will suffice. The President of the Commission is a full member of the European Council and it is far from clear if he has any voting rights.

Another unusual factor in the process envisaged under this Article is that, normally, matters coming under the Community competences which are discussed at the level of the European Council return to the Commission for it to prepare legislative proposals. In this case, and probably emphasising the sensitive governmental nature of these guidelines, no provision is made for the return of the recommendation to the Commission before its adoption by the Council.

This paragraph provides that the European Parliament is to be informed by the Council of its recommendation. This would seem to give the European Parliament no scope for any debate on the matter prior to its entry into force, and was the subject of criticism in the European Parliament in the report on the Maastricht inter-governmental conference (European Parliament Report A3-123). There is no requirement that the European Parliament be informed prior to the entry into force of the recommendation and even if there was, the notion of "informing" the European Parliament leaves it with no real power. This is in contrast to the Commission's draft, which had proposed the formal consultation of the European Parliament on general recommendations and on the adoption of recommendations specific to a Member State, but with a time-limit of two months imposed on the European Parliament's consideration of any matter under the latter heading to prevent delay (Arts. 102c/102d, see [1991] E.C. Bull., Supp. 2, at 41-42).

The ECOFIN Council has commenced a policy of having two meetings a year in respect of matters falling under the rubric of Art. 103: one in early summer, to adopt broad guidelines for submission to the European Council, and one at the end of the year to focus on multilateral surveillance (see [1994] 1-2 E.U. Bull., 1.2.3). The Commission submitted its first recommendation on economic guidelines in November 1993 (COM (93) 629), which led to the adoption of the first Council recommendation in December 1993 ([1994] O.J. L7/9). Further guidelines were adopted by the Council subsequent to the Corfu summit of the European Council, in June 1994 ([1994] O.J. L200).

Para. (3)

This deals with the so-called multilateral surveillance procedure. This surveillance, carried out by the Council on the basis of Commission reports, will assess both the Member States' economic performances and the compliance of the Member States' economic policies with the broad guidelines laid down under Art. 103(2) E.C.

Para. (4)

This contains the very limited "sanctions" envisaged for those Member States the economic policies of which "are not consistent with the broad guidelines referred to in para. 2" or more vaguely, the economic policies of which "risk jeopardising the proper functioning of economic and monetary union". In the event of a perceived breach, the Council may, by a qualified majority vote, make the necessary recommendations to the Member State involved. Any such action by the Council must be based, in the first instance, on a Commission recommendation. If the Commission makes a proposal to do so, the Council can, by qualified majority vote, make its recommendations public. Such public censure is the maximum "penalty" available in this field, and is only available where the Member State concerned has the opportunity to vote in its own defence. Unanimity in Council is required to amend a Commission proposal (see Art. 189a E.C.) but no such Treaty restraint is imposed on the Council in amending a Commission recommendation.

The President of the Council and the Commission are to report to the European Parliament on the results of the multilateral surveillance, and this is stepped up where the Council has made its recommendations public. In this situation, the President of the Council may be invited before the relevant Committee of the European Parliament. While this paragraph does not indicate any compulsion on the President to attend, it is politically very likely that he would attend, if requested. It also marks the first Treaty recognition of the important role played by Committees in the European Parliament (see also Art. 109b(3) E.C.).

Para. (5)

This lays down the procedure for the adoption of the detailed rules for the multilateral surveillance process, which is to be the co-operation procedure (Art. 189c E.C.). No specific time-frame is envisaged for this taking place.

Article 103a

1. Without prejudice to any other procedures provided for in this Treaty, the Council may, acting unanimously on a proposal from the Commission, decide upon the measures appropriate to the economic situation, in particular if severe difficulties arise in the supply of certain products.

2. Where a Member State is in difficulties or is seriously threatened with severe difficulties caused by exceptional occurrences beyond its control, the Council may, acting unanimously on a proposal from the Commission, grant, under certain conditions, Community financial assistance to the Member State concerned. Where the severe difficulties are caused by natural disasters, the Council shall act by qualified majority. The President of the Council shall inform the European Parliament of the decision taken.

GENERAL NOTE

The first paragraph permits the derogation from the co-ordination guidelines laid down above. The specific situation envisaged is serious supply difficulties as regards certain products, but derogation can apply in other situations, subject to the proviso that the measures taken be "appropriate to the economic situation". The effective limitation on any abuse of this procedure is that its application requires the unanimous vote of the Council. This replaces the analogous provisions in Art. 103 EEC on conjunctural policy. That Article permitted a limited amount of qualified majority voting in the Council, which has not been retained in the E.C. Treaty.

Paragraph 2 permits, by the same procedure, the granting of financial assistance to a Member State faced with "severe difficulties caused by exceptional occurrences beyond its control". In the event of these severe difficulties being the result of natural disasters (*e.g.* earthquakes), then qualified majority voting will apply. Paragraph 2 of this Article shall apply only from the start of the third stage (Art. 109e(3) E.C.).

The European Parliament has no formal role in measures adopted under the first paragraph and is merely informed of the outcome of the process under para. 2.

Article 104

1. Overdraft facilities or any other type of credit facility with the ECB or with the central banks of the Member States (hereinafter referred to as 'national central banks') in favour of Community institutions or bodies, central governments, regional, local or other public authorities, other bodies governed by public law or public undertakings of Member States shall be prohibited, as shall the purchase directly from them by the ECB or national central banks of debt instruments.

2. The provisions of paragaph 1 shall not apply to publicly-owned credit institutions, which in the context of the supply of reserves by central banks shall be given the same treatment by national central banks and the ECB as private credit institutions.

GENERAL NOTE

This Article, and the subsequent Arts. 104a and 104b E.C., lay down a number of practices which are to be forbidden in the field of public sector finance. These prohibitions took effect from the coming into force of the second stage of economic and monetary union on January 1, 1994 (see Art. 109e(3) E.C.). First, overdraft facilities or any other type of credit facility with the European Central Bank or the national central banks in favour of public sector bodies are to be forbidden. The direct purchase of debt instruments from the European Central Bank or national central banks by public sector bodies is also prohibited. Paragraph 2 sets out an exemption to this prohibition for publicly owned credit institutions, where the supply of reserves by central banks is concerned. For some reason, the adoption of more specific definitions as regards the prohibition in this Article, appear under Art. 104b(2) E.C. (see note on that Article. These definitions are to be decided upon by the co-operation procedure).

Article 104a

1. Any measure, not based on prudential considerations, establishing privileged access by Community institutions or bodies, central governments, regional, local or other public authorities, other bodies governed by public law or public undertakings of Member States to financial institutions shall be prohibited.

2. The Council, acting in accordance with the procedure referred to in Article 189c, shall, before 1 January 1994, specify definitions for the application of the prohibition referred to in paragraph 1.

GENERAL NOTE

This Article, applicable from the start of the second stage, seeks to prohibit the privileged access to financial institutions by national authorities. Acting under the co-operation procedure, the Council was to determine by January 1, 1994 the specific definitions for the application of this provision, determining in particular what constitute "prudential considerations". This was done by Council Reg. 3604/93, adopted in December 1993 ([1993] O.J. L332/1).

Article 104b

1. The Community shall not be liable for or assume the commitments of central governments, regional, local or other public authorities, other bodies governed by public law, or public undertakings of any Member State, without prejudice to mutual financial guarantees for the joint execution of a specific project. A Member State shall not be liable for or assume the commitments of central governments, regional, local or other public authorities, other bodies governed by public law or public undertakings of another Member State, without prejudice to mutual financial guarantees for the joint execution of a specific project.

2. If necessary, the Council, acting in accordance with the procedure referred to in Article 189c, may specify definitions for the application of the prohibitions referred to in Article 104 and in this Article.

GENERAL NOTE

This Article, again applicable from the start of the second stage, lays out the details of the so-called "no-bailing out" rule. It makes it clear that the Community shall neither be responsible for, nor assume, the commitments of central governments or other national public authorities.

A similar duty is imposed on the Member States as regards the commitments of central governments and of other national authorities in other Member States. A proviso is made in the case of both Community and national authorities, that mutual financial guarantees for the joint execution of a specific project will still be permissible. This was included because such joint guarantees constitute one of the most common means of Community funding under the Cohesion funds, etc.

Paragraph 2 asserts that definitions for this Article and for Art. 104 E.C. will be specified under the co-operation procedure. Unlike Art. 104a(2) E.C. on the adoption of specific definitions in the field of privileged access to financial institutions, the current Article does not specify any time-limit for the adoption of definitions. As both measures are due to come into force at the same time, the reason for this discrepancy is unclear.

Article 104c

1. Member States shall avoid excessive government deficits.
2. The Commission shall monitor the development of the budgetary situation and of the stock of government debt in the Member States with a view to identifying gross errors. In particular it shall examine compliance with budgetary discipline on the basis of the following two criteria:
   (a) whether the ratio of the planned or actual government deficit to gross domestic product exceeds a reference value, unless
      — either the ratio has declined substantially and continuously and reached a level that comes close to the reference value;
      — or, alternatively, the excess over the reference value is only exceptional and temporary and the ratio remains close to the reference value;
   (b) whether the ratio of government debt to gross domestic product exceeds a reference value, unless the ratio is sufficiently diminishing and approaching the reference value at a satisfactory pace.

The reference values are specified in the Protocol on the excessive deficit procedure annexed to this Treaty.

3. If a Member State does not fulfil the requirements under one or both of these criteria, the Commission shall prepare a report. The report of the Commission shall also take into account whether the government deficit exceeds government investment expenditure and take into account all other relevant factors, including the medium term economic and budgetary position of the Member State.

The Commission may also prepare a report if, notwithstanding the fulfilment of the requirements under the criteria, it is of the opinion that there is a risk of an excessive deficit in a Member State.

4. The Committee provided for in Article 109c shall formulate an opinion on the report of the Commission.

5. If the Commission considers that an excessive deficit in a Member State exists or may occur, the Commission shall address an opinion to the Council.

6. The Council shall, acting by a qualified majority on a recommendation from the Commission, and having considered any observations which the Member State concerned may wish to make, decide after an overall assessment whether an excessive deficit exists.

7. Where the existence of an excessive deficit is decided according to paragraph 6, the Council shall make recommendations to the Member State concerned with a view to bringing that situation to an end within a given period.

Subject to the provisions of paragraph 8, these recommendations shall not be made public.

8. Where it establishes that there has been no effective action in response to its recommendations within the period laid down, the Council may make its recommendations public.

9. If a Member State persists in failing to put into practice the recommendations of the Council, the Council may decide to give notice to the Member State to take, within a specified time limit, measures for the deficit reduction which is judged necessary by the Council in order to remedy the situation.

In such a case, the Council may request the Member State concerned to submit reports in accordance with a specific timetable in order to examine the adjustment efforts of that Member State.

10. The rights to bring actions provided for in Articles 169 and 170 may not be exercised within the framework of paragraphs 1 to 9 of this Article.

11. As long as a Member State fails to comply with a decision taken in accordance with paragraph 9, the Council may decide to apply or, as the case may be, intensify one or more of the following measures:
— to require that the Member State concerned shall publish additional information, to be specified by the Council, before issuing bonds and securities;
— to invite the European Investment Bank to reconsider its lending policy towards the Member State concerned;
— to require that the Member State concerned makes a non-interest-bearing deposit of an appropriate size with the Community until the excessive deficit has, in the view of the Council, been corrected;
— to impose fines of an appropriate size.

The President of the Council shall inform the European Parliament of the decisions taken.

12. The Council shall abrogate some or all of its decisions as referred to in paragraphs 6 to 9 and 11 to the extent that the excessive deficit in the Member State concerned has, in the view of the Council, been corrected.

If the Council previously has made public recommendations, it shall, as soon as the decision under paragraph 8 has been abrogated, make a public statement that an excessive deficit in the Member State concerned no longer exists.

13. When taking the decisions referred to in paragraphs 7 to 9, 11 and 12, the Council shall act on a recommendation from the Commission by a majority of two thirds of the votes of its members weighted in accordance with Article 148(2) and excluding the votes of the representative of the Member State concerned.

14. Further provisions relating to the implementation of the procedure described in this Article are set out in the Protocol on the excessive deficit procedure annexed to this Treaty.

The Council shall, acting unanimously on a proposal from the Commission and after consulting the European Parliament and the ECB, adopt the appropriate provisions which shall then replace the said Protocol.

Subject to the other provisions of this paragraph the Council shall, before January 1994, acting by a qualified majority on a proposal from the Commission and after consulting the European Parliament, lay down detailed rules and definitions for the application of the provisions of the said Protocol.

GENERAL NOTE

Para. (1)

Article 104c(1) states, in no uncertain terms, that the main task of the co-ordination of the Member States' economic policies is to be the avoidance of excessive government deficits. Article 104c(2) sets out the criteria for determining the "excessiveness" or otherwise of the deficit. The remainder of the Article concerns the procedures for sanctioning non-complying States. Unlike the procedure for the co-ordination of economic policies under Art. 103 E.C., the sanctions envisaged under this Article may, after an ascending course of adverse publicity and warnings, become punitive in nature (Art. 104c(11) E.C.). This shall take place, however, once the third stage has come into force and will apply only to States which have joined the single currency. The coming into force of the Article as a whole is somewhat convoluted. According to Art. 109e(3) E.C., Art. 104c took effect from the start of the second stage but Arts. 104c(1), (9) and (11) will come into operation only during the third stage. Articles 104c(9) and (11) deal with the punitive aspects of the process and the result is that, while the basis of the excessive deficit procedure operates during the second stage, there are less rigorous sanctions in place. As with Art. 103 E.C. the maximum penalty during the second stage is adverse publicity. The postponement of Art. 104c(1) E.C., on the other hand, frees the States from the imperative "Member States shall avoid excessive government deficits". During the second stage, the Member States have a somewhat lower target to meet. Article 109e(4) E.C. simply states that "the Member States shall *endeavour* to avoid excessive government deficits" (authors' italics).

One source of confusion is that the core provision on the punitive sanctions applicable in the third stage, Art. 104c(14), is not included under Art. 109e(3) as coming into force on the commencement of the third stage. This is probably a legislative oversight rather than an intentional omission.

Para. (2)

This paragraph sets out the criteria for assessing the scale of the government deficit and more lucidly, sets the levels at which this is deemed to become excessive. The duty to monitor the development of the budgetary situation in the Member States falls on the Commission. The Commission must pay particular heed to two factors: (a) whether the ratio of the planned or actual government deficit to Gross Domestic Product exceeds a reference value; and (b) whether the ratio of government debt to Gross Domestic Product exceeds a specific reference value. The reference values themselves are laid down in the Protocol on the Excessive Deficit Procedure. The Protocol defines these reference values as (a) 3 per cent for the ratio of planned or actual government deficit to Gross Domestic Product and (b) 60 per cent for the ratio of government debt to Gross Domestic Product.

This Article is markedly different from that in the Luxembourg draft. The latter document was seen by many Member States as being too inflexible, concentrating heavily on one year's budgetary figures. This Article allows a great deal more flexibility in the analysis. As regards the ratio of government deficit to Gross Domestic Product; even if the figure exceeds 3 per cent, if the ratio has declined substantially and continuously and reached a level that comes close to the reference value, then it will be acceptable. This is also the case where the excess over the reference value is only exceptional and temporary, and the ratio remains close to the reference value. Similar conditions apply as regards the ratio of government debt to Gross Domestic Product.

This emphasis on the direction in which the debt and borrowing levels are moving, rather than their absolute levels, might well prove essential in so far as current economic trends make rigid compliance with the figures unlikely in the near future in all but a few Member States. The latest estimates for government borrowing as a proportion of Gross Domestic Product are as follows (1993 figures followed by 1994 figures in brackets): Belgium 7.0 per cent (5.4 per cent); Denmark 4.6 per cent (4.6 per cent); France 5.7 per cent (5.6 per cent); Germany 3.3 per cent (3.1 per cent); Greece 16.3 per cent (17.9 per cent); Ireland 2.3 per cent (2.5 per cent); Italy 9.5 per cent (9.5 per cent); Luxembourg +1.4 per cent (−0.4 per cent); Netherlands 2.9 per cent (3.6 per cent); Portugal 7.2 per cent (6.2 per cent); Spain 7.3 per cent (7.2 per cent); U.K. 7.7 per cent (6.0 per cent). Source: *European Economy*, E.C. Publications, 1994, No. 58. Belgium, Greece and Italy had public debt ratios of over 100 per cent of Gross Domestic Product in 1994 and will need several years of budget surpluses to come anywhere near the 60 per cent target (see the House of Commons Library Research Paper 93/25, The Maastricht Debate: Central Banking and Monetary Union, of March 5, 1993 by Edmonds).

The downside of such subjective analysis of the compliance criteria is that the exercise of discretion becomes inevitable in what is a relatively sensitive area. The Commission will initially make such decisions but at all levels of the decision-making process some form of discretion is present. The exercise of this discretion has already been a matter of some controversy, with objections coming from the Bundesbank in respect of the treatment of a number of Member States, including Ireland. The view on the part of the Commission that an 80 per cent debt to G.D.P. ratio would be sufficient evidence of progress by Ireland towards the prescribed reference value has been criticised. Within Ireland, debate has concentrated more on the misleading nature of any national budgetary figures relative to G.D.P., which differs significantly (and in European terms, unusually) from Gross National Product because of the level of transfers abroad in public debt servicing and profit repatriation by multi-national firms.

Para. (3)

This paragraph marks the commencement of the provisions dealing with the enforcement procedure and took effect from the start of the second stage. It empowers the Commission to prepare a report where a Member State has failed to fulfil the requirements under one or both of the criteria discussed in the note on para. (2) above. This report is to take into account all other relevant factors, including the medium term economic and budgetary position of the Member State. It ensures that the next stage of the enforcement procedure is equipped with adequate background information. The exercise of some form of discretion is unavoidable in this field and the Commission is permitted, under the second paragraph of this Article, to prepare a report even where the Member State is currently complying with the criteria, "if it is of the opinion that there is a risk of an excessive deficit".

Para. (4)

The Monetary Committee, set up under Art. 109c, and which came into being on January 1, 1994, is to formulate an opinion on the report of the Commission. This is in keeping with the general role of this body, which has as its major task the review of the monetary and financial situation in the Member States (see note on Art. 109c(1) E.C.). Nowhere in this Article or in Art. 109c(1) E.C. is there any indication as to the procedures to be followed by this Committee. The only evidence which can be adduced is that it is to operate "without prejudice to Art. 151 E.C." which would suggest that it will work alongside COREPER, but sheds little light on the manner in which it will adopt the opinion expected of it under this Article. An examination of the governing provisions of the Economic and Financial Committee (Art. 109c(2) E.C.) which will take over from the Monetary Committee at the start of stage three, is equally unilluminating in this respect.

Para. (5)

This provision gives an important discretion to the Commission. The Council cannot consider whether there is an excessive deficit unless the Commission addresses an opinion to the Council. According to Fratianni, this gives the Commission a critical role in the future political economy of the Community, as it will be for the Commission to determine in the first instance whether or not a country's fiscal policy is subject to Community scrutiny. There is, however, no duty upon the Council to act upon the Commission's recommendations (Fratianni, von Hagen *et al*, "The Maastricht Way to Economic and Monetary Union", *Essays in International Finance*, No. 187, 1992, Princeton University, pp. 40–41).

Para. (6)

The Council is to decide, on a qualified majority vote, whether an excessive deficit exists in the Member State. This vote takes place after the Member State has had an opportunity to put its own case in defence. One ambiguity in this stage of the process is the type of proposal expected from the Commission. In Art. 104c(5) the Commission is to address an opinion to the Council but, under this Article, the Commission would seem to have to make a recommendation to the Council. It is not clear whether or not this is merely an unfortunate discrepancy in the use of words. If it is not it would seem to be another example of the unduly complicated nature of the process. Whether it is an opinion or a recommendation, the Council is not constrained by the Treaty as to the voting requirements for any amendments it may wish to make. It is not a Commission "proposal" and therefore the unanimity requirement for amendment is not applicable (see Art. 189a(1) E.C.). The Council acts by a qualified majority, with the "accused" State retaining a vote. The Council has a wide discretion in deciding whether an excessive deficit exists, given the wording of Art. 104c(2). If the Council has reached such a decision, then the State concerned cannot qualify to participate in the third stage of economic and monetary union (see Art. 2 of the Protocol on the Convergence Criteria and the note on Art. 109j).

Para. (7)

If the Council makes the determination that an excessive government deficit does in fact exist, then it shall make recommendations to the Member State concerned, with a view to bringing the situation to an end within a given period. This decision is to be taken in accordance with the voting procedure laid down in Art. 104c(13) (see note on that para. below).

Para. (8)

This paragraph permits the Council to make its recommendations public if it establishes that there has not been an adequate response to its recommendations in the specified period. This is the strongest sanction available during the second stage. Unlike the equivalent sanction in relation to a Member State breaching the economic guidelines, it is not contingent on a proposal from the Commission (see Art. 103(4) E.C.). The decision is to be taken in accordance with the procedure laid down in Art. 104c(13). This requires two-thirds of the votes in Council, weighted in accordance with Art. 148(2) E.C., and excluding the vote of the Member State concerned.

Para. (9)

On the coming into force of the third stage, the Council may give the Member State a specific list of measures deemed necessary by the Council for the reduction of the excessive deficit. Once again, this is to be determined in accordance with the procedure laid down in Art. 104c(13).

Para. (10)

This paragraph excludes the application of Arts. 169 and 170 E.C. from matters within the scope of paras. (1) to (9) above. The Commission is therefore precluded from its normal role as guardian of the Treaties. Under Art. 169 E.C. the Commission can bring proceedings against a Member State before the Court of Justice when it alleges in a reasoned opinion that the State has failed to fulfil its obligations under Community law and the State fails to comply with that opinion within the time-limit. In relation to Art. 104c, paras. (1) to (9) the Council takes over the Commission's powers of notification to the Member State in the event of an envisaged breach and the Court of Justice has no jurisdiction. The exclusion of Art. 170 means that other Member States are precluded from initiating proceedings before the Court where they feel that another Member State has failed to fulfil its obligations under Art. 104c(1) to (9) E.C. On Arts. 169 and 170 generally see Weatherill and Beaumont, *E.C. Law*, (1993), Chap. 7.

Para. (11)

This is the key Article once the third stage comes into force. The Council may apply, at its discretion, any of the listed sanctions to Member States persisting with an excessive deficit. The Council may apply any or all of these measures and is quite at liberty to step up the sanction if it so desires. The only requirement for the latter course of action is, as for any action taken under this heading, that the voting requirements in Art. 104c(13) are complied with. The power to impose fines on a Member State is an important one but no mechanism is provided for dealing with Member States that fail to pay the sums due. No power is given to reduce the amount paid to that State under the Common Agricultural Policy or under the structural funds. There is therefore at least a theoretical risk, that a Member State which is a party to the single currency could destabilise the currency union by failing to reduce an excessive government deficit. Such a State would find it very difficult to obtain any favourable outcomes in decisions taken by the Council which impinge on its interests.

The European Parliament is to be informed of any action taken, but has no formal role. Before any sanction may be imposed the Commission must have made a recommendation (see Art. 104c(13)) but as such a recommendation is not a "proposal" the Council is not restricted by the Treaty to making any amendments only by unanimity. The Council could choose to permit amendments to a Commission recommendation by simple or qualified majority.

Para. (12)

This paragraph makes provision for the Council to revoke an earlier decision, where it believes that an excessive deficit has been corrected. Alternatively, if the earlier decision has been made public, the Council will make a public statement to the effect that the deficit no longer exists. The voting procedure applicable to the original adoption of the sanctions against the Member State is also applicable to any revocations under this section (Art. 104c(13)).

Para. (13)

The voting procedure is to be a form of qualified majority vote, with the individual weightings determined by Art. 148(2) E.C. The requisite majority is to be two-thirds of the Member States' votes, excluding the votes of the Member State concerned. This is a relatively strict requirement but does not give any real advantage to specific Member States. If the Member State concerned were one of the big four (U.K., Germany, France or Italy) then the exclusion of its 10 votes from the equation would require 52 of the remaining 77 votes to pass any sanctioning (or revoking) measure. Thus 25 votes would be required to veto any action. If the non-compliant State were to be one of the smaller Member States with three votes, such as Ireland, then the number of votes required to veto the application of sanctions would be 29.

Para. (14)

This paragraph deals with the Protocol on the excessive deficit procedure, already referred to as regards the reference values for determining the excessive deficits under Art. 104c(2) E.C. (Art. 1 of the Protocol). The Protocol also contains: definitions of certain key concepts including "government", "investment", "deficit" and "debt" (Art. 2 of the Protocol); a reiteration of the duty of the Member States to "ensure that national procedures in the budgetary area enable them to meet their obligations deriving from the Treaty (Art. 3 of the Protocol); and finally, a provision that the statistical data to be used in the application of the Protocol is to come from the Commission (Art. 4).

The coming into force of this provision of the Treaty is left in some doubt by virtue of Art. 109e(3) which states that, while Art. 104c came into force from the start of the second stage, certain paragraphs were excluded, including Art. 104c(14). However, no provision is made in the second sentence of Art. 109e(3) that para. (14) will come into force at the start of the third stage either. This makes for a very unclear situation as regards the application of para. 14. The Protocol itself is to come into operation from the start of the second stage, and the third paragraph of this Article specifies that action be taken prior to January 1, 1994 for the adoption of the detailed rules and provisions allowing for the application of the Protocol. (This was done in Council Reg. 3605/93 [1993] O.J. L332.) Nevertheless, the second paragraph would seem to be applicable only from the start of the third stage, in so far as reference is made to the European Central Bank. This matter is far from academic, given that this paragraph permits the adoption of new measures to replace the Protocol on the excessive deficit procedure and, most importantly, permits the alteration of the reference values contained therein. The Council, acting by unanimity on a Commission proposal, is to adopt the appropriate provisions for such a replacement. The Protocol itself sheds no light on the envisaged time-scale for this taking place. Moreover, this process of replacing the provisions of the Protocol appears not to be a matter of discretion on the part of the Council but a necessary step; the wording of the paragraph appears imperative, with the requirement that the Council "shall adopt the appropriate provisions".

Chapter 2 (Monetary Policy)

Article 105

1. The primary objective of the ESCB shall be to maintain price stability. Without prejudice to the objective of price stability, the ESCB shall support the general economic policies in the Community with a view to contributing to the achievement of the objectives of the Community as laid down in Article 2.

The ESCB shall act in accordance with the principle of an open market economy with free competition, favouring an efficient allocation of resources, and in compliance with the principles set out in Article 3a.

2. The basic tasks to be carried out through the ESCB shall be:
— to define and implement the monetary policy of the Community;
— to conduct foreign exchange operations consistent with the provisions of Article 109;
— to hold and manage the official foreign reserves of the Member States;
— to promote the smooth operation of payment systems.

3. The third indent of paragraph 2 shall be without prejudice to the holding and management by the governments of Member States of foreign exchange working balances.

4. The ECB shall be consulted:
— on any proposed Community act in its fields of competence;
— by national authorities regarding any draft legislative provision in its fields of competence, but within the limits and under the conditions set out by the Council in accordance with the procedure laid down in Article 106(6).

The ECB may submit opinions to the appropriate Community institutions or bodies or to national authorities on matters within its fields of competence.

5. The ESCB shall contribute to the smooth conduct of policies pursued by the competent authorities relating to the prudential supervision of credit institutions and the stability of the financial system.

6. The Council may, acting unanimously on a proposal from the Commission and after consulting the ECB and after receiving the assent of the European Parliament, confer upon the ECB specific tasks concerning policies relating to the prudential supervision of credit institutions and other financial institutions with the exception of insurance undertakings.

The E.C. Treaty

The importance of this Article should not be underestimated. From the start of the third stage of economic and monetary union, when this provision enters into force, the European System of Central Banks is to take over the running of the Community monetary policy. While there are separate currencies, national governments have, at least in theory, a substantial degree of flexibility of action. They may keep their central banks under political control and decide their own monetary policy and dictate their own fiscal policies. With the creation of a common currency, these freedoms are vitiated. A common monetary policy is thereby required.

The overriding objective of this policy is the maintenance of price stability (Art. 105(1)). While the European System of Central Banks may look to the objectives of the Community in Arts. 2 and 3a in the determination of its actions, pursuit of these objectives must be "without prejudice to" the achievement of price stability. This policy reflects that of the *Bundesbank* on which the European Central Bank is substantially modelled, and is frequently reiterated in other provisions of the Treaty. The *Bundesbank* does not, however, have a statutory duty to maintain "price stability" but rather to safeguard the "stability of the currency", but in practice it does give much greater weight to keeping a tight rein on inflation.

The tasks of the European System of Central Banks are set out in Art. 105(2) and reflect to a large extent those encompassed in the Central Bankers' suggested draft. The European System of Central Banks is to define and implement the monetary policy of the Community (presumably in accordance with the provisions of Art. 105(1)), to conduct foreign exchange operations consistent with the provisions of Art. 109, to hold and manage the official foreign reserves of the Member States and to promote the smooth operation of the payments system.

As regards the duty to conduct foreign exchange operations, the European System of Central Banks will act as a consultative partner to the Council rather than as an autonomous agent. While the European Central Bank will have the operational responsibility, the definition of the exchange rate policy will fall to the Council (see Art. 109 E.C.). Prior to the Maastricht summit of the European Council this was one of the more contentious topics in the economic and monetary union negotiations. It is generally accepted that it is very difficult for an independent monetary authority to pursue alternative goals; either it concentrates on keeping inflation down (as the *Bundesbank* has done) or it concentrates on maintaining an exchange rate policy. The decision to make price stability the goal was taken very early on in the negotiations, and this meant that a great deal of debate centred on the institutional control of the exchange rate policy. The eventual decision to utilise the Council will make the future relations of the European Central Bank and the Council very important and often complicated.

The third task set out in para. 2 was the subject of much debate, and its final form not determined until the Maastricht summit itself. The controversy surrounded the degree of European Central Bank control over the Member States' foreign reserves. The final draft, stating that the European Central Bank shall hold and manage the foreign exchange reserves suggests that all the reserves will be under the control of the European Central Bank. The rejected version simply contained a reference to "exchange reserves". On the other hand, Art. 30.1 of the Statute of the European System of Central Banks and the European Central Bank (set out in Protocol No. 3 below) provides that the European Central Bank shall be provided, by the national central banks, with foreign reserve assets up to an amount equivalent to 50,000 million ECU. In most countries these reserves are currently held by the national governments rather than the central banks, although Germany is a well-known exception. Their transfer to the Central Bank and their pooling under its authority are essential in order to permit the European Central Bank to maintain the external value of the ECU. Article 105(3) E.C. does allow Member States to hold and manage "foreign exchange working balances"; Art. 31.2 of the European System of Central Banks and European Central Bank Statute permits the national central banks to retain some foreign reserve assets, but any operations in those assets above a certain limit are subject to approval by the European Central Bank.

Article 105(4) provides for the incorporation of the European Central Bank into the legislative arena. It is to be consulted on any proposed Community act in its field of competence. Even if this were to be interpreted relatively narrowly, the European Central Bank, given the wide scope of matters which will have a bearing on its actions, will find itself consulted on a huge variety of matters. Because this consultation process is to take place at the proposal stage, the European Central Bank is given scope for exercising its influence over the legislation in question. The Member States are also required to submit draft legislation to the European Central Bank if this legislation falls within its area of competence. This provision duplicates Art. 4 of the Statute of the European Central Bank annexed to the Treaty. Its application is to be determined by virtue of the procedure in Art. 106(6) E.C. The European Central Bank is also empowered to submit opinions to the appropriate Community institutions or national authorities on matters in its field of competence.

Article 105(5) gives the European System of Central Banks (as opposed to the European Central Bank) the duty to contribute to the smooth conduct of policies pursued by the competent authorities relating to the prudential supervision of credit institutions and the stability of the financial system. Thus the European System of Central Banks is to take an ancillary role in this field, leaving the actual supervisory duties to other unspecified bodies (but likely to be the central banks themselves). It has been suggested, however, that the European Central Bank itself will play a much stronger role in the prudential supervision as time passes. It will be the only organisation in Europe with the ability to provide sufficient funds at short notice to bail out any institution in financial difficulties (Lomax, *National Westminster Bank Quarterly Review*, May 1991). This delegation of duties to the European Central Bank in the area of prudential supervision is specifically catered for in Art. 105(6), whereby the Council, acting unanimously on a proposal from the Commission, and after receiving the assent of the European Parliament, may confer upon the European Central Bank specific tasks relating to the prudential supervision of financial and credit institutions, with the exception of insurance undertakings.

Article 105a

1. The ECB shall have the exclusive right to authorise the issue of bank notes within the Community. The ECB and the national central banks may issue such notes.

The bank notes issued by the ECB and the national central banks shall be the only such notes to have the status of legal tender within the Community.

2. Member States may issue coins subject to approval by the ECB of the volume of the issue. The Council may, acting in accordance with the procedure referred to in Article 189c and after consulting the ECB, adopt measures to harmonise the denominations and technical specifications of all coins intended for circulation to the extent necessary to permit their smooth circulation within the Community.

GENERAL NOTE

This Article contains further material consequential on the move to a single currency, specifically the issue of the new currency units. Article 16 of the Protocol on the Statute of the European Central Bank requires the European Central Bank to respect, as far as possible, existing practices regarding the issue and design of banknotes.

Article 105a(2) deals with the issue of coins. This is to be the duty of the Member States, subject to the approval of the European Central Bank. The harmonisation of the denominations and technical specifications of the coins is to be carried out under the co-operation procedure. Although this would appear at first sight to be a relatively trivial matter, it will be very complicated in practice. The coins will have to be acceptable in coin operated machines throughout the Community, as well as being sufficiently similar to prevent confusion in different Member States. It is not a field easily susceptible to the application of the subsidiarity principle (Art. 3b E.C.).

Article 106

1. The ESCB shall be composed of the ECB and of the national central banks.

2. The ECB shall have legal personality.

3. The ESCB shall be governed by the decision-making bodies of the ECB which shall be the Governing Council and the Executive Board.

4. The Statute of the ESCB is laid down in a Protocol annexed to this Treaty.

5. Articles 5.1, 5.2, 5.3, 17, 18, 19.1, 22, 23, 24, 26, 32.2, 32.3, 32.4, 32.6, 33.1(a) and 36 of the Statute of the ESCB may be amended by the Council, acting either by a qualified majority on a recommendation from the ECB and after consulting the Commission or unanimously on a proposal from the Commission and after consulting the ECB. In either case, the assent of the European Parliament shall be required.

6. The Council, acting by a qualified majority either on a proposal from the Commission and after consulting the European Parliament and the ECB, or on a recommendation from the ECB and after consulting the European Par-

liament and the Commission, shall adopt the provisions referred to in Articles 4, 5.4, 19.2, 20, 28.1, 29.2, 30.4 and 34.3 of the Statute of the ESCB.

General Note

This Article lays down certain institutional provisions relating to the European System of Central Banks and the European Central Bank. Article 106(1) indicates the composition of the European System of Central Banks. It is to consist of the European Central Bank and the national central banks, but will be governed by the decision-making bodies of the European Central Bank (Art. 106(3)). The full operative provisions governing the European System of Central Banks are to be found in the Protocol on the Statute of the European System of Central Banks and European Central Bank annexed to the Treaty. The seat of the European Central Bank will be in Frankfurt (see [1993] O.J. C323/1).

Para. (5)

Article 106(5) permits the amendment of the listed Articles of the Statute of the European Central Bank. Reflecting the vested interest of the latter body in any such amendments, two different procedures are envisaged, and the choice between the two is dependent on the degree of European Central Bank involvement. If the amendment is proposed by the European Central Bank, then the Council may adopt the measure by qualified majority; if on the other hand the proposal originates with the Commission, then unanimity is needed. In either case, the assent of the European Parliament is required.

There is no common denominator to the Articles of the Statute open to amendment. Rather, they cover a wide variety of areas and scale from the trivial to the more weighty. They include the collection of statistical information (Art. 5.1–5.3), accounts with the European Central Bank and national central banks (Art. 17), open market and credit operations (Art. 18), minimum reserves (Art. 19.1), clearing and payment systems (Art. 22), external and other operations (Arts. 23 and 24), financial accounts (Art. 26), allocation of monetary income of national central banks (Art. 32.2, 32.4 and 32.6), allocation of net profits and losses of the European Central Bank (Art. 33.1(a)) and staff provisions (Art. 36). The major features of the system, such as the organisation of the European System of Central Banks (Chap. III, Arts. 7–16), its objectives and tasks (Arts. 2–3), and the adoption of legal acts by the European Central Bank (Art. 34) are inalienable except by the normal Treaty amendment process.

Para. (6)

This paragraph, at first glance seemingly very similar to the preceding paragraph, lays out the applicable procedure for the adoption of provisions, under certain specified Articles, of the Protocol on the Statute of the European System of Central Banks. These matters, explicitly left incomplete by the E.U. Treaty, are to be dealt with by the Council, acting on a recommendation from either the European Central Bank or the Commission and subject to consultation with the other body. The Council is to act by qualified majority vote and the process is to start in all these areas immediately after the decision on the date for the beginning of the third stage is taken. This procedure is reiterated in Art. 42 of the Protocol. Matters included under this heading are: advisory functions (Art. 4); the collection of statistical information (Art. 5.4); the setting of minimum and maximum reserves levels (Art. 19.2); the scope of operational methods of monetary control imposing obligations on third parties (Art. 20); the limits on the capital of the European Central Bank (Art. 28.1); statistical data for capital subscription (Art. 29.2); the transfer of additional foreign reserve assets to the European Central Bank (Art. 30.4); and, finally, the setting of the conditions for the imposition of fines and penalty payments for failure to comply with European Central Bank regulations and decisions (Art. 34.3).

Article 107

When exercising the powers and carrying out the tasks and duties conferred upon them by this Treaty and the Statute of the ESCB, neither the ECB, nor a national central bank, nor any member of their decision-making bodies shall seek or take instructions from Community institutions or bodies, from any government of a Member State or from any other body.

The Community institutions and bodies and the governments of the Member States undertake to respect this principle and not to seek to influence the members of the decision-making bodies of the ECB or of the national central banks in the performance of their tasks.

GENERAL NOTE

This Article enjoins the absolute independence of the European System of Central Banks, the European Central Bank, the national central banks and members of their decision-making authorities, from the Community institutions, Member States or any other related body. The language is very similar to that used under Art. 157(2) E.C. to ensure the independence of the Commission. The theoretical justification for an independent central bank is that it will respect its duty to maintain price stability, whereas politicians may engineer short-term growth prior to an election, despite the long-term inflation which such a move may cause. The role model for the European Central Bank is the *Bundesbank*. Studies indicate that governments attempt to influence the *Bundesbank*'s policies at the stage of appointing its members, but cannot thereby create a bank that will engineer pre-electoral monetary expansion. The eight-year appointment period, followed in the European Central Bank, is one reason why the *Bundesbank* has not become the puppet of the German government. The chances of political control of the European Central Bank are even less than in relation to the *Bundesbank*, because the Council is made up of people whose eight year appointments are not renewable (they are renewable in the *Bundesbank*) and who are either appointed collectively by the Governments of the Member States (up to six members of the board) or by each Government (the governors of the national central banks). Given the diverse interests of the Member States, it seems inevitable that the Bank will be genuinely independent. It would hardly be able to engineer monetary expansion to suit the electoral cycle in all of the Member States, even if it wished to do so.

Article 108

Each Member State shall ensure, at the latest at the date of the establishment of the ESCB, that its national legislation including the statutes of its national central bank is compatible with this Treaty and the Statute of the ESCB.

GENERAL NOTE

This Article requires each Member State to take all necessary steps to ensure that their national legislation, including the statute of the national central bank, is compatible with the Treaty and the Statute of the European System of Central Banks. This is to take place prior to the establishment of the latter body. The degree of action required in each Member State will depend on existing national practice, especially as regards the independence of the national central bank, but the obligations imposed by the Treaty during the third stage are diverse and often complex. Ireland has not yet adopted the requisite legislation amending the Central Bank Acts, although this can of course be done by statutory instrument under the European Communities Act, 1972.

Article 108a

1. In order to carry out the tasks entrusted to the ESCB, the ECB shall, in accordance with the provisions of this Treaty and under the conditions laid down in the Statute of the ESCB:
— make regulations to the extent necessary to implement the tasks defined in Article 3.1, first indent, Articles 19.1, 22 or 25.2 of the Statute of the ESCB and in cases which shall be laid down in the acts of the Council referred to in Article 106(6);
— take decisions necessary for carrying out the tasks entrusted to the ESCB under this Treaty and the Statute of the ESCB;
— make recommendations and deliver opinions.

2. A regulation shall have general application. It shall be binding in its entirety and directly applicable in all Member States.

Recommendations and opinions shall have no binding force.

A decision shall be binding in its entirety upon those to whom it is addressed.

Articles 190 to 192 shall apply to regulations and decisions adopted by the ECB.

The ECB may decide to publish its decisions, recommendations and opinions.

3. Within the limits and under the conditions adopted by the Council under the procedure laid down in Article 106(6), the ECB shall be entitled to impose fines or periodic penalty payments on undertakings for failure to comply with obligations under its regulations and decisions.

GENERAL NOTE

This Article endows the European Central Bank with legislative powers (in the carrying out of its tasks) analogous to those of Art. 189 E.C. The European Central Bank is also given a limited power to fine undertakings for non-compliance.

The first paragraph indicates the scope of the European Central Bank's powers. It may only adopt legislative provisions in order to carry out the tasks entrusted to the European System of Central Banks and subject to the conditions laid down in the Statute. This must be read in the light of the amended Art. 173 E.C. which permits the Court of Justice to review the legality of acts of the European Central Bank. The European Central Bank legislation is subject to the usual procedures for judicial review.

The European Central Bank is permitted to pass regulations in four areas of the European System of Central Banks statutory competence, and in any other areas to be selected by the Council acting under Art. 106(6). The topics in the original category include: the definition and implementation of the monetary policy of the Community (Art. 3.1); the calculation and determination of the required minimum reserves to be held on account with the European Central Bank and national central banks by credit institutions established in the Member States (Art. 19.1); clearing and payment systems (Art. 22); and specific tasks concerning policies relating to the prudential supervision of credit institutions and other financial institutions in accordance with the powers conferred by the Council under Art. 105(6) (Art. 25.2). The Articles referred to in brackets are those of the Statute of the European System of Central Banks and of the European Central Bank contained in the third Protocol annexed to the E.C. Treaty at Maastricht (see below for the text). The definition of regulations laid down in paragraph 2 is analogous to that contained in Art. 189 E.C., which indicates that they will be binding in their entirety and directly applicable in all Member States. One of the most novel aspects of this process is that the European Central Bank can pass such measures without the necessity of a proposal or recommendation from the Commission. The principle underlying the Commission's monopoly of legislative initiative, that it will act in the interests of the Community and not specific Member States, is obviously taken as read as regards the European Central Bank.

The European Central Bank is also empowered to take decisions necessary for the carrying out of the tasks entrusted to the European System of Central Banks, and to make recommendations and deliver opinions. The major difference from Art. 189 E.C., which governs other Community institutions, is that the European Central Bank is not empowered to pass directives.

The reference to Arts. 190 to 192 E.C. signals the requirement that the European Central Bank must state the reasons upon which the regulations and decisions it promulgates are based (Art. 190 E.C.), as well as clarifying the publication requirements of regulations in the *Official Journal*. Regulations passed by the European Central Bank will be published in the *Official Journal* and come into force on the twentieth day following publication (unless specified otherwise in the regulation). Decisions of the European Central Bank must be notified to those addressed and take effect upon such notification.

Paragraph 3 is an example of a Community institution being in a position to apply sanctions for non-compliance with Community obligations (see also the Court of Justice under Art. 171 E.C. and the Commission under Regulation 17/62/EEC). The independent European Central Bank is empowered to impose fines or periodic penalty payments on undertakings. This power will be exercised in accordance with the detailed rules to be decided by the Council under Art. 106(6). Given that the European Central Bank will be acting entirely on its own discretion in the application of these sanctions, it is likely that the Member States, in setting the ground rules, will ensure that the procedure will be rigorous and the sanctions not easily enforced. Once the rules are up and running, the Member States will have no say whatsoever in their application. The Council may adopt a regulation giving the Court of Justice unlimited jurisdiction under Art. 172 E.C. to review any penalties imposed by the European Central Bank.

Article 109

1. By way of derogation from Article 228, the Council may, acting unanimously on a recommendation from the ECB or from the Commission, and after consulting the ECB in an endeavour to reach a consensus consistent with the objective of price stability, after consulting the European Parliament, in accordance with the procedure in paragraph 3 for determining the arrangements, conclude formal agreements on an exchange rate system for the ECU in relation to non-Community currencies.

The Council may, acting by a qualified majority on a recommendation from the ECB or from the Commission, and after consulting the ECB in an endeavour to reach a consensus consistent with the objective of price stability, adopt, adjust or abandon the central rates of the ECU within the exchange rate system.

The President of the Council shall inform the European Parliament of the adoption, adjustment or abandonment of the ECU central rates.

2. In the absence of an exchange rate system in relation to one or more non-Community currencies as referred to in paragraph 1, the Council, acting by a qualified majority either on a recommendation from the Commission and after consulting the ECB, or on a recommendation from the ECB, may formulate general orientations for exchange rate policy in relation to these currencies.

These general orientations shall be without prejudice to the primary objective of the ESCB to maintain price stability.

3. By way of derogation from Article 228, where agreements concerning monetary or foreign exchange regime matters need to be negotiated by the Community with one or more States or international organisations, the Council, acting by a qualified majority on a recommendation from the Commission and after consulting the ECB, shall decide the arrangements for the negotiation and for the conclusion of such agreements.

These arrangements shall ensure that the Community expresses a single position. The Commission shall be fully associated with the negotiations.

Agreements concluded in accordance with this paragraph shall be binding on the institutions of the Community, on the ECB and on Member States.

4. Subject to paragraph 1, the Council shall, on a proposal from the Commission and after consulting the ECB, acting by a qualified majority decide on the position of the Community at international level as regards issues of particular relevance to economic and monetary union and, acting unanimously, decide its representation in compliance with the allocation of powers laid down in Articles 103 and 105.

5. Without prejudice to Community competence and Community agreements as regards economic and monetary union, Member States may negotiate in international bodies and conclude international agreements.

GENERAL NOTE

This Article, applicable from the start of the third stage, lays down the procedure for the adoption and amendment of an exchange rate system for the ECU as against non-Community currencies. As noted under Art. 105 E.C., the Council has the responsibility for the adoption of such measures, acting in consultation with, or on a recommendation from, the European Central Bank in an "endeavour to reach a consensus consistent with the objective of price stability".

The creation of such an exchange rate system will necessitate the conclusion of international agreements. The first sentence of this Article recognises that the normal process for the conclusion of such agreements is that they are negotiated by the Commission (Art. 228 E.C.). In contrast, under this Article, it will be the Council which will decide how any exchange rate agreement is negotiated and the Commission need only be "fully associated" with the negotiations. Article 228 will be effectively displaced in monetary matters. The conclusion of formal arrangements is to be carried out by a unanimous vote in Council, of Member States without a derogation (Art. 109k(4)), and may be based on either a recommendation from the European Central Bank or the Commission, after consulting the European Parliament. If the recommendation comes from the Commission, then the Council must consult the European Central Bank to try to reach an agreement consistent with the objective of price stability. The procedure envisaged for the adoption, adjustment or abandonment of the central rates of the ECU within the exchange rate system is identical, except for the voting conditions in the Council. In this area a qualified majority vote will suffice. The actual definition of qualified majority will depend on the existence of "Member States with a derogation". The votes of such Member States will be suspended and the requisite majority will be two-thirds of the votes cast, weighted in accordance with Art. 148(2) (see Art. 109k(3) and (5)). The wording of Art. 109(1) is such that the Council can override the European Central Bank and adopt or change an exchange rate agreement with third countries even though the Bank thinks that the measure will endanger price stability in the Member States that have adopted the single currency.

The President of the Council shall inform the European Parliament of any adoption, adjustment or abandonment of the ECU central rates and, although it is not expressly provided for, probably will inform the Parliament of the conclusion of formal arrangements on an exchange rate system, given the scale of importance of such a decision.

A special procedure is envisaged as regards non-Community currencies with which no exchange rate system (as under para. 1 above) is in operation (para. 2). In such a situation the Council may, by a qualified majority vote, formulate general orientations for exchange rate policy in relation to these currencies. No pre-conditions are set as to the content of these orientations. Once again, the Commission and the European Central Bank are to be involved in the process. The general orientations on exchange rate policy cannot weaken the independence of the Bank in deciding on interest rates and money supply, because the Bank's primary objective remains the maintenance of price stability.

Paragraph 3 lays down the procedure for determining the arrangements for the negotiation and conclusion of agreements on foreign exchange or monetary matters. While the detailed arrangements are to be laid down by the Council, acting by a qualified majority, this paragraph lays down the pre-condition that the Commission will "be fully associated with the negotiations".

In the first three paragraphs the Commission does not make a proposal for the Council to adopt but rather a recommendation. This frees the Council from the requirement in Art. 189a(1) that it can only amend a Commission "proposal" by unanimity. It also means that the Commission is not free to alter the recommendations at any time up to the adoption of the act by the Council (*cf.* Art. 189a(2) E.C.). Clearly the idea of "recommendation" is used here, and elsewhere in the provisions on economic and monetary union, to shift the balance of power further in favour of the Council in its relationship with the Commission.

Paragraph 4 empowers the Council to decide, on a qualified majority vote of Member States without a derogation, the position which the Community should take at the international level as regards issues of particular relevance to economic and monetary union. The significance of this provision will rest on subsequent political developments. The potential afforded to open up Community decision-making in the many international fora in which the Member States are currently represented is manifest, but will depend entirely on the desire of the Member States to surrender the prestige and influence afforded by such national representation. This paragraph would operate to regulate any such surrender, but is worded to provide for much less significant developments and is awash with ambiguities. The phrase "position of the Community at international level" might well indicate that the Member States are to adopt these positions in the different international organisations, but could also be taken as a simple desire to express the Community position without a requirement that this position be adopted by the Member State in its actions. There is no analogous provision to that in Art. K.5 of the E.U. Treaty, whereby the Member States are obliged to uphold the Community common position in international negotiations.

Representation of the Community at the international level must be decided upon by unanimous vote in Council, of Member States without a derogation, and in accordance with the allocation of powers laid down in Arts. 103 and 105. The reference to Arts. 103 and 105 will mean that the roles attributed to the Community bodies will depend on the specific international body. If the body is dealing with monetary matters it would be expected, according to the tasks of the European System of Central Banks laid down in Art. 105, that the European Central Bank would be the natural Community representative. In the fora where the national central banks and national governments are currently represented, such as the Bank for International Settlements, the meetings of the Group of Seven, IMF meetings and the World Bank, the European Central Bank would seem to be the natural representative of a third stage Community. Nevertheless, this will again depend on the desire of the Member States to cede responsibility in this field. The key words in para. 5 are "without prejudice". The paragraph preserves the power of Member States to negotiate in international bodies and to conclude international agreements in the economic and monetary sphere, provided that they do not contradict Community competence and Community agreements as regards monetary union. The Court of Justice may become involved in resolving the respective competences of the Community and the Member States in this area of external relations.

Chapter 3 (Institutional Provisions)

GENERAL NOTE

This chapter, read alongside the relevant Protocols to the Treaty, lays down the institutional backdrop to the second and third stages. It does not however deal with all the specific institutions envisaged during the process to economic and monetary union. In this respect, the heading "institutional provisions" is not so much misleading as incomplete. Those provisions governing the European Monetary Institute, which is preparing the ground for the third stage, are laid down under the chapter on "Transitional Provisions" (Chapter 4) but the other new institution designed for the second stage, the Monetary Committee, is dealt with under the present chapter (Art. 109c(1)).

Article 109a

1. The Governing Council of the ECB shall comprise the members of the Executive Board of the ECB and the Governors of the national central banks.

2. (a) The Executive Board shall comprise the President, the Vice-President and four other members.

(b) The President, the Vice-President and the other members of the Executive Board shall be appointed from among persons of recognised standing and professional experience in monetary or banking matters by common accord of the Governments of the Member States at the level of Heads of State or of Government, on a recommendation from the Council, after it has consulted the European Parliament and the Governing Council of the ECB.

Their term of office shall be eight years and shall not be renewable. Only nationals of Member States may be members of the Executive Board.

GENERAL NOTE

This Article lays down the composition of the European Central Bank's governing and executive council. Given that the bank is to have legal personality (Art. 106(2)) and be independent of Community and Member State influence (Art. 107), the personnel of these bodies have a hugely important position.

The Executive Board members, including the President and Vice-President, shall be appointed by common accord of the governments of the Member States at the level of Heads of State or Government. These persons are to be independent in the pursuit of their duties and thus they are to be appointed for a non-renewable eight-year period. The eight year time-scale, uncommon in most institutions, is intended to remove the appointees from the influence of generally shorter term governmental majorities. The non-renewable term of office is designed to obviate any advantage of appeasing a governmental authority with the aim of securing another term. The Executive Board members have eight years to exercise their independent powers, free from any influence by Member State governments or any desire to be reappointed. Given that the Executive Board has a maximum of six members, the governments cannot each have their own appointee. The decision-making process will have the collective quality of the appointment of the President of the Commission, rather than the simple rubber stamping of each country's nominee(s) that happens when appointing the rest of the Commission. The Governing Council of the European Central Bank, and the European Parliament, are merely consulted on the choice made by the Member States, and the Commission is given no formal role in the process. Rule 29D of the European Parliament's Rules of Procedure (amended subsequent to the E.U. Treaty, see [1993] O.J. C268/51) provides that the candidates for President, Vice President and Executive Board members of the European Central Bank will be invited to appear before the parliamentary committee responsible. The committee will recommend to the Parliament acceptance or rejection of the candidate. If the vote is against a candidate the President of the Parliament will ask the Council to withdraw the candidate. The Council can ignore this request, but it would put any candidate in a very weak position to be appointed after being rejected by the European Parliament.

The Executive Board of the Bank will have day to day responsibility for the single currency and, unless otherwise provided, will take decisions by a simple majority, with the President having a casting vote in the event of a tie (Art. 11 of the Protocol on the Statute of the European System of Central Banks, referred to in Art. 106). The members of the Executive Board are joined by the governors of the national central banks of Member States without a derogation, to form the Governing Council of the European Central Bank, which will formulate the monetary policy of the Member States party to the single currency, including intermediate monetary objectives, key interest rates and the supply of reserves (Arts. 10 and 12 of the Protocol on the Statute of the European System of Central Banks). The Governing Council meets at least 10 times a year and, unless otherwise provided, takes decisions by a simple majority with the President having a casting vote.

Article 109b

1. The President of the Council and a member of the Commission may participate, without having the right to vote, in meetings of the Governing Council of the ECB.

The President of the Council may submit a motion for deliberation to the Governing Council of the ECB.

2. The President of the ECB shall be invited to participate in Council meetings when the Council is discussing matters relating to the objectives and tasks of the ESCB.

3. The ECB shall address an annual report on the activities of the ESCB and on the monetary policy of both the previous and current year to the European Parliament, the Council and the Commission, and also to the European Council.

The President of the ECB shall present this report to the Council and to the European Parliament, which may hold a general debate on that basis.

The President of the ECB and the other members of the Executive Board may, at the request of the European Parliament or on their own initiative, be heard by the competent Committees of the European Parliament.

GENERAL NOTE

This Article lays down the limited interaction between the European Central Bank and the other Community institutions. It reflects the necessity of some co-ordination between the bodies while maintaining respect for the independence of the monetary authority.

Therefore, the President of the Council and a member of the Commission may participate in the meetings of the Governing Council of the European Central Bank, but have no voting rights. Their influence will no doubt depend on the particular matter under discussion and upon a variety of other variables not susceptible to legal analysis. The President of the Council may submit a motion for deliberation to the Governing Council; the emphasis that the Governing Council gives it is entirely at their own discretion.

The President of the European Central Bank shall be invited to participate in Council meetings where matters within the discretion of the European Central Bank are being discussed. Again his or her influence will depend on many diverse political factors.

Further means of ensuring the accountability of the bank are laid down in para. (3). The European Central Bank is to address an annual report on the activities of the European System of Central Banks, and on the monetary policy of both the previous and current year, to the European Parliament, the Council, the Commission and also to the European Council. It is open to the European Parliament to hold a debate on the report. Although the President of the European Central Bank will present an annual report to Parliament and the President and the other Executive Board members may be heard by the competent committees of Parliament, it is not clear how forthcoming they will be in answering any questions put to them. If the European Central Bank's accountability to the political institutions were increased it might lose its independence and therefore risk losing the benefits of sustained low inflation.

Article 109c

1. In order to promote co-ordination of the policies of Member States to the full extent needed for the functioning of the internal market, a Monetary Committee with advisory status is hereby set up.

It shall have the following tasks:
— to keep under review the monetary and financial situation of the Member States and of the Community and the general payments system of the Member States and to report regularly thereon to the Council and to the Commission;
— to deliver opinions at the request of the Council or of the Commission, or on its own initiative for submission to those institutions;
— without prejudice to Article 151, to contribute to the preparation of the work of the Council referred to in Articles 73f, 73g, 103(2), (3), (4) and (5), 103a, 104a, 104b, 104c, 109e(2), 109f(6), 109h, 109i, 109j(2) and 109k(1);
— to examine, at least once a year, the situation regarding the movement of capital and the freedom of payments, as they result from the application of this Treaty and of measures adopted by the Council; the examination shall cover all measures relating to capital movements and payments; the Committee shall report to the Commission and to the Council on the outcome of this examination.
The Member States and the Commission shall each appoint two members of the Monetary Committee.
2. At the start of the third stage, an Economic and Financial Committee shall be set up. The Monetary Committee provided for in paragraph 1 shall be dissolved.
The Economic and Financial Committee shall have the following tasks:
— to deliver opinions at the request of the Council or of the Commission, or on its own initiative for submission to those institutions;
— to keep under review the economic and financial situation of the Member States and of the Community and to report regularly thereon to the Council and to the Commission, in particular on financial relations with third countries and international institutions;
— without prejudice to Article 151, to contribute to the preparation of the work of the Council referred to in Articles 73f, 73g, 103(2), (3), (4) and (5), 103a, 104a, 104b, 104c, 105(6), 105a(2), 106(5) and (6), 109, 109h, 109i(2) and (3), 109k(2), 109l(4) and (5), and to carry out other advisory and preparatory tasks assigned to it by the Council;
— to examine, at least once a year, the situation regarding the movement of capital and the freedom of payments, as they result from the application of this Treaty and of measures adopted by the Council; the examination shall cover all measures relating to capital movements and payments; the Committee shall report to the Commission and to the Council on the outcome of this examination.
The Member States, the Commission and the ECB shall each appoint no more than two members of the Committee.
3. The Council shall, acting by a qualified majority on a proposal from the Commission and after consulting the ECB and the Committee referred to in this Article, lay down detailed provisions concerning the composition of the Economic and Financial Committee. The President of the Council shall inform the European Parliament of such a decision.
4. In addition to the tasks set out in paragraph 2, if and as long as there are Member States with a derogation as referred to in Articles 109k and 109l, the Committee shall keep under review the monetary and financial situation and the general payments system of those Member States and report regularly thereon to the Council and to the Commission.

GENERAL NOTE

This Article makes provision for the creation of the Monetary Committee and its successor, the Economic and Financial Committee. The Monetary Committee (para. 1) is an advisory body with the main task of monitoring the Member States' budgetary performance and monetary situation (first indent). In addition, it can deliver opinions to the Council or the Commission on its own initiative or at their request and, at least once a year, it will look at the position regarding the freedom of movement of capital between the Member States (second and fourth indents). It will also take on a role alongside COREPER in the preparation of material for the Council in certain specified areas (third indent).

On the coming into force of the third stage, the Monetary Committee will be dissolved and replaced by the Economic and Financial Committee, provided for in para. 2. This body will take an essentially similar role to the Monetary Committee, with marginal differences regarding its make-up and its tasks. Detailed provisions are to be drawn up by the Council, acting by a qualified majority, on the composition of the Committee. All that exists at present is the assertion that the Member States, the Commission and the European Central Bank shall each appoint no more than two members of the Committee. Rules governing eligibility, periods of office and removal will be necessary. In the realm of the Monetary Committee, no provision was made for the adoption of such rules. The preconception was that the members would serve until the dissolution of the Committee. The lack of attention to detail as regards the second stage may come to be regretted, given the possibility of its prolongation.

Article 109d

For matters within the scope of Articles 103(4), 104c with the exception of paragraph 14, 109, 109j, 109k and 109l(4) and (5), the Council or a Member State may request the Commission to make a recommendation or a proposal, as appropriate. The Commission shall examine this request and submit its conclusions to the Council without delay.

GENERAL NOTE

This Article permits the Member States or the Council to request the Commission to make a recommendation or proposal. Thus the Commission's right of initiative in the specified areas is preserved, but the aforementioned parties are permitted to exercise a degree of influence over the process. This influence is however only as powerful as the Commission chooses it to be. The Commission's sole obligation is to examine any such request and report its conclusions to the Council. The areas where this prompting of the Commission is permitted include: recommendations to a Member State that its economic policies are not consistent with the broad economic guidelines laid down by Council (Art. 103(4)); the excessive deficit procedure in Art. 104c (with the exception of para. 14 on the amendment of the Protocol on the excessive deficit procedure); all matters on the external exchange rate of the ECU (Art. 109); matters relating to the convergence criteria (Art. 109j); the time-frame for the move to the third stage and the determination of Member States with a derogation (Art. 109k); and, finally, matters relating to the adoption of the conversion rates for national currencies for the change to the ECU (Art. 109l(4) and (5)). The Council already had the power to make such requests under Art. 152 EEC/E.C. but Art. 109d extends the power to each Member State in the specific cases listed.

Chapter 4 (Transitional Provisions)

GENERAL NOTE

These Articles, as the name would suggest, deal with the second stage of economic and monetary union, known as the transitional stage given its short intended life. During the second stage of economic and monetary union, the necessary steps are to be taken to permit the adoption of a single currency and an independent monetary authority overseeing the process.

Article 109e

1. The second stage for achieving economic and monetary union shall begin on 1 January 1994.
2. Before that date
(a) each Member State shall:
— adopt, where necessary, appropriate measures to comply with the prohibitions laid down in Article 73b, without prejudice to Article 73e, and in Articles 104 and 104a(1);
— adopt, if necessary, with a view to permitting the assessment provided for in subparagraph (b), multiannual programmes intended to ensure the lasting convergence necessary for the achievement of

economic and monetary union, in particular with regard to price stability and sound public finances;

(b) the Council shall, on the basis of a report from the Commission, assess the progress made with regard to economic and monetary convergence, in particular with regard to price stability and sound public finances, and the progress made with the implementation of Community law concerning the internal market.

3. The provisions of Articles 104, 104a(1), 104b(1) and 104c with the exception of paragraphs 1, 9, 11 and 14 shall apply from the beginning of the second stage.

The provisions of Articles 103a(2), 104c(1), (9) and (11), 105, 105a, 107, 109, 109a, 109b and 109c(2) and (4) shall apply from the beginning of the third stage.

4. In the second stage, Member States shall endeavour to avoid excessive government deficits.

5. During the second stage, each Member State shall, as appropriate, start the process leading to the independence of its central bank, in accordance with Article 108.

GENERAL NOTE

Para. (1)

This clearly sets the date for the coming into force of the second stage. All Member States moved to this stage together irrespective of their economic position, degree of convergence, or economic policies.

Para. (2)

This paragraph is the only indication in the Treaty of the tasks envisaged during the first stage but it operated only from November 1, 1993 to December 31, 1993.

The duties incumbent on the Member States included: the adoption of appropriate measures to ensure the removal of all restrictions on the free movement of capital between the Member States and third countries (Art. 73b; see the note on that Article); compliance with Arts. 104 and 104a on the prohibition of certain aspects of public sector finance and the adoption of multi-annual programmes, intended to ensure the lasting convergence necessary for the achievement of economic and monetary union. Paragraph 2 also makes it clear that the progress towards the single market, and in particular the implementation of the necessary Community law, was another key feature of the first stage. For an account of the requisite report, see [1993] 11 E.C. Bull., 1.2.25.

Para. (3)

This delimits those provisions of the Treaty which took effect from the start of the second stage and those which shall take effect from the commencement of the third stage.

Para. (4)

This is the key aspect of the second stage. The Member States are to endeavour to avoid excessive government deficits. This is in contrast to the third stage imperative that the Member States shall avoid such deficits (see note on Art. 104c).

Para. (5)

During the second stage, the Member States are to start the process leading to the independence of their central banks. This has not yet been done in Ireland. The words "as appropriate" would seem to have been inserted at the bequest of the U.K. as they mean that Member States with an express derogation from the third stage do not have to comply. The U.K. and Denmark are under no obligation to pursue an independent national central bank, provided that they comply with all the other provisions dealing with the progress towards the third stage.

Article 109f

1. At the start of the second stage, a European Monetary Institute (hereinafter referred to as 'EMI') shall be established and take up its duties; it shall have legal personality and be directed and managed by a Council, consisting of a President and the Governors of the national central banks, one of whom shall be Vice-President.

The President shall be appointed by common accord of the Governments of the Member States at the level of Heads of State or of Government, on a recommendation from, as the case may be, the Committee of Governors of the central banks of the Member States (hereinafter referred to as 'Committee of Governors') or the Council of the EMI, and after consulting the European Parliament and the Council. The President shall be selected from among persons of recognised standing and professional experience in monetary or banking matters. Only nationals of Member States may be President of the EMI. The Council of the EMI shall appoint the Vice-President.

The Statute of the EMI is laid down in a Protocol annexed to this Treaty.

The Committee of Governors shall be dissolved at the start of the second stage.

2. The EMI shall:
— strengthen co-operation between the national central banks;
— strengthen the co-ordination of the monetary policies of the Member States, with the aim of ensuring price stability;
— monitor the functioning of the European Monetary System;
— hold consultations concerning issues falling within the competence of the national central banks and affecting the stability of financial institutions and markets;
— take over the tasks of the European Monetary Co-operation Fund, which shall be dissolved; the modalities of dissolution are laid down in the Statute of the EMI;
— facilitate the use of the ECU and oversee its development, including the smooth functioning of the ECU clearing system.

3. For the preparation of the third stage, the EMI shall:
— prepare the instruments and the procedures necessary for carrying out a single monetary policy in the third stage;
— promote the harmonisation, where necessary, of the rules and practices governing the collection, compilation and distribution of statistics in the areas within its field of competence;
— prepare the rules for operations to be undertaken by the national central banks in the framework of the ESCB;
— promote the efficiency of cross-border payments;
— supervise the technical preparation of ECU bank notes.

At the latest by 31 December 1996, the EMI shall specify the regulatory, organisational and logistical framework necessary for the ESCB to perform its tasks in the third stage. This framework shall be submitted for decision to the ECB at the date of its establishment.

4. The EMI, acting by a majority of two thirds of the members of its Council may:
— formulate opinions or recommendations on the overall orientation of monetary policy and exchange rate policy as well as on related measures introduced in each Member State;
— submit opinions or recommendations to Governments and to the Council on policies which might affect the internal or external monetary situation in the Community and, in particular, the functioning of the European Monetary System;
— make recommendations to the monetary authorities of the Member States concerning the conduct of their monetary policy.

5. The EMI, acting unanimously, may decide to publish its opinions and its recommendations.

6. The EMI shall be consulted by the Council regarding any proposed Community act within its field of competence.

Within the limits and under the conditions set out by the Council, acting by a qualified majority on a proposal from the Commission and after consulting the European Parliament and the EMI, the EMI shall be consulted by the authorities of the Member States on any draft legislative provision within its field of competence.

7. The Council may, acting unanimously on a proposal from the Commission and after consulting the European Parliament and the EMI, confer upon the EMI other tasks for the preparation of the third stage.

8. Where this Treaty provides for a consultative rôle for the ECB, references to the ECB shall be read as referring to the EMI before the establishment of the ECB.

Where this Treaty provides for a consultative rôle for the EMI, references to the EMI shall be read, before 1 January 1994, as referring to the Committee of Governors.

9. During the second stage, the term ['ECB'] used in Articles 173, 175, 176, 177, 180 and 215 shall be read as referring to the EMI.

GENERAL NOTE

This is a comprehensive provision laying down the structure and tasks of the primary second stage body, the European Monetary Institute. At the special European Council in Brussels in November 1993, held to mark the coming into force of the E.U. Treaty, it was agreed that the European Monetary Institute would have its seat in Frankfurt (see [1993] O.J. C323/1).

Paragraph 1 lays down the organisational structure of the European Monetary Institute and designates it as having legal personality. The European Monetary Institute's role is mainly advisory: exhorting the Member States and the national central banks to strengthen their co-operation and their co-ordination of monetary policy. It can, however, take legally binding decisions under Arts. 15.1 and 15.4 of the Statute of the European Monetary Institute. Its organisation is very similar to that envisaged for the European Central Bank; its direction and management are determined by a Council, consisting of all the Governors of the national central banks and a President selected from among persons of recognised standing and appointed by common accord of the governments of the Member States. As with the members of the Executive Council of the European Central Bank, the President of the European Monetary Institute must be a national of one of the Member States. He or she is appointed on a full time basis for three years. The appointment can be renewed. The first President is Professor Alexandre Lamfalussy. The President proposes and chairs meetings of the Council of the European Monetary Institute, presents the views of the European Monetary Institute externally and is responsible for its day to day management (Art. 9 of the Statute of the European Monetary Institute). No explicit provision is made for the other members of either the European Central Bank or the European Monetary Institute governing bodies; such matters are presumably the domain of the Member State when it appoints its national governors. The detailed provisions governing the European Monetary Institute are laid down in the Protocol on the Statute of the European Monetary Institute annexed to the Treaty.

Upon the coming into force of the second stage, the Committee of Governors was dissolved. This body, established in 1964, had been the main forum for co-operation of the central banks of the Community and saw an exponential rise in its workload since the movement towards full economic and monetary union started. Its tasks have been taken over, in the first instance, by the Monetary Committee and the European Monetary Institute.

Paragraph 2 lays down the tasks of the European Monetary Institute. The emphasis is on strengthening co-operation, and monitoring and overseeing the different aspects of the second stage. It will, nevertheless, be responsible for the running of the European Monetary Co-operation Fund until its dissolution.

Paragraph 3 sets out the preparatory tasks of the European Monetary Institute in laying the groundwork for the third stage. One of the most significant tasks is to be found in the last indent of this paragraph. At the latest by December 31, 1996, the European Monetary Institute is to specify the regulatory, organisational, and logistical framework necessary for the European Central Bank to perform its tasks. In effect, the European Monetary Institute will act as a midwife for the birth of the European Central Bank.

Paragraph 4 provides for the adoption of non-binding measures by the European Monetary Institute, aimed again at the smoothing of progress towards the third stage. These measures, to be adopted by the Council of the European Monetary Institute by a two-thirds majority, are laid down in the three indents to this paragraph. They cover a broad sphere of activities and permit the addressing of opinions and recommendations to the Member States, the Council and the monetary authorities of the Member States. The Council of the European Monetary Institute may decide to publish its recommendations and opinions and thus ensure some form of adverse publicity, if it so wishes, for bodies it considers unco-operative. Whatever the motives of the European Monetary Institute, it must act by unanimity if it wishes to take this step (para. 5). In a provision mirroring the analogous European Central Bank Article, para. 6 requires that the European Monetary Institute be consulted by the Council regarding any proposed Community act within its fields of competence. Paragraph 6 also provides that the European Monetary Institute is to be consulted by the Member States on any draft national legislation in its field of competence, but this is to be subject to any limitations and conditions set by the Council, acting by a qualified majority on a proposal from the Commission. The tasks of the European Monetary Institute in the preparation for the third stage are not exhaustively listed; it is possible for the Council to add any further tasks it considers necessary, but any such addition must be decided upon by unanimity (para. 7). Although the national central banks need not be independent of their national governments during stage two, when the governors of the central banks meet in the Council of the European Monetary Institute they must act independently of their governments (see Art. 8 of the Statute of the European Monetary Institute).

Paragraph 8 highlights the close relationship between the European Central Bank and the European Monetary Institute, in that it states that references to a consultative role for the European Central Bank in the Treaty must be read as referring to the European Monetary Institute prior to the establishment of the European Central Bank. Similar provision was made for references to the European Monetary Institute in the period up to January 1, 1994 to be taken as applying to the Committee of Governors. Paragraph 9 lays out specific instances where the European Central Bank reference is to be replaced by a reference to the European Monetary Institute. This seemingly innocuous provision gives wide "hidden" powers to the European Monetary Institute in the period up till the establishment of the European Central Bank. The substitution of the reference to the European Central Bank by a reference to the European Monetary Institute in the Articles specified means that: the European Monetary Institute will be able to take Art. 173 action for the purpose of protecting its prerogatives (but most measures adopted by the European Monetary Institute will not be subject to Art. 173 review because they do not produce legal effects *vis-á-vis* third parties); the European Monetary Institute may take actions against the other institutions for failure to act and is subject to the same sanction itself (Art. 175); the European Monetary Institute must take steps to comply with any decision of the Court of Justice rendering one of its acts void or after a ruling that it has failed to act (Art. 176); and the validity and interpretation of acts of the European Monetary Institute will be open to preliminary rulings under the Art. 177 procedure. Damage caused by the European Monetary Institute or its servants in the performance of their duties will require to be made good (Art. 215) and the Court of Justice will have jurisdiction to determine the liability of the European Monetary Institute (Art. 178). Finally, this para. alludes to Art. 180 E.C., whereby the Court of Justice will have jurisdiction in disputes concerning the fulfilment by national central banks of obligations under the Statute of the European Monetary Institute. In this connection, the powers of the Council of the European Monetary Institute in respect of national central banks shall be the same as those conferred upon the Commission in respect of Member States by Art. 169. In other words, where the Governing Council of the European Monetary Institute considers that a national central bank has failed to fulfil an obligation under the statute of the European Monetary Institute, it shall deliver a reasoned opinion on the matter, after giving the bank a chance to submit its observations. Should the bank concerned not comply with this opinion within the period laid down by the European Monetary Institute, then the latter may bring the matter before the Court of Justice.

All the above provisions shall apply to the European Central Bank from the start of the third stage.

Article 109g

The currency composition of the ECU basket shall not be changed.

From the start of the third stage, the value of the ECU shall be irrevocably fixed in accordance with Article 109l(4).

GENERAL NOTE

This Article makes reference to the ECU in terms of the transitional phases. The first paragraph ensures that the currency composition of the ECU basket shall not be changed at any stage in the run-up to the adoption of the ECU as the single currency of the E.C. This measure is likely to be of limited significance; its greatest impact will be on ECU denominated deposits, loans and marketable securities. The second paragraph makes reference to the irrevocable fixing of currency values, when the single currency is adopted, under Art. 109l(4).

Article 109h

1. Where a Member State is in difficulties or is seriously threatened with difficulties as regards its balance of payments either as a result of an overall disequilibrium in its balance of payments, or as a result of the type of currency at its disposal, and where such difficulties are liable in particular to jeopardise the functioning of the Common Market or the progressive implementation of the common commercial policy, the Commission shall immediately investigate the position of the State in question and the action which, making use of all the means at its disposal, that State has taken or may take in accordance with the provisions of this Treaty.

The Commission shall state what measures it recommends the State concerned to take.

If the action taken by a Member State and the measures suggested by the Commission do not prove sufficient to overcome the difficulties which have arisen or which threaten, the Commission shall, after consulting the Committee referred to in Article 109c, recommend to the Council the granting of mutual assistance and appropriate methods therefor.

The Commission shall keep the Council regularly informed of the situation and of how it is developing.

2. The Council, acting by a qualified majority, shall grant such mutual assistance; it shall adopt directives or decisions laying down the conditions and details of such assistance, which may take such forms as:

   (a) a concerted approach to or within any other international organisations to which Member States may have recourse;

   (b) measures needed to avoid deflection of trade where the State which is in difficulties maintains or reintroduces quantitative restrictions against third countries;

   (c) the granting of limited credits by other Member States, subject to their agreement.

3. If the mutual assistance recommended by the Commission is not granted by the Council or if the mutual assistance granted and the measures taken are insufficient, the Commission shall authorise the State which is in difficulties to take protective measures, the conditions and details of which the Commission shall determine.

Such authorisation may be revoked and such conditions and details may be changed by the Council acting by a qualified majority.

4. Subject to Article 109k(6), this Article shall cease to apply from the beginning of the third stage.

GENERAL NOTE

Article 109h makes provision, effective during the second stage only, for the benefit of a Member State the balance of payments difficulties of which risk jeopardising the functioning of the common market or the progressive implementation of the common commercial policy. The Commission can investigate and recommend measures to the Member State. If these are insufficient, the Commission can recommend to the Council that it should grant mutual assistance to the Member State concerned. The Council can act by qualified majority vote. This may take one of the specified forms laid down in the Article but this would not appear to be an exhaustive list. The Commission can, as a last resort, authorise the Member State to take protective measures, the conditions and details of which the Commission shall predetermine. This is one of the Commission's more significant powers, which can be amended or overridden by the Council only if it can do so by a qualified majority.

This Article must be read in the light of the existing power under Council regulation 1969/88 of June 24, 1988, which established a single facility providing medium-term financial assistance for Member States' balance of payments. The European Monetary Institute has a function under Art. 11 of that regulation (see Art. 6.1 of the European Monetary Institute Statute).

This Article will continue to apply to Member States with a derogation after the coming into force of the third stage (Art. 109k(6)).

Article 109i

1. Where a sudden crisis in the balance of payments occurs and a decision within the meaning of Article 109h(2) is not immediately taken, the Member State concerned may, as a precaution, take the necessary protective measures. Such measures must cause the least possible disturbance in the functioning of the Common Market and must not be wider in scope than is strictly necessary to remedy the sudden difficulties which have arisen.

2. The Commission and the other Member States shall be informed of such protective measures not later than when they enter into force. The Commission may recommend to the Council the granting of mutual assistance under Article 109h.

3. After the Commission has delivered an opinion and the Committee referred to in Article 109c has been consulted, the Council may, acting by a qualified majority, decide that the State concerned shall amend, suspend or abolish the protective measures referred to above.

4. Subject to Article 109k(6), this Article shall cease to apply from the beginning of the third stage.

GENERAL NOTE

This Article is complementary to the preceding Art. 109h and gives the Member States a strictly guarded right to take autonomous measures to meet sudden crises in their balance of payments. The Council can amend or override the unilateral action of the Member State by qualified majority vote. Once again, this provision will continue to apply in the third stage only as regards Member States with a derogation.

Articles 109h and 109i are very similar to their predecessors, Arts. 108 and 109 EEC Given the removal of any limitations on the free movement of capital during the second stage of economic and monetary union, it may well be that Arts. 109h and 109i will be resorted to by the Member States.

Article 109j

1. The Commission and the EMI shall report to the Council on the progress made in the fulfilment by the Member States of their obligations regarding the achievement of economic and monetary union.

These reports shall include an examination of the compatibility between each Member State's national legislation, including the statutes of its national central bank, and Articles 107 and 108 of this Treaty and the Statute of the ESCB. The reports shall also examine the achievement of a high degree of sustainable convergence by reference to the fulfilment by each Member State of the following criteria:

— the achievement of a high degree of price stability; this will be apparent from a rate of inflation which is close to that of, at most, the three best performing Member States in terms of price stability;

— the sustainability of the government financial position; this will be apparent from having achieved a government budgetary position without a deficit that is excessive as determined in accordance with Article 104c(6);

— the observance of the normal fluctuation margins provided for by the Exchange Rate Mechanism of the European Monetary System, for at least two years, without devaluing against the currency of any other Member State;

— the durability of convergence achieved by the Member State and of its participation in the Exchange Rate Mechanism of the European Monetary System being reflected in the long-term interest rate levels.

The four criteria mentioned in this paragraph and the relevant periods over which they are to be respected are developed further in a Protocol annexed to this Treaty. The reports of the Commission and the EMI shall also take account of the development of the ECU, the results of the integration of markets, the situation and development of the balances of payments on current account and an examination of the development of unit labour costs and other price indices.

2. On the basis of these reports, the Council, acting by a qualified majority on a recommendation from the Commission, shall assess:

— for each Member State, whether it fulfils the necessary conditions for the adoption of a single currency;

— whether a majority of the Member States fulfil the necessary conditions for the adoption of a single currency,

and recommend its findings to the Council, meeting in the composition of the Heads of State or of Government. The European Parliament shall be consulted and forward its opinion to the Council, meeting in the composition of the Heads of State or of Government.

3. Taking due account of the reports referred to in paragraph 1 and the opinion of the European Parliament referred to in paragraph 2, the Council, meeting in the composition of Heads of State or of Government, shall, acting by a qualified majority, not later than 31 December 1996:

— decide, on the basis of the recommendations of the Council referred to in paragraph 2, whether a majority of the Member States fulfil the necessary conditions for the adoption of a single currency;

— decide whether it is appropriate for the Community to enter the third stage,

and if so

— set the date for the beginning of the third stage.

4. If by the end of 1997 the date for the beginning of the third stage has not been set, the third stage shall start on 1 January 1999. Before 1 July 1998, the Council, meeting in the composition of Heads of State or of Government, after a repetition of the procedure provided for in paragraphs 1 and 2, with the exception of the second indent of paragraph 2, taking into account the reports referred to in paragraph 1 and the opinion of the European Parliament, shall, acting by a qualified majority and on the basis of the recommendations of the Council referred to in paragraph 2, confirm which Member States fulfil the necessary conditions for the adoption of a single currency.

GENERAL NOTE

The date on which the transition to stage three will take place will depend upon a number of factors, but particularly on the degree of economic convergence. Article 109j, as elaborated by the Protocol on the convergence criteria, outlines the criteria by which the Member States will be judged. The Commission and the European Monetary Institute (see Art. 7 of the European Monetary Institute Statute) will have to report to the Council on the progress made by the Member States. In addition to the statistical analysis as regards the four economic criteria on which most commentators tend to concentrate, the report shall examine the compatibility of each Member State's national legislation, including the statute of the national central bank, with Arts. 107 and 108 of the Treaty and the Statute of the European System of Central Banks. Other matters to be considered are: the development of the ECU; the results of the integration of the markets; the situation and development of the balances of payments on current account; and an examination of the development of unit labour costs and other price indices. Thus, very few economic data will be excluded from consideration. This is quite in keeping with the consequences of moving to a single currency, which will have effects in all areas of economic life. Moreover, as the unification of Germany highlighted, the costs of unifying entities with divergent economic bases, even with enormous political will behind the venture, can be huge. For this reason, the Germans were very keen to ensure strict convergence criteria to keep the pain to a minimum.

The convergence criteria themselves are laid out in the four indents in this Article and developed, as mentioned previously, in the Protocol annexed to the Treaty. These convergence criteria will not be easy to achieve. At the beginning of 1992 only France and Luxembourg had fulfilled all the criteria (in relation to excessive government deficits see note on Art. 104c(2)). By 1993 only Luxembourg had met all the arithmetical targets. In 1994, only Luxembourg and

Ireland failed to receive negative reports on their progress in convergence (and the Irish position was a matter of some controversy, as noted above). The huge financial strains imposed upon the ERM in August 1993 have led to the creation of new wide 15 per cent bands in the ERM. In strictly legal terms, the opening up of this wider band means, paradoxically, that the convergence requirement is made much easier to achieve. Article 3 of the Protocol simply requires the Member State to have observed the normal fluctuation margins provided for by the ERM for at least two years without severe tensions. With a 15 per cent "normal" banding, the Member States ought not to have any difficulty observing this condition. Unfortunately, in this field economics hold sway over legal provisions. If the Member States were to secure economic union with their currencies at widely different levels, the costs might be enormous. A number of the Member States have therefore made explicit calls for a swift return to the narrow ERM bandings. Whether or not this will take place is a matter for political determination. In the meantime, however, those Member States which were formerly in the narrow band of the ERM have succeeded in maintaining that position, even though they are formally free to depart from it. This indicates a further paradox, that the widening of permitted fluctuations to 15 per cent in either direction deprives speculators of the easy target of currencies which governments are committed to maintain within very narrow fluctuation margins, thus making it easier for governments in fact to maintain such stability.

On the basis of the reports submitted to it, the Council, acting by a qualified majority on a recommendation from the Commission, shall assess, for each Member State, whether it has fulfilled the necessary conditions for the adoption of a single currency and whether or not a majority of the Member States fulfil the requisite conditions. The Council will then recommend its findings to the Council composed of the Heads of State or Government. This latter body, after having obtained the opinion of the European Parliament, will then decide by qualified majority vote whether a majority of the Member States fulfil the necessary conditions for the adoption of a single currency. This decision is to be taken no later than December 31, 1996. Even if there exists a majority of the Member States having fulfilled the necessary conditions, the Council is left with the discretion to "decide whether it is appropriate for the Community to enter the third stage". It is quite possible that this will take account of the composition of the States having fulfilled the conditions. If Germany is not one of the majority States that have fulfilled the criteria then it is very difficult to envisage any move to the third stage. If the decision is taken to move to the third stage the Council will then set the date for this occurrence.

Paragraph 4 is the fall-back provision in the event of no decision having been taken on the commencement of the third stage by the end of 1997. This is then set to take place regardless on January 1, 1999. Before July 1, 1998, the Council, acting on the basis of the reports prepared under para. 1, will determine the Member States which fulfil the necessary conditions for the adoption of the single currency. There is no minimum number of States laid down in the Treaty for commencement of the third stage but practical considerations would have to be taken into account in the event of only two or three States meeting the standards. In particular, as already suggested, it would be unlikely for any such move to the third stage to take place without the participation of Germany, no matter how many imperatives as to the irrevocable nature of the process are included in the Treaty. This commitment to a single currency on January 1, 1999 may be amended at the inter-governmental conference in 1996.

Article 109k

1. If the decision has been taken to set the date in accordance with Article 109j(3), the Council shall, on the basis of its recommendations as referred to in Article 109j(2), acting by a qualified majority on a recommendation from the Commission, decide whether any, and if so which, Member States shall have a derogation as defined in paragraph 3 of this Article. Such Member States shall in this Treaty be referred to as 'Member States with a derogation'.

If the Council has confirmed which Member States fulfil the necessary conditions for the adoption of a single currency, in accordance with Article 109j(4), those Member States which do not fulfil the conditions shall have a derogation as defined in paragraph 3 of this Article. Such Member States shall in this Treaty be referred to as 'Member States with a derogation'.

2. At least once every two years, or at the request of a Member State with a derogation, the Commission and the ECB shall report to the Council in accordance with the procedure laid down in Article 109j(1). After consulting

the European Parliament and after discussion in the Council, meeting in the composition of the Heads of State or of Government, the Council shall, acting by a qualified majority on a proposal from the Commission, decide which Member States with a derogation fulfil the necessary conditions on the basis of the criteria set out in Article 109j(1), and abrogate the derogations of the Member States concerned.

3. A derogation referred to in paragraph 1 shall entail that the following Articles do not apply to the Member State concerned: Article 104c(9) and (11), 105(1), (2), (3) and (5), 105a, 108a, 109, and 109a(2)(b). The exclusion of such a Member State and its national central bank from rights and obligations within the ESCB is laid down in Chapter IX of the Statute of the ESCB.

4. In Articles 105(1), (2) and (3), 105a, 108a, 109 and 109a(2)(b), 'Member States' shall be read as 'Member States without a derogation'.

5. The voting rights of the Member States with a derogation shall be suspended for the Council decisions referred to in the Articles of this Treaty mentioned in paragraph 3. In that case, by way of derogation from Articles 148 and 189a(1), a qualified majority shall be defined as two thirds of the votes of the representatives of the Member States without a derogation weighted in accordance with Article 148(2), and unanimity of those Member States shall be required for an act requiring unanimity.

6. Articles 109h and 109i shall continue to apply to a Member State with a derogation.

GENERAL NOTE

This Article makes provision for the "Member States with a derogation". The likely scenario of a two-speed Community when the third stage comes into being will lead to a great many questions being asked of the Treaty structure and the compatibility of actions of the derogating States with those States committed to the third stage. This Article attempts to tie up as many loose ends as possible in this respect. Nevertheless, it is possible that clashes will occur. In the economic sphere, Member States outwith the central core may see a substantial number of monetary and financial decisions taken against their interests. It is one of the key features of this Article that Member States with a derogation are excluded from the decision-making bodies of the third stage.

Para. (1)

This provides that, if a date has been set for the commencement of the third stage under Art. 109j(3), then those Member States which have not fulfilled the conditions for the move to a single currency, as determined by the Council on the basis of its recommendations under Art. 109j(2), will be classed as Member States with a derogation for the purposes of the present Article.

If the Council has confirmed under Art. 109j(4) which Member States fulfil the necessary conditions then the remainder shall constitute Member States with a derogation.

Para. (2)

At least once every two years, or at the request of a Member State with a derogation, the status of Member States with a derogation shall be reviewed. This envisages an identical procedure to Art. 109j(1), under which the Council, acting in the composition of the Heads of State or Government, may decide, by a qualified majority vote, on the suitability of the Member State concerned for the move to a single currency. If this decision is taken then the Member State shall enter forthwith into the third stage.

Para. (3)

This paragraph makes reference to those Articles of the Treaty which will not apply to the Member States with derogations. These include: the punitive measures envisaged for non-compliance with Council recommendations on the reduction of excessive government deficits (Art. 104c(9) and (11)); the provisions on the European System of Central Banks in the field of monetary policy (Art. 105(1), (2), (3) and (5)); the issue of banknotes and coinage (Art. 105a); the promulgation of legislative measures by the European Central Bank (Art. 108); the setting of and amendment of the ECU rate in an exchange rate system with third countries (Art. 109); and the appointment of the Executive Board of the European Central Bank (Art. 109a(2)(b)).

Para. (4)

   This merely gives further weight to the above paragraph. While para. 3 removed the application of certain Articles from Member States with a derogation, so this paragraph provides for a change of wording to emphasise that these Articles apply only to Member States without a derogation.

Para. (5)

   The disapplication of the Articles specified above to Member States with a derogation is to be coupled, quite naturally, with the disapplication of the voting rights of those States in these same Articles. This paragraph then goes on to specify the means of calibrating a qualified majority vote in the event of derogating States. It is to be calculated as two-thirds of the votes of the Member States without a derogation, weighted in accordance with Art. 148(2). Unanimity of these Member States will be required for an act requiring unanimity. It is likely that, as provided under Art. 148(3) E.C., abstentions by Member States without a derogation, present in person or represented at the Council, shall not prevent the adoption of acts which require unanimity.

Para. (6)

   Articles 109h and 109i, relating to balance of payments difficulties, continue to apply to all Member States with a derogation. They are, of course, inapplicable to States that have achieved the single currency.

Article 109l

   1. Immediately after the decision on the date for the beginning of the third stage has been taken in accordance with Article 109j(3), or, as the case may be, immediately after 1 July 1998:
   — the Council shall adopt the provisions referred to in Article 106(6);
   — the governments of the Member States without a derogation shall appoint, in accordance with the procedure set out in Article 50 of the Statute of the ESCB, the President, the Vice-President and the other members of the Executive Board of the ECB.
   If there are Member States with a derogation, the number of members of the Executive Board may be smaller than provided for in Article 11.1 of the Statute of the ESCB, but in no circumstances shall it be less than four.
   As soon as the Executive Board is appointed, the ESCB and the ECB shall be established and shall prepare for their full operation as described in this Treaty and the Statute of the ESCB. The full exercise of their powers shall start from the first day of the third stage.
   2. As soon as the ECB is established, it shall if necessary, take over functions of the EMI. The EMI shall go into liquidation upon the establishment of the ECB; the modalities of liquidation are laid down in the Statute of the EMI.
   3. If and as long as there are Member States with a derogation, and without prejudice to Article 106(3) of this Treaty, the General Council of the ECB referred to in Article 45 of the Statute of the ESCB shall be constituted as a third decision-making body of the ECB.
   4. At the starting date of the third stage, the Council shall, acting with the unanimity of the Member States without a derogation, on a proposal from the Commission and after consulting the ECB, adopt the conversion rates at which their currencies shall be irrevocably fixed and at which irrevocably fixed rate the ECU shall be substituted for these currencies, and the ECU will become a currency in its own right. This measure shall by itself not modify the external value of the ECU. The Council shall, acting according to the same procedure, also take the other measures necessary for the rapid introduction of the ECU as the single currency of those Member States.
   5. If it is decided, according to the procedure set out in Article 109k(2), to abrogate a derogation, the Council shall, acting with the unanimity of the

Member States without a derogation and the Member State concerned, on a proposal from the Commission and after consulting the ECB, adopt the rate at which the ECU shall be substituted for the currency of the Member State concerned, and take the other measures necessary for the introduction of the ECU as the single currency in the Member State concerned.

GENERAL NOTE

Immediately after the decision on the date for the beginning of the third stage has been taken in accordance with Art. 109j(3), or immediately after July 1, 1998; the provisions included in this Article must be implemented. Among these requirements is appointment of the President, Vice-President and other members of the Executive Board of the European Central Bank. This is to be carried out by the governments of the Member States without a derogation, acting by common accord. The recommendation is to come from the Council and the decision can only be taken at Head of State or Government level and after the European Parliament and the Council of the European Monetary Institute have been consulted. While the President shall be appointed for eight years, the Vice-President is to have the shorter period of office of four years and other members of the Executive Board periods of between five and eight years. No term of office is renewable (see Art. 50 of the European System of Central Banks Statute). Such divergent terms of office in the appointments phase are designed to create staggered eight-year appointments in the future and avoid the whole Executive Board changing at the same time, thus creating serious problems of discontinuity. The membership of the Executive Board is governed by Art. 11.1 of the Statute on the European Central Bank which provides for a President, Vice-President and four other members. This is not a set figure, and the present Article provides that membership of the Executive Board shall on no account be less than four, presumably implying a President, Vice-President and two other members. It may be less than six if there are a number of Member States with a derogation. This is a somewhat curious provision in that, even if only one Member State were to make the transition to the third stage, the only nationality requirement is that the Board members must be nationals of a Member State. The Member State could, in theory, appoint four of its own nationals.

The Executive Board will take all the necessary steps to prepare for the full operation of the European Central Bank and European System of Central Banks. Their full powers shall not, however, take effect until the start of the third stage. Upon the establishment of the European Central Bank and European System of Central Banks, the European Monetary Institute is to go into liquidation.

Para. (3)

This provision provides for the operation of the General Council of the European Central Bank as laid down in Art. 45 of the Statute on the European Central Bank. This body will consist of the President and the Vice-President of the European Central Bank and the governors of the national central banks. The other members of the Executive Board may participate, without having the right to vote, in meetings of the General Council. The General Council is to be the third decision-making body of the European Central Bank and will operate so long as there exist Member States with derogations. The General Council, by way of its make-up, permits these countries to have a say on matters crucial to the operation of the Community. This is achieved through the medium of the national central bank governors. The responsibilities of the General Council are laid down in Art. 47 of the Protocol on the Statute of the European Central Bank. They are mainly consultative and advisory, but they are to deal with a number of areas on the border of the second and third stages which are complicated by the existence of Member States with a derogation. Examples include the giving of advice in the preparation of the abrogation of the derogations provided for in Art. 109k, and, probably most importantly, the General Council is to contribute to the preparations necessary for irrevocably fixing the exchange rates of the currencies of the Member States with a derogation against the single currency (Art. 109l(5) E.C. and Art. 47.3 of the Statute of the European System of Central Banks). The General Council is to adopt its own rules of procedure.

Para. (4)

This paragraph deals with one of the fundamental elements of the move to the third stage. The Council, acting with the unanimity of the Member States without a derogation, on a proposal from the Commission and after having consulted the European Central Bank, shall adopt the conversion rates at which their currencies shall be irrevocably fixed and at which rate the ECU shall be substituted. As the provision makes clear; "the ECU will become a currency in its own right". The Council is then required to take, by the same procedure, other measures necessary for the rapid introduction of the ECU as the single currency of those Member States. Paragraph

5 then deals with the application of the single currency to Member States previously with a derogation. The procedure is essentially similar to para. 4. It appears that the introduction of a single currency replacing national legal tender may occur only after an introductory period when their exchange rates are locked, but the ECU is used immediately only in European Central Bank transactions with commercial banks, and probably soon after in the inter-bank market. National notes and coinages could then be substituted with tender of uniform value (but possibly still of distinctive national design, subject to Art. 105a) after a suitable period for trading in existing national currency.

Article 109m

1. Until the beginning of the third stage, each Member State shall treat its exchange rate policy as a matter of common interest. In so doing, Member States shall take account of the experience acquired in co-operation within the framework of the European Monetary System (EMS) and in developing the ECU, and shall respect existing powers in this field.

2. From the beginning of the third stage and for as long as a Member State has a derogation, paragraph 1 shall apply by analogy to the exchange rate policy of that Member State.

GENERAL NOTE

This Article deals with the exchange rate policies of the Member States during the second stage. They are to be treated as matters of common interest, and the desire to see some degree of convergence as laid down in Art. 109j must, therefore, be one of the primary issues here. Indeed, the present Article makes explicit reference to the "experience acquired in co-operation within the framework of the EMS".

While this Article will necessarily lapse as regards States moving to the single currency upon the coming into force of the third stage, it will continue in force in relation to Member States with a derogation. While not within the single currency system, they are not to be freed from the duty to ensure that they do not adopt exchange rate policies prejudicial to the Community. There is no mechanism for ensuring that a Member State with a derogation will treat its exchange rate policy as a matter of common interest. Member States without a single currency will be at liberty to engage in competitive devaluation if they so choose.

TITLE VII: Common Commercial Policy

GENERAL NOTE

With the physical separation of the economic and monetary union provisions in the Treaty, Arts. 110 to 116 EEC are removed from the economic policy title and appear now under the separate heading, "common commercial policy". The area itself is largely unchanged. The general principles of a common Community customs tariff and common commercial policy towards third countries remain; Art. 110 itself is unamended. The repeal of Art. 111 EEC marks its falling into desuetude; it dealt solely with the operation of the common policies up to the end of the transitional period. The majority of the other amendments follow this trend of consequential amendments and the updating of out-of-date provisions.

Article 110

By establishing a customs union between themselves Member States aim to contribute, in the common interest, to the harmonious development of world trade, the progressive abolition of restrictions on international trade and the lowering of customs barriers.

The common commercial policy shall take into account the favourable effect which the abolition of customs duties between Member States may have on the increase in the competitive strength of undertakings in those States.

Article 111

(*Repealed at Maastricht*)

Article 112

1. Without prejudice to obligations undertaken by them within the framework of other international organisations, Member States shall, before the end of the transitional period, progressively harmonise the systems whereby they grant aid for exports to third countries, to the extent necessary to ensure that competition between undertakings of the Community is not distorted.

On a proposal from the Commission, the Council, shall, acting unanimously until the end of the second stage and by a qualified majority thereafter, issue any directives needed for this purpose.

2. The preceding provisions shall not apply to such drawback of customs duties or charges having equivalent effect nor to such repayment of indirect taxation including turnover taxes, excise duties and other indirect taxes as is allowed when goods are exported from a Member State to a third country, in so far as such drawback or repayment does not exceed the amount imposed, directly or indirectly, on the products exported.

Article 113

1. The common commercial policy shall be based on uniform principles, particularly in regard to changes in tariff rates, the conclusion of tariff and trade agreements, the achievement of uniformity in measures of liberalisation, export policy and measures to protect trade such as those to be taken in case of dumping or subsidies.

2. The Commission shall submit proposals to the Council for implementing the common commercial policy.

3. Where agreements with one or more States or international organisations need to be negotiated, the Commission shall make recommendations to the Council, which shall authorise the Commission to open the necessary negotiations.

The Commission shall conduct these negotiations in consultation with a special committee appointed by the Council to assist the Commission in this task and within the framework of such directives as the Council may issue to it.

The relevant provisions of Article 228 shall apply.

4. In exercising the powers conferred upon it by this Article, the Council shall act by a qualified majority.

GENERAL NOTE

The wording which previously opened this Article, "After the transitional period has ended", is removed as it is redundant. In para. 3, the reference to "agreements with third States" is replaced by reference to "one or more States or international organisations".

The Community represents the Member States in such negotiations. The means of negotiating agreements in this sphere will remain the same post-Maastricht. The Commission makes the recommendations to the Council, which then authorises the Commission to open the necessary negotiations. The Commission then conducts these negotiations in consultation with a special committee, appointed by the Council to assist the Commission in this task. This procedure, unamended by the E.U. Treaty, must now be carried out in the light of the amended Art. 228 E.C.

There is no requirement to consult the European Parliament about agreements concluded under Art. 113(3) (see Art. 228(3)). This is a serious weakness in the powers of the Parliament.

The Council may choose to consult the European Parliament in relation to some commercial policy agreements, but it is not obliged to do so (see Bradley, (1989) 9 Y.E.L. 235, 246). One reason for not giving the Parliament a right to be consulted is the short deadlines which often operate if a commercial agreement is to be satisfactorily concluded. The position could be overcome if the Parliament were required to give its opinion within the deadlines that operate for that particular agreement.

The Commission has considerable discretion in negotiating agreements in the commercial policy field because it is only required to persuade a qualified majority of the Council (para. 4) to vote for the agreement. In that regard the position is the same as it was before the Maastricht Treaty came into force.

Article 114

(*Repealed at Maastricht*)

GENERAL NOTE

This Article is repealed because it was of purely historical interest, specifying the use of unanimity in the Council in relation to Art. 113 during the transitional period.

Article 115

In order to ensure that the execution of measures of commercial policy taken in accordance with this Treaty by any Member State is not obstructed by deflection of trade, or where differences between such measures lead to economic difficulties in one or more Member States, the Commission shall recommend the methods for the requisite co-operation between Member States. Failing this, the Commission may authorise Member States to take the necessary protective measures, the conditions and details of which it shall determine.

In case of urgency, Member States shall request authorisation to take the necessary measures themselves from the Commission, which shall take a decision as soon as possible; the Member States concerned shall then notify the measures to the other Member States. The Commission may decide at any time that the Member States concerned shall amend or abolish the measures in question. In the selection of such measures, priority shall be given to those which cause the least disturbance to the functioning of the common market.

GENERAL NOTE

Article 115 provides a procedure whereby the Member States may request authorisation to control the importation of third country goods from other Member States, where deflection of trade occurs or economic difficulties arise. The reason for the existence of this Article is the incomplete nature of the common commercial policy. The external boundaries of the Community are not identical State by State; while the external Community competence in commercial policy is, in theory, exclusive to the Community in order to achieve uniformity, it remains the case that different Member States may be permitted or empowered by the Community to impose different quotas on the importation of goods from particular third countries. There would be a risk that such concessions would be subverted if third country goods could freely enter a State which had been permitted to impose a quota, via another Member State. Therefore, the Member States have Art. 115 E.C. under which they may request authorisation to control the importation of such goods from another Member State. External disunity has thus created internal disunity. If the commercial policy was operating as envisaged, then Art. 115 E.C. would be unnecessary. The demise of Art. 115 is dependent on the establishment of a comprehensive and uniform common commercial policy. That this has not taken place is highlighted by the retention of Art. 115 by the Maastricht amendments. While it has been altered slightly, its essential basis remains. The major change concerns the adoption of urgent measures. Under the EEC Treaty, the Member States were permitted, during the transitional period, to take the necessary measures and only then notify them to the Commission and to the other Member States. This power for Member States to act unilaterally expired at the end of the transitional period. The amended Art. 115 E.C. provides for the adoption of urgent measures only after express authorisation from the Commission. As before, the Commission is free to decide at any time that the Member State concerned shall amend or abolish the measure in question.

Another difference from Art. 115 EEC is that, in the last sentence of para. 1, the Commission is no longer obliged to authorise Member States to take the necessary protective measures but it "may" do so.

The last sentence of the amended Art. 115, carried over from Art. 115 EEC, maintains an analogous principle to that of proportionality; priority will be given to the measure which will cause the least disturbance to the functioning of the common market. The sentence no longer makes reference to the need to expedite the introduction of the common customs tariff, because this has long since been introduced.

Article 116
(*Repealed at Maastricht*)

GENERAL NOTE

The repeal of Art. 116 EEC has removed the obligation on the Member States to proceed only by common action, in respect of all matters of particular interest to the common market, within the framework of international organisations of an economic character. The effects on the pursuit of a common commercial policy of this injection of national discretion will remain to be seen.

TITLE VIII: Social Policy, Education, Vocational Training and Youth

Chapter 1 (Social Provisions)

GENERAL NOTE

The European Community has always had a social dimension, encompassed primarily within Arts. 117-122 EEC. Through these provisions, a large raft of social measures have been enunciated in a wide variety of fields. Nevertheless, in recent years, pressure has grown from a number of Member States and Community institutions for the process to be made more dynamic and far-reaching. The meetings of the European Council at Hanover and Madrid (June 1988 and 1989, respectively) called for the "same importance to be given to social aspects as to economic aspects and for their development in a balanced fashion". The U.K. on the other hand has consistently argued that the development of the social arena implies increased expense for industry and thus diminished international competitiveness. The proposals put forward for the strengthening of the social provisions of the Treaty, with wider areas of Community competence and increased scope for qualified majority voting, were found acceptable by 11 of the then 12 Member States at Maastricht but not by the U.K. The result is the novel approach in which the 11 Member States, refusing to permit the watering down of the already modest developments proposed in the field simply to satisfy one Member State, annexed a Protocol to the E.C. Treaty containing an "Agreement on Social Policy concluded between the Member States of the E.C. with the exception of the U.K.". The Protocol notes that the 11 Member States (excluding the U.K.) "wish to continue along the path laid down in the 1989 Social Charter". All 12 Member States have authorised the 11 to have recourse to the "institutions, procedures and mechanisms of the Treaty for the purpose of taking and implementing decisions based on the agreement". All 12 also agreed that the U.K. "shall not take part in the deliberations and the adoption by the Council of Commission proposals" made under the agreement and that attendant "financial consequences other than administrative costs entailed for the institutions" shall not apply to the U.K. Austria, Finland and Sweden became parties to both the Protocol and the Agreement on Social Policy upon their accession to the Union on January 1, 1995. While the U.K. is excluded from participating in Council deliberations on matters considered pursuant to the Agreement on Social Policy, British M.E.P.s participate fully in the European Parliament in all such areas, as do M.E.P.s from all Member States with a derogation in respect of monetary matters (see European Parliament on the Rules of Procedure, [1994] O.J. C44).

The result of this approach is that the social provisions of the E.C. Treaty are largely unamended, although the Social Protocol annexed to the Treaty had originally been envisaged as taking the place of the Treaty provisions. Indeed, Art. 1 of the Social Policy Agreement substantially reiterates Art. 117 E.C. in laying down the policy of the 14 in this field. The greatest difference between the Treaty provisions and the Social Policy Agreement is in the scope of qualified majority voting. Under the E.C. Treaty the only area covered by qualified majority voting is that of health and safety (Art. 118a E.C.). Under the Social Policy Agreement, this is expanded to cover: working conditions; the information and consultation of workers; equality between men and women with regard to labour market opportunities and treatment at work; the integration of persons excluded from the labour market, without prejudice to Art. 127 E.C. and improvement of the working environment to protect workers' health and safety (Art. 2(1) of the Agreement). It is arguable that the Community already had the powers to legislate in the majority of these fields, but the potential for effective action is opened up by the application of qualified majority voting under the Agreement. Under Art. 118a EEC, the Community passed the Council Directives of June 12, 1989 on the introduction of measures to encourage improvements in the health and safety of workers at work (Dir. 89/391/EEC, [1989] O.J. L183/1).

The agreement now in force between the 14 Member States is declared to be "without prejudice to the provisions of this Treaty, particularly those relating to social policy" (see the preamble to the Protocol). The legal implications of the U.K. opt-out from the Social Policy Agreement are, however, somewhat unclear. The existence of two distinct sets of provisions on social policy operating side by side undoubtedly opens up the potential of legislative confusion or even conflict. One of the possible scenarios following the coming into force of the TEU was the Commission withdrawing some proposals on directives which the U.K. was blocking and re-presenting them under the Social Policy Agreement. The European parliament passed a resolution in February 1994 calling for the Agreement to be used rather than dilute measures to placate the U.K. ([1994] O.J. C77). This has occurred with the draft directive on European Works Councils (4466/91, COM (90) 581 final) which, having been first introduced under Art. 100 EEC, required unanimity for adoption. It appears that any attempt to put this draft directive before the Council using a legal basis under the E.C. Treaty that requires only qualified majority voting would have resulted in a purported U.K. "veto" under the Luxembourg compromise. It was transferred for consideration under Art. 2(2) of the Agreement on Social Policy in May 1994 ([1994] O.J. C135), and an amended Commission proposal was adopted by the Council after the second reading by the Parliament in September, as Directive 94/45/E.C. ([1994] O.J. L254).

While many of the Member States already have more protective labour laws than the U.K., the Social Protocol increases the potential of a growing divergence between the 14 and the U.K. This could create a number of awkward legal consequences. One question is whether measures adopted under the Social Policy Agreement can take supremacy over conflicting measures adopted under the E.C. Treaty. In this regard the provisions agreed under the E.C. Treaty must have supremacy in the U.K. The Protocol on Social Policy states that "this Protocol and the said Agreement are without prejudice to the provisions of this Treaty, particularly those relating to social policy which constitute an integral part of the *acquis communautaire*". The issue, however, remains open in the other 14 Member States. Secondly, if the U.K. were to sign up to the Social Policy Agreement at some later date, would it then become bound by the decisions reached by the 14 during its period of non-involvement? This would almost certainly be insisted upon by the other Member States.

Article 117

Member States agree upon the need to promote improved working conditions and an improved standard of living for workers, so as to make possible their harmonisation while the improvement is being maintained.

They believe that such a development will ensue not only from the functioning of the common market, which will favour the harmonisation of social systems, but also from the procedures provided for in this Treaty and from the approximation of provisions laid down by law, regulation or administrative action.

Article 118

Without prejudice to the other provisions of this Treaty and in conformity with its general objectives, the Commission shall have the task of promoting close co-operation between Member States in the social field, particularly in matters relating to:
— employment;
— labour law and working conditions;
— basic and advanced vocational training;
— social security;
— prevention of occupational accidents and diseases;

— occupational hygiene;
— the right of association, and collective bargaining between employers and workers.

To this end, the Commission shall act in close contact with Member States by making studies, delivering opinions and arranging consultations both on problems arising at national levels and on those of concern to international organisations.

Before delivering the opinions provided for in this Article, the Commission shall consult the Economic and Social Committee.

Article 118a

1. Member States shall pay particular attention to encouraging improvements, especially in the working environment, as regards the health and safety of workers, and shall set as their objective the harmonisation of conditions in this area, while maintaining the improvements made.

2. In order to help achieve the objective laid down in the first paragraph, the Council, acting in accordance with the procedure referred to in Article 189c and after consulting the Economic and Social Committee, shall adopt, by means of directives, minimum requirements for gradual implementation, having regard to the conditions and technical rules obtaining in each of the Member States.

Such directives shall avoid imposing administrative, financial and legal constraints in a way which would hold back the creation and development of small and medium-sized undertakings.

3. The provisions adopted pursuant to this Article shall not prevent any Member State from maintaining or introducing more stringent measures for the protection of working conditions compatible with this Treaty.

GENERAL NOTE

This Article, inserted by the S.E.A., provides for the adoption of measures aimed at the protection of the health and safety of workers. A number of directives has been passed in this field. One example is the Directive on the protection at work of pregnant women or women who have recently given birth (Dir. 92/85/EEC, [1992] O.J. L348). The E.C. Directive on Working Time was adopted on November 23, 1993 under this Article, despite U.K. opposition. David Hunt M.P., the U.K. Employment Secretary, stated that the U.K. would seek the annulment of the Directive in an action under Article 173 E.C. before the Court of Justice (see *The Times*, November 24, 1993).

The danger is that Art. 118a is used as the legal basis for measures which have only a limited connection with "health and safety" because it is the only one of the social provisions under the E.C. Treaty which allows for qualified majority voting in the Council.

The amendment to this Article simply alters the name of the co-operation procedure to the "procedure referred to in Art. 189c". No substantive amendments are made to the Article itself. On the position on health and safety implementing measures, see E.C. Commission Background Report, E.C. B3/93, November 1, 1993.

Article 118b

The Commission shall endeavour to develop the dialogue between management and labour at European level which could, if the two sides consider it desirable, lead to relations based on agreement.

Article 119

Each Member State shall during the first stage ensure and subsequently maintain the application of the principle that men and women should receive equal pay for equal work.

For the purpose of this Article, 'pay' means the ordinary basic or minimum wage or salary and any other consideration, whether in cash or in kind, which the worker receives, directly or indirectly, in respect of his employment from his employer.

Equal pay without discrimination based on sex means:
(a) that pay for the same work at piece rates shall be calculated on the basis of the same unit of measurement;
(b) that pay for work at time rates shall be the same for the same job.

Article 120

Member States shall endeavour to maintain the existing equivalence between paid holiday schemes.

Article 121

The Council may, acting unanimously and after consulting the Economic and Social Committee, assign to the Commission tasks in connection with the implementation of common measures, particularly as regards social security for the migrant workers referred to in Articles 48 to 51.

Article 122

The Commission shall include a separate chapter on social developments within the Community in its annual report to the European Parliament.

The European Parliament may invite the Commission to draw up reports on any particular problems concerning social conditions.

Chapter 2 (The European Social Fund)

Article 123

In order to improve employment opportunities for workers in the internal market and to contribute thereby to raising the standard of living, a European Social Fund is hereby established in accordance with the provisions set out below; it shall aim to render the employment of workers easier and to increase their geographical and occupational mobility within the Community, and to facilitate their adaptation to industrial changes and to changes in production systems in particular through vocational training and retraining.

GENERAL NOTE

The provisions relating to the European Social Fund are amended by enlarging the Fund's stated aims to include helping workers adapt to industrial changes and to changes in production systems, in particular through vocational training and retraining. These changes have been incorporated into the new regulations governing the operation of the structural funds as a whole from January 1, 1994 to the end of 1999 (see Reg. 2052/88 [1988] O.J. L185/9 as amended by Regs. 2081/93 and 2082/93, [1993] O.J. L193/5 and L193/20); see the note on Art. 125. The administration of the Fund by the Commission, assisted by a Social Fund Committee is retained (Article 124 E.C.).

Article 124

The Fund shall be administered by the Commission.
The Commission shall be assisted in this task by a Committee presided over by a member of the Commission and composed of representatives of Governments, trade unions and employers' organisations.

Article 125

The Council, acting in accordance with the procedure referred to in Article 189c and after consulting the Economic and Social Committee, shall adopt implementing decisions relating to the European Social Fund.

GENERAL NOTE

The detailed provisions governing the application of the Social Fund, found in Art. 125 EEC, have been replaced by a brief provision that the Council is to adopt implementing decisions in this field, using the co-operation procedure. Articles 126, 127, and 128 EEC, previously encompassing supplementary provisions as to the Social Fund and general provisions on vocational training, are removed. The repeal of these Articles does not leave a void as to the application process for the Social Fund. Since the adoption of the S.E.A., the three structural funds have been aimed at the achievement of common "priority objectives" laid down in detailed secondary legislation adopted under Art. 130d EEC (see Art. 1, Reg. 2052/88, on the task of the structural funds and on co-ordination of their activities ([1988] O.J. L185/9) as amended by Reg. 2081/93). Regulation 2052/88 lays down the framework for these three funds: the European Social Fund (see specifically Reg. 4255/88 as amended by Reg. 2084/93 [1993] O.J. L193/39); the European Regional Development Fund (see specifically Reg. 4254/88 as amended by Reg. 2083/93 [1993] O.J. L193/34); the European Agricultural Guidance and Guarantee Fund (see specifically Reg. 4256/88 as amended by Reg. 2085/93 [1993] O.J. L193/44; all three regulations in [1988] O.J. L374/1–25). Of the five objectives originally envisaged for these funds, only the European Social Fund was specifically geared to the achievement of all five. Objective one is the top priority of the funds and aims "to promote the development and adjustment of the regions whose development is lagging behind (less than 75 per cent of the Community average)".

At the Edinburgh European Council, agreement was reached in principle as to the application of the structural funds in the period January 1, 1994 to the end of 1999. These amendments provided primarily for the creation of the Cohesion Fund (see Art. 130d and the Protocol on Economic and Social Cohesion). This new fund, aimed exclusively at the four cohesion countries (Spain, Portugal, Ireland and Greece), sets out to alleviate the regional disparities between the Community countries, particularly evident in these four "poorer" States. Thus, the Cohesion Fund can be seen to be aimed at "objective one" (see Reg. 2052/88 above), which will continue to be the top priority, accounting for some 70 per cent of the total funds. This leaves the Social Fund with the primary duty of addressing what were objectives three and four of Reg. 2052/88: "the combating of long-term unemployment and facilitating the integration into working life of young people and those socially excluded from the labour market". This is in line with the E.U. Treaty amendment to the objectives of the European Social Fund laid out in Art. 123 E.C. which increases the Fund's stated aims to cover vocational training and retraining to facilitate adaptation to structural change in industry. The governing provisions in this field are now Arts. 1–9 of Reg. 2084/93 ([1993] O.J. L193/39) replacing Arts. 1–9 of Reg. 4255/88.

Any requests for financial assistance under the Fund must be submitted as operational programmes, global grant schemes or projects (Art. 5, Reg. 2084/93). This information must include specific data particular to each proposed project, as laid down in Art. 14(2) of Reg. 4253/88 and Art. 5 of Reg. 2084/93. This will include the groups targeted by the project, the number of persons and the duration of the operations. Requests for financial assistance under the Social Fund are put forward by Member States or by bodies governed by public law and the acceptance of such requests by the Commission and the Social Fund Committee can mean a reimbursement of a percentage of the expenditure incurred by the State or public sector body. Article 1 of Reg. 2084/93 lays down the type of programmes qualifying for financial assistance. These include vocational training measures designed to help the long-term unemployed, measures promoting equal opportunities for men and women, and programmes designed to facilitate the adaptation of workers to industrial change. Article 2 then sets out the expenditure eligible for reimbursement from the Social Fund.

The revised structural funds for the period 1993–1999, agreed at the Edinburgh European Council, provide for a two-fold increase in the amount of funds available compared with the previous period. From 21,277 million ECU in 1993, the funds will progressively increase to 30,000 million ECU in 1999. The figures for the cohesion fund itself are 1,500 million ECU in 1993 rising to 2,600 million ECU in 1999. This increase is primarily aimed at the cohesion needed by the time of the envisaged achievement of the third stage of economic and monetary union (see conclusions of the Presidency, S.N. 456/92, pp. 8–11).

On the Social Fund and structural funds in general see Mathijsen, *A Guide to European Union Law* (6th ed., 1995) pp. 333–40; and E.C. Commission, Background Report, B16/93, 28/5/93.

The removal of the detailed Treaty provisions on the application of the European Social Fund has provided a convenient slot for the Articles on education and culture.

Chapter 3 (Education, Vocational Training and Youth)

GENERAL NOTE

While these are, at first glance, new Community competences (save as respects vocational training, see Art. 127), the powers made available to the Community through the Council are very limited and the thrust of the new material is towards declaring Community aims while reiterating that these areas remain essentially within the responsibility of the Member States.

Article 126

1. The Community shall contribute to the development of quality education by encouraging co-operation between Member States and, if necessary, by supporting and supplementing their action, while fully respecting the responsibility of the Member States for the content of teaching and the organisation of education systems and their cultural and linguistic diversity.
2. Community action shall be aimed at:
   — developing the European dimension in education, particularly through the teaching and dissemination of the languages of the Member States;
   — encouraging mobility of students and teachers, *inter alia* by encouraging the academic recognition of diplomas and periods of study;
   — promoting co-operation between educational establishments;
   — developing exchanges of information and experience on issues common to the education systems of the Member States;
   — encouraging the development of youth exchanges and of exchanges of socio-educational instructors;
   — encouraging the development of distance education.
3. The Community and the Member States shall foster co-operation with third countries and the competent international organisations in the sphere of education, in particular the Council of Europe.
4. In order to contribute to the achievement of the objectives referred to in this Article, the Council:
   — acting in accordance with the procedure referred to in Article 189b, after consulting the Economic and Social Committee and the Committee of the Regions, shall adopt incentive measures, excluding any harmonisation of the laws and regulations of the Member States;
   — acting by qualified majority on a proposal from the Commission, shall adopt recommendations.

GENERAL NOTE

This Article incorporates into the Community Treaties for the first time an explicit legal base for the adoption of measures in the educational field. Prior to the conclusion of the E.U. Treaty, inter-governmental co-operation in this field through exchanges of information, pilot studies and non-binding resolutions were backed up by the Community's own education programmes. These programmes came about partly under the old Art. 128 EEC and partly under the Action Programme on Education agreed in 1986 ([1986] O.J. C33). ERASMUS, LINGUA and COMMETT were adopted under Arts. 128 and 235 EEC and provide for links between universities and industry (COMMETT, Decision 86/365, [1986] O.J. L222 and Decision 89/271, [1989] O.J. L13), the promotion of foreign language teaching (LINGUA, Decision 89/489, [1989] O.J. L239) and Community university exchange programmes (ERASMUS, Decision 87/327, [1987] O.J. L166). The new education Article puts this co-operation between Member States on a firmer footing.

The role of the Community in this field will be restricted to the adoption of incentive measures; with the express proviso that these shall exclude "any harmonisation of the laws and regulations of the Member States" (Art. 126(4) E.C.). These measures are to be adopted under the conciliation and veto procedure in Art. 189b E.C., and only after consultation of the Economic and Social Committee and the Committee of the Regions has taken place. This amounts to the most convoluted process for the adoption of legislation under the whole Treaty. The Council is also empowered to enact non-binding recommendations, acting by a qualified majority on a proposal from the Commission.

The principle of subsidiarity is implicit throughout this Article; phrases such as "fully respecting the responsibility of the Member States for the content and the organisation of education systems and their cultural and educational diversity" making quite clear where the balance of power is to lie. This reflects the sensitive national feelings towards any standardisation of the school curriculum, etc., which is explicitly excluded by the provisions of the Article. The insertion of this Article prevents further development of education policy by the Community under the rubric of vocational training (Art. 128 EEC, now repealed). The new process removes the scope of application of simple majority voting previously available under Art. 128 EEC. For a detailed examination of the operation of Art. 126 E.C., see the separate contributions of Verbruggen, de Groof, Lenaerts and Whelan in de Groof ed., *Subsidiarity and Education* (1994).

Article 127

1. The Community shall implement a vocational training policy which shall support and supplement the action of the Member States, while fully respecting the responsibility of the Member States for the content and organisation of vocational training.

2. Community action shall aim to:
   — facilitate adaptation to industrial changes, in particular through vocational training and retraining;
   — improve initial and continuing vocational training in order to facilitate vocational integration and reintegration into the labour market;
   — facilitate access to vocational training and encourage mobility of instructors and trainees and particularly young people;
   — stimulate co-operation on training between educational or training establishments and firms;
   — develop exchanges of information and experience on issues common to the training systems of the Member States.

3. The Community and the Member States shall foster co-operation with third countries and the competent international organisations in the sphere of vocational training.

4. The Council, acting in accordance with the procedure referred to in Article 189c and after consulting the Economic and Social Committee, shall adopt measures to contribute to the achievement of the objectives referred to in this Article, excluding any harmonisation of the laws and regulations of the Member States.

GENERAL NOTE

This Article lays down the scope of the Community vocational training policy; previously enunciated by Art. 128 EEC. In common with the provision on education above, the Community is only empowered to implement a vocational training policy in support of Member State action (Art. 127(1) E.C.). The aims of the Community action are listed under para. 2. The only role for the Council is to adopt measures under the co-operation procedure with the goal of achieving these objectives. The influence of the principle of subsidiarity is felt, with the express exclusion of "any harmonisation of the laws and regulations of the Member States" and the requirement "fully [to respect] the responsibility of the Member States for the content and organisation of vocational training".

The repeal of Art. 128 EEC removes the application of simple majority voting in Council and replaces it with qualified majority and unanimity, depending on the way the European Parliament votes in the second reading under the co-operation procedure (Art. 189c E.C.). This may allow the individual Member States to wield much greater control over the training budget.

While this Article bears a number of similarities to the preceding provision on education, it seems to permit greater scope for Community action. On the first place it is built upon an explicit pre-existing Community competence and an established process for the reimbursement of Member States for expenditure incurred in training programmes. Secondly, unlike the education provisions, the scope for Community measures in the training field is not restricted to incentive measures but to measures "contributing to the achievement of the objectives referred to in the Article". Thirdly, the Court of Justice in *Gravier v. City of Liege* (Case 293/83 [1985] E.C.R. 593), in the context of Art. 128 EEC, observed that access to vocational training is a means of bringing about the key objective of free movement of persons throughout the Community. Thus Community nationals could rely on Art. 7 EEC (now Art. 6 E.C.), to claim equality with nationals of a Member State providing training, in qualifying for access to the course. The Court in *Gravier* envisaged a very wide notion of vocational training covering "any form of education which prepares for a qualification for a particular profession, trade or employment or which provides the necessary skills and training for such a profession, trade or employment ... even if the training programme includes an element of general education" (para. 30). The Court confirmed the breadth of this principle in *Blaizot v. University of Liege* (Case 24/86 [1988] E.C.R. 379) where it stated that "only certain courses of study ... intended for persons wishing to improve their general knowledge rather than prepare themselves for an occupation" fall outside the scope of vocational training (para. 20). (See further Case 242/87, *Commission v. Council (ERASMUS)*: [1989] E.C.R. 1425.) The whole of Art. 127 E.C. must be read in the light of this case law. The duty of the Community to facilitate access to vocational training (Art. 127(2) E.C., third indent) would seem to have been achieved to a large extent by the Court of Justice. Financial assistance of non-nationals attending vocational training in another Member State is however wholly at the discretion of the Member State concerned (Case 197/86, *Brown v. Secretary of State for Scotland*: [1988] E.C.R. 3205). Financial matters will be a major consideration in any development of the Community vocational training policy under Art. 127 E.C. In this respect see the annotations on the European Social Fund under Arts. 123–125 E.C.

TITLE IX: Culture

Article 128

1. The Community shall contribute to the flowering of the cultures of the Member States, while respecting their national and regional diversity and at the same time bringing the common cultural heritage to the fore.

2. Action by the Community shall be aimed at encouraging co-operation between Member States and, if necessary, supporting and supplementing their action in the following areas:
   — improvement of the knowledge and dissemination of the culture and history of the European peoples;
   — conservation and safeguarding of cultural heritage of European significance;
   — non-commercial cultural exchanges;
   — artistic and literary creation, including in the audiovisual sector.

3. The Community and the Member States shall foster co-operation with third countries and the competent international organisations in the sphere of culture, in particular the Council of Europe.

4. The Community shall take cultural aspects into account in its action under other provisions of this Treaty.

5. In order to contribute to the achievement of the objectives referred to in this Article, the Council:
   — acting in accordance with the procedure referred to in Article 189b and after consulting the Committee of the Regions, shall adopt incen-

tive measures, excluding any harmonisation of the laws and regulations of the Member States.

The Council shall act unanimously throughout the procedures referred to in Article 189b;

— acting unanimously on a proposal from the Commission, shall adopt recommendations.

GENERAL NOTE

In line with Community competences in the field of education, the incorporation of culture into the Community sphere is subject to an array of provisos restricting the scope of Community action in this field. In this area, where national diversity is manifest, the Community is to play only a small role because the culture provisions are by far the most restrictive of Community action. Article 128 roughly follows the pattern of the preceding Articles. The Community is under a duty to "contribute to the flowering of the cultures of the Member States" and to bring "the common cultural heritage to the fore". The Community is empowered, in pursuit of the objectives laid down in Art. 128(2) E.C., to adopt incentive measures, but excluding any harmonisation of the laws and regulations of the Member States, and to adopt recommendations on the subject. The adoption of the incentive measures is to take place under the conciliation and veto procedure but with the added requirement that the Council act by unanimity throughout. This effectively renders the Art. 189b process otiose, the conciliation element is much less likely to work effectively given the unanimity requirement in Council (see note on Art. 189b E.C.). The adoption of recommendations, which are non-binding, is similarly tied to a position of unanimity in Council. The promulgation of even the limited measures envisaged under this Article is thus made very difficult. The adoption of measures in the field of "culture" in the past was achieved under Art. 235 and thus similarly required unanimity. Cultural matters have also been evident in European legislation enacted under different Community headings. The "Television Without Frontiers" Directive enacted in 1989, has, as one of its aims, the encouragement of European production of television material. In pursuit of this goal, it lays down guidelines specifying that a majority of transmission time ought, "wherever practicable", to be devoted to European works. This is then backed up by complicated statistics regarding the status of sporting, news and teletext programmes. Thus, a directive aimed at the free movement of television programmes has an inescapably cultural backdrop, and would seem to imply the inclusion of cultural affairs in the Treaty long before the Maastricht amendments came into being; moreover, the adoption of measures with cultural implications under existing Treaty provisions, Art. 100a in particular, will remain more tempting to the Commission in future given the limited scope for action under the cultural heading itself.

Usher asserts that the Community had developed a new Community policy in the culture field as early as 1988 and did so without even making reference to Art. 235. In a Resolution passed on May 27, 1988, the Council set out the future plan of action for work in this area. They called for, *inter alia*, the setting up of a committee on cultural affairs and for the Commission to implement decisions of the Council at the Community level ([1988], O.J. C197/1). See now the Commission Communication on Community action in the field of culture (COM (94) 356).

Article 128(4) states that "the Community shall take cultural matters into account in its actions under other provisions of the Treaty". While this is not as imperative a requirement as that enunciated under the analogous environmental provision, it ought to give cultural arguments greater weight. Venables has asserted that cultural considerations could well surface in many initiatives for the completion of the internal market in relation to copyright, and other measures to protect intellectual property, approximation of VAT and other indirect taxes and levies (Venables, *The Amendment of the Treaties* (1992), p. 58).

The provision under the educational title that the Committee of the Regions be consulted (Art. 127) is not duplicated here. It is arguable that co-operation among the Member States in the cultural field would have a strong regional element. The conclusion that consultation of the Committee of the Regions has been appended to a variety of Articles on an ad hoc basis is hard to avoid.

TITLE X: Public Health

Article 129

1. The Community shall contribute towards ensuring a high level of human health protection by encouraging co-operation between the Member States and, if necessary, lending support to their action. Community action shall be directed towards the prevention of diseases, in particular the major health

scourges, including drug dependence, by promoting research into their causes and their transmissions, as well as health information and education.

Health protection requirements shall form a constituent part of the Community's other policies.

2. Member States shall, in liaison with the Commission, co-ordinate among themselves their policies and programmes in the areas referred to in paragraph 1. The Commission may, in close contact with the Member States, take any useful initiative to promote such co-ordination.

3. The Community and the Member States shall foster co-operation with third countries and the competent international organisations in the sphere of public health.

4. In order to contribute to the achievement of the objectives referred to in this Article, the Council:
— acting in accordance with the procedure referred to in Article 189b, after consulting the Economic and Social Committee and the Committee of the Regions, shall adopt incentive measures, excluding any harmonisation of the laws and regulations of the Member States;
— acting by a qualified majority on a proposal from the Commission, shall adopt recommendations.

GENERAL NOTE

This provision aims to ensure a high level of health protection in the Community. This is to be achieved through the promotion of research and the sharing of information and education. In common with the rest of these "new" competences, this marks a formalisation of the Community's role in this area. The Article reflects the principle of subsidiarity both in general and in the more specific exclusion of any harmonisation of the laws and regulations of the Member States. Article 129(1) follows the pattern of the preceding Articles by laying down the role of the Community as one of encouraging co-operation between the Member States. The addition of the proviso that "if necessary", the Community may "lend support to their action" does not appear to alter the underlying balance of power in any substantial fashion. Any such "necessary" action would still have to be read in the light of Art. 129(4), explicitly excluding any harmonisation of national law.

The Commission is given the task of liaising with the Member States to co-ordinate their actions in the fields of disease prevention, drug dependence, and research into their causes and transmissions. The Council is empowered to adopt incentive measures under the conciliation and veto procedure, avoiding any harmonisation of national laws, or to enact non-binding recommendations on the basis of a Commission proposal. The latter measures are to be adopted by qualified majority, but bypass any European Parliamentary consideration.

Community measures in the field of health protection have been promulgated under a variety of different legal bases in the past; in particular Arts. 100a and 235 EEC. Council Directive 89/622 on the approximation of the laws of the Member States concerning the labelling of tobacco products was passed under Art. 100a EEC, with the preamble citing the Directive's goal as "a vital factor in the protection of public health" (see recently on this Directive Case C–11/92, *R. v. Secretary of State for Health*, in which the Court of Justice found the U.K. acted legally in demanding warnings 50 per cent bigger than stipulated by the Directive, as minimum harmonisation applied). See further Council Resolution on future action in the field of public health ([1993] O.J. C174/1).

TITLE XI: Consumer Protection

Article 129a

1. The Community shall contribute to the attainment of a high level of consumer protection through:
(a) measures adopted pursuant to Article 100a in the context of the completion of the internal market;

(b) specific action which supports and supplements the policy pursued by the Member States to protect the health, safety and economic interests of consumers and to provide adequate information to consumers.

2. The Council, acting in accordance with the procedure referred to in Article 189b and after consulting the Economic and Social Committee, shall adopt the specific action referred to in paragraph 1(b).

3. Action adopted pursuant to paragraph 2 shall not prevent any Member State from maintaining or introducing more stringent protective measures. Such measures must be compatible with this Treaty. The Commission shall be notified of them.

GENERAL NOTE

This Article would seem to afford a rather strong legislative base for the adoption of measures in the field of consumer protection. The restrictions on the subject matter and the form that Community action should take which are found in the headings on culture and health are not found in this Article. This could well be due to the fact that consumer protection has been explicitly recognised in the Community Treaty since the S.E.A., and dealt with under a variety of headings since early on in the development of the single European market. In 1975 the Council adopted a Resolution concerning a preliminary programme for a consumer protection and information policy ([1975] O.J. C92/1). This dealt with the protection of consumers' health and safety, misleading advertising, consumer information, etc. A number of legislative enactments were promulgated under these headings. In 1986, the Council adopted a Resolution setting out its policy of integration of consumer policy into other common policies of the Community ([1987] O.J. C3/1). Then Art. 100a(3) EEC, inserted by the S.E.A., empowered the Commission to make proposals for the establishment of the Single Market "concerning health, safety, environmental protection and consumer protection", and to "take as a base a high level of protection". While there was still no express Community competence in this field, consumer protection legislation continued to be passed, especially under both Arts. 100 and 100a EEC. The legislation passed in this field has often had consumer protection as a by-product of some form of internal market harmonisation but there have also been some measures exclusively aimed at consumer protection. A prime example is Council Directive 88/378 on the approximation of laws of the Member States concerning the safety of toys (on consumer safety measures in general see E.C. Commission Background Report E.C. B2/93 and Weatherill, "Consumer Safety Legislation in the U.K. and Art. 30 EEC" (1988) 13 E.L.Rev. 87). Measures recently passed in the consumer protection field include the Directive on unfair terms in consumer contracts ([1993] O.J. L95; see Brander and Ulmer, "The Community Directive on Unfair terms in Consumer Contracts: Some Critical Comments on the proposal submitted by the E.C. Commission" (1991) 28 C.M.L.Rev. 647) and the General Product Safety Directive (Dir. 92/59, [1992] O.J. L228/24).

Consumer protection legislation has now got its own legal base under Art. 129a. The Community is empowered, as before, to attempt to secure a high degree of consumer protection through the adoption of Art. 100a measures. Secondly, and more importantly, the Community is to take specific action which supports and supplements the policy of the Member States to protect the health, safety and economic interests of consumers. This suggests a very broad scope, without the proviso common to the preceding Articles that the measures shall exclude any harmonisation of national laws and regulations. This power must however be exercised in accordance with the principle of subsidiarity. The General Product Safety Directive mentioned above contains more than an element of this principle in its operative provisions. This is in line with the three year action plan of consumer policy in the EEC adopted in 1990, which made explicit reference to the subsidiarity principle and to its enunciation in the consumer protection field (COM (90) 98, at 3). Measures adopted under this heading will be by the conciliation and veto procedure. Expressly provided for in this Article is the notion of minimum harmonisation, whereby Member States can maintain or introduce more stringent measures than laid down in the secondary legislation, subject to their notifying the Commission of their existence. This is quite in keeping with the idea of subsidiarity, as well as avoiding the situation under which the pursuit of Community policies could lead to a lowering of standards in the more advanced Member States (see Goyens, "Consumer Protection in a Single European Market: What Challenge for the E.C. Agenda?", (1992) 29 C.M.L.Rev. 71).

Finally, the Community is also given the power to provide adequate information to consumers (one of the measures dropped by the Commission at the Edinburgh European Council in the name of subsidiarity concerned the compulsory nutritional labelling of foodstuffs previously proposed in [1988] O.J. C282).

TITLE XII: Trans-European Networks

GENERAL NOTE

These Articles mark something of a new departure for the internal market. The aim is to permit the citizens of the Union to "derive full benefit from the setting up of an area without any internal frontiers". This is to be achieved through Community contribution to the establishment and development of trans-European networks in the areas of transport, telecommunications, and energy infrastructures. This contribution is to be aimed at the achievement of the "objectives referred to in Arts. 7a and 130a"; in other words, the completion of the internal market and economic and social cohesion.

The scope for Community action under this heading is large. The Community, in aiming to achieve the interconnection and inter-operability of the national networks and access to such networks, is to establish guidelines on the subject, as well as implementing measures aimed at the inter-operability of the networks. The second indent of Art. 129c alludes to the adoption of measures necessary for the inter-operability of the networks, especially through the field of technical harmonisation. The adoption of the guidelines envisaged under the first indent of Art. 129c(1) is by the conciliation and veto procedure following the consultation of the Economic and Social Committee and the Committee of the Regions. The implementation of measures under the second indent is to be on the basis of the co-operation procedure. The third indent of Art. 129c is one of the more interesting provisions of the Treaty. It permits the Community to support the financial efforts made by the Member States in common projects, identified under the guidelines referred to previously. The Community is to assist the Member States in these projects through feasibility studies, loan guarantees or interest rate subsidies. Alternatively, the Community may utilise the Cohesion Fund (Art. 130d E.C.) to finance projects relating to transport infrastructure. In the adoption of guidelines or projects of common interest which relate to the territory of a Member State then the approval of that Member State shall be required (Art. 129d).

The Commission has made it clear that, although the Community will support projects of European interest, and is supporting less prosperous regions through its Regional Development Fund and the new Cohesion Fund, in view of its limited resources, it does not see itself as the major provider of finance for transport infrastructure programmes and is keen to encourage private sector investment (E.C. Commission, E.C. B10/93, at 3).

This Article also provides that "the Community may decide to co-operate with third countries to promote objects of mutual interest and to ensure the inter-operability of networks" (Art. 129c(3)). No provision is, however, made as to the procedure to be utilised in deciding to go ahead with such co-operation, nor is any mention made of the source of funding, if required.

Article 129b

1. To help achieve the objectives referred to in Articles 7a and 130a and to enable citizens of the Union, economic operators and regional and local communities to derive full benefit from the setting up of an area without internal frontiers, the Community shall contribute to the establishment and development of trans-European networks in the areas of transport, telecommunications and energy infrastructures.

2. Within the framework of a system of open and competitive markets, action by the Community shall aim at promoting the interconnection and inter-operability of national networks as well as access to such networks. It shall take account in particular of the need to link island, landlocked and peripheral regions with the central regions of the Community.

Article 129c

1. In order to achieve the objectives referred to in Article 129b, the Community:
— shall establish a series of guidelines covering the objectives, priorities and broad lines of measures envisaged in the sphere of trans-European networks; these guidelines shall identify projects of common interest;

— shall implement any measures that may prove necessary to ensure the inter-operability of the networks, in particular in the field of technical standardisation;

— may support the financial efforts made by the Member States for projects of common interest financed by Member States, which are identified in the framework of the guidelines referred to in the first indent, particularly through feasibility studies, loan guarantees or interest rate subsidies; the Community may also contribute, through the Cohesion Fund to be set up no later than 31 December 1993 pursuant to Article 130d, to the financing of specific projects in Member States in the area of transport infrastructure.

The Community's activities shall take into account the potential economic viability of the projects.

2. Member States shall, in liaison with the Commission, co-ordinate among themselves the policies pursued at national level which may have a significant impact on the achievement of the objectives referred to in Article 129b. The Commission may, in close co-operation with the Member States, take any useful initiative to promote such co-ordination.

3. The Community may decide to co-operate with third countries to promote projects of mutual interest and to ensure the inter-operability of networks.

Article 129d

The guidelines referred to in Article 129c(1) shall be adopted by the Council, acting in accordance with the procedure referred to in Article 189b and after consulting the Economic and Social Committee and the Committee of the Regions.

Guidelines and projects of common interest which relate to the territory of a Member State shall require the approval of the Member State concerned.

The Council, acting in accordance with the procedure referred to in Article 189c and after consulting the Economic and Social Committee and the Committee of the Regions, shall adopt the other measures provided for in Article 129c(1).

TITLE XIII: Industry

Article 130

1. The Community and the Member States shall ensure that the conditions necessary for the competitiveness of the Community's industry exist.

For that purpose, in accordance with a system of open and competitive markets, their action shall be aimed at:

— speeding up the adjustment of industry to structural changes;

— encouraging an environment favourable to initiative and to the development of undertakings throughout the Community, particularly small and medium-sized undertakings;

— encouraging an environment favourable to co-operation between undertakings;

— fostering better exploitation of the industrial potential of policies of innovation, research and technological development.

2. The Member States shall consult each other in liaison with the Commission and, where necessary, shall co-ordinate their action. The Commission may take any useful initiative to promote such co-ordination.

3. The Community shall contribute to the achievement of the objectives set out in paragraph 1 through the policies and activities it pursues under other provisions of this Treaty. The Council, acting unanimously on a proposal from the Commission, after consulting the European Parliament and

the Economic and Social Committee, may decide on specific measures in support of action taken in the Member States to achieve the objectives set out in paragraph 1.

This Title shall not provide a basis for the introduction by the Community of any measure which could lead to a distortion of competition.

GENERAL NOTE

Opinions on the likely effect of this Article vary markedly. It has been argued that it will provide a basis for substantial Community expenditure on matters currently financed by the Member States (U.K. Select Committee on European Legislation, (1991–1992), H.C. 24, xlvi). The opposite view is that it marks no real change from the pre-Maastricht position. The latter view appears the more cogent. Advocates of an integrationist industrial policy are, however, more likely to be thwarted by the requirement of unanimity in Council for the adoption of any measures to support Member State action under this heading than by any restraints imposed by the wording of the Article (on reputed French desire for strongly interventionist industrial policy, at least prior to the election of a centre-right government, see Maillet, "Le Double Visage de Maastricht: Achevement et Nouveau Depart", (1992) RMC 209). Any other Community action aimed at the achievement of the objectives laid down in para. 1 will be carried out under other provisions of the Treaty. (See also Bangemann, "Pour une Politique Industrielle Européenne", (1992), RMC 367.) The last sentence of Art. 130(3) gives priority to Community competition policy over its industrial policy.

Despite the tenor of this Article, which seems to be aimed at the avoidance of an interventionist industrial policy, the Delors II package on the future financing of the Community (S.N. 456/92) adopted at the Edinburgh European Council of December 1992 places some emphasis on industrial policy, but, significantly, not in the context of the present Article. Rather, it envisages the use of an increased Social Fund to protect employees in industries under threat from competitors both within and outwith the Community (see Venables, *The Amendment of the Treaties* (1992), p. 62 and notes above on Arts. 123–125 E.C.).

TITLE XIV: Economic and Social Cohesion

GENERAL NOTE

This Title, inserted by the S.E.A. with the express purpose of securing the goals laid down under Art. 130a EEC, is re-enacted with considerable extension. The overall aim remains the strengthening of economic and social cohesion and the reduction of disparities between the levels of development of the various regions (Art. 130a E.C., which makes only very small amendments to the wording of the second paragraph). The formal provisions of this Title must be read in the light of an appended Protocol laying down various policy goals (Protocol No. 15 on Economic and Social Cohesion). The major substantive amendment to this Title is the provision for the creation of a new "Cohesion Fund" to stand alongside the three existing structural funds. Article 130d, second indent, provides that "the Council shall, before December 31, 1993, set up a Cohesion Fund to provide a financial contribution to projects in the fields of the environment and trans-European networks in the area of transport infrastructure". This fund is open to the four "cohesion countries" defined as those, at the pertinent time, whose Gross National Product per capita is below 90 per cent of the Community average. The four countries which qualify in this category are Spain, Portugal, Ireland and Greece. Other amendments relate to the procedures to be applied in the adoption and amendment of the funds themselves.

Article 130a

In order to promote its overall harmonious development, the Community shall develop and pursue its actions leading to the strengthening of its economic and social cohesion.

In particular the Community shall aim at reducing disparities between the levels of development of the various regions and the backwardness of the least-favoured regions, including rural areas.

GENERAL NOTE

Paragraph 1 of the Article is unamended by the E.U. Treaty. Paragraph 2 is amended to make explicit reference to "rural areas" being included among the "least favoured regions". The appended Protocol further elaborates the goals set out in Art. 130a E.C.

Article 130b

Member States shall conduct their economic policies and shall co-ordinate them in such a way as, in addition, to attain the objectives set out in Article 130a. The formulation and implementation of the Community's policies and actions and the implementation of the internal market shall take into account the objectives set out in Article 130a and shall contribute to their achievement. The Community shall also support the achievement of these objectives by the action it takes through the Structural Funds (European Agricultural Guidance and Guarantee Fund, Guidance Section; European Social Fund; European Regional Development Fund), the European Investment Bank and the other existing financial instruments.

The Commission shall submit a report to the European Parliament, the Council, the Economic and Social Committee and the Committee of the Regions every three years on the progress made towards achieving economic and social cohesion and on the manner in which the various means provided for in this Article have contributed to it. This report shall, if necessary, be accompanied by appropriate proposals.

If specific actions prove necessary outside the Funds and without prejudice to the measures decided upon within the framework of the other Community policies, such actions may be adopted by the Council acting unanimously on a proposal from the Commission and after consulting the European Parliament, the Economic and Social Committee and the Committee of the Regions.

GENERAL NOTE

This Article continues to place responsibility for the achievement of the goals listed in Art. 130a on the Member States. They are to be assisted by Community action in the collection and distribution of the structural funds listed under this Article and the other financial institutions mentioned, specifically the European Investment Bank.

The second paragraph to this Article is new and requires the Commission, which exercises executive responsibilities in the administration of the structural funds, to submit a report every three years to the Council, European Parliament, Economic and Social Committee and the Committee of the Regions on the progress being made towards economic and social cohesion.

The third paragraph is another addition. This permits the adoption of specific actions necessary for the achievement of the goals of economic and social cohesion, in areas where the mechanism of Fund support is inappropriate or inapplicable. Such actions are to be adopted by the Council, acting by a unanimous vote on a Commission proposal. The European Parliament, Economic and Social Committee and the Committee of the Regions are all to be consulted.

Article 130c

The European Regional Development Fund is intended to help redress the main regional imbalances in the Community through participating in the development and structural adjustment of regions whose development is lagging behind and in the conversion of declining industrial regions.

GENERAL NOTE

This Article is unamended. On the European Regional Development Fund in general see Mathijsen, *A Guide to European Union Law* (6th ed., 1995), pp. 333–340 and Scott and Mansell, "European Regional Development: Confusing Quantity with Quality?" (1993) 18 E.L.Rev. 87.

Article 130d

Without prejudice to Article 130e, the Council, acting unanimously on a proposal from the Commission and after obtaining the assent of the European Parliament and consulting the Economic and Social Committee and the Committee of the Regions, shall define the tasks, priority objectives and the organisation of the Structural Funds, which may involve grouping the Funds. The Council, acting by the same procedure, shall also define the general rules applicable to them and the provisions necessary to ensure their effectiveness and the co-ordination of the Funds with one another and with the other existing financial instruments.

The Council, acting in accordance with the same procedure, shall before 31 December 1993 set up a Cohesion Fund to provide a financial contribution to projects in the fields of environment and trans-European networks in the area of transport infrastructure.

GENERAL NOTE

This Article contains the major alteration and innovation encompassed in this Title of the Treaty. From the date of the coming into force of the E.U. Treaty, all decisions concerning the tasks, priority objectives and the organisation of the structural funds will have to be adopted in accordance with the procedure laid down in this Article. This provides for the unanimous agreement of the Council, acting on a Commission proposal. The European Parliament must then give its assent to any agreement so reached. The Committee of the Regions, with its special interest in such matters, is to be consulted, as is the Economic and Social Committee. This same procedure is also applicable for the adoption of the general rules governing the funds and the provisions necessary to ensure the effectiveness and the co-ordination of the funds with one another. In other words, effectively all subsequent decisions concerning the nature of the structural funds, rather than their implementation, will be passed in accordance with the procedure laid down in this Article. The latest alterations to the Fund regulations and, in particular, Reg. 2052/88 on the tasks of the structural funds and on the co-ordination of their activities, [1988] O.J. L185/9, were carried out under the old Art. 130d EEC. It also required unanimity in the Council and provided only for European Parliamentary consultation. The aim of these new regulations was partly to improve the effectiveness of the Funds, and partly to prepare for the smooth transition to the new period of structural fund financing beginning in 1994 (see Regs. 2081/93, 2082/93, 2083/93, 2084/93, 2085/93, [1993] O.J. L193/5-47). Any subsequent decisions governing the Funds will take place under the amended procedures laid down in these regulations.

The second paragraph of this Article makes provision for the creation of a Cohesion Fund by the end of 1993: "to provide a financial contribution to projects in the fields of the environment and trans-European networks in the area of transport infrastructure". This fund came into being on April 1, 1993, before the coming into force of the E.U. Treaty. Treaty Council Regulation 792/93 established a "temporary cohesion financial instrument" in advance of the formal Cohesion Fund which was to come into existence once the E.U. Treaty was in force, [1993] O.J. L79/44. The Edinburgh European Council meeting in December 1992 was substantially concerned with the issue of the amount of cohesion funding. The Spanish Prime Minister, Felipe Gonzalez, held out for a substantial increase in the funding applicable to his country under the new Cohesion Fund. This Fund is to apply in the areas mentioned above, *i.e.* transport infrastructure and environment, and is applicable to the four cohesion countries identified prior to the Maastricht summit as having a per capita Gross National Product of less than 90 per cent of the Community average (Greece, Ireland, Portugal and Spain). The funding which was agreed to provisionally at Edinburgh and subsequently approved provides for the four cohesion countries to see their incomes from the Funds increase by over 100 per cent in the period 1994 to 1999. The precondition of this funding, in the light of the overall pursuit of economic convergence, is that the Member States concerned must maintain a programme for the attainment of economic convergence in accordance with Art. 104c E.C. (this last obligation is substantially reiterated in Reg. 792/93 setting up the temporary cohesion funding instrument; see also the Protocol on Economic and Social Cohesion). The provision of funding in the areas specified, *viz*, environmental measures and trans-European networks, will be in the manner described under the Cohesion fund regulations and subject to the conditions laid down in the relevant Articles (on trans-European networks see Art. 129b(1) and environmental measures see Art. 130s(5)).

Regulation 792/93 on the temporary cohesion financial instrument was extended by Reg. 566/94 in March 1994. The Cohesion Fund was formally established in May 1994 by Reg. 1164/94/E.C. ([1994] O.J. L130/1).

Article 130e

Implementing decisions relating to the European Regional Development Fund shall be taken by the Council, acting in accordance with the procedure referred to in Article 189c and after consulting the Economic and Social Committee and the Committee of the Regions.

With regard to the European Agricultural Guidance and Guarantee Fund, Guidance Section, and the European Social Fund, Articles 43, and 125 respectively shall continue to apply.

GENERAL NOTE

The implementing measures to be taken concerning the European Regional Development Fund are to continue to be taken on the basis of the co-operation procedure, but the Article is amended to give a right of consultation on such measures to the Economic and Social Committee and the Committee of the Regions.

The second paragraph of this Article is amended to remove the reference to Arts. 126 and 127 which are no longer relevant in the consideration of the structural fund provisions. As a result of the E.U. Treaty amendments these Articles deal with education, vocational training and youth.

TITLE XV: Research and Technological Development

GENERAL NOTE

The provisions of the EEC Treaty inserted by the S.E.A. governing the research and technological development policy of the Community were long and complex (Arts. 130f–q EEC). The amendments made at Maastricht primarily aim to redefine and extend the powers of the Community in this area. The final result is little more than a tidying up exercise. While the legislative procedures relevant to this Title have been altered, the overall regime familiar after the S.E.A. amendments to the EEC Treaty remains. This regime consists primarily of the adoption of a multiannual framework programme defining the objectives, priorities and extent of overall Community finance for the research and development programme (Art. 130i). The Council then, acting on the basis of a Commission proposal, passes specific programmes governing particular areas of research and technological development (Art. 130i(4)). These specific programmes must be geared to the achievement of the aims listed in Art. 130g, be in accordance with the multiannual framework programme, and lay down detailed rules for their implementation, duration and envisaged cost (Art. 130i(3)).

One of the most pertinent amendments made is to the procedure for the adoption of the multi-annual framework programme (Art. 130i E.C.). Under the Maastricht amendments, this is to be achieved through the conciliation and veto procedure under Art. 189b E.C. but tied to the achievement of unanimity in Council. The Commission had sought the application of qualified majority voting to this programme, and not only to the sectoral programmes adopted under it. This was provided for in both the Luxembourg and Dutch draft Treaties but removed at the Maastricht meeting itself. The Commission's support for the application of the qualified majority procedure was aimed at the alleviation of the delays caused trying to secure such unanimous agreement. The delay in the adoption of the four-year framework programme leads to related delays in the application of the sectoral programmes themselves and causes problems as to their continuity. If the Council had difficulty securing the adoption of such measures with a Council of 12, it will find it more difficult with a Community of 15 Member States (or the 20 that are projected for a few years' time). Nevertheless, the adoption of the first multiannual framework programme; requiring a unanimous vote in the Council under the old Art. 130q EEC, proceeded relatively expeditiously (Council Decision 87/516, [1987] O.J. L302/1). The right to pass the implementing measures adopted under the multiannual framework programme had also been sought by the Commission, but this right remains with the Council (Art. 130o and see E.C. Bull. Supp. 2/91, at 137). For the 1990–1994 multiannual framework programme see Decision 90/221 ([1990] O.J. L117/28). The adoption of the framework programme for 1994–1998 was the occasion of considerable muscle-flexing by the newly empowered Parliament, which forced an increase in planned expenditure (see Council and Parliament Decision 1110/94, [1994] O.J. L126/1). Under the multiannual framework programme a vast number of specific programmes has appeared in diverse fields such as energy technology (THERMIE), telecommunications (RACE), agriculture and industry (ECLAIR), etc. For a detailed breakdown of these projects, see Commission D.G. XII Catalogue, 1992.

Another important amendment is made in Art. 130f on the goals of the Community research policy. The old Art. 130f advocated research solely for the purpose of increasing the competitiveness of European industry. This has now been qualified by an acceptance that research is to be encouraged where "it is deemed necessary by virtue of other chapters of the Treaty". In this respect it is likely that the research may well continue mainly along the lines of increasing the wealth-creation potential of Community industry, but it will also have regard to the environmental impact of such increased competitiveness, and other related factors such as the quality of life.

On the Community's research and development programmes in general see Mathijsen, *A Guide to European Union Law* (6th ed., 1995), pp. 341–5, and Peterson, "Technology Policy in Europe: Explaining the Framework Programme and Eureka in Theory and Practice", 29 Journal of Common Market Studies, 269–290.

Article 130f

1. The Community shall have the objective of strengthening the scientific and technological bases of Community industry and encouraging it to become more competitive at international level, while promoting all the research activities deemed necessary by virtue of other Chapters of this Treaty.

2. For this purpose the Community shall, throughout the Community encourage undertakings, including small and medium-sized undertakings, research centres and universities in their research and technological development activities of high quality; it shall support their efforts to co-operate with one another, aiming, notably, at enabling undertakings to exploit the internal market potential to the full, in particular through the opening up of national public contracts, the definition of common standards and the removal of legal and fiscal obstacles to that co-operation.

3. All Community activities under this Treaty in the area of research and technological development, including demonstration projects, shall be decided on and implemented in accordance with the provisions of this Title.

GENERAL NOTE

The first paragraph of this Article is amended so that the Community's objective in the field of research and technological development shall also include the promotion of "all research activities deemed necessary by virtue of other chapters of the Treaty". Thus the promotion of research and development is not to be tied exclusively to the promotion of industrial competitiveness but is to be utilised for other goals. One likely area for promotion is the research and development necessary for the achievement of effective environmental protection under the strengthened Title XVI.

The third paragraph of this Article makes another important alteration to the existing provision. The new wording ties the achievement of all Community activities in the field of research and development to the procedures laid down in this title. This effectively means that action under Art. 100a E.C. or Art. 235 E.C. is effectively precluded. Both of these provisions have been used in the past to promulgate specific measures in this field (see Usher, "The Development of Community Powers under the S.E.A.", in Whyte & Smythe eds., *Current Issues in European and International Law* (1990)). It applies equally to the use of any other Treaty provision for the adoption of research and development measures, something which has been done before. The vocational training Article, Art. 128 EEC, has been used as the basis for COMETT decisions, the programme for co-operation between universities and industry regarding training in the field of technology (Council Decision 89/27, [1989] O.J. L13/28). This decision was taken under Art. 128 EEC., despite the explicit inclusion in Art. 130g EEC, as one of the goals of the research and development title, of "the stimulation of the training and mobility of researchers in the Community". While research and development programmes are now to be aimed at the achievement of other Treaty goals (Art. 130f(1)), it will not be possible to base them on any other Treaty provision. Thus, any attempt to secure a more "favourable" legal base (such as the simple majority vote which originally applied under Art. 128 EEC) will be readily susceptible to challenge under the new Art. 130f.

Article 130g

In pursuing these objectives the Community shall carry out the following activities, complementing the activities carried out in the Member States:

(a) implementation of research, technological development and demonstration programmes, by promoting co-operation with and between undertakings, research centres and universities;

(b) promotion of co-operation in the field of Community research, technological development, and demonstration with third countries and international organisations;
(c) dissemination and optimisation of the results of activities in Community research, technological development, and demonstration;
(d) stimulation of the training and mobility of researchers in the Community.

GENERAL NOTE

The activities of the Community laid out in this Article are unamended. They must, however, be read in the light of the extended Community rôle laid out in Art. 130h.

Article 130h

1. The Community and the Member States shall co-ordinate their research and technological development activities so as to ensure that national policies and Community policy are mutually consistent.
2. In close co-operation with the Member States, the Commission may take any useful initiative to promote the co-ordination referred to in paragraph 1.

GENERAL NOTE

Under the old Art. 130h, the Member States were to "co-ordinate among themselves the policies and programmes carried out at national level". The Commission was to have a liaison role in this process. The amended Article shifts the onus of action towards the Community by providing that the Community and the Member States are to co-ordinate their research so as to ensure that "national policies and Community policy are mutually consistent". This marks a significant expansion of the Community's role in this area. Moreover, the Commission is empowered to "take any useful initiative to promote such co-operation". This will permit it to act in a much broader area than was the case when it was simply a liaison body for the Member States, ensuring merely the co-ordination of national measures rather than Community and national actions.

Article 130i

1. A multiannual framework programme, setting out all the activities of the Community, shall be adopted by the Council, acting in accordance with the procedure referred to in Article 189b after consulting the Economic and Social Committee. The Council shall act unanimously throughout the procedures referred to in Article 189b.
The framework programme shall:
— establish the scientific and technological objectives to be achieved by the activities provided for in Article 130g and fix the relevant priorities;
— indicate the broad lines of such activities;
— fix the maximum overall amount and the detailed rules for Community financial participation in the framework programme and the respective shares in each of the activities provided for.
2. The framework programme shall be adapted or supplemented as the situation changes.
3. The framework programme shall be implemented through specific programmes developed within each activity. Each specific programme shall define the detailed rules for implementing it, fix its duration and provide for the means deemed necessary. The sum of the amounts deemed necessary, fixed in the specific programmes, may not exceed the overall maximum amount fixed for the framework programme and each activity.
4. The Council, acting by a qualified majority on a proposal from the Commission and after consulting the European Parliament and the Economic and Social Committee, shall adopt the specific programmes.

GENERAL NOTE

This Article lays down the means by which the measures to be adopted under this Title will come about. The two-tier approach of multiannual framework and subordinate specific programmes remains, but the procedures for their adoption are altered. Article 130i(1) dictates that the conciliation and veto procedure shall apply to the adoption of the multiannual framework programmes. This is to be tied to the requirement of unanimity in Council. The old procedure, that of unanimity in Council and the consultation of the European Parliament at least had the advantage of being relatively simple, procedurally. The conciliation and veto procedure, where it is tied to a requirement of unanimity in Council, amounts to a very significant procedural challenge to the adoption of any measures. Moreover, the procedure can last upwards of nine months. While the adoption of the multiannual framework programme is made more difficult, so the adoption of the specific programmes is simplified. The old procedure called for the adoption of such measures under the co-operation procedure, the new Art. 130i(4) simply provides for a qualified majority vote in the Council and the consultation of the European Parliament. Thus while the procedure is simplified, it also marks a downgrading of the role of the European Parliament.

In the light of the Community drive for financial efficiency, the amended Art. 130i(3) provides that the "sum of the amounts deemed necessary, fixed in the specific programmes, may not exceed the overall maximum amount fixed for the framework programme and each activity". This places a more stringent duty on the Community and Member States to keep within budget than was the case under the similarly worded Art. 130p EEC.

Article 130j

For the implementation of the multiannual framework programme the Council shall:
— determine the rules for the participation of undertakings, research centres and universities;
— lay down the rules governing the dissemination of research results.

GENERAL NOTE

While this Article is new, the matters contained therein have already been dealt with in the implementation of previous multiannual framework programmes. The Council adopted a specific programme for the dissemination and utilisation of research results (Value) (XXIII General Report of the EEC (1989), p. 164). University involvement in the research development process of the Communities has also been long recognised (Commission, D.G. XIII, Report on University and Research Interfaces in Europe, 1992). The Article merely formalises existing practice.

Article 130k

In implementing the multiannual framework programme, supplementary programmes may be decided on involving the participation of certain Member States only, which shall finance them subject to possible Community participation.

The Council shall adopt the rules applicable to supplementary programmes, particularly as regards the dissemination of knowledge and access by other Member States.

GENERAL NOTE

This, and the following Articles, simply reiterate the existing provisions of the Title, but with some consequential amendments to take account of the amended legislative procedures applicable in this field. Article 130p is the only new addition among the remaining Articles. Some reallocation of the content of the provisions in this Title has led to Art. 130q being repealed.

Article 130l

In implementing the multiannual framework programme the Community may make provision, in agreement with the Member States concerned, for participation in research and development programmes undertaken by several Member States, including participation in the structures created for the execution of those programmes.

Article 130m

In implementing the multiannual framework programme the Community may make provision for co-operation in Community research, technological development and demonstration with third countries or international organisations.

The detailed arrangements for such co-operation may be the subject of agreements between the Community and the third parties concerned, which shall be negotiated and concluded in accordance with Article 228.

Article 130n

The Community may set up joint undertakings or any other structure necessary for the efficient execution of Community research, technological development and demonstration programmes.

Article 130o

The Council, acting unanimously on a proposal from the Commission and after consulting the European Parliament and the Economic and Social Committee, shall adopt the provisions referred to in Article 130n.

The Council, acting in accordance with the procedure referred to in Article 189c and after consulting the Economic and Social Committee, shall adopt the provisions referred to in Articles 130j to 130l. Adoption of the supplementary programmes shall require the agreement of the Member States concerned.

Article 130p

At the beginning of each year the Commission shall send a report to the European Parliament and the Council. The report shall include information on research and technological development activities and the dissemination of results during the previous year, and the work programme for the current year.

GENERAL NOTE

This Article, added by the E.U. Treaty, provides for the Commission to send a report to the European Parliament and the Council on the research and development programme.

Article 130q

(Repealed at Maastricht)

TITLE XVI: Environment

GENERAL NOTE

Articles 130r to 130t E.C. on the environment are substantially amended. The environment, from being an area of Community action, is promoted to a Community policy. While the objectives of this policy remain substantially unaltered, attempts are made to include environmental considerations into other areas of Community competence (Art. 130r(2)). The principle of minimum harmonisation, applicable to the environment since its inclusion in the Treaties by the S.E.A., continues to be applicable. This principle dictates that the measures laid down by the Community with the aim of securing the goals under this heading shall not preclude the Member States from maintaining or introducing more stringent protective measures (Art. 130t E.C.). Such a provision is especially relevant as regards the environment, where levels of protection are manifestly different throughout the Member States and yet the most effective protection available is the common goal. A strict harmonising approach to the subject would lead to unattainable targets being set in certain Member States, while the more "developed" Member States would be forced to reduce the level of environmental protection previously enjoyed. Therefore, environmental protection measures were made subject to the doctrine of minimum harmonisation. The adverse effects which such an approach has on market uniformity are tempered somewhat by the requirements laid down, under Art. 130t, of Commission notification and compliance with the fundamental norms of the Community system. The necessity of such minimum harmonisation should be somewhat mitigated by the introduction of the Cohesion Fund to assist those countries to whom the fund is applicable, including Ireland, by enabling them to draw on the funds therein for environmental projects which would otherwise require them to incur disproportionate expenditure (Art. 130s(5) E.C.).

The existing environmental protection legislation enacted by the Community covers a vast range of areas and there is an ever growing corpus of Community law dealing with such matters. The Community is now active in the fields of aquatic environment, air pollution, noise abatement, control of chemicals, industrial hazards and biotechnology, conservation of the natural heritage, etc. (see Mathijsen, *A Guide to European Union Law* (6th ed., 1995), pp. 346–51). The Treaty amendments introduce the goal of securing the future sustainable growth of industry, *et al.* (Art. 2 E.C.). The concept of sustainable growth seems to be used almost interchangeably with the notion of sustainable development as espoused in the Commission document *Towards Sustainability*, E.C. Commission, Luxembourg, Office for Official Publications of the E.C. (1993). Sustainable development has been approved by the Heads of Government and of State of the Community in a Declaration of June 26, 1990, and underlays the Treaty which emerged from the United Nations Conference on Environment and Development (U.N.C.E.D.) in Rio de Janeiro on June 3–14, 1992. Whatever approach the Community is to take, the vast majority of the legislative enactments in this field are in the form of directives, and the supervision of their implementation is one of the most demanding tasks placed upon the Commission. For an excellent analysis of the rate of national compliance with Community law in this sector see Macrory, "The Enforcement of Community Environmental Laws: Some Critical Issues" (1992) 29 C.M.L.Rev. 364 (see also House of Lords, Select Committee on the E.C., Implementation and enforcement of environmental legislation, 9th Report, Session 1991–92). It is quite likely that the new principle of State responsibility enunciated in *Francovich and Bonifaci v. Italy* (Cases C–6/90 and 9/90, [1991] E.C.R. 5359 will prove most influential in this field. (See Murgatroyd, "State Liability and the European Environment: *Francovich*, Maastricht and the Question of Compensation" (1993) 1 *Environmental Liability* 11 and Crocket & Schultz, "The Integration of Environmental Policy and the E.C.: Recent Problems of Implementation and Enforcement", 29 Col. Jl. Transnational L. 169.)

Article 130r

1. Community policy on the environment shall contribute to pursuit of the following objectives:
   — preserving, protecting and improving the quality of the environment;
   — protecting human health;
   — prudent and rational utilisation of natural resources;
   — promoting measures at international level to deal with regional or worldwide environmental problems.

2. Community policy on the environment shall aim at a high level of protection taking into account the diversity of situations in the various regions of the Community. It shall be based on the precautionary principle and on the principles that preventive action should be taken, that environmental damage should as a priority be rectified at source and that the polluter should pay. Environmental protection requirements must be integrated into the definition and implementation of other Community policies.

In this context, harmonisation measures answering these requirements shall include, where appropriate, a safeguard clause allowing Member States to take provisional measures, for non-economic environmental reasons, subject to a Community inspection procedure.

3. In preparing its policy on the environment, the Community shall take account of:
   — available scientific and technical data;
   — environmental conditions in the various regions of the Community;
   — the potential benefits and costs of action or lack of action;

— the economic and social development of the Community as a whole and the balanced development of its regions.

4. Within their respective spheres of competence, the Community and the Member States shall co-operate with third countries and with the competent international organisations.

The arrangements for Community co-operation may be the subject of agreements between the Community and the third parties concerned, which shall be negotiated and concluded in accordance with Article 228.

The previous subparagraph shall be without prejudice to Member States' competence to negotiate in international bodies and to conclude international agreements.

GENERAL NOTE

The fourth indent of this Article is a new addition to the list of Community objectives in the field of the environment. However, it does little more than entrench existing practice, with the express duty imposed on the Community to promote "measures at international level to deal with regional or world-wide environmental problems". This is quite in keeping with policies adopted by the Community in the numerous environmental measures promulgated both prior to and subsequent to the S.E.A. The Community has long recognised that environmental policy must take account of such trans-boundary problems as global warming, tropical deforestation, acid rain, etc. The Community has been a party to the majority of the international initiatives in these fields, *e.g.* the Convention on International Trade in Endangered Species of Wild Flora and Fauna ([1982] O.J. L384/1, modified [1989] O.J. L66/24); see also Art. 130r(4) E.C.).

Para. (2)
Added to the first paragraph of this Article is the obligation that environmental protection requirements be integrated into the definition and implementation of other Community policies. This marks a realisation that environmental matters cannot be considered in isolation and signals a more dynamic integrative approach than that included in the old Art. 130r(2) EEC, which stated that "environmental protection requirements shall be a component of the Community's other policies". The new approach is evident in the recent Commission strategy on the common transport policy. Mirroring the current environmental buzz-words "sustainable growth", the common transport strategy is to be based on "sustainable mobility", whereby the new transport policy will aim to enhance the economic and social benefits of all means of transport whilst reducing their environmental impact (see COM (92) 48 final).

Para. (3)
This Article is unamended but, in the light of the new commitment to cohesion funding for the less developed regions of the Community, to assist with environmental projects, the second and fourth indents of this Article are given a new relevance.

Para. (4)
The old Art. 130r(4) EEC is replaced by what was the old Art. 130r(5) EEC. The repealed provision contained an implicit reference to the principle of subsidiarity, stating that "the Community shall take action relating to the environment to the extent to which objectives referred to in para. 1 can be attained better at Community level". This Article has been replaced by the general notion of subsidiarity encompassed in Art. 3b E.C. Nevertheless, the principle included in the old Art. 130r(4) EEC seems to have been worded in a manner more conducive to Community action. This Article presented the first bite of the legislative cherry to the Community, subject to the proviso that it should renounce its competence if it were proved that the action could be better achieved by the Member States. Under the new Art. 3b E.C., the burden is subtly altered with the insertion of the condition that the Community shall act, but only if and in so far as the objectives of the proposed action cannot be sufficiently achieved by the Member States. The words "only in so far as" and "sufficiently achieved" would seem to shift the presumption towards Member State action.

Article 130s

1. The Council, acting in accordance with the procedure referred to in Article 189c and after consulting the Economic and Social Committee, shall decide what action is to be taken by the Community in order to achieve the objectives referred to in Article 130r.

2. By way of derogation from the decision-making procedure provided for in paragraph 1 and without prejudice to Article 100a, the Council, acting unanimously on a proposal from the Commission and after consulting the European Parliament and the Economic and Social Committee, shall adopt:
— provisions primarily of a fiscal nature;
— measures concerning town and country planning, land use with the exception of waste management and measures of a general nature, and management of water resources;
— measures significantly affecting a Member State's choice between different energy sources and the general structure of its energy supply.

The Council may, under the conditions laid down in the preceding subparagraph, define those matters referred to in this paragraph on which decisions are to be taken by a qualified majority.

3. In other areas, general action programmes setting out priority objectives to be attained shall be adopted by the Council, acting in accordance with the procedure referred to in Article 189b and after consulting the Economic and Social Committee.

The Council, acting under the terms of paragraph 1 or paragraph 2 according to the case, shall adopt the measures necessary for the implementation of these programmes.

4. Without prejudice to certain measures of a Community nature, the Member States shall finance and implement the environment policy.

5. Without prejudice to the principle that the polluter should pay, if a measure based on the provisions of paragraph 1 involves costs deemed disproportionate for the public authorities of a Member State, the Council shall, in the act adopting that measure, lay down appropriate provisions in the form of:
— temporary derogations and/or
— financial support from the Cohesion Fund to be set up no later than 31 December 1993 pursuant to Article 130d.

GENERAL NOTE

This Article lays down the applicable legislative procedures for the adoption of Community measures in the field of environmental protection. The applicable procedure will depend on the specific type of measure envisaged. This Article, taken as a whole, is often given as an example of the convoluted legislative pattern introduced by the E.U. Treaty amendments, with the existence of widely varying legislative procedures. In Art. 130s alone, there are three different legislative procedures available. This state of affairs will no doubt lead to challenges to the legal base, especially with all too predictable divergent interpretations. When the difference between procedures is the difference between being outvoted in Council or not, or alternatively in the case of the European Parliament, the difference between mere consultation and an actual say in the legislative measure, the stakes are undeniably raised.

Para. (1)

This Article lays down the basic legislative procedure envisaged by the Treaty for the adoption of measures aimed at the securing of the objectives in Art. 130r. Such measures are to be adopted under the co-operation procedure, which opens up this area of environmental policy to the scope of qualified majority voting (previously unanimity under Art. 130s EEC). This type of voting will apply to a wide variety of legislation, given the broad legislative base of Art. 130r.

Para. (2)

This Article marks a significant broadening of the future scope of Community environmental action. The Community is to have the power to adopt measures under the three new headings listed. The most hotly debated heading was the first one, permitting the adoption of "provisions primarily of a fiscal nature". This refers to the potential imposition of so-called "energy taxes" aimed at the economic enforcement of prudent energy policies (see U.K. House of Lords, Select Committee on the E.C., Carbon/Energy Tax, 8th Report, Session 1991–92). It has long been accepted that the most efficient means of securing alternative consumer and industry compliance with environmental guidelines is through the imposition of punitive taxation on harmful and less environmentally friendly practices. This view has been supported by the experience of a higher level of taxation on leaded petrol, with the aim of transferring motorists to the more environmentally friendly lead-free variety. The first indent of this Article makes provision for the imposition of such taxes on a Community scale and in a wide variety of areas.

The inclusion of this provision marks the recognition that the achievement of the goal of "sustainability" cannot be done simply through the setting of limits on pollutants. The scope for financial legislation and broadened competences is necessary to achieve such a goal. Nevertheless, the sensitivity of this, and the other two areas under this heading, has led to their being made exceptions to the general qualified majority voting rule applicable to the other areas of environmental protection. The relevant procedure regarding the adoption of measures under these headings is unanimity in the Council following a Commission proposal; the European Parliament and the Economic and Social Committee are to be consulted on any such actions. Nevertheless, provision is made for the alteration to the qualified majority procedure for whichever of these headings the Council selects without the necessity of a further inter-governmental conference. The decision to make such a transferral is to be taken by unanimity under the procedure laid down for the adoption of measures in this field.

The energy tax proposal of the Commission has not been able to make much headway in the Council under the present unanimity requirement. The President of the Commission, Jacques Delors, remarked in December 1994 in the European Parliament just before his retirement on the "increasingly pathetic compromises" in this regard, as the Essen European Council summit provided a framework for some countries immediately to apply the tax (*Agence Europe* No. 6379, December 15, 1994), with the Commission giving guidelines to Member States on how to apply the tax.

Para. (3)

This Article makes provision for the adoption of general action programmes which will set out the priority objectives of the environmental policy. This is to be achieved under the conciliation and veto procedure. The specific action programmes to be adopted under this heading will be the subject of the procedures applicable by reference to paras. 1 and 2; therefore, if the measure concerns a fiscal provision then this will be dealt with by unanimity under para. 2, etc.

Article 130t

The protective measures adopted in common pursuant to Article 130s shall not prevent any Member State from maintaining or introducing more stringent protective measures. Such measures must be compatible with this Treaty. They shall be notified to the Commission.

GENERAL NOTE

This Article lays down the notion of minimum harmonisation whereby the existence of Community protective measures shall not prevent any Member State from maintaining or introducing more stringent protective measures. While such provisions detract from the notion of uniformity in the common market, they do reflect the notion of subsidiarity, in that they envisage the development of different levels of regulatory competence in the Community (see Bieber, (1988) 13 E.L.Rev. 147). The measures taken by the Member States must however be compatible with the Treaty itself. This inevitably involves a balancing of the relative weights of the arguments on either side. This was highlighted in the "Danish bottle" case (Case 302/86, *Commission v. Denmark* [1988] E.C.R. 4607; see Sexton, "Enacting National Environmental Laws more stringent than other States' Laws in the European Community: *Re Disposable Beer Cans: Commission v. Denmark*", 24 Cornell Int. L. J. 563).

As with the pre-existing provision under the EEC Treaty, each Member State is under an obligation to notify the Commission of national protective measures more stringent than the underlying Community rule. This gives the Commission, the body which exercises the majority of executive responsibilities in this field, the opportunity to assess the compliance of such measures with the Treaties and advise the Member State accordingly.

TITLE XVII: Development Co-operation

GENERAL NOTE

Articles 130u–130y provide a specific legal base for policies currently carried out in various ad hoc ways. The object of such policies is laid down in Art. 130u(1) and it is provided that any actions by the Community in other policy areas must always take account of these factors and the effect its actions will have on the developing countries (Art. 130v). The primary means of achieving the goals set out is the negotiation of international agreements with the third countries concerned. Article 130y provides for a link with the amended Art. 228 E.C.

Article 130u

1. Community policy in the sphere of development co-operation which shall be complementary to the policies pursued by the Member States, shall foster:
   — the sustainable economic and social development of the developing countries, and more particularly the most disadvantaged among them;
   — the smooth and gradual integration of the developing countries into the world economy;
   — the campaign against poverty in the developing countries.
2. The Community policy in this area shall contribute to the general objective of developing and consolidating democracy and the rule of law, and to that of respecting human rights and fundamental freedoms.
3. The Community and the Member States shall comply with the commitments and take account of the objectives they have approved in the context of the United Nations and other competent international organisations.

GENERAL NOTE

Paragraph 1 of this Article provides that the action of the Community in this field is to be complementary to that of the Member States. The goals at which Community policy is to aim are then set out. Paragraph 2 lays out the political motivation for the achievement of these goals, such as the consolidation of democracy and respect for human rights. The pursuit of development co-operation prior to the completion of the E.U. Treaty, in the main carried out under the Afro-Caribbean-Pacific conventions (see note on Art. 130y), always had the realisation of these goals set out in the relevant Treaties. In a joint declaration contained in Annex I to the final Act in the signature of the Third Lomé convention, the contracting parties reiterated their obligations in the field of human rights. In the absence of any sanction procedure (now incidentally provided by Art. 228a in the field of the common foreign and security policy), the inclusion of such duties will remain of purely verbal significance; certain of the contracting States have less than perfect human rights records.

Article 130v

The Community shall take account of the objectives referred to in Article 130u in the policies that it implements which are likely to affect developing countries.

Article 130w

1. Without prejudice to the other provisions of this Treaty the Council, acting in accordance with the procedure referred to in Article 189c, shall adopt the measures necessary to further the objectives referred to in Article 130u. Such measures may take the form of multiannual programmes.
2. The European Investment Bank shall contribute, under the terms laid down in its Statute, to the implementation of the measures referred to in paragraph 1.
3. The provisions of this Article shall not affect co-operation with the African, Caribbean and Pacific countries in the framework of the ACP-EEC Convention.

GENERAL NOTE

The adoption of the measures to further the objectives of this Title is to be by the co-operation procedure. Unusually, the Community is given the discretion as to whether or not the adoption of multi-annual programmes is the best means of achieving these goals. It is more than likely that some form of general programme will be laid down in this field. Paragraph 3 of this Article makes clear that the established Afro-Caribbean-Pacific-EEC agreements will continue to be applicable.

Article 130x

1. The Community and the Member States shall co-ordinate their policies on development co-operation and shall consult each other on their aid programmes, including in international organisations and during international conferences. They may undertake joint action. Member States shall contribute if necessary to the implementation of Community aid programmes.
2. The Commission may take any useful initiative to promote the co-ordination referred to in paragraph 1.

GENERAL NOTE

This Article marks, arguably, the most important part of this Title. It provides that the Member States will be obliged to co-ordinate their actions with each other and with the Community, as well as consulting each other on their aid programmes. Thus some form of "Community" action is ensured in all areas, irrespective of whether or not the Community has an agreement up and running in the area. Thus the Member States will be in a position to respond rapidly to any urgent situation without formal co-operation and this will serve to co-ordinate their actions and thus alleviate waste and unnecessary expense. The Member States are similarly required to co-ordinate their actions and consult each other in international bodies and negotiations. The Commission will exercise a general co-ordination role in this respect, the second paragraph empowering it to take any useful initiative in this field.

Article 130y

Within their respective spheres of competence, the Community and the Member States shall co-operate with third countries and with the competent international organisations. The arrangements for Community co-operation may be the subject of agreements between the Community and the third parties concerned, which shall be negotiated and concluded in accordance with Article 228.

The previous paragraph shall be without prejudice to Member States' competence to negotiate in international bodies and to conclude international agreements.

GENERAL NOTE

This Article primarily provides for the adoption of international agreements, with the purpose of securing the goals laid out in Art. 130u(1). This has been the most popular means of securing development co-operation prior to the inclusion of an explicit legal base in the Treaty. The best known of such international agreements are the three Lomé conventions which set the ground for the co-operation between the Community and the Afro-Caribbean-Pacific countries. The essential basis of these conventions is their provision for trade and commodities co-operation. The fourth Lomé convention took effect on March 1, 1990 and will continue in existence for double the period common to its predecessors, expiring in the year 2000 (first Lomé convention, [1976] O.J. L25/1; second, [1980] O.J. L347/1; third [1986] O.J. L86/3; fourth, [1990] O.J. L84/4; see on these conventions, Simmonds, "The Lomé Convention and the New International Economic Order" (1976) 13 C.M.L.Rev. 315; "The Second Lomé Convention: The Innovative Features" (1980) 17 C.M.L.Rev. 99; "The Third Lomé Convention" (1985) 22 C.M.L.Rev. 389; "The Fourth Lomé Convention" (1991) 28 C.M.L.Rev. 521). Any renegotiation of this convention in the meantime will take place under the new Art. 228 procedure, which is explicitly referred to under this heading. The same procedure is applicable for any other development agreements entered into after the coming into force of the E.U. Treaty.

PART FOUR (ASSOCIATION OF THE OVERSEAS COUNTRIES AND TERRITORIES)

Article 131

The Member States agree to associate with the Community the non-European countries and territories which have special relations with Belgium, Denmark, France, Italy, the Netherlands and the United Kingdom.

These countries and territories (hereinafter called the 'countries and territories') are listed in Annex IV to this Treaty.

The purpose of association shall be to promote the economic and social development of the countries and territories and to establish close economic relations between them and the Community as a whole.

In accordance with the principles set out in the Preamble to this Treaty, association shall serve primarily to further the interests and prosperity of the inhabitants of these countries and territories in order to lead them to the economic, social and cultural development to which they aspire.

Article 132

Association shall have the following objectives:

1. Member States shall apply to their trade with the countries and territories the same treatment as they accord each other pursuant to this Treaty.

2. Each country or territory shall apply to its trade with Member States and with the other countries and territories the same treatment as that which it applies to the European State with which it has special relations.

3. The Member States shall contribute to the investments required for the progressive development of these countries and territories.

4. For investments financed by the Community, participation in tenders and supplies shall be open on equal terms to all natural and legal persons who are nationals of a Member State or of one of the countries and territories.

5. In relations between Member States and the countries and territories the right of establishment of nationals and companies or firms shall be regulated in accordance with the provisions and procedures laid down in the Chapter relating to the right of establishment and on a non-discriminatory basis, subject to any special provisions laid down pursuant to Article 136.

Article 133

1. Customs duties on imports into the Member States of goods originating in the countries and territories shall be completely abolished in conformity with the progressive abolition of customs duties between Member States in accordance with the provisions of this Treaty.

2. Customs duties on imports into each country or territory from Member States or from the other countries or territories shall be progressively abolished in accordance with the provisions of Articles 12, 13, 14, 15 and 17.

3. The countries and territories may, however, levy customs duties which meet the needs of their development and industrialisation or produce revenue for their budgets.

The duties referred to in the preceding subparagraph shall nevertheless be progressively reduced to the level of those imposed on imports of products from the Member State with which each country or territory has special relations. The percentages and the timetable of the reductions provided for under this Treaty shall apply to the difference between the duty imposed on a product coming from the Member State which has special relations with the country or territory concerned and the duty imposed on the same product coming from within the Community on entry into the importing country or territory.

4. Paragraph 2 shall not apply to countries and territories which, by reason of the particular international obligations by which they are bound, already apply a non-discriminatory customs tariff when this Treaty enters into force.

5. The introduction of or any change in customs duties imposed on goods imported into the countries and territories shall not, either in law or in fact,

give rise to any direct or indirect discrimination between imports from the various Member States.

Article 134

If the level of the duties applicable to goods from a third country on entry into a country or territory is liable, when the provisions of Article 133(1) have been applied, to cause deflections of trade to the detriment of any Member State, the latter may request the Commission to propose to the other Member States the measures needed to remedy the situation.

Article 135

Subject to the provisions relating to public health, public security or public policy, freedom of movement within Member States for workers from the countries and territories, and within the countries and territories for workers from Member States, shall be governed by agreements to be concluded subsequently with the unanimous approval of Member States.

Article 136

For an initial period of five years after the entry into force of this Treaty, the details of and procedure for the association of the countries and territories with the Community shall be determined by an Implementing Convention annexed to this Treaty.

Before the Convention referred to in the preceding paragraph expires, the Council shall, acting unanimously, lay down provisions for a further period, on the basis of the experience acquired and of the principles set out in this Treaty.

Article 136a

The provisions of Articles 131 to 136 shall apply to Greenland, subject to the specific provisions for Greenland set out in the Protocol on special arrangements for Greenland, annexed to this Treaty.

PART FIVE (INSTITUTIONS OF THE COMMUNITY)

TITLE I: Provisions Governing the Institutions

Chapter 1 (The Institutions)

Section 1: The European Parliament

Article 137

The European Parliament, which shall consist of representatives of the peoples of the States brought together in the Community, shall exercise the powers conferred upon it by this Treaty.

GENERAL NOTE

The amendment to this Article marks an acknowledgement of the developing powers of the European Parliament. The introduction of the conciliation and veto procedure (Art. 189b E.C.), while far from perfect, marks the first time that the European Parliament has had the opportunity to veto legislation approved by the Council. The Maastricht Treaty has also strengthened or formalised the role of the Parliament in other areas, such as the appointment of the Commission. There is still, however, some distance to go before the democratic deficit in the Community is addressed: in other words, powers transferred from national parliaments to the European level are not yet subject to adequate control by a democratically elected body in the

European legislative process (see European Parliament Report on the Democratic Deficit in the E.C., rapporteur M. Toussaint, European Parliament Document A2–276/87 and Lodge, *The Democratic Deficit and the European Parliament*, Fabian Society, 1991). The Maastricht amendments do however mark the greatest single increase in the powers of the European Parliament since the establishment of the Community. In this respect, the wording of the old Art. 137 EEC alluding to the "advisory and supervisory powers" of the European Parliament was somewhat out of date. The new Article reflects the broader scope of European Parliament influence, making reference simply to the "powers conferred upon it by this Treaty" (see Bradley, "Better Rusty than Missin': The Institutional Reforms of the Maastricht Treaty and the European Parliament", in O'Keeffe & Twomey eds. *Legal Issues of the Maastricht Treaty* (1994) p. 193).

Article 138

(Paras. 1 and 2 as replaced by Direct Elections Act, Arts. 1 and 2)

1. The representatives in the European Parliament of the peoples of the States brought together in the Community shall be elected by direct universal suffrage.

2. The number of representatives elected in each Member State is as follows:

Austria	21
Belgium	24
Denmark	16
Finland	16
Germany	81
Greece	24
Spain	60
France	81
Ireland	15
Italy	81
Luxembourg	6
Netherlands	25
Portugal	24
Sweden	22
United Kingdom	81

3. The European Parliament shall draw up proposals for elections by direct universal suffrage in accordance with a uniform procedure in all Member States.

The Council shall, acting unanimously after obtaining the assent of the European Parliament, which shall act by a majority of its component members, lay down the appropriate provisions, which it shall recommend to Member States for adoption in accordance with their respective constitutional requirements.

GENERAL NOTE

One amendment to this Article is made not by the TEU but by the decision taken at the Edinburgh European Council to increase the number of M.E.P.'s, primarily to take account of German reunification. Article 138(2) was amended accordingly. The number of seats is now as follows (pre-Edinburgh summit figures in brackets): Belgium 25 (24); Denmark 16 (16); Germany 99 (81); Greece 25 (24); Spain 64 (60); France 87 (81); Ireland 15 (15); Italy 87 (81); Luxembourg 6 (6); Netherlands 31 (25); Portugal 25 (24) and U.K. 87 (81). (Conclusions of the Presidency, point 26 and Decision of February 1, 1993, [1993] O.J. L33/15). These changes helped to give better representation to the more populous Member States. The smaller Member States, such as Ireland, are still significantly over-represented, on the ratio of M.E.P.s to head of population. One significant aspect of the new allocation of M.E.P.s is that Germany now has more of them than the other major states (France, Italy and U.K.). This reflects the fact that East Germany has been absorbed into Germany and needed to be represented in the European Parliament without diminishing West German representation, and that unification had given Germany a population significantly larger than the three next largest Member States.

Further amendments were made to provide for the accession of the new Member States. Austria will be represented by 20 M.E.P.s, Finland by 16 and Sweden by 21.

Para. (3)

The first sentence of para. (3) remains unchanged. The basic principle still remains that the European Parliament is to draw up proposals for elections by direct universal suffrage, in accordance with a uniform electoral procedure in all Member States. This is the sole Article in the Treaty giving the Parliament the right to propose legislative measures, a power otherwise almost exclusively vested in the Commission (however, see also Art. 138e(4) E.C. which provides that the European Parliament is to propose the detailed rules governing the Ombudsman's duties).

The European Parliament has been attempting for years to put forward proposals acceptable in all Member States, but without success. The primary obstacle has been the U.K.'s refusal to accept any form of proportional representation. The latest development in the saga was the European Parliament Resolution on draft electoral procedure for the election of M.E.P.s ([1993] O.J. C115/121). These proposals, put forward by the Dutch M.E.P., Karel de Gucht, called for the introduction throughout the Community of a limited form of proportional representation prior to the then forthcoming European Parliament elections of 1994. The resolution simply adopts certain principles about the electoral procedure, rather than proposing a particular electoral system. The two core features of the European Parliament's principles are proportional representation and some use, at least, of a list system. No new electoral procedure was adopted in time for the 1994 European Parliament elections.

The procedure for the eventual adoption of the electoral procedure was amended at Maastricht. Unanimity in the Council has been preserved, as well as the requirement that the Member States adopt the measure in accordance with their respective constitutional requirements. Under Art. 138(3) EEC, the European Parliament was given no formal role in the adoption of the measure; this has now been upgraded to a power of veto. The European Parliament must give its assent, acting by a majority of its component Members, to the procedure agreed by the Council.

Article 138a

Political parties at European level are important as a factor for integration within the Union. They contribute to forming a European awareness and to expressing the political will of the citizens of the Union.

GENERAL NOTE

This Article is a political declaration of intent more suited to inclusion in the preamble than in the body of the Treaty. The formation of truly European political parties standing on a uniform ticket throughout the Community in the European Parliament elections is seen as a major factor in increasing European awareness. The situation at present, with groupings of like-minded national parties coming together in the European Parliament is one step towards such an occurrence, but still represents the European Parliament as a place where national interests are vented as opposed to European ones.

Article 138b

In so far as provided in this Treaty, the European Parliament shall participate in the process leading up to the adoption of Community acts by exercising its powers under the procedures laid down in Articles 189b and 189c and by giving its assent or delivering advisory opinions.

The European Parliament may, acting by a majority of its members, request the Commission to submit any appropriate proposal on matters on which it considers that a Community act is required for the purpose of implementing this Treaty.

GENERAL NOTE

As with all of Articles 138a-e E.C., this Article was added by the E.U. Treaty, and marks a further limited improvement of the European Parliament's position in the legislative process. The first paragraph simply emphasises the new diverse role which the European Parliament is to play in the varying legislative procedures now available for the adoption of Community legislation.

The second paragraph is only comprehensible if one looks at the reasoning behind its inclusion in the Treaty. In the run-up to the inter-governmental conference, the European Parliament had called for a limited right of legislative initiative. One of the fundamental principles of the Community is that the Commission holds the monopoly of legislative initiative: the idea is that the Commission will act in accordance with the spirit of the Treaty in developing the Community in the interests of all the Member States, not just the larger ones. The European Parliament accepted this basic principle but asked for "the right to initiate legislative proposals in cases where the Commission fails to respond within a specified deadline to a specific request adopted by a majority of M.E.P.s" ("Martin II" report, [1990] O.J. C231/97). This was strenuously opposed by the Commission, who saw it as the thin end of the wedge as regards its monopoly in this field. Thus, the present Article was drafted, whereby the European Parliament may request the Commission to submit a legislative proposal, but the European Parliament has no right to act should the Commission fail to take up the European Parliament's request. This gives the European Parliament a very similar right to that which the Council has always had under Art. 152 EEC/E.C., but marks little more than an entrenchment of the previously utilised mechanism of "own initiative reports" drawn up by the European Parliament. Nevertheless, these reports were generally aimed at publicity for a particular issue rather than any real push for legislative influence and were treated as such by the Commission. The more direct legislative power encompassed in this Article ought to focus the European Parliament more towards its legislative function, in keeping with its development under Maastricht. Rule 36B of the European Parliament's Rules of Procedure (as amended subsequent to the E.U. Treaty, see [1993] O.J. C268/51) states that any resolution requesting the Commission to submit a legislative proposal must be based on an own-initiative report, state the legal basis for the measure and give detailed recommendations as to the content of the proposal. The Commission and the European Parliament have generally enjoyed a cordial relationship in the past; since March 1988 they have agreed upon the annual legislative timetable at the beginning of each year. The European Parliament thus has a degree of influence over the legislative proposals to be passed in that period. This influence will only have increased with the greater involvement of the European Parliament in the legislative process post-Maastricht. The threat of European Parliament rejection, or at least the delay, of certain proposals in what is always a full legislative calendar has never been measured but is likely to be substantial.

Article 138c

In the course of its duties, the European Parliament may, at the request of a quarter of its members, set up a temporary Committee of Inquiry to investigate, without prejudice to the powers conferred by this Treaty on other institutions or bodies, alleged contraventions or maladministration in the implementation of Community law, except where the alleged facts are being examined before a court and while the case is still subject to legal proceedings.

The temporary Committee of Inquiry shall cease to exist on the submission of its report.

The detailed provisions governing the exercise of the right of inquiry shall be determined by common accord of the European Parliament, the Council and the Commission.

GENERAL NOTE

This provision marks the formalisation of a pre-existing European Parliament power. Since the advent of direct elections the European Parliament has increasingly used such committees as a means of highlighting issues of political concern and bringing them into the spotlight for public scrutiny (*e.g.*, Report by the Committee of Inquiry into Racism and Xenophobia A3–0195/90 which led to a number of Council and Commission initiatives on the subject).

At present there is no obligation upon the members of national governments, the Council or Commission to appear before such committees. For the latter two bodies, attendance is the norm. Whether or not such attendance is to be made compulsory is important as regards the democratic scrutiny of the whole Union structure. Should the European Parliament acquire the right to require the members of, for example, the Political Committee under the common foreign and security pillar to appear before its committees, this would be a major coup for parliamentary democracy at the European level. Whether or not this will take place is to be the subject of an inter-institutional agreement under Art. 138c, third indent, whereby the detailed rules governing the exercise of the right of inquiry are to be determined by the common accord of the institutions. (For the text of the Draft Act establishing the Procedures for Exercising the Right of Inquiry adopted by Common Accord of the Institutions see [1993] O.J. C21/147).

As was the case prior to the Maastricht Treaty, such a committee will be set up if requested by one-quarter of the members of the European Parliament (pre-Maastricht, see Rule 109/3 of the

European Parliament Rules of Procedure). The avoidance of matters which are *sub judice*, respected tacitly prior to Maastricht, is now formalised. Subsequent to the coming into force of the TEU, a new Rule of Procedure, Rule 109A, regulates a temporary committee of inquiry, see [1993] O.J. C268/51.

Article 138d

Any citizen of the Union, and any natural or legal person residing or having its registered office in a Member State, shall have the right to address, individually or in association with other citizens or persons, a petition to the European Parliament on a matter which comes within the Community's fields of activity and which affects him, her or it directly.

GENERAL NOTE

The addition of the right of Union citizens and other natural or legal persons resident in a Member State to petition the European Parliament adds very little to current practice. This right has been available since 1953 (Rule 128 of European Parliament Rules of Procedure). Its constitutionalisation may well lead to greater use being made of a procedure that is becoming an increasingly popular means of redress by disaffected citizens (fewer than 100 in 1979 to approximately 800 by 1989, and 1083 in the parliamentary year 1993–94. The increased popularity of this process led to the creation in 1987 of a European Parliament Committee with exclusive competence to hear petitions. The Petitions Committee prepares an annual report on its work which is submitted to the European Parliament for debate in plenary session.

The Treaty does not specify any remedy for cases found by the European Parliament to merit some form of consideration. Thus, the satisfaction of the individual's claim depends on the existence of pre-existing remedies under the Treaty. If the matter concerns a failure to implement Community law in a Member State, then the European Parliament may notify the Commission, or it can similarly communicate its findings to the relevant body. In one important respect, the right of petition can be seen to be having somewhat of an effect. As a direct result of petitions to the European Parliament, and the subsequent notification of the Commission, a relatively large number of Art. 169 EEC proceedings have been initiated for failure of a Member State to comply with Community law. In session 1989-90 alone, eight Art. 169 proceedings were initiated as a result of petitions to the European Parliament (see Bradley (1990) 10 Y.E.L. 367, at 384). The right of petition has also been supplemented by an inter-institutional agreement reached between the European Parliament, Council and Commission which encourages "Member States to give as clear and swift replies as possible to those questions which the Commission might decide, after due examination, to forward to the Member States concerned" (see Bradley (1989) 9 Y.E.L. 235, at 251).

This right is given express enunciation under the new citizenship heading in the Treaty at Art. 8d E.C. This is somewhat deceptive, in that the right is available to a much broader group than Union citizens *per se*, including resident natural persons and legal persons with a statutory seat in a Member State. Any petition must come from a person with the requisite *locus standi*; the case must involve "matters affecting him, her or it directly".

The right to petition would seem to have been intentionally circumscribed to exclude petitions concerning the new inter-governmental pillars of the Union. Article 138d restricts the area of competence of petitions to "matters within the Community's fields of activity" (Closa, "The Concept of Citizenship in the Treaty on European Union" (1992) 29 C.M.L.Rev. 1137, at 1164).

Article 138e

1. The European Parliament shall appoint an Ombudsman empowered to receive complaints from any citizen of the Union or any natural or legal person residing or having its registered office in a Member State concerning instances of maladministration in the activities of the Community institutions or bodies, with the exception of the Court of Justice and the Court of First Instance acting in their judicial rôle.

In accordance with his duties, the Ombudsman shall conduct inquiries for which he finds grounds, either on his own initiative or on the basis of complaints submitted to him direct or through a member of the European Parliament, except where the alleged facts are or have been the subject of legal proceedings. Where the Ombudsman establishes an instance of maladministration, he shall refer the matter to the institution concerned, which shall have a period of three months in which to inform him of its views.

The Ombudsman shall then forward a report to the European Parliament and the institution concerned. The person lodging the complaint shall be informed of the outcome of such inquiries.

The Ombudsman shall submit an annual report to the European Parliament on the outcome of his inquiries.

2. The Ombudsman shall be appointed after each election of the European Parliament for the duration of its term of office. The Ombudsman shall be eligible for reappointment.

The Ombudsman may be dismissed by the Court of Justice at the request of the European Parliament if he no longer fulfils the conditions required for the performance of his duties or if he is guilty of serious misconduct.

3. The Ombudsman shall be completely independent in the performance of his duties. In the performance of those duties he shall neither seek nor take instructions from any body.

The Ombudsman may not, during his term of office, engage in any other occupation, whether gainful or not.

4. The European Parliament shall, after seeking an opinion from the Commission and with the approval of the Council acting by a qualified majority, lay down the regulations and general conditions governing the performance of the Ombudsman's duties.

GENERAL NOTE

This Article gives voice to the decision at Maastricht to set up the office of Community Ombudsman to investigate instances of maladministration within the Community bodies. This is included in the section on the European Parliament because the independent Ombudsman is to be appointed by the European Parliament. The appointment of the first Ombudsman has in fact been deferred to 1995 because of political disagreement between the Socialist and European Peoples' Party (Christian Democrat) groups. The Ombudsman has the power to act on his own initiative or at the instance of a direct complaint from a Union citizen or a legal entity or person resident in one of the Member States. Complaints may also be directed through an M.E.P. The Ombudsman will then conduct inquiries into the matter and, should any instance of maladministration be discovered, the institution concerned will be informed of the decision; the institution has a period of three months to inform the Ombudsman of its views. The Ombudsman then forwards a report to the European Parliament and to the institution concerned. The person lodging the complaint is to be informed of the outcome of these inquiries, but nowhere in the procedure is there any sanction envisaged for the discovery of an instance of maladministration. The only recourse will take place as a result of the institution concerned deciding to remedy the problem itself.

The Ombudsman lacks any punitive sanctioning power and any influence exercised will be based on extra-legal considerations, such as the institution's desire to avoid any adverse publicity on the matter, or its respect for the fairness of the Ombudsman's adjudication. Whether the office of Ombudsman will amount to a useful addition to the Community remains to be seen. The European Parliament itself is not confident; its Committee on Petitions views the move as "an unwarranted and unnecessary increase in bureaucracy in an area where various mechanisms for complaint are already in existence" (*European Parliament News*, June 10–14, 1991). Its existence alongside the pre-existing right to address petitions to the European Parliament would appear to be somewhat of a duplication of effort, unless the complaint is against the European Parliament, which causes confusion to citizens wanting to make a valid complaint about some aspect of the Community.

The detailed rules governing the performance of the Ombudsman's duties are to be proposed by the European Parliament. This it has done, in the European Parliament Decision on the Regulations and General Conditions governing the Performance of the Ombudsman's Duties (Decision 94/262/E.C., [1994] O.J. L113/15). This dictates that, *inter alia*, the Community institutions shall be obliged to supply the Ombudsman with the information requested and give him access to the files concerned; refusal on the grounds of confidentiality is precluded (Art. 3(2)). A similar duty is applied to the Member States, and officials and servants of the Community are to appear before the Ombudsman at his request (Art. 3(3)). Other provisions provide for a close relationship between the Ombudsman and the European Parliament Petitions Committee, as well as co-operation with the national ombudsmen (Arts. 2 and 5 respectively). Both the Commission and the Council have taken decisions on access to documents in pursuance of the Ombudsman's enquiries (for the Commission, see [1994] O.J. L54/25; for the Council, [1993] O.J. L46/58). The procedures for the appointment and dismissal of the Ombudsman are set out in Rules 130A and 130B of the European Parliament's Rules of Procedure, as amended subsequent to the TEU ([1993] O.J. C268/51). Rule 130C provides that the detailed powers of the Ombudsman are to be laid down in a special annex to the Parliament's Rules of Procedure.

Article 139

The European Parliament shall hold an annual session. It shall meet, without requiring to be convened, on the second Tuesday in March.

The European Parliament may meet in extraordinary session at the request of a majority of its members or at the request of the Council or of the Commission.

Article 140

The European Parliament shall elect its President and its officers from among its members.

Members of the Commission may attend all meetings and shall, at their request, be heard on behalf of the Commission.

The Commission shall reply orally or in writing to questions put to it by the European Parliament or by its members.

The Council shall be heard by the European Parliament in accordance with the conditions laid down by the Council in its rules of procedure.

Article 141

Save as otherwise provided in this Treaty, the European Parliament shall act by an absolute majority of the votes cast.

The rules of procedure shall determine the quorum.

Article 142

The European Parliament shall adopt its rules of procedure, acting by a majority of its members.

The proceedings of the European Parliament shall be published in the manner laid down in its rules of procedure.

Article 143

The European Parliament shall discuss in open session the annual general report submitted to it by the Commission.

Article 144

If a motion of censure on the activities of the Commission is tabled before it, the European Parliament shall not vote thereon until at least three days after the motion has been tabled and only by open vote.

If the motion of censure is carried by a two-third majority of the votes cast, representing a majority of the members of the European Parliament, the members of the Commission shall resign as a body. They shall continue to deal with current business until they are replaced in accordance with Article 158. In this case, the term of office of the members of the Commission appointed to replace them shall expire on the date on which the term of office of the members of the Commission obliged to resign as a body would have expired.

GENERAL NOTE

The power of the European Parliament to dismiss the whole Commission, by a vote of censure carried by a two-thirds majority, is retained under the Maastricht amendments. This power has never been used, although its use has been threatened on a number of occasions (an excellent example was the motion on the Commission's handling of the GATT negotiations with the U.S. on agricultural matters (B3–1676/92; for vote see O.J. [1993] C21/124)). As with all such motions in the past, it failed to secure the requisite majority (see Weatherill and Beaumont, *E.C. Law* (1993), p. 85). Its non-use has a great deal to do with the fact that it amounts to a very blunt instrument; the European Parliament can only remove the whole Commission rather than individual Commissioners. The generally cordial nature of the relationship between these two bodies, both of which pursue essentially similar pro-European goals, means that the European Parliament is very rarely sufficiently dissatisfied with the Commission to prompt recourse to such a draconian sanction. Moreover, such an action would not make for such cordiality between the bodies in future. Another reason for the non-utilisation of this procedure may have been that there was nothing to stop the Member States appointing a new Commission with views equally opposed to the European Parliament's, or even consisting of the same, recently sacked, members; the only remedy would then be the dismissal of this "new" Commission and so on. It was highly unlikely that the Member States would have risked sparking such a prolonged period of appointment and dismissal of the Commission for fear of leaving the running of the Community in effective limbo. After the Maastricht amendments the European Parliament does have a role in the appointment process (see Art. 158(2) E.C.) but still lacks the key power to block the appointment of individual Commissioners.

The E.U. Treaty adds a new last sentence to the second paragraph of this Article. This simply clarifies the position should the European Parliament actually successfully censure the Commission.

It provides that the new Commission appointed to replace the Commission sacked by the European Parliament is appointed only for the remainder of the latter's term of office (see Art. 158 E.C.). This was also made necessary by the novel two year period to be served by the Commission appointed in 1993. It is to cease operation in 1995 to make way for the utilisation of a new investiture process. Any censure of the short-term Commission could not have been allowed to postpone the taking of office of the new Commission in 1995, as this date was selected specifically to ensure the tying together of the periods of office of the European Parliament and the Commission (see Art. 158 E.C.).

A Dutch proposal prior to the Maastricht summit was that the European Parliament should be empowered to remove individual Commissioners, as opposed to the removal of the whole body (letter from the Dutch Prime Minister, Mr Lubbers, to the Rome European Council meeting of December 12, 1990, see Laursen and Finn, *The Intergovernmental Conference on Political Union*, (1992), p. 315). The aim of such a process would be to strengthen the accountability of the Commission to the European Parliament, a form of ministerial responsibility. It could, however, undermine the collegiate nature of the Commission and its commitment to collective responsibility. The proposal was nevertheless not taken up by the Inter-governmental Conference which chose instead to concentrate on the process of appointment of the Commission.

SECTION 2: The Council

Article 145

To ensure that the objectives set out in the Treaty are attained, the Council shall, in accordance with the provisions of this Treaty:
— ensure co-ordination of the general economic policies of the Member States;
— have power to take decisions;
— confer on the Commission, in the acts which the Council adopts, powers for the implementation of the rules which the Council lays down. The Council may impose certain requirements in respect of the exercise of these powers. The Council may also reserve the right, in specific cases, to exercise directly implementing powers itself. The procedures referred to above must be consonant with principles and rules to be laid down in advance by the Council, acting unanimously on a pro-

posal from the Commission and after obtaining the Opinion of the European Parliament.

Article 146

The Council shall consist of a representative of each Member State at ministerial level, authorised to commit the government of that Member State.
[The office of President shall be held in turn by each Member State in the Council for a term of six months, in the order decided by the Council acting unanimously.]

GENERAL NOTE

The original Art. 146 EEC was repealed by the Merger Treaty of April 8, 1965, which laid down similar rules with respect to the institutions existing separately at that time under the three Community Treaties. The newly added Art. 146 E.C. is essentially a reworded Art. 2 of the Merger Treaty.

The first paragraph of the new Article has caused something of a debate. Article 2 of the Merger Treaty provided that "The Council shall consist of representatives of the Member States. Each government shall delegate to it one of its members". The second sentence of Art. 2 of the Merger Treaty left it open to the Member States to send a member of the government. This implied a member of the national rather than the regional government but did not specify that the person was at ministerial level nor that he or she must be authorised to commit the national government of that State. It has been suggested that the broadened reference in the new Art. 146 to "a representative of each Member State at ministerial level" indicates that the Member States are not obliged to be represented at the national level. It has thus been interpreted as meaning that regional ministers could attend as a matter of course.

The second paragraph was amended by the Act of Accession [1994] O.J. CC241/08.

Article 147

The Council shall meet when convened by its President on his own initiative or at the request of one of its members or of the Commission.

GENERAL NOTE

This Article replicates Art. 3 of the Merger Treaty and, as with several of the other Articles relating to the Council and to the Commission, reintegrates the material into the E.C. Treaty. On the Council in general see Weatherill and Beaumont, *E.C. Law* (1993), Chap. 3; Hartley, *Foundations of European Community Law* (3rd ed., 1994), pp. 17–23.

Article 148

1. Save as otherwise provided in this Treaty, the Council shall act by a majority of its members.
2. Where the Council is required to act by a qualified majority, the votes of its members shall be weighted as follows:

Belgium	5
Denmark	3
Germany	10
Greece	5
Spain	8
France	10
Ireland	3
Italy	10
Luxembourg	2
Netherlands	5
[Austria	4]
Portugal	5
[Finland	3]
[Sweden	4]
United Kingdom	10

For their adoption, acts of the Council shall require at least:
 — 54 votes in favour where this Treaty requires them to be adopted on a
proposal from the Commission,
 — 54 votes in favour, cast by at least eight members, in other cases.
 3. Abstentions by members present in person or represented shall not prevent the adoption by the Council of acts which require unanimity.

<small>GENERAL NOTE</small>

 Article 148(2) was amended by the Act of Accession [1994] O.J. C241/08; [1995] O.J. L1/1.

Article 149

(*Repealed at Maastricht*)

Article 150

 Where a vote is taken, any member of the Council may also act on behalf of
not more than one other member.

Article 151

 1. A committee consisting of the Permanent Representatives of the Member States shall be responsible for preparing the work of the Council and for
carrying out the tasks assigned to it by the council.
 2. The Council shall be assisted by a General Secretariat, under the direction of a Secretary-General. The Secretary-General shall be appointed by
the Council acting unanimously.
 The Council shall decide on the organisation of the General Secretariat.
 3. The Council shall adopt its rules of procedure.

<small>GENERAL NOTE</small>

 The original Art. 151 EEC was repealed by the Merger Treaty of April 8, 1965; Art. 4 of which
had formalised the role of COREPER in the Community system. Article 151 E.C. adds nothing
new to current practice; para. 1 of the present Article is an exact replica of the existing Art. 4 of
the Merger Treaty. Paragraph 2, on the other hand, gives Treaty status to the General Secretariat, the body of Community civil servants with the task of assisting the Council in its day to
day work and providing a permanent service to the rotating presidency and the working groups
thereunder. The provision in the present Article that the Secretary-General shall be appointed
by the Council acting unanimously was in the Council's Rules of Procedure (see [1979] O.J.
L268, as amended by [1987] O.J. L291, Art. 17(1)) as was the power of the Council to decide on
the organisation of the General Secretariat (Art. 17(2)). The General Secretariat must be distinguished from COREPER, which consists of national civil servants/diplomats and operates in
a manner analogous to the Council itself. It prepares the ground for Council meetings; a positive
decision on a matter in the preceding COREPER meeting usually leads to its adoption at full
Council without debate. The General Secretariat on the other hand, composed of Community
civil servants, is not attributed such widespread powers. On COREPER and the General Secretariat generally see Hartley, *Foundations of European Community Law* (3rd ed., 1994),
pp. 18–19).
 The Council adopted new Rules of Procedure by a Decision of December 6, 1993, [1993] O.J.
L304/1, which entered into force on December 7, 1993. The Council styles itself the "Council of
the European Union" (see Art. 13 of the Rules of Procedure). Article 6 specifies that the policy
debates on the Presidency's six-month work programme will be televised, but that other debates
will be televised only if unanimity is obtained in the Council. Another important development is
that Art. 7(5) of the Rules prescribes in detail when the record of the votes in the Council will be
made public.

Article 152

 The Council may request the Commission to undertake any studies the
Council considers desirable for the attainment of the common objectives,
and to submit to it any appropriate proposals.

Article 153

The Council shall, after receiving an opinion from the Commission, determine the rules governing the committees provided for in this Treaty.

Article 154

The Council shall, acting by a qualified majority, determine the salaries, allowances and pensions of the President and members of the Commission, and of the President, Judges, Advocates General and Registrar of the Court of Justice. It shall also, again by a qualified majority, determine any payment to be made instead of remuneration.

GENERAL NOTE

This Article is a carbon copy of its predecessor, Art. 6 of the Merger Treaty. It is now restored to its proper place within the E.C. Treaty.

SECTION 3: The Commission

The Commission
The relevant Articles with regard to the Commission were in great need of attention, having been substantially altered by the provisions of the Merger Treaty. Articles 156 to 163 EEC, repealed by the Merger Treaty, are re-enacted with some modifications, although the role of the Commission post-Maastricht remains relatively unchanged. The primary amendment in the institutional sphere relates to its appointment (Art. 158 E.C.). On the Commission in general, see Weatherill and Beaumont, *E.C. Law* (1993), Chap. 2 and Hartley, *Foundations of European Community Law* (3rd ed., 1994), pp. 11–17.

Article 155

In order to ensure the proper functioning and development of the common market, the Commission shall:
— ensure that the provisions of this Treaty and the measures taken by the institutions pursuant thereto are applied;
— formulate recommendations or deliver opinions on matters dealt with in this Treaty, if it expressly so provides or if the Commission considers it necessary;
— have its own power of decision and participate in the shaping of measures taken by the Council and by the European Parliament in the manner provided for in this Treaty;
— exercise the powers conferred on it by the Council for the implementation of the rules laid down by the latter.

Article 156

The Commission shall publish annually, not later than one month before the opening of the session of the European Parliament, a general report on the activities of the Community.

GENERAL NOTE

Articles 156 to 163 EEC were repealed by the Merger Treaty of 1965 and replaced by the detailed provisions enclosed in the latter document. The re-enactment of these Articles by the

E.U. Treaty marks an attempt at greater clarity in the provisions governing the operation of the Commission. This has been achieved to a great extent by the movement of the pertinent provisions of the Merger Treaty back into the body of the E.C. Treaty.

The present Art. 156 E.C. is an example of this; simply inserting Art. 18 of the Merger Treaty into the new E.C. Treaty. Its insertion thus has no effect upon current practice; the Commission is required to publish an annual general report on the activities of the Community, at least one month before the opening session of the European Parliament.

Article 157

1. The Commission shall consist of [20] members, who shall be chosen on the grounds of their general competence and whose independence is beyond doubt.

The number of members of the Commission may be altered by the Council, acting unanimously.

Only nationals of Member States may be members of the Commission.

The Commission must include at least one national of each of the Member States, but may not include more than two members having the nationality of the same State.

2. The members of the Commission shall, in the general interest of the Community, be completely independent in the performance of their duties.

In the performance of these duties, they shall neither seek nor take instructions from any government or from any other body. They shall refrain from any action incompatible with their duties. Each Member State undertakes to respect this principle and not to seek to influence the members of the Commission in the performance of their tasks.

The members of the Commission may not, during their term of office, engage in any other occupation, whether gainful or not. When entering upon their duties they shall give a solemn undertaking that, both during and after their term of office, they will respect the obligations arising therefrom and in particular their duty to behave with integrity and discretion as regards the acceptance, after they have ceased to hold office, of certain appointments or benefits. In the event of any breach of these obligations, the Court of Justice may, on application by the Council or the Commission, rule that the member concerned be, according to the circumstances, either compulsorily retired in accordance with Article 160 or deprived of his right to a pension or other benefits in its stead.

GENERAL NOTE

This Article essentially reiterates Art. 10 of the Merger Treaty. The Commission now consists of 20 members (Act of Accession, [1994] O.J. C241/08; [1995] O.J. L1/1), chosen on the grounds of general competence rather than specialist expertise. The number of Commissioners may be altered by the Council, acting unanimously. The issue of the number of Commissioners has surfaced recently, particularly in the debates over the enlargement of the Community. A proposal to the Inter-governmental Conference that the number of Commissioners be reduced from 17 to 12 (*i.e.* one per Member State) was postponed. A declaration appended to the E.U. Treaty stated that a review of the number of Commissioners (and of M.E.P.s) would begin "no later than the end of 1992" and be completed prior to the 1994 elections (Declaration No.15). It was further postponed during the negotiation of the accession agreements with the new Member States, but the accession was accompanied by a declaration by the Member States that the questions of the number of members of the Commission, and of voting weights in the Council, would be examined in the Inter-governmental Conference to be convened in 1996. The Treaty still includes the proviso that the Commission "must include at least one national of each of the Member States" and not more than two from one Member State. It is quite possible that even one Commissioner per Member State will become untenable by around the end of the decade, with a second wave of new Central European Member States after the year 2000. After the latter have joined, membership will rise to around 20 and this excludes other potential applicants, such as the Baltic States, and some of the existing applicants, like Malta, Cyprus and Turkey. The effects throughout the institutional structure of the Community will be manifest; a prime difficulty is the number of working languages which would be necessitated, given the expense at present of maintaining the existing official languages. It is possible that the situation will eventually be reached where the Commissioner chairs are passed in rotation between the Member States, perhaps with the larger States having a guaranteed appointee and the smaller States figuring in the rotation (as in the appointment of Advocates General to the Court of Justice). This would be strenuously opposed by the Irish Government, which sees the Commission (as do most smaller Member States) as a protector of their interests from Great Power intrigue in the Council. See further on this question Ungerer, "Institutional Consequences of Broadening and Deepening the Community", (1993) 30 C.M.L.Rev. 71.

The remainder of Art. 157(1) lays down the conditions for the post of Commissioner. These are not based on any professional qualification, but simply on a nationality criteria. The notion of Union citizenship does not seem to have percolated into the institutional provisions; the simple requirement that the Commissioners be nationals of a Member State is retained.

Article 157(2) lays down the principles enjoining the Commissioners' independence in the performance of their duties. The Member States are to undertake to respect this principle. To further ensure their independence, the Commissioners are prohibited from engaging in any other occupation during their period of office. The duties continue after their term ends, with the obligation that they "behave with integrity and discretion". Any breach of these duties could lead to compulsory retirement or, alternatively, the suspension of any pension or other post-employment rights. The former sanction is to be carried out in accordance with the procedure enunciated in Art. 160 E.C. (previously Art. 13 of the Merger Treaty). It is highly likely that the decision to suspend the pension rights of an ex-Commissioner would be similarly carried out under the "serious misconduct" procedure of Art. 160 E.C. There has not yet been an example of such an action.

Article 158

1. The members of the Commission shall be appointed, in accordance with the procedure referred to in paragraph 2, for a period of five years, subject, if need be, to Article 144.

Their term of office shall be renewable.

2. The governments of the Member States shall nominate by common accord, after consulting the European Parliament, the person they intend to appoint as President of the Commission.

The governments of the Member States shall, in consultation with the nominee for President, nominate the other persons whom they intend to appoint as members of the Commission.

The President and the other members of the Commission thus nominated shall be subject as a body to a vote of approval by the European Parliament. After approval by the European Parliament, the President and the other members of the Commission shall be appointed by common accord of the governments of the Member States.

3. Paragraphs 1 and 2 shall be applied for the first time to the President and the other members of the Commission whose term of office begins on 7 January 1995.

The President and the other members of the Commission whose term of office begins on 7 January 1993 shall be appointed by common accord of the governments of the Member States. Their term of office shall expire on 6 January 1995.

GENERAL NOTE

Prior to the Maastricht summit, the European Parliament had called for a role in the appointment of the Commission, something which was lacking in the existing Treaties. The Martin report to the Inter-governmental Conference requested that the European Parliament have the power to elect the President of the European Commission, acting on a proposal of the European Council (European Parliament Doc A3–166/90; [1990] O.J. C231). Such an election would come about immediately after the European Parliamentary elections, allowing the electorate to see a direct result of their vote in the composition of the executive. In order to make this feasible, it was proposed that the term of office of the Commission be increased from four to five years and chronologically linked to the parliamentary term.

The agreement reached at Maastricht followed the European Parliament's wishes, in that the Commission's term of office is to be altered to five years to link with that of the European Parliament. This means that the Commission appointed in January 1993 served only a two-year period of office (Art. 158(3) E.C.). The new procedure came into force after the European

Parliament elections of summer 1994. The new Commission took office from January 7, 1995. The delay between the European Parliament elections and the investiture of the new Commission has advantages and drawbacks. In practical terms, it permits the use of the autumn months to go through the new procedures. On the other hand, it distances the vote in the European elections from the appointment of the Commission. Whether or not this was an intention of the Member States negotiating at Maastricht is unclear. The slightly increased democratic legitimisation of the Commission weakens the claim that the Commission is the unaccountable bureaucracy of the Communities.

Instead of the right to elect the President of the Commission, the European Parliament has gained the right to be consulted on the appointment. However, as widely predicted, this consultation has turned out to be tantamount to an election. Any person nominated by the Member States would be very reluctant to take up office in the face of rejection by an elected body with which he or she would have to work closely (Corbett, "The Inter-governmental Conference on Political Union" (1992) 30 Journal of Common Market Studies 294). In practice, the Enlarged Bureau of the European Parliament has been consulted on the appointment of a new Commission President in the past. The European Parliament has amended its Rules of Procedure subsequent to the E.U. Treaty (see [1993] O.J. C268/51). The Enlarged Bureau has been replaced by the Conference of Presidents (Rule 23), *i.e.* the President of the Parliament and the chairmen of the political groups. Rule 29 now governs the procedure for the appointment of the Commission President. The nominee will be invited to make a statement to the Parliament, and this will be followed by a vote where a simple majority of the votes cast is sufficient. It is difficult to imagine the Governments appointing the nominee, or that person continuing to seek appointment, in the face of an adverse vote in the European Parliament. This was certainly the view taken by most commentators on likely developments had the consultation process on M. Santer's nomination as President of the Commission ended in a negative vote. It was what Wellington would have called "a close-run thing". Santer was saved from defeat by the defection from the Socialist opposition line by M.E.P.s for Socialist parties in government in some of the Member States. He was approved by 260 votes to 238, with 23 abstentions ([1994] 8 E.U. Bull. 7, 1.6.3).

The other proposal of the European Parliament which was taken up at Maastricht was the formalisation of the vote of confidence in the Commission as a whole after its appointment by the common accord of the Member States (Art. 158(2), third indent). Since 1982, the European Parliament has held a debate and a vote of confidence on the incoming Commission when it presents itself to the European Parliament with its legislative programme. This was recognised by the national governments in the Stuttgart Solemn Declaration on European Union of 1983 (see [1983] 6 E.C. Bull., 2.3.5) and the Delors Commissions have waited until they received this vote of confidence before taking their oath of office before the Court of Justice. This is an important gesture on the part of the Commission and strengthens the public perception of the European Parliament. The result of a "no" vote in the European Parliament is not explicitly laid out but the wording of Art. 158(3) makes it apparent that the appointment of the President and other members of the Commission may only take place after such a positive vote is forthcoming. Rule 29A of the Parliament's Rules of Procedure (see [1993] O.J. C268/51) provides that the persons nominated to serve on the Commission will be invited to appear before the "appropriate committees according to their prospective fields of responsibility". The committees of Parliament involved in this process report to the Parliament before it votes on whether to approve the Commission as a whole by a majority of the votes cast. The Commission nominees subjected themselves to scrutiny by the appropriate committees of Parliament in early 1995. They are not obliged to do so, but the implied threat of the Rules of Procedure is that the Commission as a whole will not be approved if nominees do not submit to a hearing before the relevant committee. In the event, a number of Commissioners (including the Irish Commissioner, Mr Flynn) were subjected to strong criticism for their attitude to the Parliament, their (lack of) command of their briefs, or for their substantive views on matters within their prospective responsibilities. Another element of this system is that it presupposes that the portfolios of the new members of the Commission will be agreed while they are still simply the nominees of their governments. The European Parliament cannot compel the nascent Commission to do this unless it is prepared to vote against approving the Commission over this issue.

This new two-tier investiture process thus marks both a formalisation and a strengthening of the role of the European Parliament in the appointment of the Commission. Nevertheless, the Member States were reluctant to allow the Commission's appointment to be drawn any further from their influence. This could be seen in the rejection of the European Parliament's proposal that the President-elect of the Commission be engaged in a joint decision-making process with the Member States as to the selection of the other members of the Commission. Instead, the President-elect will be consulted on the incoming Commissioners, but no more (this merely confirms existing practice, Weatherill and Beaumont, *E.C. Law* (1993), p. 42, and Van Miert,

(1973) 10 C.M.L.Rev. 257). This shows that, despite Treaty declarations as to the obligation on the Member States not to seek to influence the members of the Commission in the performance of their duties (Merger Treaty Art. 10(2), now Art. 157(2), second indent), these Member States are reluctant to lessen their hold over the appointment of individual Commissioners. While opinions as to their independence varies, there can be little doubt that Commissioners' ideologies play a very large part in their appointment and reappointment, as each Member State can identify its own criteria of selection. The ability of Member States to reappoint Commissioners (retained in Art. 158(1), second indent) entails the risk that the Member States will fail to reappoint Commissioners who are no longer in favour, as opposed to exercising this discretion on more satisfactory grounds, such as diminished administrative ability (the refusal of Mrs Thatcher to reappoint Lord Cockfield as one of the U.K. Commissioners is the most oft-cited example of the potential for misuse of this provision, see George, *An Awkward Partner: Britain in the European Community* (1990), p.197). The non-renewable term of employment of the European Central Bank executive board signals the direction which perhaps ought to have been followed. On the other side of the coin, this would entail the enforced loss of valuable and skilled Commissioners after a certain period, regardless of their ability.

Article 159

Apart from normal replacement, or death, the duties of a member of the Commission shall end when he resigns or is compulsorily retired.

The vacancy thus caused shall be filled for the remainder of the member's term of office by a new member appointed by common accord of the governments of the Member States. The Council may, acting unanimously, decide that such a vacancy need not be filled.

In the event of resignation, compulsory retirement or death, the President shall be replaced for the remainder of his term of office. The procedure laid down in Article 158(2) shall be applicable for the replacement of the President.

Save in the case of compulsory retirement under the provisions of Article 160, members of the Commission shall remain in office until they have been replaced.

GENERAL NOTE

Previously Art. 12 of the Merger Treaty, Art. 159 E.C. lays down the procedure should any of the Commissioners die, resign or be dismissed (compulsorily retired). The vacancy thus created shall be filled for the remainder of the member's term of office by a new member, appointed by the common accord of the Member States. The Council could, if agreed to unanimously, decide not to fill the vacancy. In the absence of a subsequent unanimous decision that the number of Commissioners remain permanently reduced, this vacancy would have to be filled when the new Commission took office.

Article 160

If any member of the Commission no longer fulfils the conditions required for the performance of his duties or if he has been guilty of serious misconduct, the Court of Justice may, on application by the Council or the Commission, compulsorily retire him.

GENERAL NOTE

This Article was previously Art. 13 of the Merger Treaty and its substance is unchanged. In order to ensure the independence of the Commission, there are only two means of removing

Commissioners against their will. The first is through a European Parliament motion of censure under Art. 144 E.C. The other is provided for in the present Article, and is the only means by which an individual Commissioner may be removed. The Court of Justice, acting on an application by the Commission or the Council, may decide to remove a Commissioner "if he no longer fulfils the conditions required for the performance of his duties or if he has been guilty of serious m isconduct". This provision has been utilised only once, to replace a critically and terminally ill Commissioner (see Decision 76/619 [1976] O.J. L201/31). The phrase "serious misconduct" has yet to be tested.

Article 161

The Commission may appoint a Vice-President or two Vice-Presidents from among its members.

GENERAL NOTE

This Article marks an alteration to the Merger Treaty provision, which required the appointment of six vice-presidents of the Commission (Art. 14 as amended by the Act of Accession, 1985, which provided that the Council could, acting by a unanimous vote, amend the number of vice-presidents). The present Article alludes simply to the potential appointment of up to two Commission vice-presidents. The provision agreed at Maastricht recognised the reality of the situation that no more than two people are needed to deputise for the President in chairing Commission meetings.

Article 162

1. The Council and the Commission shall consult each other and shall settle by common accord their methods of co-operation.
2. The Commission shall adopt its rules of procedure so as to ensure that both it and its departments operate in accordance with the provisions of this Treaty. It shall ensure that these rules are published.

GENERAL NOTE

This Article simply reiterates the provisions of Arts. 15 and 16 of the Merger Treaty in paragraphs one and two of the present Article respectively.

In common with the other major political institutions of the Community (the European Parliament and the Council), the Commission is empowered to adopt its own rules of procedure. This is a major power and permits the adoption of the most favourable conditions possible under the leeway afforded by the Treaty itself. The European Parliament has proven most adept at manipulating this restricted freedom to its best effect. The Commission's current rules of procedure are published as the Provisional Rules of Procedure of July 6, 1967 ([1967] O.J. Spec. ed. 2nd. Ser. (VII) 14), subsequently much amended (see Toth, *The Oxford Encyclopaedia of Community Law* (1990), Vol. 1, pp. 67-68). These rules of procedure must be adhered to. In *BASF A.G. v. Commission* (Case T-79/89, subsequently C-137/92) Art. 12 of the Rules of Procedure, which requires the original text of Commission measures to be annexed to the minutes in which their adoption was recorded, was not complied with in adopting Commission Decision 89/190. The Commission was unable to produce an authenticated version of the decision, which was then declared non-existent by the Court of First Instance. The Commission appealed to the Court of Justice and Advocate General van Gerven recommended to the Court that the Court of First Instance decision should be overturned.

Article 163

The Commission shall act by a majority of the number of members provided for in Article 157.

A meeting of the Commission shall be valid only if the number of members laid down in its rules of procedure is present.

GENERAL NOTE

This Article relates to the normal working procedures of the Commission (repeating identical Art. 17 of the Merger Treaty). The Commission acts collectively by simple majority vote. This is the case whatever function it is exercising, be it executive or legislative. All Commissioners have an equal standing and weight in the voting process.

SECTION 4: The Court of Justice

Amendments to the institutional structure of the European Court of Justice are relatively minimal. The greatest alteration arises under Art. 171(2) E.C. whereby the Court of Justice has acquired the right to impose fines on Member States who fail to fulfil their obligations under the Treaty. This is a fundamental innovation and gives the court unlimited discretion to apply penalties for non-compliance. Another major change is a widening of the category of case that the Council can decide to transfer from the jurisdiction of the Court of Justice to the Court of First Instance (Art. 168a E.C.). Other alterations to the role of the Court of Justice may well result from the coming into force of the E.U. Treaty. These may arise out of its interpretative jurisdiction. Sooner or later the court will have to rule on subsidiarity challenges. It will probably also have to deal with the thorny implications of the U.K. opt-out from the Social Policy Agreement appended to the Treaty. That the Court of Justice will accept such an overtly constitutional role was made all the more likely by its 1991 Opinion on the E.C./European Free Trade Association Agreement on the European Economic Area. The court found this agreement incompatible with the existing Community legal system, and thereby unconstitutional (see Opinion 1/91 [1991] E.C.R. 6079). The result of this decision was the revision and postponement of the European Economic Area agreement (see (1992) 29 C.M.L.Rev. 991).

Article 164

The Court of Justice shall ensure that in the interpretation and application of this Treaty the law is observed.

Article 165

The Court of Justice shall consist of [15] Judges.
[The Court of Justice shall sit in plenary session. It may, however, form chambers, each consisting of three, five or seven Judges, either to undertake certain preparatory inquiries or to adjudicate on particular categories of cases in accordance with rules laid down for these purposes.] The Court of Justice shall sit in plenary session when a Member State or a Community institution that is a party to the proceedings so requests. Should the Court of Justice so request, the Council may, acting unanimously, increase the number of Judges and make the necessary adjustments to the second and third paragraphs of this Article and to the second paragraph of Article 167.

GENERAL NOTE

The amendment to the third indent of this Article marks a "watering down" of the mandatory requirement that the Court of Justice should meet in plenary session in cases brought by a Member State or a Community institution. The new Art. 165 E.C. provides that a plenary bench need only convene in such cases if so requested by the Member State or Community institution concerned. This power to request a plenary session is, however, extended by Art. 165 E.C. to instances where the case is against a Member State or Community institution. This is a regrettable decrease in the ability of the Court of Justice to reduce its backlog of cases by using a Chamber rather than a plenary session. The aim should be to prevent the time wasted in an already crowded schedule when a plenary bench is called upon to sit in, for example, a case against a Member State for failure to comply with its Community law obligations, where no defence of substance is lodged. Such cases are better dealt with by a chamber of three or five judges, as more than one chamber can then sit at a time. Unfortunately, Art. 95(2) of the revised E.C.J. Rules of Procedure ([1991] O.J. L176/7) permits a Member State or Community institution to insist on a plenary session of the Court of Justice even where they are only intervening in the case or making written observations in a preliminary ruling.

The constitution of the Court of Justice was amended from 13 judges to 15 by the Act of Accession [1994] O.J. C241/08; [1995] L1/1. The amendments in para. 2 were also made by the Act of Accession.

Article 166

[The Court of Justice shall be assisted by eight Advocates General. However, a ninth Advocate General shall be appointed as from the date of accession until 6 October 2000.]

It shall be the duty of the Advocate General, acting with complete impartiality and independence, to make, in open court, reasoned submissions on cases brought before the Court of Justice, in order to assist the Court in the performance of the task assigned to it in Article 164.

Should the Court of Justice so request, the Council may, acting unanimously, increase the number of Advocates General and make the necessary adjustments to the third paragraph of Article 167.

GENERAL NOTE

Paragraph 1 was substituted by the Act of Accession [1994] O.J. C241/08; [1995] O.J. L1/1.

Article 167

The Judges and Advocates General shall be chosen from persons whose independence is beyond doubt and who possess the qualifications required for appointment to the highest judicial offices in their respective countries or who are jurisconsults of recognised competence; they shall be appointed by common accord of the Governments of the Member States for a term of six years.

[Every three years there shall be a partial replacement of the Judges. Eight and seven Judges shall be replaced alternately.]

[Every three years there shall be a partial replacement of the Advocates General. Four Advocates General shall be replaced on each occasion.]

Retiring Judges and Advocates General shall be eligible for reappointment.

The Judges shall elect the President of the Court of Justice from among their number for a term of three years. He may be re-elected.

GENERAL NOTE

The amendments in paras. 1 and 2 were made by the Act of Accession [1994] O.J. C241/08; [1995] O.J. L1/1.

Article 168

The Court of Justice shall appoint its Registrar and lay down the rules governing his service.

Article 168a

1. A Court of First Instance shall be attached to the Court of Justice with jurisdiction to hear and determine at first instance, subject to a right of appeal to the Court of Justice on points of law only and in accordance with the conditions laid down by the Statute, certain classes of action or proceeding defined in accordance with the conditions laid down in paragraph 2. The Court of First Instance shall not be competent to hear and determine questions referred for a preliminary ruling under Article 177.

2. At the request of the Court of Justice and after consulting the European Parliament and the Commission, the Council, acting unanimously, shall determine the classes of action or proceeding referred to in paragraph 1 and

the composition of the Court of First Instance and shall adopt the necessary adjustments and additional provisions to the Statute of the Court of Justice. Unless the Council decides otherwise, the provisions of this Treaty relating to the Court of Justice, in particular the provisions of the Protocol on the Statute of the Court of Justice, shall apply to the Court of First Instance.

3. The members of the Court of First Instance shall be chosen from persons whose independence is beyond doubt and who possess the ability required for appointment to judicial office; they shall be appointed by common accord of the governments of the Member States for a term of six years. The membership shall be partially renewed every three years. Retiring members shall be eligible for reappointment.

4. The Court of First Instance shall establish its rules of procedure in agreement with the Court of Justice. Those rules shall require the unanimous approval of the Council.

GENERAL NOTE

This Article, inserted by the S.E.A., provides for the creation and subsequent operation of the new Court of First Instance attached to the Court of Justice. The Council, acting on the basis of this Article, made provision for the setting up of the Court of First Instance on October 24, 1988 (see Decision 88/591, [1988] O.J. L319/1 and [1989] O.J. C215/1 (corrected version)).

In the original Art. 168a EEC, the jurisdiction of the Court of First Instance was to be determined by the Council, but specifically excluded actions brought by Member States or Community institutions, and questions referred for preliminary rulings under Art. 177. Such cases account for about two-thirds of the case-load of the Court of Justice. Within the limited area of the jurisdiction of the Court of Justice which could be transferred to the Court of First Instance, the Council decided not to transfer jurisdiction in cases brought by legal entities or persons under Arts. 173 and 175 relating to measures to protect trade within the meaning of Art. 113 of the Treaty in the case of dumping and subsidies. The Court of Justice had requested that the Court of First Instance be given such jurisdiction, but the Council merely promised to re-examine the Court of Justice's proposal after two years of operation of the Court of First Instance (Decision 88/591, Art. 3(3)). The Council did confer jurisdiction upon the Court of First Instance in relation to staff cases (*i.e.* disputes between servants of the Community and its institutions under Art. 179) and in actions brought against a Community institution by natural or legal persons under Arts. 173 and 175 EEC relating to the implementation of competition rules as regards undertakings.

In the run-up to the Maastricht inter-governmental conference, the Court of First Instance suggested that "a point has been reached beyond which, unless care is taken, the law's delays will be such as to discourage those who seek the law's protection" (see "Reflections on the Future Development of the Community Judicial System" (1991) 16 E.L.Rev. 175). The Court of First Instance, set up to alleviate some of the burden on the Court of Justice, had not had sufficient effect; the average length of proceedings before the Court of Justice in preliminary rulings was 17.5 months in 1988 and 18.5 months in 1991. In direct actions, the figures were even worse: 23.7 months in 1988 and 24.2 months in 1991. It was therefore agreed at Maastricht to amend Art. 168a E.C., whereby the Council, acting unanimously on a request from the European Court of Justice and after consulting the Commission and the European Parliament, can transfer any area of the Court of Justice's jurisdiction to the Court of First Instance, except for preliminary rulings under Art. 177. The Court of Justice attaches a great deal of importance to Art. 177, because it is the mechanism by which it can ensure the uniform application of Community law. In Council Decision 93/350 (amending 88/591), the Council has conferred jurisdiction on the Court of First Instance in all direct actions concerning legal entities or persons (Art. 1 of the Decision; [1993] O.J. L144/21, which took effect from August 1, 1993) except that the jurisdiction in anti-dumping and subsidy cases was to remain with the Court of Justice, subject to a future unanimous vote to transfer such competences. On September 27, 1993, 515 cases were transferred from the Court of Justice to the Court of First Instance as a consequence of Decision 93/350. The vast majority of the cases relate to the non-contractual liability of the Community arising from, and/or the illegality of, Community measures concerning milk quotas. The Decision has since been amended to extend the jurisdiction of the Court of First Instance over actions over measures to protect trade, which jurisdiction became effective on March 15, 1994 (E.U. Bull. 1–2/94, 1.7.19).

On the Court of First Instance in general see: Weatherill and Beaumont, *E.C. Law* (1993), pp. 158–164; Due, "The Court of First Instance" (1987) 7 Y.E.L. 1; Kennedy, "The Essential Minimum: The Establishment of the Court of First Instance" (1989) 14 E.L.Rev. 7; Vesterdorf,

"The Court of First Instance of the E.C. after Two Full Years in Operation" (1992) 29 C.M.L.Rev. 897 and Millett, *The Court of First Instance* (1990).

Article 169

If the Commission considers that a Member State has failed to fulfil an obligation under this Treaty, it shall deliver a reasoned opinion on the matter after giving the State concerned the opportunity to submit its observations.

If the State concerned does not comply with the opinion within the period laid down by the Commission, the latter may bring the matter before the Court of Justice.

Article 170

A Member State which considers that another Member State has failed to fulfil an obligation under this Treaty may bring the matter before the Court of Justice.

Before a Member State brings an action against another Member State for an alleged infringement of an obligation under this Treaty, it shall bring the matter before the Commission.

The Commission shall deliver a reasoned opinion after each of the States concerned has been given the opportunity to submit its own case and its observations on the other party's case both orally and in writing.

If the Commission has not delivered an opinion within three months of the date on which the matter was brought before it, the absence of such opinion shall not prevent the matter from being brought before the Court of Justice.

Article 171

1. If the Court of Justice finds that a Member State has failed to fulfil an obligation under this Treaty, the State shall be required to take the necessary measures to comply with the judgment of the Court of Justice.

2. If the Commission considers that the Member State concerned has not taken such measures it shall, after giving that State the opportunity to submit its observations, issue a reasoned opinion specifying the points on which the Member State concerned has not complied with the judgment of the Court of Justice. If the Member State concerned fails to take the necessary measures to comply with the Court's judgment within the time-limit laid down by the Commission, the latter may bring the case before the Court of Justice. In so doing it shall specify the amount of the lump sum or penalty payment to be paid by the Member State concerned which it considers appropriate in the circumstances. If the Court of Justice finds that the Member State concerned has not complied with its judgment it may impose a lump sum or penalty payment on it. This procedure shall be without prejudice to Article 170.

GENERAL NOTE

The amendment to this Article marks a fundamental shift in the means available for securing the effective implementation of Community law. The EEC Treaty provided only for weak remedies should the Member States fail to fulfil their obligations under that Treaty. While the Court of Justice had jurisdiction under Arts. 169 and 170 EEC to rule on the Member States' failures, the only subsequent remedy relied on the State taking "the necessary measures to comply with the Court's judgments" (Art. 171 EEC). The Court's judgments in infringement proceedings were declaratory and, though they are binding on the Member State concerned, the Court of Justice had no further powers. The result was that some Member States were slow to comply with the Court's judgments. Indeed, by the end of 1992, 90 of the Court's judgments had not been complied with. Considering that 244 cases of infringement of Community law by the Member States were decided by the Court of Justice between 1988 and the end of 1992, non-compliance in 90 cases is an unacceptably high proportion (see the *Tenth Annual Report on Commission Monitoring of the Application of Community Law*, [1993] O.J. C233/68 and 207). The only remedy, prior to the Maastricht Treaty, was for the Commission to initiate new infringement proceedings against the Member State. This required the whole of the Art. 169 process to be gone through again, a very cumbersome procedure with an uncertain outcome (see further Weatherill and Beaumont, *E.C. Law* (1993), pp. 180–2). Indeed, by the end of 1992, the Court of Justice had been forced to give a second decision against a Member State on a repeat infringement proceeding on 12 occasions.

This problem has been addressed by the E.U. Treaty. Following a proposal from the U.K. Government, which initially received a lukewarm reception from the Commission (see [1991] E.C. Bull. Supp. at 81 and 151–2), Art. 171 was amended to provide that the Court of Justice may impose penalties on Member States which fail to comply with its judgments under Arts. 169 and 170 E.C. This is a very important step in the enforcement of Community law, but will not be without difficulties in its application. One major problem seems to be that the process leading up to the imposition of the sanction will be very lengthy. The procedure under either Arts. 169 or 170 must first be satisfied before Art. 171 itself comes into play. Under the latter Article, it will fall to the Commission to determine whether or not the Member State has taken measures to alleviate its breach. It will then request the Member State concerned to give its observations, and issue a reasoned opinion specifying the nature of the State's non-compliance with the Court's judgment and giving a time-limit for compliance. The Commission will then, if it considers that the State has failed to take the necessary measures to comply with the Court's judgment within the time-limit, bring the case before the Court of Justice with a recommendation as to the level of fine that should be imposed. At all stages of the proceedings, the Commission has a discretion whether or not to proceed with the case. The full process requires two references to the Court of Justice and two reasoned opinions from the Commission, followed by responses from the Member State concerned. This could take upwards of three years from the outset of the proceedings! One other factor mitigating against its effective application is the absence of any proviso providing for the retention of Community funds due to the Member State concerned. This would make for a very effective sanction, as the Member State would not have to be pursued for the amount of the fine because it is simply docked from its allocation. Under Art. 88 of the European Coal and Steel Community Treaty, the Commission, with the assent of the Council acting by a two-thirds majority, may suspend the payment of any sums which the Community may be liable to pay to the State in question. It appears that this procedure has never been used.

Another potential problem arises from the failure of Art. 171 E.C. to permit the tailoring of the sanction to fit the breach, for example, the imposition of an injunction on a Member State. The scope of the phrase "lump sum or penalty payment" is unclear. Could it mean that the court has to choose between these alternative penalties, as a literal interpretation would suggest, or could it apply a penalty payment for every day that a Member State fails to pay the lump sum ordered by the Court (see Curtin, "The Constitutional Structure of the Union: A Europe of Bits and Pieces" (1993) 30 C.M.L.Rev. 17, at 32–34). There is always the chance that a state will fail to pay a lump sum or penalty payment. What the Community could do in that situation is far from clear, but would no doubt rest on extra-legal considerations.

Nevertheless, the new procedure under Art. 171, while far from perfect does mark a significant departure for the European Community. Empowering a Community institution to adopt a penal sanction on a Member State is a significant surrender of national sovereignty. Ironically, the loss of sovereignty caused by this centralising "federal" measure was proposed by the same U.K. Government which so strongly resisted the inclusion of the "f" word in the E.U. Treaty and trumpeted its opt-outs from the third stage of economic and monetary union and from the Social Policy Agreement.

There are, of course, other mechanisms for enforcing Community law, that have been developed by the Court of Justice. With the lack of formal sanctions in the EEC Treaty for non-compliance with Community law, it fell on the Court to secure its uniform application. This was evident from the development of the principles of direct applicability (see Case 26/62, *Van Gend en Loos*: [1963] E.C.R. 1) and supremacy of Community law (see Case 6/64, *Costa v. ENEL*: [1964] E.C.R. 585). These principles were to be embellished and built upon throughout the subsequent decades, in particular to secure the effective application (*effet utile*) of directives throughout the Member States. Firstly, by giving vertical direct effect to directives in *Van Duyn v. Home Office* (Case 41/74, [1975] Chap. 358) and in *Publico Ministero v. Ratti* (Case 148/78, [1979] E.C.R. 1629). Secondly, by developing the Art. 5 obligation to encompass the national courts in the interpretation of national law in accordance with Community obligations (indirect effects) (see Case 14/83, *Von Colson and Kamann v. Land Nordrhein-Westfalen*: [1984] E.C.R. 1891 and Case C-106/89, *Marleasing SA v. La Comercial Internacional de Alimentation SA*: [1990] E.C.R. 4135). (See generally: Curtin, "The Effectiveness of Judicial Protection of Individual Rights" (1990) 27 C.M.L.Rev. 709; Steiner, "From Direct Effects to *Francovich*: Shifting the Means of Enforcement of Community Law" (1993) 18 E.L.Rev. 2; and de Búrca, "Giving Effect to European Community Directives" (1992) 55 M.L.R. 215).

The jurisprudence reached its zenith with the now famous *Francovich and Boniface v. Italy* (Cases C–6, C–9/90 [1991] E.C.R. 535 9, noted by Bebr (1992) 29 C.M.L.Rev. 57 and Duffy (1992) 17 E.L.Rev. 133). This laid down the principle of State liability, whereby a Member State is, in certain circumstances, obliged to make good damage to individuals arising from non-implementation of a directive. The application of the principle in this case arose in a clear and blatant case of non-implementation. Francovich and Boniface were employees of an undertaking that became insolvent, leaving substantial arrears of salary unpaid. They brought proceedings in the Italian courts for the recovery of the compensation provided for by Directive 80/987 on the protection of employees in the event of the insolvency of their employer, or, in the alternative, damages. Italy had, however, failed to implement this Directive by the envisaged date of October 23, 1983 and had even been found guilty of this breach before the Court of Justice in *Commission v. Italian Republic* (Case 22/87, [1989] E.C.R. 143). The Italian courts sought a preliminary ruling from the Court of Justice. The court first considered whether the relevant provisions of Directive 80/987 were directly effective. The court applied the usual test for establishing direct effect: whether or not the provisions were unconditional and sufficiently precise. The Directives provided guarantees for the payment of unpaid remuneration in the case of the insolvency of the employer. These guarantees were sufficiently precise and unconditional in relation to their content and the persons entitled to them, but not in relation to the person or persons obliged to pay the guaranteed sums. Thus the applicants could not rely on the direct effect of the Directive against the State, even though the time-limit had run out.

Given that Directive 80/987 was not sufficiently precise in establishing who was liable to pay the guarantees contained in it, Community law, prior to the *Francovich* case, would have been of no avail to the applicants. The court, however, decided that the principle of liability of a Member State for damage caused to individuals by infringements of Community law for which it was responsible was inherent in the scheme of the E.E.C. Treaty. In particular, the obligation stemmed from Art. 5 of the Treaty which provides that "Member States shall take all appropriate measures, whether general or particular, to ensure fulfilment of the obligations arising out of the Treaty". The court also argued that the "full effectiveness" of Community rules might be called into question and the protection of the rights that they conferred would be weakened if individuals could not obtain compensation where their rights were infringed by a breach of Community law imputable to a Member State. It is a matter for each Member State to determine the competent courts and appropriate procedures for legal actions intended to enable individuals to obtain damages from the State. The European Court has indicated that these procedures must be no less favourable to applicants than those relating to similar claims under internal law, and must not be so organised as to make it practically impossible or excessively difficult to obtain damages from the state.

The result of this principle is that Member States will find themselves subject to potentially unlimited damages payments for non-implementation of directives, potentially restricted only by the number of applicants who can claim less. Moreover, rather than the centralised enforcement procedure envisaged by Art. 171, the Member State will find it almost impossible to ignore a judgment from a domestic court. The Court of Justice was well aware of this when it enunciated this principle (on what are admittedly shaky foundations: see Weatherill and Beaumont, *E.C. Law* (1993), pp. 301–4). The result is a very powerful tool in the hands of the Court of Justice and domestic courts to secure the implementation of Community directives. It puts the onus for securing the effective implementation of Community law onto interested parties rather than relying on absolute Commission discretion (see Evans, "The Enforcement Procedure of Article 169: Commission Discretion" (1979) 4 E.L.Rev. 442 and Weatherill and Beaumont, *E.C. Law* (1993), pp. 171–2). There is still some doubt as to the scope of the *Francovich* principle. The breach of Community law in that case was blatant, having been the subject of an infringement proceeding before the Court of Justice. Cases concerning less clearcut breaches of Community law, where the State's "fault" is not so palpable, will determine just how far reaching the *Francovich* principle is, but it has been argued that it gives "claws and teeth that are far sharper and more incisive than those concocted by the authors of the Maastricht Treaty" (Mancini and Keeling, "From CILFIT to E.R.T.: The Constitutional Challenge Facing the European Court" (1991) 11 Y.E.L. 1, 10). However, this remedy will not be available in relation to all violations of Community law by Member States. The conditions laid down in *Francovich* will not be met in all cases, the conditions being: (a) the result laid down in the Directive must involve the attribution of rights attached to individuals; (b) the content of the rights must be capable of being identified from the provisions of the Directive; and (c) there must be a causal link between the failure by the Member State to fulfil its obligations and the damage suffered by the individual. Where *Francovich* does not apply Art. 171 might well be used as an effective back-stop.

Article 172

Regulations adopted jointly by the European Parliament and the Council, and by the Council, pursuant to the provisions of this Treaty, may give the Court of Justice unlimited jurisdiction with regard to the penalties provided for in such regulations.

GENERAL NOTE

This Article is consequentially amended to take account of the fact that under the new conciliation and veto procedure, legislative measures are adopted jointly by the Council and the European Parliament. The substantive content of the Article is unaltered.

Article 173

The Court of Justice shall review the legality of acts adopted jointly by the European Parliament and the Council, of acts of the Council, of the Commission and of the ECB, other than recommendations and opinions, and of acts of the European Parliament intended to produce legal effects *vis-à-vis* third parties.

It shall for this purpose have jurisdiction in actions brought by a Member State, the Council or the Commission on grounds of lack of competence, infringement of an essential procedural requirement, infringement of this Treaty or of any rule of law relating to its application, or misuse of powers.

The Court shall have jurisdiction under the same conditions in actions brought by the European Parliament and by the ECB for the purpose of protecting their prerogatives.

Any natural or legal person may, under the same conditions, institute proceedings against a decision addressed to that person or against a decision which, although in the form of a regulation or a decision addressed to another person, is of direct and individual concern to the former.

The proceedings provided for in this Article shall be instituted within two months of the publication of the measure, or of its notification to the plaintiff, or, in the absence thereof, of the day on which it came to the knowledge of the latter, as the case may be.

GENERAL NOTE

The first paragraph of this Article was amended at Maastricht to permit the review by the Court of Justice of acts "adopted jointly by the European Parliament and the Council ... and of acts of the European Parliament intended to produce legal effects *vis-à-vis* third parties". The former provision applies to measures adopted under the conciliation and veto procedure laid down in Art. 189b E.C., while the latter provision is merely a recognition of existing Court case law on the interpretation of Art. 173 EEC (Case 294/83, *Les Verts v. European Parliament* [1986] E.C.R. 1339).

The second paragraph is amended, partly to formalise the Court's decision that the European Parliament ought to be permitted to take actions under this Article "for the purposes of protecting its own prerogatives" (Case C–70/88, *European Parliament v. Council (Chernobyl)* [1990] E.C.R. I–2041) and partly to attribute a similar right of action to the European Central Bank.

This Article thus gives Treaty status to the European Parliament's ability to bring actions for annulment. This was a matter on which some debate had been raised, thanks to two divergent decisions of the Court of Justice on the matter. In Case 302/87, *European Parliament v. Council (Comitology)* [1988] E.C.R. 5615, the Court of Justice, sitting with 13 judges, took a literal approach to the interpretation of Art. 173 EEC and refused the European Parliament any *locus standi* under this provision. However, a nine judge Court was prepared in the *Chernobyl* case to grant the limited *locus standi* now recognised by Art. 173 E.C. (See Bebr, "The Standing of the European Parliament in the Community System of Legal Remedies" (1990) 10 Y.E.L. 171.)

Article 174

If the action is well founded, the Court of Justice shall declare the act concerned to be void.

In the case of a regulation, however, the Court of Justice shall, if it considers this necessary, state which of the effects of the regulation which it has declared void shall be considered as definitive.

Article 175

Should the European Parliament, the Council or the Commission, in infringement of this Treaty, fail to act, the Member States and the other institutions of the Community may bring an action before the Court of Justice to have the infringement established.

The action shall be admissible only if the institution concerned has first been called upon to act. If, within two months of being so called upon, the institution concerned has not defined its position, the action may be brought within a further period of two months.

Any natural or legal person may, under the conditions laid down in the preceding paragraphs, complain to the Court of Justice that an institution of the Community has failed to address to that person any act other than a recommendation or an opinion.

The Court of Justice shall have jurisdiction, under the same conditions, in actions or proceedings brought by the ECB in the areas falling within the latter's field of competence and in actions or proceedings brought against the latter.

GENERAL NOTE

This Article is amended, as with Art. 173 to which it is closely related, to take account of existing Court of Justice jurisprudence on the status of the European Parliament and to attribute analogous rights to the European Central Bank on its coming into operation. It has always been clear from Art. 175 EEC that the European Parliament has *locus standi* to bring actions for failure to act against the Council or the Commission (utilised for the first time in Case 13/83, *European Parliament v. Council* [1985] E.C.R. 1513). The amendment of the Article recognises the right of the other institutions to challenge the European Parliament over its failure to act. The last paragraph of Art. 175 E.C. has been inserted to enable actions for failure to act to be brought against the European Central Bank. The Bank can bring an action for failure to act against the Commission, Council and European Parliament but only in areas falling within the Bank's "field of competence".

Article 176

The institution or institutions whose act has been declared void or whose failure to act has been declared contrary to this Treaty shall be required to take the necessary measures to comply with the judgment of the Court of Justice.

This obligation shall not affect any obligation which may result from the application of the second paragraph of Article 215.

This Article shall also apply to the ECB.

GENERAL NOTE

The amendment to this Article simply consists of the addition of the third paragraph to take account of the legislative role envisaged for the European Central Bank in the third stage of economic and monetary union. Substantively, the Article is unaltered.

Article 177

The Court of Justice shall have jurisdiction to give preliminary rulings concerning:
(a) the interpretation of this Treaty;
(b) the validity and interpretation of acts of the institutions of the Community and of the ECB;
(c) the interpretation of the statutes of bodies established by an act of the Council, where those statutes so provide.

Where such a question is raised before any court or tribunal of a Member State, that court or tribunal may, if it considers that a decision on the question is necessary to enable it to give judgment, request the Court of Justice to give a ruling thereon.

Where any such question is raised in a case pending before a court or tribunal of a Member State against whose decisions there is no judicial remedy under national law, that court or tribunal shall bring the matter before the Court of Justice.

GENERAL NOTE

The new Art. 177 is amended consequentially to take account of the coming into being of the European Central Bank in the third stage of economic and monetary union. A reference to the European Central Bank is appended to paragraph (b).

Article 178

The Court of Justice shall have jurisdiction in disputes relating to compensation for damage provided for in the second paragraph of Article 215.

Article 179

The Court of Justice shall have jurisdiction in any dispute between the Community and its servants within the limits and under the conditions laid down in the Staff Regulations or the Conditions of Employment.

Article 180

The Court of Justice shall, within the limits hereinafter laid down, have jurisdiction in disputes concerning:
(a) the fulfilment by Member States of obligations under the Statute of the European Investment Bank. In this connection, the Board of Directors of the Bank shall enjoy the powers conferred upon the Commission by Article 169;
(b) measures adopted by the Board of Governors of the European Investment Bank. In this connection, any Member State, the Commission or the Board of Directors of the Bank may institute proceedings under the conditions laid down in Article 173;
(c) measures adopted by the Board of Directors of the European Investment Bank. Proceedings against such measures may be instituted only by Member States or by the Commission, under the conditions laid down in Article 173, and solely on the grounds of non-compliance with the procedure provided for in Article 21(2), (5), (6) and (7) of the Statute of the Bank.
(d) the fulfilment by national central banks of obligations under this Treaty and the Statute of the ESCB. In this connection the powers of the Council of the ECB in respect of national central banks shall be the same as those conferred upon the Commission in respect of Member States by Article 169. If the Court of Justice finds that a national central bank has failed to fulfil an obligation under this Treaty, that bank shall be required to take the necessary measures to comply with the judgment of the Court of Justice.

GENERAL NOTE

Paragraph (d) is added to this Article to give the Court of Justice jurisdiction in cases where the fulfilment by the national central banks of their obligations under the Treaty or under the Statute of the European System of Central Banks is in question. The Council of the European Central Bank is declared to have the same powers as the Commission under Art. 169 E.C. where the actions of the national central banks are concerned (see also Art. 35.6 of the Statute of the

European System of Central Banks). The wording of Article 180 does not seem to preclude the Commission from also taking steps under Art. 169 regarding the national central banks. Thus, in this area there are two entities given the task of ensuring compliance with the E.C. Treaty, a role previously carried out by the Commission. In paragraphs (b) and (c) the words "European Investment" have been added, to indicate that the Bank referred to is not the European Central Bank.

Article 181

The Court of Justice shall have jurisdiction to give judgment pursuant to any arbitration clause contained in a contract concluded by or on behalf of the Community, whether that contract be governed by public or private law.

Article 182

The Court of Justice shall have jurisdiction in any dispute between Member States which relates to the subject matter of this Treaty if the dispute is submitted to it under a special agreement between the parties.

Article 183

Save where jurisdiction is conferred on the Court of Justice by this Treaty, disputes to which the Community is a party shall not on that ground be excluded from the jurisdiction of the courts or tribunals of the Member States.

Article 184

Notwithstanding the expiry of the period laid down in the fifth paragraph of Article 173, any party may, in proceedings in which a regulation adopted jointly by the European Parliament and the Council, or a regulation of the Council, of the Commission or of the ECB is at issue, plead the grounds specified in the second paragraph of Article 173 in order to invoke before the Court of Justice the inapplicability of that regulation.

GENERAL NOTE

This Article is amended simply to take account of alterations made in Arts. 173 and 189b of the Treaty. The references to the relevant paras. of Art. 173 are updated to take account of the additions made thereto, while the potential of legislative measures being adopted jointly by the Council and the European Parliament (Art. 189b E.C.) is also accounted for.

Article 185

Actions brought before the Court of Justice shall not have suspensory effect. The Court of Justice may, however, if it considers that circumstances so require, order that application of the contested act be suspended.

Article 186

The Court of Justice may in any cases before it prescribe any necessary interim measures.

Article 187

The judgments of the Court of Justice shall be enforceable under the conditions laid down in Article 192.

Article 188

The Statute of the Court of Justice is laid down in a separate Protocol. The Council may, acting unanimously at the request of the Court of Justice

and after consulting the Commission and the European Parliament, amend
the provisions of Title III of the Statute.

The Court of Justice shall adopt its rules of procedure. These shall require
the unanimous approval of the Council.

SECTION 5: The Court of Auditors

GENERAL NOTE

With the Court of Auditors being attributed the status of an institution by the Maastricht
Treaty amendments (see Art. 4 E.C.), the substantive provisions governing this body have been
moved from Arts. 206 and 206a EEC, into the institutional chapter of the E.C. Treaty. Thus, a
new section 5 is appended to the institutional heading and the material from the old Articles is
substantially reiterated in Arts. 188a–188c E.C.

Article 188a

The Court of Auditors shall carry out the audit.

GENERAL NOTE

This is a new provision stating in simple terms the Court of Auditors' main task, that of carrying out the audit of the Community's finances.

Article 188b

[1. The Court of Auditors shall consist of 15 members.]

2. The members of the Court of Auditors shall be chosen from among
persons who belong or have belonged in their respective countries to external audit bodies or who are especially qualified for this office. Their independence must be beyond doubt.

3. The members of the Court of Auditors shall be appointed for a term of
six years by the Council, acting unanimously after consulting the European
Parliament.

However, when the first appointments are made, four members of the
Court of Auditors, chosen by lot, shall be appointed for a term of office of
four years only.

The members of the Court of Auditors shall be eligible for reappointment.

They shall elect the President of the Court of Auditors from among their
number for a term of three years.

The President may be re-elected.

4. The members of the Court of Auditors shall, in the general interest of
the Community, be completely independent in the performance of their
duties.

In the performance of these duties, they shall neither seek nor take instructions from any government or from any other body. They shall refrain from
any action incompatible with their duties.

5. The members of the Court of Auditors may not, during their term of
office, engage in any other occupation, whether gainful or not. When entering upon their duties they shall give a solemn undertaking that, both during
and after their term of office, they will respect the obligations arising therefrom and in particular their duty to behave with integrity and discretion as
regards the acceptance, after they have ceased to hold office, of certain
appointments or benefits.

6. Apart from normal replacement, or death, the duties of a member of the
Court of Auditors shall end when he resigns, or is compulsorily retired by a
ruling of the Court of Justice pursuant to paragraph 7. The vacancy thus
caused shall be filled for the remainder of the member's term of office.

Save in the case of compulsory retirement, members of the Court of Auditors shall remain in office until they have been replaced.

7. A member of the Court of Auditors may be deprived of his office or of his right to a pension or other benefits in its stead only if the Court of Justice, at the request of the Court of Auditors, finds that he no longer fulfils the requisite conditions or meets the obligations arising from his office.

8. The Council, acting by a qualified majority, shall determine the conditions of employment of the President and the members of the Court of Auditors and in particular their salaries, allowances and pensions. It shall also, by the same majority, determine any payment to be made instead of remuneration.

9. The provisions of the Protocol on the Privileges and Immunities of the European Communities applicable to the Judges of the Court of Justice shall also apply to the members of the Court of Auditors.

GENERAL NOTE

This Article duplicates the provisions previously enclosed in Art. 206(2) to (10) EEC. No substantive amendments are made to any of these paras. but they are renumbered as (1) to (9). The appointment of members of the court and the conditions surrounding their period of office is thereby unaltered. The old para. (1) is deleted because it referred to the establishment of the Court of Auditors, which is now done by Art. 4 E.C.

The amendment in para. 1 was made by the Act of Accession [1994] O.J. C241/08; [1995] O.J. L1/1.

Article 188c

1. The Court of Auditors shall examine the accounts of all revenue and expenditure of the Community. It shall also examine the accounts of all revenue and expenditure of all bodies set up by the Community in so far as the relevant constituent instrument does not preclude such examination.

The Court of Auditors shall provide the European Parliament and the Council with a statement of assurance as to the reliability of the accounts and the legality and regularity of the underlying transactions.

2. The Court of Auditors shall examine whether all revenue has been received and all expenditure incurred in a lawful and regular manner and whether the financial management has been sound.

The audit of revenue shall be carried out on the basis of the amounts established as due and the amounts actually paid to the Community.

The audit of expenditure shall be carried out on the basis both of commitments undertaken and payments made.

These audits may be carried out before the closure of accounts for the financial year in question.

3. The audit shall be based on records and, if necessary, performed on the spot in the other institutions of the Community and in the Member States. In the Member States the audit shall be carried out in liaison with the national audit bodies or, if these do not have the necessary powers, with the competent national departments. These bodies or departments shall inform the Court of Auditors whether they intend to take part in the audit.

The other institutions of the Community and the national audit bodies or, if these do not have the necessary powers, the competent national departments, shall forward to the Court of Auditors, at its request, any document or information necessary to carry out its task.

4. The Court of Auditors shall draw up an annual report after the close of each financial year. It shall be forwarded to the other institutions of the Community and shall be published, together with the replies of these institutions to the observations of the Court of Auditors, in the Official Journal of the European Communities.

The Court of Auditors may also, at any time, submit observations, particularly in the form of special reports, on specific questions and deliver opinions at the request of one of the other institutions of the Community.

It shall adopt in its annual report, special reports or opinions by a majority of its members.

It shall assist the European Parliament and the Council in exercising their powers of control over the implementation of the budget.

GENERAL NOTE

As with the preceding Articles on the Court of Auditors, the present Article is largely unaltered from the old Art. 206a EEC. One alteration is the addition of a new second indent to para. 1. The assertion contained therein must be read in the light of the new Art. 209a E.C., which provides that the Member States are to take "the same measures to counter fraud affecting the financial interests of the Community as they take to counter fraud affecting their own financial interests". In paras. (3) and (4) the word "other" is inserted before "institutions'", because the Court of Auditors was elevated to institutional status in Art. 4 E.C. Paragraph (4) empowers the Court of Auditors to prepare "special reports" when asked to do so by any of the other institutions of the Community.

Chapter 2 (Provisions Common to Several Institutions)

Article 189

In order to carry out their task and in accordance with the provisions of this Treaty, the European Parliament acting jointly with the Council, the Council and the Commission shall make regulations and issue directives, take decisions, make recommendations or deliver opinions.

A regulation shall have general application. It shall be binding in its entirety and directly applicable in all Member States.

A directive shall be binding, as to the result to be achieved, upon each Member State to which it is addressed, but shall leave to the national authorities the choice of form and methods.

A decision shall be binding in its entirety upon those to whom it is addressed.

Recommendations and opinions shall have no binding force.

GENERAL NOTE

This Article is amended to take account of the new decision-making process under Art. 189b E.C. whereby some Community acts are to be adopted jointly by the European Parliament and the Council. This apart, the Article is unaltered.

Article 189a

1. Where in pursuance of this Treaty, the Council acts on a proposal from the Commission, unanimity shall be required for an act constituting an amendment to that proposal, subject to Article 189b(4) and (5).

2. As long as the Council has not acted, the Commission may alter its proposal at any time during the procedures leading to the adoption of a Community act.

GENERAL NOTE

This Article, previously Art. 149(1) and (2) EEC, is amended to account for the new conciliation and veto procedure under Art. 189b E.C. The first of the basic principles previously encompassed in Art. 149(1) EEC, that the Council, acting on the basis of a Commission proposal must act by unanimity if it wishes to adopt an act constituting an amendment to the Commission proposal, is watered down with regard to the conciliation stage under Art. 189b E.C. During this part of the procedure, the Commission is relegated to the role of honest broker, and the Council and the European Parliament members, meeting in the conciliation committee, may adopt an act different from the original Commission proposal. In certain legislative areas this will be done by qualified majority voting in Council (for example, the adoption of legislation under Art. 100a E.C.). Whether or not this will amount to a significant diminution of power for the Commission is uncertain. It is likely that the role of the Commission in taking "all the necessary initiatives with a view to reconciling the positions of the European Parliament and the Council" will be significant, but all will depend on subsequent practice. The Commission's powers are only diluted if a conciliation committee is convened under Art. 189b(4) and (5) E.C. The normal rule continues to apply to amendments to the Commission proposal prior to this. Thus, the Council must act by unanimity to accept any amendments of the European Parliament on which the Commission has expressed a negative opinion or to put forward its own amendments (Art. 189b (3) E.C.). Nevertheless, as soon as a conciliation committee is convened, the Council may adopt amendments to the Commission proposal by qualified majority vote. Hartley suggests that the Council may well simply wait for the three-month period under Art. 189b(3) E.C. to elapse, without approving any European Parliament amendments, and when the conciliation committee is thereby convened, adopt any amendments it desires by qualified majority vote. The Commission's loss is thereby the European Parliament's gain; for the first time it can have its amendments, opposed by the Commission, adopted by qualified majority vote (Hartley, "Constitutional and Institutional Aspects of the Maastricht Agreement" (1993) 42 I.C.L.Q. 213, at 225).

One factor justifying the amendment to this Article is that the usefulness of the conciliation process under Art. 189b E.C. would be prejudiced by the necessity of unanimity, its purpose being the securing of compromises between the European Parliament and the Council. Such compromises are much more unlikely where one body is required to take certain of its decisions by unanimity (see note on Art. 189b E.C.).

The second paragraph of Art. 189a is unaltered from its original form under Art. 149(2) EEC.

Article 189b

1. Where reference is made in this Treaty to this Article for the adoption of an act, the following procedure shall apply.

2. The Commission shall submit a proposal to the European Parliament and the Council.

The Council, acting by a qualified majority after obtaining the Opinion of the European Parliament, shall adopt a common position. The common position shall be communicated to the European Parliament. The Council shall inform the European Parliament fully of the reasons which led it to adopt its common position. The Commission shall inform the European Parliament fully of its position.

If, within three months of such communication, the European Parliament:

    (a) approves the common position, the Council shall definitively adopt the act in question in accordance with that common position;

    (b) has not taken a decision, the Council shall adopt the act in question in accordance with its common position;

    (c) indicates, by an absolute majority of its component members, that it intends to reject the common position, it shall immediately inform the Council. The Council may convene a meeting of the Conciliation Committee referred to in paragraph 3 to explain further its position. The European Parliament shall thereafter either confirm, by an absolute majority of its component members, its rejection of the common position, in which event the proposed act shall be deemed not to have been adopted, or propose amendments in accordance with subparagraph (d) of this paragraph;

    (d) proposes amendments to the common position by an absolute majority of its component members, the amended text shall be forwarded to the Council and to the Commission, which shall deliver an opinion on those amendments.

3. If, within three months of the matter being referred to it, the Council, acting by a qualified majority, approves all the amendments of the European Parliament, it shall amend its common position accordingly and adopt the act in question; however, the Council shall act unanimously on the amendments

on which the Commission has delivered a negative opinion. If the Council does not approve the act in question, the President of the Council, in agreement with the President of the European Parliament, shall forthwith convene a meeting of the Conciliation Committee.

4. The Conciliation Committee, which shall be composed of the members of the Council or their representatives and an equal number of representatives of the European Parliament, shall have the task of reaching agreement on a joint text, by a qualified majority of the members of the Council or their representatives and by a majority of the representatives of the European Parliament. The Commission shall take part in the Conciliation Committee's proceedings and shall take all the necessary initiatives with a view to reconciling the positions of the European Parliament and the Council.

5. If, within six weeks of its being convened, the Conciliation Committee approves a joint text, the European Parliament, acting by an absolute majority of the votes cast, and the Council, acting by a qualified majority, shall have a period of six weeks from that approval in which to adopt the act in question in accordance with the joint text. If one of the two institutions fails to approve the proposed act, it shall be deemed not to have been adopted.

6. Where the Conciliation Committee does not approve a joint text, the proposed act shall be deemed not to have been adopted unless the Council, acting by a qualified majority within six weeks of expiry of the period granted to the Conciliation Committee, confirms the common position to which it agreed before the conciliation procedure was initiated, possibly with amendments proposed by the European Parliament. In this case, the act in question shall be finally adopted unless the European Parliament, within six weeks of the date of confirmation by the Council, rejects the text by an absolute majority of its component members, in which case the proposed act shall be deemed not to have been adopted.

7. The periods of three months and six weeks referred to in this Article may be extended by a maximum of one month and two weeks respectively by common accord of the European Parliament and the Council. The period of three months referred to in paragraph 2 shall be automatically extended by two months where paragraph 2(c) applies.

8. The scope of the procedure under this Article may be widened, in accordance with the procedure provided for in Article N(2) of the Treaty on European Union, on the basis of a report to be submitted to the Council by the Commission by 1996 at the latest.

GENERAL NOTE

This Article sets out the new conciliation and veto procedure hammered out at Maastricht. The procedure is simply referred to throughout the E.C. Treaty as "the procedure referred to in Article 189b". The alternative term contended for, "co-decision", would have been something of a misnomer, in so far as the procedure does not confer a true right of co-decision on the European Parliament in the adoption of Community legislation. Rather, it provides for the convening of a conciliation committee of equal numbers of M.E.Ps and Council members, or their representatives, to meet and attempt to resolve their differences if divergences in their positions exist (the conciliation facet). If the conciliation committee reaches agreement, the resulting text has to be approved by the appropriate majorities in both the Council and the European Parliament. If, however, no agreement is reached in the conciliation committee, the two institutions are not in an equal position. The Council can adopt its common position, perhaps with some of the European Parliament's amendments if it so desires, and the European Parliament only has the options of accepting it or vetoing it. Nonetheless, for the first time the European Parliament enjoys the right to block legislation upon which the Council has expressed a positive opinion.

This procedure is some distance from the right of co-decision requested by the European Parliament in the run-up to the Inter-governmental Conference ([1990] O.J. C231/97 at point 31). The European Parliament took the view that it was only through such a process that the democratic deficit in the Community could be properly addressed. Despite the fact that a majority of the Member States were in favour of conferring such positive powers upon the European Parliament a vocal minority ensured that such a sea change in the Community balance of powers was not going to be achieved at Maastricht (see Laursen and Finn eds., *The Inter-governmental*

Conference on Political Union (1992), Chap. 2—Italy, Greece, Spain and France expressed support for full co-decision). The procedure which was agreed at Maastricht therefore, unsurprisingly, bears the scars of compromise, not just as regards its name.

Rather than describe the complex process in segments relating to the individual paras. of Art. 189b, it will be easier to follow in one overall assessment, with references to the corresponding paras. of the Article.

The process commences, as with the majority of Community legislation, with a Commission proposal (Art. 189b(2)). As with the co-operation procedure introduced by the S.E.A. (Art. 49(2) EEC, now Art. 189c E.C.), this is forwarded to the European Parliament and the Council. The Council then, acting by a qualified majority, adopts a common position on the proposal, after receiving the opinion of the European Parliament. The Council and the Commission must then inform the European Parliament of their positions on the matter; in the Council's case this amounts to a statement of reasons underlying its common position. This again is similar to the co-operation procedure.

The next stage of the process involves the European Parliament's reaction to the common position. This amounts to the second reading by the European Parliament, but it is constrained by a three month time-limit in which to operate (although this may be extended in accordance with Art. 189b(7) on the common accord of the Council and the European Parliament). The European Parliament has four alternative courses of action. It can approve the common position, in which case the Council will adopt the act as it stands (Art. 189b(2)(a)). Secondly, if the European Parliament fails to act within the requisite time period, the Council can again adopt the act in accordance with the common position (Art. 189b(2)(b)). Thus far, the procedure is very similar to that under the existing co-operation procedure, the differences become manifest only where the European Parliament signals its intention to reject the common position or proposes amendments of its own. With regard to the former scenario, the decision of the European Parliament, by an absolute majority of its members (as opposed to a majority of votes cast), to reject the common position, is not determinative (Art. 189b(2)(c)). The last sentence of Art. 189b(7) provides that, in the event of the European Parliament giving notification of its intention to reject, the three month time period will be automatically extended by two months. Such a motion is taken as a notice of intention to the Council. The Council may then convene a meeting of the conciliation committee, provided for in Art. 189b(4), to further explain its position. Once this has taken place, the European Parliament may confirm its rejection, again acting by an absolute majority of its members, or it may propose amendments to the common position. If the European Parliament rejects the measure a second time then the act is deemed not to have been adopted. This is not quite as simple as may at first sight appear. The mustering of an absolute majority of M.E.Ps is no mean feat, and this is even more difficult to achieve twice. The European Parliament, in its resolution on the procedure, indicated the difficulties it would face in this respect but also that it would not permit such procedural difficulties from preventing it rejecting "unacceptable" legislative proposals ([1992] O.J. C21/138, at 139).

Should the European Parliament propose amendments to the common position either at second reading or subsequent to a notification of intent to reject, Art. 189b(2)(d) applies. According to this procedure, the European Parliament, by an absolute majority of its members, may propose amendments to the common position; these are then forwarded to the Commission and the Council. The Council acts by qualified majority in relation to the amendments on which the Commission has not expressed a negative opinion, but by unanimity in relation to those amendments where the Commission has expressed such an opinion (see note on Art. 189a(1)). In the likely event that the Council does not adopt all Parliament's amendments, the President of the Council, must, in agreement with the President of the European Parliament, convene a meeting of the conciliation committee (Art. 189b(3)).

This committee is to consist of an equal number of members of the European Parliament and the Council or its representatives and its aim is to reach agreement on a joint text. It would seem to be unlikely that government ministers will attend many, if any, conciliation committees. The Council will probably be represented by the Member States' Permanent Representatives and Deputy Permanent Representatives who sit in COREPER. The composition of Parliament's delegation to the conciliation committee is regulated by Rule 52B of the Rules of Procedure (as amended subsequent to the TEU, see [1993] O.J. C268/51). For the first 12 months of the operation of Art. 189b, Parliament's delegation will include three Vice-Presidents as permanent members. The President of the Parliament, or one of the three permanent members, will lead the delegation. Other members of the delegation will include the chairman and rapporteur of the Parliamentary committee responsible for handling the legislative proposal under discussion. The choice of the remaining M.E.Ps to attend the conciliation committee will be made by the political groups under the direction of the Conference of Presidents (*i.e.* the President of the Parliament and the chairmen of the political groups). Most, if not all, of those selected will be members of the committee responsible for dealing with the piece of legislation in issue during its first and second reading. By ensuring that three or four of Parliament's leaders attend all the conciliation committees, Parliament has indicated the high level of commitment that it is making to this process. The Commission is not attributed its usual rights under Art. 189a(1) E.C., but instead will "take all necessary initiatives with a view to reconciling the positions of the European Parliament and the Council" (Art. 189b(4)). The European Parliament supports the Commission's involvement because the European Parliament and the Council may come together in the conciliation committee with widely divergent positions. The Commission has vast experience in such inter-institutional matters. As Curtin states, the Council has little experience of a direct institutional dialogue with the European Parliament as envisaged by the conciliation committee procedure (Curtin, "The Constitutional Structure of the Union: A Europe of Bits and Pieces" (1993) 30 C.M.L.Rev. 17, at 37). The Commission will still have the power to alter the proposed act where this may assist the process of conciliation (Art. 189a(2) E.C.). The European Parliament has also highlighted that it wishes as much as possible of the negotiating to take place either prior to the commencement of the procedure, or during the first reading, when all of the institutions may interact in accordance with their normal prerogatives. In other words, the stated aim of the European Parliament is to reach agreement on legislative provisions as soon as possible and to avoid having to go through the stages of what is a very complicated and potentially time-consuming legislative process ([1992] O.J. C21/138, at 139). The prospect of increased inter-institutional discussion may well be one positive and necessary result of this complicated procedure.

Returning to the question of amendments in the conciliation committee. If, within a period of six weeks following the convening of the committee, a joint text is approved, the European Parliament and the Council have a further six weeks in which to approve it (once more subject to extension in accordance with Art. 189b(7)). In general, the Council acts by qualified majority, while the European Parliament acts by a majority of votes cast. This is, however, not always the case. In two specific areas, the Council is bound to act by unanimity. These are measures under Art. 128(5) in the field of culture and Art. 130i on research and technological development. Articles 128(5) and 130i E.C. state that "the Council shall act unanimously throughout the procedures referred to in Art. 189b". This will make the achievement of workable compromises very difficult, given that the Council side can have its progress halted by one dissenting voice.

One area of the procedure which has caused real controversy is the final stage of the process, should the European Parliament or the Council fail to reach agreement in the conciliation committee. Article 189b(6) provides that the Council may, acting by a qualified majority, adopt its own common position, possibly with amendments approved by the European Parliament. The onus then falls upon the European Parliament positively to reject such a text within six weeks; failure to achieve the requisite absolute majority of members within this time leads to the act coming into force. The risk inherent in this procedure is that the Council may simply go through the motions of the conciliation committee without reaching agreement, and then adopt its common position thereafter. The European Parliament must then muster an absolute majority of its members, not just a majority of votes cast, to veto the Council's text. Moreover, it leads to the European Parliament taking full blame for the long drawn out legislative process coming to an end without any result. It would appear that unsuccessful attempts were made by Chancellor Kohl of Germany to alter this stage of the procedure during the Maastricht negotiations. While the Art. 189b E.C. procedure gives the impression of co-decision between the European Parliament and the Council (for example the act is jointly signed into being by the Presidents of the Council and the European Parliament (Art. 191 E.C.)), the reality is that the balance of power is still with the Council. Nevertheless, for the first time the European Parliament is given the right to veto legislation approved by the Council, albeit within a very complex procedure.

One very important factor concerns the scope of the new procedure. It will at first apply to 13 different legislative bases; these are Art. 49 on legislation on the free movement of workers, Art. 54(2) on directives on the freedom of establishment, Art. 56(2) on the co-ordination of Member State constraints on the freedom of establishment, Art. 57(1) and (2) on the mutual recognition of diplomas and co-ordination of Member State provisions on the taking up of activities by self-employed persons respectively, Art. 100a on the adoption of internal market harmonisation measures, Art. 126(4) on the adoption of incentive measures in the field of education, Art. 128 (5) for incentive measures in the field of culture, Art. 129(4) on the adoption of incentive measures in the field of public health, Art. 129a(2) on consumer protection measures, Art. 129d(1) on guidelines in the field of trans-European networks, Art. 130 i(1) on the multi-annual framework programmes for research and technological development and Art. 130s(3) on general action programmes regarding environmental policy.

This coverage is far from what the European Parliament had sought in the run-up to the Inter-governmental Conference and, as a rule, avoids the vast majority of nationally sensitive areas as well as all constitutional matters. It does, however, cover a wider number of legislative bases than the co-operation procedure did when introduced by the S.E.A. The co-operation procedure, with a more limited scope, had a significant impact on the role of the European Parliament in the legislative process, and the conciliation and veto procedure should have an even greater impact. Thanks to pressure from States not happy with the range of bases to which the conciliation and veto procedure applies, Art. 189b(8) provides that the next Inter-governmental Conference is to look at the widening of this procedure's scope.

In conclusion, the new procedure marks an important development in the legislative powers of the European Parliament and thus in the democratic legitimacy of the Community. Unfortunately, the process is very complicated, and thus will make the adoption of legislation both time-consuming and lacking in transparency to an outside observer. This is to be regretted on both counts. Whether or not the more dramatic predictions that its complexity could paralyse the Community's decision-making structure will be borne out is a matter of some doubt, but actual practice in its application will prove very important; not least the degree to which the institutions can adapt to the new tri-partite system and achieve meaningful three-way dialogues.

Article 189c

Where reference is made in this Treaty to this Article for the adoption of an act, the following procedure shall apply:

   (a) The Council, acting by a qualified majority on a proposal from the Commission and after obtaining the Opinion of the European Parliament, shall adopt a common position.

   (b) The Council's common position shall be communicated to the European Parliament. The Council and the Commission shall inform the European Parliament fully of the reasons which led the Council to adopt its common position and also of the Commission's position.

     If, within three months of such communication, the European Parliament approves this common position or has not taken a decision within that period, the Council shall definitively adopt the act in question in accordance with the common position.

   (c) The European Parliament may, within the period of three months referred to in point (b), by an absolute majority of its component members, propose amendments to the Council's common position. The European Parliament may also, by the same majority, reject the Council's common position. The result of the proceedings shall be transmitted to the Council and the Commission.

     If the European Parliament has rejected the Council's common position, unanimity shall be required for the Council to act on a second reading.

   (d) The Commission shall, within a period of one month, re-examine the proposal on the basis of which the Council adopted its common position, by taking into account the amendments proposed by the European Parliament.

     The Commission shall forward to the Council, at the same time as its re-examined proposal, the amendments of the European Parliament which it has not accepted, and shall express its opinion on them. The Council may adopt these amendments unanimously.

   (e) The Council, acting by a qualified majority, shall adopt the proposals as re-examined by the Commission.

     Unanimity shall be required for the Council to amend the proposal as re-examined by the Commission.

   (f) In the cases referred to in points (c), (d) and (e), the Council shall be required to act within a period of three months. If no decision is taken within this period, the Commission proposal shall be deemed not to have been adopted.

   (g) The periods referred to in points (b) and (f) may be extended by a maximum of one month by common accord between the Council and the European Parliament.

GENERAL NOTE

This Article, previously Art. 149(2) EEC contains the co-operation procedure introduced by the S.E.A. The procedure itself remains unchanged, but the scope of application of the procedure, which has been widely used, is somewhat increased, despite the majority of the internal market provisions being promoted to the conciliation and veto procedure. For further details on which Treaty provisions the co-operation procedure applies to (before and after the E.U. Treaty amendments) and how it has worked in the first few years of operation, see Weatherill and Beaumont, *E.C. Law* (1993), pp. 97–102.

Article 190

Regulations, directives and decisions adopted jointly by the European Parliament and the Council, and such acts adopted by the Council or the Commission, shall state the reasons on which they are based and shall refer to any proposals or opinions which were required to be obtained pursuant to this Treaty.

GENERAL NOTE

This Article has been amended in a way that recognises that some Community legislation will be adopted jointly by the European Parliament and the Council under the new conciliation and veto procedure (Art. 189b). The Article continues to make the stating of reasons essential for all binding Community legislation. For a brief analysis of Art. 190 see Weatherill and Beaumont, *E.C. Law* (1993), pp. 122–3 and 215–6.

Article 191

1. Regulations, directives and decisions adopted in accordance with the procedure referred to in Article 189b shall be signed by the President of the European Parliament and by the President of the Council and published in the Official Journal of the Community. They shall enter into force on the date specified in them or, in the absence thereof, on the 20th day following that of their publication.

2. Regulations of the Council and of the Commission, as well as directives of those institutions which are addressed to all Member States, shall be published in the Official Journal of the Community. They shall enter into force on the date specified in them or, in the absence thereof, on the 20th day following that of their publication.

3. Other directives, and decisions, shall be notified to those to whom they are addressed and shall take effect upon such notification.

GENERAL NOTE

The first paragraph was added by the E.U. Treaty as it applies to binding legislative measures adopted under the new conciliation and veto procedure provided for in Art. 189b E.C. All such measures must be published in the *Official Journal*. Given their binding nature they will in practice be published in the "L" series of the *Official Journal*. The paragraph adopts the traditional time for regulations to come into force, *i.e.* when stated in the regulation or, if no date is specified, 20 days after publication (see Art. 191(1) EEC), but extends its application to directives and decisions.

Paragraph two is an amended version of Art. 191(1) EEC. The requirement of publication in the *Official Journal* has been extended to apply to directives which are applicable to all Member States.

Paragraph three replicates the old Art. 191(2) EEC with the insertion of "Other" at the beginning. This change is necessitated by the fact that directives and decisions adopted under the Art.

189b procedure, and directives addressed to all Member States, are for the first time subject to a requirement to be published in the *Official Journal*. It is unfortunate that all decisions which are addressed to all the Member States are not subject to the same publication requirement. Such decisions are binding and could have direct effect, so they should be readily available to lawyers and the general public. In practice, it is likely that such decisions will be published in the *Official Journal*, but a Treaty requirement would have been more satisfactory.

Article 192

Decisions of the Council or of the Commission which impose a pecuniary obligation on persons other than States, shall be enforceable.

Enforcement shall be governed by the rules of civil procedure in force in the State in the territory of which it is carried out. The order for its enforcement shall be appended to the decision, without other formality than verification of the authenticity of the decision, by the national authority which the Government of each Member State shall designate for this purpose and shall make known to the Commission and to the Court of Justice.

When these formalities have been completed on application by the party concerned, the latter may proceed to enforcement in accordance with the national law, by bringing the matter directly before the competent authority.

Enforcement may be suspended only by a decision of the Court of Justice. However, the courts of the country concerned shall have jurisdiction over complaints that enforcement is being carried out in an irregular manner.

Chapter 3 (The Economic and Social Committee)

Article 193

An Economic and Social Committee is hereby established. It shall have advisory status.

The Committee shall consist of representatives of the various categories of economic and social activity, in particular, representatives of producers, farmers, carriers, workers, dealers, craftsmen, professional occupations and representatives of the general public.

Article 194

The number of members of the Committee shall be as follows:

Belgium	12
Denmark	9
Germany	24
Greece	12
Spain	21
France	24
Ireland	9
Italy	24
Luxembourg	6
Netherlands	12
[Austria	12]
Portugal	12
[Finland	9]
[Sweden	12]
United Kingdom	24

The members of the Committee shall be appointed by the Council, acting unanimously, for four years. Their appointments shall be renewable.

The members of the Committee may not be bound by any mandatory instructions. They shall be completely independent in the performance of their duties, in the general interest of the Community.

The Council, acting by a qualified majority, shall determine the allowances of members of the Committee.

GENERAL NOTE

The last two sentences of this Article have been inserted by the E.U. Treaty. They reinforce the independence of members of the Economic and Social Committee. Previously they could not be bound by any mandatory instructions but now they must also be "completely independent" like members of the Commission (Art. 157(2)) and of the Committee of the Regions (Art. 198a). The symmetry with the new provisions on the Committee of the Regions is reflected in a common size (compare Arts. 194 and 198a) and common support staff in Brussels (see Protocol No. 16 below). However, the provisions governing the two Committees are not identical. Curiously enough the Maastricht Treaty has amended Art. 194 so that the Council, by qualified majority, can decide what allowances Economic and Social Committee members will get, but there is no express provision on the point for the new Committee of the Regions.

Further amendments were made by the Act of Accession [1994] O.J. C241/08; [1995] O.J. L1/1.

Article 195

1. For the appointment of the members of the Committee, each Member State shall provide the Council with a list containing twice as many candidates as there are seats allocated to its nationals.

The composition of the Committee shall take account of the need to ensure adequate representation of the various categories of economic and social activity.

2. The Council shall consult the Commission. It may obtain the opinion of European bodies which are representative of the various economic and social sectors to which the activities of the Community are of concern.

Article 196

The Committee shall elect its chairman and officers from among its members for a term of two years.

It shall adopt its rules of procedure.

The Committee shall be convened by its chairman at the request of the Council or of the Commission. It may also meet on its own initiative.

GENERAL NOTE

The only change to this Article is the addition of the last sentence. The Economic and Social Committee can now meet on its own initiative, not just when requested by the Council or Commission. This mirrors the right given to the Committee of the Regions in Art. 198b. This may well lead to more meetings held at the Community taxpayer's expense. As the Committee has an unconstrained power to adopt its own rules of procedure, it could make it possible for its meetings to be called by relatively few members. Since the Committee is purely advisory and is made up of members appointed by the Council the case is sometimes for its elimination as opposed to an expanded role (see Weatherill and Beaumont, *E.C. Law* (1993), p. 129, but contrast Smith (1989) Stat. L. Rev. 56 at 68).

Article 197

The Committee shall include specialised sections for the principal fields covered by this Treaty.

In particular, it shall contain an agricultural section and a transport section, which are the subject of special provisions in the Titles relating to agriculture and transport.

These specialised sections shall operate within the general terms of reference of the Committee. They may not be consulted independently of the Committee.

Sub-committees may also be established within the Committee to prepare on specific questions or in specific fields, draft opinions to be submitted to the Committee for its consideration.

The rules of procedure shall lay down the methods of composition and the terms of reference of the specialised sections and of the sub-committees.

Article 198

The Committee must be consulted by the Council or by the Commission where this Treaty so provides. The Committee may be consulted by these institutions in all cases in which they consider it appropriate. It may [take the initiative of issuing an opinion] in cases in which it considers such action appropriate.

The Council or the Commission shall, if it considers it necessary, set the Committee, for the submission of its opinion, a time limit which may not be less than one month from the date on which the chairman receives notification to this effect. Upon expiry of the time limit, the absence of an opinion shall not prevent further action.

The opinion of the Committee and that of the specialised section, together with a record of the proceedings, shall be forwarded to the Council and to the Commission.

GENERAL NOTE

In some versions of the treaty the words in brackets read "issue an opinion on its own initiative".

The last sentence of the first paragraph is an amendment introduced by the E.U. Treaty. It gives the Economic and Social Committee the power to give an opinion on its own initiative whenever it wishes to do so. The same right is given to the Committee of the Regions in Art. 198c. In both cases this is a recipe for the Committee pontificating about all aspects of Community policy and doing so by proliferating their meetings (see note on Art. 196 above). It is questionable whether these own initiative opinions will prove to be helpful in the development of the Community.

In paragraph two the Economic and Social Committee's delaying power has been increased from 10 days to one month. This change avoids the necessity of the Committee having to meet more than once a month and is therefore to be welcomed.

Chapter 4 (The Committee of the Regions)

Article 198a

A Committee consisting of representatives of regional and local bodies, hereinafter referred to as the 'Committee of the Regions,' is hereby established with advisory status.

[The number of members of the Committee of the Regions shall be as follows:

Belgium	12
Denmark	9
Germany	24
Greece	12
Spain	21
France	24
Ireland	9
Italy	24
Luxembourg	6
Netherlands	12
[Austria	12]
Portugal	12
[Finland	9]
[Sweden	12]
United Kingdom	24]

The members of the Committee and an equal number of alternate members shall be appointed for four years by the Council acting unanimously on proposals from the respective Member States. Their term of office shall be renewable.

The members of the Committee may not be bound by any mandatory instructions. They shall be completely independent in the performance of their duties, in the general interest of the Community.

GENERAL NOTE

The provision is very similar to Art. 194 concerning the Economic and Social Committee. One difference between the two Articles is mentioned in the note on Art. 194. In addition, the Council is required to appoint alternate members to the Committee of the Regions but not to the Economic and Social Committee.

The amendments were made by the Act of Accession [1994] O.J. C241/08; [1995] O.J. L1/1.

Article 198b

The Committee of the Regions shall elect its chairman and officers from among its members for a term of two years.

It shall adopt its rules of procedure and shall submit them for approval to the Council, acting unanimously.

The Committee shall be convened by its chairman at the request of the Council or of the Commission. It may also meet on its own initiative.

GENERAL NOTE

This provision is identical to Art. 196 concerning the Economic and Social Committee, except that the Committee of the Regions cannot control its own rules of procedure but must have them approved unanimously by the Council.

Article 198c

The Committee of the Regions shall be consulted by the Council or by the Commission where this Treaty so provides and in all other cases in which one of these two institutions considers it appropriate.

The Council or the Commission shall, if it considers it necessary, set the Committee, for the submission of its opinion, a time-limit which may not be less than one month from the date on which the chairman receives notification to this effect. Upon expiry of the time-limit, the absence of an opinion shall not prevent further action.

Where the Economic and Social Committee is consulted pursuant to Article 198, the Committee of the Regions shall be informed by the Council or the Commission of the request for an opinion. Where it considers that specific regional interests are involved, the Committee of the Regions may issue an opinion on the matter.

It may [take the initiative of issuing an opinion] in cases in which it considers such action appropriate.

The opinion of the Committee, together with a record of the proceedings, shall be forwarded to the Council and to the Commission.

GENERAL NOTE

In some versions of the Treaty the words in brackets read "issue an opinion on its own initiative".

The substance of this Article is very similar to Art. 198 concerning the Economic and Social Committee. Many more Treaty Articles require mandatory consultation of that body than require consultation of the Committee of the Regions (Arts. 49, 54, 63, 75, 79, 84, 99, 100, 100a, 118a, 121, 126, 127, 129, 129a, 129d, 130, 130b, 130d, 130e, 130i, 130o and 130s compared with Arts. 126, 128, 129, 129d, 130b, 130d and 130e). Paragraph two requires the Committee of the Regions to be informed whenever the Economic and Social Committee is asked for an opinion (whether mandatory or optional). The Committee of the Regions can then choose to give its own opinion on the proposed legislation.

It is likely that any failure to consult the Committee of the Regions (or the Economic and Social Committee) in cases where the Treaty requires such consultation would mean that if an action was competently brought before the European Court under Art. 173, the legislation would be annulled (*cf.* the analogous requirement to consult the European Parliament in Case 139/79, *Roquette Fréres v. Council* [1980] E.C.R. 3333).

Chapter 5 (European Investment Bank)

Article 198d

The European Investment Bank shall have legal personality.

The members of the European Investment Bank shall be the Member States.

The Statute of the European Investment Bank is laid down in a Protocol annexed to this Treaty.

GENERAL NOTE

This Article repeats what was formerly in Art. 129 E.E.C. with the exclusion of any reference to the establishing of the European Investment Bank, as it has been established since the founding of the Community.

Article 198e

The task of the European Investment Bank shall be to contribute, by having recourse to the capital market and utilising its own resources, to the balanced and steady development of the common market in the interest of the Community. For this purpose the Bank shall, operating on a non-profit-making basis, grant loans and give guarantees which facilitate the financing of the following projects in all sectors of the economy:

(a) projects for developing less-developed regions;

(b) projects for modernising or converting undertakings or for developing fresh activities called for by the progressive establishment of the common market, where these projects are of such a size or nature that they cannot be entirely financed by the various means available in the individual Member States;

(c) projects of common interest to several Member States which are of such a size or nature that they cannot be entirely financed by the various means available in the individual Member States.

In carrying out its task, the Bank shall facilitate the financing of investment programmes in conjunction with assistance from the structural funds and other Community financial instruments.

GENERAL NOTE

This provision is identical to its predecessor, Art. 130 EEC, except for the addition of the last paragraph. This explicit reference to the work of the European Investment Bank in the context of the structural funds, ties in with the reference to the Bank in Art. 130b (introduced by the S.E.A.) as a means by which the Community can take action to support the objectives associated with economic and social cohesion set out in Art. 130a (see note on that Article). In the Protocol on Economic and Social Cohesion the Member States reaffirmed their conviction that the European Investment Bank should "continue to devote the majority of its resources to the promotion of economic and social cohesion, and declare their willingness to review the capital needs of the

European Investment Bank as soon as this is necessary for that purpose". The Act of March 25, 1993 amending the Protocol on the Statute of the Investment Bank, enabling the establishment of a European Investment Fund, is noted in the annotation of the European Communities Act, 1972 above.

TITLE II: Financial Provisions

Article 199

All items of revenue and expenditure of the Community, including those relating to the European Social Fund, shall be included in estimates to be drawn up for each financial year and shall be shown in the budget.

The administrative expenditure occasioned for the institutions by the provisions of the Treaty on European Union relating to common foreign and security policy and to co-operation in the [spheres] of justice and home affairs shall be charged to the budget. The operational expenditure occasioned by the implementation of the said provisions may, under the conditions referred to therein, be charged to the budget.

The revenue and expenditure shown in the budget shall be in balance.

GENERAL NOTE

In some versions of the text the word in square brackets is fields.

The second paragraph was added by the TEU. The administrative expenditure relating to the common foreign and security policy and justice and home affairs pillars is to be charged to the E.C. budget. This gives the European Parliament a significant financial role in constraining the cash allocated to the operation of the two inter-governmental pillars, even though it has a very limited role in the decision-making process as regards the substantive issues under those pillars. The degree of influence the European Parliament will depend on whether the expenditure is categorised as compulsory or non-compulsory. Articles J.11(2) and K.8(2) of the TEU lay down the procedure whereby the Council charges the operating expenditure of the common foreign and security policy and justice and home affairs either to the E.C. budget or to the Member States. It requires a unanimous decision for the Council to charge operational expenditure to the E.C. budget. It is not as clear as to which voting procedure applies in relation to a decision to charge the Member States. Logically, it should be less than unanimity because some mechanism for paying operational expenditure must be agreed, and if it has to be done unanimously there is a danger that no mechanism will be agreed. On the other hand, Arts. J.8(2) and K.4(3) E.U. provide that in these pillars the Council is to act unanimously "except on matters of procedure". Therefore unanimity will be required unless the Council regards the question as to who must pay for operational expenditure as a procedural matter.

Article 200

GENERAL NOTE

This Article has been repealed. It was long overdue for repeal, as it related to the financial contributions of the six original Member States to the Community budget revenue. Article 201 EEC had envisaged the replacement of Art. 200 by a Community measure laying down a system of the Community's own resources. This was done first of all in the Council Decision on the Replacement of Financial Contributions from Member States by the Community's Own Resources (Decision 70/243 of April 21, [1970] J.O.; [1970] L94/19; O.J. Dec. [1970] (I) 224). Later, it was replaced by Council Decision 85/257 ([1985] O.J. L128/15). This in turn was replaced by Council Decision 88/376 of June 24, 1988 ([1988] O.J. L185/24).

Article 201

Without prejudice to other revenue, the budget shall be financed wholly from own resources. The Council, acting unanimously on a proposal from the

Commission and after consulting the European Parliament, shall lay down provisions relating to the system of own resources of the Community, which it shall recommend to the Member States for adoption in accordance with their respective constitutional requirements.

GENERAL NOTE

The procedure whereby decisions about the Community's own resources can be taken, is the same as that provided in Art. 201 EEC. The change that has been made is the removal of references to the possibility of moving from Member States financing the Community by contributions, to the system of own resources. The latter is, of course, an accepted fact of Community life and the new Art. 201 is able to declare that the budget shall be financed wholly from own resources. The old Art. 201 explicitly referred to revenue from the common customs tariff as a possible own resource. The new Article does not specify what the constituent elements of the own resource are or should be. The last major change to the system of own resources, first established by Decision 70/243 (see note on Art. 200 above), was taken following the European Council meeting in Brussels in February 1988 ([1988] 2 E.C. Bull., 13 *et seq.* and [1988] 3 E.C. Bull., 105). Council Decision 88/376 added a fourth source of revenue, based on a Gross National Product scale, to the three sources first established in the 1970 Decision (agricultural levies, common customs tariff and a percentage of VAT). For a short account of the Community's own resources see Mathijsen, *A Guide to European Union Law* (6th ed., 1995), pp. 129–31. For a fuller analysis see Kapteyn and Verloren van Themaat, *Introduction to the Law of the European Communities* (2nd ed., 1990), pp. 215–9.

Article 201a

With a view to maintaining budgetary discipline, the Commission shall not make any proposal for a Community act, or alter its proposals, or adopt any implementing measure which is likely to have appreciable implications for the budget without providing the assurance that that proposal or that measure is capable of being financed within the limit of the Community's own resources arising under provisions laid down by the Council pursuant to Article 201.

GENERAL NOTE

This is a new Article, inserted into the Treaty. For the first time, the idea of maintaining budgetary discipline has been embedded in the Treaty. The three political institutions, Commission, Council and Parliament, had earlier entered into an inter-institutional agreement on budgetary discipline and improvement of the budgetary procedure (see [1988] O.J. L185) and Zangl, "The Inter-institutional Agreement on Budgetary Discipline and Improvement of the Budgetary Procedure" (1989) 26 C.M.L.Rev. 675). The new Article places the onus on the Commission not to make proposals which would have the effect of breaching the limit of finances available from own resources. In the agreement on own resources in 1988, an overall ceiling on own resources was set at 1.2 per cent of total Community Gross National Product for payments. The inter-institutional agreement attempts to ensure that the own resources ceilings are not overstepped, but it does not have binding legal force. A new Interinstitutional Agreement on budgetary discipline and improvement of the budgetary procedure was adopted on October 29, 1993 (see [1993] O.J. C333/1). It covers the 1993 to 1999 financial perspective agreed at the Edinburgh European Council in December 1992.

Article 202

The expenditure shown in the budget shall be authorised for one financial year, unless the regulations made pursuant to Article 209 provide otherwise.

In accordance with conditions to be laid down pursuant to Article 209, any appropriations, other than those relating to staff expenditure, that are unexpended at the end of the financial year may be carried forward to the next financial year only.

Appropriations shall be classified under different chapters grouping items of expenditure according to their nature or purpose and subdivided, as far as may be necessary, in accordance with the regulations made pursuant to Article 209.

The expenditure of the European Parliament, the Council, the Commission and the Court of Justice shall be set out in separate parts of the budget, without prejudice to special arrangements for certain common items of expenditure.

Article 203

1. The financial year shall run from 1 January to 31 December.
2. Each institution of the Community shall, before 1 July, draw up estimates of its expenditure. The Commission shall consolidate these estimates in a preliminary draft budget. It shall attach thereto an opinion which may contain different estimates.

The preliminary draft budget shall contain an estimate of revenue and an estimate of expenditure.

3. The Commission shall place the preliminary draft budget before the Council not later than 1 September of the year preceding that in which the budget is to be implemented.

The Council shall consult the Commission and, where appropriate, the other institutions concerned whenever it intends to depart from the preliminary draft budget.

The Council, acting by a qualified majority, shall establish the draft budget and forward it to the European Parliament.

4. The draft budget shall be placed before the European Parliament not later than 5 October of the year preceding that in which the budget is to be implemented.

The European Parliament shall have the right to amend the draft budget, acting by a majority of its members, and to propose to the Council, acting by an absolute majority of the votes cast, modifications to the draft budget relating to expenditure necessarily resulting from this Treaty or from acts adopted in accordance therewith.

If, within 45 days of the draft budget being placed before it, the European Parliament has given its approval, the budget shall stand as finally adopted. If within the period the European Parliament has not amended the draft budget nor proposed any modifications thereto, the budget shall be deemed to be finally adopted.

If within this period the European Parliament has adopted amendments or proposed modifications, the draft budget together with the amendments or proposed modifications shall be forwarded to the Council.

5. After discussing the draft budget with the Commission and, where appropriate, with the other institutions concerned, the Council shall act under the following conditions:

(a) The Council may, acting by a qualified majority, modify any of the amendments adopted by the European Parliament;

(b) With regard to the proposed modifications:

— where a modification proposed by the European Parliament does not have the effect of increasing the total amount of the expenditure of an institution, owing in particular to the fact that the increase in expenditure which it would involve would be expressly compensated by one or more proposed modifications correspondingly reducing expenditure, the Council may, acting by a qualified majority, reject the proposed modification. In the absence of a decision to reject it, the proposed modification shall stand as accepted;

— where a modification proposed by the European Parliament has the effect of increasing the total amount of the expenditure of an institution, the Council may, acting by a qualified majority, accept this proposed modification. In the absence of a decision to accept it, the proposed modification shall stand as rejected;

— where, in pursuance of one of the two preceding subparagraphs, the Council has rejected a proposed modification, it may, acting by a qualified majority, either retain the amount shown in the draft budget or fix another amount.

The draft budget shall be modified on the basis of the proposed modifications accepted by the Council.

If, within 15 days of the draft being placed before it, the Council has not modified any of the amendments adopted by the European Parliament and if the modifications proposed by the latter have been accepted, the budget shall be deemed to be finally adopted. The Council shall inform the European Parliament that it has not modified any of the amendments and that the proposed modifications have been accepted.

If within the period the Council has modified one or more of the amendments adopted by the European Parliament or if the modifications proposed by the latter have been rejected or modified, the modified draft budget shall again be forwarded to the European Parliament. The Council shall inform the European Parliament of the results of its deliberations.

6. Within 15 days of the draft budget being placed before it, the European Parliament, which shall have been notified of the action taken on its proposed modifications, may, acting by a majority of its members and three-fifths of the votes cast, amend or reject the modifications to its amendments made by the Council and shall adopt the budget accordingly. If within this period the European Parliament has not acted, the budget shall be deemed to be finally adopted.

7. When the procedure provided for in this Article has been completed, the President of the European Parliament shall declare that the budget has been finally adopted.

8. However, the European Parliament, acting by a majority of its members and two-thirds of the votes cast, may, if there are important reasons, reject the draft budget and ask for a new draft to be submitted to it.

9. A maximum rate of increase in relation to the expenditure of the same type to be incurred during the current year shall be fixed annually for the total expenditure other than that necessarily resulting from this Treaty or from acts adopted in accordance therewith.

The Commission shall, after consulting the Economic Policy Committee, declare what this maximum rate is as it results from:

— the trend, in terms of volume, of the gross national product within the Community;

— the average variation in the budgets of the Member States; and

— the trend of the cost of living during the preceding financial year.

The maximum rate shall be communicated, before 1 May, to all the institutions of the Community. The latter shall be required to conform to this during the budgetary procedure, subject to the provisions of the fourth and fifth subparagraphs of this paragraph.

If, in respect of expenditure other than that necessarily resulting from this Treaty or from acts adopted in accordance therewith, the actual rate of increase in the draft budget, established by the Council is over half the maximum rate, the European Parliament may, exercising its right of amendment, further increase the total amount of that expenditure to a limit not exceeding half the maximum rate.

Where the European Parliament, the Council or the Commission consider that the activities of the Communities require that the rate determined according to the procedure laid down in this paragraph should be exceeded, another rate may be fixed by agreement between the Council, acting by a qualified majority, and the European Parliament, acting by a majority of its members and three-fifths of the votes cast.

10. Each institution shall exercise the powers conferred upon it by this Article, with due regard for the provisions of the Treaty and for acts adopted in accordance therewith, in particular those relating to the Communities' own resources and to the balance between revenue and expenditure.

Article 204

If at the beginning of a financial year, the budget has not yet been voted, a sum equivalent to not more than one-twelfth of the budget appropriations for the preceding financial year may be spent each month in respect of any chapter or other subdivision of the budget in accordance with the provisions of the Regulations made pursuant to Article 209; this arrangement shall not, however, have the effect of placing at the disposal of the Commission appropriations in excess of one-twelfth of those provided for in the draft budget in course of preparation.

The Council may, acting by a qualified majority, provided that the other conditions laid down in the first subparagraph are observed, authorise expenditure in excess of one-twelfth.

If the decision relates to expenditure which does not necessarily result from this Treaty or from acts adopted in accordance therewith, the Council shall forward it immediately to the European Parliament; within 30 days the European Parliament, acting by a majority of its members and three-fifths of the votes cast, may adopt a different decision on the expenditure in excess of the one-twelfth referred to in the first subparagraph. This part of the decision of the Council shall be suspended until the European Parliament has taken its decision. If within the said period the European Parliament has not taken a decision which differs from the decision of the Council, the latter shall be deemed to be finally adopted.

The decisions referred to in the second and third subparagraphs shall lay down the necessary measures relating to resources to ensure application of this Article.

Article 205

The Commission shall implement the budget, in accordance with the provisions of the regulations made pursuant to Article 209, on its own responsibility and within the limits of the appropriations, having regard to the principles of sound financial management.

The regulations shall lay down detailed rules for each institution concerning its part in effecting its own expenditure.

Within the budget, the Commission may, subject to the limits and conditions laid down in the regulations made pursuant to Article 209, transfer appropriations from one chapter to another or from one sub-division to another.

GENERAL NOTE

The last clause of the first paragraph: "having regard to the principles of sound financial management" has been added by the E.U. Treaty. This is a very minor change that acts as a reminder to the Commission to implement the budget in a financially prudent way. It is difficult to see how this clause might successfully be invoked against the Commission in any claim that it had imprudently implemented the budget. The Commission merely has to have regard to the principles referred to, and it is not at all clear what these principles are.

Article 205a

The Commission shall submit annually to the Council and to the European Parliament the accounts of the preceding financial year relating to the implementation of the budget. The Commission shall also forward to them a financial statement of the assets and liabilities of the Community.

Article 206

1. The European Parliament, acting on a recommendation from the Council which shall act by a qualified majority, shall give a discharge to the Commission in respect of the implementation of the budget. To this end, the Council and the European Parliament in turn shall examine the accounts and the financial statement referred to in Article 205a, the annual report by the Court of Auditors together with the replies of the institutions under audit to the observations of the Court of Auditors and any relevant special reports by the Court of Auditors.

2. Before giving a discharge to the Commission, or for any other purpose in connection with the exercise of its powers over the implementation of the budget, the European Parliament may ask to hear the Commission give evidence with regard to the execution of expenditure or the operation of financial control systems. The Commission shall submit any necessary information to the European Parliament at the latter's request.

3. The Commission shall take all appropriate steps to act on the observations in the decisions giving discharge and on other observations by the European Parliament relating to the execution of expenditure, as well as on comments accompanying the recommendations on discharge adopted by the Council.

At the request of the European Parliament or the Council, the Commission shall report on the measures taken in the light of these observations and comments and in particular on the instructions given to the departments which are responsible for the implementation of the budget. These reports shall also be forwarded to the Court of Auditors.

GENERAL NOTE

The first paragraph of Art. 206 is derived from Art. 206b EEC with the addition of the last clause: "and any relevant special reports by the Court of Auditors".

Paragraphs 2 and 3 are new material added by the TEU. Paragraph 2 gives the Parliament explicit, Treaty-based, power to glean any necessary information from the Commission on its execution of expenditure or the operation of financial control systems. Paragraph 3 requires the Commission to "take all appropriate steps" to carry out the observations of the European Parliament and Council in relation to the discharge. This does not seem to require the Commission to do what the other institutions say, but does require it to do what it regards as "appropriate" to comply with the wishes of the other institutions. The Commission has to report on the actions it takes to the other institutions and the Court of Auditors. It is difficult to see how the Commission can be compelled to take the steps that the Parliament and Council want.

These two paragraphs were part of the attempt at Maastricht to bring the Commission under even closer scrutiny by the Parliament and to tighten up the financial discipline and prudence in the Community.

Article 206a

(Repealed at Maastricht)

Article 206b

(Repealed at Maastricht)

GENERAL NOTE

These Articles were repealed by the E.U. Treaty. Article 206a EEC concerned the Court of Auditors and an amended version can now be found in Art. 188c E.C. Article 206b EEC has been absorbed into Art. 206 E.C. (see the note on that Article).

Article 207

The budget shall be drawn up in the unit of account determined in accordance with the provisions of the regulations made pursuant to Article 209.

The financial contributions provided for in Article 200(1) shall be placed at the disposal of the Community by the Member States in their national currencies.

The available balances of these contributions shall be deposited with the Treasuries of Member States or with bodies designated by them. While on deposit, such funds shall retain the value corresponding to the parity, at the date of deposit, in relation to the unit of account referred to in the first paragraph.

The balances may be invested on terms to be agreed between the Commission and the Member State concerned.

The regulations made pursuant to Article 209 shall lay down the technical conditions under which financial operations relating to the European Social Fund shall be carried out.

GENERAL NOTE

This Article is not amended by the E.U. Treaty. This is unfortunate given that the second sentence contains a reference to Art. 200 which was repealed by the E.U. Treaty. Hopefully, this discrepancy will be removed at the next inter-governmental conference in 1996.

Article 208

The Commission may, provided it notifies the competent authorities of the Member States concerned, transfer into the currency of one of the Member States its holdings in the currency of another Member State, to the extent necessary to enable them to be used for purposes which come within the scope of this Treaty. The Commission shall as far as possible avoid making such transfers if it possesses cash or liquid assets in the currencies which it needs.

The Commission shall deal with each Member State through the authority designated by the State concerned. In carrying out financial operations the Commission shall employ the services of the bank of issue of the Member State concerned or of any other financial institution approved by that State.

Article 209

The Council, acting unanimously on a proposal from the Commission and after consulting the European Parliament and obtaining the opinion of the Court of Auditors, shall:
- (a) make Financial Regulations specifying in particular the procedure to be adopted for establishing and implementing the budget and for presenting and auditing accounts;
- (b) determine the methods and procedure whereby the budget revenue provided under the arrangements relating to the Community's own resources shall be made available to the Commission, and determine the measures to be applied, if need be, to meet cash requirements;
- (c) lay down rules concerning the responsibility of financial controllers, authorising officers and accounting officers, and concerning appropriate arrangements for inspection.

GENERAL NOTE

Only para. (c) has been amended, by the insertion of the words "financial controllers" before "authorising officers". This is a very minor amendment.

Article 209a

Member States shall take the same measures to counter fraud affecting the financial interests of the Community as they take to counter fraud affecting their own financial interests.

Without prejudice to other provisions of this Treaty, Member States shall co-ordinate their action aimed at protecting the financial interests of the Community against fraud. To this end they shall organise, with the help of the Commission, close and regular co-operation between the competent departments of their administrations.

GENERAL NOTE

This is a new practice designed to help the fight against fraudulent use of Community finances. The obligation in the first paragraph is one of parallelism; the Member States are to be just as vigilant in countering fraud against Community finances as they are in dealing with fraud affecting their own interests. The symbolism of this paragraph is positive, but it is not apparent that it can be readily enforced.

The second paragraph imposes on Member States a requirement to co-ordinate their anti-fraud activities. This may be of some help in the battle against fraud, but it is questionable whether such co-ordination is sufficient. Commission Decision 94/140/E.C. established the Advisory Committee for Co-ordination of Fraud Prevention ([1994] O.J. L61). The Commission has also published a Communication to the Council, Parliament and Court of Auditors on its anti-fraud strategy (COM (94) 92). It has proposed in the pillar of co-operation in the fields of judicial and home affairs a Convention for the Protection of the Communities' Financial Interests, which would create common fraud offences (COM (94) 214).

PART SIX (GENERAL AND FINAL PROVISIONS)

Article 210

The Community shall have legal personality.

Article 211

In each of the Member States, the Community shall enjoy the most extensive legal capacity accorded to legal persons under their laws; it may, in particular, acquire or dispose of movable and immovable property and may be a party to legal proceedings. To this end, the Community shall be represented by the Commission.

Article 212

(as replaced by Merger Treaty, Art. 24(1))

24(1). The officials and other servants of the European Coal and Steel Community, the European Economic Community and the European Atomic Energy Community shall, at the date of entry into force of this Treaty, become officials and other servants of the European Communities and form part of the single administration of those Communities.

The Council shall, acting by a qualified majority on a proposal from the Commission and after consulting the other institutions concerned, lay down the Staff Regulations of officials of the European Communities and the Conditions of Employment of other servants of those Communities.

Article 213

The Commission may, within the limits and under conditions laid down by the Council in accordance with the provisions of this Treaty, collect any information and carry out any checks required for the performance of the tasks entrusted to it.

Article 214

The members of the institutions of the Community, the members of committees, and the officials and other servants of the Community shall be required, even after their duties have ceased, not to disclose information of the kind covered by the obligation of professional secrecy, in particular information about undertakings, their business relations or their cost components.

Article 215

The contractual liability of the Community shall be governed by the law applicable to the contract in question.

In the case of non-contractual liability, the Community shall, in accordance with the general principles common to the laws of the Member States, make good any damage caused by its institutions or by its servants in the performance of their duties.

The preceding paragraph shall apply under the same conditions to damage caused by the ECB or by its servants in the performance of their duties.

The personal liability of its servants towards the Community shall be governed by the provisions laid down in their Staff Regulations or in the Conditions of Employment applicable to them.

GENERAL NOTE

Paragraph 2 concerning the non-contractual liability of the Community has been extended by paragraph three to cover damage caused by the European Central Bank or by its servants, in the performance of their duties. For a brief summary of the Court's jurisdiction in relation to Art. 215(2), provided for by Art. 178, see Weatherill and Beaumont, *E.C.* Law (1993), pp. 269–73.

Article 216

The seat of the institutions of the Community shall be determined by common accord of the Governments of the Member States.

Article 217

The rules governing the languages of the institutions of the Community shall, without prejudice to the provisions contained in the rules of procedure of the Court of Justice, be determined by the Council, acting unanimously.

Article 218
(*as replaced by Merger Treaty, Art. 28(1)*)

28(1). The European Communities shall enjoy in the territories of the Member States such privileges and immunities as are necessary for the performance of their tasks, under the conditions laid down in the Protocol annexed to this Treaty. The same shall apply to the European Investment Bank.

Article 219

Member States undertake not to submit a dispute concerning the interpretation or application of this Treaty to any method of settlement other than those provided for therein.

Article 220

Member States shall, so far as is necessary, enter into negotiations with each other with a view to securing for the benefit of their nationals:
— the protection of persons and the enjoyment and protection of rights under the same conditions as those accorded by each State to its own nationals;

— the abolition of double taxation within the Community;
— the mutual recognition of companies or firms within the meaning of the second paragraph of Article 48, the retention of legal personality in the event of transfer of their seat from one country to another, and the possibility of mergers between companies or firms governed by the laws of different countries;
— the simplification of formalities governing the reciprocal recognition and enforcement of judgments of courts or tribunals and of arbitration awards.

Article 221

Within three years of the entry into force of this Treaty, Member States shall accord nationals of the other Member States the same treatment as their own nationals as regards participation in the capital of companies or firms within the meaning of Article 58, without prejudice of the other provisions of this Treaty.

Article 222

This Treaty shall in no way prejudice the rules in Member States governing the system of property ownership.

Article 223

1. The provisions of this Treaty shall not preclude the application of the following rules:
   (a) No Member State shall be obliged to supply information the disclosure of which it considers contrary to the essential interests of its security;
   (b) Any Member State may take such measures as it considers necessary for the protection of the essential interests of its security which are connected with the production of or trade in arms, munitions and war material; such measures shall not adversely affect the conditions of competition in the common market regarding products which are not intended for specifically military purposes.
2. During the first year after the entry into force of this Treaty, the Council shall, acting unanimously, draw up a list of products to which the provisions of paragraph 1(b) shall apply.
3. The Council may, acting unanimously on a proposal from the Commission, make changes in this list.

Article 224

Member States shall consult each other with a view to taking together the steps needed to prevent the functioning of the common market being affected by measures which a Member State may be called upon to take in the event of serious internal disturbances affecting the maintenance of law and order, in the event of war, serious international tension constituting a threat of war, or in order to carry out obligations it has accepted for the purpose of maintaining peace and international security.

Article 225

If measures taken in the circumstances referred to in Articles 223 and 224 have the effect of distorting the conditions of competition in the common market, the Commission shall, together with the State concerned, examine how these measures can be adjusted to the rules laid down in this Treaty.

By way of derogation from the procedure laid down in Articles 169 and 170, the Commission or any Member State may bring the matter directly before the Court of Justice if it considers that another Member State is making improper use of the powers provided for in Articles 223 and 224. The Court of Justice shall give its ruling *in camera.*

Article 226

1. If, during the transitional period, difficulties arise which are serious and liable to persist in any sector of the economy or which could bring about serious deterioration in the economic situation of a given area, a Member State may apply for authorisation to take protective measures in order to rectify the situation and adjust the sector concerned to the economy of the common market.

2. On application by the State concerned, the Commission shall, by emergency procedure, determine without delay the protective measures which it considers necessary, specifying the circumstances and the manner in which they are to be put into effect.

3. The measures authorised under paragraph 2 may involve derogations from the rules of this Treaty, to such an extent and for such periods as are strictly necessary in order to attain the objectives referred to in paragraph 1. Priority shall be given to such measures as will least disturb the functioning of the common market.

Article 227

[1. This Treaty shall apply to the Kingdom of Belgium, the Kingdom of Denmark, the Federal Republic of Germany, the Hellenic Republic, the Kingdom of Spain, the French Republic, Ireland, the Italian Republic, the Grand Duchy of Luxembourg, the Kingdom of the Netherlands, the Republic of Austria, the Portuguese Republic, the Republic of Finland, the Kingdom of Sweden and the United Kingdom of Great Britain and Northern Ireland.]

2. With regard to the French overseas departments, the general and particular provisions of this Treaty relating to:
— the free movement of goods;
— agriculture, save for Article 40(4);
— the liberalisation of services;
— the rules on competition;
— the protective measures provided for in Articles 109h, 109i and 226;
— the institutions,
shall apply as soon as this Treaty enters into force.

The conditions under which the other provisions of this Treaty are to apply shall be determined, within two years of the entry into force of this Treaty, by decisions of the Council, acting unanimously on a proposal from the Commission.

The institutions of the Community will, within the framework of the procedures provided for in this Treaty, in particular Article 226, take care that the economic and social development of these areas is made possible.

3. The special arrangements for association set out in Part Four of this Treaty shall apply to the overseas countries and territories listed in Annex IV to this Treaty.

This Treaty shall not apply to those overseas countries and territories having special relations with the United Kingdom of Great Britain and Northern Ireland which are not included in the aforementioned list.

4. The provisions of this Treaty shall apply to the European territories for whose external relations a Member State is responsible.

5. Notwithstanding the preceding paragraphs:

(a) This Treaty shall not apply to the Faeroe Islands.
(b) This Treaty shall not apply to the Sovereign Base Areas of the United Kingdom of Great Britain and Northern Ireland in Cyprus.
(c) This Treaty shall apply to the Channel Islands and the Isle of Man only to the extent necessary to ensure the implementation of the arrangements for those islands set out in the Treaty concerning the accession of new Member States to the European Economic Community and to the European Atomic Energy Community signed on 22 January 1972.
[(d) This Treaty shall not apply to the Åland islands. The Government of Finland may, however, give notice, by a declaration deposited when ratifying this Treaty with the Government of the Italian Republic, that the Treaty shall apply to the Åland islands in accordance with the provisions set out in Protocol No. 2 to the Act concerning the conditions of accession of the Republic of Austria, the Republic of Finland and the Kingdom of Sweden and the adjustments to the Treaties on which the European Union is founded. The Government of the Italian Republic shall transmit a certified copy of any such declaration to the Member States.]

GENERAL NOTE

Only two amendments have been made to this Article by the TEU. Paragraph 2 no longer applies to Algeria, and para. 5 now simply declares that the Treaty does not apply to the Faeroe Islands. Article 227(5) of the EEC Treaty had given Denmark the power to declare that the Treaty would apply to the Faeroe Islands, but this option expired on December 31, 1975. Thus, the amendment simply removes some dead wood from the Treaty.

The amendments in para. 1 were made by and and new para. 5(d) added by the Act of Accession [1994] O.J. C241/08; [1995] O.J. L1/1.

Article 228

1. Where this Treaty provides for the conclusion of agreements between the Community and one or more States or international organisations, the Commission shall make recommendations to the Council, which shall authorise the Commission to open the necessary negotiations. The Commission shall conduct these negotiations in consultation with special committees appointed by the Council to assist it in this task and within the framework of such directives as the Council may issue to it.

In exercising the powers conferred upon it by this paragraph, the Council shall act by a qualified majority, except in the cases provided for in the second sentence of paragraph 2, for which it shall act unanimously.

2. Subject to the powers vested in the Commission in this field, the agreements shall be concluded by the Council, acting by a qualified majority on a proposal from the Commission. The Council shall act unanimously when the agreement covers a field for which unanimity is required for the adoption of internal rules, and for the agreements referred to in Article 238.

3. The Council shall conclude agreements after consulting the European Parliament, except for the agreements referred to in Article 113(3), including cases where the agreement covers a field for which the procedure referred to in Article 189b or that referred to in Article 189c is required for the adoption of internal rules. The European Parliament shall deliver its Opinion within a time limit which the Council may lay down according to the urgency of the matter. In the absence of an Opinion within that time limit, the Council may act.

By way of derogation from the previous subparagraph, agreements referred to in Article 238, other agreements establishing a specific institutional framework by organising co-operation procedures, agreements having important budgetary implications for the Community and agreements entailing amendment of an act adopted under the procedure referred to in

Article 189b shall be concluded after the assent of the European Parliament has been obtained.

The Council and the European Parliament may, in an urgent situation, agree upon a time limit for the assent.

4. When concluding an agreement, the Council may, by way of derogation from paragraph 2, empower the Commission to approve modifications on behalf of the Community where the agreement provides for them to be adopted by a simplified procedure or by a body set up by the agreement; it may attach specific conditions to such empowerment.

5. When the Council envisages concluding an agreement which calls for amendments to this Treaty, the amendments must first be adopted in accordance with the procedure laid down in Article N of the Treaty on European Union.

6. The Council, the Commission or a Member State may obtain the opinion of the Court of Justice as to whether an agreement envisaged is compatible with the provisions of this Treaty. Where the opinion of the Court of Justice is adverse, the agreement may enter into force only in accordance with Article N of the Treaty on European Union.

7. Agreements concluded under the conditions set out in this Article shall be binding on the institutions of the Community and on Member States.

GENERAL NOTE

The procedure whereby the Community can enter into different international agreements is set out in this, greatly extended, version of Art. 228. The procedure whereby agreements under the common commercial policy and association agreements were arrived at was previously set out under Arts. 113 and 238 EEC, respectively.

Para. (1)

This has adopted the procedure prescribed by Art. 113 EEC for concluding international agreements in the context of the common commercial policy, and extended it to all international agreements. Previously, these other international agreements were required to be negotiated by the Commission (Art. 228(1) EEC), but no provision was made for the Council to set up Committees which the Commission has to consult during the negotiations. More importantly, the Council was not explicitly authorised to constrain the negotiating mandate of the Commission within the framework of Council directives.

Para. (2)

This clarifies the voting procedure in the Council in relation to all international agreements. Agreements under the common commercial policy will continue to be reached by qualified majority (*cf.* Art. 113(4) EEC) and association agreements will still require unanimity (*cf.* Art. 238 EEC). Since the landmark decision of the European Court of Justice in the *E.R.T.A.* case (Case 22/70, *Commission v. Council* [1971] E.C.R. 263) the Community has had implied powers to enter into international agreements in any area where it has power to legislate internally (see also Opinion 1/78, *Natural Rubber* [1979] E.C.R. 2871). Article 228 EEC was silent on the voting procedure to be adopted in the Council, therefore it was unclear what voting requirements applied to international agreements falling within the Community's implied powers. It was at least arguable that the silence of Art. 228 EEC in regard to how the Council was to conclude such agreements implied that a simple majority was sufficient (see Art. 148(1) EEC/E.C. which states that: "Save as otherwise provided in this Treaty, the Council shall act by a majority of its members"). Paragraph 2 of Art. 228 E.C. should remove any doubt. International agreements require at least a qualified majority vote in the Council, and where internal rules can be adopted only by unanimity, then international agreements must be adopted on the same basis.

Para. (3)

This clarifies the role of the European Parliament in relation to international agreements. The Parliament is still given no formal role in relation to international agreements under the common commercial policy (see the note on Art. 113 above). As previously required by Art. 238 EEC, the Parliament must give its assent to an association agreement, but that paragraph does not lay down any requirement as to the majority needed in Parliament. Under Art. 238 EEC an absolute majority of Parliament's component members was required, but now under Rule 33(7) of the European Parliament's Rules of Procedure (as amended subsequent to the TEU, see [1993] O.J. C268/51) assent can be given by a majority of votes cast. In relation to other international agreements, the Parliament has now been given a comprehensive right to be consulted. This is advantageous for the Parliament in relation to agreements where internal Community rules could be adopted without any consultation of the European Parliament (see Weatherill and Beaumont, *E.C. Law* (1993), pp. 796–7). Article 228 EEC gave a right to Parliament to be consulted about the adoption of an international agreement only "where required by this Treaty". However, in the context of matters adopted internally under the co-operation procedure (Art. 189c) or the conciliation and veto procedure (Art. 189b), consulting the Parliament gives it much less influence and power in external agreements than it has been granted over internal rules. This is a potential means to circumvent Parliament's internal veto under Art. 189b. Where the international agreement requires an amendment to an act adopted under the conciliation and veto procedure, the Parliament must give its assent.

In two other areas the Parliament has been given, for the first time, the power to block an international agreement. First, where the agreement has important budgetary implications for the Community. That is an appropriate, if somewhat belated, change reflecting the fact that the Community's budget has been adopted jointly by the Council and Parliament since the Budgetary Treaties of the 1970's. Secondly, where the agreement establishes a specific institutional framework by organising co-operation procedures. It is not at all clear what is meant by "co-operation procedures".

Where the Parliament has a right to be consulted, the Council is given a new right to set a time-limit, within which Parliament must give its Opinion. If the Opinion is not given within the time-limit, then the Council is free to act. This is a sensible provision to prevent the Parliament turning a right to be consulted into a veto, by indefinitely failing to give an Opinion. The only danger is that the Council may set an unrealistically short deadline. In such circumstances the Court might declare the Agreement void, due to failure to give Parliament sufficient time to give its Opinion. Where the Parliament's assent is required then the Council cannot unilaterally impose a time-limit on the Parliament. The two institutions may agree a time-limit. Parliament may delay giving its assent in order to try to force concessions from the Council (see Bradley, (1988) 8 Y.E.L. 189, at 198–9).

Para. (4)

This is a new provision authorising the Council to delegate to the Commission the power to modify an international agreement, without having to go through the full procedure. This would remove the Parliament's right to be consulted or to give its assent and the Council's right to vote on its adoption by qualified majority or unanimity. This new power to delegate in the field of international agreements echoes the long-standing power of the Council to delegate internal legislative power to the Commission (see Art. 145 indent 3 EEC/E.C.). In the internal context the Council has delegated a lot of legislative power to the Commission in terms of quantity but very little in terms of quality. The Council has developed an elaborate committee structure to monitor the Commission's delegated powers (see Weatherill and Beaumont, *E.C. Law* (1993), pp. 51–4, and Council Decision 87/373 [1987] O.J. L197/33). It will be interesting to see if the Council makes use of this power to delegate to the Commission in the context of international agreements, and if it sets up management or regulatory committees to monitor the delegated power, relying on its discretion to "attach specific conditions to such authorisation".

Para. (5)

The substance of this provision was formerly in Art. 238(3) EEC (see note on that Article). Paragraph 5 has a much wider scope than its predecessor, in that it applies to all international agreements and not just association agreements. The paragraph effectively bars any attempt to amend the E.C. Treaty by the devious route of concluding an international agreement with another State. Such agreements can be adopted by qualified majority in the Council and do not necessarily require the assent of the Parliament: these are much lower requirements than those provided for by Art. N, E.U. on Treaty amendments.

Para. (6)

This provision replicates its predecessor in Art. 228 EEC, except that the reference to Art. 236 EEC has been replaced by a reference to Art. N, E.U. The former has been repealed and the latter now regulates the Treaty amendment procedure (see the note on the repeal of Art. 236). For a brief treatment of the Court's power to give Opinions under Art. 228, see Weatherill and Beaumont, *E.C. Law* (1993), pp. 275–7.

Para. (7)

This provision is carried over from Art. 228 EEC. It impliedly makes international agreements entered into by the Community a higher source of law than any legislation adopted by the Community.

Article 228a

Where it is provided, in a common position or in a joint action adopted according to the provisions of the Treaty on European Union relating to the common foreign and security policy, for an action by the Community to interrupt or to reduce, in part or completely, economic relations with one or more third countries, the Council shall take the necessary urgent measures. The Council shall act by a qualified majority on a proposal from the Commission.

GENERAL NOTE

This provision provides an intersection between the E.C. Treaty and the common foreign and security policy pillar established by the E.U. Treaty. If a foreign policy decision is taken to impose economic sanctions on a third State, then this requires to be followed up by a measure under the E.C. Treaty. Clearly any severance, or reduction, of trade with a non-Member State represents a change in the Community's common commercial policy, and thus E.C. legislation is called for. Article 228a for the first time creates a specific mechanism to deal with the problem. The Commission makes a proposal, which the Council passes by qualified majority vote. The European Parliament is not given any role in the legislative process, presumably because these measures often require to be passed very quickly.

Article 228a is a new solution but the problem is not a new one. Under European Political Co-operation, the predecessor of common foreign and security policy, formalised in the S.E.A., it was recognised that there needed to be consistency between "[t]he external policies of the European Community and the policies agreed in European Political Co-operation" (Article 30(5) S.E.A.). The problem is often further complicated by the fact that the economic sanctions are imposed by the United Nations and then specific Community legislation is needed to implement the sanctions. This legislation may permit exceptions to the sanctions which may be taken up in some Member States and not in others.

Almost as soon as the E.U. Treaty entered into force, Art. 228a was used as the legal basis for Regulations 3274/93 and 3275/93 concerning sanctions in relation to Libya, following various U.N. Security Council Resolutions (see [1993] O.J. L295). These were implemented in Ireland by Statutory Instruments No. 384 and No. 385 of 1993, under the European Communities Act, 1972, which set out the criminal penalties applicable in the case of breach of the economic sanctions.

Article 229

It shall be for the Commission to ensure the maintenance of all appropriate relations with the organs of the United Nations, of its specialised agencies and of the General Agreement on Tariffs and Trade.

The Commission shall also maintain such relations as are appropriate with all international organisations.

Article 230

The Community shall establish all appropriate forms of co-operation with the Council of Europe.

Article 231

The Community shall establish close co-operation with the Organisation for Economic Co-operation and Development, the details of which shall be determined by common accord.

GENERAL NOTE

This Article was long overdue for amendment. The version in the EEC Treaty referred to the Community establishing "close co-operation with the Organisation for European Economic Co-operation". That body was a relatively weak inter-governmental institution set up after the Second World War to disburse the very substantial amount of money given by the United States for the development of Europe in the Marshall Plan. By 1961 the Organisation for European Economic Co-operation had evolved into the Organisation for Economic Co-operation and

Development. The latter is based in Paris but is not a European international institution. It is concerned with monitoring economic performance in its member countries, and with helping to improve the economies of developing countries.

Article 232

1. The provisions of this Treaty shall not affect the provisions of the Treaty establishing the European Coal and Steel Community, in particular as regards the rights and obligations of Member States, the powers of the institutions of that Community and the rules laid down by that Treaty for the functioning of the common market in coal and steel.

2. The provisions of this Treaty shall not derogate from those of the Treaty establishing the European Atomic Energy Community.

Article 233

The provisions of this Treaty shall not preclude the existence or completion of regional unions between Belgium and Luxembourg, or between Belgium, Luxembourg and the Netherlands, to the extent that the objectives of these regional unions are not attained by application of this Treaty.

Article 234

The rights and obligations arising from agreements concluded before the entry into force of this Treaty between one or more Member States on the one hand, and one or more third countries on the other, shall not be affected by the provisions of this Treaty.

To the extent that such agreements are not compatible with this Treaty, the Member State or States concerned shall take all appropriate steps to eliminate the incompatibilities established. Member States shall, where necessary, assist each other to this end and shall, where appropriate, adopt a common attitude.

In applying the agreements referred to in the first paragraph, Member States shall take into account the fact that the advantages accorded under this Treaty by each Member State form an integral part of the establishment of the Community and are thereby inseparably linked with the creation of common institutions, the conferring of powers upon them and the granting of the same advantages by all the other Member States.

Article 235

If action by the Community should prove necessary to attain, in the course of the operation of the common market, one of the objectives of the Community and this Treaty has not provided the necessary powers, the Council shall, acting unanimously on a proposal from the Commission and after consulting the European Parliament, take the appropriate measures.

Article 236

(Repealed at Maastricht)

Article 237

(Repealed at Maastricht)

GENERAL NOTE

Article 236 EEC was the provision which outlined the mechanism by which the Treaty could be amended. It has been replaced by Art. N, E.U. The latter is very similar to the former. Article N, E.U. provides a common method for amending all the Treaties on which the Union is founded (*i.e.* the ESCS, E.C. and Euratom Treaties, as well as the E.U. Treaty). The one substantive change in the procedure for Treaty amendment, introduced by Art. N, E.U. is that the European Central Bank is to be "consulted in the case of institutional changes in the monetary area".

Paragraph 2 of Art. N, E.U. provides that an Inter-governmental Conference shall be convened in 1996 to examine those provisions of the Treaties for which revision is provided. Article 189b(8) E.C. provides that the scope of the procedure laid down under that Article—conciliation and veto—may be widened at the 1996 Inter-governmental Conference. The Commission is to submit a report to the Council on this matter by 1996. Article J(4) E.U., concerning security and defence policy, is to be considered for revision at the 1996 Inter-governmental Conference. The Council is to submit a report to the European Council concerning Art. J(4) by 1996. Doubtless the 1996 Inter-governmental Conference will consider other Treaty amendments, including the possibility of establishing an appropriate hierarchy between the different categories of Community acts (see Declaration No. 16 below).

Article 237 EEC dealt with the procedure by which a State could become a member of the Community. Article O, E.U. applies to the method by which a State becomes a member of the European Union. The substance of the two Articles is identical, except that by becoming a member of the Union a State becomes a member of the three Communities which form part of the Union, including the E.C., as well as the two inter-governmental pillars of the common foreign and security policy and co-operation in the fields of justice and home affairs.

Article 238

The Community may conclude with one or more States or international organisations agreements establishing an association involving reciprocal rights and obligations, common action and special procedures.

GENERAL NOTE

Paragraphs 2 and 3 of Art. 238 EEC have been repealed. The substance of para. 2 is now found in Art. 228(3) E.C. The Council still requires unanimity and the Parliament still has to give its assent to any agreement adopted under Art. 238. Two minor reforms to the old para. 2 have been made. First, it is no longer specified that an absolute majority of the component members of the Parliament must vote for the agreement for Parliament's assent to be given. Secondly, the Council and the European Parliament may, in an urgent situation, agree upon a time-limit for the latter's assent. A revised version of para. 3 of Art. 238 EEC is now found in Art. 228(5) E.C. No substantive change has been made. If the agreement calls for amendments to the E.C. Treaty, then the amendments must first be adopted in accordance with the procedure laid down for amending the Treaty in Article N, E.U.

The first paragraph of Art. 238 E.C. still refers to the adoption of association agreements. The wording is altered only marginally from paragraph 1 of Art. 238 EEC. The words "conclude with a third state, a union of states or an international organisation" have been replaced with "conclude with one or more states or international organisations". The key change here is that an association agreement may be entered into with more than one State or international organisation.

Article 239

The Protocols annexed to this Treaty by common accord of the Member States shall form an integral part thereof.

Article 240

This Treaty is concluded for an unlimited period.

SETTING UP OF THE INSTITUTIONS

Article 241

The Council shall meet within one month of the entry into force of this Treaty.

Article 242

The Council shall, within three months of its first meeting, take all appropriate measures to constitute the Economic and Social Committee.

Article 243

The Assembly shall meet within two months of the first meeting of the Council, having been convened by the President of the Council, in order to elect its officers and draw up its rules of procedure. Pending the election of its officers, the oldest member shall take the chair.

Article 244

The Court of Justice shall take up its duties as soon as its members have been appointed. Its first President shall be appointed for three years in the same manner as its members.

The Court of Justice shall adopt its rules of procedure within three months of taking up its duties.

No matter may be brought before the Court of Justice until its rules of procedure have been published. The time within which an action must be brought shall run only from the date of this publication.

Upon his appointment, the President of the Court of Justice shall exercise the powers conferred upon him by this Treaty.

Article 245

The Commission shall take up its duties and assume the responsibilities conferred upon it by this Treaty as soon as its members have been appointed.

Upon taking up its duties, the Commission shall undertake the studies and arrange the contacts needed for making an overall survey of the economic situation of the Community.

Article 246

1. The first financial year shall run from the date on which this Treaty enters into force until 31 December following. Should this Treaty, however, enter into force during the second half of the year, the first financial year shall run until 31 December of the following year.

2. Until the budget for the first financial year has been established, Member States shall make the Community interest-free advances which shall be deducted from their financial contributions to the implementation of the budget.

3. Until the Staff Regulations of officials and the Conditions of Employment of other servants of the Community provided for in Article 212 have been laid down, each institution shall recruit the Staff it needs and to this end conclude contracts of limited duration.

Each institution shall examine together with the Council any question concerning the number, remuneration and distribution of posts.

FINAL PROVISIONS

Article 247

This Treaty shall be ratified by the High Contracting Parties in accordance with their respective constitutional requirements. The instruments of ratification shall be deposited with the Government of the Italian Republic.

This Treaty shall enter into force on the first day of the month following the deposit of the instrument of ratification by the last signatory State to take this step. If, however, such deposit is made less than 15 days before the beginning of the following month, this Treaty shall not enter into force until the first day of the second month after the date of such deposit.

Article 248

This Treaty, drawn up in a single original in the Dutch, French, German and Italian languages, all four texts being equally authentic, shall be deposited in the archives of the Government of the Italian Republic, which shall transmit a certified copy to each of the Governments of the other signatory States.

PROTOCOLS 1–16

PROTOCOLS[1]

PROTOCOL ON THE ACQUISITION OF PROPERTY IN DENMARK

(Annexed to E.C. Treaty)

Notwithstanding the provisions of this Treaty, Denmark may maintain the existing legislation on the acquisition of second homes.

PROTOCOL CONCERNING ARTICLE 119 OF THE TREATY ESTABLISHING THE EUROPEAN COMMUNITY

(Annexed to E.C. Treaty)

For the purposes of Article 119 of this Treaty, benefits under occupational social security schemes shall not be considered as remuneration if and in so far as they are attributable to periods of employment prior to 17 May 1990, except in the case of workers or those claiming under them who have before that date initiated legal proceedings or introduced an equivalent claim under the applicable national law.

PROTOCOL ON THE STATUTE OF THE EUROPEAN SYSTEM OF CENTRAL BANKS AND OF THE EUROPEAN CENTRAL BANK

(Annexed to E.C. Treaty (Article 4a))

CHAPTER I: Constitution of the ESCB

Article 1 (The European System of Central Banks)

1.1. The European System of Central Banks (ESCB) and the European Central Bank (ECB) shall be established in accordance with Article 4a of this Treaty; they shall perform their tasks and carry on their activities in accordance with the provisions of this Treaty and of this Statute.

1.2. In accordance with Article 106(1) of this Treaty, the ESCB shall be composed of the ECB and of the central banks of the Member States ('national central banks'). The Institut Monétaire Luxembourgeois will be the central bank of Luxembourg.

CHAPTER II: Objectives and Tasks of the ESCB

Article 2 (Objectives)

In accordance with Article 105(1) of this Treaty, the primary objective of the ESCB shall be to maintain price stability.

Without prejudice to the objective of price stability, it shall support the general economic policies in the Community with a view to contributing to the achievement of the objectives of the Community as laid down in Article 2 of this Treaty.

The ESCB shall act in accordance with the principle of an open market economy with free competition, favouring an efficient allocation of resources, and in compliance with the principles set out in Article 3a of this Treaty.

Article 3 (Tasks)

3.1. In accordance with Article 105(2) of this Treaty, the basic tasks to be carried out through the ESCB shall be:

---

[1] The preambles to most of the Protocols have been omitted.

— to define and implement the monetary policy of the Community;
— to conduct foreign exchange operations consistent with the provisions of Article 109 of this Treaty;
— to hold and manage the official foreign reserves of the Member States;
— to promote the smooth operation of payment systems.

3.2. In accordance with Article 105(3) of this Treaty, the third indent of Article 3.1 shall be without prejudice to the holding and management by the governments of Member States of foreign exchange working balances.

3.3. In accordance with Article 105(5) of this Treaty, the ESCB shall contribute to the smooth conduct of policies pursued by the competent authorities relating to the prudential supervision of credit institutions and the stability of the financial system.

Article 4 (Advisory functions)

In accordance with Article 105(4) of this Treaty:
(a) the ECB shall be consulted:
    — on any proposed Community act in its fields of competence;
    — by national authorities regarding any draft legislative provision in its fields of competence, but within the limits and under the conditions set out by the Council in accordance with the procedure laid down in Article 42;
(b) the ECB may submit opinions to the appropriate Community institutions or bodies or to national authorities on matters in its fields of competence.

Article 5 (Collection of statistical information)

5.1. In order to undertake the tasks of the ESCB, the ECB, assisted by the national central banks, shall collect the necessary statistical information either from the competent national authorities or directly from economic agents. For these purposes it shall co-operate with the Community institutions or bodies and with the competent authorities of the Member States or third countries and with international organisations.

5.2. The national central banks shall carry out, to the extent possible, the tasks described in Article 5.1.

5.3. The ECB shall contribute to the harmonisation, where necessary, of the rules and practices governing the collection, compilation and distribution of statistics in the areas within its fields of competence.

5.4. The Council, in accordance with the procedure laid down in Article 42, shall define the natural and legal persons subject to reporting requirements, the confidentiality regime and the appropriate provisions for enforcement.

Article 6 (International co-operation)

6.1. In the field of international co-operation involving the tasks entrusted to the ESCB, the ECB shall decide how the ESCB shall be represented.

6.2. The ECB and, subject to its approval, the national central banks may participate in international monetary institutions.

6.3. Articles 6.1 and 6.2 shall be without prejudice to Article 109(4) of this Treaty.

CHAPTER III: Organisation of the ESCB

Article 7 (Independence)

In accordance with Article 107 of this Treaty, when exercising the powers and carrying out the tasks and duties conferred upon them by this Treaty and this Statute, neither the ECB, nor a national central bank, nor any member of their decision-making bodies shall seek or take instructions from Community institutions or bodies, from any government of a Member State or from any other body. The Community institutions and bodies and the governments of the Member States undertake to respect this principle and not to seek to influence the members of the decision-making bodies of the ECB or of the national central banks in the performance of their tasks.

Article 8 (General principle)

The ESCB shall be governed by the decision-making bodies of the ECB.

Article 9 (The European Central Bank)

9.1. The ECB which, in accordance with Article 106(2) of this Treaty, shall have legal personality, shall enjoy in each of the Member States the most extensive legal capacity accorded to legal persons under its law; it may, in particular, acquire or dispose of movable and immovable property and may be a party to legal proceedings.

9.2. The ECB shall ensure that the tasks conferred upon the ESCB under Article 105(2), (3), and (5) of this Treaty are implemented either by its own activities pursuant to this Statute or through the national central banks pursuant to Articles 12.1 and 14.

9.3. In accordance with Article 106(3) of this Treaty, the decision-making bodies of the ECB shall be the Governing Council and the Executive Board.

Article 10 (The Governing Council)

10.1. In accordance with Article 109a(1) of this Treaty, the Governing Council shall comprise the members of the Executive Board of the ECB and the Governors of the national central banks.

10.2. Subject to Article 10.3, only members of the Governing Council present in person shall have the right to vote. By way of derogation from this rule, the Rules of Procedure referred to in Article 12.3 may lay down that members of the Governing Council may cast their vote by means of tele-conferencing. These rules shall also provide that a member of the Governing Council who is prevented from voting for a prolonged period may appoint an alternate as a member of the Governing Council.

Subject to Articles 10.3 and 11.3, each member of the Governing Council shall have one vote. Save as otherwise provided for in this Statute, the Governing Council shall act by a simple majority. In the event of a tie, the President shall have the casting vote.

In order for the Governing Council to vote, there shall be a quorum of two-thirds of the members. If the quorum is not met, the President may convene an extraordinary meeting at which decisions may be taken without regard to the quorum.

10.3. For any decisions to be taken under Articles 28, 29, 30, 32, 33 and 51, the votes in the Governing Council shall be weighted according to the national central banks' shares in the subscribed capital of the ECB. The weights of the votes of the members of the Executive Board shall be zero. A decision requiring a qualified majority shall be adopted if the votes cast in favour represent at least two thirds of the subscribed capital of the ECB and represent at least half of the shareholders. If a Governor is unable to be present, he may nominate an alternate to cast his weighted vote.

10.4. The proceedings of the meetings shall be confidential. The Governing Council may decide to make the outcome of its deliberations public.

10.5. The Governing Council shall meet at least ten times a year.

Article 11 (The Executive Board)

11.1. In accordance with Article 109a(2)(a) of this Treaty, the Executive Board shall comprise the President, the Vice-President and four other members.

The members shall perform their duties on a full-time basis. No member shall engage in any occupation, whether gainful or not, unless exemption is exceptionally granted by the Governing Council.

11.2. In accordance with Article 109a(2)(b) of this Treaty, the President, the Vice-President and the other Members of the Executive Board shall be appointed from among persons of recognised standing and professional experience in monetary or banking matters by common accord of the governments of the Member States at the level of the Heads of State or of Government, on a recommendation from the Council after it has consulted the European Parliament and the Governing Council.

Their term of office shall be eight years and shall not be renewable.

Only nationals of Member States may be members of the Executive Board.

11.3. The terms and conditions of employment of the members of the Executive Board, in particular their salaries, pensions and other social security benefits shall be the subject of contracts with the ECB and shall be fixed by the Governing Council on a proposal from a Committee comprising three members appointed by the Governing Council and three members appointed by the Council. The members of the Executive Board shall not have the right to vote on matters referred to in this paragraph.

11.4. If a member of the Executive Board no longer fulfils the conditions required for the performance of his duties or if he has been guilty of serious misconduct, the Court of Justice may, on application by the Governing Council or the Executive Board, compulsorily retire him.

11.5. Each member of the Executive Board present in person shall have the right to vote and shall have, for that purpose, one vote. Save as otherwise provided, the Executive Board shall act by a simple majority of the votes cast. In the event of a tie, the President shall have the casting vote. The voting arrangements shall be specified in the Rules of Procedure referred to in Article 12.3.

11.6. The Executive Board shall be responsible for the current business of the ECB.

11.7. Any vacancy on the Executive Board shall be filled by the appointment of a new member in accordance with Article 11.2.

Article 12 (Responsibilities of the decision-making bodies)

12.1. The Governing Council shall adopt the guidelines and take the decisions necessary to ensure the performance of the tasks entrusted to the ESCB under this Treaty and this Statute. The Governing Council shall formulate the monetary policy of the Community including, as appropriate, decisions relating to intermediate monetary objectives, key interest rates and the supply of reserves in the ESCB, and shall establish the necessary guidelines for their implementation.

The Executive Board shall implement monetary policy in accordance with the guidelines and decisions laid down by the Governing Council. In doing so the Executive Board shall give the necessary instructions to national central banks. In addition the Executive Board may have certain powers delegated to it where the Governing Council so decides.

To the extent deemed possible and appropriate and without prejudice to the provisions of this Article, the ECB shall have recourse to the national central banks to carry out operations which form part of the tasks of the ESCB.

12.2. The Executive Board shall have responsibility for the preparation of meetings of the Governing Council.

12.3. The Governing Council shall adopt Rules of Procedure which determine the internal organisation of the ECB and its decision-making bodies.

12.4. The Governing Council shall exercise the advisory functions referred to in Article 4.

12.5. The Governing Council shall take the decisions referred to in Article 6.

Article 13 (The President)

13.1. The President or, in his absence, the Vice-President shall chair the Governing Council and the Executive Board of the ECB.

13.2. Without prejudice to Article 39, the President or his nominee shall represent the ECB externally.

Article 14 (National central banks)

14.1. In accordance with Article 108 of this Treaty, each Member State shall ensure, at the latest at the date of the establishment of the ESCB, that its national legislation, including the statutes of its national central bank, is compatible with this Treaty and this Statute.

14.2. The statutes of the national central banks shall, in particular, provide that the term of office of a Governor of a national central bank shall be no less than five years.

A Governor may be relieved from office only if he no longer fulfils the conditions required for the performance of his duties or if he has been guilty of serious misconduct.

A decision to this effect may be referred to the Court of Justice by the Governor concerned or the Governing Council on grounds of infringement of this Treaty or of any rule of law relating to its application. Such proceedings shall be instituted within two months of the publication of the decision or of its notification to the plaintiff or, in the absence thereof, of the day on which it came to the knowledge of the latter, as the case may be.

14.3. The national central banks are an integral part of the ESCB and shall act in accordance with the guidelines and instructions of the ECB. The Governing Council shall take the necessary steps to ensure compliance with the guidelines and instructions of the ECB, and shall require that any necessary information be given to it.

14.4. National central banks may perform functions other than those specified in this Statute unless the Governing Council finds, by a majority of two thirds of the votes cast, that these interfere with the objectives and tasks of the ESCB. Such functions shall be performed on the responsibility and liability of national central banks and shall not be regarded as being part of the functions of the ESCB.

Article 15 (Reporting commitments)

15.1. The ECB shall draw up and publish reports on the activities of the ESCB at least quarterly.

15.2. A consolidated financial statement of the ESCB shall be published each week.

15.3. In accordance with Article 109b(3) of this Treaty, the ECB shall address an annual report on the activities of the ESCB and on the monetary policy of both the previous and the current year to the European Parliament, the Council and the Commission, and also to the European Council.

15.4. The reports and statements referred to in this Article shall be made available to interested parties free of charge.

Article 16 (Bank notes)

In accordance with Article 105a(1) of this Treaty, the Governing Council shall have the exclusive right to authorise the issue of bank notes within the Community.

The ECB and the national central banks may issue such notes. The bank notes issued by the ECB and the national central banks shall be the only such notes to have the status of legal tender within the Community.

The ECB shall respect as far as possible existing practices regarding the issue and design of bank notes.

CHAPTER IV: Monetary Functions and Operations of the ESCB

Article 17 (Accounts with the ECB and the national central banks)

In order to conduct their operations, the ECB and the national central banks may open accounts for credit institutions, public entities and other market participants and accept assets, including book-entry securities, as collateral.

Article 18 (Open market and credit operations)

18.1. In order to achieve the objectives of the ESCB and to carry out its tasks, the ECB and the national central banks may:
— operate in the financial markets by buying and selling outright (spot and forward) or under repurchase agreement and by lending or borrowing claims and marketable instruments, whether in Community or in non-Community currencies, as well as precious metals;
— conduct credit operations with credit institutions and other market participants, with lending being based on adequate collateral.

18.2. The ECB shall establish general principles for open market and credit operations carried out by itself or the national central banks, including for the announcement of conditions under which they stand ready to enter into such transactions.

Article 19 (Minimum reserves)

19.1. Subject to Article 2, the ECB may require credit institutions established in Member States to hold minimum reserves on accounts with the ECB and national central banks in pursuance of monetary policy objectives. Regulations concerning the calculation and determination of the required minimum reserves may be established by the Governing Council. In cases of non-compliance the ECB shall be entitled to levy penalty interest and to impose other sanctions with comparable effect.

19.2. For the application of this Article, the Council shall, in accordance with the procedure laid down in Article 42, define the basis for minimum reserves and the maximum permissible ratios between those reserves and their basis, as well as the appropriate sanctions in cases of non-compliance.

Article 20 (Other instruments of monetary control)

The Governing Council may, by a majority of two thirds of the votes cast, decide upon the use of such other operational methods of monetary control as it sees fit, respecting Article 2.

The Council shall, in accordance with the procedure laid down in Article 42, define the scope of such methods if they impose obligations on third parties.

Article 21 (Operations with public entities)

21.1. In accordance with Article 104 of this Treaty, overdrafts or any other type of credit facility with the ECB or with the national central banks in favour of Community institutions or bodies, central governments, regional, local or other public authorities, other bodies governed by public law or public undertakings of Member States shall be prohibited, as shall the purchase directly from them by the ECB or national central banks of debt instruments.

21.2. The ECB and national central banks may act as fiscal agents for the entities referred to in Article 21.1.

21.3. The provisions of this Article shall not apply to publicly-owned credit institutions which, in the context of the supply of reserves by central banks, shall be given the same treatment by national central banks and the ECB as private credit institutions.

Article 22 (Clearing and payment systems)

The ECB and national central banks may provide facilities, and the ECB may make regulations, to ensure efficient and sound clearing and payment systems within the Community and with other countries.

Article 23 (External operations)

The ECB and national central banks may:
— establish relations with central banks and financial institutions in other countries and, where appropriate, with international organisations;
— acquire and sell spot and forward all types of foreign exchange assets and precious metals; the term 'foreign exchange asset' shall include securities and all other assets in the currency of any country or units of account and in whatever form held;
— hold and manage the assets referred to in this Article;
— conduct all types of banking transactions in relations with third countries and international organisations, including borrowing and lending operations.

Article 24 (Other operations)

In addition to operations arising from their tasks, the ECB and national central banks may enter into operations for their administrative purposes or for their staff.

CHAPTER V: Prudential Supervision

Article 25 (Prudential supervision)

25.1. The ECB may offer advice to and be consulted by the Council, the Commission and the competent authorities of the Member States on the scope and implementation of Community legislation relating to the prudential supervision of credit institutions and to the stability of the financial system.

25.2. In accordance with any decision of the Council under Article 105(6) of this Treaty, the ECB may perform specific tasks concerning policies relating to the prudential supervision of credit institutions and other financial institutions with the exception of insurance undertakings.

CHAPTER VI: Financial Provisions of the ESCB

Article 26 (Financial accounts)

26.1. The financial year of the ECB and national central banks shall begin on the first day of January and end on the last day of December.

26.2. The annual accounts of the ECB shall be drawn up by the Executive Board, in accordance with the principles established by the Governing Council.

The accounts shall be approved by the Governing Council and shall thereafter be published.

26.3. For analytical and operational purposes, the Executive Board shall draw up a consolidated balance sheet of the ESCB, comprising those assets and liabilities of the national central banks that fall within the ESCB.

26.4. For the application of this Article, the Governing Council shall establish the necessary rules for standardising the accounting and reporting of operations undertaken by the national central banks.

Article 27 (Auditing)

27.1. The accounts of the ECB and national central banks shall be audited by independent external auditors recommended by the Governing Council and approved by the Council.

The auditors shall have full power to examine all books and accounts of the ECB and national central banks and obtain full information about their transactions.

27.2. The provisions of Article 188b of this Treaty shall only apply to an examination of the operational efficiency of the management of the ECB.

Article 28 (Capital of the ECB)

28.1. The capital of the ECB, which shall become operational upon its establishment, shall be 5,000 million ECUs.

The capital may be increased by such amounts as may be decided by the Governing Council acting by the qualified majority provided for in Article 10.3, within the limits and under the conditions set by the Council under the procedure laid down in Article 42.

28.2. The national central banks shall be the sole subscribers to and holders of the capital of the ECB. The subscription of capital shall be according to the key established in accordance with Article 29.

28.3. The Governing Council, acting by the qualified majority provided for in Article 10.3, shall determine the extent to which and the form in which the capital shall be paid up.

28.4. Subject to Article 28.5, the shares of the national central banks in the subscribed capital of the ECB may not be transferred, pledged or attached.

28.5. If the key referred to in Article 29 is adjusted, the national central banks shall transfer among themselves capital shares to the extent necessary to ensure that the distribution of capital shares corresponds to the adjusted key.

The Governing Council shall determine the terms and conditions of such transfers.

Article 29 (Key for capital subscription)

29.1. When in accordance with the procedure referred to in Article 109l(1) of this Treaty the ESCB and the ECB have been established, the key for subscription of the ECB's capital shall be established. Each national central bank shall be assigned a weighting in this key which shall be equal to the sum of:

— 50 per cent of the share of its respective Member State in the population of the Community in the penultimate year preceding the establishment of the ESCB;

— 50 per cent of the share of its respective Member State in the gross domestic product at market prices of the Community as recorded in the last five years preceding the penultimate year before the establishment of the ESCB;

The percentages shall be rounded up to the nearest multiple of 0·05 per cent points.

29.2. The statistical data to be used for the application of this Article shall be provided by the Commission in accordance with the rules adopted by the Council under the procedure provided for in Article 42.

29.3. The weightings assigned to the national central banks shall be adjusted every five years after the establishment of the ESCB by analogy with the provisions laid down in Article 29.1.

The adjusted key shall apply with effect from the first day of the following year.

29.4. The Governing Council shall take all other measures necessary for the application of this Article.

Article 30 (Transfer of foreign reserve assets to the ECB)

30.1. Without prejudice to Article 28, the ECB shall be provided by the national central banks with foreign reserve assets, other than Member States' currencies, ECUs, IMF reserve positions and SDRs, up to an amount equivalent to 50,000 million ECUs. The Governing Council shall decide upon the proportion to be called up by the ECB following its establishment and the amounts called up at later dates.

The ECB shall have the full right to hold and manage the foreign reserves that are transferred to it and to use them for the purposes set out in this Statute.

30.2. The contributions of each national central bank shall be fixed in proportion to its share in the subscribed capital of the ECB.

30.3. Each national central bank shall be credited by the ECB with a claim equivalent to its contribution.

The Governing Council shall determine the denomination and remuneration of such claims.

30.4. Further calls of foreign reserve assets beyond the limit set in Article 30.1 may be effected by the ECB, in accordance with Article 30.2, within the limits and under the conditions set by the Council in accordance with the procedure laid down in Article 42.

30.5. The ECB may hold and manage IMF reserve positions and SDRs and provide for the pooling of such assets.

30.6. The Governing Council shall take all other measures necessary for the application of this Article.

Article 31 (Foreign reserve assets held by national central banks)

31.1. The national central banks shall be allowed to perform transactions in fulfilment of their obligations towards international organisations in accordance with Article 23.

31.2. All other operations in foreign reserve assets remaining with the national central banks after the transfers referred to in Article 30, and Member States' transactions with their foreign exchange working balances shall, above a certain limit to be established within the framework of Article 31.3, be subject to approval by the ECB in order to ensure consistency with the exchange rate and monetary policies of the Community.

31.3. The Governing Council shall issue guidelines with a view to facilitating such operations.

Article 32 (Allocation of monetary income of national central banks)

32.1. The income accruing to the national central banks in the performance of the ESCB's monetary policy function (hereinafter referred to as 'monetary income') shall be allocated at the end of each financial year in accordance with the provisions of this Article.

32.2. Subject to Article 32.3, the amount of each national central bank's monetary income shall be equal to its annual income derived from its assets held against notes in circulation and deposit liabilities to credit institutions. These assets shall be earmarked by national central banks in accordance with guidelines to be established by the Governing Council.

32.3. If, after the start of the third stage, the balance sheet structure of the national central banks do not, in the judgment of the Governing Council, permit the application of Article 32.2, the Governing Council, acting by a qualified majority, may decide that, by way of derogation from Article 32.2, monetary income shall be measured according to an alternative method for a period of not more than five years.

32.4. The amount of each national central bank's monetary income shall be reduced by an amount equivalent to any interest paid by that central bank on its deposit liabilities to credit institutions in accordance with Article 19.

The Governing Council may decide that national central banks shall be indemnified against costs incurred in connection with the issue of bank notes or in exceptional circumstances for specific losses arising from monetary policy operations undertaken for the ESCB.

Indemnification shall be in a form deemed appropriate in the judgment of the Governing Council; these amounts may be offset against the national central banks' monetary income.

32.5. The sum of the national central banks' monetary income shall be allocated to the national central banks in proportion to their paid-up shares in the capital of the ECB, subject to any decision taken by the Governing Council pursuant to Article 33.2.

32.6. The clearing and settlement of the balances arising from the allocation of monetary income shall be carried out by the ECB in accordance with guidelines established by the Governing Council.

32.7. The Governing Council shall take all other measures necessary for the application of this Article.

Article 33 (Allocation of net profits and losses of the ECB)

33.1. The net profit of the ECB shall be transferred in the following order:
- (a) an amount to be determined by the Governing Council, which may not exceed 20 per cent of the net profit, shall be transferred to the general reserve fund subject to a limit equal to 100 per cent of the capital;
- (b) the remaining net profit shall be distributed to the shareholders of the ECB in proportion to their paid-up shares.

33.2. In the event of a loss incurred by the ECB, the shortfall may be offset against the general reserve fund of the ECB and, if necessary, following a decision by the Governing Council, against the monetary income of the relevant financial year in proportion and up to the amounts allocated to the national central banks in accordance with Article 32.5.

CHAPTER VII: General Provisions

Article 34 (Legal acts)

34.1. In accordance with Article 108a of this Treaty, the ECB shall:
- — make regulations to the extent necessary to implement the tasks defined in Article 3.1, first indent, Articles 19.1, 22 or 25.2 and in cases which shall be laid down in the acts of the Council referred to in Article 42;
- — take decisions necessary for carrying out the tasks entrusted to the ESCB under this Treaty and this Statute;
- — make recommendations and deliver opinions.

34.2. A regulation shall have general application. It shall be binding in its entirety and directly applicable in all Member States.

Recommendations and opinions shall have no binding force.

A decision shall be binding in its entirety upon those to whom it is addressed.

Articles 190 and 192 of this Treaty shall apply to regulations and decisions adopted by the ECB.

The ECB may decide to publish its decisions, recommendations and opinions.

34.3. Within the limits and under the conditions adopted by the Council under the procedure laid down in Article 42, the ECB shall be entitled to impose fines or periodic penalty payments on undertakings for failure to comply with obligations under its regulations and decisions.

Article 35 (Judicial control and related matters)

35.1. The acts or omissions of the ECB shall be open to review or interpretation by the Court of Justice in the cases and under the conditions laid down in this Treaty.

The ECB may institute proceedings in the cases and under the conditions laid down in this Treaty.

35.2. Disputes between the ECB, on the one hand, and its creditors, debtors or any other person, on the other, shall be decided by the competent national courts, save where jurisdiction has been conferred upon the Court of Justice.

35.3. The ECB shall be subject to the liability regime provided for in Article 215 of this Treaty.

The national central banks shall be liable according to their respective national laws.

35.4. The Court of Justice shall have jurisdiction to give judgment pursuant to any arbitration clause contained in a contract concluded by or on behalf of the ECB, whether that contract be governed by public or private law.

35.5. A decision of the ECB to bring an action before the Court of Justice shall be taken by the Governing Council.

35.6. The Court of Justice shall have jurisdiction in disputes concerning the fulfilment by a national central bank of obligations under this Statute.

If the ECB considers that a national central bank has failed to fulfil an obligation under this Statute, it shall deliver a reasoned opinion on the matter after giving the national central bank concerned the opportunity to submit its observations.

If the national central bank concerned does not comply with the opinion within the period laid down by the ECB, the latter may bring the matter before the Court of Justice.

Article 36 (Staff)

36.1. The Governing Council, on a proposal from the Executive Board, shall lay down the conditions of employment of the staff of the ECB.

36.2. The Court of Justice shall have jurisdiction in any dispute between the ECB and its servants within the limits and under the conditions laid down in the conditions of employment.

Article 37 (Seat)

Before the end of 1992, the decision as to where the seat of the ECB will be established shall be taken by common accord of the governments of the Member States at the level of Heads of State or of Government.

Article 38 (Professional secrecy)

38.1. Members of the governing bodies and the staff of the ECB and the national central banks shall be required, even after their duties have ceased, not to disclose information of the kind covered by the obligation of professional secrecy.

38.2. Persons having access to data covered by Community legislation imposing an obligation of secrecy shall be subject to such legislation.

Article 39 (Signatories)

The ECB shall be legally committed to third parties by the President or by two members of the Executive Board or by the signatures of two members of the staff of the ECB who have been duly authorised by the President to sign on behalf of the ECB.

Article 40 (Privileges and immunities)

The ECB shall enjoy in the territories of the Member States such privileges and immunities as are necessary for the performance of its tasks, under the conditions laid down in the Protocol on the Privileges and Immunities of the European Communities annexed to the Treaty establishing a Single Council and a Single Commission of the European Communities.

CHAPTER VIII: Amendment of the Statute and Complementary Legislation

Article 41 (Simplified amendment procedure)

41.1. In accordance with Article 106(5) of this Treaty, Articles 5.1, 5.2, 5.3, 17, 18, 19.1, 22, 23, 24, 26, 32.2, 32.3, 32.4, 32.6, 33.1(a) and 36 of this Statute may be amended by the Council, acting either by a qualified majority on a recommendation from the ECB and after consulting the Commission, or unanimously on a proposal from the Commission and after consulting the ECB. In either case the assent of the European Parliament shall be required.

41.2. A recommendation made by the ECB under this Article shall require a unanimous decision by the Governing Council.

Article 42 (Complementary legislation)

In accordance with Article 106(6) of this Treaty, immediately after the decision on the date for the beginning of the third stage, the Council, acting by a qualified majority either on a proposal from the Commission and after consulting the European Parliament and the ECB, or on a recommendation from the ECB and after consulting the European Parliament and the Commission, shall adopt the provisions referred to in Articles 4, 5.4, 19.2, 20, 28.1, 29.2, 30.4 and 34.3 of this Statute.

CHAPTER IX: Transitional and Other Provisions for the ESCB

Article 43 (General Provisions)

43.1. A derogation as referred to in Article 109k(1) of this Treaty shall entail that the following Articles of this Statute shall not confer any rights or impose any obligations on the Member State concerned: 3, 6, 9.2, 12.1, 14.3, 16, 18, 19, 20, 22, 23, 26.2, 27, 30, 31, 32, 33, 34, 50 and 52.

43.2. The central banks of Member States with a derogation as specified in Article 109k(1) of this Treaty shall retain their powers in the field of monetary policy according to national law.

43.3. In accordance with Article 109k(4) of this Treaty, 'Member States' shall be read as 'Member States without a derogation' in the following Articles of this Statute: 3, 11.2, 19, 34.2 and 50.

43.4. 'National central banks' shall be read as 'central banks of Member States without a derogation' in the following Articles of this Statute: 9.2, 10.1, 10.3, 12.1, 16, 17, 18, 22, 23, 27, 30, 31, 32, 33.2 and 52.

43.5. 'Shareholders' shall be read as 'central banks of Member States without a derogation' in Articles 10.3 and 33.1.

43.6. 'Subscribed capital of the ECB' shall be read as 'capital of the ECB subscribed by the central banks of Member States without a derogation' in Articles 10.3 and 30.2.

Article 44 (Transitional tasks of the ECB)

The ECB shall take over those tasks of the EMI which, because of the derogations of one or more Member States, still have to be performed in the third stage.

The ECB shall give advice in the preparations for the abrogation of the derogations specified in Article 109l of this Treaty.

Article 45 (The General Council of the ECB)

45.1. Without prejudice to Article 106(3) of this Treaty, the General Council shall be constituted as a third decision-making body of the ECB.

45.2. The General Council shall comprise the President and Vice-President of the ECB and the Governors of the national central banks. The other members of the Executive Board may participate, without having the right to vote, in meetings of the General Council.

45.3. The responsibilities of the General Council are listed in full in Article 47 of this Statute.

Article 46 (Rules of procedure of the General Council)

46.1. The President or, in his absence, the Vice-President of the ECB shall chair the General Council of the ECB.

46.2. The President of the Council and a member of the Commission may participate, without having the right to vote, in meetings of the General Council.

46.3. The President shall prepare the meetings of the General Council.

46.4. By way of derogation from Article 12.3, the General Council shall adopt its Rules of Procedure.

46.5. The Secretariat of the General Council shall be provided by the ECB.

Article 47 (Responsibilities of the General Council)

47.1. The General Council shall:
— perform the tasks referred to in Article 44;
— contribute to the advisory functions referred to in Articles 4 and 25.1.

47.2. The General Council shall contribute to:
— the collection of statistical information as referred to in Article 5;
— the reporting activities of the ECB as referred to in Article 15;
— the establishment of the necessary rules for the application of Article 26 as referred to in Article 26.4;
— the taking of all other measures necessary for the application of Article 29 as referred to in Article 29.4;
— the laying down of the conditions of employment of the staff of the ECB as referred to in Article 36.

47.3. The General Council shall contribute to the necessary preparations for irrevocably fixing the exchange rates of the currencies of Member States with a derogation against the currencies, or the single currency, of the Member States without a derogation, as referred to in Article 109l(5) of this Treaty.

47.4. The General Council shall be informed by the President of the ECB of decisions of the Governing Council.

Article 48 (Transitional provisions for the capital of the ECB)

In accordance with Article 29.1 each national central bank shall be assigned a weighting in the key for subscription of the ECB's capital.

By way of derogation from Article 28.3, central banks of Member States with a derogation shall not pay up their subscribed capital unless the General Council, acting by a majority representing at least two thirds of the subscribed capital of the ECB and at least half of the shareholders, decides that a minimal percentage has to be paid up as a contribution to the operational costs of the ECB.

Article 49 (Deferred payment of capital, reserves and provisions of the ECB)

49.1. The central bank of a Member State whose derogation has been abrogated shall pay up its subscribed share of the capital of the ECB to the same extent as the central banks of other Member States without a derogation, and shall transfer to the ECB foreign reserve assets in accordance with Article 30.1. The sum to be transferred shall be determined by multiplying the ECU value at current exchange rates of the foreign reserve assets which have already been transferred to the ECB in accordance with Article 30.1, by the ratio between the number of shares subscribed by the national central bank concerned and the number of shares already paid up by the other national central banks.

49.2. In addition to the payment to be made in accordance with Article 49.1, the central bank concerned shall contribute to the reserves of the ECB, to those provisions equivalent to reserves, and to the amount still to be appropriated to the reserves and provisions corresponding to the balance of the profit and loss account as at 31 December of the year prior to the abrogation of the derogation. The sum to be contributed shall be determined by multiplying the amount of the reserves, as defined above and as stated in the approved balance sheet of the ECB, by the ratio between the number of shares subscribed by the central bank concerned and the number of shares already paid up by the other central banks.

Article 50 (Initial appointment of the members of the Executive Board)

When the Executive Board of the ECB is being established, the President, the Vice-President and the other members of the Executive Board shall be appointed by common accord of the governments of the Member States at the level of Heads of State or of Government, on a recommendation from the Council and after consulting the European Parliament and the Council of the EMI. The President of the Executive Board shall be appointed for eight years. By way of derogation from Article 11.2, the Vice-President shall be appointed for four years and the other members of the Executive Board for terms of office of between five and eight years. No term of office shall be renewable. The number of members of the Executive Board may be smaller than provided for in Article 11.1, but in no circumstance shall it be less than four.

Article 51 (Derogation from Article 32)

51.1. If, after the start of the third stage, the Governing Council decides that the application of Article 32 results in significant changes in national central banks' relative income positions, the amount of income to be allocated pursuant to Article 32 shall be reduced by a uniform percentage which shall not exceed 60 per cent in the first financial year after the start of the third stage and which shall decrease by at least 12 percentage points in each subsequent financial year.

51.2. Article 51.1 shall be applicable for not more than five financial years after the start of the third stage.

Article 52 (Exchange of bank notes in Community currencies)

Following the irrevocable fixing of exchange rates, the Governing Council shall take the necessary measures to ensure that bank notes denominated in currencies with irrevocably fixed exchange rates are exchanged by the national central banks at their respective par values.

Article 53 (Applicability of the transitional provisions)

If and as long as there are Member States with a derogation Articles 43 to 48 shall be applicable.

PROTOCOL ON THE STATUTE OF THE EUROPEAN MONETARY INSTITUTE

(Annexed to the E.C. Treaty)

Article 1 (Constitution and name)

1.1 The European Monetary Institute (EMI) shall be established in accordance with Article 109f of this Treaty; it shall perform its functions and carry out its activities in accordance with the provisions of this Treaty and of this Statute.

1.2. The members of the EMI shall be the central banks of the Member States ('national central banks'). For the purposes of this Statute, the Institut Monétaire Luxembourgeois shall be regarded as the central bank of Luxembourg.

1.3. Pursuant to Article 109f of this Treaty, both the Committee of Governors and the European Monetary Co-operation Fund (EMCF) shall be dissolved. All assets and liabilities of the EMCF shall pass automatically to the EMI.

Article 2 (Objectives)

The EMI shall contribute to the realisation of the conditions necessary for the transition to the third stage of Economic and Monetary Union, in particular by:
— strengthening the co-ordination of monetary policies with a view to ensuring price stability;
— making the preparations required for the establishment of the European System of Central Banks (ESCB), and for the conduct of a single monetary policy and the creation of a single currency in the third stage;
— overseeing the development of the ECU.

Article 3 (General principles)

3.1. The EMI shall carry out the tasks and functions conferred upon it by this Treaty and this Statute without prejudice to the responsibility of the competent authorities for the conduct of the monetary policy within the respective Member States.

3.2. The EMI shall act in accordance with the objectives and principles stated in Article 2 of the Statute of the ESCB.

Article 4 (Primary tasks)

4.1. In accordance with Article 109f(2) of this Treaty, the EMI shall:
— strengthen co-operation between the national central banks;
— strengthen the co-ordination of the monetary polices of the Member States with the aim of ensuring price stability;
— monitor the functioning of the European Monetary System (EMS);
— hold consultations concerning issues falling within the competence of the national central banks and affecting the stability of financial institutions and markets;
— take over the tasks of the EMCF; in particular it shall perform the functions referred to in Articles 6.1, 6.2 and 6.3;
— facilitate the use of the ECU and oversee its development, including the smooth functioning of the ECU clearing system.
The EMI shall also:
— hold regular consultations concerning the course of monetary policies and the use of monetary policy instruments;
— normally be consulted by the national monetary authorities before they take decisions on the course of monetary policy in the context of the common framework for *ex ante* co-ordination.

4.2. At the latest by 31 December 1996, the EMI shall specify the regulatory, organisational and logistical framework necessary for the ESCB to perform its tasks in the third stage, in accordance with the principle of an open market economy with free competition. This framework shall be submitted by the Council of the EMI for decision to the ECB at the date of its establishment.

In accordance with Article 109f(3) of this Treaty, the EMI shall in particular:
- prepare the instruments and the procedures necessary for carrying out a single monetary policy in the third stage;
- promote the harmonisation, where necessary, of the rules and practices governing the collection, compilation and distribution of statistics in the areas within its field of competence;
- prepare the rules for operations to be undertaken by the national central banks in the framework of the ESCB;
- promote the efficiency of cross-border payments;
- supervise the technical preparation of ECU bank notes.

Article 5 (Advisory functions)

5.1. In accordance with Article 109f(4) of this Treaty, the Council of the EMI may formulate opinions or recommendations on the overall orientation of monetary policy and exchange rate policy as well as on related measures introduced in each Member State. The EMI may submit opinions or recommendations to governments and to the Council on policies which might affect the internal or external monetary situation in the Community and, in particular, the functioning of the EMS.

5.2. The Council of the EMI may also make recommendations to the monetary authorities of the Member States concerning the conduct of their monetary policy.

5.3. In accordance with Article 109f(6) of this Treaty, the EMI shall be consulted by the Council regarding any proposed Community act within its field of competence.

Within the limits and under the conditions set out by the Council acting by a qualified majority on a proposal from the Commission and after consulting the European Parliament and the EMI, the EMI shall be consulted by the authorities of the Member States on any draft legislative provision within its field of competence, in particular with regard to Article 4.2.

5.4. In accordance with Article 109f(5) of this Treaty, the EMI may publish its opinions and its recommendations.

Article 6 (Operational and technical functions)

6.1. The EMI shall:
- provide for the multilaterisation of positions resulting from interventions by the national central banks in Community currencies and the multilateralisation of intra-Community settlements;
- administer the very short-term financing mechanism provided for by the Agreement of 13 March 1979 between the central banks of the Member States of the European Community laying down the operating procedures for the European Monetary System (hereinafter referred to as 'EMS Agreement') and the short-term monetary support mechanism provided for in the Agreement between the central banks of the Member States of the European Economic Community of 9 February 1970, as amended;
- perform the functions referred to in Article 11 of Council Regulation 1969/88 of 24 June 1988 establishing a single facility providing medium-term financial assistance for Member States' balances of payments.

6.2. The EMI may receive monetary reserves from the national central banks and issue ECUs against such assets for the purpose of implementing the EMS Agreement. These ECUs may be used by the EMI and the national central banks as a means of settlement and for transactions between them and the EMI. The EMI shall take the necessary administrative measures for the implementation of this paragraph.

6.3. The EMI may grant to the monetary authorities of third countries and to international monetary institutions the status of 'Other Holders' of ECUs and fix the terms and conditions under which such ECUs may be acquired, held or used by Other Holders.

6.4. The EMI shall be entitled to hold and manage foreign exchange reserves as an agent for and at the request of national central banks. Profits and losses regarding these reserves shall be for the account of the national central bank depositing the reserves.

The EMI shall perform this function on the basis of bilateral contracts in accordance with rules laid down in a decision of the EMI.

These rules shall ensure that transactions with these reserves shall not interfere with the monetary policy and exchange rate policy of the competent monetary authority of any Member State and shall be consistent with the objectives of the EMI and the proper functioning of the Exchange Rate Mechanism of the EMS.

Article 7 (Other tasks)

7.1. Once a year the EMI shall address a report to the Council on the state of the preparations for the third stage. These reports shall include an assessment of the progress towards convergence in the Community, and cover in particular the adaptation of monetary policy instruments and the preparation of the procedures necessary for carrying out a single monetary policy in the third stage, as well as the statutory requirements to be fulfilled for national central banks to become an integral part of the ESCB.

7.2. In accordance with the Council decisions referred to in Article 109f(7) of this Treaty, the EMI may perform other tasks for the preparation of the third stage.

Article 8 (Independence)

The members of the Council of the EMI who are the representatives of their institutions shall, with respect to their activities, act according to their own responsibilities. In exercising the powers and performing the tasks and duties conferred upon them by this Treaty and this Statute, the Council of the EMI may not seek or take any instructions from Community institutions or bodies or governments of Member States.

The Community institutions and bodies as well as the governments of the Member States undertake to respect this principle and not to seek to influence the Council of the EMI in the performance of its tasks.

Article 9 (Administration)

9.1. In accordance with Article 109f(1) of this Treaty, the EMI shall be directed and managed by the Council of the EMI.

9.2. The Council of the EMI shall consist of a President and the Governors of the national central banks, one of whom shall be Vice-President. If a Governor is prevented from attending a meeting, he may nominate another representative of his institution.

9.3. The President shall be appointed by common accord of the governments of the Member States at the level of Heads of State or of Government, on a recommendation from, as the case may be, the Committee of Governors or the Council of the EMI, and after consulting the European Parliament and the Council.

The President shall be selected from among persons of recognised standing and professional experience in monetary or banking matters. Only nationals of Member States may be President of the EMI.

The Council of the EMI shall appoint the Vice-President. The President and Vice-President shall be appointed for a period of three years.

9.4. The President shall perform his duties on a full-time basis. He shall not engage in any occupation, whether gainful or not, unless exemption is exceptionally granted by the Council of the EMI.

9.5. The President shall:
— prepare and chair the meetings of the Council of the EMI;
— without prejudice to Article 22, present the views of the EMI externally;
— be responsible for the day-to-day management of the EMI.

In the absence of the President, his duties shall be performed by the Vice-President.

9.6. The terms and conditions of employment of the President, in particular his salary, pension and other social security benefits, shall be the subject of a contract with the EMI and shall be fixed by the Council of the EMI on a proposal from a Committee comprising three members appointed by the Committee of Governors or the Council of the EMI, as the case may be, and three members appointed by the Council. The President shall not have the right to vote on matters referred to in this paragraph.

9.7. If the President no longer fulfils the conditions required for the performance of his duties or if he has been guilty of serious misconduct, the Court of Justice may, on application by the Council of the EMI, compulsorily retire him.

9.8. The Rules of Procedure of the EMI shall be adopted by the Council of the EMI.

Article 10 (Meetings of the Council of the EMI and voting procedures)

10.1. The Council of the EMI shall meet at least ten times a year. The proceedings of Council meetings shall be confidential. The Council of the EMI may, acting unanimously, decide to make the outcome of its deliberations public.

10.2. Each member of the Council of the EMI or his nominee shall have one vote.

10.3. Save as otherwise provided for in this Statute, the Council of the EMI shall act by a simple majority of its members.

10.4. Decisions to be taken in the context of Articles 4.2, 5.4, 6.2 and 6.3. shall require unanimity of the members of the Council of the EMI.

The adoption of opinions and recommendations under Articles 5.1 and 5.2, the adoption of decisions under Articles 6.4, 16 and 23.6 and the adoption of guidelines under Article 15.3 shall require a qualified majority of two thirds of the members of the Council of the EMI.

Article 11 (Interinstitutional co-operation and reporting requirements)

11.1 The President of the Council and a member of the Commission may participate, without having the right to vote, in meetings of the Council of the EMI.

11.2. The President of the EMI shall be invited to participate in Council meetings when the Council is discussing matters relating to the objectives and tasks of the EMI.

11.3. At a date to be established in the Rules of Procedure, the EMI shall prepare an annual report on its activities and on monetary and financial conditions in the Community. The annual report, together with the annual accounts of the EMI, shall be addressed to the European Parliament, the Council and the Commission and also to the European Council.

The President of the EMI may, at the request of the European Parliament or on his own initiative, be heard by the competent Committees of the European Parliament.

11.4. Reports published by the EMI shall be made available to interested parties free of charge.

Article 12 (Currency denomination)

The operations of the EMI shall be expressed in ECUs.

Article 13 (Seat)

Before the end of 1992, the decision as to where the seat of the EMI will be established shall be taken by common accord of the governments of the Member States at the level of Heads of State or of Government.

Article 14 (Legal capacity)

The EMI, which in accordance with Article 109f(1) of this Treaty shall have legal personality, shall enjoy in each of the Member States the most extensive legal capacity accorded to legal persons under their law; it may, in particular, acquire or dispose of movable or immovable property and may be a party to legal proceedings.

Article 15 (Legal acts)

15.1. In the performance of its tasks, and under the conditions laid down in this Statute, the EMI shall:
— deliver opinions;
— make recommendations;
— adopt guidelines, and take decisions, which shall be addressed to the national central banks.

15.2. Opinions and recommendations of the EMI shall have no binding force.

15.3. The Council of the EMI may adopt guidelines laying down the methods for the implementation of the conditions necessary for the ESCB to perform its functions in the third stage. EMI guidelines shall have no binding force; they shall be submitted for decision to the ECB.

15.4. Without prejudice to Article 3.1, a decision of the EMI shall be binding in its entirety upon those to whom it is addressed. Articles 190 and 191 of this Treaty shall apply to these decisions.

Article 16 (Financial resources)

16.1. The EMI shall be endowed with its own resources. The size of the resources of the EMI shall be determined by the Council of the EMI with a view to ensuring the income deemed necessary to cover the administrative expenditure incurred in the performance of the tasks and functions of the EMI.

16.2. The resources of the EMI determined in accordance with Article 16.1 shall be provided out of contributions by the national central banks in accordance with the key referred to in Article 29.1 of the Statute of the ESCB and be paid up at the establishment of the EMI. For this purpose, the statistical data to be used for the determination of the key shall be provided by the Commission, in accordance with the rules adopted by the Council, acting by a qualified majority on a proposal from the Commission and after consulting the European Parliament, the Committee of Governors and the Committee referred to in Article 109c of this Treaty.

16.3. The Council of the EMI shall determine the form in which contributions shall be paid up.

Article 17 (Annual accounts and auditing)

17.1. The financial year of the EMI shall begin on the first day of January and end on the last day of December.

17.2. The Council of the EMI shall adopt an annual budget before the beginning of each financial year.

17.3. The annual accounts shall be drawn up in accordance with the principles established by the Council of the EMI. The annual accounts shall be approved by the Council of the EMI and shall thereafter be published.

17.4. The annual accounts shall be audited by independent external auditors approved by the Council of the EMI. The auditors shall have full power to examine all books and accounts of the EMI and to obtain full information about its transactions.

The provisions of Article 188b of this Treaty shall only apply to an examination of the operational efficiency of the management of the EMI.

17.5. Any surplus of the EMI shall be transferred in the following order:
  (a) an amount to be determined by the Council of the EMI shall be transferred to the general reserve fund of the EMI;
  (b) any remaining surplus shall be distributed to the national central banks in accordance with the key referred to in Article 16.2.

17.6. In the event of a loss incurred by the EMI, the shortfall shall be offset against the general reserve fund of the EMI. Any remaining shortfall shall be made good by contributions from the national central banks, in accordance with the key as referred to in Article 16.2.

Article 18 (Staff)

18.1. The Council of the EMI shall lay down the conditions of employment of the staff of the EMI.

18.2. The Court of Justice shall have jurisdiction in any dispute between the EMI and its servants within the limits and under the conditions laid down in the conditions of employment.

Article 19 (Judicial control and related matters)

19.1. The acts or omissions of the EMI shall be open to review or interpretation by the Court of Justice in the cases and under the conditions laid down in this Treaty. The EMI may institute proceedings in the cases and under the conditions laid down in this Treaty.

19.2. Disputes between the EMI, on the one hand, and its creditors, debtors or any other person, on the other, shall fall within the jurisdiction of the competent national courts, save where jurisdiction has been conferred upon the Court of Justice.

19.3. The EMI shall be subject to the liability regime provided for in Article 215 of this Treaty.

19.4. The Court of Justice shall have jurisdiction to give judgment pursuant to any arbitration clause contained in a contract concluded by or on behalf of the EMI, whether that contract be governed by public or private law.

19.5. A decision of the EMI to bring an action before the Court of Justice shall be taken by the Council of the EMI.

Article 20 (Professional secrecy)

20.1. Members of the Council of the EMI and the staff of the EMI shall be required, even after their duties have ceased, not to disclose information of the kind covered by the obligation of professional secrecy.

20.2. Persons having access to data covered by Community legislation imposing an obligation of secrecy shall be subject to such legislation.

Article 21 (Privileges and immunities)

The EMI shall enjoy in the territories of the Member States such privileges and immunities as are necessary for the performance of its tasks, under the conditions laid down in the Protocol on the Privileges and Immunities of the European Communities annexed to the Treaty establishing a Single Council and a Single Commission of the European Communities.

Article 22 (Signatories)

The EMI shall be legally committed to third parties by the President or the Vice-President or by the signatures of two members of the staff of the EMI who have been duly authorised by the President to sign on behalf of the EMI.

Article 23 (Liquidation of the EMI)

23.1. In accordance with Article 109l of this Treaty, the EMI shall go into liquidation on the establishment of the ECB.

All assets and liabilities of the EMI shall then pass automatically to the ECB.

The latter shall liquidate the EMI according to the provisions of this Article.

The liquidation shall be completed by the beginning of the third stage.

23.2. The mechanism for the creation of ECUs against gold and US dollars as provided for by Article 17 of the EMS Agreement shall be unwound by the first day of the third stage in accordance with Article 20 of the said Agreement.

23.3. All claims and liabilities arising from the very short-term financing mechanism and the short-term monetary support mechanism, under the Agreements referred to in Article 6.1, shall be settled by the first day of the third stage.

23.4. All remaining assets of the EMI shall be disposed of and all remaining liabilities of the EMI shall be settled.

23.5. The proceeds of the liquidation described in Article 23.4 shall be distributed to the national central banks in accordance with the key referred to in Article 16.2, 23.6.

The Council of the EMI may take the measures necessary for the application of Articles 23.4 and 23.5.

23.7. Upon the establishment of the ECB, the President of the EMI shall relinquish his office.

PROTOCOL ON THE EXCESSIVE DEFICIT PROCEDURE

(Annexed to E.C. Treaty (Article 104c))

Article 1

The reference values referred to in Article 104c(2) of this Treaty are:
— 3 per cent for the ratio of the planned or actual government deficit to gross domestic product at market prices;

— 60 per cent for the ratio of government debt to gross domestic product at market prices.

Article 2

In Article 104c of this Treaty and in this Protocol:
— government means general government, that is central government, regional or local government and social security funds, to the exclusion of commercial operations, as defined in the European System of Integrated Economic Accounts;
— deficit means net borrowing as defined in the European System of Integrated Economic Accounts;
— investment means gross fixed capital formation as defined in the European System of Integrated Economic Accounts;
— debt means total gross debt at nominal value outstanding at the end of the year and consolidated between and within the sectors of general government as defined in the first indent.

Article 3

In order to ensure the effectiveness of the excessive deficit procedure, the governments of the Member States shall be responsible under this procedure for the deficits of general government as defined in the first indent of Article 2. The Member States shall ensure that national procedures in the budgetary area enable them to meet their obligations in this area deriving from this Treaty. The Member States shall report their planned and actual deficits and the levels of their debt promptly and regularly to the Commission.

Article 4

The statistical data to be used for the application of this Protocol shall be provided by the Commission.

PROTOCOL ON THE CONVERGENCE CRITERIA REFERRED TO IN ARTICLE 109J OF THE TREATY ESTABLISHING THE EUROPEAN COMMUNITY

(Annexed to E.C. Treaty (Article 109j))

Article 1

The criterion on price stability referred to in the first indent of Article 109j(1) of this Treaty shall mean that a Member State has a price performance that is sustainable and an average rate of inflation, observed over a period of one year before the examination, that does not exceed by more than 1½ percentage points that of, at most, the three best performing Member States in terms of price stability. Inflation shall be measured by means of the consumer price index (CPI) on a comparable basis, taking into account differences in national definitions.

Article 2

The criterion on the government budgetary position referred to in the second indent of Article 109j(1) of this Treaty shall mean that at the time of the examination the Member State is not the subject of a Council decision under Article 104c(6) of this Treaty that an excessive deficit exists.

Article 3

The criterion on participation in the Exchange Rate Mechanism of the European Monetary System referred to in the third indent of Article 109j(1) of this Treaty shall mean that a Member State has respected the normal fluctuation margins provided for by the Exchange Rate Mechanism of the European Monetary System without severe tensions for at least the last two years before the examination. In particular, the Member State shall not have devalued its currency's bilateral central rate against any other Member State's currency on its own initiative for the same period.

Article 4

The criterion on the convergence of interest rates referred to in the fourth indent of Article 109j(1) of this Treaty shall mean that, observed over a period of one year before the examination, a Member State has had an average nominal long-term interest rate that does not exceed by more than 2 percentage points that of, at most, the three best performing Member States in terms of price stability. Interest rates shall be measured on the basis of long term government bonds or comparable securities, taking into account differences in national definitions.

Article 5

The statistical data to be used for the application of this Protocol shall be provided by the Commission.

Article 6

The Council shall, acting unanimously on a proposal from the Commission and after consulting the European Parliament, the EMI or the ECB as the case may be, and the Committee referred to in Article 109c, adopt appropriate provisions to lay down the details of the convergence criteria referred to in Article 109j of this Treaty, which shall then replace this Protocol.

PROTOCOL AMENDING THE PROTOCOL ON THE PRIVILEGES AND IMMUNITIES OF THE EUROPEAN COMMUNITIES

(*Annexed to E.C. Treaty*)

Sole Article

The Protocol on the Privileges and Immunities of the European Communities, annexed to the Treaty establishing a Single Council and a Single Commission of the European Communities, shall be supplemented by the following provisions:

Article 23

This Protocol shall also apply to the European Central Bank, to the members of its organs and to its staff, without prejudice to the provisions of the Protocol on the Statute of the European System of Central Banks and the European Central Bank.

The European Central Bank shall, in addition, be exempt from any form of taxation or imposition of a like nature on the occasion of any increase in its capital and from the various formalities which may be connected therewith in the State where the bank has its seat. The activities of the Bank and of its organs carried on in accordance with the Statute of the European System of Central Banks and of the European Central Bank shall not be subject to any turnover tax.

The above provisions shall also apply to the European Monetary Institute. Its dissolution or liquidation shall not give rise to any imposition.

PROTOCOL ON DENMARK

(Annexed to E.C. Treaty)

The provisions of Article 14 of the Protocol on the Statute of the European System of Central Banks and of the European Central Bank shall not affect the right of the National Bank of Denmark to carry out its existing tasks concerning those parts of the Kingdom of Denmark which are not part of the Community.

PROTOCOL ON PORTUGAL

(Annexed to E.C. Treaty)

1. Portugal is hereby authorised to maintain the facility afforded to the Autonomous Regions of Azores and Madeira to benefit from an interest-free [credit] facility with the Banco de Portugal under the terms established by existing Portuguese law.

2. Portugal commits itself to pursue its best endeavours in order to put an end to the abovementioned facility as soon as possible.

PROTOCOL ON THE TRANSITION TO THE THIRD STAGE OF ECONOMIC AND MONETARY UNION

(Annexed to E.C. Treaty)

THE HIGH CONTRACTING PARTIES,

Declare the irreversible character of the Community's movement to the third stage of Economic and Monetary Union by signing the new Treaty provisions on Economic and Monetary Union.

Therefore all Member States shall, whether they fulfil the necessary conditions for the adoption of a single currency or not, respect the will for the Community to enter swiftly into the third stage, and therefore no Member State shall prevent the entering into the third stage.

If by the end of 1997 the date of the beginning of the third stage has not been set, the Member States concerned, the Community institutions and other bodies involved shall expedite all preparatory work during 1998, in order to enable the Community to enter the third stage irrevocably on 1 January 1999 and to enable the ECB and the ESCB to start their full functioning from this date.

PROTOCOL ON CERTAIN PROVISIONS RELATING TO THE UNITED KINGDOM OF GREAT BRITAIN AND NORTHERN IRELAND

(Annexed to E.C. Treaty)

THE HIGH CONTRACTING PARTIES,

RECOGNISING that the United Kingdom shall not be obliged or committed to move to the third stage of Economic and Monetary Union without a separate decision to do so by its government and Parliament,

NOTING the practice of the government of the United Kingdom to fund its
   borrowing requirement by the sale of debt to the private sector,
HAVE AGREED the following provisions,
   1. The United Kingdom shall notify the Council whether it intends to move
to the third stage before the Council makes its assessment under Article 109j
(2) of this Treaty.
   Unless the United Kingdom notifies the Council that it intends to move to
the third stage, it shall be under no obligation to do so.
   If no date is set for the beginning of the third stage under Article 109j(3) of
this Treaty, the United Kingdom may notify its intention to move to the third
stage before 1 January 1998.
   2. Paragraphs 3 to 9 shall have effect if the United Kingdom notifies the
Council that it does not intend to move to the third stage.
   3. The United Kingdom shall not be included among the majority of Member States which fulfil the necessary conditions referred to in the second
indent of Article 109j(2) and the first indent of Article 109j(3) of this Treaty.
   4. The United Kingdom shall retain its powers in the field of monetary
policy according to national law.
   5. Articles 3a(2), 104c(1), (9) and (11), 105(1) to (5), 105a, 107, 108, 108a,
109, 109a(1) and (2)(b) and 109l(4) and (5) of this Treaty shall not apply to
the United Kingdom. In these provisions references to the Community or the
Member States shall not include the United Kingdom and references to
national central banks shall not include the Bank of England.
   6. Articles 109e(4) and 109h and i of this Treaty shall continue to apply to
the United Kingdom. Articles 109c(4) and 109m shall apply to the United
Kingdom as if it had a derogation.
   7. The voting rights of the United Kingdom shall be suspended in respect
of acts of the Council referred to in the Articles listed in paragraph 5. For this
purpose the weighted votes of the United Kingdom shall be excluded from
any calculation of a qualified majority under Article 109k(5) of this Treaty.
   The United Kingdom shall also have no right to participate in the appointment of the President, the Vice-President and the other members of the
Executive Board of the ECB under Articles 109a(2)(b) and 109l(1) of this
Treaty.
   8. Articles 3, 4, 6, 7, 9.2, 10.1, 10.3, 11.2, 12.1, 14, 16, 18 to 20, 22, 23, 26, 27, 30
to 34, 50 and 52 of the Protocol on the Statute of the European System of
Central Banks and of the European Central Bank ('the Statute') shall not
apply to the United Kingdom.
   In those Articles, references to the Community or the Member States shall
not include the United Kingdom and references to national central banks or
shareholders shall not include the Bank of England.
   References in Articles 10.3 and 30.2 of the Statute to 'subscribed capital of
the ECB' shall not include capital subscribed by the Bank of England.
   9. Article 109l(3) of this Treaty and Articles 44 to 48 of the Statute shall
have effect, whether or not there is any Member State with a derogation,
subject to the following amendments:
   (a) References in Article 44 to the tasks of the ECB and the EMI shall
       include those tasks that still need to be performed in the third stage
       owing to any decision of the United Kingdom not to move to that
       stage.
   (b) In addition to the tasks referred to in Article 47 the ECB shall also give
       advice in relation to and contribute to the preparation of any decision
       of the Council with regard to the United Kingdom taken in accordance
       with paragraphs 10(a) and 10(c).
   (c) The Bank of England shall pay up its subscription to the capital of the
       ECB as a contribution to its operational costs on the same basis as
       national central banks of Member States with a derogation.

10. If the United Kingdom does not move to the third stage, it may change its notification at any time after the beginning of that stage. In that event:

(a) The United Kingdom shall have the right to move to the third stage provided only that it satisfies the necessary conditions. The Council, acting at the request of the United Kingdom and under the conditions and in accordance with the procedure laid down in Article 109k(2) of this Treaty, shall decide whether it fulfils the necessary conditions.

(b) The Bank of England shall pay up its subscribed capital, transfer to the ECB foreign reserve assets and contribute to its reserves on the same basis as the national central bank of a Member State whose derogation has been abrogated.

(c) The Council, acting under the conditions and in accordance with the procedure laid down in Article 109l(5) of this Treaty, shall take all other necessary decisions to enable the United Kingdom to move to the third stage.

If the United Kingdom moves to the third stage pursuant to the provisions of this protocol, paragraphs 3 to 9 shall cease to have effect.

11. Notwithstanding Articles 104 and 109e(3) of this Treaty and Article 21.1 of the Statute, the government of the United Kingdom may maintain its Ways and Means facility with the Bank of England if and so long as the United Kingdom does not move to the third stage.

PROTOCOL ON CERTAIN PROVISIONS RELATING TO DENMARK

(Annexed to E.C. Treaty)

THE HIGH CONTRACTING PARTIES,

TAKING INTO ACCOUNT that the Danish Constitution contains provisions which may imply a referendum in Denmark prior to Danish participation in the third stage of Economic and Monetary Union,

HAVE AGREED on the following provisions,

1. The Danish Government shall notify the Council of its position concerning participation in the third stage before the Council makes its assessment under Article 109j(2) of this Treaty.

2. In the event of a notification that Denmark will not participate in the third stage, Denmark shall have an exemption. The effect of the exemption shall be that all Articles and provisions of this Treaty and the Statute of the ESCB referring to a derogation shall be applicable to Denmark.

3. In such case, Denmark shall not be included among the majority of Member States which fulfil the necessary conditions referred to in the second indent of Article 109j(2) and the first indent of Article 109j(3) of this Treaty.

4. As for the abrogation of the exemption, the procedure referred to in Article 109k(2) shall only be initiated at the request of Denmark.

5. In the event of abrogation of the exemption status, the provisions of this Protocol shall cease to apply.

PROTOCOL ON FRANCE

(Annexed to E.C. Treaty)

France will keep the privilege of monetary emission in its overseas territories under the terms established by its national laws, and will be solely entitled to determine the parity of the CFP franc.

The E.C. Treaty

(Annexed to E.C. Treaty)

THE HIGH CONTRACTING PARTIES,

NOTING that 11 Member States, that is to say the Kingdom of Belgium, the Kingdom of Denmark, the Federal Republic of Germany, the Hellenic Republic, the Kingdom of Spain, the French Republic, Ireland, the Italian Republic, the Grand Duchy of Luxembourg, the Kingdom of the Netherlands, the Portuguese Republic, wish to continue along the path laid down in the 1989 Social Charter; that they have adopted among themselves an Agreement to this end; that this Agreement is annexed to this Protocol; that this Protocol and the said Agreement are without prejudice to the provisions of this Treaty, particularly those which relate to social policy which constitute an integral part of the *'acquis communautaire'*:

1. Agree to authorise those 11 Member States to have recourse to the institutions, procedures and mechanisms of the Treaty for the purposes of taking among themselves and applying as far as they are concerned the acts and decisions required for giving effect to the abovementioned Agreement.

2. The United Kingdom of Great Britain and Northern Ireland shall not take part in the deliberations and the adoption by the Council of Commission proposals made on the basis of this Protocol and the abovementioned Agreement.

By way of derogation from Article 148(2) of the Treaty, acts of the Council which are made pursuant to this Protocol and which must be adopted by a qualified majority shall be deemed to be so adopted if they have received at least 44 votes in favour.

The unanimity of the members of the Council, with the exception of the United Kingdom of Great Britain and Northern Ireland, shall be necessary for acts of the Council which must be adopted unanimously and for those amending the Commission proposal.

Acts adopted by the Council and any financial consequences other than administrative costs entailed for the institutions shall not be applicable to the United Kingdom of Great Britain and Northern Ireland.

AGREEMENT ON SOCIAL POLICY CONCLUDED BETWEEN THE MEMBER STATES OF THE EUROPEAN COMMUNITY WITH THE EXCEPTION OF THE UNITED KINGDOM OF GREAT BRITAIN AND NORTHERN IRELAND

The undersigned 11 HIGH CONTRACTING PARTIES, that is to say the Kingdom of Belgium, the Kingdom of Denmark, the Federal Republic of Germany, the Hellenic Republic, the Kingdom of Spain, the French Republic, Ireland, the Italian Republic, the Grand Duchy of Luxembourg, the Kingdom of the Netherlands and the Portuguese Republic (hereinafter referred to as 'the Member States'),

WISHING to implement the 1989 Social Charter on the basis of the *'acquis communautaire,'*

CONSIDERING the Protocol on social policy,

HAVE AGREED as follows:

Article 1

The Community and the Member States shall have as their objectives the promotion of employment, improved living and working conditions, proper social protection, dialogue between management and labour, the development of human resources with a view to lasting high employment and the combating of exclusion. To this end the Community and the Member States shall implement measures which take account of the diverse forms of national practices, in particular in the field of contractual relations, and the need to maintain the competitiveness of the Community economy.

Article 2

1. With a view to achieving the objectives of Article 1, the Community shall support and complement the activities of the Member States in the following fields:
   — improvement in particular of the working environment to protect workers' health and safety;
   — working conditions;
   — the information and consultation of workers;
   — equality between men and women with regard to labour market opportunities and treatment at work;
   — the integration of persons excluded from the labour market, without prejudice to Article 127 of the Treaty establishing the European Community (hereinafter referred to as 'the Treaty').

2. To this end, the Council may adopt, by means of directives, minimum requirements for gradual implementation, having regard to the conditions and technical rules obtaining in each of the Member States.

Such directives shall avoid imposing administrative, financial and legal constraints in a way which would hold back the creation and development of small and medium-sized undertakings.

The Council shall act in accordance with the procedure referred to in Article 189c of the Treaty after consulting the Economic and Social Committee.

3. However, the Council shall act unanimously on a proposal from the Commission, after consulting the European Parliament and the Economic and Social Committee, in the following areas:
   — social security and social protection of workers;
   — protection of workers where their employment contract is terminated;
   — representation and collective defence of the interests of workers and employers, including co-determination, subject to paragraph 6;
   — conditions of employment for third-country nationals legally residing in Community territory;
   — financial contributions for promotion of employment and job-creation, without prejudice to the provisions relating to the Social Fund.

4. A Member State may entrust management and labour, at their joint request, with the implementation of directives adopted pursuant to paragraphs 2 and 3.

In this case, it shall ensure that, no later than the date on which a directive must be transposed in accordance with Article 189, management and labour have introduced the necessary measures by agreement, the Member State concerned being required to take any necessary measure enabling it at any time to be in a position to guarantee the results imposed by that directive.

5. The provisions adopted pursuant to this Article shall not prevent any Member State from maintaining or introducing more stringent preventive measures compatible with the Treaty.

6. The provisions of this Article shall not apply to pay, the right of association, the right to strike or the right to impose lock-outs.

Article 3

1. The Commission shall have the task of promoting the consultation of management and labour at Community level and shall take any relevant measure to facilitate their dialogue by ensuring balanced support for the parties.

2. To this end, before submitting proposals in the social policy field, the Commission shall consult management and labour on the possible direction of Community action.

3. If, after such consultation, the Commission considers Community action advisable, it shall consult management and labour on the content of the envisaged proposal. Management and labour shall forward to the Commission an opinion, or, where appropriate, a recommendation.

4. On the occasion of such consultation, management and labour may inform the Commission of their wish to initiate the process provided for in Article 4. The duration of the procedure shall not exceed nine months, unless the management and labour concerned and the Commission decide jointly to extend it.

Article 4

1. Should management and labour so desire, the dialogue between them at Community level may lead to contractual relations including agreements.

2. Agreements concluded at Community level shall be implemented either in accordance with the procedures and practices specific to management and labour and the Member States or, in matters covered by Article 2, at the joint request of the signatory parties, by a Council decision on a proposal form from the Commission.

The Council shall act by qualified majority, except where the agreement in question contains one or more provisions relating to one of the areas referred to in Article 2(3), in which case it shall act unanimously.

Article 5

With a view to achieving the objectives of Article 1 and without prejudice to the other provisions of the Treaty, the Commission shall encourage co-operation between the Member States and facilitate the co-ordination of their action in all social policy fields under this Agreement.

Article 6

1. Each Member State shall ensure that the principle of equal pay for male and female workers for equal work is applied.

2. For the purpose of this Article, 'pay' means the ordinary basic or minimum wage or salary and any other considerations, whether in cash or in kind, which the worker receives directly or indirectly, in respect of his employment, from his employer.

Equal pay without discrimination based on sex means:
(a) that pay for the same work at piece rates shall be calculated on the basis of the same unit of measurement;
(b) that pay for work at time rates shall be the same for the same job.

3. This Article shall not prevent any Member State from maintaining or adopting measures providing for specific advantages in order to make it easier for women to pursue a vocational activity or to prevent or compensate for disadvantages in their professional careers.

Article 7

The Commission shall draw up a report each year on progress in achieving the objectives of Article 1, including the demographic situation in the Community. It shall forward the report to the European Parliament, the Council and the Economic and Social Committee.

The European Parliament may invite the Commission to draw up reports on particular problems concerning the social situation.

DECLARATIONS

1. Declaration on Article 2(2)

The 11 High Contracting Parties note that in the discussions on Article 2(2) of the Agreement it was agreed that the Community does not intend, in laying down minimum requirements for the protection of the safety and health of employees, to discriminate in a manner justified by the circumstances against employees in small and medium-sized undertakings.

2. Declaration on Article 4(2)

The 11 High Contracting Parties declare that the first of the arrangements for application of the agreements between management and labour Community-wide—referred to in Article 4(2)—will consist in developing, by collective bargaining according to the rules of each Member State, the content of the agreements, and that consequently this arrangement implies no obligation on the Member States to apply the agreements directly or to work out rules for their transposition, nor any obligation to amend national legislation in force to facilitate their implementation.

PROTOCOL ON ECONOMIC AND SOCIAL COHESION

(Annexed to E.C. Treaty)

THE HIGH CONTRACTING PARTIES,

RECALLING that the Union has set itself the objective of promoting economic and social progress, *inter alia*, through the strengthening of economic and social cohesion;

RECALLING that Article 2 of this Treaty includes the task of promoting economic and social cohesion and solidarity between Member States and that the strengthening of economic and social cohesion figures among the activities of the Community listed in Article 3;

RECALLING that the provisions of Part Three, Title XIV, on economic and social cohesion as a whole provide the legal basis for consolidating and further developing the Community's action in the field of economic and social cohesion, including the creation of a new fund;

RECALLING that the provisions of Part Three, Title XII on trans-European networks and Title XVI on environment envisage a Cohesion Fund to be set up before 31 December 1993;

STATING their belief that progress towards Economic and Monetary Union will contribute to the economic growth of all Member States;

NOTING that the Community's Structural Funds are being doubled in real terms between 1987 and 1993, implying large transfers, especially as a proportion of GDP of the less prosperous Member States;

NOTING that the European Investment Bank is lending large and increasing amounts for the benefit of the poorer regions;

NOTING the desire for greater flexibility in the arrangements for allocations from the Structural Funds;

NOTING the desire for modulation of the levels of Community participation in programmes and projects in certain countries;

NOTING the proposal to take greater account of the relative prosperity of Member States in the system of own resources,

REAFFIRM that the promotion of economic and social cohesion is vital to the full development and enduring success of the Community, and underline the importance of the inclusion of economic and social cohesion in Articles 2 and 3 of this Treaty;

REAFFIRM their conviction that the Structural Funds should continue to play a considerable part in the achievement of Community objectives in the field of cohesion;

REAFFIRM their conviction that the European Investment Bank should continue to devote the majority of its resources to the promotion of economic and social cohesion, and declare their willingness to review the capital needs of the European Investment Bank as soon as this is necessary for that purpose;

REAFFIRM the need for a thorough evaluation of the operation and effectiveness of the Structural Funds in 1992, and the need to review, on that occasion, the appropriate size of these Funds in the light of the tasks of the Community in the area of economic and social cohesion;

AGREE that the Cohesion Fund to be set up before 31 December 1993 will provide Community financial contributions to projects in the fields of environment and trans-European networks in Member States with a per capita GNP of less than 90 per cent of the Community average which have a programme leading to the fulfilment of the conditions of economic convergence as set out in Article 104c;

DECLARE their intention of allowing a greater margin of flexibility in allocating financing from the Structural Funds to specific needs not covered under the present Structural Funds regulations;

DECLARE their willingness to modulate the levels of Community participation in the context of programmes and projects of the Structural Funds, with a view to avoiding excessive increases in budgetary expenditure in the less prosperous Member States;

RECOGNISE the need to monitor regularly the progress made towards achieving economic and social cohesion and state their willingness to study all necessary measures in this respect;

DECLARE their intention of taking greater account of the contributive capacity of individual Member States in the system of own resources, and of examining means of correcting, for the less prosperous Member States, regressive elements existing in the present own resources system.

DECLARATIONS 1–26

DECLARATIONS

GENERAL NOTE

The declarations are statements of intent by the Member States of the European Union but they are not an integral part of the E.C. Treaty or of the E.U. Treaty. The declarations are not enforceable in the E.C.J.

DECLARATION ON CIVIL PROTECTION, ENERGY AND TOURISM

The Conference declares that the question of introducing into the Treaty establishing the European Community Titles relating to the spheres referred to in Article 3(t) of that Treaty will be examined, in accordance with the procedure laid down in Article N(2) of the Treaty on European Union, on the basis of a report which the Commission will submit to the Council by 1996 at the latest.

The Commission declares that Community action in those spheres will be pursued on the basis of the present provisions of the Treaties establishing the European Communities.

DECLARATION ON NATIONALITY OF A MEMBER STATE

The Conference declares that, wherever in the Treaty establishing the European Community reference is made to nationals of the Member States, the question whether an individual possesses the nationality of a Member State shall be settled solely by reference to the national law of the Member State concerned. Member States may declare, for information, who are to be considered their nationals for Community purposes by way of a declaration lodged with the Presidency and may amend any such declaration when necessary.

DECLARATION ON PART THREE, TITLES III AND VI, OF THE TREATY ESTABLISHING THE EUROPEAN COMMUNITY

The Conference affirms that, for the purposes of applying the provisions set out in Part Three, Title III, Chapter 4 on capital and payments, and Title VI on economic and monetary policy, of this Treaty, the usual practice, according to which the Council meets in the composition of Economic and Finance Ministers, shall be continued, without prejudice to Article 109j(2) and (4) and Article 109k(2).

DECLARATION ON PART THREE, TITLE VI, OF THE TREATY ESTABLISHING THE EUROPEAN COMMUNITY

The Conference affirms that the President of the European Council shall invite the Economic and Finance Ministers to participate in European Council meetings when the European Council is discussing matters relating to Economic and Monetary Union.

DECLARATION ON MONETARY CO-OPERATION WITH NON-COMMUNITY COUNTRIES

The Conference affirms that the Community shall aim to contribute to stable international monetary relations.

To this end the Community shall be prepared to co-operate with other European countries and with those non-European countries with which the Community has close economic ties.

DECLARATION ON MONETARY RELATIONS WITH THE REPUBLIC OF SAN MARINO, THE VATICAN CITY AND THE PRINCIPALITY OF MONACO

The Conference agrees that the existing monetary relations between Italy and San Marino and the Vatican City and between France and Monaco remain unaffected by the Treaty establishing the European Community until the introduction of the ECU as the single currency of the Community.

The Community undertakes to facilitate such renegotiations of existing arrangements as might become necessary as a result of the introduction of the ECU as a single currency.

DECLARATION ON ARTICLE 73D OF THE TREATY ESTABLISHING THE EUROPEAN COMMUNITY

The Conference affirms that the right of Member States to apply the relevant provisions of their tax law as referred to in Article 73d(1)(a) of this Treaty will apply only with respect to the relevant provisions which exist at the end of 1993.

DECLARATION ON ARTICLE 109 OF THE TREATY ESTABLISHING THE EUROPEAN COMMUNITY

The Conference emphasises that use of the term 'formal agreements' in Article 109(1) is not intended to create a new category of international agreement within the meaning of Community law.

DECLARATION ON PART THREE, TITLE XVI, OF THE TREATY ESTABLISHING THE EUROPEAN COMMUNITY

The Conference considers that, in view of the increasing importance of nature conservation at national, Community and international level, the Community should, in exercising its powers under the provisions of Part Three, Title XVI, take account of the specific requirements of this area.

DECLARATION ON ARTICLES 109, 130R AND 130Y OF THE TREATY ESTABLISHING THE EUROPEAN COMMUNITY

The Conference considers that the provisions of Article 109(5), Article 130r(4), second subparagraph, and Article 130y do not affect the principles resulting from the judgment handed down by the Court of Justice in the AETR case.

DECLARATION ON THE DIRECTIVE OF 24 NOVEMBER 1988 (EMISSIONS)

The Conference declares that changes in Community legislation cannot undermine the derogations granted to Spain and Portugal until 31 December 1999 under the Council Directive of 24 November 1988 on the limitation of emissions of certain pollutants into the air from large combustion plants.

DECLARATION ON THE EUROPEAN DEVELOPMENT FUND

The Conference agrees that the European Development Fund will continue to be financed by national contributions in accordance with the current provisions.

DECLARATION ON THE ROLE OF NATIONAL PARLIAMENTS IN THE EUROPEAN UNION

The Conference considers that it is important to encourage greater involvement of national Parliaments in the activities of the European Union.

To this end, the exchange of information between national Parliaments and the European Parliament should be stepped up. In this context, the governments of the Member States will ensure, *inter alia*, that national Parliaments receive Commission proposals for legislation in good time for information or possible examination.

Similarly, the Conference considers that it is important for contacts between the national Parliaments and the European Parliament to be stepped up, in particular through the granting of appropriate reciprocal facilities and regular meetings between members of Parliament interested in the same issues.

DECLARATION ON THE CONFERENCE OF THE PARLIAMENTS

The Conference invites the European Parliament and the national Parliaments to meet as necessary as a Conference of the Parliaments (or 'Assises').

The Conference of the Parliaments will be consulted on the main features of the European Union, without prejudice to the powers of the European Parliament and the rights of the national Parliaments. The President of the European Council and the President of the Commission will report to each session of the Conference of the Parliaments on the state of the Union.

DECLARATION ON THE NUMBER OF MEMBERS OF THE COMMISSION AND OF THE EUROPEAN PARLIAMENT

The Conference agrees that the Member States will examine the questions relating to the number of members of the Commission and the number of members of the European Parliament no later than at the end of 1992, with a view to reaching an agreement which will permit the establishment of the necessary legal basis for fixing the number of members of the European Parliament in good time for the 1994 elections. The decisions will be taken in the light, *inter alia*, of the need to establish the overall size of the European Parliament in an enlarged Community.

DECLARATION ON THE HIERARCHY OF COMMUNITY ACTS

The Conference agrees that the Intergovernmental Conference to be convened in 1996 will examine to what extent it might be possible to review the classification of Community acts with a view to establishing an appropriate hierarchy between the different categories of act.

DECLARATION ON THE RIGHT OF ACCESS TO INFORMATION

The Conference considers that transparency of the decision-making process strengthens the democratic nature of the institutions and the public's confidence in the administration. The Conference accordingly recommends that the Commission submit to the Council no later than 1993 a report on measures designed to improve public access to the information available to the institutions.

DECLARATION ON ESTIMATED COSTS UNDER COMMISSION PROPOSALS

The Conference notes that the Commission undertakes, by basing itself where appropriate on any consultations it considers necessary and by strengthening its system for evaluating Community legislation, to take account in its legislative proposals of costs and benefits to the Member States' public authorities and all the parties concerned.

DECLARATION ON THE IMPLEMENTATION OF COMMUNITY LAW

1. The Conference stresses that it is central to the coherence and unity of the process of European construction that each Member State should fully

and accurately transpose into national law the Community directives addressed to it within the deadlines laid down therein. Moreover, the conference, while recognising that it must be for each Member State to determine how the provision of Community law can best be enforced in the light of its own particular institutions, legal system and other circumstances, but in any event in compliance with Article 189 of the Treaty establishing the European Community, considers it essential for the proper functioning of the Community that the measures taken by the different Member States should result in Community law being applied with the same effectiveness and rigour as in the application of their national law.

2. The Conference calls on the Commission to ensure, in exercising its powers under Article 155 of this Treaty, that Member States fulfil their obligations. It asks the Commission to publish periodically a full report for the Member States and the European Parliament.

DECLARATION ON ASSESSMENT OF THE ENVIRONMENTAL IMPACT OF COMMUNITY MEASURES

The Conference notes that the Commission undertakes in its proposals, and that the Member States undertake in implementing those proposals, to take full account of their environmental impact and of the principle of sustainable growth.

DECLARATION ON THE COURT OF AUDITORS

The Conference emphasises the special importance it attaches to the task assigned to the Court of Auditors by Articles 188a, 188b and 206 of the Treaty establishing the European Community.

It requests the other Community institutions to consider, together with the Court of Auditors, all appropriate ways of enhancing the effectiveness of its work.

DECLARATION ON THE ECONOMIC AND SOCIAL COMMITTEE

The Conference agrees that the Economic and Social Committee will enjoy the same independence with regard to its budget and staff management as the Court of Auditors has enjoyed hitherto.

DECLARATION ON CO-OPERATION WITH CHARITABLE ASSOCIATIONS

The Conference stresses the importance, in pursuing the objectives of Article 117 of the Treaty establishing the European Community, of co-operation between the latter and charitable associations and foundations as institutions responsible for social welfare establishments and services.

DECLARATION ON THE PROTECTION OF ANIMALS

The Conference calls upon the European Parliament, the Council and the Commission, as well as the Member States, when drafting and implementing Community legislation on the common agricultural policy, transport, the internal market and research, to pay full regard to the welfare requirements of animals.

DECLARATION ON THE REPRESENTATION OF THE INTERESTS OF THE OVERSEAS COUNTRIES AND TERRITORIES REFERRED TO IN ARTICLE 227(3) AND (5)(A) AND (B) OF THE TREATY ESTABLISHING THE EUROPEAN COMMUNITY

The Conference, noting that in exceptional circumstances divergences may arise between the interests of the Union and those of the overseas countries and territories referred to in Article 227(3) and (5)(a) and (b), agrees that the Council will seek to reach a solution which affords with the position of the Union. However, in the event that this proves impossible, the Conference agrees that the Member State concerned may act separately in the interests of the said overseas countries and territories, without this affecting the Community's interests. The Member State concerned will give notice to the Council and the Commission where such a divergence of interests is likely to occur and, when separate action proves unavoidable, make it clear that it is acting in the interests of an overseas territory mentioned above.

This declaration also applies to Macao and East Timor.

DECLARATION ON THE OUTERMOST REGIONS OF THE COMMUNITY

The Conference acknowledges that the outermost regions of the Community (the French overseas departments, Azores and Madeira and Canary Islands) suffer from major structural backwardness compounded by several phenomena (remoteness, island status, small size, difficult topography and climate, economic dependence on a few products), the permanence and combination of which severely restrain their economic and social development.

It considers that, while the provisions of the Treaty establishing the European Community and secondary legislation apply automatically to the outermost regions, it is nonetheless possible to adopt specific measures to assist them inasmuch and as long as there is an objective need to take such measures with a view to the economic and social development of those regions. Such measures should have as their aim both the completion of the internal market and the recognition of the regional reality to enable the outermost regions to achieve the average economic and social level of the Community.

INDEX

ANGLO-IRISH AGREEMENT,
  constitutionality, 46–47, 48
ARTICLE 177 EC, 17–24
  abortion information, and, 21–22
  Article 26 of Constitution, and, 21–24
  Bills allegedly contrary to Community law,
    21–22
  constitutionality of Bills, and, 21
  discretion of judge, and, 18
  integrity of Community law in Ireland, and,
    17–24
  intervention of Court of Justice, and, 24
  litigation *inter partes*, and, 22
  national procedural rules, and, 23–24
  part of Irish law, as, 19
  protection of integrity of Community legal
    order, 23
  purpose of, 18
  references to Court of Justice, and, 22–23
  relationship between Irish and Community
    law, and, 20
  renvoi prejudiciel, and, 21–24
AUSTRIA,
  cessation of sovereign authority, 45

CITIZENSHIP OF EUROPEAN UNION,
  "essential scope and objectives", and, 41–42
COMMON DEFENCE POLICY,
  "essential scope and objectives", and, 41
COMMUNITY AND UNION TREATIES,
  amendment, 39–42
    constitutional amendment, and, 39–42
    "essential scope and objectives". 39–40
  citizenship of European Union, 41–42
  common defence policy, 41
  voting rights in national elections, 41–42
COMMUNITY COMPETENCE, 79–87
  declaration, 83
  international agreements, 81
  mixed agreements. *See* MIXED AGREEMENTS
  nature of, 79
  participation, 83
  respective competences of states, and, 85
COMMUNITY PATENT CONVENTION,
  ratification, 37–38
CONSTITUTION ACT,
  Eleventh Amendment 1992, 160–162. *See
    also* ELEVENTH AMENDMENT
  provision for membership of European
    Communities and European Union, 5
  Tenth Amendment 1987, 159–160
  Third Amendment 1972, 155–157
CONSTITUTION OF IRELAND,
  Article 29.4.3–6, 5
CONSTITUTIONAL INTERPRETATION, 121–142
  abortion information, 129–130
  analysis of options, 133

CONSTITUTIONAL INTERPRETATION—*cont.*
  approaches, 121–122
  conflict between Community law and Irish
    constitutional law, 130–131
  current domestic constitutional test for
    reception of Community law obli-
    gations, 142
  fundamental national constitutional prin-
    ciples, and, 139
  harmonious approach, 123–124, 134–135
  historical approach, 124–126
  literal approach, 122–123
  natural law approach, 126–128
  "necessitated" measures, 131–132
  normative conflict, and, 121–142
  objective historical approach, 136
  Preamble of Constitution, and, 135
  principles, 121–128
  requirement of unanimity, and, 137
  teleological approach, 123
CONSTITUTIONAL REQUIREMENTS,
  meaning, 33–35
CONVERGENCE CRITERIA, 463–464
Crotty v. Taoiseach, 25–49
  exceptional nature of case, 48
  facts, 25–26
  freedom to conduct foreign policy, 42–49
  "necessitated" measures, 30–38
  Supreme Court judgment, 26–30

DECLARATIONS, 473–477
  Article 73 E.C. Treaty, 474
  Article 109 E.C. Treaty, 474
  Articles 109, 130r and 130y, E.C. Treaty,
    474
  assessment of environmental impact of
    Community measures, 476
  civil protection, energy and tourism, 473
  Conference of Parliament, 475
  co-operation with charitable associations,
    476
  Court of Auditors, 476
  Directive of 24 November 1988, 474
  Economic and Social Committee, 476
  estimated costs under Commission pro-
    posals, 475
  European Development Fund, 474
  hierarchy of Community acts, 475
  implementation of Community law,
    475–476
  monetary co-operation with non-Com-
    munity countries, 473–474
  monetary relations with San Marino, Vat-
    ican and Monaco, 474
  nationality of Member State, 473
  number of Members of Commission and
    European Parliament, 475
  outermost regions of Community, 477

Index

DECLARATIONS—*cont.*
  Part Three E.C. Treaty, 473, 474
  protection of animals, 476
  representation of interests of overseas countries and territories, 476–477
  right of access to information, 475
  role of national parliaments in European Union, 474–475
DELEGATED LEGISLATION,
  adoption, 57

ECONOMIC AND MONETARY UNION, 215–218
ECONOMIC AND SOCIAL COHESION, 471–472
ELEVENTH AMENDMENT, 89–120
  direct applicability, and, 106–109
  European Court of Justice, and, 116–119
  European Union, and, 89–120
  force of law in State, and, 106–109
  Union acts and obligations, 90–109
ESSENTIAL SCOPE AND OBJECTIVE,
  meaning, 39–40
EUROPEAN CENTRAL BANK, 442–455
EUROPEAN COMMUNITIES ACTS 1972–1995, 165–166
EUROPEAN COMMUNITIES ACT 1972, 166–181
  confirmation of regulations, 177–181
  definitions, 167–171
  effect of regulations, 177–181
  general provisions, 171–175
  Joint Committee on European Affairs, 178–181
  power to make regulations, 175–177
  regulations to have statutory effect, 178
EUROPEAN COMMUNITIES (AMENDMENT) ACT 1972, 182–183
EUROPEAN COMMUNITIES (AMENDMENT) ACT 1977, 183–184
EUROPEAN COMMUNITIES (AMENDMENT) ACT 1979, 184–185
EUROPEAN COMMUNITIES (AMENDMENT) ACT 1985, 185–186
EUROPEAN COMMUNITIES (AMENDMENT) (NO. 2) ACT 1985, 186–187
EUROPEAN COMMUNITIES (AMENDMENT) ACT 1986, 187–188
EUROPEAN COMMUNITIES (AMENDMENT) ACT 1992, 189–190
EUROPEAN COMMUNITIES (AMENDMENT) ACT 1993, 190–195
  definitions, 191
  extension of time limit to two years, 194–195
  Meagher, response to, 193–194
EUROPEAN COMMUNITIES (AMENDMENT) ACT 1994, 195–196
EUROPEAN COMMUNITIES (AMENDMENT) ACT 1995, 196, 197
EUROPEAN COMMUNITIES (CONFIRMATION OF REGULATIONS) ACT 1983, 181–182
E.C. TREATY, 243 *et seq.*
  acquisition of property in Denmark, 442
  agriculture, 283–288
  approximation of laws, 311–316

E.C. TREATY—*cont.*
  Association of the Overseas Countries and Territories, 381–383
  citizenship of the Union, 267–275
  Commission, 393–399
  Committee of the Regions, 420–422
  common commercial policy, 352 *et seq.*
  Community policies, 275 *et seq.*
  competition, 306–310
    aids granted by states, 308–310
    dumping, 308
    tax provisions, 310–311
    undertakings, 306–308
  consumer protection, 364–366
  Council, 390–393
  Court of Auditors, 409
  Court of Justice, 399–409
  culture, 362–363
  customer union, 276–283
  development co-operation, 379–381
  economic and monetary policy, 316 *et seq.*
    institutional provisions, 337–340
    transitional provisions, 340–352
  economic and social cohesion, 368–371
  Economic and Social Committee, 418–420
  economic policy, 319–329
  education, 355–362
  elimination of customs duties between Member States, 276–278
  environment, 375–379
  European Investment Bank, 422–423
  European Parliament, 383–390
  European Social Fund, 358–360
  final provisions, 440–441
  free movement of goods, 275–283
  free movement of persons, services and capital, 288–303
    capital, 293–303
    payments, 293–303
    right of establishment, 289–292
    services, 292–293
    workers, 288–289
  general provisions, 430–440
  industry, 367–368
  institutions of the Community, 383 *et seq.*
    financial provisions, 423–430
    provisions common to, 411–418
  monetary policy, 329–337
  principles, 254–267
  Protocol concerning Article 199, 442
  Protocol on Denmark, 465, 467
  Protocol on France, 467
  Protocol on Portugal, 465
  Protocol relating to U.K., 465–467
  Protocols, 442–472
  public health, 363–364
  research, 371–375
  setting up of common customs tariff, 278–283
  setting up of institutions, 439–440
  social policy, 355–362
  technological development, 371–375
  trans-European networks, 366–367
  transport, 303–306

Index

E.C. Treaty—*cont.*
  vocational training, 355–362
  youth, 355–362
European Council, 95–96
  decision 1992, 96–97
European Court of Human Rights, 113–116
  collective liability of Member States, and, 114
  exclusion of jurisdiction, 116
  jurisdiction, 113–116
  supervision by, 113–116
  transfer of powers by state, and, 115–116
European Court of Justice, 116–119
  Eleventh Amendment, and, 116–119
  exclusion of, 116–119
    "external Constitution", and, 117–118
    national courts, and, 118
    national fundamental rights supervision, 117
    "necessitated" clause, and, 117
    vires, and, 118–119
European Monetary Institute, 217, 456–462
European Parliament, 211–212
European Social Fund, 358–360
European System of Central Banks, 442–455
  amendment of Statute, 453–455
  complementary legislation, 453–455
  constitution, 442
  financial provision, 448–451
  general provisions, 451–453
  monetary functions and operations, 447–448
  objectives, 442–443
  organisation, 443–447
  prudential supervision, 448
  tasks, 442–443
European Union,
  acting through institutions "borrowed" from Communities, 102
  acts, 90–109
  acts of Council under treaty, 98–99
  acts of Member States, and, 98–106
  acts of Members treated as acts of, whether, 104–105
  agreements involving charge on public funds, 105–106
  capacity, 102–103
  common foreign and security policy, 93–95
    implementation, 94
  common provisions of Treaty, 95–98
  competence, 99–100
  co-operation in fields of judicial and home affairs, 91–93
  Court of Justice, role of, 97
  direct applicability, 106–109
  distinct decision-making power, whether, 99
  effect of Treaty amendments and accessions, 97–98
  elements, 89
  Eleventh Amendment, and, 89–120. *See also* Eleventh Amendment
  final provisions of Treaty, 95–98
  force of law in state, and, 106–109

European Union—*cont.*
  fundamental rights, and, 109–116
    enforcement, 109–110
    judicial protection, 110
  immunities, 102
  impetus for development, 95
  implied obligation of solidarity, 93
  international identity, 100
  international legal personality, 99–100
  joint position, 92
  joint position on political offences, 107–108
  limited legal personality, 103
  measures implementing joint action, 107
  obligations, 90–109
  observance of conventions after ratification, 93
  operational expenditure, 94–95
  personality, 90–91
  pillars, 89–90
  powers derived from Communities, 104
  privileges, 102
  process of European integration, and, 100
  secondary legal obligations, imposition of, 97
  secondary obligations under Treaty, 91–98
  single institutional framework, 101
  treaty-making, 105
  unincorporated international agreements, 108
  varying degrees of international personality, and, 103
Excessive deficit procedure, 462–463

Foreign policy, 42–49
  freedom to conduct, 42–49
  Germany, 44
  Permanent Court of International Justice, and, 45
  Single European Act, and, 28–29
  United Kingdom, 43
Fundamental rights, 109–116
  enforcement, 109–110
  European Union, and, 109–116
  injunctions or prohibiting power of Council, 111
  judicial protection, 110
  judicial scrutiny of government positions, 112
  national "prior restraint" jurisdiction, 113
  policy options, 110
  pre-emptive judicial role, 111
  "prior restraint" of government, 110–113
  protection, 69–70
  supervision by European Court of Human rights, 113–116. *See also* European Court of Human Rights

Germany,
  constitution, 44
  foreign policy, 44

481

IMPLEMENTATION OF COMMUNITY LAW, 51–67
assessment of machinery, 60–61
choice of mode by state, 53
discretion as to means, 54
Meagher v. Minister for Agriculture, and, 51–67
omnibus bills, 54–55
IMPLEMENTING MEASURES, 69–78
"according to procedures to be determined", 72
actual and legal obligation, 76
actual necessity, 76–77
alternative scheme, 77
"consequent on", 71
demands of two distinct legal systems, 70
feasible alternatives, 75–76
"legal obligation" test, 71–72
national judges, and, 74
"nature of content", 69
"necessary machinery", 78
"necessity", 70–71
necessity test, 69
optional schemes, 72–73
procedure, and, 74
proportionality, 76–77
reasonableness, 73–74
review of content, 69–78
social welfare legislation, 75
subsidiary jurisdiction, 77
supervisory jurisdiction of courts, 78
two-tier test for judicial scrutiny, 74–75

JOINT COMMITTEE ON EUROPEAN AFFAIRS ROLE, 55

MAASTRICHT TREATY. *See also* TREATY ON EUROPEAN UNION
Protocol No. 17, 143–154. *See also* PROTOCOL No. 17 to Maastricht Treaty
Meagher v. Minister for Agriculture, 51–67
assessment of machinery for implementation of Community law, 60–61
High Court, 58–60
implementation of Community law, and, 51–67
Supreme Court, 60–67
appropriateness, concept of, 63–64, 65
double construction rule, 61–62
ministerial implementation, and, 65–66
nature of E.C. directives, 64
significance, 66
time limit for prosecutions, 62
validity of ministerial regulations, 62
MEMBER STATE OBLIGATION, 79–87
MINISTERS,
law-making power, 51
MIXED AGREEMENTS, 79–87
allocation of responsibility under, 84
Community as party to part of, 83
Community law, and, 80–84
Community responsibility, and, 84–87
effect, 81–82
forms, 82

MIXED AGREEMENTS—*cont.*
interpretation, 85–86
Irish Constitution, and, 83–84
meaning, 80
nature of, 79
obligations distinguished, 86–87
obligatory quality, 80
"responsibility", 86
responsibility for breach, 86
scope, 81

NATIONAL ELECTIONS,
voting rights in, 41–42
NORMATIVE CONFLICT, 121–142
abortion information, 129–130
constitutional interpretation, and, 121–142
fundamental national constitutional principles, and, 139
implied amendment, and, 134–135
interpretative role of Irish courts, and, 128–141
legal obligation test, and, 133
literal readings of Constitution, and, 134–135
measures outside jurisdiction of E.C.J., 132–133
"necessitated" measures, 131–132
requirement of unanimity, and, 137

OMNIBUS BILLS, 54–55

PROTOCOL NO. 17,
abortion, and, 143–144
Community law, and, 144–151
Declaration of 1 May 1992, and, 149–150
effect, 145–146
European Court of Justice, and, 149
Irish constitutional law, and, 147
Irish *renvoi*, and, 144
part of Union law, whether, 151–152
renvoi in reverse, and, 143–154
restriction of travel and information, and, 148
scope, 144–145
Treaty on European Union, and, 151–154
PRIVILEGES AND IMMUNITIES OF EUROPEAN COMMUNITIES, 464–465
PROPORTIONALITY,
nature of principle, 76–77

RECEPTION OF E.C. LAW IN IRISH LAW, 7–16
competence of European Communities, 9
concrete claims of community law, 11
divisible sovereignty, doctrine of, 9–10
federal nature of Community legal system, and, 8
immunity clauses, 13
judicial interpretations, and, 7
multiple sources of sovereign authority, and, 9
national courts, and, 10
natural law, and, 14–15
normative conflict, 12
obligation of membership of Communities, and, 14

RECEPTION OF E.C. LAW IN IRISH LAW—*cont.*
"principle of the mirror image", 11–12
ratification of Treaties, and, 7–8
status of constitutional law, and, 14–15
terminology, 16
"the force of law in the State", 15
transfers of sovereignty, and, 10

SEPARATION OF POWERS,
erosion, 52
SINGLE EUROPEAN ACT, 25–49
admission of new Member States, 28
constitutionality of national action, and,
30–31
contents, 25
*Crotty v. An Taoiseach. See Crotty v. An
Taoiseach*
essential objectives, 25–49
foreign policy co-operation, 28–29
intended objective, 48–49
invocation of domestic impediments to
treaty-making competence, 32
Irish constitutional requirements, and,
33–34
legal obligation, 25–49
legal obligation of membership of Communities, and, 30
"necessitated by the obligations of membership of the Communities", 36
political commitment to ratify, 25
qualified majority voting, 27
ratification of amendments, and, 31–32
special status of Community and Union
Treaties under Constitution, 32–33
SOCIAL POLICY, 468–471
STABILITY PACT FOR EUROPE, 153–154

TRANSITION TO THIRD STAGE OF ECONOMIC AND
MONETARY UNION, 465
Treaty of Rome
amendments to, 206–211
TREATY ON EUROPEAN UNION. *See also* MAAS-
TRICHT TREATY
amendment, 236–237
amendments to E.C.S.C. Treaty, 229
amendments to Euratom Treaty, 229
amendments to Treaty of Rome, 206–211
applications of new membership, 237
background, 199–201
Commission, 212
Committee of the Regions, 213
common foreign and security policy,
230–233
common provisions, 226–229
consistency and continuity of Union objectives, 226

TREATY ON EUROPEAN UNION—*cont.*
co-operation in fields of justice and home
affaris, 233–236
Council of Ministers, 213
declaration on asylum, 241
declaration on Constitution of Ireland, 238
declaration on disputes between E.C.B.
and E.M.I., 242
declaration on police co-operation,
241–242
declaration on practical arrangements in
field of common foreign and security
policy, 238–239
declaration on use of language in field of
common foreign and security policy,
239
declaration on voting in field of common
foreign and security policy, 238
economic and monetary union, 215–218
enlargement of Union, 218–219
entry into force, 237
establishment of European Union, 226
European Council, 227
European Court of Justice, 213
European Parliament, 211–212
foreign policy, 202–205
home affairs, 202–205
institutional reforms, 211
institutions governed by provisions in E.C.
Treaty, 227
justice, 202–205
languages of authentic text, 237–238
legislative procedures, 213–215
limitation of extent of application of European Court's powers, 236
negotiation process, 198–199
1996, 218–219
objectives of Union, 226
provisions amending E.E.C. Treaty, 229
ratification, 237
respect for national identities and fundamental rights, 227
scheme, 206
security policy, 202–205
structure of new Union, 201–202
text, 220 *et seq.*
unlimited period of, 237

UNITED KINGDOM,
foreign policy, 43
UNITED NATIONS,
powers of Security Council, 46

VOTING RIGHTS,
national elections, in, 41–42

WESTERN EUROPEAN UNION, 239–241